MASTERPLOTS II

POETRY SERIES
REVISED EDITION

MASTERPLOTS II

POETRY SERIES
REVISED EDITION

1
"A"–Brief Pause in the Organ Recital

Editor, Revised Edition
PHILIP K. JASON

Project Editor, Revised Edition
TRACY IRONS-GEORGES

Editors, Supplement
JOHN WILSON   **PHILIP K. JASON**

Editor, First Edition
FRANK N. MAGILL

SALEM PRESS

Pasadena, California   Hackensack, New Jersey

Editor in Chief: Dawn P. Dawson
Project Editor: Tracy Irons-Georges   *Research Supervisor:* Jeffry Jensen
Production Editor: Cynthia Beres   *Research Assistant:* Jeff Stephens
Copy Editor: Lauren Mitchell   *Acquisitions Editor:* Mark Rehn

Some of the essays in this work originally appeared in *Masterplots II, Poetry Series*, ed-
ited by Frank N. Magill (Pasadena, Calif.: Salem Press, Inc., 1992), and in *Masterplots II,
Poetry Series Supplement*, edited by John Wilson and Philip K. Jason (Pasadena, Calif.:
Salem Press, Inc., 1998).

∞ The paper used in these volumes conforms to the American National Standard for
Permanence of Paper for Printed Library Materials, Z39.48-1992 (R1997).

Library of Congress Cataloging-in-Publication Data
Masterplots II. Poetry series.— Rev. ed. / editor, Philip K. Jason ; project editor, Tracy
   Irons-Georges
      p. ; cm.
   Rev. ed.: Masterplots two / Frank Northen Magill, 1992-1998.
   Includes bibliographical references and indexes.
      ISBN 1-58765-037-1 (set : alk. paper) — ISBN 1-58765-038-X (vol. 1 : alk. paper) —
   1. Poetry — Themes, motives. I. Title: Masterplots two. II. Title: Masterplots 2. III.
Jason, Philip K., 1941-   . IV. Irons-Georges, Tracy.

PN1110.5 .M37 2002
809.1—dc21

                                                                2001055059

Second Printing

TABLE OF CONTENTS

TABLE OF CONTENTS

TABLE OF CONTENTS

PUBLISHER'S NOTE

The original seven volumes of *Masterplots II, Poetry Series* (1992) examined works by some of the most important poets throughout history and around the world. A three-volume supplement published in 1998 updated and extended the original series' coverage. This eight-volume *Masterplots II: Poetry Series, Revised Edition* contains 1,386 essays, incorporating 1,115 entries from the previous editions and 271 entirely new entries.

Individual poems, both short and long, are emphasized in the *Masterplots II* series, although some collections receive coverage as well. The titles found here are the ones most often taught in classrooms and featured in poetry anthologies. To eliminate duplication, poetry covered in the twelve-volume *Masterplots, Revised Second Edition* (1996) is not found in this set, including 21 entries previously published in *Masterplots II*; for readers' convenience, a list of all poetry titles in *Masterplots, Revised Second Edition* is provided at the end of volume 8.

The *Revised Edition* adds important poems by both classic writers (such as Geoffrey Chaucer, John Milton, Anne Bradstreet, Henry Wadsworth Longfellow, William Butler Yeats, Edna St. Vincent Millay, Walt Whitman, Wilfred Owen, and Allen Ginsberg) and contemporary poets (such as Philip Levine, Jimmy Santiago Baca, Lorna Dee Cervantes, Robert Bly, Gary Soto, Sharon Olds, Garrett Kaoru Hongo, Maya Angelou, Adrienne Rich, Amiri Baraka, Margaret Atwood, and N. Scott Momaday). Of the 433 poets whose works are covered here, 99 are women and 29 have never before appeared in the *Masterplots II, Poetry Series*. For the first time, readers will find such well-known poems as W. H. Auden's "The Shield of Achilles," Lewis Carroll's "Jabberwocky," Robert Frost's "Out, Out—," Langston Hughes's "Mulatto" and "Trumpet Player," Randall Jarrell's "The Death of the Ball Turret Gunner," Elizabeth Bishop's "Filling Station" and "Sestina," William Carlos Williams's "This Is Just to Say," and Audre Lorde's "The Night-Blooming Jasmine."

Each article begins with ready-reference information that includes the author's name and date of birth (and death, if applicable) and the date of the poem's first publication. For poems first published in a foreign language, the original title and date are given, as well as the name and date of the original collection and of the English translation. A summary called "The Poem" is followed by two sections that explore the work in depth. "Forms and Devices" examines the poetic devices employed and explores language choice, meter, rhyme, point of view, symbolism, and another literary techniques. "Themes and Meanings" analyzes the main focus of the poetry and the poet's overriding concerns; this section often provides context by relating the work at hand to the poet's larger body of work. All essays carry a byline.

The articles in *Masterplots II: Poetry Series, Revised Edition* are arranged alphabetically by title. Four indexes at the end of volume 8 are designed to assist the reader in selecting articles of interest. The Title Index locates specific poems and collections, including alternate foreign-language and English titles. The Author Index lists all poets and their entries in the set, including any alternate names. A new feature for the *Masterplots II, Poetry Series* is the Geographical and Ethnic Index, which categorizes the covered poets by country as well as under the headings "Gay and Lesbian" and "Women"; the United States is broken down further into the ethnic groups African American, Asian American, Latino, and Native American. The Type of Poem Index lists the titles under the following categories: ballad, dramatic monologue, elegy, epic, epistle/letter in verse, lyric, meditation, mock epic, mock pastoral, narrative, ode, pastoral, poetic sequence, satire, sonnet, sonnet sequence, verse drama, and verse essay. Volume 8 also offers a Glossary of poetic terms and a Bibliography; the latter first appeared in the 1992 set and has been thoroughly updated with the latest scholarship on poetry in general and major poets in particular.

We would like to thank the many academicians and other writers who contributed to this set. A list of their names and affiliations appears at the beginning of volume 1. Special mention must also be made of Editor Philip K. Jason, Professor of English at the United States Naval Academy in Annapolis, Maryland, who applied his expert knowledge to the shaping of the set's contents.

CONTRIBUTING REVIEWERS

H. McCrea Adams
Independent Scholar

Howard C. Adams
Frostburg State University

Michael Adams
Fairleigh Dickinson University

Susan S. Adams
Northern Kentucky University

Amy Adelstein
Independent Scholar

Opal Palmer Adisa
California College of Arts

A. Jay Adler
Los Angeles Southwest College

Kathleen Aguero
Pine Manor College

Patricia Alkema
Independent Scholar

Betty Alldredge
Angelo State University

Diane M. Almeida
University of Massachusetts, Boston

Daniel Altamiranda
Universidad de Buenos Aires

David J. Amante
University of North Carolina at Charlotte

Christopher Ames
Oglethorpe University

Phillip B. Anderson
University of Central Arkansas

Candace E. Andrews
San Joaquin Delta College

Terry L. Andrews
Independent Scholar

Anu Aneja
Ohio Wesleyan University

Andrew J. Angyal
Elon College

Raymond M. Archer
Indiana University at Kokomo

Stanley Archer
Texas A&M University

Frank Ardolino
University of Hawaii at Manoa

Dorothy B. Aspinwall
University of Hawaii at Manoa

Bryan Aubrey
Independent Scholar

Edmund August
Jefferson Community College

William Baer
University of Evansville

Jim Baird
University of North Texas

James J. Balakier
University of South Dakota

JoAnn Balingit
University of Delaware

Thomas Banks
Ohio Northern University

Linda Bannister
Loyola Marymount University

Stephen M. Baraban
Independent Scholar

Judith Barban
Winthrop College

Jack V. Barbera
University of Mississippi

Henry J. Baron
Calvin College

Terry Barr
Presbyterian College

David Barratt
Independent Scholar

Melissa E. Barth
Appalachian State University

Kathleen M. Bartlett
University of Central Florida

Elise Bartosik-Vélez
University of Illinois, Urbana-Champaign

Sharon Bassett
California State University, Los Angeles

Robert Bateman
Concord College

Cynthia S. Becerra
Humphreys College

Carol F. Bender
Alma College

Todd K. Bender
University of Wisconsin-Madison

Alma Bennett
Clemson University

Gaymon L. Bennett
Northwest Nazarene University

Richard P. Benton
Trinity College

Stephen Benz
Barry University

James J. Berg
Independent Scholar

Gordon N. Bergquist
Creighton University

Dorothy M. Betz
Georgetown University

David Biespiel
University of Maryland

John Biguenet
Loyola University, New Orleans

Cynthia A. Bily
Adrian College

xiii

Margaret Boe Birns
New York University

Nicholas Birns
New School University

Richard Bizot
University of North Florida

Neil Blackadder
Princeton University

Robert G. Blake
Elon College

Keisha Blakely
*California State University,
Fresno*

Pegge Bochynski
Salem State College

Bernadette Lynn Bosky
Independent Scholar

Nila M. Bowden
Morgan State University

Gerard Bowers
Willamette University

Kevin Boyle
Elon College

Trisha M. Brady
University of Pittsburgh

Douglas Branch
*Southwest Tennessee
Community College*

Colin Brayton
*University of California,
Berkeley*

Marie J. K. Brenner
Bethel College

Carol Breslin
Gwynedd-Mercy College

Hans-Peter Breuer
University of Delaware

William D. Brewer
Appalachian State University

Wesley Britton
*Grayson County Community
College*

Patricia Pollock Brodsky
*University of Missouri-
Kansas City*

Marlene Broemer
Independent Scholar

David Bromige
Sonoma State University

C. L. Brooke
Cleveland State University

Keith H. Brower
Dickinson College

James S. Brown
Charleston Southern University

Mary Hanford Bruce
Monmouth College

Carl Brucker
Arkansas Tech University

Paul James Buczkowski
Eastern Michigan University

Maria Budisavljević-
Oparnica
Arizona State University

Paul Budra
*Simon Fraser University,
Vancouver, B.C., Canada*

Michael Burns
*Southwest Missouri State
University*

Della Burt-Bradley
Harold Washington College

Susan Butterworth
Independent Scholar

Edmund J. Campion
University of Tennessee

William Carroll
Independent Scholar

Linda M. Carter
Morgan State University

Caroline Carvill
*Rose-Hulman Institute of
Technology*

Mary LeDonne Cassidy
South Carolina State University

Thomas J. Cassidy
*University of Wisconsin—
Marshfield*

Christine R. Catron
St. Mary's University

Carole A. Champagne
*University of Maryland Eastern
Shore*

John Steven Childs
Polytechnic University

Balance Chow
Rollins College

Paul Christensen
Texas A&M University

C. L. Chua
*California State University,
Fresno*

Norris B. Clark
University of Akron

Steven Clotzman
Independent Scholar

David W. Cole
*University of Wisconsin Center-
Baraboo*

Judith Collins
University of Kentucky

Richard Collins
Louisiana State University

David Conde
*Metropolitan State College of
Denver*

Sandra Cookson
Canisius College

Laura Cowan
University of Maine

Beverly Coyle
Vassar College

Bill Coyle
Salem State College

George Craddock
Concord College

Christopher E. Crane
*United States Naval Academy,
Annapolis*

CONTRIBUTING REVIEWERS

Stephen H. Crane
University of South Florida

Barry Crawford
University of California, Riverside

Peter Crawford
Independent Scholar

Vance Crummett
University of Wisconsin— Milwaukee

Thomas M. Curley
Bridgewater State College

Marsha Daigle-Williamson
Spring Arbor College

Koos Daley
Adams State College

Richard Damashek
Illinois Benedictine College

Robert Darling
Keuka College

Jonathan Daunt
University of California, Davis

Dean Davies
Mesa State College

Anita Price Davis
Converse College

Delmer Davis
Andrews University

Jo Culbertson Davis
Williams Baptist College

Todd Davis
Goshen College

William V. Davis
Baylor University

Frank Day
Clemson University

Dennis R. Dean
University of Wisconsin— Parkside

Cameron K. Deaver
Independent Scholar

Bill Delaney
Independent Scholar

Francine Dempsey
College of Saint Rose

Scott D. Denham
Davidson College

Louise A. DeSantis Deutsch
Cape Cod Community College

Joseph Dewey
University of Pittsburgh- Johnstown

Carolyn F. Dickinson
Columbia College

Shoshanah Dietz
La Sierra University

Matts Djos
Mesa State College

Margaret A. Dodson
Independent Scholar

Susan Dominguez
Oberlin College

Gene Doty
University of Missouri, Rolla

Barbara Drake
Linfield College

William Ryland Drennan
University of Wisconsin- Baraboo

John Drury
University of Cincinnati

Gloria Duarte-Valverde
Angelo State University

Stefan R. Dziemianowicz
Independent Scholar

Doris Earnshaw
University of California, Davis

Robert Eddy
Fayetteville State University

K Edgington
Towson University

Bruce L. Edwards
Bowling Green State University

Clifford Edwards
Fort Hays State University

Eduardo F. Elías
University of Utah

David L. Elliott
Keystone College

Robert P. Ellis
Independent Scholar

Edmund L. Epstein
City University of New York, Queens College

David Lawrence Erben
University of South Florida

Thomas L. Erskine
Salisbury State University

Angela M. Estes
California Polytechnic State University, San Luis Obispo

Carrie Etter
University of California, Irvine

Jo N. Farrar
San Jacinto College

Beth Ann Fennelly
University of Arkansas

Brian C. Ferguson-Avery
Independent Scholar

John W. Fiero
University of Southwestern Louisiana

Edward Fiorelli
St. John's University

Sandra K. Fischer
State University of New York— Albany

T. A. Fishman
Purdue University

Ray Fleming
Pennsylvania State University

Thomas C. Foster
University of Michigan, Flint

Joseph Francavilla
Columbus State University

June M. Frazer
Western Illinois University

Tom Frazier
Cumberland College

Terri Frongia
*University of California,
Riverside*

Janice Moore Fuller
Catawba College

Joe B. Fulton
Dalton College

Robert L. Gale
University of Pittsburgh

Jeffery Galle
Northeast Louisiana University

Jo K. Galle
Northeast Louisiana University

Ann D. Garbett
Averett College

Keith Garebian
Independent Scholar

Samuel B. Garren
*North Carolina A&T State
University*

Joshua Alden Gaylord
New York University

Michelle Gibson
University of Cincinnati

Jill B. Gidmark
University of Minnesota

Erlis Glass
Rosemont College

Laurie Glover
Claremont Graduate School

Nancy D. Goldfarb
University of Michigan

Lois Gordon
Fairleigh Dickinson University

Sidney Gottlieb
Sacred Heart University

Carla Graham
*University of Wisconsin,
La Crosse*

James Green
Arizona State University

Jeffrey Greer
Western Michigan University

Glenn Grever
Illinois State University

Louise Grieco
Independent Scholar

Gary Grieve-Carlson
Lebanon Valley College

William Grim
Ohio University

Jeffrey D. Groves
Harvey Mudd College

Tasha C. Haas
University of Kansas

H. George Hahn
Towson University

Robert Haight
*Kalamazoo Valley Community
College*

James Hale
Central Washington University

Jay L. Halio
University of Delaware

William T. Hamilton
*Metropolitan State College of
Denver*

Michael W. Hancock
University of Kansas

Katherine Hanley
St. Bernard's Institute

Tina Hanlon
Concord College

Eugene Kenneth Hanson
College of the Desert

Betsy P. Harfst
Kishwaukee College

Susan Tetlow Harrington
*University of Maryland Eastern
Shore*

Sandra Hanby Harris
Tidewater Community College

Betty L. Hart
University of Southern Indiana

Jack Hart
University of Rio Grande

Robert D. Harvey
University of Nevada, Reno

Nelson Hathcock
Saint Xavier University

John C. Hawley
Santa Clara University

David M. Heaton
Ohio University

Hartmut Heep
*University of Illinois at Urbana-
Champaign*

Terry Heller
Coe College

Greig Henderson
University of Toronto

Diane Andrews Henningfeld
Adrian College

Andrew C. Higgins
American University

John Hildebidle
*Massachusetts Institute of
Technology*

Paula Hilton
University of New Orleans

Joseph W. Hinton
Independent Scholar

William Hoagland
Northwest College

Mary Ann Hoegberg
Independent Scholar

Alan Holder
Hunter College

W. Kenneth Holditch
University of New Orleans

Hilary Holladay
*University of North Carolina—
Chapel Hill*

Sandra J. Holstein
Southern Oregon University

Gregory D. Horn
*Southwest Virginia Community
College*

George F. Horneker
Arkansas State University

Whitney Hoth
Fort Hays State University

Kenneth L. Houghton
Independent Scholar

W. Scott Howard
University of Denver

Patricia J. Huhn
Trinidad State Junior College

Mary Hurd
East Tennessee State University

Ed Ingebretsen
Georgetown University

Charles Isenberg
Reed College

Miglena Ivanova
University of Illinois at Urbana-Champaign

Maura Ives
Texas A&M University

Barry Jacobs
Montclair State College

Helen Jaskoski
California State University, Fullerton

Michael Jeffrys
Independent Scholar

Jeffry Jensen
Independent Scholar

Christopher D. Johnson
Francis Marion University

Geri Johnson
Loyola University, New Orleans

Sheila Golburgh Johnson
Independent Scholar

William Jolliff
George Fox University

Ralph Robert Joly
Asbury College

Ginger Jones
Lincoln University-Missouri

Kirkland Jones
Texas Southern University

Marlene Kadar
York University

Leela Kapai
Prince George's Community College

Robert Kaplan
University of Arizona

Daven M. Kari
California Baptist College

Cynthia Lee Katona
Ohlone College

Heidi Kelchner
University of South Florida

Sherrill Keller
Central Washington University

Steven G. Kellman
University of Texas, San Antonio

W. P. Kenney
Manhattan College

Frank L. Kersnowski
Trinity University

Gunilla Theander Kester
University of North Carolina—Chapel Hill

Claire Keyes
Salem State College

Mabel M. Khawaja
Hampton University

Kimberley H. Kidd
King College
East Tennessee State University

Judith Kitchen
State University of New York, Brockport

Judith Kleck
Central Washington University

Elaine Laura Kleiner
Indiana State University

Kathleen L. Komar
University of California, Los Angeles

Paula Kopacz
Eastern Kentucky University

Robin Kornman
Princeton University

Dave Kuhne
Texas Christian University

Kathryn Kulpa
Independent Scholar

Donald D. Kummings
University of Wisconsin-Parkside

Paul R. La Chance
Frostburg State University

Christine de Lailhacar
State University of New York Maritime College

R. Scott LaMascus
Oklahoma Christian University

R. T. Lambdin
University of South Florida

Daniel W. Landes
East Central University

Joshua Landy
Princeton University

R. Parks Lanier, Jr.
Radford University

Kathleen Margaret Lant
California Polytechnic State University, San Luis Obispo

Peter Lapp
Queen's University, Kingston, Ontario, Canada

Carlota Larrea
Pennsylvania State University

Eugene Larson
Los Angeles Pierce College

Terry Lass
Columbia College

William T. Lawlor
University of Wisconsin-Stevens Point

Jacqueline Lawson
University of Michigan, Dearborn

Anne K. LeCroy
East Tennessee State University

Linda Ledford-Miller
University of Scranton

L. L. Lee
Western Washington University

Steven Lehman
John Abbott College

Bruce H. Leland
Western Illinois University

Elisabeth Anne Leonard
Kent State University

Jordan Leondopoulos
St. John's University

Holli G. Levitsky
Loyola Marymount University

Leon Lewis
Appalachian State University

Thomas Lisk
North Carolina State University

James Livingston
Northern Michigan University

Alexander Long
The Johns Hopkins University

Russell Lord
Plymouth State College

Elizabeth Losh
University of California, Irvine

Bernadette Flynn Low
*Community College of
    Baltimore County, Dundalk
    Campus*

Sara Lundquist
University of Toledo

Loretta McBride
*State Technical Institute,
    Memphis*

Janet McCann
Texas A&M University

Joanne McCarthy
Tacoma Community College

Clarence McClanahan
Diablo Valley College

James McCorkle
*Hobart and William Smith
    Colleges*

Andrew Macdonald
Loyola University

Gina Macdonald
Loyola University

Gardner McFall
*The Cooper Union for the
    Advancement of Science and
    Art, New York*

Ron McFarland
University of Idaho

Richard D. McGhee
Kansas State University

Edythe M. McGovern
West Los Angeles College

S. Thomas Mack
*University of South Carolina-
    Aiken*

Edgar V. McKnight, Jr.
Gardner-Webb University

Joseph McLaren
Hofstra University

A. L. McLeod
Rider University

Kevin McNeilly
*Queen's University, Kingston,
    Ontario, Canada
University of Western Ontario,
    Canada*

Mary E. Mahony
*Wayne County Community
    College*

Lois A. Marchino
University of Texas, El Paso

Tony A. Markham
*State University of New York,
    Delhi*

Donald G. Marshall
University of Illinois at Chicago

Kathleen Bonann Marshall
Northwestern University

Laura Martin
Emory University

Paula M. Martin
University of New Orleans

Wayne Martindale
Wheaton College

Thomas Matchie
North Dakota State University

H. A. Maxson
Wesley College

Clark Mayo
*California State University, San
    Bernardino*

Aparajita Mazumder
*University of Illinois at Urbana-
    Champaign*

Laurence W. Mazzeno
Alvernia College

Kenneth W. Meadwell
*University of Winnipeg,
    Manitoba, Canada*

Patrick Meanor
*State University of New York,
    Oneonta*

Muriel Mellown
*North Carolina Central
    University*

Michael J. Meyer
Concordia University Wisconsin

Julia M. Meyers
Duquesne University

Michael R. Meyers
North Carolina State University

Vasa D. Mihailovich
*University of North Carolina—
    Chapel Hill*

Jane Ann Miller
Dartmouth College

Paula M. Miller
Biola University

Timothy C. Miller
Millersville University

Maureen W. Mills
Central Michigan University

Judith N. Mitchell
Rhode Island College

CONTRIBUTING REVIEWERS

Christian H. Moe
Southern Illinois University at Carbondale

Scott E. Moncrieff
Andrews University

Robert A. Morace
Daemen College

Bernard E. Morris
Independent Scholar

Sherry Morton-Mollo
California State University, Fullerton

Charmaine Allmon Mosby
Western Kentucky University

Dean de la Motte
Guilford College

Roark Mulligan
Christopher Newport University

Russell Elliott Murphy
University of Arkansas at Little Rock

Thomas Mussio
University of Michigan

John M. Muste
Ohio State University

Stephen V. Myslinski
Salve Regina University

Susan Nagel
Independent Scholar

D. Gosselin Nakeeb
Pace University

Joseph M. Nassar
Rochester Institute of Technology

Arthur A. Natella, Jr.
Independent Scholar

William Nelles
University of Massachusetts, Dartmouth

Elizabeth Nelson
St. Peter's College

Cynthia Nichols
North Dakota State University

Robert Niemi
St. Michael's College

Emma Coburn Norris
Troy State University

George O'Brien
Georgetown University

Bruce Olsen
Alabama State University

Peter D. Olson
Hillsdale College

Edward F. Palm
Glenville State College

Janet Taylor Palmer
Caldwell Community College

James Panabaker
Queen s University, Kingston, Ontario, Canada

Matthew Parfitt
Boston University

Jay Paul
Christopher Newport University

Pamela Pavliscak
University of North Carolina— Chapel Hill

David Peck
California State University, Long Beach

Ted Pelton
Lakeland College

Thomas Amherst Perry
Texas A&M University, Commerce

Marion Petrillo
Bloomsburg University

Rhonda Pettit
Northern Kentucky University

John R. Pfeiffer
Central Michigan University

Allene Phy-Olsen
Austin Peay State University

Carol Lawson Pippen
Towson University

Scott D. Vander Ploeg
Madisonville Community College

Francis Poole
University of Delaware

Joseph Powell
Central Washington University

Verbie Lovorn Prevost
University of Tennessee at Chattanooga

Jonathan L. Price
California State University, Sacramento

Victoria Price
Lamar University

Norman Prinsky
Augusta State University

Charles Pullen
Queen's University, Kingston, Ontario, Canada

Nicolas Pullin
Loyola University Chicago

Gregory J. Racz
Parsons School of Design

Dean Rader
State University of New York at Binghamton

Philip Raisor
Old Dominion University

Jerrald Ranta
University of Wyoming

Ralph Reckley, Sr.
Morgan State University

Robin Anne Reid
Texas A&M University, Commerce

Rosemary M. Canfield Reisman
Charleston Southern University

Donald Revell
University of Denver

Mark Rich
Independent Scholar

Janine Rider
Mesa State College

Jeanette A. Ritzenthaler
New Hampshire College

Len Roberts
Independent Scholar

Claire Robinson
*Maharishi International
University*

Danny Robinson
Bloomsburg University

Larry Rochelle
*Johnson County Community
College*

Paulette Roeske
College of Lake County

Jill Rollins
*University of New Brunswick,
Quebec, Canada*

Carl Rollyson
*Baruch College, City University
of New York*

Heather Rosario-Sievert
*Hostos Community College,
City University of New York*

Paul Rosefeldt
Delgado Community College

Joseph Rosenblum
*University of North Carolina—
Greensboro*

Robert L. Ross
University of Texas—Austin

Stan Sanvel Rubin
*State University of New York,
College at Brockport*

Nicholas Ruddick
University of Regina

Lynn Sager
Alverno College

Christine F. Sally
University of South Florida

Scott Samuelson
Ricks College

Mark Sanders
College of the Mainland

Alexa L. Sandmann
The University of Toledo

Roy Scheele
Doane College

Phyllis J. Scherle
*Indiana University at
Indianapolis*

Karin Schestokat
Oklahoma State University

Peter A. Schneider
College of Saint Elizabeth

Beverly Schneller
Millersville University

Kathleen Schongar
The May School

Marilyn Schultz
*California State University,
Fullerton*

Jeffrey Schwartz
Greenwich Academy

Daniel M. Scott III
Rhode Island College

James Scruton
Bethel College

Rita M. Scully
Chestnut Hill College

Lisa A. Seale
*University of Wisconsin Center,
Marathon County*

Paul Serralheiro
Dawson College

D. Dean Shackelford
Concord College

Helen Shanley
Independent Scholar

Chenliang Sheng
Northern Kentucky University

Julie Sherrick
St. Bonaventure University

Agnes A. Shields
Chestnut Hill College

Anne Shifrer
Utah State University

R. Baird Shuman
*University of Illinois at Urbana-
Champaign*

Anne W. Sienkewicz
Independent Scholar

Thomas J. Sienkewicz
Monmouth College

Karla Sigel
Eastern Kentucky University

Charles L. P. Silet
Iowa State University

Carl Singleton
Fort Hays State University

Genevieve Slomski
Independent Scholar

Marjorie Smelstor
*University of Wisconsin, Eau
Claire*

David P. Smith
Naval War College

Katherine Snipes
Eastern Washington University

Jean M. Snook
*Memorial University of
Newfoundland*

Valerie C. Snyder
Independent Scholar

Steven P. Sondrup
Brigham Young University

George Soule
Carleton College

Anca Mitroi Sprenger
Brigham Young University

Scott M. Sprenger
Brigham Young University

Brian Stableford
King Alfred's College

Isabel B. Stanley
East Tennessee State University

Virginia Starrett
*California State University,
Fullerton*

CONTRIBUTING REVIEWERS

Thomas J. Steele
Regis University

Karen F. Stein
University of Rhode Island

Eric Sterling
Auburn University Montgomery

Ingo Roland Stoehr
University of Texas—Austin

Stefan Stoenescu
Independent Scholar

Sue Storm
Independent Scholar

Gerald H. Strauss
Bloomsburg University

Elisabeth Strenger
Brandeis University

Michael Stuprich
Ithaca College

Ernest Suarez
Catholic University of America

Thomas F. Suggs
University of Kentucky

Alvin Sullivan
Southern Illinois University—Edwardsville

James Sullivan
California State University, Los Angeles

David Sundstrand
Citrus College

Charlene E. Suscavage
University of Southern Maine

Catherine Swanson
Independent Scholar

Roy Arthur Swanson
University of Wisconsin, Milwaukee

James Tackach
Roger Williams University

Marie Gerenday Tamas
Rutgers University

James T. F. Tanner
University of North Texas

Judith K. Taylor
Northern Kentucky University

Lorenzo Thomas
University of Houston-Downtown

Betty Taylor-Thompson
Texas Southern University

Jonathan L. Thorndike
Rocky Mountain College

John H. Timmerman
Calvin College

Christine D. Tomei
Allegheny College

Tony Trigilio
Northeastern University

Veta Smith Tucker
Grand Valley State University

Richard Tuerk
Texas A&M University-Commerce

Lewis Turco
State University of New York, College at Oswego

Linda Turzynski
Rutgers University

Von E. Underwood
Cameron University

Julia A. Urla
University of Michigan

J. K. Van Dover
Lincoln University

J. Don Vann
University of North Texas

Dennis Vannatta
University of Arkansas, Little Rock

Paul Varner
Oklahoma Christian University

Martha Modena Vertreace-Doody
Kennedy-King College

Mark Vogel
Appalachian State University

Albert Wachtel
Pitzer College

Steven C. Walker
Brigham Young University

Sue B. Walker
University of South Alabama

Jaquelyn W. Walsh
McNeese State University

Amy R. Walter
Independent Scholar

Kathryn A. Walterscheid
University of Missouri-St. Louis

Qun Wang
California State University, Monterey Bay

Gladys J. Washington
Texas Southern University

Dennis L. Weeks
University of Great Falls

Ron Welburn
Western Connecticut State University

Tiffany Werth
Portland State University

Lana J. White
West Texas A&M University

Julia Whitsitt
Texas Tech University

Barbara Wiedemann
Auburn University at Montgomery

Albert E. Wilhelm
Tennessee Technological University

Thomas Willard
University of Arizona

Judith Barton Williamson
Sauk Valley Community College

John Wilson
Independent Scholar

Sharon K. Wilson
Fort Hays State University

Rosemary Gates Winslow
The Catholic University of America

Michael Witkoski
University of South Carolina

Anna M. Wittmann
Medicine Hat College, Alberta, Canada

Cynthia Wong
Western Illinois University

Qingyun Wu
California State University, Los Angeles

Jennifer L. Wyatt
Civic Memorial High School

Scott Yarbrough
Charleston Southern University

Joanna Yin
University of Hawaii

Howard Young
Pomona College

John Young
Independent Scholar

Harry Zohn
Brandeis University

MASTERPLOTS II

POETRY SERIES
REVISED EDITION

"A"

Author: Louis Zukofsky (1904-1978)
Type of poem: Poetic sequence
First published: 1932-1978; complete poem collected in *"A,"* 1978

The Poem

"A" is one of the longest poems in the English language, numbering more than eight hundred pages. It was written over a forty-six-year period (1928-1974) and is divided into twenty-four sections (referred to as movements) that differ widely in length, from the single page of "A"-16 to the 242 pages of "A"-24. *"A"* is generally considered to be the greatest poetic achievement of the twentieth century Objectivist school of poetry, which was led by Louis Zukofsky and included George Oppen, Lorine Niedecker, Charles Reznikoff, and Carl Rakosi.

The title *"A"* is significant in that it is not only the first word of the poem but also an indefinite pronoun and as such is a response to Zukofsky's earlier poem, "Poem beginning 'the'" (1926). The twenty-four movements of *"A"* suggest the twenty-four hours of the day—that is, the solar day representing the totality of human civilization. The *a* of *"A"* is also the first step in the poet's attempt to comment upon this process literally from *a* to *z* (the *z* of Zukofsky, that is).

"A"-1 begins with a description of a performance of Johann Sebastian Bach's *St. Matthew's Passion* at Carnegie Hall in New York City on April 5, 1928. The dichotomy between intellect and emotions is examined and is continued in "A"-2, in which the narrator Zukofsky engages in a debate with the eponymous character Kay. The death of one Ricky (in reality, the suicide of Ricky, the brother of Whittaker Chambers, who was one of Zukofsky's fellow students at Columbia University) is mentioned in "A"-3. "A"-4 is concerned with origins, and specific references are made to the poetry of Yehoash (the pen name of the Yiddish poet Solomon Bloomgarden). The dichotomy between intellect and emotions that was first seen in "A"-1 and "A"-2 is rehashed in "A"-5. "A"-6 constitutes a reexamination of "A" 1-5, which the reader now discovers to have been only a preamble to the central aesthetic question posed by the poet: *"Can/ The design/ Of the fugue/ Be transferred/ To poetry?"* (page 38).

"A"-7 and "A"-8 concern themselves with the worsening conditions of the Great Depression and constitute Zukofsky's effort to examine the roles of the individual and society within the contexts of three intellectual constructs that strive for universal validity and will only be fully revealed in "A"-12: Marxist economics, Einsteinian physics, and Pythagorean music theory. The interweaving of these and other ideas is a poetic approximation of the interplay of musical lines in the fugue. "A"-8 functions, then (as do "A"-12 and "A"-24), as a summation and amalgamation of all that has transpired so far in the poem.

"A"-9 provides lyrical relief from the literary pyrotechnics of the preceding movement and is the poet's paean to memory, the recollection of love as well as musical themes. In "A"-9, music is equated with action, action being remembrance, a necessary prerequisite, in Zukofsky's mind, for the existence of love. By the time of "A"-10, the Great Depression is over, and the Nazi occupation of Paris and the regime of Marshall Pétain are being examined.

"A"-11 and "A"-12 both examine the tightly knit and loving relationships among the members of Zukofsky's immediate family, including the poet, his composer wife Celia, and their violinist son Paul. The 135 pages of "A"-12 are longer than the previous eleven sections of the poem combined. In "A"-12, the specific nature of the relationships or harmony among the members of the Zukofsky family is examined in universalizing contexts symbolized by the many references to the works of those who strove for the totality or "universal harmony" of artistic creation, such as Pythagoras, J. S. Bach, Arnold Schönberg, William Shakespeare, James Joyce, and Johann Wolfgang von Goethe.

"A"-13 and "A"-14 are movements that signal Zukofsky's retreat into a very personal and hermeneutic poetic world. "A"-13 is an attenuated description of a walking tour of New York City taken by the poet and his son. In "A"-14, which mostly consists of three-line stanzas with two or three words per stanza, Zukofsky limits his syntax so severely that the words become direct images rather than metaphors of the objects and ideas they are trying to describe. "A"-15, "A"-16, and "A"-17 are concerned with Zukofsky's musings on history and his appropriation of the literary montage techniques utilized by William Carlos Williams in *Paterson* (1946-1958). "A"-15 contains an English approximation of the Hebrew of the Book of Job and describes the tragic events of the early 1960's: the assassination of President Kennedy, the Bay of Pigs fiasco, and the deepening American involvement in the Vietnam War. "A"-17 includes a chronology of the writing of *"A"* and the rest of Zukofsky's canon, as well as an extended tribute to the poetry of Williams.

"A"-18 and "A"-19 provide an interesting contrast. The former movement concerns itself with the theme of societal decline. Zukofsky makes additional references to the Vietnam War as well as to Edward Gibbon's *The History of the Decline and Fall of the Roman Empire* (1776-1788) and works by Henry Brooks Adams, including *Degradation of Democratic Dogma* (1919) and *The Education of Henry Adams* (1907). "A"-19, however, is concerned with renewal—specifically, Paul Zukofsky's very promising career as a concert violinist, which is given impetus by his participation in the Paganini Violin Competition, held in Italy. Paul Zukofsky's career as one of the foremost performers of avant-garde music forms the topic of "A"-20.

"A"-21 is Zukofsky's idiosyncratic English translation of Plautus's Latin play *Rudens*. The play within the poem is indicative of Zukofsky's efforts at translation (particularly the poetry of Catullus) and is somewhat analogous to the literary influence of Shakespeare, a lifelong infatuation for Zukofsky. *Rudens* is a recognition comedy, set outdoors for the most part, which contains a storm scene; as such, it is reminiscent of Shakespeare's play *The Tempest* (1611). "A"-21 is connected to the rest of the poem not thematically but as a testimony to the literary work in which Zukofsky was engaged and as a symbol of the past as present and the permanence of art as opposed to the vagaries of history.

"A"-22 and "A"-23 are perhaps the most densely textured, difficult to comprehend, and personal sections of the poem. They constitute Zukofsky's attempt to resolve the many themes of the poem, to seek the unity and totality of human existence. "A"-22 and "A"-23 point toward the resolution of Zukofsky's aesthetic dilemma in "A"-24 and also make oblique references to his final poetic work, *80 Flowers* (1978). Zukofsky's poem, therefore, progresses from poem as music (music in both the literal and the Pythagorean sense) to a resolution of the "music" of humanity with that of nature.

"A"-24 is a summa of Zukofsky's entire poetic career. Here the "music" of Zukofsky's poetry leaves the abstract Pythagorean realm and becomes literal music. The implied counterpoint of the earlier sections of the poem becomes actual musical counterpoint. "A"-24 also reveals how inextricably linked were Zukofsky's work and family life; this section is and is not a work of Zukofsky's. As a birthday present, Celia Zukofsky gave her husband a work entitled "L. Z. Masque," which became "A"-24. This work consists of four different texts by Louis Zukofsky that are set to selections from George Frideric Handel's *Pièces pour le clavecin*. The result is a five-part "score" in which music (Handel's pieces), thought (Zukofsky's book of essays entitled *Prepositions*), drama (Zukofsky's play, *Arise, Arise*), story (the poet's short story "It was"), and poetry (excerpts from earlier sections of "A") are simultaneously presented. The gift of "L. Z. Masque" delighted the poet, who realized that it contained the solution to the resolution of his lifetime's work.

Forms and Devices

"A"-24 exhibits a dazzling display of poetic forms and devices, many of which are derived from musical procedures. Leitmotifs—that is, short recurring phrases—occur throughout the poem. "A"-8, "A"-12, and "A"-24 are long movements in which poetic approximations of the musical fugue are attempted. One of Zukofsky's common "fugue" themes is the use of Bach's name as an acrostic. Bach's name was used by the composer himself and many others as the theme of musical fugues (in German musical notation, B-A-C-H equals the notes B flat-A-C-B natural). Zukofsky uses Bach's name in "A"-12, "A"-23, and several other movements of the poem as an acrostic representing the words *B*lest-*A*rdent-*C*elia-*H*appy. This acrostic is later transformed into a representation of *B*aruch Spinoza (Hebrew *baruch*, blessed)-*A*ristotle-*C*elia-*H*ohenheim (the last name of the medieval scientist Paracelsus).

The sonnet is a favorite poetic form of Zukofsky's. "A"-7 is very close to being a crown of sonnets, in which seven sonnets are linked; the last line of each of the first six sonnets becomes the first line of the next sonnet, and the last line of the seventh sonnet repeats the first line of the first sonnet. "A"-9 is a double canzone, two sets of five sonnets, in which the last word of each line of the first set is used as the last word of each corresponding line of the second set. "A"-9 also employs the standard musical canzona rhythm of long, short, short.

Unusual forms and devices abound in "A." "A"-10 approximates a medieval troped

Mass, in which words and music were added to the text and music of the original Gregorian chants of the Mass. Zukofsky calls "A"-13 a partita (a baroque musical suite, a collection of instrumental dance pieces in varying moods and tempi), and he divides this movement into five subsections that in meter and spirit are roughly analogous to the allemande, courante, sarabande, gigue, and chaconne of the baroque dance suite. "A"-19 consists of two-word lines. This section is concerned with Paul Zukofsky's appearance in the Paganini Violin Competition in Italy; therefore, the two-word lines are meant to represent the up and down motions of bowing the violin. "A"-20 makes references to Paul Zukofsky's interest in modern music, particularly dodecaphonic (or twelve-tone) music. This movement consists of four twelve-line stanzas with introduction and epilogue and is meant to approximate the variations on the tone row of a dodecaphonic musical composition.

"A"-22 and "A"-23 are similarly structured, each consisting of one thousand lines in which twenty five-line stanzas (with five words per line) precede and follow a main body of eight hundred lines. Both movements begin with the word "an," continuing the precedent of the "An" songs found in "A"-14 and displaying once again the wealth of meaning Zukofsky found in simple words.

Themes and Meanings

It is not surprising that the themes and meanings of a work as long and complicated as *"A"* cannot be distilled into a neat package. The meaning of *"A"* is really the meaning of life itself, whether or not there is a unity or unifying force by means of which the entire universe may be understood or into which it may be subsumed. The thematic structure of *"A"* is therefore correspondingly dense. A cursory (and very incomplete) list of the thematic material of *"A"* includes the music and life of J. S. Bach, birds, flowers, horses, labor, love, eyes (both the subjective "I" and the objective seeing "eye"), Zukofsky's family, Spinoza, Aristotle, Paracelsus, Pythagoras, Karl Marx, leaves, light, and Shakespeare.

The creation of the twenty-four movements of *"A"* was designed by Zukofsky to occupy a lifetime of work and to be a commentary on the lifetime that was being occupied by the process of creating the poem. Zukofsky's fascination with the linguistic possibilities of small and seemingly insignificant words such as pronouns is an attempt to extrapolate the universal from the microcosmic or the individual, and is influenced by the *Cantos* of Ezra Pound (1917-1970) and James Joyce's *Ulysses* (1922). The Pythagorean and Boethian concept of the harmony of the spheres (the tripartite categorization of actual musical harmony, the "harmony" among individual human beings, and the cosmic "harmony" linking everything in the universe) is omnipresent in *"A."* By utilizing an extremely dense structure of themes or leitmotifs, Zukofsky presents analogues of universal harmony in his examinations of himself (as poet attempting to find an individual poetic voice) and of his relationships with his wife and son.

Also present throughout the poem is the tension arising from the dichotomy between historical determinism and the contingent nature of art. The indefinite articles "a" and "an," therefore, seem to represent the unlimited possibilities of art, as opposed to the definite article "the," which symbolizes the eschatology of historical forces represented by Marxist thinking and Judeo-Christian theology, both of which Zukofsky ultimately rejected.

History and art become somewhat reconciled for Zukofsky in *"A"* in that both are acts of remembrance. The historian "remembers" events that have already transpired while the artist seeks the remembrance of the eternal verities implicit in the autonomous work of art. Memory, the human capacity for the self-understanding of recurring (or even contingent) patterns of existence, found its analogue not only in the casual repetitions of the poetic refrain but also in the more organic type of repetition found in musical forms. The evolutionary "musicalization" of *"A,"* from the report of a musical performance in "A"-1 to the actual notated musical score of "A"-24, is a process whereby Zukofsky equates music with the human (and humane) capacity for remembrance.

At the end of *"A,"* Zukofsky has found no ultimate resolution or single key to the understanding of the interconnectivity of the individual with his fellow humans, of humankind with nature, or of the present with the past and future. Unlike the similarly grandiose *Cantos* of Pound, however, which deal with similar ideas and end on a note of defeat, Zukofsky's *"A"* is triumphant, life-affirming, and open-ended, implying poetic and human possibilities left to be examined. Zukofsky's conclusion is that there is neither a hermeneutic key to understanding existence nor a grand Hegelian synthesis of the disparate elements of the cosmos. There remains, however, the universal "fugue" in which each voice sounds its music simultaneously. Understanding the individual life, the nature of art, the history of humankind, or the cosmos will always be, in Zukofskian terms, a close and objective examination of the particularities of existence as they appear before the poet's eye.

William Grim

THE ACHE OF MARRIAGE

Author: Denise Levertov (1923-1997)
Type of poem: Lyric
First published: 1962; collected in *O Taste and See: New Poems*, 1964

The Poem

"The Ache of Marriage" is part of a Denise Levertov collection entitled *O Taste and See: New Poems*. In the title poem and others in the collection, Levertov moves outward from the sensual and immediate to the wider implications of actions or concepts. The poems are filled with rich physical detail, which the poet uses in this particular poem to present the essential qualities of a marriage. Levertov had written about marriage in earlier poems such as "The Marriage, I" and "The Marriage, II" (in her 1958 and 1960 collections), but those love poems are somewhat more conventional and romantic than her work in *O Taste and See*. In this collection she achieves a new sense of immediacy, coupling personal experience with myth. These qualities are evident in such poems as "Abel's Bride" and "Divorcing" as well as in "The Ache of Marriage." In *O Taste and See* Levertov seems to have found her personal poetic voice.

"The Ache of Marriage" is a short poem in free verse, its thirteen lines divided into irregular stanzas of one, three, three, three, and two lines. The title, which is repeated as the first line, establishes the essential conflict and dilemma of the poem: the yearning for a total communion within marriage that is probably not attainable. The poem uses the first-person-plural point of view, suggesting that both the man and the woman are searching for joy but are finding that joy tempered with sadness. As is true in most lyric poetry, there is no noticeable distinction made between the author and the speaker (part of the "we").

The poem employs a series of sensual images to convey both joy and pain: thigh, tongue, throbbing teeth, the belly of the leviathan, and the ark. The images progress from the highly personal to the archetypal and biblical—moving from the familiar and sensual to the universal. The speakers (the partners in the marriage) are expressing the aching quality of a marriage through the senses rather than through spoken words of love.

The last image of the poem is the ark, with the two marriage partners aboard—safe and removed from the outside world yet not happy. The phrase "The ache of it" echoes the first line and concludes the poem, leaving both the speakers and the reader unsatisfied with the knowledge that marriage continues to embody both joy and pain and probably does not allow total communion.

Forms and Devices

Born and reared in England, Levertov moved to the United States after World War II as the bride of an American soldier. Her work was much influenced by American poets, especially William Carlos Williams, Robert Creeley, and Robert Duncan.

Added to her traditional British poetic experience, the American influence encouraged Levertov to adopt innovative forms.

The poetic devices most important to the poem in achieving both immediacy and voice are the seemingly unstructured free-verse form, the heavy use of sensual imagery, and the use of biblical myth. Levertov used what could be called organic form in "The Ache of Marriage." As she has indicated in interviews and writing, she lets the content or subject matter of a poem determine its form. Free verse, with its irregular meter and irregular line and stanza lengths, gives her the freedom of prose combined with the intensity of poetry. The term "projective verse" could also be applied to her work in this poem. Projective verse regards meter and form as artificial constraints and seeks to "project" a voice through the content and the pauses for breath that determine the line. The result in this case is a poem of fragmented prose poetry that expresses, through its lack of strict form, the quality of a marriage as being both a yearning for and an inability to communicate fully. Both partners are reaching out but are almost clumsily unable to reach each other.

Since the poem is composed primarily of a series of images linked by abstract concepts, the reader can perhaps best understand the poem by looking at the images separately. The first group of images includes thigh, tongue, and teeth—the last one seeming incongruous until it is examined in context. Thigh and tongue are clearly sensual, suggesting lovemaking by the marital partners. The use of the words "beloved" and "throbs" also contributes to this sense of physical love. However, the "throbs" goes on to include "in the teeth." One clearly sees an added image here—a toothache.

These images are followed by a stanza of abstract statement expressing the couple's yearning for commitment. Then the following stanza uses one major image—the leviathan and "we in its belly." Adding "belly" to the image clarifies the fact that this is a biblical allusion, referring to the story of Jonah, who was swallowed by a sea monster, or leviathan (whale). In this image the couple is depicted as having been swallowed by something they welcome yet cannot escape. They are still searching for some kind of "joy, some joy not to be known outside of it."

The final image in the cluster is the ark, again a biblical allusion, suggesting qualities similar to the belly of the whale: The ark is a safe haven for the couple ("two by two"), yet no escape is in sight. The cluster of images Levertov uses in this poem work together to form a progression from the personal to the universal. By incorporating the biblical images, the poet moves the concerns of marriage into the mystical and spiritual realm. The biblical images also add a quality of timelessness. Myth in literature makes concrete and particular a perception of human beings or human institutions. In this case, the "ache" of the institution of marriage is made concrete.

Themes and Meanings

The poem's two primary themes are expressed immediately: the simultaneous longing for total communication and the knowledge that such communication is probably not possible. Love and marriage have been subjects for poets throughout the centuries, so Levertov is certainly not tackling a new subject. Yet she breaks from tradition by presenting her themes from both a twentieth century and a timeless perspective.

Levertov is often discussed as a feminist poet, but her reflections on love, marriage, and even divorce are never occasions for "male bashing." Rather, she suggests that both men and women have difficulty in functioning wholly either within or outside marriage. In "Divorcing" she writes, "We were Siamese twins,/ Our blood's not sure/ it can circulate,/ now we are cut apart." In the poems in *O Taste and See* she presents a realistic rather than a romantic picture of love and marriage. Twentieth century works (with the exception of romance novels) do not romanticize love and marriage with a "happily ever after" conclusion. They are honest in their sometimes puzzling conclusions. Levertov, like other modern poets, leaves the reader feeling both hope and despair.

Betty Alldredge

ACQUAINTED WITH THE NIGHT

Author: Robert Frost (1874-1963)
Type of poem: Sonnet
First published: 1928, in *West-Running Brook*

The Poem

Robert Frost's "Acquainted with the Night" is a sonnet written in terza rima, a rhyme scheme that generally suggests a continual progression. The poem examines the poet's relationship with himself and with society. Consisting of seven complete sentences, each beginning with the words "I have," the poem relates Frost's journey from the "furthest city light" into the dark night.

The first stanza introduces the poet's relationship with the night as an acquaintance. The idea that the poet is "one acquainted with the night" acts as the glue holding the poem together. Indeed, the first and last lines are identical, emphasizing the poet's assertion that he is acquainted with the night, and between these lines Frost clarifies the nature of the relationship. The first stanza also implies that his acquaintance with the night is a journey. He has both "walked out in rain—and back in rain" and has "outwalked the furthest city light." His journey into the night and into the rain is also, for the poet, a journey to self-knowledge.

In the second stanza, the poet looks out at society—"down the saddest city lane"— as he leaves the confines of the city and, thus, society. Because he covets the time alone that he will have outside the city, he passes "the watchman on his beat," but he makes no eye contact with the watchman, nor does he desire any contact with him. The need for solitude is so strong that he wants nothing to detain him. In effect, he is ignoring society in his quest for the night, for solitude.

It becomes clear in the third and fourth stanzas that the poet feels that just as he ignores society, so society ignores him. In line seven, he says that he had "stood still and stopped the sound of feet," in effect pausing on his journey and becoming a silent observer of the sounds and activities of the city. In his silence he remains outside society, neither taking part in nor being noticed by the world around him.

He then hears "an interrupted cry . . . from another street" but has no knowledge of why the cry is sounded or what it means. By becoming a silent observer on the outskirts of the city, he is no longer a part of the rhythms of city life, nor are they a part of him. Life continues, and he knows that the cry is not intended to "call [him] back or say good-by." He willingly leaves society behind in order to seek solitude. Then, in the distance, he sees "at an unearthly height/ One luminary clock against the sky." It is the "luminary clock" that provides the only light on the poet's trip out of the city since he passed beyond the city light at the beginning of his journey.

In the final couplet, the poet states that the clock "proclaimed the time was neither wrong nor right." The clock, which may be a symbol of the moon or of time itself, gives a sense of the ambiguity of time in the poet's existence—that it is neither wrong nor right. Nevertheless, in the final line of the poem, the poet confidently restates his original assertion—"I have been one acquainted with the night." Although he feels isolated to some extent from both himself and from society, and though he feels a sense of uncertainty about time and life, he at least retains some sense of who he is: someone who is still on a journey to know himself better.

Forms and Devices

Frost uses symbolism and imagery to set a mood of not just isolation and loneliness but also quiet and solitude. Themes such as rain, night, unearthly height, and sad city lanes evoke these feelings of both isolation and quietness. Yet, as Frost represents these images, they also seem to promote a feeling of reflection in his escape from the city to the quiet darkness of the surrounding countryside.

The "luminary clock" is symbolic of time, either natural or as constructed by humanity. This clock, which the poet sees at "an unearthly height," can be interpreted as either the moon or a clock in a tower situated high above the city. Yet whether the clock is natural or human-made, it has much to say to the poet as he observes it from the dark outskirts of town. When he says that the clock "proclaimed the time was neither wrong nor right," he is given pause to consider his life and all its questions and possibilities. Characterizing the time as not right but also not wrong suggests a certain relativity or ambiguity concerning time and life.

Frost also uses the journey motif in this poem. When he speaks of going into the rain and coming back again, he suggests that he is on a journey, one that is not yet complete. In this poem, the night represents his destination—the poet's own inner life, possibly self-knowledge. The poet, then, feels at least partially alienated from himself in much the same way that the night promotes a feeling of alienation from other people.

Because Frost characterizes the night—his own inner life—as something he does not fully know, something he is only acquainted with, the reader knows that the journey is still incomplete; full self-knowledge has not yet been achieved. The poet's journey takes him beyond the "city light" or society itself. Because he presents himself as a silent observer of the sounds and activities of the city, it is also evident that the poet feels alienated from society as well as from himself. The poet does not seem to be looking for a better understanding of society, though, since he refuses to make eye contact with the city watchman. He is more concerned with going out into the night, to learn more about himself. Yet, he does not seem to be in a hurry; the luminary clock itself tells him that the time for self-knowledge is "neither wrong nor right." The journey in this poem ends as it begins, with the poet's statement that he "is one acquainted with the night." The poet seems content to continue the journey, perhaps sensing that it is a journey that will continue throughout his life.

Another device that Frost uses in this poem is a conversational tone. The sonnet is simple and direct, giving the reader a sense of identification with the poet. Frost speaks directly to the reader, relating his thoughts and feelings in straightforward, easily understood diction. Only in his use of symbols and images does he attach unusual meanings and associations to the words he chooses to convey his ideas.

Themes and Meanings

In "Acquainted with the Night" Frost embraces the night as an entity with which he is familiar. The phrase "acquainted with the night" itself is an unusual one in that an acquaintance is usually not considered a close friend but someone or something that is known only superficially. However, in this poem, the tone is one of quiet acceptance of the night as, if not an intimate friend, at least a familiar aspect of his life, and thus it appears that the night symbolizes more than just isolation or loneliness. It represents the poet's inner self as well, a self with which he is acquainted but does not know well. The poet's journey into the night, then, can be seen as ongoing and continual, progressing to a more complete self-knowledge.

If the poet does not know himself, then his acquaintance with society, as symbolized by the city light, is even more tenuous. He listens to the sounds of the city but is not a part of it; he sees the city watchman but avoids any contact with him.

Frost's poetry often contains darkness, whether it be dark woods or the dark night. For Frost, the darkness evokes a sense of quiet and calm. Embracing the solitude and isolation of night and its accompanying darkness, the poet illustrates that for him the world is a dichotomy. There is the dark and quiet world beyond the "furthest city light," and there is the city itself, with its watchman, its clock, and its responsibilities. The poet, seeking self-knowledge and the solitude he obviously treasures, journeys out into the night, where he is sure to find these things. While for many people the night and its accompanying sense of isolation is a melancholy and lonely time, Frost welcomes it as a time of introspection, willingly journeying out to meet it.

Furthermore, Frost knows that he has a foot in both worlds—in his own inner, personal world, symbolized by the night, and in society, symbolized by the city lights and the clock—as do most poets. Knowing the importance of being alone in order to produce his poetry, he also knows he must return to society with its time constraints and its responsibilities. He instinctively understands that he must obtain a balance between these two opposing worlds. As a poet, these temporal considerations detract from his creativity, but as a productive member of society, he knows he must function within the confines of that society. Frost ends his poem in the only possible way, by reiterating his initial assertion about himself: "I have been one acquainted with the night."

Kimberley H. Kidd

ADAM'S CURSE

Author: William Butler Yeats (1865-1939)
Type of poem: Lyric
First published: 1902; collected in *In the Seven Woods*, 1903

The Poem

William Butler Yeats's "Adam's Curse," written in six uneven stanzas of iambic pentameter rhymed couplets, recounts one of the poet's meetings with Maud Gonne, a free-spirited Irish patriot and sometime actress who was just returning from an extended trip abroad. Maud's sister, the "beautiful mild" Kathleen, was the third person present, but the personal situation is mildly altered in the poem. Maud, identified only as "you," is said to be the younger woman's "close friend" rather than sister.

After setting the scene—three friends at twilight on a late summer evening—the poem turns to a conversation that took place between the poet and his beloved's beautiful young woman friend. He remembers observing that although the writing of poetry is more difficult than physical work, the product of a poet's labors has to appear effortless. The friend, gentle of voice, with the kind of mild, seemingly natural attractiveness destined to break men's hearts, responded that the beauty of women is also the product of studied effort. That observation led the poet to remark that all human accomplishments since the biblical fall of Adam have entailed hard labor. Even love was once regarded as an exalted experience that required the gathering of precedents from the old poetic world of chivalry. It was treated as a profound matter, to be studied and approached reverently. Now, like the writing of poetry, it is considered idle.

Maud, referred to only as "you," remained silent, and the word "love" silenced the speakers. The three watched the vestiges of daylight fade. The moon, apparently hollowed out by time's tide breaking in waves of days and years over the earth, drew the poet's special attention.

In that silence, he later confessed, he thought "you" beautiful. He wanted to love Maud chivalrously. Once, loving her had seemed joyous and fortunate, but now, like the hollow moon, she and he were exhausted by love.

Forms and Devices

There is a sense that "Adam's Curse," like one of William Wordsworth's meditative poems—"Tintern Abbey," for example—resulted from the contemplation in tranquility of powerful emotions that accompanied an important but seemingly trivial event. That sense places the poem in a Romantic tradition Wordsworth made explicit in his preface to the second edition (1800) of *Lyrical Ballads*, but with a crucial difference.

Wordsworth and his fellow poet Samuel Taylor Coleridge first published *Lyrical Ballads* in 1798, a little more than a hundred years before Yeats's poem. The nineteenth century was about to begin, and English Romanticism was on the rise, replacing the comparatively stiff neoclassicism of the previous century. Wordsworth and Coleridge were attempting to introduce deep feeling and natural expression into poetry because the work of the neoclassical poets seemed to them too cerebral and formal. At the start of the twentieth century, Yeats was troubled that apparently natural emotions and appearances are illusory.

Yeats's conversational tone appears relaxed. However, as his seemingly easy observation that poetry—unless it seems "a moment's thought,/ Our stitching and unstitching has been naught"—reveals by its technical perfection, studied labor is required in order to produce the appearance of ease, in the Renaissance called *sprezzatura*.

There is in "Adam's Curse" a subtle invocation of courtly Renaissance sonnet-making and challenges to it. The overriding issue in William Shakespeare's *Sonnets* (1609) is a love triangle. The sonnet writer's female lover seduces his young male friend. In Yeats's poem, there is no such deception, but the poet, though in love with the older woman, is clearly attracted to the younger woman's voice and beauty. The importance of her presence between two mature lovers is underscored by his anticipation of the effect she will have on other men. Obviously, there was some such effect on the person who predicts the future.

There is also in the poem the echo of a specific Shakespearean sonnet, the seventy-third. In that sonnet, as in "Adam's Curse," a season (in Shakespeare's case, autumn) and day are ending, but once again with crucial differences. The poet of the sonnet contemplates the positive intensifying effect that the coming end of his life has on his friend. His love has become "more strong,/ To love that well which [he] must leave ere long." The powerful emotion that informs Yeats's poem is negative, the overwhelming waning, the hollowing-out, of romantic lovers.

Like romantic love, the couplets and stanzas of iambic pentameter in the poem are throwbacks. As modernism emerged from late Victorian Romanticism, those technical features of poetry were being displaced by free verse, which had been invented by the American poet Walt Whitman in the mid-nineteenth century. As if to acknowledge that formal verse is of a piece with the fading season, day, and love itself in "Adam's Curse," Yeats's couplets are diminished in effect, sometimes because they are parts of separate sentences. At other times, a thought flows through a rhyme to the next line, hiding both the rhyme and meter by not pausing as the line ends. Some rhymes are kept intentionally inexact, as slant or off-rhymes: "strove"-"love," "grown"-"moon." And because of the odd number of lines in some stanzas, three of the couplets are separated from one another by the gaps of thought between stanzas. The stanzas are not merely of different lengths, but in addition the second stanza ends partway through a line, and the third begins with the completion of that line, producing both a hemistiched line and hemistiched stanzas. In short, though the poem uses fixed forms of verse, it so uses them as to reinforce its suggestion that things are falling apart. Not only is the season ending; not only is day ending; but the forms of verse themselves are being diminished just like love.

The sense of loss, the close of something important, begins with the title of the poem, "Adam's Curse," invoking the loss of Eden and the condemnation of humanity to hard labor for all gains. This use of an earlier story or myth to enhance the reader's understanding of a contemporary situation anticipates what Yeats's fellow Irishman and novelist James Joyce would do in patterning the experiences of the people of *Ulysses* (1922) after those of the ancient Greek hero Odysseus. The "mythical method," the poet and critic T. S. Eliot called it in *"Ulysses*, Order, and Myth" (1923), providing posterity with a useful critical term while mistakenly crediting Joyce with the invention of a technique that has been used for millennia. This much in any case is clear about Yeats's poem: In its awareness of the craft that supports apparent natural-ness, in its challenge to formal verse, even as it uses it, in its allusive approach to con-tent, and in its clear-eyed disillusionment with romantic love, "Adam's Curse" is modernist, written as though it were near the dawn of the period.

Themes and Meanings

In form, style, material content, and meaning, "Adam's Curse" is about the end of a certain set of values and the need for another. Both temporal ends in the poem, the conclusion of summer and the close of the day, mark the waning of something else, the poet's chivalric love of "you" (Maud) that remains unspecified until the last stanza. Almost twenty years before the disillusionment of World War I set in, Yeats was disillusioned. Love, which the high Victorian poet Mathew Arnold in "Dover Beach" (1867) thought a safe harbor for those troubled by religious doubt and disillu-sionment with what were once seen as promising industrial and political revolutions, strikes Yeats as empty, as hollow as the rest.

For a dozen years, Yeats had been cherishing an unrequited romantic love of Maud, who steadfastly rejected his proposals, but as the twentieth century dawned he was growing more realistic. His poetry, originally characterized by dreamy ideals, mysti-cism, and a heroic Celtic past, replete with great kings, legendary leaders, deep loves, tragic events, and fairies, was becoming specific in its references and more earthy in its vision. Though he went on proposing marriage to Maud and even her daughter in the years that followed, in "Adam's Curse" Yeats reveals an awareness that what he dreamt of would not materialize. The poem sets this awareness in the poet's recollec-tion of a discussion during their meeting of what it takes to produce fine poetry and beauty in this fallen world.

Humans, whether by God or simply as a result of the natural state of things, are con-demned to labor "like an old pauper, in all kinds of weather." Those in control of capi-tal, those in control of what officially passes for knowledge, and those who claim to have insight into the spiritual issues of human life denigrate poets, the real seekers af-ter truth and creators of beauty in this fallen world. In accordance with their awareness of the condition of the world in which they find themselves, Yeats implicitly asserts, poets must mute their instruments and present images that accord with the nature of what they perceive, in language that fits their perceptions. Yet, still, the accurate pre-sentation of that world in words and with images that bring it vividly before the senses, no matter how disillusioning, is beautiful, and the recognition of the painful truths of the human condition is liberating and exhilarating.

Albert Wachtel

ADONAIS

Author: Percy Bysshe Shelley (1792-1822)
Type of poem: Elegy
First published: 1821

The Poem

   Adonais is a long poem, running 495 lines in fifty-five Spenserian stanzas. As the poet states in his subtitle, it is "An Elegy on the Death of John Keats." The younger Keats, an acquaintance and fellow Romantic poet whom Percy Bysshe Shelley had invited to visit with him in Italy, had been seeking warmer climes to relieve the tuberculosis which eventually took his life, at the age of twenty-six, on February 23, 1821.

   The poem's title requires the reader to pause and reflect momentarily on Shelley's highly conscious design. In keeping with the conventions of the pastoral elegy, Adonais is the fictive name which Shelley assigns John Keats. Readers familiar with Greek mythology will certainly hear an echo of Adonis in the name; he was the decidedly handsome youth whom the goddess Venus loved and who also died a tragic and early death, being killed by a wild boar. One familiar with Judaic traditions might also hear Adonai in Shelley's choice of name. Adonai in Hebrew means God or Lord, and is a substitute for the ineffable name which even the name Jehovah only betokens.

   If it seems presumptuous for Shelley to hint at a godlike quality to the young man whose death he is mourning, it is easier to see an intended symmetry: As a poet, Keats shares a spiritual identity both with a mortal beloved of the gods and with the godhead itself, and he is the inheritor of both the classical and biblical traditions that compose Western culture—an heir, that is, of the ages.

   The poem opens boldly with a single, undeniable fact and the poet's response to it: "I weep for Adonais—he is dead!" Stanzas 2 through 35 will present a parade of mourners who, with the poet, have come to grieve. The poet pitifully urges the fallen Adonais's mother, Urania, to awaken to lead the mourners at his bier; in her, Shelley combines both the Venus of the Adonis myth (Venus Urania is one of the goddess's titles) and Urania, the muse of astronomy. That latter may seem an odd choice unless one knows that Adonais's ultimate destiny is an eternity represented by the stars.

   For the moment, however, there is only despair, and readers are urged to "weep for Adonais—he is dead!" Stanza 9 brings as leaders of the solemn procession the dead shepherd/poet's "flocks"—his dreams and inspirations. Continuing through stanza 13, there is a cataloging of the personifications of all those thoughts and feelings, attitudes and skills, which made his genius, as they view the corpse in shocked disbelief. Awakened by the grieving poet as well as by the figure Misery, Urania appears in stanza 22, and the poet repeats his lament: "He will awake no more, oh, never more!" In the wild distraction of her grief she urges her son to arise, to awake; her pleas are in vain.

   Stanzas 30 through 34 bring a select group of human mourners. The "Pilgrim of

Eternity," to anyone familiar with Byron's first great work, *Childe Harold's Pilgrim-age* (1812-1818), is George Gordon, Lord Byron. The next is the Irish poet Thomas Moore, whose themes also comment on the sorrows and losses wrought by time's passage. Finally, stanzas 31 through 34 present a Shelleyan self-portrait: "one frail Form" who has "fled astray," "his branded and ensanguined brow," a brow "like Cain's or Christ's."

This image is not simply of himself but of the poetic soul in general as a gentle, high-strung creature who, as an outcast, survives the darts of his callous fellow mortals with dignity and a quiet grace. The image spurs a substantial shift in the poet's attitude toward Adonais's death.

To this point, the poet has lamented his and others' helplessness to make sense of that death. In stanza 37, however, the poet reflects on a fit punishment for the "nameless worm" and "noteless blot" who is the anonymous and highly critical reviewer of Keats's *Endymion* (1818), who, in Shelley's eyes, drove John Keats/Adonais to an early grave. The worst punishment that Shelley can contrive is that such a scoundrel should live: "Live thou, whose infamy is not thy fame!/ Live!" Faced with the contradiction that he would wish a long life upon the miscreant who took his hero's life, in stanza 38 the poet bursts open the gates of consolation that are required of the pastoral elegy: "Nor let us weep that our delight is fled/ Far from these carrion kites."

Adonais "is not dead . . ./ He hath awakened from the dream of life." Shelley turns his grief from Adonais to "we" who must live on and "decay/ Like corpses in a charnel," and after a series of stanzas (39-49) in which he celebrates the richer and fuller life that Adonais must now be experiencing, the poet becomes mindful that he is in Rome, itself a city rife with visible records of loss and decay. Moreover, he is in the Protestant cemetery there, where Shelley's three-year-old son is buried as well; and yet, as if mocking all despair, a "light of laughing flowers along the grass is spread." Nature does not abhor death and decay, he sees; it is humans, who fear and hate in the midst of life, who do.

"What Adonais is, why fear we to become?" he asks in stanza 51. The reversal of attitude is completed, and in stanza 52 Shelley makes the most profound profession of faith in the everlasting and transcendent to be found in all English poetry. It is life's worldly cares—that obscuring and distracting "dome of many-coloured glass"—not Death that is the enemy and the source of human despair. "Follow where all is fled," he urges, and he goads his own heart into having the courage to face not extinction but "that Light whose smile kindles the Universe." The poem concludes by imagining Adonais to be a part of "the white radiance of Eternity." As the poem ends, "like a star," the soul of the dead poet "Beacons from the abode where the Eternal are."

Forms and Devices

Adonais is a pastoral elegy, a highly stylized composition adhering to rules, or conventions, that hark back at least two thousand years to such Greek poets as Theocritus, Moschus, and Bion. Shelley had in fact translated into English Bion's *Lament for Adonis* and Moschus's *Lament for Bion*; he would have been familiar with the form, even had he never studied those classical sources, through the seventeenth century English masterpiece, John Milton's "Lycidas."

In general, the pastoral deals with an idyllic imaginative landscape where it is always May and the pastures and hills are always green. Despite renowned uses of pastoral conventions in poems from the late sixteenth century such as Edmund Spenser's *The Shepheardes Calendar* (1579) and Sir Walter Raleigh's "The Nymph's Reply to the Shepherd," by Shelley's own time the pastoral mode had fallen into disuse among serious English poets. Some of this development was attributable to changing social conditions; pasture lands had been fenced off, and the Industrial Revolution was making England a less bucolic nation. The eighteenth century critic Samuel Johnson had also poked fun at the pastoral's sanitized view of the lives of shepherds, pointing out that they generally smelled quite bad; in 1798, William Wordsworth had pointedly subtitled *Michael* (published in 1800), his realistic narrative of an elderly shepherd struggling to make ends meet, "a pastoral," as if to sound the death knell, in English poetry, of this long-standing literary tradition.

Indeed, it may seem strange that Shelley should choose to lament Keats's death in such an artificial and constrained format as the pastoral requires. If his feelings of grief were genuine, one might ask, why not have expressed them in plain, or at least far less contrived terms. The pastoral allows the poet to exercise, nevertheless, the option of poeticizing the event. From that perspective, Shelley, who was quite capable of using a wide range of poetic styles and expression, was first of all doing his fellow poet a high honor by eulogizing him in a structure unique to poetic discourse.

Also, Keats's own poetry often harked back to pastoral themes if not actual modes. "Ode on a Grecian Urn" is only one outstanding example, and all of Keats's poetry is rich in an appreciation of life's simple pleasures and beauties—and of the pain that their loss can cause.

Shelley adheres to all the traditional formal pastoral constraints—and more—in producing his elegy. In keeping with the tradition, he does not identify the characters by their actual names, but by their shepherd names or by characteristics typical of natural rather than social environs. Since the tradition is Greek, he harks back to classical myth and imagery. Keats's poetic efforts, as noted previously, are his flocks. The procession of mourners is appropriately arrayed in flowers and other vestiges of spring; even in the depths of his grief, the poet never fails to remind the reader that it is in fact the springtime of the year.

Themes and Meanings

In his preface to *Adonais*, Shelley called Keats one of the writers "of the highest genius who have adorned our age." Shelley saw in the tragedy of Keats's untimely death a comment on the mindless cruelty that the world inflicts upon the sensitive soul. Shelley imagined that Keats's illness and death were the direct result of an anonymous and vituperative review of Keats's ambitious poem *Endymion*. That review, which is now known to have been written by an individual named John Wilson Croker, had been published in the influential *Quarterly Review* for April, 1818. Shelley was not alone in his opinion that the negative reaction had broken the young Keats's heart; Byron was of the same opinion.

Shelley's poem is therefore a sincere act of public mourning and reaffirmation in the face of an apparently needless and certainly tragic death; yet it is also a literary broadside of the first order. Its pointed and feeling attack on the pettiness of the quarterly reviewers in the face of the poetry which Shelley and his fellow Romantics were producing (and in the process, altering the nature of English poetry for generations to come) itself follows a long tradition harking back at least as far as John Dryden's *Mac Flecknoe* (1682) and Alexander Pope's *The Dunciad* (1728-1743). With typical Romantic *élan*, nevertheless, Shelley turns both the pastoral elegy and the literary satire into a stirring commentary on the larger purpose of death in an unfeeling and violent physical universe.

Shelley's decision to utilize the pastoral mode is particularly telling. In its earliest formulations, it was an Edenic vision, a harking back to greener, happier, sunnier times. It is likely that no one has ever imagined that the pastoral described, or was intended to describe, a true human condition. Only the most coldhearted, however, can fail to hear in its eternal springtime optimism the dearest longings of the human heart for peace, ease, and contentment.

In this regard, even the elegaic pastoral is compelled to render the experience positive by poem's end, for while no poet can deny the undeniable reality of bodily death, the pastoral's very idealizations require one to imagine a transcendent reality as the true locus of all human hopes and aspirations. In its spirited exultation that light shall triumph over darkness, that the true shall endure the violence done them through hatred and spite, and that all of nature conspires yearly to reward humankind with renewals and resurrections that can take the breath away, *Adonais* reaffirms life in the very act of lamenting an individual's death.

Russell Elliott Murphy

ADVICE TO A PROPHET

Author: Richard Wilbur (1921-   )
Type of poem: Lyric
First published: 1961, in *Advice to a Prophet and Other Poems*

The Poem

"Advice to a Prophet" is composed of nine quatrains with an *abba* rhyme scheme. The formal structure of the poem is appropriate to its serious content. Richard Wilbur begins the poem by addressing a hypothetical prophet who needs to appear in reality to persuade the human race to eliminate the weapons of twentieth century warfare, which can annihilate life on earth. The poet imagines that the prophet, when he states this danger, will be "mad-eyed" from being ignored. Consequently, the prophet needs the poet's advice on how to tell the truth in effective language.

The poet imagines that the prophet will not speak of humanity's "fall," like the prophets of the Old Testament, but will beg people in "God's name" to have self-pity. The poet begins to offer advice in stanza 2, telling the prophet not to speak of the "force and range" of weapons, because people cannot imagine numbers so large or the destructive power to which they refer. Similarly, the poet explains in stanza 3, the prophet's talk about the death of the human race will have no effect, because humanity is incapable of imagining an unpeopled world.

Instead, the poet recommends in stanza 4, the prophet should speak of the changes the use of weapons would cause in the natural world. These are comprehensible because they are familiar. Humanity has witnessed changes brought about by natural processes, such as a cloud dispersing or a vine killed by frost. Also, the poet states in stanza 5, people have watched deer flee into a forest and birds fly away, disturbed by human presence. A pine tree growing at a cliff's edge, its roots half-exposed, about to fall, is also a familiar sight. The poet returns to the effects of war on nature in stanza 6, providing an example from history. The ancient city of Xanthus was burned so severely in war that the debris of the Xanthus river caught on fire, stunning the trout.

After focusing attention on changes in the natural world, the poet recommends, in stanza 7, that the prophet ask what humanity would be without nature. The poet explains that nature is a "live tongue," giving images, such as "the dolphin's arc, the dove's return," that people use to express their own thoughts and feelings. The poet gives more examples in stanza 8: the rose, representing love, and the shell of a locust, expressing the idea of the soul leaving a body at death. Images from nature also enable people to represent ideal selves—perhaps graceful like the dolphin or faithful like the dove. In the concluding stanza, the poet asks if human language would be possible without the images of nature. He tells the prophet to ask if human hearts would "fail" if people had only the "worldless rose." Without the oak tree, could there be ideas like "lofty" and "long standing"?

Forms and Devices

In "Advice to a Prophet," Wilbur uses a variety of verbal devices, most of which exemplify ways in which human language and nature depend on each other for meaning. He uses personification to show how human characteristics are projected onto things in the natural world. The leaves are "untroubled," the stone has a "face," and the locust is "singing." Nature, itself, is a "live tongue." In this construction, "tongue" is also a metaphor for nature. The poet uses "glass," or a mirror, as another metaphor to represent nature. Wilbur also draws a metaphor from the language of weaponry, in "rocket the mind," where "rocket" means to go beyond the mind's capacity to imagine, as well as to destroy the mind.

In this context, other words take on double meanings. The phrase "death of the race" refers to the human race but also suggests the arms race. If people do not end the arms race, the human race itself may end. "The locust of the soul unshelled" implies the shells of weaponry as well as the literal shell of a locust. Some double meanings in the poem are expressed in puns. When the poet refers to ways nature "alters," he evokes the "altars" of religious worship, indicating that nature should be treated with reverence. Similarly, he puns on "arc" in "the dolphin's arc, the dove's return," making an allusion to Noah's "ark" and the story of the first destruction of the world by flood.

Wilbur makes other allusions to the Bible. When he writes that the prophet will not speak of humanity's "fall," he refers to the fall of Adam and Eve in the garden of Eden. He also evokes Old Testament prophecies of coming plagues of locusts. The historical allusion to the destruction of Xanthus by fire reminds the reader of the biblical prophecy that the second destruction of the world will be by fire. It is likely that the poet intends the reference to Xanthus to evoke modern parallels—the destruction of Nagasaki and Hiroshima by the fires of atomic explosion. These events made it clear that the destruction of the world by fire is possible. In this context, the phrase "the dreamt cloud" brings to mind the mushroom cloud accompanying the explosion of atomic and nuclear weapons.

When Wilbur writes that nature may become a "glass obscured" by the use of such weapons, he alludes to the biblical idea that in this world people see as through a glass, darkly. By using variations of the word "dream" as a metaphor representing human perception, the poet implies a need for clear vision. Wilbur's prophet, himself a figure of biblical tradition, hopes to clarify human sight.

Themes and Meanings

By giving advice to the prophet, Wilbur thereby becomes the prophet, obliquely assuming one of the poet's traditional roles. Just as the prophet is "mad-eyed from stating the obvious" without being listened to, the poet in the modern world is for the most part unread, his role as prophet forgotten. It is ironic that the poet is speaking to himself. By addressing the prophet as "you," however, he calls on the reader to become the prophet and to pass on the word of the poet's vision. Wilbur's view of life on Earth is summarized in the titles of two of his other poems: "A World With-out Objects Is a Sensible Emptiness" and "Love Calls Us to the Things of This World."

The first of those titles finds expression in the poet's idea of a "worldless rose." There can be no world without objects. If there were, it would be a sensible emptiness: nothing there to see, touch, smell, taste, or hear, and no one there to do these things. There can be no "worldless" human beings. The poet believes this is obvious, perhaps so obvious that it has been forgotten. How else can he explain why human beings allow weapons to exist that are capable of destroying the world?

The other title mentioned above, "Love Calls Us to the Things of This World," expresses the attitude Wilbur believes people should have toward all things of nature, including themselves. Love is the opposite of war. The things of this world are exemplified throughout "Advice to a Prophet"—the lark and the dove, the horse and the deer, the dolphin and the trout, the rose and the vine, the jack-pine and the oak tree and its locust. By viewing these things as "words" spoken to us by the "living tongue" of nature, Wilbur draws on the transcendental tradition of Ralph Waldo Emerson, Walt Whitman, and Henry David Thoreau.

For these writers every natural fact is a symbol of a spiritual fact. The "living tongue" of nature speaks the language of God; spirit is incarnate in nature. Humanity can have heaven on Earth and save its collective soul if it answers the poet-prophet's "call" and "believes" in nature—which is "God's name." If this were so, people would not allow weapons to exist. The world might become one modeled on Wilbur's poem "The Baroque Wall-Fountain in the Villa Sciarra," in which he envisions Saint Francis of Assisi's desire for the "dreamt land/ Toward which all hungers leap, all pleasures pass." The imagined land is Eden, and Wilbur believes humanity can return to it—if people do not destroy it first.

James Green

ADVICE TO KING LEAR

Author: Turner Cassity (1929-   )
Type of poem: Lyric
First published: 1986, in *Hurricane Lamp*

The Poem

"Advice to King Lear" is a short lyric poem of thirteen lines that are divided into two stanzas. The first stanza has six lines, and the second stanza has seven; the same end rhyme is employed for all thirteen lines. Turner Cassity has made his reputation by writing structured verse. "Advice to King Lear" was included in his 1986 collection *Hurricane Lamp*. Like many poems in this collection, "Advice to King Lear" is a compressed creation in which Cassity wryly combines the profound past with the seemingly ordinary present. The poem combines the Shakespearean tragedy *King Lear* (c. 1605-1606) and the bizarre Texas setting in which it is being staged.

Cassity reprints as an epigraph a description from *San Antonio: A Pictorial Guide*, which states that the Arneson River Theatre is unique because its stage stands on one side of the San Antonio River, but its grass seats are located on the other side. The final comment of the guide notes that "Occasional passing boats enhance audience enjoyment." This particular setting fits well with Cassity's use of the ironic. As the title states, the narrator of the poem will be advising King Lear. The first word of the poem is "Unlikely," which—as becomes evident as the poem progresses—is a definite understatement; the unlikely and the unusual are common in Cassity's poems. (Other poems in *Hurricane Lamp* that illustrate this theme include "News for Loch Ness," "A Dialogue with the Bride of Godzilla," and "Scheherazade in South Dakota.") After the "Unlikely," Cassity contrasts the locale where the play is being staged and the artificial weather that must be created in order to produce *King Lear* correctly. The San Antonio area is a "semi-desert," and on the night of the play, the night is "azure." To create the illusion that there is a storm on stage, the crew must resort to the use of a wind machine. Through it all, "Advice to King Lear" juxtaposes King Lear's tragedy against the almost silly notion of staging the play in a place where the locale, not Shakespeare's instructions, dictates the ending.

With King Lear's situation becoming increasingly desperate, the freak coincidence happens, and "Pleasure craft now part the placid water." The stage weather has become "glummer" with each succeeding act, but the poet interjects that no matter where *King Lear* is staged, a "mummer's still a mummer." A mummer is an actor, and therefore the opening has been created for something "unlikely" to happen in this particular production of *King Lear*. Circumstances allow King Lear to alter his fate, if he wishes, and take the advice finally given to him as the "pleasure craft" passes: "Get on the boat, Old Man, and go to summer."

Forms and Devices

Cassity structures his poetry in a traditional manner. His subjects may vary greatly, but he adds power to his point of view by compressing his observations into poems that usually employ metered lines and dense syntax. Cassity is a disciplined poet who has been compared with such poets as Yvor Winters and Alexander Pope. Cassity's technique and socially conscious themes link him with Winters's formalist school of poetry, and he is like the eighteenth century poet Pope in his reliance on wit and the frequent use of satire. In "Advice to King Lear," he makes use of his varied poetic strengths without seeming overcontrived.

Since the rhyme scheme is the same throughout the poem, Cassity adds variation by means of alliteration. The first four lines of the poem end with words that end in *ure*. Each of these words—"azure," "seizure," "pressure," and "foreclosure"—has a strong *s* sound, which unites the words. The last two lines of the first stanza and the first two of the second stanza have final words that end with *ter*. Each of these words— "matter," "stutter," "glitter," and "water"—draws its power from the pronounced *t* sound. Four of the last five lines of the poem finish with words that end in *mer*. The one line that does not stop with a word ending in *mer* ends with the word "dumber." Since the *b* is silent in "dumber," the sound effect for all five lines is the same. The sound that is made by the words ending these lines—"glummer," "mummer," "dumber," "drummer," and "summer"—is the lazy *um*, which could be described as a trance-inducing sound. Each of the sound choices that Cassity has used heightens the total emotional impact of "Advice to King Lear."

Cassity does not write easy poems, but there is a payoff if they are closely read. He is never obscure for obscurity's sake; the reader of "Advice to King Lear" should be somewhat familiar with Shakespeare's *King Lear*. The correct emotional response to the poem will come out of an intellectual understanding and appreciation of Western literary tradition. It is also necessary to appreciate Cassity's sense of playfulness in combining literary tradition and rather absurd contemporary circumstances. The charm of "Advice to King Lear" comes from the poet's dextrous wit. In the end, the winning quality of the poem is its ability to seem sophisticated without taking itself too seriously.

Themes and Meanings

The Arneson River Theatre is almost too good a creation to be true for a poet like Cassity. He recognized the possibility of exploiting its unique setting in order to expand the choices for a more spontaneous solution to the tragedy of *King Lear*. In the first stanza, the reader is introduced to the connection between the desertlike setting of the theater and the gloomy weather conditions that must be artificially generated. The poem opens up at this point to be more than merely contrast; it is also about what it takes to stage the play and keep the financial backers from worrying about "foreclosure." By the end of the first stanza, the reader has been introduced to the difficulty of staging a tragedy that is occurring on the heath, both logistically and financially.

Cassity, by writing about the staging of a Shakespeare play, also suggests the playwright's habit of occasionally having the characters step outside their roles to make offhand remarks about being in a play. Cassity does this himself in "Advice to King Lear." By the middle of the second stanza—after the "Pleasure craft" have already appeared—the poet inserts the line "Outdoors or in, a mummer's still a mummer," which refers to the fact that actors are merely playing roles; if the situation presents itself, actors can step out of their written characters and expand plot solutions. The narrator of the poem speaks to Lear and presents the mounting evidence for him to act on his own, for him to reject his gloomy end. The narrator mentions that his "fool can only grow forever dumber" and that his heirs will "march one to their different drummer." Since this is the case, the passing of a pleasure craft is a wonderful opportunity for Lear to follow the narrator's advice: "Get on the boat . . . and go to summer." The boat becomes a marvelous theatrical prop. Whereas the wind machines were used to impose a prescribed set of circumstances, the local boat serves to make *King Lear*—the dusty old tragedy—new and alive in the present. The situation is liberating not only for the players, but also for the viewing audience. In witnessing the staging of *King Lear* at this particular theater in San Antonio, the audience must rely on illusion for the play to seem comprehensible, but the river between the stage and the seats has allowed the unusual to happen. "Advice to King Lear" is a fine example of Cassity's poetic gifts: Structure and content work together to make the poem wholly balanced in terms of tone, which allows Cassity's wit to shine through.

Michael Jeffrys

ADVICE TO MY SON

Author: Peter Meinke (1932-   )
Type of poem: Lyric
First published: 1991, in *Liquid Paper: New and Selected Poems*

The Poem

Peter Meinke's "Advice to My Son" is, as the title suggests, a poem on how to live one's life, from the perspective of one who is older and more experienced. In a fashion both witty and wise, the parent advises the son, and by extension the reader, on the dangers and delights life holds in store. In only twenty-three lines, Meinke conveys a powerful sense of the multiple and often opposing aspects of life: the practical and the idealistic, the physical and the spiritual, the temporal and the long-term, the sensual and the intellectual, the secular and the religious, the aesthetic and the mundane. He does this both directly and indirectly, through contradictory statements as well as sudden and at first seemingly incongruous shifts in imagery, diction, rhyme, and tone. He suggests that the key to a successful life lies in the ability to reconcile, or at least accept and cope with, very different desires and needs. A sense of humor helps, too.

The narrator, who is never specifically identified as the mother or father, begins by suggesting, somewhat paradoxically, that the son should both live for the moment and plan for the future. Because the days "go fast," he is told to live them "as if each one may be your last." Yet only a few lines later the reader is told that they "go slow" and it is necessary to "plan long range." The narrator admits it is a "trick" to pull this off, implying that there is a danger if one does not do both. Indeed, the violent imagery of the first half of the poem suggests that just coping with the sharp turns of fortune may require more than a few tricks. Reaching "heaven or hell" depends on one's ability to "survive" such catastrophes as "the shattered windshield and the bursting shell."

The second stanza, lines 11-21, begins with sound advice to balance the desire for the beautiful and the ideal with attention to the practical, the commonplace necessities of daily life. People cannot exist solely on the "peony and the rose"; they must also "plant squash and spinach." Although the former "saves," the latter provides "stronger sustenance." Here the poem seems to take its own advice by acknowledging the importance of the two sides of human nature. Both are vital; too much attention to either could upset a delicate balance. Almost as if he had produced a syllogism, the narrator then goes on, with a presumptuous "therefore," to give advice on marriage (fall in love, but be careful), work relationships (be both trusting and cautious), and the need to keep things in proper perspective (serve both bread and wine).

Forms and Devices

For such a brief poem, "Advice to My Son" employs an impressive array of poetic skills. The modern, seemingly casual, offhand tone artfully disguises a sophisticated use of poetic technique. The poem itself reflects the advice it gives: It presents a delightful mix of traditional and innovative rhyme, rhythm, imagery, and diction, as well as an effective blend of seriousness and humor, which keeps the reader off-balance just enough to maintain the element of surprise throughout, even after multiple readings.

This contrast between the traditional and the new, the formal and the casual, begins with the first line. After the rather stately title "Advice to My Son," a traditional poetic title and topic, the tone shifts dramatically with the first three words of the poem, "The trick is," almost as if the parent is giving the son a secret on how to get by rather than broad general advice on how to live and build character. The tone shifts again a few lines later when readers learn that "young men lose their lives" in violent ways. The description of how they do so, by way of "the shattered windshield and the bursting shell," is itself a sharp contrast to the abstract statement three lines earlier that they are lost in "strange and unimaginable ways."

This mix of traditional and modern in the first stanza is reinforced by the irregular rhyme scheme. Although there is standard end rhyme, it is not evenly spaced; lines 1 and 4 rhyme, as do lines 3, 6, and 8, as well as 7 and 10. The odd rhyme scheme, combined with the varied line length—from ten words in line 3 to two words in line 22— creates an irregular syncopated feeling that echoes the overall tone and theme of the poem.

The second stanza, which also contains this juggling of traditional and idiosyncratic rhyme, diction, and tone, shows Meinke firmly in control of his form. After the apocalyptic imagery at the end of the first stanza, Meinke begins the second with a return to colloquial language of the beginning, "To be specific." He then employs common everyday imagery to represent a broad philosophical approach to life: "between the peony and the rose/ plant squash and spinach, turnips and tomatoes." Lest the reader get too comfortable in the garden, the author abruptly shifts from the vernacular to the abstract phrase, "beauty is nectar."

The second half of this stanza, which is the third sentence in this four-line poem, consists of three aphorisms, such as "marry a pretty girl/ after seeing her mother." Thus, throughout the poem Meinke blends the graphic with the bland, the abstract with the concrete, traditional rhyme with irregular rhyme and rhythm. The effect on the reader, a feeling of randomness as well as control, echoes the sense of the world and the advice that the parent seeks to give to the son. The final two lines, which comprise the whole last stanza, snap the poem shut with a humorous wink at the reader, leaving little doubt that the author is fully in control of his medium.

Themes and Meanings

"Advice to My Son" is an invigorating and successful poem because it conveys some age-old advice in a fresh dynamic way. Many who might not be inclined to listen to advice might find it difficult to resist such a cleverly camouflaged homily. The contradictory statements, the graphic images, the platitudes and insights, the shifting tone and diction, the unusual rhythm and rhyme scheme, all come together to produce a unified effect, with just enough ambiguity, ambivalence, and humor to invite the reader back for another reading.

The advice poem, often from father to son, has a long history in English poetry. Meinke draws on this tradition even as he alters it slightly to suit his purposes. He realizes that if the poet or parent were to pontificate directly on the truths of life it might strike the modern reader, accustomed to being skeptical of absolute statements on the nature of reality and morality, as rather pompous. His task is to convey a sense of the dangers and rewards of life without coming across as either cynical or naïve—or dogmatic.

Meinke often writes of domestic relationships and introspective musings. Here he is more successful than usual, in part because he refuses to gloss over the darker realities of daily life. Yet neither does he focus on them exclusively. Life is a serious, even dangerous affair, full of accidents, warfare, misleading appearances, and deception. However, it is not so serious that one should neglect what is beautiful and inspiring. People need those things in life that are fragile, lovely, and intoxicating: the peony, rose, nectar, honied vine, pretty girls, truth, and wine. This is emphasized as the negative, violent imagery of the first stanza is gradually, although not completely, replaced by the more positive language of the last two stanzas. Once the son—and the reader—accepts that life is a mixed blessing, that it is both earthy and spiritual, practical and idealistic, he has learned the trick mentioned in the first line of the poem. It is true that "the stomach craves stronger sustenance/ than the honied vine," but the soul still seeks beauty, the "nectar, in a desert." A mixed blessing is still a blessing. The son can toast to that if he follows the advice of the last line to "always serve wine."

Danny Robinson

AENEAS AT WASHINGTON

Author: Allen Tate (1899-1979)
Type of poem: Dramatic monologue
First published: 1933; collected in *The Mediterranean and Other Poems,* 1936

The Poem

"Aeneas at Washington" is a thirty-nine-line poem in blank verse. It utilizes an oc-casional Alexandrine or six-beat line, very likely in oblique tribute to the hexameter line of the Latin poetic source, Vergil's *Aeneid* (c. 29-19 B.C.E.) for Allen Tate's hero/speaker, Aeneas.

The poem opens with Aeneas in medias res, recounting an episode from Vergil's epic. In this particular episode, Vergil borrows from a narrative technique used in one of his Homeric sources, the *Odyssey* (c. 800 B.C.E.). In that far more ancient epic, Homer, rather than directly relating to the audience Odysseus's adventures on his re-turn voyage, has Odysseus himself tell his hosts, the Phaiakians, the story of his trav-els. In the same way, Vergil, who is writing for a Roman audience to celebrate Impe-rial Roman values, has his hero, Aeneas, tell Queen Dido of Carthage the story of the night Troy finally fell to the Greek forces which had been besieging the city for nine years. So, too, Tate begins with Aeneas virtually in midsentence as he is describing the horribly bloody moment in which Neoptolemus, the son of the dead hero Achilles, mercilessly slaughters the Trojan king, Priam, and his queen, Hecuba, along with their children, as they huddle near the altar to Athena.

As the title informs the reader, however, while this Aeneas may be the man of whose exploits Vergil sang, those ancient times and places are far behind him now; he is instead in Washington, D.C., the capital of a modern, industrial state whose institu-tions are in many ways modeled on those of imperial Rome. If Tate brings Aeneas into the modern world, he nevertheless does not update him. That is to say, this Aeneas is the same hero found in the *Aeneid*, embodying and espousing the same value struc-ture: "I bore me well," he says, "[a] true gentlemen, valorous in arms/ Disinterested and honourable." Details are missing, but this speaker is indeed the mythic hero whose devotion to family and duty is his foremost attribute, along with his acquies-cence to the demands of destiny and the will of the gods.

If there is something vital missing from Tate's hero, it is an upbeat attitude. For one thing, the poem is entirely in the past tense. Aeneas is looking back, true, but even the contemporary world is cast in terms that are past, as if some irrevocable closure has gripped the Republic. While the Aeneas who first encounters Dido in Vergil's epic is bone-weary from his travails, in Tate's hands Aeneas has become a world-weary, per-haps even cynical or skeptical figure. He is not the forward-looking hero who will bring his refugee followers to a new home in Italy; now he says that their "hunger" ul-timately was fit for "breeding calculation/ And fixed triumphs" out of the "vigor of prophecy," as if the results were not worth the centuries-long promise and the effort.

In lines that seem to echo popular patriotic songs such as "America the Beautiful," one hears how Aeneas views those results in this later New World, America, itself the supposed flower of the same ancient Greco-Roman culture that bred Vergil and his epic hero. The "glowing fields of Troy" become "hemp ripening/ And tawny gold, the thickening Blue Grass," reminders of Tate's native Kentucky, positive enough images surely; nevertheless, "the towers that men/ Contrive," rather than the towers of Ilium, are, one must imagine, the skyscrapers of commerce and smokestacks of industry, cluttering the skies.

Aeneas closes by relating how he stood once "far from home at nightfall/ By the Potomac" and, seeing the Capitol's "great Dome" lit up at night and reflected in those waters, could no longer recognize "The city my blood had built"; instead, he thought of that older city, Troy, and "what we had built her for."

Forms and Devices

In "Aeneas at Washington," Tate weaves a web of literary and historical allusion so tightly that the poem cannot profitably be explored without bringing to it a measure of the literary and cultural erudition the poet does. It is as if Aeneas traverses the intervening centuries in the course of the poem, beginning in ancient Carthage but simultaneously setting sail from Troy for America as well as for Italy. The British spelling of "honourable" and the Elizabethan "victualing," for example, give the reader a sense that he or she might be in an intervening heroic era—Shakespearean England—which coincides with the time during which the New World was first being explored and settled.

A devoted student and practitioner of modern poetry, Tate knew that in adept hands, as T. S. Eliot had vividly demonstrated in poems such as *The Waste Land* (1922), the literary device of allusion could give a semblance of order and meaning to contemporary events and crises which otherwise might seem chaotic, random, and pointless. For example, in the poem, Tate applies a single extended historical and literary allusion to comment on a complex sociocultural and political process, very much as if the allusive element were a musical counterpoint to the unfolding surface theme.

To appreciate the allusion, readers must realize that Vergil's Aeneas is not a Greek or Trojan but a Roman hero. One also needs to know that Vergil wrote not to celebrate Homeric Greece but imperial Rome, specifically in the person of the emperor Caesar Augustus. Furthermore, one needs to know that America's founding fathers modeled many of the republic's concepts and institutions, including the very notion of representative democracy, on Roman precedents, particularly the Roman Senate. Finally, one must keep in mind that the Capitol building in Washington, D.C., is modeled after an ancient Roman temple to Jupiter situated on the Capitoline hill and that it was Jupiter who saw to it, in Vergil's epic, that Aeneas abandon his private life and get down to the business of fulfilling a destiny that would be a public, not a private, boon and accomplishment.

Through this tangled series of connections the poet is commenting with a compounded in irony on an America founded on the principle of individual liberty yet now serving the cause of collectivity and realpolitik. In this way, Tate is able to utilize as innocuous a device as the historical/literary allusion to comment on the crisis of individuality and self-fulfillment in the banal anonymity of the modern industrial state.

Themes and Meanings

If "Aeneas at Washington" has a single theme, it is the corruption of an ideal. This ideal is, in Tate's view, so pervasive and ancient that he cannot attempt to describe its corruption except in sweeping cultural and mythic terms.

During the 1930's, the Great Depression was both undermining America's faith in the free enterprise system and threatening the tenuous balance between urban and rural segments of society. Even without this economic crisis, the increasing industrialization and urbanization of American culture, along with the United States having become entangled in Old World affairs as a result of World War I, was increasingly provoking debate about the national purpose. Some were insisting that the republican virtues upon which America had been founded—respect for the individual, for the common man, for self-sufficiency and self-reliance—were in danger of succumbing to the hollow necessities of internationalism.

A leading force in this call for a restoration of those republican virtues was a group of Southern thinkers and writers who called themselves the Agrarians. The Agrarian movement included such important literary figures as John Crowe Ransom, Robert Penn Warren, John Gould Fletcher, and Kentucky-born, Tennessee-educated Allen Tate. Despite its harking back to the classical past, "Aeneas at Washington" is a product of the Agrarian movement. It sees in the present-day corruption of traditional values and ideals a national dilemma that transcends contemporary issues.

At the heart of the problem, Tate is saying, is the concept of the city and what it represents. In this regard, the provincial beauty of Troy is the civilized ideal against which the crass materialism and imperial vainglory of ancient Rome and its present-day counterpart, Washington, D.C., pale in comparison—yet the irony is that Rome was the result of the mythic attempt to rebuild Troy. Finally, then, the poem suggests that human history has become a devolutionary process amid which the ideals of a golden age, with its pastoral myth, remain only to taunt humankind into regret at how low it has fallen despite high aims.

Russell Elliott Murphy

AFFLICTION (I)

Author: George Herbert (1593-1633)
Type of poem: Meditation
First published: 1633, in *The Temple*

The Poem

"Affliction" (I) is a lyric poem of eleven six-line stanzas. The rhyme scheme is *ababcc*. Lines 1, 3, 5, and 6 are generally iambic pentameter, with lines 2 and 4 using iambic trimeter. The poem is part of a collection entitled *The Temple*. George Herbert, a priest in a country parsonage, is said to have given the manuscript to a friend as he (Herbert) lay near death. The message accompanying the manuscript called the work "a picture of the many spiritual conflicts that have past betwixt God and my Soul, before I could subject mine to the will of Jesus my Master, in whose service I have now found perfect freedom." Whether Herbert did indeed speak these words or they were put into his mouth by a devoted biographer, they well describe the movement in the collection of poems and effectively introduce the reader to "Affliction." Called "Affliction" (I) because there are four other poems in *The Temple* with the same title, the poem relates the speaker's personal journey in the spiritual life. The speaker tells readers that, captivated early by the beauty of serving God, he responded with great eagerness and dedication. The first three stanzas are exuberant, unrealistic. The speaker finds joy in God's service and a certain payback in the satisfaction he derives from his efforts to live in a holy manner. Serving God, "the King," is sufficient. His spirituality is sincere but superficial and self-seeking.

The fourth stanza introduces a shift: "But with my yeares sorrow did twist and grow." Suddenly the spiritual life, formerly a source of deep peace, becomes painful and difficult to bear. The speaker experiences even physical discomfort: "My flesh began unto my soul in pain." The poem does not indicate the cause of the depression but suggests that God simply removes himself from the speaker's consciousness.

The letdown is predictable. The poem continues its description of the spiritual and physical pain in which the speaker lives, without hope or joy. Searching for some meaning in life, he turns to the life of the mind and becomes an academic, studying at a university. Here, "academick praise" sustains him for a time and gives him the joy he sought. Knowing on some level that this respite is also temporary, he nevertheless pursues this course until illness again overtakes him. The last two stanzas show the speaker in distress, in sadness, in "affliction," but turned toward God, patient in his distress and willing to endure God's will for him, however difficult that might be. He cries to God: "Now I am here, what thou wilt do with me/ None of my books will show." As the poem finishes he displays an act of faith and love: "Ah my deare God! Though I am clean forgot,/ Let me not love thee, if I love thee not."

Although it is possible that this poem reflects an actual struggle experienced by Herbert regarding his priesthood, it is more probable that the poem describes a general inner struggle to be faithful to God's designs and plans. The speaker is more concerned with the why of his actions—his motives—than with the *what*, or the literal decisions.

Forms and Devices

"Affliction" (I) is a fine example of Herbert's writing. As do most of his poems, it uses the first person throughout, giving a reader the sense that the spiritual experience is actually taking place. The poem reads like a cross between a journal entry and a biblical psalm, reviewing the speaker's spiritual life and coming to a conclusion that accepts God's actions in his life.

The affliction of the title works on several levels. The speaker early sees God as afflicting him with suffering and discouragement. He eventually realizes, however, that the real afflictions are those of the world: self-seeking, vanity, and earthly pleasure.

Herbert is considered a writer of the Metaphysical school, of which his contemporary John Donne was the originator and remains its most famous example. Like Donne, Herbert uses ordinary language, the rhythms of conversation, explosive outbursts, a deeply personal approach to God, and daring figures of speech. Describing his first religious fervor, he says, "There was no month but May." He also exaggerates for effect: "consuming agues dwell in ev'ry vein,/ And tune my breath to grones." Herbert's vocabulary, though some of it may seem stilted to the modern reader, is in fact conversational, even colloquial at times. "Affliction" is not a formal prayer so much as a dialogue with God.

Like Donne, Herbert uses a formal structure, keeping to his iambic rhythms and firm rhyme scheme. The intense struggles of the spiritual life are played against this careful structure so that the reader perceives both order and chaos simultaneously. Similarly, the speaker is both disordered in his efforts to run away from God and supported by God's care for him.

Schooled in classical rhetoric, Herbert combines a conversational tone with elegant figures. The last line of the poem, "Let me not love thee if I love thee not," is a chiasmas. This term means "cross," and the placement of "love," "thee," "thee," and "love" makes an *x*, or cross, when the poem is diagrammed. A key influence on Herbert was the Psalms, with their frequent cries to God for mercy, deliverance, and salvation. Like many of the Psalms, "Affliction" uses past tense to review the speaker's actions up to the present moment, moving then to the present tense as the speaker describes his current spiritual state.

Themes and Meanings

"Affliction" (I) relates a classic part of the traditional spiritual journey. Descriptions of such journeys were particularly common in poetry of Herbert's period, but they recur in almost every century. A good nineteenth century example is Francis Thompson's "The Hound of Heaven." Herbert's religious training for his ordination as a priest had given him a great sensitivity to God's actions in his life. The poem may be autobiographical, but it also mirrors the experience of countless others who aspire to a life of holiness.

The early stanzas show the stage of a spiritual life common to beginners, those in an early fervor in which everything is joyful, grace-filled, even easy. It is a traditional spiritual high point, and it is followed, not surprisingly, by a massive letdown in which the speaker finds the spiritual life not only difficult but also meaningless and distasteful. This state is also traditional, even predictable, in the spiritual life. The movement is from consolation to desolation, from first fervor to letdown. Countless believers have experienced this passage, each believing that he or she is the only one encountering these difficulties.

When the speaker seeks solace or refuge in the academic life, he follows a common path: He substitutes another good for the difficult and often unrewarding good of serving God. Here he falls prey to inappropriate motives, sustained by praise and the easy recognition of the university. Though the intellectual life is a good one, the temptation to intellectual pride is too great. Once again sickness overtakes him.

The end of the poem shows the speaker in another classic state: experiencing the "dark night of the soul." Herbert does not use this phrase, but the great mystic John of the Cross, who coined the term, described it as helplessness, lack of consolation, and feelings of uselessness, joined with a conviction that God is somehow involved in the entire process. This helpless waiting is the first step toward true conversion of heart. The speaker confronts his self-seeking, even in good endeavors, and opens his life to God's activity and power. (Some later writers have noted the similarity of this state to the first of the "twelve steps" of Alcoholics Anonymous and similar programs.) Having handed over his power to God, the speaker can now grow in the spiritual life. This is not a one-time conversion of heart but a central part of the journey.

It should be noted that the speaker's description of his turning from God's service does not imply turning to a life of sin. Like most spiritual poems, "Affliction" shows a good person turning toward a deeper life. The speaker is not struggling with affirming the existence of God; rather, he is a devout believer who freely engages in conversation with God. The poem is written *after* the most intense struggle, not during it. The speaker is firm in his conviction that God does indeed care for him, however remote God may seem at times.

Another term for the stage that the poem depicts is the Purgative Way, the way of conversion and formation. It is followed by the Illuminative Way, in which God instructs the soul in the ways of holiness, and the Unitive Way, in which God and the soul are united in holiness.

Reading George Herbert requires an appreciation of both his theology and his seventeenth century approach to the spiritual life. It is not always an easy task for the modern reader, but the effort can be richly repaid as Herbert's poems unfold. "Affliction" and many other poems in *The Temple* will stand with other literature of Herbert's period as a rich record of struggle, sorrow, and surrender in the journey toward spiritual peace. The later poems in the volume depict the soul progressing in the spiritual life toward deep contemplation and joy in the presence of God.

Katherine Hanley

AFFLICTION (IV)

Author: George Herbert (1593-1633)
Type of poem: Lyric
First published: 1633, in *The Temple*

The Poem

George Herbert includes five poems entitled "Affliction" in the first half of his collection of lyrics. Perhaps this is one way of emphasizing how difficult and yet important it is to understand the experience of affliction fully. These poems form a loosely linked sequence, and together they dramatize a variety of responses to suffering and propose several ways of connecting human with divine grief. "Affliction" (I) is perhaps the most well-known and successful of these poems, particularly because it seems to be deeply autobiographical, dramatizing what many critics interpret to be the pains and frustrations that inescapably plagued Herbert in both his secular and his devotional life. In some ways, though, "Affliction" (IV) is equally powerful: It narrates a life of pain and disappointment from the inside, focusing not on the steps of a persona's career in the "world of strife," as in "Affliction" (I), but on a nearly hallucinatory vision of one's self being fragmented, tortured, and then miraculously reformed.

The five six-line stanzas are addressed to God, but at the beginning of the poem, the speaker is so guilt-ridden and disoriented that he approaches God fearfully. "Broken in pieces," he imagines God as a tormentor hunting him, and he seeks not help but oblivion. Twice he speaks of himself as a "wonder," underscoring the fact that the "normal" perception of one's place in the world—indeed, in the cosmos—has given way to a "tortured" sense of being stretched between heaven and earth.

The poem shifts rapidly from one image of distress to another. As in so many other poems by Herbert, one of the great afflictions of life is a heightened consciousness, and in stanza 2, the speaker is figuratively attacked by his thoughts, imagined as knives that wound body and soul alike. The self in extreme pain can only interpret experience in terms of that pain: Even the potentially promising image of a vessel watering flowers is part of a nightmarish vision of continual assault.

For the rest of the poem, the speaker's distress is presented in terms of a violent rebellion that disrupts life on all levels: personal, political, and cosmic. Order, obedience, and control seem to have vanished, and everything seems dangerously unstable. Chaos is self-destructive, leading to the death of the rioting "attendants" and "elements" as well as the speaker, and it is also murderous, threatening even God, who is closely bound up in the life of the persona. The only hope is that God will intervene and scatter "All the rebellions of the night."

It is only in the last stanza that the speaker can envision some "relief." Through God's powerful action, the rebellious forces of grief can be brought back to work to praise God and help rebuild the persona's damaged self. The poem ends with a description of order restored and the self reintegrated, on the way to "reach heaven, and much more, thee." This is, however, only a plea, and although the end of the poem is much more calm and assured than the beginning, the imagined security of the conclusion is not yet an accomplished fact.

Forms and Devices

Herbert is a master at using poetic form to underscore his themes. At the beginning of "Affliction" (IV), the shape and sound of the lines embody the fragmentation and nervousness of the speaker. Iambic meter is Herbert's basic unit here, but he varies it to add emphasis of different kinds. For example, he opens with a trochaic substitution—that is, the first word is accented on the first syllable rather than the second, as it would be in an iambic pattern. This not only dramatically accentuates the key word "Broken" but also disrupts the rhythm of the entire first line so that it is halting and jerky rather than smoothly flowing. A similar substitution in line 4 places an accentual stress on "Once," and thereby heightens the rhetorical contrast between what he was previously—a "poor creature," but presumably less miserable—and what he is "now"— a "wonder." Other subtle touches make the first stanza even more irregular and unstable. Lines 1 and 4 each contain nine syllables instead of eight, the norm for the other stanzas, and since the last syllable in each is unaccented, they form a so-called "feminine" rhyme, a technique often used to weaken the closure usually conveyed by rhyme. Finally, by repeating the word "wonder," Herbert adds a kind of eerie echo effect that underscores the speaker's obsessive concentration on his pain.

By the last stanza, though, the form of the poem helps underscore the dramatic improvement in the speaker's state of mind. The repeated words are not "wonder" and "wound," as they are earlier, but "day by day," conveying a new sense of patience and trust in time as allied with progress, not decay. Metrical substitutions accent words that are encouraging rather than frightening: "Labor," for example, which situates the speaker in a world of "praise" rather than pain. Finally, the rhymes are strong and subtly reinforce the transformation of "grief" into "relief" and the restored intimacy of "me" and "thee."

The state of mind of the speaker of "Affliction" (IV) is expressed not only by his speech patterns but also by the imagery that he uses. Through most of the poem, he seems to be ransacking his vocabulary to seize upon as many figures of pain and chaos as he can find: He is broken, hunted, forgotten, and tortured. Much of the energy of the poem comes from the rapid shifts among images and metaphors as he tries to give coherent representation to a self he feels is under attack, but ironically, what he brings to life in most of the poem is a picture of unruly "attendants" and "elements" that threaten to destroy the world. The crucial turn in "Affliction" (IV) comes when he shifts suddenly to a deeply felt plea to God and a description of God's role in this "strife." The comparison of God to a "sun" is commonplace but powerful, and the vision of the "light" dispersing "All the rebellions of the night" is infinitely refreshing to the troubled speaker. For all the implied militancy of this simile, Herbert is careful to end on a gentle note. The sun—and he presumably has Christ in mind as well, the "son" of God—tames and rebuilds rather than destroys. This is crucial because the rebellious powers are not so much inveterate and external enemies, but rather parts of the persona's self—"My thoughts," "my attendants." He is consoled and redeemed by transforming affliction from a rebellious power into part of a process ending in praise of God.

Themes and Meanings

"Affliction" (IV) is a meditation on the experience of human suffering and its role in one's devotional life. Like many of the Psalms, to which Herbert alludes repeatedly throughout *The Temple*, this poem suggests that one of the key tasks in life is not to eradicate suffering—an impossibility—but to understand how it can deepen, not dissolve, one's faith, and how it can be balanced by the deep joys of that faith. Herbert is one of the great poetic analysts of physical and spiritual pain, and "Affliction" (IV) acutely voices the thoughts of a person leading a life based on the premise "I suffer, therefore I am." At its darkest moments, this poem shows that suffering leads to more suffering, but in its much more optimistic conclusion, it suggests that suffering is the preparation for a return to intimacy with God. Herbert's other poems titled "Affliction" focus more directly on the way in which human suffering is linked to the far greater sacrificial suffering of Christ. This is implicit rather than explicit in "Affliction" (IV), where Herbert emphasizes not Christ's agony but his ability to turn all "grief" to "relief." Because of Christ's power, manifested every day like the sun, human suffering is endurable and meaningful. The poem does not—and perhaps cannot—dramatize exactly how this works, but its presentation of the miracle of recovery is stirring: The opening plea to stay hidden from the Lord gives way to the concluding plea to grow ever closer to "heaven" and "thee."

What is at stake in "Affliction" (IV) is not only the self but, the speaker would have the reader believe, the entire world. The first two stanzas are a meditation on personal suffering, but the next two stanzas suddenly introduce terms that turn the internal struggle into a microcosmic focal point of all the chaos and disorder of the world at large. Many of the writers of the early seventeenth century were painfully aware of the turbulence of their times and brooded over what seemed to be increasing social, religious, political, and even cosmic instability. John Donne's comments on how "new philosophy" calls everything into doubt are well known, but Herbert's poems also tend to picture a world in which (to use Donne's words) all coherence is threatened. To use an even more compelling example, "Affliction" (IV) is as close as Herbert comes to William Shakespeare's grim vision of life in *King Lear* (c. 1605-1606). Like Lear, Herbert's speaker is bound upon a wheel of fire, stretched "Betwixt this world and that of grace," and his mental distress is a mirror of an external world of strife, plots, rebellions, and the threat of nothingness. "Nothing" is a key word in *King Lear*; it is also a word Herbert places at almost the exact center of this poem.

If the world of "Affliction" (IV) temporarily pivots on nothingness, however, it does not end there. The miracle that does not happen in *King Lear* does happen—or is at least powerfully imagined—in Herbert's poem. The true "wonder" is not, as the speaker first thinks, the way affliction tortures but, as he finally learns, how it elevates.

Sidney Gottlieb

AFTER A STRANGER CALLS TO TELL ME
MY MOTHER'S BEEN HIT BY A CAR IN FRONT
OF THE BUDDHIST CHURCH

Author: James Masao Mitsui (1940-1996)
Type of poem: Lyric
First published: 1986; collected in *From a Three-Cornered World: New and Selected Poems*, 1997

The Poem

"After a Stranger Calls to Tell Me My Mother's Been Hit By a Car in Front of the Buddhist Church" is written from the first-person point of view. It consists of forty lines divided into four stanzas: a six-line introductory stanza, followed by a twenty-two-line stanza and two concluding stanzas of six lines each. The title notes the event and subject that inspired the poem and prepares the reader for the tone and voice of the narrator, who is easily assumed to be the poet, James Mitsui.

The poem begins dramatically in the present tense with the narrator entering a hospital setting. Mitsui's images in the initial stanza plunge the reader *in medias res* into the experience. Flashes of color combine with the image of gurneys being pushed "through swinging doors" to re-create the sense of panic one feels when rushing into the hospital upon hearing of an injured loved one.

After this dramatic entry, the poem takes a more retrospective turn with a stanza-long flashback in past tense. Written as if it were a film or theater script, it creates the impression that the mother is a character who is being forced to play a set role. This "script" has directed her through four significant and difficult moves in her life, the most traumatic being the hasty move to Tule Lake, a World War II relocation camp for Japanese Americans. This move is described with vivid details and highlights the fact that the narrator's mother was constantly compelled to reinvent her life and identity to fit unforeseen and undesired circumstances.

After revealing the mother's past, the poet returns to the present in the last two stanzas. He depicts her as being more assertive than in his previous description. By this time in her life, she has learned to swear and complain in broken English. Although the physical trauma of the automobile accident is limited to a small bruise, the incident serves as a metaphor for many events in her past. Mitsui writes: "There are no answers./ No cause./ No driver saying he's sorry." As the title implies, she was leaving church, a place of tranquillity and spirituality, and was run down by a stranger who showed no remorse. The final image of the poem portrays a woman who has suffered many indignities in her life, not the least among them being American society's view of her as little more than a cipher written on vinyl.

Forms and Devices

Readers familiar with classical East Asian poetry will recognize that Mitsui's long-winded title signals a particular kind of lyric, the occasional poem. (One such poem is Chinese poet Han Yü's "Demoted I Arrive at Lan-T'ien Pass and Show This Poem to My Brother's Grandson Han Hsiang," from the ninth century.) Their seemingly cumbersome titles are actually licenses for immediacy; they free their authors from providing prosaic background introductions, allowing them direct entry into the essential action or meaning they wish to communicate. Often the occasions of such poems then become points of departure or objective correlatives for observations about life.

This poem's title also appears to encode an allusive irony, a device used repeatedly throughout the poem. It is ironic that the mother is struck by a callous hit-and-run *vehicle* in front of a Buddhist church. Readers acquainted with Buddhism will recall that its two major denominations (analogous to Christianity's Catholicism and Protestantism) are the Hinayana and Mahayana, Sanskrit for "Lesser Vehicle" and "Greater Vehicle." All Buddhists seek nirvana (salvation), but Hinayana Buddhists believe in achieving a personal salvation, whereas Mahayana Buddhists believe in seeking a common salvation (for the self and others). Hence Mahayana Buddhists revere bodhisattvas, who (like some saints) are qualified to enter nirvana but compassionately stay to help their more benighted fellows. The hit-and-run driver, out to save himself or herself, must have been in a much lesser vehicle—no bodhisattva he (or she).

Mitsui also chooses words carefully for their symbolic value. For instance, when the mother was released from her relocation camp, she settled in a region of the United States "surrounded by cheatgrass and rattlesnakes"—words that contain connotations of treachery and danger and that quietly characterize the environment into which America's dominant majority has historically situated its ethnic minorities.

Situational irony occurs in Mitsui's description of the mother's hospital setting. The care the mother receives in the hospital conjures up her memories of the degradation and dehumanization of the relocation camp. Thus her bed curtains remind her of the blankets used in the camp barracks to designate families' quarters. The nurses' ministrations remind her of the camp's dearth of privacy, with its doorless privies and partitionless showers. Finally, the hospital's "vinyl I.D. bracelet" on her wrist forms an ironic image contrasting the preciousness ("bracelet") of her identity with cheapness ("vinyl"), symbolizing the low regard society has of it.

The second stanza's shift from present action to past memory is entirely natural. When one loses or is about to lose a close friend or relative, that person's character and significance pass in review before the mind's eye. Thus the flashback in the second stanza serves to evoke the hard life and indomitable character of the mother. Her life is described as a "script," a course determined by family and society. She performs her scripted role as if following the inevitabilities of her karma, spelling out the characteristics of her ordained dharma as victim (of family circumstance), wife, cook, victim (of a racist society), homemaker, and again victim (of an automobile accident). Through it all, her integrity, undaunted courage, and fierce will to survive shine steadfast. The hard knocks life dealt her would have broken a brittler spirit, but hers is resilient and adamant—in the end, she has merely sustained "a bruise on her wrist."

Themes and Meanings

Many occasional poems not only convey a vivid impression of the fleeting event but also make an observation about the larger human experience—hence Ben Jonson's "Inviting a Friend to Supper" (1616) is not only a dinner invitation but also a model of Elizabethan taste and civility. In Mitsui's poem, the shock and anxiety occasioned by the mother's automobile accident become also a poetic vehicle to appraise the woman's character and thereby apprise the reader of the historical experience of her ethnic group in twentieth century America: The individual woman becomes an exemplar of her ethnic genus, the Japanese Americans.

The heart of Mitsui's poem, the lengthy flashback of the second stanza remembering the mother's "script"-like life, contains two highlighted events: immigration and incarceration. Both reveal the quality of the woman's character and strike key themes of Japanese American history. She emigrated to the United States not by individual choice but because her family decided to make a marriage of convenience between her and a previous Japanese American immigrant, the widower of her elder sister. (One may gather from another of Mitsui's poems, "Katori Maru, October 1920," that this occurred to Mitsui's own mother in 1920.) Somewhat like the so-called picture brides of that era who came from Japan and Korea to marry immigrant men known to them only through photographs, the mother emigrated to the United States to replace her sister in a female variant of a leviratic marriage. In her patriarchal Asian society, her preferences were not consulted. She confronted her destiny with a stoic, can-do determination and a denial of self-gratification. In this spirit she created a home and a family for a new generation of Americans.

Wrongful incarceration was also writ large into the script of this mother's life, as it was into the lives of the nearly 120,000 Japanese Americans who were rudely relocated from their homes and put into "concentration camps" (President Franklin Roosevelt's term) during World War II. Mitsui's family was actually relocated in 1942 from their home in Washington State to the exceptionally harsh Tule Lake camp named in the poem. However, like the Japanese Americans of her generation, the mother in Mitsui's poem survived this indignity and injustice perpetrated by her government and her society, but she could not forget. Hence, being hospitalized after her accident, removed from home, deprived of privacy—with only a curtain demarcating her personal space and with her identity reduced to a vinyl band cuffing her wrist—all these circumstances provoke a flood of frightening associations with her experience of the wartime camp. This brave woman thus cries out to be free, to go home. The reader may well see this frail-bodied but tough-spirited woman laid low by a callous and conscienceless driver as emblematic of her ethnic coevals whose human freedoms were trampled by the political machinery of racism and xenophobia in the land of the free.

C. L. Chua and Keisha Blakely

AFTER APPLE-PICKING

Author: Robert Frost (1874-1963)
Type of poem: Meditation
First published: 1914, in *North of Boston*

The Poem

Robert Frost preferred to write within the traditional forms and patterns of English poetry, scorning free verse, comparing its lack of form and metrical regularity to playing tennis without a net. "After Apple-Picking" is not free verse, but it is among Frost's least formal works. It contains forty-two lines, varying in length from two to eleven syllables, with a rhyme scheme that is also highly irregular; many of the rhyme lines are widely separated. There are no stanza breaks. Frost intends to evoke a mood of hesitation and drowsiness, as if the speaker were about to drop off to sleep and is no longer fully in control of his thoughts.

The poem is written in the first person; the speaker is someone who has worked long and hard but is now on the verge of being overwhelmed by fatigue and the depth of the experience. The details of his activity are recalled in contemplating the dream he expects to have. The poem is filled with images drawn from the speaker's experience with the pastoral world; the events he remembers all took place on a farm, specifically in an apple orchard. He has climbed a ladder to pick apples; even when he has finished, he can almost feel the rungs of the ladder beneath his feet. The smell of the apples is pervasive, and he can still hear the sound of the wagons carrying loads of apples into the barn.

All the sensory images are pleasant, but they have become distorted, as if the pleasant dream could become a nightmare. The speaker finds that the large harvest for which he had wished has become excessive: He has "had too much/ Of apple-picking." He recalls the details of the work with pleasure, but he is half afraid of the sleep he feels coming on. On the edge of sleep, he remembers not only the ripe apples successfully picked but also those that fell and were considered damaged and had to be sent to the cider mill. He knows that his sleep will be troubled by the failures more than by the successes. He is not sure about the nature of the sleep he is about to drop into—whether it will be ordinary sleep, more like a hibernation, or more like death.

Forms and Devices

The irregularities of line length and rhyme scheme, so unusual in a Frost poem, are noteworthy; they provide an almost staggering effect to "After Apple-Picking," as if the speaker were literally reeling with fatigue. More important, the meters are highly irregular, especially in the frequent short lines: "As of no worth," for example, where two unaccented syllables precede two stressed syllables, or "Were he not gone," in which every syllable receives almost equal emphasis.

Reinforcing this impression of fatigue is the sense of disorientation which affects his senses: Images of smell, sight, movement, hearing and touch are all used. The speaker's vision is compared to looking at the world through a thin sheet of ice which would distort and cloud what was seen. He has been off the ladder for a while, but he still can feel its rungs under his feet as well as its swaying. The apples he will see in his dreams are distorted, magnified to show every mark. He still hears the sound of the wagons.

As is often the case in Frost's poems, the language is poetic without being stilted. It is not really the language of common speech—no colloquial language is used—but with the carefully planned metrics, the language conveys the sense of someone speaking aloud. The richness of the imagery, reinforcing the drowsiness of the speaker's mood, also contributes to this effect.

The entire poem is a kind of extended metaphor, in which the activity of harvesting apples represents other kinds of activity, but Frost avoids metaphorical imagery, choosing instead precise images and rhythmic patterns which tend to fall, reinforcing the dominant theme of the fatigue of the narrator: "For all/ That struck the earth,/ No matter if not bruised or spiked with stubble,/ Went surely to the cider-apple heap/ As of no worth." The language also supports the sense that the experience being described has become excessive: "There were ten thousand thousand fruit to touch,/ Cherish in hand, lift down, and not let fall."

Themes and Meanings

Much of Frost's poetry, like "After Apple-Picking," describes ordinary events taking place in a rural setting, often on the kind of farm where he lived for many years. Many poems also use such settings to pose broad questions concerning the meaning of human life and the relations between man and the natural world. Few of these poems are as clearly allegorical as this one.

The lessons of "After Apple-Picking" could be applied to almost any line of endeavor which the participant loves and enjoys but finds exhausting, partly because of the loving effort required. For Frost himself, the poem most likely is intended to describe his feelings about poetry, after writing it over a period of years.

There is an anomaly in this, for "After Apple-Picking" was written when Frost was thirty-nine, still a relatively young man, while the poem seems to represent an old man's feelings. The explanation may be that the poem was composed in 1913, immediately after *A Boy's Will* (1913), his first book, had been published. The book had come out after many years of struggle and had received little favorable notice. "After Apple-Picking" may have been a response to that disappointment, an expression of his uncertainty about his future as a poet.

In any case, the speaker had wished for a full and productive life in poetry, and he feels that he has had that. Never having desired any other kind of life, he has given all of his devotion to poetry and is able to believe that he has succeeded; the harvest has been a full one, perhaps even fuller than he had hoped for or expected. He has written a large number of poems and can feel confident that they are good.

Now, however, he is forced to realize that the experience has drained him. He cannot forget any aspect of it, nor does he regret having lived as he has, but he has no desire to continue. Furthermore, his mind focuses on the failures, symbolized by the fallen apples: the poems he started and could not find a way to finish, the ideas which would never find clear expression in his poems, perhaps even the poems which he finished but was dissatisfied with and had to discard. What should have been an entirely satisfying experience turns out to have left him dissatisfied, less proud of what he achieved than concerned about his failures.

Having come to the end of an experience, he is also troubled by uncertainty about what lies ahead. He uses the image of the hibernating woodchuck to symbolize this question. Perhaps the sleep he goes to will be only an ordinary "human sleep," from which the speaker will arise, presumably refreshed and ready to go on with his life. Perhaps, however, it will be a sleep like the animal's hibernation, an oblivion extending over a long period of time and ending in a world entirely different from the one the sleeper left. The questions also raise an issue that Frost was often concerned with— that of what, if anything, may lie beyond death. In a poem entitled "The Onset," he uses the cycle of seasons to suggest that death is only temporary, like winter, but in "After Apple-Picking" he provides no such assurances. The early hopeful image of the ladder pointing "Toward heaven" is not confirmed by the conclusion of the poem.

It is typical of Frost's approach to the larger questions of life that he does not provide or even suggest an answer to the questions he raises, preferring to leave the reader to find the way to his or her own answers. The poem finally leaves the impression that the sensory enjoyment of the endeavor provides its true justification, but that the larger issues it implies are beyond human understanding.

John M. Muste

AFTER GREECE

Author: James Merrill (1926-1995)
Type of poem: Meditation
First published: 1961; collected in *Water Street*, 1962

The Poem

James Merrill's "After Greece" is a surrealist narrative meditation upon reality or authentic being. It addresses the human means to apprehend that reality, both as mortal individuals mired in the narrative development of personal consciousness and as persons aware of a cultural and historical matrix in which they participate. The title of the volume in which this poem appears is *Water Street*, the address in Stonington, Connecticut, where Merrill settled when not at his other home in Athens, Greece. The action of "After Greece" examines his awareness of interesting changes as he returns from his Athens flat to his American house on Water Street, a return from ancient to contemporary, from a foreign to his own country.

In the first fifteen lines, set in Greece, the poet reflects upon the country's ruined glory, both as glory and as ruin. Having sailed for "home"—in America—he feels disoriented and depressed at this failing season of the year (autumn), having to entertain uninvited guests, and finds his mood, like his liquor bottles, filled with spleen. His dream confuses Athens and Water Street, Greek sculptures with his great-great-grandmothers, and abstract ideals with simple concrete essentials. Clearly, his unconscious is hard at dreamwork to seek resolution. Then his depression lifts: "Stay then. Perhaps the system/ Calls for spirits." The system must be some cosmic order that includes himself. He lifts his glass in salute to a new spiritual recognition that his divided homes, like his own divided nature, can come together in a stable, permanent identity within his existential personality as a poet.

Merrill acknowledges several mentors in his works; here, most obviously, his mentors are Marcel Proust and Dante. Like Proust's, Merrill's voice in this poem wanders through memory and desire, dream and waking, to achieve resolution in the poet's transformation of life's contingencies into the beauty of literature. Another poem near this one in *Water Street*, "For Proust," presents Proust doing precisely that. Like Dante in the opening of his *Divina Commedia* (c. 1320; *The Divine Comedy*, 1802), that pilgrimage through *Inferno* and *Purgatorio* to *Paradiso*, Merrill finds himself at thirty-five "midway this life of ours," as Dante says, wondering, "But where is home—these walls?/ These limbs?" He sees his likeness in "the very spaniel underfoot [who]/ Races in sleep, toward what?" As Thoreau said, "Be it life or death, we crave only reality." Merrill's confusion about "home" is a confusion about where lies what is most real for him. The poem's fifty-five lines strive to provide an answer—however short of paradise—that will suffice for a human being in the twentieth century.

Forms and Devices

Merrill's entire œuvre is an encyclopedia of strictly formal stanzaic forms and intricate rhyme schemes (sonnets, villanelles, ballads), but in "After Greece" he displays a mastery of blank verse. It is very irregular blank verse, varying in line length from four to twelve syllables, from two to seven stresses, dancing around the regular iambic pentameter of ten syllables and five stresses. Many lines wrench the regular pattern by piling up two or three stressed syllables in a row. This use of spondaic and pyrrhic rather than iambic feet creates a highly energized if not downright panicky voice, revealing the anxiety of the speaker's concerns: the rage and sorrow over conflicts of past and present, concrete and abstract modes of perception, and feeling and thought, which threaten the stability of personal identity in the midst of historical awareness of destruction and death.

Along with the extreme irregularity of the verse, one becomes aware of a shifting of perception through flamboyant leaps of Merrill's voice from the objective, intellectual, and abstract ("Art, Public Spirit/ Ignorance, Economics, Love of Self/ Hatred of Self. . . .") to the subjective, sensual, and concrete ("salt, wine, olive, the light, the scream—"). Merrill moves from external objects to personal, psychological reality. Indeed, his voice slips from external awareness of "real" objects ("The rest/ Lay spilled, their fluted drums half sunk in cyclamen/ Or deep in water's biting clarity") to inward dream ("I some days flee in dream. . . .").

To add to the surrealist confusion of his stream of consciousness, one comes to see that sensory experience, whether in direct and personal awareness or in dream and memory, may, when one attempts to verbalize it, merge abstract and concrete, thought and feeling. The fraught question then arises: What happens to animal instinctive sensual experience when, in human consciousness, linguistic manipulation intervenes? Can people know what they think—or feel—without language? Does language ineluctably distort humans' "original" animal instinctive experience? Can the poet in his verse merge and unify the concrete and abstract, the animal and the human, in an authentic spiritual vision of reality?

Themes and Meanings

Perhaps now the poem's full action can reveal itself as a process from confusion and anxiety toward enlightenment and acceptance of a human history in a natural world. Merrill begins his poem with "Light into the olive entered/ And was oil," a wonderful image that in fact contains the poem's action: The movement of light into the natural world (olive) produces the possibility of further light, as human beings process the light-generated olives into olive oil for cooking (human physical sustenance) and lamp oil to penetrate night's darkness (human spiritual awareness).

Edgar Allan Poe's "The glory that was Greece," as every schoolchild knows, is but a remnant of a destroyed past. Socrates drank the hemlock; Athens fell to Sparta and then to Alexander and then to Rome and then to the Turks; the Parthenon's miraculous beauty of proportioned structure was blown up three hundred years ago, and to see the temple's great Elgin marbles, even in broken majesty, one needs to go to the British

Museum. The reality of Greece's glory is more memory than actuality. Modern humans are all "after Greece." Yet so is the poet Merrill, who lives part of the year in Athens and part on Water Street in Stonington, Connecticut, founded not by ancient Greek aesthetic and philosophical genius, but by the dour hardihood of Merrill's Calvinist American ancestors. Where, then, is home?

When he recalls the elegant little temple on the Acropolis next to the Parthenon's ruin—the Erectheum—he suddenly dreams those caryatids (Aeschylus's vengeful Furies from the *Oresteia* (458 B.C.E.; English trans., 1777) transformed into the strong but gentle maidens symbolizing Athenian law) are to his dream mind his own American great-great-grandmothers, worrying in their nineteenth century bourgeois way about holding on to their property. Merrill explains to them ("How I distrust them . . . those ladies") in his dream that the twentieth century horrors he has managed to live through—the Great Depression, World War II, the Holocaust, the atomic bomb dropped on Hiroshima, the Cold War—he has had his irons in the fire (a nice bit of American demotic: Having several irons in the fire signifies having several motives burning for action). However, his capitalized list is one of abstract ideals that deny each other ("Art, Public Spirit/ Ignorance, Economics, Love of Self/ Hatred of Self"). The move here from abstract public notions to that ambiguous personal self is significant. Now the poet realizes the inadequacy of such ideals and turns to "Essentials: salt, wine, olive, the light, the scream," moving from external facts to an inward and psychological reality. In naming those "essentials" he has turned them, too, into abstract ideas that, like the Parthenon and the Erectheum's caryatids, are subject to decay and destruction.

Now comes the epiphany and the poem's conclusion. Earlier in his disorientation in Stonington he has wondered about those uninvited "guests, windy and brittle, who drink my liquor." Now he wishes the "essentials" to be turned into "spirits" that can nurture his new awareness of how abstract and concrete, past and present, and personal and historical can produce (like the poem's olive) light and enlightenment. Merrill's very American pun on "spirits" (angels and booze) may, he wishes, allow him to survive the world's tangled meanings, as well as his own. Merrill reveals in this poem a voice capable at once of profound philosophical investigation and a wholly unpretentious personal freshness and humor.

Robert D. Harvey

AFTER OUR WAR

Author: John Balaban (1943-   )
Type of poem: Lyric
First published: 1974; collected in *Blue Mountain*, 1982

The Poem

"After Our War" is a twenty-five-line poem in free verse. John Balaban uses the first-person plural point of view, thereby including and implicating the reader in the horror of the Vietnam War. Although the poem appears to be one stanza, internal divisions marked by structure, sense, and tense divide the poem into three eight-line sections, followed by a one-line concluding question. The first and last lines begin with the phrase "After our war." This phrase therefore frames the poem, returning the reader at the end of the poem to its beginning. This device reminds the reader that the implications of the war continue long after the soldiers returned home.

The poem opens with a horrific, surreal listing of the "dismembered bits" of those killed and wounded in the Vietnam War. Balaban credits the body parts with movement of their own; they "came squinting, wobbling, jabbering back." This series of verbs gives ghastly movement to the poem, as does the image of "genitals . . ./ inching along roads like glowworms and slugs."

The second eight-line section turns to a description of the "ghosts" of the war, the "abandoned souls" of those who died. It seems likely that these ghosts are Vietnamese dead, because they appear "in the city streets,/ on the evening altars, and on the doorsills of cratered homes," all images of Vietnam. The ephemeral ghosts stand in contrast to the physical fragments of the first eight lines. Thus there is a marked shift from physical disembodiment in the opening lines to the spiritual disembodiment in the second section. Lines 14-16 return to the dismembered body parts, depicting their arrival in the United States. The first sixteen lines are unified by the poet's use of the past tense, letting the reader understand that he speaks of events "after our war" but before the present.

In line 17, Balaban shifts into the present tense, telling the reader how fragments of the war have lodged themselves in the present in the United States as an "extra pair of lips glued and yammering" on the cheek of a "famous man" or as a "hard keloidal scar" on "your daughter's breast." The shift to present tense signals the poet's conviction that the remnants of the war continue to blight the present. In line 22 the poet once again shifts tenses, moving toward an uncertain future. The uncertainty is underscored by Balaban's use of three questions that close the poem.

The movement of the poem, then, is from past to future, from grotesque specificity to abstract reflection. This movement reminds the reader that the war, which happened in the past, continues into the present, and it raises questions about the possibility of meaning in the future.

Forms and Devices

Balaban's use of imagery in this poem is both startling and complex. Visual images abound; genitals look like "glowworms and slugs," ghosts appear like "swamp fog," homes are "cratered." There is also the image of *not* looking. The fragments that attach themselves to friends and famous men make it difficult to shake hands, make it "better, sometimes, not to look another in the eye."

Imagery is not limited to visual descriptions, however; Balaban also uses auditory images, kinesthetic images that create a sense of movement, and tactile images. Lip fragments are "jabbering" and "yammering," for example, making meaningless noise, unable to make sense of their current situation. Kinesthetic images such as genitals "inching along roads" and body parts "squinting" and "wobbling" create a particular sense of movement in the poem. Although these "snags and tatters" might be better left in Vietnam, they make their jerky, uneven movement home, arriving in the United States.

Finally, the reader's sense of touch is addressed early in the poem by such images as "pierced eyes," "jaw splinters," and "gouged lips." The graphic adjectives, derived from verbs, evoke physical pain. Balaban turns again to tactile imagery toward the end of the poem with the handshake, a symbol of friendship and accord. Now, after the war, handshakes are "unpleasant." With the phrase "at your daughter's breast thickens a hard keloidal scar," Balaban uses a tactile image to push the images of the Vietnam War into the next generation.

A second device that Balaban uses skillfully is literary allusion, a figure of speech that makes brief reference to some earlier literary figure or work. In lines 22 and 23 Balaban writes, "After the war, with such Cheshire cats grinning in our trees,/ will the ancient tales still tell us new truths?" The Cheshire cat is an obvious allusion to Lewis Carroll's *Alice's Adventures in Wonderland*, a nineteenth century children's book. Here, however, Wonderland is invoked not for its appeal to children but rather for the violent, irrational, upside-down world that Alice finds when she slips down the rabbit hole. In Wonderland, meanings are topsy-turvy, truths change with the moment, and the Cheshire cat fades in and out of view as Alice tries unsuccessfully to make sense of a world in which she finds herself. Likewise, Balaban suggests, after the Vietnam War, people must try to make sense of a world that seems to have lost rationality and meaning.

A second, less obvious allusion is to Balaban's own earlier poem "Carcanet: After Our War," the title poem of his first major collection of poetry, published in 1974. Balaban used the phrase again in his 1991 autobiographical account of his time as a conscientious objector in Vietnam, *Remembering Heaven's Face: A Moral Witness in Vietnam* (as both section and chapter titles). That Balaban continues to return to this phrase suggests his concern with finding meaning in a changed world.

Themes and Meanings

"After Our War" is about the possibility of meaning in the world, about a generation of people who question whether either meaning or love is possible after the Vietnam

War. Balaban's use of lips in lines 3 and 18 suggests that speech or words are inadequate for expressing the experience of the war. The closing four lines of the poem raise questions about this inadequacy:

> After the war, with such Cheshire cats grinning in our trees,
> will the ancient tales still tell us new truths?
> Will the myriad world surrender new metaphor?
> After our war, how will love speak?

Balaban questions whether "ancient tales" can hold adequate answers for the world after the war. Although he looks for new truths, it seems unlikely that the texts and language that spoke so eloquently in the past will have anything to say in this new world. In this questioning, Balaban seems to connect himself to World War I poet Wilfred Owen, who rejected the "old lie," that it is fitting and sweet to die for one's country, in his poem "Dulce et Decorum Est." In line 24 Balaban introduces the notion of "metaphor," which is a figure of speech. Again, he questions whether the world, in all its variety, will offer language capable of describing life and capable of imparting meaning after our war.

Finally, in the last question, Balaban wonders whether love will find language to express itself. By its placement in the poem, this line signals Balaban's most important concern and his conviction that meaning in the world is a product of love. Further, the introduction of love at this last possible moment requires the reader to look again at the entire poem. Love "speaks," metaphorically and physically, through the birth of a child. Yet when one returns to the opening lines of the poem, one reads not only of lips and tibias but also of disembodied, destroyed genitals—a reminder that many men came home from the war impotent from either physical or emotional wounds.

Still others came home from Vietnam unknowingly made sterile through their exposure to the defoliant Agent Orange (a topic Balaban addresses in other poems). Both Vietnamese and Americans exposed to Agent Orange also had genetic damage that was passed on to their surviving offspring in the form of devastating deformities. (Balaban reveals in *Heaven's Face* that his wife Lonnie suffered a miscarriage while they were in Vietnam in 1971; they were unable to conceive again for sixteen years.) The "extra pair of lips" and the "hard keloidal scar" take on terrible significance in this context. Thus, the literal and metaphorical toxicity of the war makes even procreation, birth, and rebirth questionable. Love, Balaban seems to be saying, is what repopulates and regenerates the world, but the offspring of war are dismemberment, death, sterility, scars, and deformity.

Diane Andrews Henningfeld

AFTER SOMEONE'S DEATH

Author: Tomas Tranströmer (1931-   )
Type of poem: Lyric
First published: 1966, as "Efter en döda," in *Klanger och spår*; English translation
  collected in *Selected Poems*, 1981

The Poem

"After Someone's Death" is a poem of three stanzas of four lines each. As in many of Tomas Tranströmer's poems, this one begins with the appearance of a story, but by the end, the series of disconnected images do not seem to add up to a coherent narrative. It is the speaker's visual (rather than organic) ordering of things that holds the poem's various images together. The title suggests the discontinuity between life and death; it is the time after someone's death that the poem considers. The speaker is not identified as the one who specifically experiences the death of another person, and this general detachment may allow the speaker to talk of a more universal condition. It is not uncommon for people to experience the death of another person. The reference to "us" in the first stanza may therefore refer to all people.

In the following two stanzas, the speaker addresses more directly a "you" in the poem. The other person is depicted in familiar situations such as shuffling on skis on a winter's day and feeling his or her "heart throbbing." In these depictions, the speaker seems to be consoling the other person by reminding him or her of activities in which the living and breathing human body can still engage.

The speaker assumes some responsibility for the emotional well-being of the person who has possibly experienced someone's death. Tranströmer establishes the mood of this situation in the first stanza when he makes note of the "shock" that follows death. The "cold drops" here suggest the numbness induced by shock. The repetition of "cold" and the way it "consumes" the living warmth in the second stanza reinforce this idea.

The third stanza highlights the difference between being dead and feeling dead. When someone literally dies, the one who remains often feels deadened by this fact. The latter, suffering from the cold truth of death, must be reminded of the blood that still pulses in his or her own self. Nevertheless, the speaker is sympathetic toward this apparent lack of emotional feeling and understands that the other person is gripped by a sense of unreality. It is at this time that "the shadow feels more real than the body" or, in other words, when the gloominess is the actuality.

The last two lines shift away from the interpersonal concerns. The image of a samurai and his armor made of "black dragon-scales" ends the poem, and it seems peculiar to the more cosmic and humanist concerns of the earlier lines. As well as being disconnected from the rest of the poem, this last image may even be considered shocking. In this respect, the lines contribute to the mood or effect of the poem, rather than provide a satisfying closure to the never-ending pain that the death of another person causes.

Forms and Devices

At one time Tranströmer was a practicing psychologist, and his work enables him to employ many strategies to speak about the unspeakable. How else do humans come to understand what death means unless they first realize what psychological and emotional effects visit them after someone else dies?

The poem does not appear to be logically developed because the grief caused by death forces one to reconsider the outside world. After death, the world is transformed; it is irrational, since everything seems inexplicable. If the poem develops in discontinuous fashion, it is the poet's attempt to correspond the reality of the experience to the unreality of death. The speaker of the poem acts as a kind of mediator between the fact of death and the emotional impact of the one who remains after the dead. The world is seen through the eyes of the other who is suffering, and the pain is interpreted through the components of the physical world. If objects are transposed in this presentation, this may be caused by the way in which personal affliction has filtered the images.

The poem begins with the effect of the "shock"; it takes the form of "a long pallid glimmering comet's tail." Already, the poem establishes the sense of lifelessness in the cosmic metaphor. Unfortunately, this lack of vitality is all-encompassing ("It contains us") and alters even inconsequential things such as television sets. The movement from the personal (grief) to the universal (comets) and then to the quotidian (televisions and aerials) suggests the rapidness with which the shock of death affects all aspects of existence. The reference to the passive act of watching blurred television pictures speaks of a psychological condition as well. One does not have heart for much else, and rather than be left with one's own pain, it is easier to displace it by letting external images flicker across one's consciousness.

In the second stanza, the cosmic and technological realms transpose into a natural one; it is as though the speaker requests that the one suffering get up and go outdoors to refresh the body and the mind. The speaker gently paints this picture: "You can still shuffle along on skis in the winter sun" indicates that once, perhaps as a past joyous activity, "you" used to be uplifted by skiing in the woods.

In the second half of the stanza, however, the speaker returns to the sympathetic tone and considers how the innocent act of skiing itself could have drastic consequences. The comparison of the remaining tree leaves to "old telephone directories" suggests that one might think again of dead things or of things that have since passed away.

By the third stanza, the speaker acknowledges the endlessness of pain itself and, again, gently reminds the other that it is "still beautiful" to be alive. Like the groves with bare trees, though, one feels the vast emptiness: Even the "samurai looks insignificant beside his armor." What was once plenitude and substance becomes devoid of meaningful substance.

Themes and Meanings

"After Someone's Death" is a poem that depicts the emotional shock that people experience as a psychological condition after someone has died. Against the lurid pain itself, the poem offers a message of consolation without denying the inevitable fact of mortality.

After a death, everything feels unreal and unnatural. The poem encapsulates this mood by presenting images and situations that do not bear obvious, or organic, relation to one another. A way to interpret this strategy of discontinuous images is to consider the manner in which the mind's eye perceives the world when one is going through an emotional upheaval. The constant shifts in perception signify disturbances in the normal or usual order of experience.

Despite the overwhelming sensation of grief, the poem emphasizes everyday or familiar situations, both to show how these are transformed by the fact of death and to urge one to return to these things since they constitute life. Beyond that, the poem suggests that the natural course of life always ends with death and that all things are changed by this fact. Not surprisingly, then, the images share a common trait: The comet's tail, the television pictures, the skiing, "last year's leaves" on the trees, and the throbbing heart are all things that move or are in motion. If the shock renders one incapacitated, the poem focuses on movement or mobility to depict the inevitability of things changing.

While the poem's tone is gentle, even consoling, the message resists being glib or appearing naïve. The poet Tranströmer, who understands the archipelago of his native Stockholm, perceives the complexities of the human mind as well. Death, the poem reveals, invades emotional life in much the same way modern technology has embedded itself in daily life—both disorder the images of experience. In television, for example, news reports, commercials, and entertainment programs appear in irrelevant order, but one is not unduly troubled by these jumps. If the poem seems fragmented and random in the way images appear, Tranströmer is expressing the conditions of modern experience in some of its disjointed facets.

The poem does not pretend to offer unprecedented wisdom about death; neither does it attempt to discredit the pain that death can cause to those still living. It does attempt, however, to suggest that death is a part of all life, no matter how unreal one feels after it has occurred to someone else. It is usually after someone else's death that one is reminded of his or her own impending death.

On this note, the poem ends enigmatically with the image of the samurai beside his armor. This image suggests that, in the end, all humans are but warriors beside the apparel they don to face (or to fight or confront) the world. Finally, one rests alongside the things that contained one in life, as one also departs from that which was once himself or herself.

Cynthia Wong

AFTER THE NOISE OF SAIGON

Author: Walter McDonald (1934-   )
Type of poem: Lyric
First published: 1986; collected in *After the Noise of Saigon*, 1988

The Poem

Walter McDonald's "After the Noise of Saigon" consists of nine three-line stanzas that present a lyrical, first-person description of a hunting trip. The prey is ostensibly a wounded cougar, but more significant, the speaker is creating a space to confront a wounded part of himself. That crazed, wounded aspect of his psyche, the result of his Vietnam experience, must be faced alone and in the wilderness. Though little hope for complete healing is suggested, the poem convincingly portrays a veteran doing what he must do to persevere in the present.

The poem begins with a conditional sentence that focuses attention on the reason behind this particular strenuous pursuit: "If where we hunt defines us," the speaker posits, "then stalking this steep hillside/ dark with spruce makes sense." The hunt, then, is in part for self-definition, and to that end it makes more sense than the speaker's other way of experiencing his past: the dreams he has "floundered in/ for years" and which have left him only "disgusted." However, progress is difficult. When he looks back for any "spoor" (blood from the wounded animal) he might have missed, he is flipped in the face by switches. When he swings his head "face-forward for clues," he is stung by evergreen needles.

"The strangest nightmare of all," more threatening even than the ardent struggle of the hunt, is the fact that he has chosen a method of hunting that places him in mortal danger. He is pursuing not with a rifle but with a bow, and he intends to get as close to the creature as possible, though his "aim with a bow/ is no better at twenty yards/ than forty." The difficulty and the danger are essential to his purposes, and he continues for hours even as the climbing makes him dizzy.

Purposeful though the hunt may be, the role of the woods and his place among them remains somewhat ambiguous even to the speaker himself. "These blue trees," he tells readers, "have nothing/ and all to do with what I'm here for/ after the noise of Saigon." At the least, they provide the isolation and the struggle that he needs; they may even recall another experience of stalking through dense foliage. Though his reasoning is not precise, the "noise of Saigon" has clearly left a "bitter sap" that rises within him, "bad blood" that he needs to spill alone and in the forests. By persevering through the woods—and possibly by shedding blood—he can address his own woundedness. There he may, without endangering his friends or their perceptions of him, allow himself to meet or even to become that "damned/ madman stumbling for his life." Recalling the first line—the proposition that "where we hunt defines us"—it is clear that, because of "the noise of Saigon," this madman is an intrinsic part of the speaker, as much so as the respectable man who sometimes goes hunting alone.

Forms and Devices

The point of view of the poem is that of a first-person narrator relating immediate experience. The present continuing verb in line 8 ("Switches . . . keep flipping me") grounds the experience in the here and now and causes the rest of the present-tense verbs to do likewise. In contrast, the speaker's Vietnam experience is presented as the distant past: He has dreamed of it "for years." This temporal distance reveals the seriousness of his struggle. Though it began in his distant past, it maintains a grave significance in his present.

McDonald writes tightly controlled free verse. His lines contain three or four accented syllables each, arranged in a loosely iambic pattern frequently varied with dactyls and anapests. His stanzas do not break with the meaning, but instead often break against the sentence structure. In this way they work like measures of music. As a result of such techniques, his work is deeply rhythmic, but with the subtle pulse and flow of speech. The rhythm is complemented by the poet's consistent attention to sound. Internal rhyme is a frequent enhancement, sometimes full, as in "Switches dripping sap/ keep flipping me," "needles sting when I swing my head"; and sometimes partial, as in "knowing my aim with a bow" and "see me as a friend, not some damned/ madman." More pervasive are assonance ("simple" and "bitter," "strangest nightmare," "climbing until I'm dizzy"), consonance ("dark" and "makes," "no better at twenty," "simple bitter sap"), and alliteration ("stalking" and "steep," "might have missed," "cougar" and "climbing"). In concert, these devices create a lush tapestry of interwoven sound.

The poem is also rich in metaphor. The speaker's fruitless dreams are compared to floundering in deep water, and because they too are a way of experiencing the past, they are also compared to this hunt. The "noise of Saigon," or the effect of it, is likened to the energy force in the trees, the "simple bitter sap that rises" in the speaker. The metaphor is compounded by comparing that sap to "bad blood" that the speaker needs "to spill/ out here alone in the silence." "Bad blood" may be understood in two complementary ways. If understood as an ongoing grudge, it is between two aspects of the speaker's self: the sane, respectable citizen and the "damned madman." "Bad blood" may also be understood as an evil strain fundamental to an individual, something dark and violent at the very core. Such an understanding would suggest that "after the noise of Saigon," a dark tendency persists in the narrator that he cannot exorcise and can barely control. A war continues within, and keeping the darker self from striking out seems to be the purpose of the hunt. If he must spill blood, he will do so "far from people [he] know[s]."

McDonald's syntax also presents an engaging ambiguity in stanzas 7-9. Read strictly, the last two stanzas are an appositive that defines "the noise of Saigon" of the seventh stanza. If so, that "noise" is the bitter sap that rises within the poet. The stanza may also be read as referring to "what I'm here for/ after the noise of Saigon." If this is the case, the "what I'm here for" is the bitter sap caused by the noise of Saigon. Either way, the effects of his Vietnam experience have driven him to the woods. Just as sap rises in the blue spruce, a "simple bitter sap" rises in the narrator, and he must confront it. The poem ends, then, exactly where its suggestive opening line ("If where we hunt defines us") directed: The narrator has discovered a definition. He is both a respectable "friend" and a "damned/ madman stumbling for his life."

Themes and Meanings

McDonald is not a confessional poet—his poems are fictions, and his mask remains intentionally in place. He is, however, a jet pilot and a Vietnam veteran, and he has drawn upon his war experience extensively in both his poetry and fiction. He is also a regionalist who writes of rugged outdoor activities such as hunting and ranching in the American West. It is not surprising then that these inner regions would come together in the story of a man, home from the war, who is trying to define himself. It is typical of McDonald's work that the narrator is acting with courage under intense psychological distress: He is facing the fact of who he is, and he is coping with that fact—even with the fact of evil within.

The divided self, the war within between evil and good, is one of the most ancient and persistent themes in literature. In this poem, the interior struggle is enhanced and objectified through the pursuit of the cougar. At first the wounded cat seems little more than a formal necessity: If the speaker is stalking, he needs to be stalking something. Yet it is thematically significant that two hunts are taking place. The narrator is hunting for the cougar, but he is also hunting for some post-Vietnam understanding of himself. Both hunts take place in rough terrain: The cougar is hunted on a steep and thickly wooded hillside; the self is hunted through years of dreams and inner turmoil. Both are seeking a wounded prey that leaves a difficult trail—the cougar was wounded by the hunter and is tracked by spoor on the brush; the self was wounded by its Vietnam experience and is tracked by its sometimes irrational, violent action. Finally, both are dangerous when wounded. A cougar, generally little threat to humans, is likely to attack when wounded; similarly, the wounded self the hunter seeks must remove himself from his friends, lest they see—and maybe suffer at the hands of—the "damned madman."

The poem offers no simple or even permanent solution for what must be done after the noise of Saigon. The struggle to adjust is continual, and no end is coming into sight. McDonald provides only a glimpse of how one former soldier deals with the violent strains of his woundedness, doing his best not to hurt others and working hard to come to terms with who he is now. If he finds self-definition, it is only this: He is a man who, by the most strenuous perseverance, can function in society and even be a good friend, but he is also a man who sometimes must remove himself from society and exert himself in the strenuous and violent spilling of "bad blood."

William Jolliff

AFTER THE SURPRISING CONVERSIONS

Author: Robert Lowell (1917-1977)
Type of poem: Epistle/letter in verse
First published: 1946, in *Lord Weary's Castle*

The Poem

"After the Surprising Conversions" is a forty-six-line poem on a historical event in colonial New England, a common subject for Robert Lowell. The title indicates that the poem takes places after the conversions and destructive religious enthusiasm that swept southern New England in the wake of the sermons of Jonathan Edwards. Edwards is explaining and, in a sense, justifying the origins and development of the event to an unknown correspondent.

The speaker of the poem is Edwards himself; the poem is based upon his letter of 1736, "A Faithful Narrative of the Surprising Work of God in the Conversion of Many Hundred Souls in Northhampton and the Neighboring Towns and Villages." The tone of Lowell's re-creation of the letter is very different from the fervor that occasioned it. Edwards comments matter-of-factly on the suicides and on how "it began to be more sensible"—it can now be sorted out and understood more fully.

The origins of the religious awakening began with one man, who "came of melancholy parents." There were, however, signs of hope in his life. He would watch the wind touch a tree and think of God's beneficent creation. He was predisposed to "loving," but "he durst/ Not entertain much hope of his estate/ In heaven." Edwards preached one Sunday on Kings, a historical book of the Bible that is an unlikely source for such momentous events. Immediately after, the melancholy gentleman, Josiah Hawley, who was in fact the uncle of Edwards, "showed concernment for his soul." This concern immediately leads him to preach the difficulty of salvation to others, and he "dreamed/ That he was called to trumpet Judgment Day/ to Concord." In May, he "cut his throat." Edwards seems to ascribe the cause of this suicide to the nature and family background of Hawley; it is a means by which Edwards justifies his own role in the episode.

After this event, others suddenly began to fear for their spiritual state, cutting their throats after urging others to do the same. A madness and despair about God's grace seized them; the only answer was suicide. Edwards ascribes these terrible events to Satan and, curiously, to God: "God/ Abandoned us to Satan." The religious gains that had been achieved earlier by Edwards are now undone in the religious madness that follows. It is interesting that Edwards seems to deny or attenuate his own responsibility for the suicides and passes the responsibility to God. The God who empties the land and allows Satan to take over is not Jesus, but Jehovah, the God of wrath.

The last lines of the poem deal with teeming and fecund nature. The fullness of the unpicked apple trees and the spawn of the bass are a rebuke to those who have lost themselves in abstract and abstruse religious speculation. Nature is life-giving, and the way of Edwards's God leads only to self-destruction.

Forms and Devices

The poem is written in a loose iambic pentameter that does not call attention to itself, although the pattern is regular and the syllables are exact. There are a few significant changes in the iambic pattern; the spondees of line 42 (" 'Cut your own throat. Cut your own throat. Now! Now!' ") consciously violate the established meter, reflecting the violence of the awakening. The variation of the meter at the beginning of line 40, "Jumped at broad noon, as though some peddler groaned," also supports the changed view of those who once took their salvation for granted.

The poem consists of run-on couplets that hide their formal nature. Since the couplets consistently run on, the reader is hardly aware that they are couplets until he or she closely examines the poem. So there is an underlying recurrence that gives order to the seemingly casual conversational style of the letter and the violent events that it describes. The interaction between a fixed form and terrible and irrational events provides a tension that is not resolved until the end of the poem, when nature returns as a presence.

There are some interesting opposing images in the poem. The melancholy man broods on "terror," but earlier "loving shook him like a snake." Love gives way to death, and the landscape that was a sign of God's goodness seems to disappear until the end of the poem. The demand to "Cut your own throat" is described in a strange but appropriate simile "as though some peddler groaned/ At it in its familiar twang." Death has, in Lowell's strange reformulation of Edwards, become a commodity to be sold to those gullible or guilty enough to buy. Even the time period of the events, "Hard on our Lord's Ascension," contrasts with the later lines, "The breath of God had carried out a planned/ And sensible withdrawal from this land." The beneficent Jesus who has completed his mission of redemption and ascends to heaven is transformed later in the poem into a wrathful Jehovah.

The last image pattern is very different from what has gone before. Images of nature return to stand against the cutting of throats. The visual and aural images of the cracking apple trees filled with "unpicked apples" and the "small-mouth bass" breaking water, "gorged with spawn," are a counterpoint to the selling of death and the despair that leads to suicide.

Edwards's actual words make up about one-third of the poem. Lowell borrows phrases and occasionally whole sentences and surrounds them with his own language, so the poem filters the spirit of Jonathan Edwards through the mind and art of Robert Lowell. The extensive use of such historical elements in a poem is very unusual. Lowell manages to preserve the integrity of these elements, but they have been turned into an artistic creation, a unified poem; this is not merely a historical curiosity.

Themes and Meanings

Robert Lowell was a member of the famous Lowell family, prominent in Boston society. In this poem, he seems to feel that he must explore the Puritan past of New England to discover guilt and transgressions that will help him and his readers come to better terms with the heritage of the past. Lowell does not falsify that earlier and very different world. He does, however, focus on the irrationality and terror of early America rather than the repression that so many others have noted. Moreover, he has recovered the voice of that early world, and the Puritans condemn themselves in their own words.

At the time when the poem was written, Lowell was a devout Catholic convert with a history of manic-depressive illness. *Lord Weary's Castle* is a testament to that newfound faith. It is clear that Lowell believed that his madness did not come from his religion, as it does in "After the Surprising Conversions": For him, religious conversion was a way to overcome madness.

The Puritan God in the poem seems to be a destroyer, not a preserver: "The breath of God had carried out a planned/ And sensible withdrawal from this land." If he is not leveling the land, he is abandoning it to Satan to do with as he will. It is the fear that they cannot appease this God that leads Josiah Hawley and those who follow him to take refuge in suicide. The Catholic deity is very different for Lowell; for example, in the sixth section of "The Quaker Graveyard in Nantucket," he speaks of "Our Lady of Walsingham," whose shrine holds out hope to man and the world. The virgin is an intercessor for man and is very different from a wrathful Jehovah.

The overt meaning of the poem in the story of the conversions and suicides is supported by the imagery. The passages on nature at the end of the poem are especially significant. This section, one of Lowell's additions to Edwards's letter, speaks in a tone that is very different from that of the preceding sections. The descriptions and images suggest the continuation of nature: "Sir, the bough/ Cracks with the unpicked apples, and at dawn/ The small-mouth bass breaks water, gorged with spawn." Man ignores the goodness of nature, since the apples are "unpicked," and the sexual suggestion of the bass's "spawn" is a principle of life, not the self-willed death and life denial of religious terror. Lowell clearly believed that his new religion, Catholicism, was life-giving, and he continually associates it with natural images. The Puritans do not pick the fruit, but let it rot; the Garden of Eden has been abandoned.

James Sullivan

AFTERWORD

Author: Joseph Brodsky (1940-1996)
Type of poem: Lyric
First published: 1987, as "Posleslovie," in *Uraniia*; English translation collected in *To Urania*, 1988

The Poem

"Afterword" is a poem of forty lines divided into five numbered sections of eight lines each (two quatrains, in the English translation). As the title suggests, it is a look backward, but, in this case, over a life still in progress rather than a finished work. It is written in the first person. The speaker, at first, seems to be talking to himself or to no one in particular. By the end, he seems to be talking to a single interlocutor, but the "you" could be the distant reader just as easily as the person across the table. This move from singular experience to common fate is at the heart of much lyric poetry, but here the change takes on material form: The self, with time and age, becomes not merely something else, but everything else.

The first section begins with the most general of lyrical-elegiac observations: "The years are passing." The speaker observes their passage around him almost as if he is sitting at a café table. A palace facade is cracking and the Holy Family, whether on a relief, a painting, or a calendar, moves ever-so-slightly closer to Egypt. The world is crowded with the living, the city is full of lights, and the astronomer counts up his "sparkling tips."

The next section shifts from the general to the particular. The pronoun "I" appears for the first time and notes rather dispassionately, seemingly without complaint, that it can no longer remember exactly when or where events took place. The speaker also observes that the events themselves cannot remember anything, so that whoever was involved ("saved or fled") is away and clear.

The next step is both logical and crucial to the poem. The speaker defines what all this means—he, the individual, is, with time, becoming part of the whole. Life, in general, is a "rustling . . . fabric," and now his individual skin is taking on the look of what enwraps it. His profile could be a wrinkle, a patch, or a leaf, all visible things that could be wholes or parts in themselves. Whether whole or part, however, they have always been something apart from him, and anything outside of himself can be "ignored, coveted, stood in fear of."

If the previous stanzas are addressed to the reader—or someone—in general, the next two stanzas narrow the focus. "Touch me—and you'll touch dry burdock stems" might be figuratively addressed to the reader in general but, by virtue of that imperative, sounds more immediate. By touching the speaker, one also touches whatever and whomever one has seen or known.

The final section moves from sight to sound, or rather speech. "I am speaking to you, and it's not my fault/ if you don't hear." However, the listener is not at fault either.

Rather, like the cracked wall or the gaunt Holy Family, the vocal cords wear out. The voice is muffled and hard to distinguish from other sounds around it. The speaker, however, does not complain about losing his voice on top of all the other losses; that loss makes it easier for the listener to hear those other sounds, which are part of life's rhythm—the rooster's crow, the ticking sound made by a needle on a record. The poem ends with a twist on the story of Red Riding Hood: "The better to hear you with, my dear," says the wolf when the girl tells him what big ears he has. Here, the line is, "the better for you not to notice when my talk stops," and it is anyone's guess who is the wolf and who is not.

Forms and Devices

For Joseph Brodsky, poetry was always a process of thought more than an exploration of emotion or music. That is not to say that he ignored the latter two, but "Afterword" is a good example of poetic logic at work.

The translation follows the original Russian's rhyme scheme (*abab cdde*, with some variations) and rhythm without observing a strict metrical pattern. There is also a good deal of internal rhyme and alliteration, while the end rhymes used in the translation themselves are often near, rather than full, rhymes. Still, for the English-speaking reader, what ties the poem together is image and metaphor rather than sound.

Each section represents a shift in focus and direction: The first three are linked by imagery of accumulation and profusion. The first abounds in visual images: the passage of time expressed in space, the palace facade cracking, the eyeless seamstress finally threading her needle, the Holy Family inching its way toward Egypt. Important, too, is what occupies the space. The emphasis is on "the visible world" and its multitudes, its numbers upon numbers of living beings, its bright and "extraneous" light, its quantity of "sparkling tips" that strain the astronomer's eyes. When the speaker begins questioning his own memory of events, there follows a list of possible times and places, and, after that, a list of almost generic events, "an explosion, or say, a flood,/ the lights of the Kuzbas derricks or some betrayal." The transition from section 2 to section 3 introduces the paradox that drives the poem: Events themselves cannot remember, so, when those who "were saved or fled" lose track, that means their tracks are covered. Therefore, loss, in some way, equals survival.

The answer section 3 offers is not an answer to individual questions of what, where, or who, much less how or why. Rather, it is a statement of what all this, taken together, now undifferentiated, means. The poet, too, can no longer be set apart from the surrounding shapes and objects, the "fractions or wholes," or their more abstract effects or the feelings they evoke. This section contains another list, this time combining physical objects, actions, and emotions.

Touch dominates section 4—the first stanza contains images of dryness and dampness, while the second stanza returns to a list that ends with the word "loss." In the final stanza, sense of hearing replaces sense of touch, with the addition of time ("The sum of days") again equated with subtraction of sound ("when my talk stops").

Themes and Meanings

Pure elegies, or elegiac lyrics on the transience of life, may start out with someone else's life and death but, more often than not, work their way around to the poet's own—something Brodsky himself pointed out in "Footnote to a Poem," his essay on Marina Tsvetaeva's elegy for German poet Rainer Maria Rilke. Mourning oneself through others is a time-honored tradition in lyric poetry, with the tone of the lament ranging from defiant (Dylan Thomas's "Do Not Go Gentle into That Good Night") to nobly hopeful of immortality in some other form. The poet may be losing hair and teeth, but the consolation is a permanent place in art and memory.

The standard elegiac themes of time passing, age, and loss run through "Afterword"; what makes the poem interesting is not so much their presence but their relationship. Brodsky has often written about exile and loss, and the themes have often taken the form of meditations on separation forced either by history or geography—in other words, by time or space. In Brodsky's poetry, those are not abstract notions but things that can be smelled, touched, seen, felt, and heard.

Here, Brodsky's speaker is not so much mourning as he is musing over an observable, tangible process. The tone is both philosophical and wry. Mortality itself is a process, not an event: In his singular version of the law of preservation of matter, life reclaims its own in segments, increments, and fractions. That includes speech, because words, like the body, have their own mass and gravity. The moment at which the body is dispersed or reclaimed, when the sound of someone muttering can no longer be heard, is also called death—a word that is nowhere in this poem. It is also, mercifully, hard for the listener to pinpoint.

An afterword is meant to comment on what has come before, to present conclusions, to sum it all up. The controlling irony here is that the sum is actually a remainder: The more miles a car has on it, the more rust it accumulates, the more it becomes "a heap," the less it is a car. So it goes with the body and its voice. Still, the transformation of one kind of matter into another somehow clears the way for another form of being, one that is truly eternal. How much comfort that provides is another question.

Jane Ann Miller

AGAINST CONFIDENCES

Author: Donald Davie (1922-1995)
Type of poem: Meditation
First published: 1958; collected in *New and Selected Poems*, 1961

The Poem

Formally, "Against Confidences" consists of eight quatrains, with very short lines of between three and five syllables and an exact alternating rhyme scheme of *abab*. The poem argues against the modern popularity of pouring forth intimate details, whether in tell-all books, confessional poetry, psychoanalysis, or personal relationships. In a humorous and satiric tone, the poem explains how "Candour," one of the poem's series of personified abstractions reminiscent of the British neoclassical verse that Donald Davie esteemed, has changed in its relationship to "loose lips" (stanza 1) or "mouths that now/ Divulge, divulge" (stanza 8).

In the present time—the present being emphasized by the repetition of the word "now" in the opening and closing stanzas—loose lips or divulging mouths describe Candour, in Davie's British spelling, as "friend." This situation suggests that would-be confidants, whether in writing or in personal relationships, confuse the indiscriminate spilling of confidential details with frankness and truth.

Moving from a third-person objective point of view to the first-person plural, the poem's speaker asserts that the genuine revelation of (or quest for) truth signified by Candour cannot exist in the apparently heedless flow of expression in an environment created or distorted by "our compulsive/ Needs" on "couches" where "we sleep, confess,/ Couple." The word "couches" may signify the bed as the site of an individual's dreaming or a couple's lovemaking as well as the psychiatrist's couch. All these are spheres in which self-interest undermines the ultimate truthfulness of what appears to be candid outpouring.

Returning to the third-person point of view, the speaker defines the main facets of Candour as "reticence" or restraint, the subjection of all talk and feeling to actual test and intellectual examination, and toleration of a degree of privacy, hazy belief, or half-illuminated conviction but discouragement of self-indulgent and deceptive effusiveness.

Forms and Devices

The poem's notable compression in its grammar and in its short lines reflects as well as expresses the idea of truth and meaning inherent in "reticence" rather than its opposite. Likewise, multiple meanings are compacted into several puns and wordplays. The confidences of the title may refer to intimate details; to the state of feeling confident, which would be misplaced in dreaming, lovers' talk, confessional writing, or psychoanalysis; and to the duplicity of a confidence game, since the apparent candor of flowing expression may not be what it seems.

In contrast, reticence is Candour's "practise"—a word whose primary meaning is habitual operation but whose secondary meaning of intrigue contrasts Candour's honesty with the deceptiveness of "loose lips." This deceptiveness is conveyed by the oxymoron of the "pleased distress" (stanza 3) that people experience on their various "couches." The distress in turn suggests a discrepancy between the surface of the dream, confessional writing or talk, lovers' intimate conversations, and the true meanings or feelings that underlie them. Thus, in the midst of an anguished confessional poem, a sense may be conveyed of the poet's pleasure in his or her pain, in the act of complaining about the causes of the pain, or in the accomplishment of a literary work about the subject.

Several features of neoclassical verse also contribute to the poem's warning against effusiveness. Its precise and straightforward rhymes and rhyme scheme suggest the poem's emphasis on exactitude and forthrightness. Also, the several balanced antitheses in grammar signaled by the repeated "Not . . . , But . . . " constructions convey the speaker's thoughtful weighing, comparing, and defining of aspects of candor and effusiveness. That is, the poem is patterned to show that Candour does not reside in particular values or activities but does reside in other values and activities. The synecdoches for effusiveness, "loose lips" and "mouths" that "divulge," help suggest the absence of intellect, as if the anatomy of the effusive person were working by itself, without the brain. In contrast, the synecdoche characterizing Candour's disapproval of "loose lips" and "mouths" that "divulge," Candour's "brow" that is clear (stanza 1) or clouded (stanza 8), conveys not only a facial expression but also the anatomical location of intelligence and thought. Finally, use is made of the proverbial metaphor of the light of reason and truth contrasting with the darkness or shade of irrationality and error. This metaphor is subtly linked to the etymology of the word *candor*, from the Latin words meaning "white" and "shine." Like the circular form of the poem, whose first and last stanzas repeat, the recurrent imagery of light and dark suggests the inevitability of the poem's truths about its subject.

The "shade" of the couches of sleep, confession, and coupling (stanzas 2-3), and of "shy belief/ Too bleakly lit" (stanza 7), in which Candour cannot "live," is a metaphor not only of the darkness of weakened rationality and truth but also of the comfort provided by avoiding the harsh glare of both Candour and intelligence, particularly the latter. Candour will "respect/ Conviction's plight" in "Intellect's/ Hard equal light" (stanzas 5-6). Candour is thus humane and makes some allowances for emotional and spiritual truths, whereas the intellect is harsher. Likewise, in the concluding two stanzas, Candour's brow is not "clouded" by permitting "To shy belief/ Too bleakly lit,/ The shade's relief"; rather, what clouds Candour's brow is "to indulge/ These mouths that now/ Divulge, divulge."

Themes and Meanings

"Against Confidences" focuses on two main areas: the development of personal relationships and the modern popularity of effusiveness in print, speech, psychiatric treatment, and some social relationships. The repeated word "now" may apply to the development of personal (especially romantic) relationships, in which the participants may wrongly believe that a complete, uncritical outpouring of the self is mandated. Such an outpouring, the poem implies, will probably be warped by the romantic partners' deep-seated fears of injury to their self-esteem or by concerns about damage to the relationship.

The repeated word "now" may also point to modern times. Against the modern popularity of self-indulgently telling all, Davie's speaker counterposes the precise, vaguely archaic literary word for despising or scorning, "contemned" (stanza 1). In the 1950's and early 1960's, when "Against Confidences" was published, highly autobiographical, confessional poetry was gathering momentum in American and British literature. Confessional poetry is perhaps best exemplified by the work of a group of talented American poets that includes Robert Lowell, W. D. Snodgrass, Anne Sexton, Sylvia Plath, Allen Ginsberg, Adrienne Rich, Theodore Roethke, and John Berryman. This strand of modern poetry, which extends back to the poetry of Walt Whitman and William Wordsworth, continues to the present.

Davie's "Against Confidences," far from the vividly specific word choice and autobiographical imagery of confessional poetry, employs austerely general and abstract word choices and imagery as well as figurative language reminiscent of classical sculpture and neoclassical verse. Davie's poem remains a polished refutation of confessional poetry, as do perceptive remarks in his books of literary criticism *Purity of Diction in English Verse* (1952), *Articulate Energy: An Enquiry into the Syntax of English Poetry* (1955), and *Under Briggflatts: A History of Poetry in Great Britain, 1960-1988* (1989). The purity of diction and word choice in "Against Confidences" provides a fitting parallel to the title of Davie's first important book of literary criticism, which, like the poem, continues to be a touchstone of English literature.

Norman Prinsky

AGAINST THE EVIDENCE

Author: David Ignatow (1914-1997)
Type of poem: Lyric
First published: 1968, in *Rescue the Dead*

The Poem

"Against the Evidence," a thirty-three-line meditative poem, is characteristic of the autobiographical nature of much of David Ignatow's poetry. In free verse, it presents the contrast between the "estrangement among the human race" and the narrator's determination to live.

The poem opens with a seven-line stanza in which the narrator attempts to "close each book/ lying open on my desk" but is attacked by the books themselves as they "leap up to snap" at his fingers, causing pain. The action suggests a mutiny of the books against the speaker, although they have obviously been a significant part of his life.

The conflict is heightened when, in the second, longer stanza, the poet reflects on his heretofore harmonious relationship with books. He has "held books in my hands/ like children, carefully turning/ their pages." This harmony has resulted in a close identification of the poet with what he reads: "I often think their thoughts for them." Following this benign reflection, a jarring shift occurs as the narrator plunges into the dark message of his musing: "I am so much alone in the world." The books, which have been such a dominant part of his world are not, after all, human beings. Their mutiny at the beginning of the poem seems to suggest that the speaker is becoming estranged even from them. The poet mourns the loneliness of his preoccupation with inanimate elements such as stars or steps. He then links humans with these cold, unfeeling objects: "I can look at another human being/ and get a smile, knowing/ it is for the sake of politeness."

He has finally arrived at the core of his sadness and disillusionment, "estrangement/ among the human race," about which "Nothing must be said." In fact, "nothing is said at all" because to speak about estrangement might begin to break it down. The evidence has been building throughout the poem. It seems as though the poet has taken refuge in inanimate objects such as his books. Despite all this evidence, however, and despite his troubles, the poet asserts: "Against the evidence, I live by choice."

Forms and Devices

David Ignatow's language is deceptively simple, his images spare, and his metaphors often obscure. Like William Carlos Williams, he uses few typically poetic devices. Rather, his language carries his message. Initially in this poem Ignatow personifies his books. As he attempts to close them, they "leap up to snap" at his fingers. As realization explodes upon him, he is weakened and must sit down.

The uprising of his books seems to jar his whole existence. He reflects on the prior harmony he felt with his books, which might almost be considered symbiotic: "All my life/ I've held books in my hands/ like children." One wonders whether this means that he holds them as he holds children or as children hold books. In either case, he implies a nurturing relationship. However, the books betray him, unable to fulfill his need for community.

Juxtaposed with his comfortable perception of the books in his life is the alienation that breaks into verse 2: "I am so much alone." He reinforces his aloneness with a series of sterile images: "the stars," "the breeze," and the "steps/ on a stair" that he can count as he climbs and descends them. When he speaks of other human beings, they are no more communicative, for he feels that their smiles are only "for the sake of politeness." He pinpoints his apparent despair in the word "estrangement."

The feelings of alienation, separation, and estrangement are further expressed in the unresponsive images of familiar objects around him: "I stroke my desk,/ its wood so smooth, so patient and still." Despite all this "evidence" of his isolation and lack of community, the poet finishes with a note of affirmation that belies the note of despair in the poem: "I live by choice."

In addition to metaphor and imagery, the poet uses the arrangement of lines and stanzas to reinforce his consciousness of estrangement. The mutiny portrayed in the first seven lines of the poem in a single stanza shatters the comfortable life that many people experience with books and catches the poet in the knowledge of his own isolation. The beginning of stanza 2 lulls the reader into that former life. However, in line 15, a jarring change occurs. The suddenness of this change heightens the mood of separation, although no separation in format occurs in the stanza arrangement.

Themes and Meanings

David Ignatow has been called the "most autobiographical of writers" by the *Dictionary of American Biography.* "Against the Evidence" bears this out, as do many of his other poems. Rather than create a persona as narrator, Ignatow himself is obviously the speaker, confronting life and the human condition. In another poem, "Communion," he sees little in human experience to inspire communion.

> Then let us be friends, said Walt, and the graves
> were opened and coffins laid on top
> of one another for lack of space
> It was then the gravediggers slit
> their throats being alone in the world
> Not a friend to bury.

In "Communion" he creates an ironic contrast between himself and nineteenth century American poet Walt Whitman, who greatly influenced him. However, Ignatow considers Whitman optimistic and his own view of life realistic. Although he regards language as paramount in his writing, he also regards his work as a vehicle for moral leadership in that it points out—in his own words—"the terrible deficiencies in man.

Whitman spent his life boosting the good side. My life will be spent pointing out the bad." "Against the Evidence" reflects on the harsh realities of life, yet it reiterates the poet's choice of life over death or defeat. Ignatow has said, "My avocation is to stay alive. My vocation is to write about it."

The spare, direct images of William Carlos Williams also exerted a strong influence over Ignatow. Ignatow has noted that what he appreciates most in Williams's work is the "language of hard living." In "Against the Evidence," the evidence to which the poet refers consists of elements of hard living, especially "estrangement." His alienation is represented by the direct, though unresponsive, images of his books, the stars, the breeze, the steps, and the polite smile on the face of a fellow human. He also develops this theme in the poem "Wading Inside," in which he bemoans the dearth of human interaction: "Guilty, my oppressor/ and I go separate ways/ though we could relieve each other/ by going together as Whitman wrote/ With our arms around each other."

While much of Ignatow's poetry carries a message similar to that of "Against the Evidence," it often does so in a darker, angrier manner. In "Epitaph" he speaks of his father: "There were not hidden motives to his life,/ he is remembered for his meanness." He contrasts love and life in "Rescue the Dead," picturing love as a kind of madness: "To love is to be led away/ into a forest where the secret grave/ is dug, singing, praising darkness/ under the trees." Life itself, on the other hand, is sanity: "To live is to sign your name,/ is to ignore the dead,/ is to carry a wallet/ and shake hands."

"Against the Evidence" is, at first glance, relatively mild. When one considers elements of nature such as the stars and the breeze, one is lulled into a placid, almost peaceful mood. Only when one thinks of these images as sterile and uncommunicative, when they are joined with the "polite" but uncaring smile, does one experience the stark isolation that the poet confronts in the rest of the poem. The poem is a model of understatement; however, this very understatement underscores the aloneness of the narrator and the despair that grips all humanity at different times. Although he experiences this loneliness, he struggles to take action:

> I stroke my desk,
> its wood so smooth, so patient and still.
> I set a typewriter on its surface
> and begin to type
> to tell myself my troubles.
> Against the evidence, I live by choice.

Patricia J. Huhn

THE AGE

Author: Osip Mandelstam (1891-1938)
Type of poem: Lyric
First published: 1922, as "Vek"; in *Tristia*, second edition 1923; English translation
  collected in *Modern Russian Poetry*, 1967

The Poem

"The Age" consists of four stanzas of eight-syllable lines, which are rhymed *ababcdcd* throughout. The title refers to the age in which Osip Mandelstam lived and which he addresses in the poem. It is one of several poems with a related theme—the poet's running dialogue (indeed, an argument) with his own age.

In the very first line, the poet addresses his age directly and immediately equates it with a beast ("My age, my beast"). This equation sets the tone for the entire poem. He expresses his puzzlement about his age by wondering who can fathom its true nature and who will be able to glue together the two centuries, the preceding and the present one, both of which the poet has witnessed. He sees that the present world is being built of blood; it is gushing from the throat of earthly things, so that only a parasite is trembling in expectation of good things on the threshold of new days.

In stanza 2, the poet maintains that every creature must carry its backbone and that every wave plays with this invisible spine. He calls the present age an infant and equates it with the tender cartilage of a baby. Because of the age's infancy, the cranium of life has once again been sacrificed like a lamb. To what cause the sacrifice is to be made, the poet does not state explicitly, although at the beginning of the third stanza he speaks of captivity. If one is to liberate himself from this captivity, one must "tie the knotty elbows/ Of days together with a flute," clearly hinting at a power that can accomplish the liberation. The poet again refers to the nature of the age as one of anguish: A viper in the grass becomes its measure.

In the last stanza, the poet seems to rejoice in a possible liberation, when the buds would swell again and the green shoots would spurt, but he quickly reminds himself that the backbone of the age is broken. He ruefully calls his age beautiful but pitiful, cruel and weak, looking at the past with a senseless smile—as a beast, once supple, looks at the tracks of its own paws. The poem ends on a resigned note, seemingly without a solution to the dilemma postulated at the beginning and explored in the middle of the poem.

Forms and Devices

"The Age" is built predominantly of metaphors. There is an intricate system of metaphors designed to hold together the structure (organism) of the entire poem. The principal metaphor is a beast standing for the age in which the poet lives. Other, smaller metaphors reinforce the main one. Several refer to the physical nature of the beast: pupils, the vertebrae, blood, backbone, the cranium, paws. Just as the beast is a live being, so is the age.

Other metaphors are also taken from the living world. Blood, the essence of life, is referred to as a substance that builds, a substance which can cement "the vertebrae of two centuries." It can also signify a loss of life, however, indicating that it can rip asunder, as well as cement ("gushing through the throat of things upon the earth"). A creature that must carry its own backbone is another example. A parasite referred to in the first stanza is also a live being depending for its existence on another living being. The tender age is compared to baby's cartilage, which is sacrificed like a lamb—another young being. Days have "knotty elbows," which must be tied if one is to find a solution. Finally, when the solution gleams as a possibility (although a fleeting one), the rebirth is metaphorized by buds and green sprouts.

The poet refers to the age as a living being, calling it at one point "the age of the infant earth." It rocks the wave of human anguish. Other references to the age/beast also reveal the connection with a living being. The age is addressed almost as a human being: "My beautiful, pitiful age." It can look backward; it can smile. It can also be cruel and weak.

Built into this system of metaphors is Mandelstam's depiction of the phenomena of life and death. The repeated references to a broken backbone allude to the possibility of, or nearness to, death. When the poet asks at the very beginning who will look into the age's pupils, he refers to an agelong method of checking whether life has turned to death. The mention of the sacrifice of a lamb is another age-old expression connected with death. The poem, in fact, is filled with metaphors that refer now to life, now to death. The separation of the one state from the other is tenuous; indeed, the beast is mortally wounded, and the end is only a matter of time. Finally, two additional metaphors should be mentioned. One is the wave, which stands for water or the sea and which can be interpreted as a metaphor for life. The other is a flute, which clearly refers to art and, more specifically, to lyric poetry.

Themes and Meanings

The overriding theme in "The Age" is Mandelstam's argument with the age in which he lived. The poem therefore makes it difficult to agree completely with those critics who have characterized him as aloof and unconcerned with happenings around him. On the contrary, he was very much concerned with the life outside of his admittedly secluded poetic world, as attested by direct references in this and many other poems.

"The Age" was written in 1922, only a few years after the beginning of the October Revolution in Russia and, more important, only two years after the "new age" in the Soviet Union had begun to take shape. Mandelstam was directly affected by the revolution, but only as a bystander—even as such, he was on one or two occasions close to losing his life. The external manifestations of change, danger, and loss were not so much on his mind as were the more important potential losses—those of human dignity and artistic freedom. For this reason, his characterization of his age as a beast refers primarily to the possible destruction of both of those values, which were always more precious to him than anything else.

In this light, the mood of the poem is essentially pessimistic. This is underscored primarily by the use of the beast metaphor, which usually carries dangerous and destructive connotations. The fact that the beast is young and dying, and is therefore a victim itself, does not diminish its destructive role. When coupled with the damage it has wrought, it is not surprising that the poet considers his age in mostly negative terms.

Mandelstam's hopelessness is relieved only for a moment when, in the third stanza, he allows for a possibility of a solution. He sees this possibility in the healing and rejuvenating power of art, as symbolized by a flute. He says clearly that, in order to lead life out of captivity and start anew, "one must tie the knotty elbows/ Of days together with a flute." Tying the knotty elbows of days simply means joining the old and the new, rather than rejecting the old or destroying it.

Throughout his life, Mandelstam believed in the high mission of art, and particularly of poetry. Amid the horrors of destruction and the rejection of everything that was different from the accepted dogma, he still hoped for a moment that art could save humankind. The hope is fleeting. The beast that was once "beautiful" and "supple"—a reference to the unfulfilled promises of the revolution—can now only look at the tracks of its own paws; "the cranium of life has been sacrificed" once again.

Vasa D. Mihailovich

THE AIRY TOMB

Author: R. S. Thomas (1913-   )
Type of poem: Narrative
First published: 1946, in *The Stones of the Field*

The Poem

"The Airy Tomb" begins with the phrase "Twm was a dunce at school" and describes in the first stanza what Twm cared for instead of school: the noise and motion of birds and the land around him. Though the first stanza contains the word "I," thus establishing the presence of a speaker who is narrating the poem, the speaker remains largely absent from the poem, occasionally asking the reader for a judgment but for the most part describing what Twm did and what his world was like. The language is simple, consisting of phrases with nouns and strong verbs rather than extensive descriptive adjectives or metaphor.

The poem's second stanza describes Twm's work on a farm among the hills once he leaves school; he is more comfortable among the animals and the harsh working conditions than he was in the classroom. The third stanza tells of his father's death, and the fourth of his mother's. In the fifth stanza the poem shifts slightly from the narrative of what has happened and asks the reader to participate; the first lines are, "Can you picture Tomos now, in the house alone,/ The room silent, and the last mourner gone/ Down the hill pathway?" This question is followed by two others asking what Twm did, a device that allows the reader to imagine Twm's feelings and options rather than being told by the speaker what they are. The stanza then moves back into a narrative of Twm's life, alone on the farm.

The sixth stanza continues the description of his life, but it emphasizes how alone he is after his parents' death; one of the stanza's final images links the "Hearts and arrows" that symbolize love to his "school fractions"; Twm remains separated from other people. The poem's tone becomes somewhat fiercer and grimmer. In the last two and a half lines, "the one language he knew/ Was the shrill scream in the dark, the shadow within the shadow,/ The glimmer of flesh, deadly as mistletoe," the sense conveyed is one of the harshness of life and Twm's closeness to the tough lives of animals.

The final stanza states that Twm was desired by some of the girls around him but that he did not respond. His separation from other people leads to his becoming almost a local legend. The narrator again speaks to the reader, saying, "you, hypocrite reader, . . . are you not also weary/ Of this odd tale, preferring the usual climax?" The speaker goes on to suggest that surely there was someone whom Twm loved, but then steps back to say that there was not. The title's meaning is revealed in the final lines, with a description of Twm's body decomposing in the open air before he is finally found.

Forms and Devices

R. S. Thomas's use of rhyme and rhythm is not consistent throughout the poem, but he does use both. In the first stanza, for example, the first line does not rhyme with anything, but the second line rhymes with the third, the fourth with the fifth, and the sixth with the eleventh. While the lines tend to be about the same length, they are not always. Most of Thomas's words are one or two syllables, with the stresses falling rather unevenly, giving the poem the rhythm of someone speaking instead of an obviously metrical beat. Thomas makes use of iambic rhythms, as in the lines, "And then at fourteen term ended and the lad was free," and "And coax the mare that dragged the discordant plough," but the lines do not contain an equal number of feet and do contain additional syllables that break up the rhythm. Thomas also uses the device of enjambment; his sentences and clauses are as likely to end in the middle of the line as at the end.

In terms of imagery, Thomas relies largely on nouns and verbs; even his metaphors are free of adjectives. When he describes a dead hawk whose "weedy entrails" are "Laced with bright water," his language achieves its power through the unusual juxtaposition of two ordinary things: weeds and entrails, lace and water. The images are startling because unexpected, but the words themselves are quite ordinary. This adds a conversational tone to the poem; it also provides very specific and vivid descriptions for the reader, thus focusing the reader's attention on the scene.

Thomas's addresses to the reader are perhaps the most interesting formal aspects of the poem. By asking the reader to imagine Twm's circumstances, and later by accusing the reader of being complicit with those of Twm's neighbors who mock him, Thomas compels the reader to think about his or her expectations for both a poem and a person. He summons the socially comfortable ideas of romance and conformity, only to replace them with the image of a man who is very much alone and who wants to be so. He pushes readers to make a judgment and then to reconsider that judgment, a device that asks readers both to see the poem without the assumptions they might have brought to it and to reexamine their own attitudes toward other people. "Hypocrite reader" is a phrase used by the French poet Charles Baudelaire in his 1857 book *Les Fleurs du Mal* (*Flowers of Evil*, 1931), and one taken up in the French by T. S. Eliot in *The Waste Land* (1922); it therefore resounds with literary associations in the midst of a poem that is otherwise simple and grounded in unliterary language. By using it, Thomas calls further attention to the readers' position as readers and to their difference from Twm, the dunce at school.

Themes and Meanings

The title "The Airy Tomb" is almost an oxymoron; one expects a tomb to be closed and stuffy, rather than airy. The poem continues to overturn expectations and surprise the reader. One can initially read it as idealizing the working man or the peasant, as much Romantic poetry did, but Thomas is careful to keep the poem from becoming a soft pastoral. He describes the harshness of the Welsh farmer's life, using images such as rotting sheep or "Deadly as leprosy." In the last stanza, he writes, "you must face the fact/ Of his long life alone in that crumbling house," lines that do not allow the reader to see Twm's life as anything but desolate without human company.

The poem is about place; Twm belongs on the farm, not in school or town. When people attempt to force him out of himself in his early years at school, the attempt does not work. The only poems he can read, the only language he can understand, is that of animals. "The Airy Tomb" is also about being alone. When Twm's father dies, his mother does not live through the next winter. He is left therefore to keep the farm in much the way his father did, making a place for himself with the land. Other of Thomas's poems speak of the relationship between the Welsh peasant and the land; the farmer is often portrayed as part of the landscape, but the landscape itself is bleak and unyielding. Thomas is aware of the poverty and the difficulty of farming on the rocky and cold mountains of Wales. One cannot make a living under those harsh conditions if one does not give oneself entirely to the work. Twm's relationship with the land and the animals is what causes his solitude, but it is also necessary for his survival.

This is also a poem about mortality. Thomas represents humans as having moved away from the cycle of life and death in which the animals and the rest of the natural world participate. Animals die under the sky, but humans are buried in confining coffins that separate them from the earth. Twm, however, is able to become part of the rhythm to which the animals belong; his grief for his parents subsides into his work and into the coming of spring; life goes on. Unlike other people, he dies with the sheep under the sky. In his solitude and separation from other people, he is able to enter the natural cycle of life and death as other humans cannot. "The Airy Tomb" does not romanticize nature as something beautiful and sweetly pleasant, but it does suggest that a closer connection to the natural world and the solitude that such a connection entails can enable one to have a better death.

Elisabeth Anne Leonard

AJANTA

Author: Muriel Rukeyser (1913-1980)
Type of poem: Meditation
First published: 1944, in *Beast in View*

The Poem

"Ajanta" is a long poem written in five subtitled parts: "The Journey," "The Cave," "Les Tendresses Bestiales," "Black Blood," and "The Broken World." The poem, written in free verse, is given form by the progression of the journey it describes, in which the poet goes into herself in search of a sense of the unity of life. It is an exploration of her spirit, mind, and body.

"Ajanta" is named for the great painted caves in India, famous for their magnificent religious frescoes painted by Buddhist monks. Muriel Rukeyser uses this setting in her poem to suggest the sacredness of her own interior places, her Ajanta, both psychic and physical. The figures of gods, men, and animals in the poem are accurate descriptions of the caves' artwork.

Part I provides an emotional setting for the poem; it also describes Rukeyser's life in the midst of war and annihilation (the poem was written during World War II). The poet, in her "full youth," wants "my fullness and not a field of war" and sets out on a journey "to the midnight cave." Profoundly disturbed to be living in a world that "considered annihilation," a world with "the dead boiling up in the ground," the poet resolves to travel alone to find "This cave where the myth enters the heart again." The "myth" is, in a sense, herself.

Actually, the cave is a metaphor for the place within, where she can evaluate experience and be at peace with herself. Although the frustrations and upheaval of war are almost overwhelming ("All the way to the cave, the teeming forms of death . . . "), she makes the "expiation journey" alone. It is her solitary quest to make amends, perhaps, for what she feels is her inability to prevent the dying happening or her inability to rechannel her frustration over the war. On the way, she performs a private ritual: "I blessed my heart . . ./ For it had never been unable to suffer." The blessing is both a talisman for safekeeping and confession of her own frustration with life. To free herself from this debilitating state, the poet seeks to know herself and find possibilities of renewal.

In part 1, the star under which she travels is called "Wormwood." The wormwood plant, which contains a bitter oil used to make absinthe (a nineteenth century drink so strong it was purported to cause forgetfulness and hallucinations), has been associated by name with any unpleasant or mortifying experience. The war's profound effect on the poet's psyche is emphasized by the name Wormwood, but her belief in the vitalizing natural rhythms of the body is also alluded to: Wormwood was used in plant lore as an aphrodisiac.

Part 2, "The Cave," begins with a description of the cave, a description both literal and metaphorical. The "interlaced gods, animals, and men," religious representations painted on the walls, suggest the interconnectedness or vital union of things in a peaceful world. Because union is what the poet seeks in herself, these figures provide for her evidence that serenity is possible in a chaotic world: "The figures hold their peace/ In a web of movement."

The artwork at the Ajanta caves has been described as overwhelming; in the poem, the descriptive onslaught of things—earth, crystal, water, "pillars and prisms," riders, horses, and "Red Cow . . . running through the world"—overwhelms the reader. The cave is a place of intense feeling and emotion.

In the cave, where "the world comes forward in flaming sequences," the poet-traveler possesses her world at its most fulfilling:

> There is no frustration
> Every gesture is taken, everything yields connection . . .
> Water to sound, fire to form, life flickers
> Uncounted into the supple arms of love.

The unity she attempts to describe is conveyed in sexual images, but transcends the sexual; it cannot be confined to "the spaces of the body," which are "suddenly limit-less." The idea of union, however, is best conveyed in the imagery of the body and its physical rhythms. The last ten lines of "The Cave" are an energetic and sensuous evo-cation of the life force consecrating itself: physical action transformed into timeless, boundless energy "in the web of time."

Part 3, "Les Tendresses Bestiales" (brutish caresses), describes a return to frustra-tion (part of life's rhythm). Rukeyser examines her reaction to the frustration of lost love, one who has died, presumably in the war. The sequence is written from the per-spective of a mariner on the water, peering at the sky to chart the way. She sees the constellations reconfigure to form a "body shining."

The images come into port next: the dark streets, the faceless whore, the whispering "checkered men," "The dice and the alcohol and the destruction," and finally the "Broken bottle of loss" are images of squandering and despair. Unchecked, these im-pulses can lead to self-destruction—"the glass/ turned bloody into the face."

She compares dealing with her emotions to trying to keep a ship's wheel steady in a storm: Losing control of the wheel as "the wave turns," she sees "the world bearing my grave,/ And your eyes open in earth." The loss of her love is still very vivid. In deep mourning, the poet envisions the world as a hostile place and finds herself sink-ing into it. Her search for "the midnight cave"—her place of healing—becomes more urgent than ever.

"Black Blood," part 4, is a brief and mysterious interlude in the poem. Her attempt to return to the cave pauses at a deserted harbor, a sinister place where a "woman laced into a harp/ screams and screams" (the poet unable to sing her song?) and "The Floating Man" (the moon?) "rides on the ragged sunset." Still grieving for her love and the world's destruction, the poet realizes that her "armored ghost of rage" is "powerless" and so implores: "touch my blood again." This request shaken out of sor-row is a turning point in her journey back to harmony. The advice coming from her innermost voice to "Try to live as if there were a God" is cautious and ironic, but nevertheless more hopeful than her previous state of mind.

The final part of the poem, "The Broken World," is a return to the cave; it ends the poem with two realizations. First, the poet reaches her Ajanta, "The real world where everything is complete." She has cast off her debilitating grief and now stands shadowless "on summer earth." Shadows, "the forms of incompleteness," stand for illusion, the mere outline one so often perceives of something without seeing what the thing really is. In the cave, though, shadows do not exist: "Here everything is itself."

The "Animals arrive,/ Interlaced, and gods/ Interlaced, and men/ Flame-woven." All things are connected, both peacefully and fruitfully. In Ajanta, at last, the poet can say "I stand and am complete." Her transformation into a unified being has come out of her great loss and her sense of the world's loss. Out of the cave (her search, herself), she has been reborn.

The second realization is that although the world is and always will be a broken world, people must live in it, for there is no way to be whole unless one's world "Enters the heart again"—even with its shadows and its "old noise of tears." The poet's rebirth has allowed her to welcome back the broken world and accept the struggles of living in it.

Forms and Devices

Rukeyser's energetic experiments in poetry were considered by many critics of the 1940's and 1950's to be loose in form and disorganized. During that time, traditional prosodic forms were more acceptable to many poets and critics, but Rukeyser was more interested in a poetry in which the material could generate its own form. She did not believe in grafting predetermined structures, such as metered patterns, onto her experiences for the sake of technical unity.

She seeks to convey the wholeness of experience. Thus, in "Ajanta," as many critics did not recognize, the sexual images not only serve as thematic unifiers but also help to weave the structural fabric of the poem. In "Ajanta," and many of the poems in *Beast in View*, sex becomes an organizing force as Rukeyser attempts to reproduce in language and sound and rhythm the rhythms of the body. She later praised Walt Whitman's poetry, in which "physical rhythms are the base of every clear line. . . . He remembered his body as other poets of his time remembered English verse." Such rhythms in "Ajanta" are especially apparent in the last ten lines of part 2, "The Cave," and in the "Animals arrive" sequence in part 5, "The Broken World." At the poem's climax, the rhythm suggests one trying to catch her breath, then slowly relaxing as the feverish pace calms toward the last line of the poem.

"Ajanta" conveys the force of sexual impulse—the need and desire for union, which is what the poet seeks in herself and with the world. The sexual impulse becomes a metaphor for unity at all levels of existence. Built into the poem are journeys toward a number of unions: the poet seeking the cave to enter it, the heart seeking its myth, the bereft lover seeking whatever will relieve her sorrow, the reborn traveler taking the world into her heart again.

The image of the cave, the poem's central extended metaphor, also unifies the poem. Besides its thematic importance, the cave image frames the poem. The first lines of parts 1 and 5 echo each other: "Came in my full youth to the midnight cave" and "Came to Ajanta cave." The repetition shows that the journey has come full circle, a closing device that indicates the poet has completed the journey.

The journey motif is crucial to the poem's unity. Each section finds the traveler in another phase of self-examination; that is, in another place, more or less close to her desired goal. The nautical terms used to describe certain legs of the journey (the deserted harbor, "night sailing the river," "the foghorn's word") also help unify the poem and indicate the elemental nature of the voyage.

Themes and Meanings

By choosing to make her journey by water, Rukeyser consciously uses the time-honored symbolism of water and sea voyaging. Water is the source of life, what we are born out of; it flows beneath the surface of things; it is the element of fertility, and it is always moving and changing. It is a favorite symbol, also, to indicate female life force and women's physical transformations. This poem is about transformation and nurturing new life, or rebirth.

"Ajanta" opens *Beast in View*, Rukeyser's fourth book of poems. The "beast" she hunts on her spiritual voyage is not always in view—in "Ajanta" it remains hidden from her until her final reconciliation in the cave to which it has led her. The beast is her innermost self, what makes her who she is, what is vital to her being. The thematic energy of "Ajanta" is devoted to capturing the beast—herself in her own myth of herself—so that she can be a whole person again. Because the poem is about transformation, and adapting to changes in life and the world, the beast in "Ajanta" often appears in disguises. All these masks are part of the poet's personality and her changes. She seeks to unify them and accept them all: "the whore with the dying red hair,/ the child myself who is my murderer . . . " and later "the panther with its throat along my arm" and "the silver derelict wearing fur and claws."

The search for self-identity in "Ajanta," however, is not an end in itself. Beginning with descriptions of war atrocities, the poem reminds readers that to know oneself is vital also for the sake of the world in which one lives. The poet seeks the strong armor of self-knowledge, rather than the armor of rage, in order to know better how to aid the struggles of those who have been betrayed or who are suffering loss. The "world of the shadowed and alone" is a place in which the conscientious must fight for those in need and confront "the struggles of the moon." In "Letter to the Front" (also from *Beast in View*), Rukeyser praises the healing power that women can offer the world, especially in time of war. She envisioned female sensibilities transforming traditional man, or the traditional masculine ideal. This vision laid a path for later women poets, such as Adrienne Rich, who continue to explore similar themes.

The cave is a symbol for female sensibility, mystery, and strength. It is a dark interior, a place of hiding or hibernation, a place of meditation, a vault from which one emerges reborn, as did Jesus. It is also a source of life: Its watery, quiet space nurtures, like a womb. Its interior can be mysterious yet comforting, black, and frightening, or cool and beckoning. "Ajanta," says Kenneth Rexroth (1905-1982), is "an exploration . . . of her own interior—in every sense." That is, as a poet and a woman, Rukeyser is interested in her mind and in her body's flesh and form and how they shape her quest for fulfillment. The beauty, complexity, and energy of "Ajanta" has made it one of her most famous and powerful poems.

JoAnn Balingit

ALEXANDER'S FEAST
Or, The Power of Music, an Ode in Honor of St. Cecilia's Day

Author: John Dryden (1631-1700)
Type of poem: Ode
First published: 1697

The Poem

John Dryden's *Alexander's Feast: Or, The Power of Music* is, as its subtitle informs the reader, *An Ode in Honor of St. Cecilia's Day.* It is, in fact, Dryden's second poem in honor of this saint, the patron saint of music and, according to tradition, the inventor of the pipe organ. Therefore, the poem is not merely a tribute to the saint, but also a poem about the power of music. It has been set to music three times, the third and definitive setting that of George Frideric Handel.

The narrative framework is suggested by Plutarch's "Alexander," in which the author describes Alexander's feast for his officers, celebrating the defeat of Persia. At this feast, according to Plutarch, Alexander's mistress, Thais, persuaded Alexander to burn the Persian capitol in revenge for the Persians' burning of her home city of Athens. Dryden gives the story a very different emphasis.

The first stanza introduces Alexander and his mistress sitting in state. In the second, Alexander's musician, Timotheus, with his lyre inspires Alexander to a sense of divine power, singing the story told by Alexander's mother, Olympia, that Alexander's actual father was Zeus who, in the form of a great dragon, had impregnated her. In stanza 3 Timotheus shifts to the pleasures of drink. In stanza 4, seeing the mood of mellow intoxication becoming drunken belligerence, he next shifts the mood to one of sorrow, singing of the fall of kings, boldly choosing as his example Darius, king of Persia, whose defeat is being celebrated. In stanza 5, having already aroused the softer emotions, Timotheus moves from sorrow to thoughts of love, and then in stanza 6 to anger and revenge, inspiring Alexander to burn Persia's capital, Persepolis.

The motivations Plutarch gives Alexander, intoxication and a desire to please his mistress, however, are unrelated to the power of music. The opening lines of the sixth stanza make the desire for revenge a result of Timotheus's music, though no reason is given for the musician to desire such an outcome. The fact that this stanza follows the one about love, as well as the lines, "Thais led the way,/ To light him to his prey,/ And, like another Helen, fir'd another Troy," suggest that Thais is responsible. That, however, would seem to contradict the rest of the stanza, and to be irrelevant to the poem's theme, the power of music. The reader might suppose that Thais takes advantage of the mood Timotheus creates, though one may still wonder at the irresponsibility of raising anger and thoughts of revenge in the mind of someone already intoxicated. Such questions, however, go largely unnoticed, for readers are caught up in the mythic resonance of the burning of a great city and the analogy with Troy that concludes the narrative part of the poem.

The final stanza introduces the patron saint of music, stating that Cecilia goes beyond the nearly magical power of Timotheus's music, because she "Enlarg'd the former narrow bounds/ And added length to solemn sounds," and so either takes the prize, or at least must share it, for "He rais'd a mortal to the skies;/ She drew an angel down." This final line echoes Dryden's earlier "Song for St. Cecilia's Day," which explicitly states that the beauty of Cecilia's music causes the angel to mistake earth for heaven. The angel visitor is a part of the saint's legend, but Dryden, for the purposes of his poem, has changed the cause of the visit from Cecilia's virtue to her music. Samuel Johnson complained of the impropriety of a shared prize when the exultation of Alexander to godhead is only metaphoric, while the angelic visitor is real. However, Cecilia's advantage in the comparison is great enough that Dryden can afford to leave the judgment to the reader. Further, a divided prize introduces the sense of balance. Each of the earlier stanzas represents an extreme of emotion, so that the neat balance and antithesis at the end gives the conclusion a sense of harmonious coming together.

Forms and Devices

Alexander's Feast is a Pindaric ode. This uniquely English form, actually little related to the poetry of the Greek poet Pindar, is an ode written in irregularly rhymed free verse and was probably chosen by Dryden because the flexibility it allowed in sound patterns could better approximate the effect of music than the more rigid traditional forms. Because they are of unequal length and varying pattern of rhyme, the seven stanzas of the poem could more properly be called verse paragraphs. Each ends in a chorus of four to seven lines, which is a repetition of the last lines of the stanza. The "Grand Chorus" at the end of the poem repeats ten lines, giving the concluding stanza more weight than the others.

The one feature this ode does share with those of Pindar, and which may have been inspired by Pindar, is the fact that Saint Cecilia is glorified less through elaboration of her own life and deeds than through being placed in relationship to a grand mythic or legendary narrative. This is a convention that works to Dryden's advantage, since the saint's sketchily reported life offers little to work with.

The poem not only is about music, but also was intended from the first to be set to music. Each stanza employs every poetic resource of sound pattern and rhythm to create speed, force, hardness, softness, smoothness, or abruptness. It is as much, or more, a libretto for music than a poem praising music, and it provides instructions for any musician who would set it to music. The second stanza mentions the lyre, a stringed instrument. The third, the praise of Bacchus, introduces trumpets, drums, and hautbois. The sixth stanza goes back to the lyre.

Much of the poem's appeal is the exuberance of the language. Even the softest and most melancholy passages have a quickness and energy that hurry the reader along to the last stanza. In these parts Dryden employs one resource he has been holding back. The choice and arrangement of vowels and consonants give the lines a gravity and resonance appropriate to the pipe organ.

Music and poetry in the ancient world were less distinct from one another than in later times. Dryden takes advantage of the traditional connection to make his effects poetic as well as musical, for at least part of Timotheus's effect comes from narrative, as in the stories of Alexander's birth and of Darius's fall. The ode in praise of Saint Cecilia, the pipe organ, and the power of music is also an ode in praise of the power of poetry and of the rich classical tradition out of which so much of Western poetry arises.

Themes and Meanings

Alexander's Feast is about the power of music to raise, quell, and shift emotions. It illustrates emotion through the effective use of sound and rhythm as well as through content. What it does not do is express the emotion in a way that truly involves either the author or the reader. When a drunken Alexander mentally refights all his battles and thrice slays the slain, readers are more inclined to smile with the author than to grow bloody-minded with the warrior.

The reader accustomed to the personal intensities of the odes of the Romantic era may well be put off by Dryden's distance and objectivity. Dryden's era and the century that immediately follows are often called the Age of Reason. Yet even in this age Dryden stands out as a poet of wit and intellect rather than of emotion. It is impressive that he can illustrate emotions so effectively without involving himself or asking involvement on the reader's part. Emotion, so valued by the Romantics, can be seen as delusion as well as a dangerous and even negative force in the poem. Alexander is deluded in his assumption of godhead, vain in his reliving of his martial exploits, and wantonly angry in his burning of Persepolis. The Miltonic grandeur of Alexander's initial appearance, "Aloft in awful state/ The godlike hero sate/ On his imperial throne" is undercut throughout by the ease with which Timotheus manipulates him. The theme of the poem, however, is not Alexander's greatness, but the power of music, and even the great conqueror becomes a trophy of that power.

If one looks for themes, there is the undying luster of the classical world, its arts, its history, its myths and legends. There is the authority and allusive richness of a musical and poetic tradition that reaches back to antiquity. There is the dangerous power of the emotions and the irrational. These, however, are less themes than assumptions of Dryden's age, which he embodies and expresses better than anyone else. Ultimately, there is one real theme, and that is stated in the poem's alternate title.

Jack Hart

ALL BREAD

Author: Margaret Atwood (1939-   )
Type of poem: Lyric/meditation
First published: 1978, in *Two-Headed Poems*

The Poem

"All Bread" is a short poem in free verse, comprising four stanzas of uneven length. The poem's central premise is the interdependence of humans and the earth and the cyclical rhythms of that relationship. A parallel interdependence between males and females is also implicit in this premise. Bread is the archetypal product of the earth, both the "staff of life" and an element of sacrifice and sacrament. The mundane yet important ritual of making and consuming bread shapes the poem and provides its central metaphor.

The poem's four stanzas trace the stages in the bread-making process, moving from field to kitchen to consumption, from drudgery to communion. Stanza 1 describes the growing grain which comprises all the elements of earth, vegetable and animal, living and dead. Humans plant and harvest the grain; they assemble the wood and water necessary to mill and cook it; the cook shapes it into loaves. Stanza 2 describes the baking process, evoking the moist heat and the aroma that gives bread-making its appeal. Stanza 3 defines bread's taste on the individual's tongue; and stanza 4 invokes perhaps the most meaningful part of the bread-making process: sharing bread.

The poem is written in the first person. Its tone is personal and intimate, as if a kitchen-table conversation were taking place while bread is being shared in a daily family or neighborly ritual. Stanza 4, though, takes on the cadence of a priest intoning the rites of Eucharist: "Together/ we eat this earth" is the benediction that closes the poem.

Forms and Devices

As is typical in Margaret Atwood's poetry and much of her prose, "All Bread" is permeated with the imagery of elemental, primordial life with which Atwood believes humankind is intimately bound. The poem's language is bare. Its words are largely monosyllabic, sparse and direct, very Anglo-Saxon, sometimes gross—the speech and imagery of peasants and laborers bound, often unwillingly, to the earth: "All bread is made of wood,/ cow dung, packed brown moss,/ the bodies of dead animals." These materials are obtained by "nine strokes/ of the axe." The making and consumption of bread is the shaping metaphor for Atwood's unoriginal vision of the life cycle as binding life and death irrevocably. At the poem's conclusion, Atwood's usually pessimistic outlook is leavened by an uncharacteristic optimism. Homely, rustic rituals, performed in field and kitchen, affirm humans' community with other humans and with the earth. Says critic Kathleen Vogt: "The bread of communion is the bread baked in the kitchen; it is a part of the processes of nature, which include death and life. These processes are a kind of sacrament in 'All Bread.'"

The intricate interweaving of death and life, destruction and creation, is suggested in the poem's juxtaposed images of ancient sacrificial rituals (especially of humans to pagan gods) and of the fecund warmth of pregnancy and birth evident in the description of the bread's rising and baking:

> nine strokes
> of the axe, skin from a tree,
>
> . . . .
>
> the row
> of white famine bellies
> swollen and taut in the oven,
> lungfuls of warm breath stopped
> in the heat from an old sun.

Sacramental ceremony is also suggested by "a silver dish" in which the loaves are offered to the oven.

Salt is the dominant image in stanza 3: "Good bread has the salt taste/ of your hands after nine/ strokes of the axe, the salt/ taste of your mouth. . . . " The ambivalence expressed through the rest of the poem's imagery is sustained here. Indispensable bread is indeed the salt of the earth but conversely requires the saltiness of blood, sweat, and tears expended in the labor of sustaining life. Despite this imagery of sacrifice, a tone of fulfillment is also discernible in stanza 3.

This tone carries the reader into stanza 4, where diction and mood become more quietly exalted. For the first time, more complex and connotative words occur, recalling the solemn, splendid liturgy of the Eucharist (or Communion) ritual. "Lift," "ashes," "devour," "consecrate," "broken," and "shared" all evoke Christ's devotions to his followers at the Last Supper: "Now as they were eating, Jesus took bread, and blessed, and broke it, and gave it to the disciples and said, 'Take, eat; this is my body'" (Matthew 26:26). The poem's final lines—". . . Together/ we eat this earth"—bring it full circle, back to the earth where the residues of death and the elements of life are equally contained, and where the making and eating of humble bread is a reminder to humankind of its place in the cycle.

Themes and Meanings

"All Bread" expresses the core of Atwood's vision: humankind's love-hate relationship with the natural world, as well as with the dichotomies of its own nature. This vision is delineated through a voice that is ironic in tone, suitable for exploring the conflicts and ambiguities of humankind's struggles to survive both physically and psychically.

In an earlier poem, "Progressive Insanities of a Pioneer" (*The Animals in That Country*, 1968), Atwood defines the power struggle between humans and nature as "the tension/ between subject and object." Part of this tension lies in humans' recognition of nature as mainly predatory, and of human existence as a struggle both to survive and also to subvert these same predatory tendencies in the human character. The very real struggles of early Canadian settlers from Europe, many of whom were unsuited to the harsh Canadian climate and landscape, have provided Atwood with the perfect metaphor for exploring the nature-humankind relationship. In her own study, *Survival: A Thematic Guide to Canadian Literature* (1972), Atwood concludes the chapter "Nature the Monster" by observing, "Nature is a monster, perhaps, only if you come to it with unreal expectations or fight its conditions rather than accepting them or learning to live with them."

The speaker of "All Bread" begins by expressing outright distaste for natural processes: "All bread is made of . . .// the bodies of dead animals, the teeth/ and backbones, what is left/ after the ravens." Soon comes acknowledgment of how human labor on the earth can be consecrated by nature: "good water which is the first/ gift, four hours." Finally, there is a quiet acceptance of the relationship between humankind and nature: "to know what you devour/ is to consecrate it,/ almost." Critic Jean Mallinson observes, " 'All Bread' . . . records a kind of reconciliation with the muck of the world, the ooze and dung and dirt of it, which is part of the poet's dispraise of life in other poems."

Secondary in "All Bread" is a parallel aspect of conflict that also informs Atwood's vision: the power struggle between the sexes. As with the struggle between humanity and nature, the perspective of the poem evolves from forceful and ironic to calm and accepting. In the course of the poem, the speaker (whose tone and point of view are almost certainly female) makes reference to shared physical work and to the exclusively female pain of childbirth. Female imagery abounds in stanza 2, where the inextricable interweaving of death and life is strongest in the metaphors used to describe the bread baking. "Live burial under a moist cloth,/ . . . the row/ of white famine bellies," while somewhat glibly and gratuitously evoking the ovens of concentration camps, above all suggests the joyful pain of childbirth labor: "swollen and taut in the oven,/ lungfuls of warm breath stopped." References in stanza 3, where the tone becomes more intimate with the use of the second-person "you," are to shared sexual love—". . . the salt taste/ of your hands after nine/ strokes of the axe, the salt/ taste of your mouth." Finally, in stanza 4, Atwood refers to the shared ceremony that celebrates life's sacraments such as marriage.

"All Bread" may be viewed as a personal epiphany, or revelation, in which the speaker contemplates, at first with ironic distaste but finally with benign acceptance, the paradoxical truth of existence: that death and life are inextricably entwined, and that human relationships, especially between the sexes, are founded on the same interdependence. In this poem, the sanctity of life, despite its elements of grossness and drudgery, is celebrated.

Jill Rollins

ALL MY PRETTY ONES

Author: Anne Sexton (1928-1974)
Type of poem: Lyric
First published: 1962, in *All My Pretty Ones*

The Poem

"All My Pretty Ones" is the title poem of Anne Sexton's intensely confessional second book of poetry, *All My Pretty Ones* (1962), and it reflects that volume's absorption with loss and death. This poem consists of five ten-line stanzas and resembles the form of most of the companion poems in the volume. The poem's title comes from William Shakespeare's *Macbeth* (1606), when Macduff mourns the loss of his wife and children. In March of 1959, Anne Sexton's mother died, followed in June of the same year by Sexton's father. "All My Pretty Ones" is a monologue addressed to Sexton's dead father as she sorts through her parents' possessions.

In the first stanza, Sexton looks over her father's meager "leftovers": a key, some stock certificates, clothing, a car, his will, and a box of photographs. She is recording a moment that many children must endure: the closing of a parent's affairs, the moment when the living children must literally discard artifacts not only of their parents' lives but also of their own. She sees her task as one of helping her father to free himself from the tangles of his now past life. The stanza concludes with her decision to throw away the items that she has found.

In the second stanza, Sexton continues to gaze on the photographs in the box, wondering at the images she sees, unable to identify many of the now long-dead people with any degree of certainty. She looks at a picture of a small boy in a christening gown—is it her father? She wonders if another picture is her great-grandfather. She concludes that her father's own death renders her search for names irrelevant; now she can never know, because the person who could have told her the importance of each face in the pictures has died. She ends the stanza by locking them—entombing them—in the album and throwing it away.

Stanza 3 continues the sifting and sorting process with a scrapbook that her father had begun the year Sexton was born. It contains memorabilia of historical events such as Prohibition and the crash of the *Hindenburg*. It also enables Sexton to recall some of her father's own history, such as his financial good fortune as a result of the war. Sexton swings the focus of the poem back to her father in the stanza's concluding three lines when she remembers her father's intention to marry a second time—only months after her mother's death—and her own distraught response. Her father died three days later.

This reflection forms the bridge to stanza 4, in which Sexton looks at pictures of her parents, photographs that reflect family history as well as family wealth. It is clear from these images that Sexton led a privileged life, yet she concludes this section with a reference to her father's alcoholism. The final stanza continues this reflection: Sexton finds her mother's diary, which elliptically records three years of her father's drinking. This, like the family pictures in stanza 4, Sexton decides to keep; they are artifacts that she hopes, in the poem's final three lines, will enable her to come to terms with her own mixed feelings about her father.

Forms and Devices

By using a fairly open line in "All My Pretty Ones," Sexton achieves a conversational tone in this interior monologue. The rhyme scheme is *ababcdcdee*, which gives a strict form to the poem, but a form whose meter and structure does not intrude on what could be termed the rhythm of everyday speech. By making individual lines within a stanza fairly long, Sexton adds to the somber tone of this encounter with her dead father, his dead past, and the end of her childhood. This form also makes the lines and stanzas heavy: Sentences continue for several lines, weighing the poem down and adding to the feeling of sadness that Sexton achieves in her description of what may be her first articulation of being an adult orphan. Controlled form plays an important part in Sexton's early poetry; the more difficult the emotional event, the tighter the form. In "All My Pretty Ones," she uses the structure to give an external control to a powerful moment.

Of equal importance is the strong visual sense that Sexton imparts to the poem. Much of what she describes relates to seeing: images of her dead parents, artifacts that symbolize aspects of her father's personality and life, pictures that freeze moments in her ancestors' lives and in her immediate family's past. Sexton offers a balanced description of these artifacts, allowing the reader to decide their importance to the woman who is sorting through the remnants of her parents' lives. It is the choice of things rather than what Sexton says about those things that makes the commentary poignant and powerful. Sexton frequently reports rather than analyzes, as in the case of her mother's diary in the poem's final stanza. Much like this older woman's account of her husband's alcoholism, "telling all she does not say," Sexton's poem shows rather than explains. In this regard, the photographs she sifts through in stanzas 2 through 4 do the same thing for the poet: They offer images, but they fail to explain why they were important ones to the man who kept them for all those years.

The power of "All My Pretty Ones" rests partly in its twofold focus. The poet reflects on her father's life and tries to make sense of it, as the reader does listening to her "conversation" with her now-dead parent. Also, in sorting out her father's world, Sexton is also sorting out her feelings for this man, someone who obviously was difficult for her to love unconditionally. The actions of the daughter move from discarding images and things in the first two stanzas to keeping images and artifacts "to love or look at later." The final stanza concludes this transformation, and the last couplet resolves the tension that Sexton has been building. She offers her dead father forgiveness. This final line repeats an image of enfolding that she used to conclude the previous stanza when she refolded the pictures of her father; in the last line of the poem, Sexton herself bends down over the material scraps that her father has left behind and forgives him.

Themes and Meanings

"All My Pretty Ones" is a poem about loss, about love, and about an adult daughter's relationship to her parents, in particular to her father. It also reflects the tone and focus of the book for which it is the title piece; in *All My Pretty Ones*, Sexton attempts to deal with her preoccupation with death, pain, and bereavement. An intensely personal poet, Sexton is generally described as a confessional poet, an artist whose own life provides much if not all of the material for her poetry. In the case of *All My Pretty Ones*, it is Sexton's emotions relating to her family and to God that are the foundation for the poems. Poems such as "All My Pretty Ones" are painful for the reader because of their intensely personal revelations and because the subject matter touches on fears, griefs, and disappointments that many readers will share.

The title of the book and the poem is taken from Shakespeare's *Macbeth*, in which Macduff expresses shock and grief over the murder of his entire family and makes the point relevant to Sexton's book that he cannot stop remembering the things "That were most precious to me." This is precisely what Sexton does in this poem and in the other pieces in the book. Not only does the book's epigram from *Macbeth* set the stage, but also her choice of an additional quotation from Franz Kafka establishes the book's purpose: In the passage, Kafka says that "a book should serve as the ax for the frozen sea within us." "All My Pretty Ones" is certainly an example of the catalytic function of memory and objects, not only books, for it is the poet's sifting through the artifacts of her parents' lives that breaks down her resistance and enables her to express her true feelings for her father. The act of closing her father's house gives her the opportunity to bring closure to her relationship with him: At the poem's conclusion, she has moved toward forgiveness and acceptance.

Melissa E. Barth

ALL SOULS' NIGHT

Author: William Butler Yeats (1865-1939)
Type of poem: Meditation
First published: 1921; collected in *The Tower,* 1928

The Poem

"All Souls' Night" is the last poem in William Butler Yeats's most important collection of poetry, *The Tower* (1928). Organized into ten stanzas of ten lines each, it is a meditation, during All Souls' Night, on several friends who have died. A subtitle indicates that the poem is an epilogue to Yeats's book *A Vision* (1925), which is the codification of his theories of magic and history that were given to him by "Unknown Instructors" in the form of automatic writing transcribed by his wife Georgia. As such, the poem is meant to comment on and to celebrate this achievement. The first stanza is primarily descriptive as it sets the scene for the rest of the poem. It is midnight and the "great Christ Church bell" of Oxford University and other lesser bells "sound through the room." In this special and sacred time, a "ghost may come" to drink of the fumes of the wine that the poem's speaker has placed there. The ghost is so refined by death that he can only drink the "wine-breath."

In the next stanza, the speaker explains that he needs a mind that is armed against the "cannon sound" and other intrusions of the world, a mind that "can stay/ Wound in mind's pondering,/ As mummies in the mummy-cloth are wound." The description of souls being wound in the "mummy-cloth" comes from another of Yeats's important poems, "Byzantium." He needs this special mind or soul because he has "a marvellous thing to say/ a certain marvellous thing/ None but the living mock." That "marvellous thing" is contained in his book *A Vision.*

In the third and fourth stanzas, the speaker calls on the spirit of William Thomas Horton, a mystical painter and illustrator who was a casual friend of Yeats a number of years before the poem was written. What he discovers in Horton's life is a refusal to accept loss and tragedy as something mortals must bear. This refusal to accept such losses is crucial to *A Vision*, in which Yeats claims to have discovered a system that could explain the mysteries of life and death. Horton refuses to accept the death of his "lady," and nothing can console him: "Nothing could bring him, when his lady died,/ Anodyne for his love." The only hope remaining to him is that the "inclemency/ Of that or the next winter would be death." In the fourth stanza, Yeats amusingly describes how Horton's thought is "so mixed up" that he cannot tell "Whether of her or God he thought the most." When Horton turns his mind's eye upward, it falls "on one sole image," a vision that makes him "Wild with divinity" and illuminates heaven, "the whole/ Immense miraculous house/ The Bible promised us." Horton's vision thus achieves one of the central aims of *A Vision:* to unite the two disparate worlds of heaven and hell.

The next ghost that Yeats calls up is Florence Farr Emery, an actress of great beauty who, when she grew old and was about to lose that beauty, went to "teach a school" in Africa so those who had known and loved her would not see her decay. She had discovered "the soul's journey" from a "learned Indian," in which the soul would find a place where it could be "free and yet fast,/ Being both Chance and Choice." As Horton had unified heaven and hell, Emery had discovered the final unity that the soul would achieve.

The last ghost called up is a lesser and more controversial one, McGregor Mathers. Yeats describes him as "half a lunatic, half knave." Although he did not discover any occult knowledge, his "meditations on unknown thought" made "human intercourse grow less and less." So he, like the others, removed himself from the world to seek occult knowledge. The last part of the poem is Yeats's celebration of his own achievement in *A Vision*. He has "mummy truths to tell," and, wound within these truths, he needs "no other thing." They stand before the assault of the world and of both heaven and hell.

Forms and Devices

The ten-line stanza is one of the most important formal devices in the poem. The rhyme scheme is *abcabcdeed*, and the middle lines are iambic trimeter while the first and last lines are iambic pentameter. Yeats maintains this difficult pattern through each stanza and still manages to make the verse appear conversational and casual. Its complex arrangement mirrors that of *A Vision* to which it is connected. There are a number of sound images in the poem, including "the great Christ Church Bell" and the many "lesser" bells that "sound through the room" in the first stanza. These insistent sound images define the hostile outside world of the living who mock Yeats's vision; the sounds are contrasted to the quiet of Yeats's meditation upon the familiar ghosts who, through their quests for occult knowledge, managed to escape the world.

Although "All Souls' Night" is sparing in its use of the traditional devices of poetry, there are several important metaphors in the poem, the most significant being the comparison of the "mind's pondering" with being wound "As mummies in the mummy-cloth are wound." This suggests that the speaker has knowledge possessed by no one else but the dead. Another metaphor is the "soul's journey" in the Florence Emery section. She has discovered how the soul whirls around the moon (the cycles of the moon are central to *A Vision*) and then plunges "into the sun" where it can "sink into its own delight at last." These metaphors are ways of describing the spiritual truths that these seekers have discovered.

Yeats's verse portraits of his friends in the middle sections of the poem act as structural parallels and counterpoints to his own visionary achievement. The use of his dead friends in such a manner is a staple that also appears in such poems as "In Memory of Major Robert Gregory" and "The Municipal Gallery Revisited." "All Souls' Night," then, acts as a meditation on those friends who helped Yeats's spiritual search in his early life and provided an example of dedication to the occult. However, Yeats outdid those efforts of his friends to discover the system explained in *A Vision*.

Themes and Meanings

"All Souls' Night" functions as an epilogue to and something of a defense of *A Vision*. The book uses the phases of the moon and other mystical symbols to organize human character into cycles. Furthermore, it places these cycles into historical cones. It is therefore clear why Yeats insists in "All Souls' Night" that he has marvelous things to say. The ghosts that Yeats calls up in the poem are symbolic of the ability of Yeats's system to connect the living and the dead. The ghosts provide an example of the poet's success, and they join him in celebrating his creation of a system that provides all the answers about time, humanity, and history.

One important theme is the claim that Yeats has united heaven and hell, a concept that he learned from English poet William Blake. At the end of the poem, Yeats speaks of how his meditation can both defy the world and penetrate "To where the damned have howled away their hearts,/ And where the blessed dance." His vision is capable of encompassing both parts of the afterlife and reconciling these opposites. Yeats's vision also involves a rejection of the world, which remains outside the ceremony of calling up the ghosts. However, he describes Horton as achieving a reunion with his lost beloved. The reunion must be in the afterlife. This brings to mind Yeats's assertions of a union with Maud Gonne, a woman who spurned him and his proposals of marriage, in the other world if not this world. The reconciliation of "Chance and Choice" is another important theme in Yeats's work. The reconciliation that is claimed in "All Souls' Night" is a symbol for "Unity of Being," a state that Yeats sought all his life. In a note to his play *Calvary* (1921), Yeats said that the union of "Chance and Choice" was only to be found in God. In "All Souls' Night," it is a discovery made by Emery and is comparable to the reconciliation of opposites that Yeats achieves in both the poem and *A Vision*.

James Sullivan

ALTARWISE BY OWL-LIGHT

Author: Dylan Thomas (1914-1953)
Type of poem: Poetic sequence
First published: 1935, 1936; collected as "Poems for a Poem," in *Twenty-five Poems,*
1936

The Poem

"Altarwise by Owl-Light" is a sequence of ten sonnets. The title is taken from the opening of the first sonnet, which describes the birth of Christ as producing an era of owl-like wisdom through the light of His altar. The last sonnet returns to vary the image of "altarwise" as a celebration of the effects Christianity has had on the history of the world: It has followed "the tale's sailor from a Christian voyage/ Atlaswise."

In the first sonnet, Dylan Thomas says that Jesus descended from Adam into the grave of life, the house of the flesh, which he made wise as the owl in the twilight of history. He is a gentle man who is the sun (Son) moving between the Tropic of Capricorn (the goat/life) in the Southern Hemisphere, on December 22, and the Tropic of Cancer (the crab/death) in the Northern Hemisphere, on June 22. He does battle with Abaddon as Satan/death by hanging on the cross by a nail. He is also the cock who announces a new day, hanging on his cross on one leg like a weather-vane rooster.

The second sonnet continues to present the complexities of the Christian Nativity, when death was made into a metaphor of spiritual rebirth. The child at a mother's breast is Christ whose mother is self-sacrificing, like the pelican who feeds her young with her own blood; Christ is the pelican itself, shedding his blood for others. As the sun/Son, Christ is a child of the Milky Way, and he moves through circles of the heavens, as up a ladder (Jacob's ladder, made from the crossed bones of death) from the cave of mortality.

Sonnet 3 shows the birth of the sacrificial lamb, the one who pays the debt of death incurred by the old bellwether, the old Adam. The new lamb butts down death when Christ is sacrificed on Golgotha, the place of skulls. At the crucifixion, Christ speaks out like Rip Van Winkle, who wakes from a long sleep to become a new person. The next sonnet voices eight questions asked by the young child (Christ?), ranging from how the Word can be measured to whether God is a man or a woman. The energy of "genesis" charges a spark of light to show love projected through history, shot across the great flood of time itself.

The Annunciation of Christ's coming occurs when the angel Gabriel comes like a sheriff with two guns in sonnet 5. He plays a trick on death, and he plays cards with time. He pulls three cards from his sleeve: God, the "king of spots," king over death; Jesus, the jack (of all trades), and Mary, with the great heart. Gabriel is drunk on his message of salvation, and he tells a strange story of his travels: from Adam out of Eden, across the ocean as Ahab-Noah-Jonah, to the place of the frozen angel (Satan in

Dante's hell of ice), where death as a "black medusa" dwells and the sirens lure sailors into the Sargasso Sea.

The sixth sonnet is a cartoon of what God did in creating the universe, as described in Genesis, the book of life. It all began with the "word," as do all poems. The word is also Christ, the Word, who as the great rooster-cock of love pecks out the eye of the medusa—death. Still, the sirens sing to seduce the Adam of the flesh into their Sargasso Sea of sin. The genesis of sonnet 6 yields to the gospel of sonnet 7, where the Lord's Prayer is stamped "on a grain of rice," because rice must be planted in water to grow, like birth in the womb and rebirth in baptism. The leaves of the Bible grow from the tree of Calvary until spiritual wind turns death into life, words into poetry.

Sonnet 8 contemplates the crucifixion and passion of the suffering Christ, as viewed by his mother, Mary, and by himself. Jesus is the wound of Mary's womb, who is herself bent by the wound of the world. The rainbow of God's promise to Noah is repeated as the colors of the Trinity arching over the breasts of Mother Nature and Mary. In the last four lines, Jesus speaks as the thief of time and the physician who heals death. The next sonnet (9) is a contrast to sonnet 8. Whereas Christian burial is a way to eternal life, Egyptian burial is a futile effort to preserve the flesh in mummies and arks of parchment. The only resurrection for Egyptian mummies is the work of scholars who break into their tombs to study their dusty remains.

The final sonnet, sonnet 10, shows that the wise altar of sonnet 1 is the cross of the crucifixion ("the rude, red tree"). Here the Christian voyager has crossed the atlas to become wise enough not to be wrecked in the "dummy bay" of a false harbor. He is guided by Peter into a safe harbor, to which he holds the key ("quay"). Peter asks questions about the "tall fish" and the "rhubarb man," symbolic images of Jesus, who has restored the garden of Eden for all.

Forms and Devices

The sonnets of "Altarwise by Owl-Light" are lyrics of fourteen lines, divided into two logical parts: a sestet of six lines, followed by an octave of eight (a reversal of the conventional Italian sonnet). The rhyme scheme is *abcbac, dedefgfg*, but the rhymes are rarely exact; instead, they are slant rhymes or sight rhymes, as in the opening sonnet: "house" rhymes with "news," "furies" with "fairies," and "Adam" with "scream."

The sonnets are held together by the repetition of certain images, such as "altar," "cock," "bones," "cradle," and voyaging by water. Some of these images, such as Capricorn and Cancer, are drawn from astrology; others, such as mandrakes and pelicans, are from folklore. The sequence is dense; it rings with puns and obscure allusions. There are puns such as "genesis" and "gender" for biblical and sexual beginnings; sun for Son; and "rude, red" for "rood, read." Besides using frequent biblical allusions, the sequence employs numerous other literary allusions, such as Rip Van Winkle, and Herman Melville's Ishmael and the whale from *Moby Dick* (1851). Biblical anecdotes are mixed with contemporary events to create surrealistic effects. Sonnet 4 describes the Nativity of Christ with imagery of modern photography; sonnet 5 describes the Annunciation as an episode from a Western film made in Hollywood.

Determined by a biblical chronology that passes from Genesis to Revelation, the sequence is a series of figurative snapshots which interpret Christian images as creative (sexual and literary) symbols.

Themes and Meanings

In "Altarwise by Owl-Light," Thomas weaves together several themes to produce a richly layered meaning of personal and universal experience. Most prominent of its themes are the surrealistic events of Christian history, the trials of human sexuality, and the joyful labors of poetic creativity. In the end, all are one and the same, identified by the mysterious force of language itself.

Christian history is portrayed as very individual, as the speaker of the sonnets may sometimes be the poet, sometimes Christ, and sometimes the mother of Christ. Crucial episodes of history are taken as moments of illumination for all time, past, present, and future: the Nativity of Christ is a significant repetition of the genesis of the world, of the creation of Adam, and it is significantly repeated in the birth of every person; the Crucifixion of Christ repeats the Fall of Adam, and every person's pain/ death is a reenactment of the Fall and the Crucifixion; the Resurrection confirms the promise of new birth and new life for all, a return to Eden (the "flying garden") of the Old Adam through the New Adam of Christ.

Wherever there is creation, there is also some pain and, sometimes, there is comedy. The sequence follows the ironies and paradoxes of sexuality as blessing and curse: from the "hangnail cracked from Adam," to "the gender's strip," "marrow ladle," and "manwax," masculine crosses feminine sexuality with its "shapeless country," "milky mushrooms," and "house of bread." The theme of poetic creation crosses all with its elaboration of the major pun on the "Word" as the Beginning of All; hence, there is a "walking word," a "book of water," "medusa's scripture," "my fork tongue," and "a rocking alphabet." To create babies and poems is to create the world anew, to renew paradise and triumph over death; to joy in re-creation is to be wise, converting the atlas of the world into an altar of renewal.

Richard D. McGhee

AMAZING GRACE IN THE BACK COUNTRY

Author: Robert Penn Warren (1905-1989)
Type of poem: Narrative
First published: 1977; collected in *Now and Then: Poems, 1976-1978*, 1978

The Poem

In "Amazing Grace in the Back Country," the aging Robert Penn Warren looks back with nostalgia and wry amusement at a revivalist camp meeting he attended in rural Kentucky when he was twelve years old. Although he was quite convinced at that age that he was indeed sinful, he "hardened his heart" and refused the "amazing grace" offered by the revivalists. The tone is ironic throughout, and the poem implies that human behavior is not noticeably different after repentance. Nevertheless, this poem is not contemptuous of the yearning for redemption and hope.

The first stanza presents an unflattering analogy between the meager trappings of the traveling evangelists and the half-bankrupt carnivals that pitched their tents in the same spot. The fat lady, the geek, the moth-eaten lion, the boa constrictor that eats calves, and the aging whores demonstrate the quality of entertainment available in the backcountry. Those who lingered with the whores were likely to acquire syphilis as an added price for their fun.

The boy sits with the others listening as "an ex-railroad engineer/ Turned revivalist shouted the Threat and the Promise." An old woman in worn-out black silk kneels beside the boy and determines to save him. "She wept and she prayed, and I knew I was damned,/ Who was guilty of all short of murder,/ At least in my heart." He remembers how he once walked down the street after dark "Uttering, 'Lust—lust—lust,'/ Like an invocation, out loud."

The boy gazes in mounting alarm at the rising hysteria around him. At last, he bolts from the tent, runs into the forest, and vomits while leaning against a tree. He crouches there "knowing damnation" until the ecstatic congregation, now singing triumphantly of "amazing grace," straggles back to the village. Each singer "Found bed and lay down,/ And tomorrow would rise and do all the old things to do,/ Until that morning they would not rise, not ever."

Meanwhile, the boy lies in the forest with his hand in the spring where he rinsed his mouth after being sick and wonders what grace he will ever find. The poem ends with the thoughtful reminder "But that was long years ago. I was twelve years old then." Warren was in his seventies when he wrote the poem.

Forms and Devices

The poem uses the natural cadence of speech, avoiding rhyme and consistent meter. Both lines and stanzas vary in length. The last line stands alone, suggesting the pause, pregnant with unspoken memories of the person who looks backward at scenes a lifetime away, yet still vivid in detail. The tone is carefully modulated to fit the emotional content.

Sometimes the diction is jocular, colloquial, and disrespectful, like that used by one who remembers the language of the time and place: "one/ Boa constrictor for two bits seen/ Fed a young calf; plus a brace/ Of whores to whom menopause now/ Was barely a memory." (One can imagine the country storyteller sharing a laugh with the farmers in the general store.) Yet even here, the colloquial diction quickly fades to the more circumspect wording of the older, wiser man who remembers the tragic possibilities of coarse fun with whores: "A new and guaranteed brand of syphilis handy—yes."

The tent-meeting scene again zooms in with the immediacy of only yesterday when the boy was confused about how sinful he really was. The reader must smile at the boy's discovery of "lust" as a newly minted word, somehow equivalent to some secret sin not yet clearly understood. It is appropriate for a poet to appreciate the evocative power of words. After all, in a theological sense, the boy was not wrong in realizing that the intent of the heart is morally significant.

The poem makes an unobtrusive but thematically suggestive use of symbols. It begins with attention to the setting by the woods "where oaks of the old forest-time/ Yet swaggered and hulked over upstarts." The "old forest-time" is a reminder that these villagers have not yet completely dominated the surrounding wild country, just as they have not successfully indoctrinated the boy.

In stanza 7 through stanza 9, the protagonist is observing the worshipers and listening to them from the viewpoint of the woods. "I stared/ Through interstices of black brush to the muted gold glow/ Of God's canvas." The boy stays in the woods until all the voices are silent, and the lights are out in the tent, and the stars "Had changed place in the sky, I yet lay/ By the spring with one hand in the cold black water/ That showed one star in reflection, alone." The wheeling stars, with their connotations of time and fate, support the implication that the single star reflected in the water may symbolize the protagonist's fate. Moreover, the boy keeps his hand in the spring where the star appears, suggesting that the spring is a natural symbol of an alternate source of inspiration for the person who has refused "amazing grace." The twelve-year-old persona is not necessarily sure of that choice or what it portends for the welfare of his soul. The older Warren who tells the story has the wisdom of hindsight, but he does not make a moral judgment in the matter.

Themes and Meanings

Contemporary writers who, like Warren, were born at the beginning of the twentieth century have lived through the most rapid and spectacular social changes of any comparable period of history. This is particularly true for the South, which lingered in the rural, agrarian mode longer than other areas of the United States. Presumably at least, the backcountry does not even exist anymore. There is no place quite so isolated in its social choices, so insulated from information about the outside world, and so limited in its resources for entertainment or inspiration.

Although this poem provides a humorous commentary on the limitations of life in the backcountry, particularly the emotional poverty that at times led to what some would call religious hysteria, Warren approaches this time with a gentle and tolerant mood. Warren was and remained an unbeliever of strict fundamentalist religion. Yet he recognized that it answered a need that all people have, especially those who cannot distract themselves with the toys of a modern industrial society.

No matter what the excesses of revivalist camp meetings, these emotional encounters renewed a dream of salvation in lives that were often grim and repetitive. They assuaged what the poet calls "The late-season pain gnawing deep at the human bone."

Traveling preachers in the backcountry were often totally untrained for their calling. It was literally a calling—that is, they responded to a personal call from God, leaving behind whatever mode of life or occupation they had devised to make a living. They probably read the Bible, at least superficially, but they excelled mostly in fire-and-brimstone oratory. With the threat of damnation, these preachers sought to coerce sinners into accepting the "amazing grace" of a forgiving God.

This poem suggests that the young Warren was more frightened than inspired by the Christian message. Whether this rejection stemmed from rebellion, from a renewed devotion to sin as the boy dimly perceived it, or from an unconscious covenant with another source of inspiration remains somewhat ambiguous. Considering the subdued implication of the star and the spring, one may assume that Warren felt closer to God in the woods than he ever did in the revivalists' tent.

Some of Warren's other meditative poems written late in his life indicate that the moral and theological questions of religion continued to be live issues. Perhaps he was not immune to "The late-season pain gnawing deep at the human bone." Such poems as "A Way to Love God" and "Trying to Tell You Something" suggest that the fear is gone but that the mystery of fate remains. The imagery of these poems comes more from nature than from organized religion to provide insight into meaning and human fate.

There are no answers in the sense of doctrine or easy promises for future bliss. There is only the tremendous reality of experience and the overwhelming drive in the poet to give that experience adequate expression. Yet there is a certain hope, not exactly of salvation, but of some new remarkable insight that comes only, perhaps, at the point of death.

Katherine Snipes

THE AMBASSADOR DIARIES OF
JEAN DE BOSSCHÈRE AND EDGAR POE

Author: Norman Dubie (1945-   )
Type of poem: Lyric
First published: 1977; collected in *The City of the Olesha Fruit*, 1979

The Poem

"The Ambassador Diaries of Jean de Bosschère and Edgar Poe" has three sections, the first and third containing twelve stanzas each, the second containing five. Each stanza consists of six free-verse lines. Although Norman Dubie's title refers to Edgar Allan Poe and poet Jean de Bosschère, the poem is about Conrad Aiken (1889-1973). From childhood on, Aiken loved Poe's work, and he admired the poetry of Bosschère. Like these poets, Aiken was an orphan. The word "ambassador" comes from one of the passages in Aiken's poem "Time in the Rock," parts of which Dubie used as epigraphs in this poem, and Aiken referred to his *Preludes for Memmon* (1931) as a "spiritual diary."

In section 1, Dubie addresses Aiken and then narrates an anecdote based on Aiken's poem "And in the Hanging Gardens," whose characters—a king, a princess, and a knave—were derived from Aiken and his parents. Dubie combines the king and the knave in a single figure and provides a historical name, King Henry VIII. The young king has thrown his drinking cup from a window of his castle and goes out in the rain, cursing it and his mother, to find it. When he does, he lies down at the edge of a meadow to sleep, but servants are coming to return him to his mother, who waits with dry linens. Dubie says that the king's quest reflects a desire to be down in the muddy fields, dreaming of a castle in the air. Referring to Aiken's fear of inheriting his father's insanity, Dubie asks if his king is sane. When Aiken was eleven, his father shot Aiken's mother and then committed suicide. Dubie pictures the boy going from his dollhouse in the garden to his parents' bedroom and discovering the bodies. It begins to rain, and the walls of the dollhouse become "walls of terror, everywhere."

In section 2, Dubie quotes from Aiken's "Goya"—"Why wake the ones who sleep, if awake they/ Can only weep." Positive change will not occur in the world unless disturbing truths about human nature and the human condition are brought to consciousness. One such truth is the finality of death. Referring to Aiken's "Cliff Meeting," Dubie would like to think such a meeting of lovers will come after death for the woman who has died, but the most he will say is that it will be an "absence" of everything that is "not pretty."

In section 3, Dubie pictures Aiken writing poetry to heal the wound caused by his parents' deaths. Although Aiken won a Pulitzer Prize and Sigmund Freud considered his novel *Great Circle* (1933) a masterpiece, Dubie tells Aiken: "They no longer read your poems." Suggesting a reason, Dubie says Aiken disgusted the sheriff with details about his parents' deaths—"You told the truth." After asking Aiken if he hated women, Dubie states that the "government of children is left to women," with "the Fathers leaving us" from the beginning. These lines relate to Aiken's poem "Landscape West of Eden," in which Eve wants to stay in Eden and Adam wants to explore beyond it. Dubie suggests that some children become "orphan-poets" because of this conflict; he wrote his first poem when he was age eleven. Referring to another of his poems, "Elegies for the Ochre Deer on the Walls at Lascaux," which includes three suicides, Dubie says he once compared "the heads of two/ Bald priests" to the "buttocks/ Of lovers fleeing into the trees." This image, combined with those of rain in the poem (collected in a reference to the biblical flood), suggests a new beginning. Love and poetry offer the possibility of a new Eden.

Forms and Devices

In addition to his use of literary and historical allusions, Dubie employs parallels in diction and syntax, including images of color and clothing, to establish relationships among characters and incidents in the poem. In section 1, he refers to a "dark courtesan" with "white braids" and to the "dark room that morning" where Aiken's parents died. In section 2, he tells of the "lady in white" who "fell down this morning" and to the child who ran to her aid, as Aiken ran to his mother's. The lady addresses the child as Peter, saying she had never felt so "carefree." Aiken believed that his mother, although dead, spoke to him. Dubie renders this in a passage derived, as was the name "Peter," from Aiken's poem "The Coming Forth of Osiris Jones": "There was a voice speaking" of a handkerchief, of a flower.

Dubie establishes another link with a color image when he refers to Aiken's "red-eyed dolls" and to children who are kept "scrubbed and red/ And crying" by their mothers. This also connects with King Henry's mother, waiting with dry linens, and with Aiken's mother, who "had washed" his legs. Dubie creates another parallel with the color yellow. King Henry has "yellow sleeves," and the Nazis burned *Great Circle* because they considered it a "yellow-book, decadent," which is ironic, because it was Henry VIII and the Nazis who were decadent. They parallel the "princes and priests" who wanted to "pickle Goya's feet" as well as the priests of literature who have banished Aiken's work from the canon of accepted texts. The reference to priests also connects with the bald-headed priests who contrast with the lovers of the poem's final stanza.

Also, in contrast to the king's "yellow sleeves," Goya "wore out the elbows of his sleeves." The king "sweeps" his slipper through the grass, whereas Poe, "wearing a shawl," coughs while "sweeping snow." Dubie contrasts the opulence of kings with the poverty of poets and artists. In another reference to clothing, Aiken's father "paused, while dressing," to murder Aiken's mother. Henry VIII lives on in infamy because he had two of his wives beheaded. Dubie writes that the king left "both the children and the women." Aiken, himself, was divorced from his first two wives and left his children with their mother. In another comparison, the king has "wild-pig in his beard" and Goya "drew a pig on a wall." In his fictionalized autobiography,

Ushant (1952), Aiken tells of his mother drawing a pig to entertain her children, and in *Great Circle* he relates his nightmare about a crucified pig.

The study of these and other parallels in "The Ambassador Diaries of Jean de Bosschère and Edgar Poe" and the reading of works alluded to by Dubie in the poem do much to provide further insights into the works of both writers.

Themes and Meanings

Dubie's primary intention in "The Ambassador Diaries of Jean de Bosschère and Edgar Poe" is to draw attention to the work of Aiken. The epigraphs prefacing sections 1 and 3 of the poem give the reader a taste of Aiken's poetry—twelve lines of it—taken from one of Aiken's major works, "Time in the Rock." The numerous allusions to works by Aiken constitute an act of literary criticism: Dubie is saying that these works are important and should not be forgotten. Dubie's poem also expresses ideas that are central to Aiken's prose and poetry.

The focus on Aiken's life reflects Dubie's belief that the writer should engage in a sort of self-psychoanalysis to become aware of the forces that have determined or influenced his or her attitudes, beliefs, and actions. This consciousness provides the writer with the wisdom to avoid destructive patterns of behavior. Dubie shows Aiken beginning this process in the line of verse he writes following his parents' deaths— "Why did they whip poor Will?" Aiken was mentally and physically abused by his father, who would not have committed murder and suicide, Aiken believed, if he had developed such a consciousness. Aiken's father was one of those "who sleep," unaware of subconscious motivations. By mentioning the Nazis, Dubie reminds the reader of what can happen when an entire nation is "asleep."

Aiken believed that poetry not only allowed the poet to increase his or her individual consciousness but also served to advance the consciousness of the human race. By embodying the process of achieving self-knowledge and presenting the discoveries of the poet, it leaves a record for others to learn from and build on. As Aiken wrote in one of the passages from "Time in the Rock" that Dubie uses as an epigraph, the writer's job is "To be the ambassador/ Of all you are to all that is not you!" This sentiment raises the issue of literary tradition.

In "The Ambassador Diaries of Jean de Bosschère and Edgar Poe," Dubie writes that Aiken has been made a "childless" ambassador, meaning that his work has been relegated to the provinces of literary history, away from the mainstream of tradition, where it will not foster successors. By writing his poem about Aiken, however, Dubie means to correct this situation. Dubie becomes an inheritor of Aiken's work. As his allusions to Aiken's works demonstrate, Dubie has assimilated Aiken's consciousness, just as Aiken assimilated the consciousness of Poe and as future poets will assimilate the consciousness of Dubie. Many other writers also are the spiritual ancestors of these poets; in this way, the consciousness of the human race is increased.

James Green

AMERICA

Author: Allen Ginsberg (1926-1997)
Type of poem: Verse essay
First published: 1956, in *Howl and Other Poems,* 1956

The Poem

Allen Ginsberg's "America" presents a sharp critique of American culture delivered by someone who has almost wholly repudiated its values. The poem's speaker addresses America directly, as if he were delivering a lecture or a sermon to the nation itself, rather than to its people. The nation's aggressive anticommunist foreign policy and its culture of materialism and conformity are the primary targets of the speaker's harsh attack.

The poet emphatically denounces America's Cold War foreign policy. "America when will we end the human war?" he asks in the poem's fourth line. He follows that question with "Go [expletive] yourself with your atom bomb." The communists are not this speaker's enemies. Ginsberg's speaker informs America that he used to be a communist as a child and is not sorry for it; his mother took him to Communist cell meetings where "the speeches were free" and "everybody was angelic and sentimental about the workers." Now he brags about reading the works of Karl Marx. Near the end of the poem, the speaker satirizes America's fear of a takeover by the Soviet Union: "America you don't really want to go to war./ America it's them bad Russians./ Them Russians them Russians and them Chinamen. And them Russians./ The Russia wants to eat us alive. The Russia's power mad. She wants to take our cars from out our garages./ Her wants to grab Chicago. Her needs a Red *Reader's Digest.* Her wants our auto plants in Siberia."

American materialism also comes under attack in "America." The speaker begins the poem by declaring himself virtually bankrupt: "America I've given you all and now I'm nothing./ America two dollars and twentyseven cents January 17, 1956." He asks, "When can I go into the supermarket and buy what I need with my good looks?" He wonders when America will send its eggs to India and care for its "millions of underprivileged who live in my flowerpots under the light of five hundred suns." He jokingly asserts that he will make his living composing strophes and selling them as America peddles its Ford automobiles: "$2500 apiece $500 down on your old strophe." He condemns an America economy designed to "turn lathes in precision parts factories."

In the view of Ginsberg's speaker, *Time* magazine represents America's cultural values. "Are you going to let your emotional life be run by Time Magazine?" he asks. *Time* magazine is "always telling me about responsibility. Businessmen are serious. Movie producers are serious. Everybody's serious but me." The speaker sets himself apart from the culture of *Time* magazine. "I smoke marijuana every chance I get," he asserts. "I sit in my house for days on end and stare at the roses in the closet." He experiences "mystical visions and cosmic vibrations" and refuses to say the Lord's Prayer. Ginsberg's narrator will not join the Army or work in a factory because he is "nearsighted and psychopathic." His heroes are individuals who lived outside mainstream American culture and suffered for it: the labor leader Tom Moody, imprisoned for murder in 1916 and pardoned twenty-three years later; the socialist activists Nicola Sacco and Bartolomeo Vanzetti, executed for murder on weak evidence in 1927; and the Scottsboro boys, African American adolescents falsely accused and tried for rape during the 1930's.

Forms and Devices

Ginsberg delivers his critique of American culture in a rambling seventy-three-line free-verse poem. He eschews rhyme. His poetic ancestor is Walt Whitman, whose free-verse poems first appeared in the 1850's. Like Whitman, Ginsberg, in most of his poems, presents his message in a series of emotional outbursts, seemingly delivered in a random order. The effect, however, is often prayerlike. In "America," and in other poems in the *Howl* collection, the speaker resembles an Old Testament prophet chanting a savage critique of the values of his people.

Ginsberg uses some words not found in the Bible, however. He complains that when he visits Chinatown he gets drunk but "never get[s] laid." He announces that America's national resources include "two joints of marijuana" and "millions of genitals." Ginsberg's use of such terms in "America" and in other poems included in the *Howl* collection resulted in federal obscenity charges being brought against Lawrence Ferlinghetti, the owner of City Lights Books in San Francisco, which first published *Howl*. Ginsberg and Ferlinghetti, however, successfully defended *Howl*, and the federal government lost its case in court. By using such language in his poems, Ginsberg was attacking America's Victorian sexual mores and testing the limits of America's literary standards. Before the publication of *Howl*, explicit sexual language rarely appeared in serious literary works. Ginsberg's use of such language, his rejection of traditional poetic forms, and the sharpness of his critique of American culture partly explain why America's literary culture, which was dominated by academics during the 1950's, failed to embrace Ginsberg when *Howl* was published.

Ginsberg employs both humor and satire in "America." Some of the humor is self-deprecating: "I'm obsessed by Time Magazine./ I read it every week./ Its cover stares at me every time I slink past the corner candystore./ I read it in the basement of the Berkeley Public Library." Some of the humor results from puns: "Asia is rising against me./ I haven't got a chinaman's chance." Ginsberg's use of satire is evident in his depiction of Russia as a power-hungry nation intending to "eat us alive," confiscate Americans' cars from their driveways, take over Chicago, and transplant automobile plants to Siberia.

Themes and Meanings

Howl and Other Poems became the bible of the Beat generation, the group of counterculture writers who surfaced in the United States during the 1950's. The Beats, who included Ginsberg, Ferlinghetti, Jack Kerouac, Gary Snyder, Gregory Corso, and others, criticized the conformity and materialism that they saw developing in American culture during the post-World War II years. During a time when many young Americans enrolled in colleges or corporate training programs, married and started families, and purchased homes in the suburbs, the Beats and their followers drank to excess, experimented with illegal drugs, engaged in nontraditional sexual practices, worked odd jobs (mainly to support their fondness for travel), and condemned America's corporate culture. The Beats were cultural rebels.

"America" is a Beat anthem. In this poem, Ginsberg presents the Beat critique of a nation gone wrong—an entire culture obsessed with waging war, making money, and fostering a stifling conformity. Ginsberg's speaker sets himself against this cultural tide. He will not join the Army or take a job in a precision parts factory. He will not allow his own cultural values to be set by *Time* magazine. He will continue to engage in activities frowned upon by individuals within the mainstream culture—engaging in sex, smoking marijuana, reading Marx. The speaker in "America" represents the disillusioned youths of post-World War II American society.

Yet Ginsberg's poem is not wholly anti-American. His jeremiad contains the sincere hope that his nation will change its ways. "America when will you be angelic?/ When will you take off your clothes?" Ginsberg asks early in the poem. "America why are your libraries full of tears?" he asks a few lines later. He interrupts his critique of America to remind it that "the plum blossoms are falling." He wants the nation to take notice of its natural beauties. Ginsberg is serious when he says, "America after all it is you and I who are perfect not the next world," as well as when he admits, "It occurs to me that I am America." He pleads with America to commit itself to justice—to free Tom Mooney, spare Sacco and Vanzetti, and recognize the Scottsboro boys' innocence. He knows that America does not really want to go to war against the Russians. Ginsberg wants America to change its ways; he does not want to destroy the nation. He is actually a patriot in the tradition of Henry David Thoreau, the nineteenth century philosopher who recognized America's many wonders yet pointed critically to its shortcomings.

"America" anticipates the critique leveled against the United States by the 1960's counterculture. The poem, along with Ginsberg's other poetry, became popular during that decade, when young Americans protested America's Vietnam policy, condemned the nation's corporations, experimented with sex and drugs, and rejected the values of mainstream society. During the 1960's, Ginsberg became a leading counterculture figure, reading his poems before large crowds at leading American universities and participating in anti-Vietnam War rallies. By the time of his death in 1997, Ginsberg had been embraced by the literary culture that once looked at him as a radical and an outsider.

James Tackach

AMERICA: A PROPHECY

Author: William Blake (1757-1827)
Type of poem: Narrative
First published: 1793

The Poem

America: A Prophecy is a narrative poem consisting of two parts, a 37-line section titled "Preludium" and a longer, 226-line section entitled "A Prophecy." It is written in long, unrhymed lines that seem to have been inspired in their shape both by the epic meter of Homer and by the iambic pentameter of John Milton, but that conform to neither.

The poem takes the American Revolution as its inspiration, but, even though George Washington and other founding fathers appear in it, the poem is by no means an attempt to write a history of the event. Rather, this poem is an attempt to create an extended metaphor glorifying the spirit of the revolution.

In *America*, William Blake is developing a cosmology of deities, some of whom had appeared in his earlier poems and many of whom were to appear in later ones, such as the poem "The Four Zoas." When the poem begins, Orc, a deity associated with fire and rebellion, based very much on the myth of Prometheus, has been chained by Urthona, who is a blacksmith and associated with the earth. He is being fed by the virgin daughter of Urthona, a sympathetic spirit also associated with the earth. Inspired by her presence, Orc breaks free of his chains to embrace her; she, in turn, is inspired to speak for the first time, and, at the end of this prelude, tells him of the struggle under way on "my American plains."

The main section of the poem, "A Prophecy," concerns the struggle between the Angel of Albion (England) and a number of characters and deities associated with the American colonies. George Washington early makes an impassioned speech to warn Americans that the Angel of Albion is on his way to imprison them, but after that, he and the other founding fathers named in the poem (including Thomas Jefferson, Benjamin Franklin, and Thomas Paine) have little to do. Most of the battle is between Orc and the Angel of Albion.

Orc arrives in a fiery burst to intervene between the Angel of Albion and the American colonists. The Angel of Albion recognizes him and demands to know what he is doing. Orc declares that he is defending the principle that "everything that lives is holy" against the idea that lives can be ranked according to their importance, which he sees the Angel of Albion as trying to enforce.

Beginning in line 76, the Angel of Albion tries to rally his "Thirteen Angels," representing the spirits of the original thirteen colonies. Led by Boston's Angel, who refuses to pay any more obedience to Albion, the Thirteen Angels throw down their scepters and stand united with Washington and other founding fathers. In line 142, the human governors of the thirteen colonies meet and, unable to break the mental chains binding them to England, surrender to Washington rather than join him.

The Angel of Albion sends plagues to defeat the colonies of America, but Orc intervenes and sends the plagues back onto the English. The plagues defeat the Angel of Albion, and Blake shows what he thinks of the official English poetry of his day by having a "cowl" of flesh and scales grow over the Bard of Albion (a stand-in for any of several British poet laureates of Blake's lifetime), who has hidden in a cave.

Then Urizen, at this point the most powerful of Blake's deities, appears. Urizen is described as old, pale, and bearded, and in this poem is associated with clouds and ice. He puts a stop to the revolt against Albion by trapping Orc in a white cloud for twelve years—possibly referring to the period between the end of the American Revolution and the execution of the king of France in 1793. The poem ends with a prophecy of the time when the five gates, meaning the five senses, will be burned away and humankind will be able to perceive infinity directly, the ultimate outcome Blake sees to the French and American revolutions.

Forms and Devices

Although Blake displays a rich feel for the rhythms and sounds of language in *America*, as he does in all of his work, in this poem he does not try to conform his poetic lines to any rigid structure. Typically, though, each line will have seven or eight hard stresses. Many lines have an iambic rhythm (every second syllable stressed), but usually it is interrupted by at least one other type of poetic foot (for example, two—or three—hard stresses in a row) at some point in the line. The effect is that every line seems to reflect the conflict of forces at work in the poem in general.

The larger accomplishment of this poem is that it weaves elements from mythology, from Milton's *Paradise Lost* (1667, 1674), and from the history of the American Revolution into an original cosmology of Blake's own making. If the chained figure of Orc introduced at the beginning of the poem is derivative of Prometheus, the god in Greek mythology who defied the other gods by bringing fire to man and was therefore chained to a mountain by Zeus, he also owes much to Milton's Satan, condemned to the fires of hell for leading angels in revolt. Thus, when Orc tells the Angel of Albion, "I am Orc, wreathed round the accursed tree" (line 59), he is identifying himself with the serpent in the Garden of Eden, and more generally identifying himself with Lucifer when he refers to the "fiery Joy, that Urizen perverted to ten commands," meaning the Ten Commandments (line 61). Further, Orc identifies the rebellious spirit of the American colonies with his own rebellious spirit.

The poem, however, does not at any point become a meticulous allegory of the American Revolution. Although Orc's imprisonment may be read as a poetic rendering of the end of the war of independence, the events of the poem, such as the turning back of the plague meant for America onto the cities of Bristol and London, do not generally correspond to specific historical events. This is not a poem about the people and events of the revolution (and in fact, the Americans who are named and alluded to throughout the poem have little to do besides watch the main conflict) but about the spirit of the revolution. As such, its aim is to put this revolution into a context of revolt not only against political tyranny—the type of revolt Washington calls for in his brief but powerful speech—but generally against any tyranny that represses the potential for life.

This is why the poem is a "prophecy." It sees the American Revolution as part of a larger spiritual cleansing that will ultimately create a new world.

Themes and Meanings

America is a poem less about the importance of overthrowing political tyranny (though that is one of its concerns) than it is about the importance of overthrowing the ways of thinking and perceiving that Blake associates with political as well as spiritual tyranny.

In many ways, Orc's speech to the Angel of Albion in lines 59-75 is at the center of the meaning of the poem. In this section, Orc prophesies that he shall stamp the "stony law" of the commandments "to dust, and scatter religion abroad" (line 63), because they have served to shelter humanity from the "fiery joy" of living. This type of fire is only threatening to those (such as the Angel of Albion, and Urizen) who hide from it. Orc foresees a time when "Fires enwrap the globe, yet man is not consumed" (line 73), but in fact is transformed by the fire into a being who gleams like precious metals.

True to the spirit of Romantic poets such as Percy Bysshe Shelley and Lord Byron, with whom Blake is often associated, Blake uses fire as a basic metaphor for creativity. To someone who is afraid of it, it appears destructive. To someone who is not afraid of it, it is constructive. Religion has to be overthrown, according to Orc, because it prevents people from experiencing their own fires directly.

In fact, it is clear that for Orc this creative fire is the basic essence of life. Thus, when this fire is released through the destruction of religion, deserts will blossom. Those seeking "virginity," a term Blake does not use literally but understands as an innocent enjoyment of life's pleasures, "May find it in a harlot" (line 69). Orc's basic principle is that "every thing that lives is holy, life delights in life" (line 71). There are no isolated holy temples; everything that lives is a holy temple.

In view of such a high principle, the destruction that Orc unleashes may seem at first glance to be contradictory, but a closer examination shows that it is not Orc but the Angel of Albion who is responsible for this destruction. Orc does not create the plagues that rack London and Bristol; he merely deflects them from attacking the colonies. The Angel of Albion and his charges pay the price for trying to destroy the creative spirit of others.

The poem is called *America* because it is the revolt of the American colonies, its creative spirit, that receives Orc's attention. The revolution that the poem foresees at its end, when Orc frees himself again, is a much larger revolution, however: one that will free the human spirit throughout the world.

Thomas J. Cassidy

AMERICAN CHANGE

Author: Allen Ginsberg (1926-1997)
Type of poem: Meditation
First published: 1961; collected in *Reality Sandwiches*, 1963

The Poem

"American Change" is Allen Ginsberg's meditation on the figurative and literal meanings and values of money. Written in 1958, as Ginsberg was returning to the United States from a stint in the merchant marine, the narrative of the poem traces the speaker's changing attitudes toward his country as he reflects on the American coins in his pockets. Without their value as American currency, these coins were only souvenirs when the speaker was at sea, but as the poem plots his return to New York, he removes the change from his pocket and revalues it.

The poem is structured in a free-verse form in the breath-unit line structure that Ginsberg popularized. In such a structure, each line represents what Ginsberg once termed "one-speech-breath thought," fusing each line with equal emphasis on body, speech, and mind, a poetic concern Ginsberg borrowed from his Buddhist practice. "American Change" is divided into five stanzas, each organized according to the particular piece of money the speaker takes as his subject matter. Stanza 1 is devoted to the speaker's meditation on an Indian-head nickel; in stanza 2 the speaker explores the cultural meanings of a dime; stanza 3 is occasioned by a quarter. The poet takes a five-dollar bill as his subject matter in the fourth stanza, and the last stanza is devoted to a meditation and description of the cultural significance of a one-dollar bill.

The speaker immediately contrasts the symbolic money of his country with the sacred potential of the land. The movement from materialism to idealism is appropriate, given that two of Ginsberg's greatest influences, Walt Whitman and William Blake, perceived the United States as an idealistic answer to the threats to liberty inherent in monarchical systems of government. Ginsberg's speaker, however, sees the Native American on the front of the nickel as a "vanished man" and the buffalo on the back of the nickel as a prophetic "vanishing beast of Time." Ginsberg commonly synthesizes several religious traditions in his poetry, and "American Change" is no exception. The Native American is a "Rabbi Indian" whose "visionary gleam" has been swallowed by modern consumer capitalism. This "candy-store nostalgia of the redskin" is "dead on silver coin," and the sacredness of his culture is "gone into the great slot machine of Kansas City, Reno—." Ginsberg cuts off the line at "Reno," suggesting that a continued list of empty, consumerist cities would only be redundant.

"American Change" is framed by this contrast between the sacred and the material. With every new coin or bill, the speaker finds that the visionary origins of the United States have been swallowed by a "Vision of Money." This monetary vision is portrayed as a dead end; this path produces failure at both the figurative and literal registers of the poem. Figuratively, the money produces a "sexless," impotent erasure of vision, leaving the speaker with nothing but a "poor pile of coins." At the literal level, too, the poem dramatizes the "Vision of Money" as a futile one. The speaker reminds himself that the same money he took with him when he left the United States will buy much less now upon his return. Even when he attempts to be materialistic, the speaker despairs: "Money, money, reminder, I might as well write poems to you." He "might as well" do so because he is returning to an America that has transformed the visionary into the material, and in doing so has left the imagination as a reminder of loss, incapable of originality.

Forms and Devices

As with two other poems of the same period in his career, "America" (*Howl and Other Poems*, 1956) and "Death to Van Gogh's Ear!" (*Reality Sandwiches*, 1963), Ginsberg builds "American Change" on a shifting foundation of despairing and ironic statements. In the first stanza, the speaker opens with nostalgic articulations of home; yet as he meditates upon his return, he sadly realizes that the home he yearns for never existed. He longs for an ideal, and the tiny nickel in his hand contains within it all the deadness that prevents this ideal from coming into being. The next stanza introduces a dime, with its "sexless cold & chill." The George Washington quarter in the following stanza is "snub-nosed" and reflects the wishes of a designer who idealized Washington as a "sexless Father."

The speaker becomes miserable in the next stanza, emphasizing in the five-dollar bill "Lincoln's sour black head moled and wrinkled." The poem shifts to an ironic tone in this stanza. The speaker addresses his American change as the "dear American money" he clutches at his arrival at the Statue of Liberty. He accedes that he might as well dedicate his poetry to money—as if he, too, has been consumed by American materialism. Irony links this stanza to the final stanza, which begins with mock joy. His return to the United States is reflected in his return in the poem to George Washington—this time Washington on the face of a dollar bill: "Ahhh! Washington again, on the Dollar, same poetic black print, dark words, The United States of America, innumerable numbers." The speaker reminds himself that the words "Legal Tender" actually signify the opposite of tenderness in a consumer capitalist culture and that the sacrifice of American idealism to American economics is as absurd as his own characterization of the country's wealth as a collection of "innumerable numbers."

Irony and despair combine in the poet's final rumination on the dollar. He reflects on its unitary value—its currency as the singular dollar—by closing the poem with one word: "ONE." Ironically, the unity of his country depends upon the suppression of difference and the extinguishing of passion. The speaker remarks that the back of the bill is dominated by the "Great Seal of our Passion," a seal which indeed seals (contains) passion from further growth. The Treasury Department's attempt to prevent counterfeit bills symbolizes how cultural practices outside the norm—outside the "ONE"—cannot achieve cultural currency in the country to which he returns. What remains, for the speaker, are empty symbols of mysticism robbed of their visionary claims: the American eagle and "halo of stars," and the Masonic and Swedenborgian influences that early American leaders saw fit to adapt as images on their currency. Irony and despair combine in this final statement of "ONE" in "American Change," suggesting ultimately that, for the speaker, America has changed from a visionary land to a culture that contains and restricts dynamic American "change."

Themes and Meanings

For Ginsberg, the privilege granted to economics in American culture robs the imagination of cultural currency as it emphasizes the importance of actual hard currency itself. In "American Change," as in much of Ginsberg's work, American economic and imperial expansionism devalue the individual spirit as they increase national wealth. Discourses of history and culture are complicit in this movement away from individual freedom. The fate of the individual is much like that of the buffalo in the first stanza of "American Change": A pluralist convergence of individual identities is reduced to a "hoar body rubbed clean of wrinkles and shining like polished stone." The gleam is deceptive, just as it is when the speaker reveals that the nearly baroque illuminations on the dollar bill are merely safeguards against counterfeit currency rather than artistic renderings of the creative imagination.

The literal value of money, too, is reduced in "American Change." From *Howl* onward, Ginsberg's poetry concerned itself with both the materialist and the visionary consequences of contemporary social injustice. Thus, as the visionary potential of the country fades in the poem, so does material value. In the midst of the third stanza, the speaker counts the coins he has thus far described—a nickel, dime, and quarter—and states: "Quarter, remembered quarter, 40¢; in all—What'll you buy me when I land—one icecream soda?" He is more explicit in the next stanza, where he argues that the "immense promise" of what can be bought with five dollars shrinks with each new day.

Ginsberg's conception of visionary and creative imagination is predicated upon divine images that are fully desired and desiring. Therefore, the emptied passion of the cultural figures in the poem symbolizes the deadening of spirit in the America that occasions the poem. Much of this movement from passion to coldness is fueled by Ginsberg's attention to the potential for multiple meanings in poetic language. The "fathers" of the country—from Washington to Dwight D. Eisenhower (president at the time of the poem's writing)—no longer father (produce) anything of the imagination. They are figures of "sexless" discipline who debase the idealistic, sacred moment of the country's founding. Ginsberg reflects this debasing in language that invokes, then parodies, the power of religious language and syntax: "O Eisenhower & Washington—O Fathers—No movie star dark beauty—O thou Bignoses—." The speaker reminds the reader that Washington's image on the quarter is "naked down to his neck." However, the naked spirit of Washington is contained by the stiffness rendered on the quarter. This stiff image of Washington emphasizes only "falsetooth ideas." Thus, despite the speaker's attempt to coin a visionary body from this meditation, all that remains for him is the threat of "foul counterfeit" and the reality of diminished desire.

Tony Trigilio

AMERICAN PRIMITIVE

Author: William Jay Smith (1918-   )
Type of poem: Ballad
First published: 1957, in *Poems, 1947-1957*

The Poem

William Jay Smith's "American Primitive" is a contemporary ballad of three quatrains describing the scene of a suicide in the voice of a child narrator. Smith's title warns the reader that the poem may engage with unsophisticated content, be untrained in style, or perhaps even be crude in nature. Both content and style fulfill this promise, as a tragic scene is revealed in bits and pieces that contribute to a growing sense of mystery and horror. Only gradually do readers come to understand who and what is "primitive" in this American scene, but the issue is heightened by a compelling sense of urgency in the voice of the narrator. The child seems almost to shout the rhyming lines in defense of "my Daddy."

The poem's first stanza begins with a directive: "Look at him there in his stovepipe hat." The character being described wears not only a fine hat but also high-topped shoes and a "handsome collar." Such clothing takes the reader back in time, associating the character with a much earlier era when gentlemen were thus dressed. The child's loyalty emerges in the line, "Only my Daddy could look like that," a proclamation that the father is exceptional, very much to be admired. The child goes on to declare love for the father, love equal to the way the father loves money: "And I love my Daddy like he loves his Dollar." Thus emerges a conflict of values, a representation of a segment of American culture in which concern with money outranks parental obligations to care for the child. Subtle suggestions in the style of the language and in the limited content contribute to the reader's sense that something shady or even illegal has happened.

After creating a visual image of the father and establishing the young narrator's loyalty in the first stanza, the poem moves quickly through the remaining two stanzas. Readers hear a screen door that sounds "so funny" when it bangs and see coins littering the floor "in a shower of gold" and folding money extruding from the pockets of the father. The suicide is revealed almost casually as readers learn that the father's lips are blue and his hands are cold. In the final stanza the father "hangs in the hall" as "ladies faint." The ending of the poem repeats the comparison that the child loves the father like the father loves money. The poem utilizes death to portray forcefully that necessary yet disappointing stage of maturation in which children must confront their parents' fallibility and mortality. The narrator's feverish gaiety suggests just how painful this stage can be.

Forms and Devices

Much of the impact of the poem derives from its musical quality; an accentual rhythm and a set of simple rhymes create a sense of stability that asserts control over the tragedy being described. Ballads are often short and generally structured in four-line stanzas, as is the case with "American Primitive." The meter of a ballad is clearly heard, and in this case the rhythm of a jump-rope rhyme is also woven in. The poem begins with a dactyl, the stressed first word, "Look," followed by the unstressed "at him." This combination calls forth the understood subject "you" to command the reader's involvement. With the next accent on "there" the line continues with the unstressed "in his" equal to the previous "at him." The line ends with three heavy stresses, "stovepipe hat."

Smith has enjambed the meter of a traditional ballad by placing the usual second-line trimeter at or near the end of many lines without a line break. This produces a jumpy or staccato effect, a series of short jabs that provoke an incongruous display of power in the narrator's voice.

The accentual rhythm combines with an even rhyme scheme in making the poem a ballad. The rhyme pattern is initially *abab*, proceeding to *cdcd*, and returning to *abab* in the final stanza. In the essay "A Frame for Poetry," which appeared in his volume of selected criticism *The Streaks of the Tulip: Selected Criticism* (1972), Smith explains that he had originally included many stanzas (actually verses or "ballad bits") in the style of a "Mississippi River guitar tune—absolutely mechanical in its rhythm." Rhythm and rhyme in "American Primitive" combine to form a tightly bound structure, creating a flat innocence of style that contrasts ironically with the horror of the scene.

Further contributing to the irony of the poem, Smith's narrator speaks in the vernacular. The child refers to a "stovepipe" rather than a man's tall silk hat. The shoes are "hightop" rather than high-topped. Occurring as they do in the first stanza, these expressions alert the reader to a dichotomy—the upper-class clothing of the father is not matched by the child's diction. Later in the poem, the father's pockets are "stuffed" with paper money and the reader hears the children "holler." The vernacular language used in the poem was common in the American South where Smith grew up; Smith has even been known to read the poem using a southern accent.

Although "American Primitive" is often mistaken for a quickly written creation, Smith was not satisfied with it until he hit upon the verb "hangs" for the first line of the last stanza, "He hangs in the hall by his black cravat." This is an example of Smith's repeated assertion that "poetry is all in verbs, in verbs and nouns."

Themes and Meanings

The primary goal of "American Primitive" is to portray tragedy as central to human life, while at the same time lightening the load by using a humorous tone, one that is uniquely American. Smith's narrator functions within a larger tradition of the self-reliant child, particularly the literary American child who demonstrates a resilience and strength of character equal to even the most difficult of situations. American literature and biography include a mythos of this child as stalwart and vigorous in the face of many tumultuous events—including those resulting from the Civil War, frontier settlement, the Great Depression, and so on.

Although "American Primitive" borrows from a childhood incident in the poet's life, the ballad quality of the poem derives from its portrait of the personal in the context of the societal. In this case, members of the crowd react to the suicide, expressing the emotions the child narrator rejects—women swoon and children cry out. While discovering a father's suicide is not a common childhood experience, the loss of innocence is.

It should be noted that the poem is not entirely autobiographical—Smith's father did not commit suicide. Smith writes in his autobiography *Army Brat: A Memoir* (1980) of a time when his father, a man whose gambling regularly disturbed the peace and security of his family, stayed out all night after payday. Having searched the local hangouts for him unsuccessfully, the boy and his mother returned home late in the afternoon to discover their porch riddled by bullet holes and Smith's father asleep on the floor inside, surrounded by money won at cards. This event provided Smith with a catalyst for writing about a certain type of opportunistic American character, in this poem a father who comes off much like a carpetbagger.

"American Primitive" not only celebrates the American spirit but also represents Smith's independence as he persisted in writing formal poetry during a time when free verse dominated the American poetry scene. In his first three volumes of verse, Smith published short, lyrical poems admired for their combination of elegant forms, clarity of content, and extraordinary verbal facility. Recognizing his accomplishment, the Library of Congress named him consultant in poetry from 1968 to 1970. Smith also drew lifelong acclaim for his interest and expertise in writing light verse and children's poetry. He credits his involvement as a writer and editor of the latter with keeping imagination at the forefront of his writing and with helping him develop themes he used later in his adult poetry. The satirical tone he demonstrates in "American Primitive" and similar works has even been compared to the wit characteristic of classical Greek verse. Drawing upon these strengths, Smith has contributed to the reestablishment of humor as a valued asset in American poetry.

Margaret A. Dodson

THE AMERICAN WAY OF LIFE

Author: Claribel Alegria (1924-   )
Type of poem: Narrative
First published: 1989, bilingually in *Woman of the River*

The Poem

Claribel Alegria's "The American Way of Life" is a nonstanzaic, 206-line poem about the poet-speaker's visit to three American states: California, Pennsylvania, and New York. The speaker, who does not live in the United States, had visited America once before, but so long ago that she "nearly forgot" what the country and its people were like. The poem offers commentary on several aspects of American life and ends with the speaker's personification of America as a "bitch" who "chews up" minorities as if they were "Chiclets." The American way of life, the poet predicts, will be destroyed.

The poem opens as the speaker is "swallowed" by the state of California's "hypnotic tangle/ of freeways" viewed from an airplane. An escort who drives the speaker from the airport asks if the speaker has forgotten *"the American way of life?"* The speaker visits "the Sanctuary," where she is "presented" to her "'compatriots'" who come to America without papers ("the 'eternally undocumented'"). These "undocumented" people are "transparent" as "they slide through Mission Heights" or work as servants in a wealthy San Francisco Bay area neighborhood. After work, the immigrants gather together in "unsafe" houses, or houses where they can be found, to watch Americans riding in pleasure boats around the island of Alcatraz. The speaker's escort explains that "three hundred undocumented" are found each week by the "Migra," or border patrol agents.

The speaker visits the campus of the University of California, Berkeley, where, in the square near the "Campanile" she notes "a festive touch of anarchy." Students are protesting "the dinosaurs/ of the Establishment." The students are "Joshuas dressed in blue jeans" sounding their trumpets "amid the sacred walls/ of Jericho" or the university, so that "the walls shuddered/ and the deans trembled." From Berkeley, the speaker travels along the Pacific Coast Highway to Los Angeles. Along the way, she is warned that the "Edenic beaches" are "full of tar" from offshore drilling rigs. In East Los Angeles the speaker watches "jobless steelworkers/ walk back and forth," protesting in front of a Bethlehem Steel plant.

A quick flight to Gettysburg, Pennsylvania, and the "neon signs" that "mark the way/ to General Eisenhower's farm" remind the speaker of American military intervention in Guatemala and the attempt at intervention in Cuba ("the Bay of Pigs"). "Finally" in "New York," amid the old and new skyscrapers, the speaker observes young men on skateboards who remind her of the 1930's Olympic ice skating star Sonja Henie. On the sidewalks of New York, the speaker sees a homeless woman and a young ballerina crying. The speaker finds that she responds like native New Yorkers, who "pass by" these representations of poverty and despair "with scarcely a glance." The poem closes with the speaker prophesying that the American way of life will be destroyed by "a rain of fire/ and ashes" as Saint John the Divine prophesies in the New Testament Book of Revelation that Babylon will be destroyed.

Forms and Devices

"The American Way of Life" is a didactic narrative poem. The poet describes particular personal experiences that lead her to her revelation that the American way of living is doomed. Alegria persistently alludes to the Bible, beginning with a reference to the battle of Jericho, from the Book of Joshua. Santa Barbara, California, beaches are referred to as "Edenic," and the word "Bethlehem" is punned in line 103. Finally, the poet's vision of the destruction of the American way of life draws heavily on the Book of Revelation (17:6 and 6:13), because New York City reminds the speaker of the whore of Babylon as well as Babylon itself.

As with most of the poems in the collection *Woman of the River*, the poet uses short lines and iambic meter. The varying line lengths (usually one to three feet, but occasionally even a five-foot line) contribute to the drama of the poem. The lines of the poem are sparsely punctuated, and most of them are end-stopped—the sense of the words is found in the line.

Alegria is expert at presenting brief, strong images, and images in "The American Way of Life" are no exception. The reader moves quickly from an aerial view of San Francisco Bay to the bell tower on the campus of the University of California, Berkeley, to "the chained gates of Bethlehem Steel" in East Los Angeles to young skateboarders the speaker watches from the sidewalks of New York. In this poem, Alegria presents her images with little explanation or comment, although a second voice in the poem, that of the speaker's escort or tour guide, provides social and political commentary. However, when readers come to the poet's final image, her presentation of America as "drunk with blood/ with her diadem of rubies/ and her drugstore stink" chewing up Salvadorans, Nicaraguans, Lebanese, and Chicanos as if they were chewing gum, the speaker's political perspective is quite unmistakable.

The juxtaposition of the speaker's voice with that of her tour guide, whose words are written in italics, allows the reader to dismiss the guide's bitter and angry commentary. However, because the speaker records only what she sees—and so becomes a kind of seer and thus a prophet—the reader can trust the vision at the close of the poem. The reader's trust is further deepened because the speaker mentions precise landmarks and place names (Mission Heights, Alcatraz, Berkeley's Campanile, Rockerfeller Center), some famous, others known only locally.

Alegria's preciseness extends to her use of concrete language and her implied metaphors. For example, the bridges across San Francisco Bay are "floating spiderwebs" that "arch between Berkeley/ and San Francisco," and "two boys" in New York skate in between automobiles described as "sharks/ with chrome teeth." Alegria's metaphors offer the imaginative jump necessary for understanding her vision of the American way of life.

Themes and Meanings

Claribel Alegria is an enduring voice for the rights of Latin American people. One primary focus of her artistic work is to show how those in power exploit those who have little power. Certainly "The American Way of Life" is a strong example of Alegria's central point, but the poem speaks to more than the powerful Americans who live the life Alegria illustrates. The poem speaks to those minorities who seek the American way of life, including immigrants, displaced workers, the poor, and those who, like university students, seek to change the American way of life.

The poet speaks to immigrants when she describes the "three hundred undocumented" who are deported weekly, turned in by border patrol agents ("the Migra"). The illegal immigrants come to the United States to seek a better way of life, but Alegria reminds immigrants that those who are deported are "returned to their deaths" or to where they have no hope of a better life. The poet also takes note of those legally allowed to work in the United States, but who have no jobs. Alegria finds irony in the name of a factory, Bethlehem Steel, that causes the lives of its "jobless steelworkers" to become "suddenly as empty" as the plant in which they used to work. Christians have long associated the name Bethlehem with hope for a better future. In this instance, the name is associated with a corporation that has wreaked havoc in people's lives and caused them to feel helpless.

One university campus, Berkeley, represents the nation's institutions of higher learning when the poem mentions that "anarchy" in the form of "banners and slogans" mocks "the cloisters" or covered walks that are usually found around campus quadrangles. Students are "Joshuas" on this sacred ground. They are the chosen who will, like Joshua, lead their followers in the realization of the promise of land, in this case, the promise of America. Students "knew" as the speaker "knew" that they were having an impact because the "walls shuddered/ and the deans trembled."

In the poet's vision, the poor in the United States suffer most. Impoverished natives of El Salvador, Nicaragua, and Lebanon, as well as Chicanos, are chewed up "as if they were Chiclets." The simile here refers to the first chewing gum mass-marketed in North America. Chewing gum was produced on Staten Island, New York, in the 1870's from the sap of the Mexican chiclezapote tree. For centuries, the people of Central and South America had been chewing chicle from their native trees. Even today most chewing gum is made from the sapodilla trees of Central and South America. Alegria compares the exploitation of Latin Americans with the widely known American habit of consuming chewing gum. Alegria's compatriots, like the product that grows naturally in their countries, are as disposable as wads of gum. The poet prophesies that America's habit of exploitation will lead to its own destruction.

Ginger Jones

AMONG SCHOOL CHILDREN

Author: William Butler Yeats (1865-1939)
Type of poem: Meditation
First published: 1927; collected in *The Tower*, 1928

The Poem

William Butler Yeats's "Among School Children" is written in eight eight-line stanzas that follow a precise rhyme scheme. Along with the straightforward title, stanza I establishes the immediate context of the action in deliberately prosaic language. The speaker is visiting a schoolroom, and "a kind old nun," his guide for the day or perhaps the classroom teacher, is answering his matter-of-fact questions in a rapid, matter-of-fact way.

The tone and mood of the poem take a sharp turn in the couplet ending the first stanza, however; the speaker suddenly sees himself through the children's eyes as they "In momentary wonder stare upon/ A sixty-year-old smiling public man." The speaker is almost certainly Yeats himself; as a member of the Irish Senate, Yeats, just turned sixty, did in fact visit schools as a part of his official duties.

Seeing himself through the children's eyes inspires a reverie. He thinks of a child, a girl, whom he knew in his own childhood or youth. The facts are not quite clear, for the reader is told of a "childish day" but also of "youthful sympathy." Nevertheless, the young female is generally identified as Maud Gonne, with whom the poet first became acquainted and fell in love when she was in her late teens and he was in his twenties.

The reverie ends, but his eyes light upon one of the children, who looks amazingly like Maud when she was that age: "She stands before me as a living child." Seeing her as she looked then reminds him of what she looks like now, after the passage of nearly forty years. "Her present image" is of someone whom life has wasted and exhausted; she is "Hollow of cheek" as if she "drank the wind" and ate "a mess of shadows for [her] meat."

Thoughts of her then and now lead to thoughts of himself then and now. The years have not been kind in his case either, and, back in the present in the schoolroom, he decides that it is best to keep up a brave front and "smile on all that smile."

Yet he cannot shake the thought that human life appears to be a process of diminishment and gradual dispossession, if not outright defeat. He imagines what a mother—perhaps his own—would think, just having given birth, could she see that infant after he has lived through "sixty or more winters." Would she, he wonders, think the result worth the pain of her labor and of all her coming anxieties over her helpless infant's welfare?

In the final three stanzas, the personal note that has pervaded the poem is dropped as the speaker explores in rapid order the breadth and scope of all human thought and endeavor—from Plato to Aristotle and Pythagoras, from nuns to mothers to youthful lovers—seeking some solace for the tragic unraveling of dreams and hopes that human life seems to be. In a sudden burst of anger, the speaker excoriates all those images that people set before their mind's eyes to goad themselves and others into succeeding only at failing, and he tries instead to see human life as it is truly lived.

The vision that emerges is one in which neither devotion to others (motherhood) nor devotion to God (the nun) nor devotion to fulfilling selfhood (Maud Gonne) can alone be enough, for "Labour is blossoming or dancing." It is an ongoing process, not any final product. Therefore, one cannot isolate the individual from the passing moment by trying to imagine that at any one instant there is some greater or lesser being there; like the chestnut tree, a human life is all one piece, so one should be wary of trying to "know the dancer from the dance."

Forms and Devices

Yeats's is a poetry rich in complex webs of both personal and public symbols and allusions, and "Among School Children" is no exception. An example of this complexity can be found by examining the source of something as apparently superficial as the rhyme scheme. Ottava rima was introduced into English prosody by the early nineteenth century poet George Gordon, Lord Byron, who used it to great comic effect in poems such as his satiric masterpiece, *Don Juan* (1819-1824).

The Yeats poem is hardly satiric and is comic only by the broadest definition of the term, as one uses it when speaking of Dante's *The Divine Comedy* (c. 1320). Like Dante, whose great poem begins with the otherwise unremarkable discovery that he has lost his way, Yeats uses a rather commonplace incident—a public official's visit to a classroom while touring a school—to explore the larger meaning and purpose of human life in general.

Because of the complexity of Yeats's technique, making such connections is not as farfetched as one might suspect. A symbol, like the allusion to outside texts and sources of information, can point in any number of directions, but it will always make a connection. The poet must connect private and public symbols and allusions in a careful order and to some greater thematic purpose.

Yeats's use of the myth of Leda and the swan offers a fine example. In the ancient Greek myth, Zeus came as a swan to rape the mortal Leda; from that union came Helen of Troy. Yeats's "Ledaean body," however, is something more than a knowledge of the myth alone can betoken. In his poem "Leda and the Swan," he sees in the myth a comment on the dangerous consequences of mixing divine elements with something as fragile as human nature. Furthermore, in other poems, Yeats identifies Maud Gonne with Helen of Troy as representatives of that beauty which is destructive.

That Leda also brings to mind childbearing and childrearing in a poem that focuses on children, childhood, labor, and birth suggests still further possibilities of meaning and illustrates that the apparent opacity of the poem is actually the result of combining a wide literary heritage with a compelling richness and interconnectedness of thought, feeling, and experience.

Themes and Meanings

The central themes of "Among School Children" are best exemplified in the central action: A sixty-year-old official is visiting with elementary school children. The age-old poetic themes of innocence versus experience, naïveté versus wisdom, and youth versus age permeate every stanza of the poem.

Yeats, who in his youthful work frequently dealt with incidents of passing and loss, virtually became obsessed with those themes as he became older and faced his own mortality in more real, less abstract terms. By this point in his career, Yeats was examining the consequences and effects of time's passage not only on the human body but also on the human spirit—both for the individual and for the race as a whole—invariably basing his meditations on personal experience.

In Yeats's hands, these timeless themes take on a profound significance, because while he views human life as tragic, his vision is not nihilistic. He never does actually enunciate what purpose human life may serve, but he does believe that there is a purpose. "Among School Children" illustrates how the individual might frustrate that purpose by imagining either that he is the master of his own destiny or that there is no such thing as destiny.

Maud Gonne serves as a prime example of this frustration of purpose. The poet, who is condemned to remember the brightness and promise of her youth, must live with the meaningless fruits of her actions now that the heartbreak and frustrations of her commitment to revolutionary Irish political causes have taken their toll both on herself and others. By cutting her fulfillment short, she has cut all the rest of humankind short.

Nor will Yeats exclude himself and others from the same condemnation. All fail in their choices and actions to face squarely the one insurmountable reality: Flesh ages, spirits flag, and human dreams wither. He thus accuses himself of having given up or given in ("I . . . had pretty plumage once" but now am "a comfortable kind of old scarecrow") and accuses nuns and mothers, as much as the Helens and Mauds of the world, of betraying the innocent, childlike spirit that fosters dreams and compels human choices.

People unwittingly create false images of what it is to be human, thereby creating false hopes and expectations. Yeats suggests that since there is no choice but to move forward, one should imagine the fullness of each moment as having an inextricable harmony with all others. Life is like a dance that does exist independent of a dancer but has no shape or form without the dancers.

Russell Elliott Murphy

ANCESTOR

Author: Jimmy Santiago Baca (1952-   )
Type of poem: Dramatic monologue
First published: 1979, in *Immigrants in Our Own Land*

The Poem

Jimmy Santiago Baca's "Ancestor" is an unrhymed lyric poem that ultimately offers to the reader an invitation to partake of the "sacred ceremony" of life. Contained within the invitation is the warning that the way to the celebration is often blocked by the artifice and soullessness of those who do not recognize or who ignore the invitation issued to all by life itself and by its celebrants. The poem presents the story, in the musings of one of the sons, of three children whose unconventional father instilled in that son and his siblings the true meaning of life. Implicit in the telling of the story are society's values that are too often believed to be the only of life's values.

The literal ancestor first introduced by the speaker of the poem is the father of the two sons and a daughter. The only suggestion of the children's mother, or of more than one mother of the three children, is that young women responded positively to the masculinity of their father: they "plucked from him sweet fruit." The traditional mother figure of this family is the children's grandmother.

The father of the children is in no way a traditional father. He neither mends the crumbling walls of the home nor ministers to the physical or emotional scrapes and bruises of his children. Society's judgment is first suggested in the poem's opening line, which says that "they were afraid of him." Recognition of society's values are reflected in the son's acknowledgment that his father was not ever-present to mind the home fires. Yet the son, rather than fearful or judgmental, is awestruck. He watches for and after and he wonders at his father. He says that what his father gave was "beyond the coordinated life" and "Beyond the ordinary love."

This father is a gypsy. He appears and disappears without signal, sign, or trace. When present, he absorbs his children's unspoken thoughts and fills their home "with love and safety, for a moment." While he does not give his continued presence or material things to the children, he "made [them] grow up quick and romantic"; he gives them "true freedom." When present, he does not try to instill society's values in his children. He does not speak to them or others of their intelligence or of their future wealth. He says that they are good, and he loves them beyond society's capacity to love.

The grandmother—whether paternal or maternal is not specified—often looks long at him and says nothing; she only prays and guides "down like a root in the heart of the earth." The children look after him and "find nothing,/ not a stir, not a twig displaced from its bough." They only see him march away, "going somewhere like a child/ with a warrior's heart."

The grandmother, rooted in the earth, is shown to embrace the sunlight and the rains. The father, like a tree, is shown to offer his children to the wind, the mountains, and the skies. The son concludes his monologue with the proclamation that he, his brother, and his sister, having arisen "out of the long felt nights and days of yesterday" and having partaken of "the sacred ceremony of living," blossom.

Forms and Devices

Baca employs natural imagery to represent the supernatural, as the indigenous peoples, among whom he counts himself, believe the natural to be the language of the divine. The speaker's ancestor is said to be "like the orange tree" from which women pluck sweet fruit. The father is shown to offer his children to the wind, the mountains, and the skies. The grandmother prays and guides "down like a root" into the earth, embracing the sunlight and the rains. In addition, the children are said to be "A threefold blossom." As offspring of nature, they become "three distinct hopes, three loves." The reader is thus shown that the children, "through sacred ceremony of living, daily living," are among life's holy.

The son speaks of his father's "mystique." He shows his mystical ancestor appearing "Half covered in shadows and half in light." When the father offers his children to the elements, he is a priest pronouncing the ordinary divine in his sacred ceremony. The ultimate image is that of transubstantiation: The children are made holy in the father's and life's light. The father infuses quickness of soul into them, as he gives quickness of life to each child.

While the poem is presented as beautiful tribute to a father, its opening image is not a beautiful one. Rather, it imposes the concept of unnatural human destruction onto a natural creature. The father, first said to have been feared, is next said to be a "horse/ with broken knees no one would shoot." In the poem's context it is society's view that this father of these flourishing children is useless to society's purposes. He hauls none of its loads or baggage. Yet a grudging respect is suggested in no one's shooting or seeking to destroy one whom they might be expected to destroy and in the "Then again," which introduces the image of women enjoying his sweet fruits.

There is an overriding mythic quality to "Ancestor." The title is abstract and bestows a temporal reverence upon the father even before the father (in past tense) is introduced. The first words echo but elevate a fairy tale's familiar "Once upon a time" to "It was a time." The father is shown to appear out of nowhere and to disappear just as mysteriously. He is elevated by the speaker and by the poem as he is shown to elevate life and his children to the realm of the sacred. The story brings to its reader the sense of awe and wonder that the lore of the indigenous peoples brings to its readers. The poem's central figure is shown to represent the human and the divine origin and potential of each member of the human family.

Themes and Meanings

Baca's unpretentious poems are presented by him as mirrors that send signals to his readers as the Western films of his youth showed groups signaling each other with mirrors. In the movies, he saw lives depending upon the receipt and the understanding of the signals. Baca's belief that his life was literally saved by poetry is inherent in his attempt to signal salvation to others in his poem "Ancestor."

Baca, an unconventional poet of Chicano and Apache heritage who found the poetry of his salvation in prison, presents in this poem an unconventional father figure who gives both life and salvation to his children. The poet Baca is priest as the father is priest: Both perform a natural and sacred ritual. Transubstantiation is the experience of this poem—the natural is rendered divine on the altar and in the scripture of life.

As he holds the children of his body and his blood up for the world to see, the father of the children says, "Here are my children!" The priest, father or pastor of his congregation, during Mass says, "This is my body" and "This is my blood." Baca, likewise, is a priest in offering his poem as lifeblood for the consumption of his congregation of readers. The venue of each priest is both different and the same. The father offers his children to "the wind,/ to the mountains, to the skies of autumn and spring," asking that they be cared for and infused with the holiness of life. The priest offers his sacrament to God, asking that it be infused with the essence of Christ in order that his congregation be cared for and infused with the holiness of Christ.

Baca offers his poem as communion to and with his readers in order that they might be moved by a glimpse of life's divinity and might, having received, go forth thereafter to celebrate the sacred ceremony of living. In the mystic tradition joy is to be found in the mundaneness of life and by the most humble of human beings; the experiences of life are transformed into overriding joy. So in this poem the gypsy scorned by society touches his children with love, and, with his simple touch or word, he brings realization of their holiness to those children. The man seen by some as an orange tree and seen by others as a horse useless to the task of horses is a carrier of joy to women and children. Baca, in his depiction of rude family life—the children work in the cotton fields and live in a crude, dilapidated shelter—demonstrates the receipt and understanding and the flowering of joy in his subjects.

The mirror signal of "Ancestor" is meant to deflect the kind of signal those who fear the poem's father send. Baca's belief is that the literature of indigenous peoples can bring life to a culture grown away from life. In "Ancestor," in showing a simple holy man bringing holiness to his children, this indigenous poet means to bring life and meaning to his reader. With the presentation of this family, he signals all of humankind in showing that each human being is a child of "the earth and whatever god our religion may give us." He admonishes each member of the human family to celebrate life—daily—as the sacred ceremony he shows it to be.

Judith K. Taylor

ANCIENT AUTUMN

Author: Charles Simic (1938-   )
Type of poem: Lyric
First published: 1986, in *Unending Blues*

The Poem

Charles Simic's "Ancient Autumn" consists of four free-verse stanzas that simultaneously present a landscape and call the scene into question. While the view presented is one of everyday existence from an earlier time, subtle hints within the scene present both a cynical and comical view of human life.

The poem presents an Old World landscape where a "foolish youth" is perched in an apple tree sawing the branch that he is seated on. The orchard echoes the sound, and the few remaining apples on the tree sway from the saw's motion. As the young man looks out over the landscape from his vantage point, he can see the wisps of smoke from the village's chimneys blowing in the breeze. As he pauses to rest, he smokes a long-stemmed pipe. Below him, a chimney sweep cleans a chimney. A woman pins diapers to a clothesline and then relieves herself behind a bush, hiking her skirts high enough to show "a bit of whiteness." Closer to the center of town, "humpbacked" men roll a barrel filled with hard cider or beer. Cattle graze beyond them, and a group of children march as they play soldier.

The wind is blowing away from the youth, so he cannot hear the sound of the children's shouted commands. Likewise, a "black horseman" appears silently. This horseman is seen to be riding toward the youth in one instant, but he either changes directions quickly or is so far away that the young man has not accurately determined in which direction he is riding.

In the final stanza of the poem, the poet claims that the silence of the scene causes the youth to meditate upon the meaning of the things before him, even to the point of melancholy. The lessons these things teach are "vague" as well as "dumb." The youth's thoughts occupy him so much that he is not aware that he has begun to saw the branch again nor that the "big red sun" that illuminates the whole scene has nearly gone down. The readers of the poem have encountered the same scene as the youth in the tree, and with little direction from the poet, they too must feel some melancholy at a scene that presents no lesson and promises only increasing darkness.

Forms and Devices

"Ancient Autumn" begins with three questions that seem to provide a comic tone and present a scene transparently. "Is that foolish youth still sawing/ The good branch he's sitting on?" The poet then asks if the sound of the saw's "wheeze" fills the orchard and hill, and if the youth is able to see the village below him "The way a chicken hawk would."

The scene that follows appears with painterlike clarity. Apart from labeling the youth as "foolish"—an evaluation that most readers are likely to agree with—the poem's descriptions are objective. They appear with the perspective of a painting, as they begin with the youth in the foreground and gradually fade into the very distant sight of the horseman. He almost seems to have been captured on canvas, as he is described as leaving "forever in a hurry." Beyond him, the scene disappears into an ellipsis.

The events described are those of the commoner's everyday existence, but they have an ancient quality to them consistent with the title. Simic's choice of details— hard cider, long-stemmed pipes, line-dried diapers, a woman relieving herself outdoors, a man on a horseback, cobbled roads, and houses warmed by wood fires—all suggest an era gone by. His word choice occasionally suggests a European setting as well, as the town is called a "village" and its center park is a "commons." Both the long-gone European setting and its painterly quality call to mind a scene portrayed by the artist Pieter Bruegel the Elder. Simic has claimed an affinity for this Flemish artist whose paintings of daily life in Renaissance Europe often served as the backdrop for important historical events that were placed insignificantly within the scene.

Readers are carried along into the certainty of the scene with other subtle word choices. The poet speaks of the scene with assertion. For instance, "that foolish youth" is named as if he had previously been identified by the poet. Most of the people within the scene are described using indefinite articles; however, as the poem nears its end and the scene gains a familiarity with its readers, the horseman is introduced ("the black horseman") as if he were actually being glimpsed by both poet and readers.

However, because the poem opens with questions that cast doubt on the presence of the youth, the sound of his saw, and his view of the village, Simic creates ambiguity in a scene made up of otherwise straightforward images. If the answer is "no" to any of the initial questions, then there is no scene—and therefore, no poem. What begins as a set of rhetorical questions ultimately serves as a device to lead readers into uncertainty.

There is no sound in the poem, as the wind carries the noises away from the youth. Except for the saw's "wheeze," which is challenged by the poet's opening questions, all aspects of the scene can be perceived only through vision. In some cases, such as with the black horseman, whose direction is not immediately apparent, this vision is faulty, perhaps because of the distance. However, the point of view comes under more question when one realizes that the youth may be mentally challenged (to provide a euphemism for the poet's old-fashioned term "foolish"). The scene is laid out with careful clarity and perspective, but if one cannot trust the source of that point of view, then the poem's scene may place its readers in great uncertainty.

Themes and Meanings

Because "Ancient Autumn" describes an ordinary scene that can easily be imagined having taken place a long time ago, the scene brings to mind the aspects of readers' own mundane lives. There is work to be done, children to be taken care of, and places to travel, and most of this happens without anyone stopping to take notice of it.

Simic shows a fairly wide spectrum of everyday life in this scene. The men haul a barrel full of an alcoholic beverage, suggesting what may be used as pleasure, yet they are "humpbacked" from the work itself. The woman pins diapers and relieves herself, yet the suggestion of a baby and a white thigh allude to two more pleasurable aspects alongside the necessity of chores and defecation. The children play, but their play is warlike. These aspects—often contradictory within the same action—show aspects of human existence that continue in modern times. Simic's description of human life shows how little has changed over the course of human history.

The poem may even provide a more cynical view of human existence. While day-to-day existence has continued from the poem's "ancient" times to today, Simic's choice of season may suggest that certain aspects of the human condition threaten its own existence. The children who "play soldiers and march in step" are placed as the final image of the second stanza, and it is for their commands that the youth listens. Following this picture of innocence playing at the game of killing is the appearance of the dark horseman. The rider may be "coming" or "leaving forever." Simic may be suggesting a more austere future for those who play at war, as it is never made clear whether this shadowy figure is arriving or leaving, or even where or whom he is approaching or leaving.

If readers try to make such figures into symbols, Simic frustrates this kind of interpretation by calling them "dumb shows with their vague lessons." As the foolish youth grows pensive with the scene below him, so do the readers of the poem. No explicit meanings are offered for what the youth or the readers are seeing. As the youth continues to saw the branch that he is perched on, his action seems to strengthen the comic yet cynical view that portrays the destructive behavior of so much of humanity. The sun continues to set, which promises to bring darkness; consequently, even the youth's vision will be hampered.

However, not all of the poem may be meant to make readers "thoughtful and melancholy." The poem begins with a comic tone, and that aspect is echoed as the youth continues to saw his branch. The woman who relieves herself behind the bush is slightly comic, as are the figures of the misshapen men who haul the barrel on the commons. Such scenes provide a type of comic relief to what may be a cynical pronouncement on human nature. However, that existence of comic and tragic elements side by side adds even more ambiguity to this poem. Ultimately, that uncertainty is both humorous and depressing, depending on one's own view of human perspective: Are humans awful beings who create their own destruction, or are they silly creatures who continually surprise themselves? In "Ancient Autumn," Simic seems to present and even favor both perspectives.

Brian C. Ferguson-Avery

AN ANCIENT GESTURE

Author: Edna St. Vincent Millay (1892-1950)
Type of poem: Lyric
First published: 1954, in *Mine the Harvest*

The Poem

Edna St. Vincent Millay's "An Ancient Gesture" gives the reader a glimpse into a world of personal distress and a reflection on a tradition related to that distress. While the exact nature of the distress is never revealed, the poem's meditation on a motif from a classical story suggests its outlines.

The "I," or speaker, of "An Ancient Gesture" tells only one detail about the present moment of the poem: "I wiped my eyes on the corner of my apron." On this one detail, the reader must base all understanding of the thoughts that follow and must guess the speaker's dilemma. The reader assumes the poem's speaker to be of the feminine gender, not from the poet's own gender, nor from the association of the apron with housework, which was more often the exclusive province of women at the time of the poem's composition, in the middle years of the twentieth century. The assumption comes from the classical and literary association that arises in the speaker's mind. She thinks of Penelope, wife of Ulysses. Although the connection is never stated, the poem implies that Penelope's situation might parallel the situation of the similarly distressed speaker. Penelope is keeper of a household, she is surrounded by people who want from her what she will not give, and she is awaiting the return of a long-absent husband, of whose whereabouts she has no clue. Her wait has been a long one.

Penelope's distress has not reached the point of despair. Her faith remains unshaken that her husband will eventually return. Patience, courage, and fortitude are certainly among her traits. Yet still she feels distress and sorrow at her situation. Her distress is represented in part by the gesture she shares with the speaker of the poem: the wiping away of her tears. It is also expressed by her act of weaving by day and undoing those same labors by night. She does this because she is daily tested, being surrounded by suitors who want her, or want her estate. She weaves, then unweaves, as a means of holding these unwanted men at bay. Were she to finish her weaving, it would be a sign to them that her waiting had ended.

While the poem's speaker makes one gesture, she thinks of Penelope, who makes two, first in the wiping of the tear, and second in her act of weaving. The first is a true gesture, since it reflects her inner state. The second is a false one, to deceive the men courting her in the absence of Ulysses.

That the speaker in Millay's poem finds herself reminded of both truthful and deceptive gestures deepens the significance of the occurrence in the second stanza, when Ulysses does return, for he employs a gesture himself. He, too, wipes away a tear. The gesture was a truthful one when used by Penelope, and presumably also when used by the poem's speaker. It may be a truthful one for Ulysses as well. He may be using it to express his own feelings. Yet Ulysses is by reputation a trickster and a canny employer of falsehoods to accomplish his ends. His appropriation of Penelope's gesture, his public use of it before "the assembled throng," and the poet's final emphasis that Penelope "really cried," as if to imply that Ulysses did not, leads the reader and perhaps the poem's speaker to the realization that the original gesture has changed. Gestures, arising from the need for personal expression, are a combination of outward sign and inward significance. Ulysses demonstrates that the sign can be removed from its significance.

Once removed, moreover, that sign can be passed down through time, as a part of social culture. The poem's speaker establishes this through the sheer act of association: She engages in the gesture and finds the past rising to her, unbidden. The realization of this tie to the past seems a reassurance to her. In using the gesture she is no longer alone, because Penelope and Ulysses did this too.

Forms and Devices

In writing "An Ancient Gesture," Millay followed the traditions of lyric poetry in limiting herself to a single, emotional theme and in using language that is conspicuously musical. In both focus and language, however, she exercised great subtlety. The predominant emotional mood—of distressed sadness—goes unstated, being suggested only through a parallel from classical literature and through the rhetorical technique of stirring in the audience what the speaker of the poem may be feeling:

> Your arms get tired, and the back of your neck gets tight;
> And along towards morning, when you think it will never be light
> And your husband has been gone, and you don't know where,
>   for years,
> Suddenly you burst into tears.

The musicality of the poem's language also receives deft treatment. Unlike in most traditional lyrics, the rhythmic length of the lines and the placement of their end rhymes are irregular, giving the reader the initial impression that "An Ancient Gesture" might be an example of unusually graceful free verse. At least in part, this gracefulness does arise from a rhythmic structure, however. This structure lies hidden, clothed in language that is not heightened with literary tricks. As is the case with much free verse, the poem's lines have a relaxed, natural, and conversational flavor. The lines contain either five stresses or three, with five-stress lines predominating and pairs of three-stress lines closing each of the two stanzas.

While the rhymes are used in an irregular pattern, they are used purposefully. The succession of the three rhymes "night," "tight," and "light" in the first stanza gives a sense of building toward the poem's most emotional moment, which is itself emphasized by rhymes (". . . for years,/ Suddenly you burst into tears"). The last line of the poem, "Penelope, who really cried," is also given weight by rhyme, especially because the line with which it rhymes, "But only as a gesture,—a gesture which implied," is central to understanding the poem as a whole.

Millay used the repetition of words and phrases for emphasis and to enhance the unity of her work. The initial line of the first stanza, "I thought, as I wiped my eyes on the corner of my apron," reappears at the beginning of the second stanza, with the simple addition of an initial conjunction. The repetition creates an illusion of duration and of depth. To the reader, the distress appears to be of the sort that will not quickly pass.

Two lines in the poem, the only three-stress lines not placed at the ends of stanzas, are clearly parallel: the second line of the first stanza, "Penelope did this too," and the fourth line of the second stanza, "Ulysses did this too." These two short lines effectively cement the stanzas, and their separate thoughts, firmly together. Their parallel assertions also reinforce the importance of their message, affirming the speaker's connection to tradition through her use of a gesture.

Themes and Meanings

Although she was writing a lyric poem, Millay chose a title, "An Ancient Gesture," that would signal her intention of speaking about more than an emotional state, however powerful an emotion it might be. The title itself serves as a kind of gesture, indicating to the reader that the topic will be not the tears themselves but the act of wiping them away. Although gestures are often seen in a negative light, as in the common phrase "an empty gesture," Millay never does other than emphasize the importance and positive value of the gesture: "There is simply nothing else to do." The gesture is valid unto itself, a pure act arising out of social and cultural traditions. It is "authentic, antique,/ In the very best tradition, classic, Greek." In recognizing this validity, Millay suggests that people need the gesture, because of those times when "there is simply nothing else to do." Being the only response to a situation, it becomes the necessary response.

In a real sense Millay is talking about the inheritance of culture in "An Ancient Gesture." Evoking Penelope's use of the loom, one of the most important tools in domestic culture from ancient times, signals that she is speaking of the gesture as being similarly central to social culture. By revealing that her speaker's gesture is "in the very best tradition," she reaffirms this. She then shows how the tradition came to be passed down: Ulysses learns it from "Penelope, who really cried"—from Penelope, who gave the gesture its meaning. While the speaker identifies first with Penelope's use of the gesture, the reader is left with the impression that she also identifies with that of Ulysses.

"An Ancient Gesture" is important in demonstrating the possible range of the lyric poem. It shows how the form not only can carry emotional content but also be a vehicle for the exploration of deeper themes. As a specific literary work, "An Ancient Gesture" commands respect for its effective combination of structural rigor and informal yet musical language, as well as for the compelling development of its theme. It remains one of the capping works of one of America's most lyrical poets.

Mark Rich

AND DEATH SHALL HAVE NO DOMINION

Author: Dylan Thomas (1914-1953)
Type of poem: Lyric
First published: 1933; collected in *Twenty-five Poems*, 1936

The Poem

"And Death Shall Have No Dominion" is a poem in three nine-line stanzas of sprung rhythm. Each of the stanzas begins and ends with the title line, which echoes Romans 6:9 from the King James translation of the Christian New Testament: "Death hath no more dominion." The title and the refrain give the theme of the poem—resurrection—and introduce its characteristic rhythm and solemn tone.

The poem is built on repetition, and not merely of the title. Once the meaning of the first line is grasped, the entire poem is understood. Each of the intervening lines and images is simply another way of saying that the life force is immortal—that people's bodies may die but their spirits live on in the world.

The speaker of the poem is a grand and disembodied voice. There is no particular representative intended; there is no character whose words these are taken to be. The poem is an oratory; it is truth spoken out of the air.

The first stanza deals with the dead, who shall be made whole again at the end of time. The unity and wholeness of the universe is hinted at by an arresting rearrangement of elements that Dylan Thomas creates in the third line: "the man in the wind and the west moon." Man in the moon, man in the wind, west wind, west moon—it does not matter how the parts are arranged because all is one.

When dead men reach the final reckoning, therefore, even though their bodies are gone, "they shall have stars at elbow and foot." The paradox of having elbows and feet and yet no body reiterates the poem's theme of resurrection. More important than the body is the spirit or the life force. "Though lovers be lost," the poet says, "love shall not." It is not people but people's spiritual force that shall endure.

There is much religious-sounding language in the first stanza, particularly many echoes of the language of the King James Bible: "naked they shall be one," "stars at elbow and foot," and "they shall rise again." There is no Christianity here, however. God is never mentioned, there is no talk of souls or of salvation, and the moment at which all shall or shall not happen is not specified as any sort of Judgment Day. Whatever happens to people happens because that is the nature of things, not because a supreme being has ordained it.

In the second stanza, Thomas treats the pain of life and death. Even if the pain should be bad enough for people's faith to "snap in two," they will still not suffer a final death. It is nature, not faith, that determines one's ultimate fate.

The last stanza connects one's life force to that of other natural beings—the birds and flowers. When people die, their life force may enter a daisy or the sun, but it will not simply end. Death shall have no dominion.

Forms and Devices

As is often the case with Thomas's poetry, much of the power of this poem comes from the sound of it. It should be read aloud to be fully appreciated. "And Death Shall Have No Dominion" is one of his poems that Thomas himself chose to record. When one listens to the poem, one is immediately struck by its rhythm. Gerard Manley Hopkins coined the term "sprung rhythm" to describe his own poetry in which the rhythm is based not on metrical feet, but simply on the number of stressed syllables in a line. The term is apt here. Two different readers reciting this poem are likely to stress different syllables within any given line, yet both readers will create the same effect of wavelike rhythm—strong, regular, and insistent.

Thomas creates this powerful rhythm by the careful selection of words and the crafting of lines. Nearly all of the words in the poem are monosyllabic and contain explosive consonants that create a sharp separation between words.

One line from the first stanza demonstrates this: "When their bones are picked clean and the clean bones gone." The combinations of consonants make it nearly impossible to elide words in this line. In "picked clean," the two hard *k* sounds demand to be sounded separately; in "clean bones gone," each of the three words begins with an explosive consonant, and the repetition of the *n* creates the effect of stress and echo. The line must be read slowly, distinctly, and rhythmically.

Most of the lines in the poem are punctuated at the end, and much of this punctuation is in the form of periods and semicolons. Again, this forces the reader to pause at regular intervals, enhancing the rhythm.

Repetition also aids rhythm in this poem. The most obvious example of this is the title line, which occurs six times in the poem, creating a rhythm of larger units that recede and echo back.

Repetition operates on a smaller scale as well. In the first stanza, three lines are structured to echo one another: "Though they go mad they shall be sane,/ Though they sink through the sea they shall rise again;/ Though lovers be lost love shall not." In the first two lines, repetition of the word "they" helps to create the wavelike effect, as do the words "lovers" and "love" in the third line.

Thomas has not created rhythm for its own sake, although his body of work clearly demonstrates that he was much taken by the beauty inherent in spoken language. This poem's rhythm, reminiscent of a Christian prayer or sermon, reinforces the solemnity and importance of its theme.

Thomas chooses to echo religious oratory, not to deliver a Christian message, but to offer his idea of resurrection in a ritual style that Christians will understand.

Themes and Meanings

The central issue in this poem is the nature of resurrection and, therefore, the essential nature of the life force being resurrected. By using echoes of the Christian Bible throughout the poem, Thomas demands that his views be seen in contrast to the Christian tradition in which he was reared.

Thomas has often been referred to as a pantheist. The word "pantheism" comes from the Greek *pan*, meaning all, and *theos*, meaning God. In other words, God and the universe are one, or God and nature are one. Although it is unlikely that Thomas ever used the term to describe himself, pantheism does seem to capture much of his system of belief. This idea is demonstrated in this poem as well as others, including "A Refusal to Mourn the Death, by Fire, of a Child in London" and "The Force That Through the Green Fuse Drives the Flower."

When Saint Paul said in his letter to the Romans that "death hath no more dominion," he meant that those who had chosen salvation would not suffer eternal damnation and spiritual death. Instead, they would be resurrected on the Day of Judgment and given new spiritual bodies.

Thomas makes it clear from the beginning that he sees things differently. When he states (and restates) that "death shall have no dominion," he carefully and deliberately leaves out the word "more." For Thomas, it is not a matter of death ceasing to have power—death has never been the end of life.

When people die, the poem says, their spirits live on. The issue of bodies is moot. When people die their spirits may next inhabit a flower ("Heads of the characters hammer through daisies") or something else, but their spirits will continue to live.

Faith, Thomas says in stanza 2, has nothing to do with it. Some may lose their faith ("Faith in their hands shall snap in two") as a result of the suffering inherent in life. Perhaps like Thomas they might turn away from the traditional faith of their childhood toward something else. Whatever they decide about God and the universe, their life force will not die because it is not the nature of this force to die.

Thomas does not use biblical echoes in "The Force That Through the Green Fuse Drives the Flower," even though its theme is similar to "And Death Shall Have No Dominion." If the essential message of the former poem is that human life and death are simply part of the natural cycle, then "And Death Shall Have No Dominion" takes this message one step further.

The use of biblical language forces the reader to juxtapose the two systems of belief. "And Death Shall Have No Dominion" is not only an oratory celebrating a pantheistic view—it is also an overt rejection of Christian beliefs.

Cynthia A. Bily

AND THERE IS ALWAYS ONE MORE STORY

Author: Simon J. Ortiz (1941-   )
Type of poem: Narrative
First published: 1977, in *A Good Journey*

The Poem

"And there is always one more story" begins with an italicized preface that places the poem within a long line of oral narration. Simon J. Ortiz declares "It must be an old story" since it eventually came to him from his mother, who heard a woman "telling/ about her grandson who was telling the story/ which was told to him by somebody else." The chain of connection is linked by "All/ these voices," Ortiz says, establishing the generational process of transmission that provides the material for the poem.

Continuing the personal tone that his introduction has initiated, the story begins with the classic opening "One time," but Ortiz displays the operation of oral transmission by parenthetically inserting his daughter Rainy's comment, "You're sposed to say, 'Onesa ponsa/ time,' Daddy," before actually moving into the tale. There is a shift into another realm as the central characters of the poem, "some Quail Women grinding corn" and Tsuushki ("Coyote Lady") are presented, with a final authorial comment about Tsuushki—"I don't know why she wasn't grinding corn too"—before the world that the story creates completely absorbs the poet's attention.

The details of the narration continue in a mix of description ("It was a hot, hot day, very hot"), dialogue, and action. The nearest water is "at the top of a tall rock pinnacle," and the women lend Tsuushki feathers so she can fly with them. Once there, they decide to reverse familiar practice by playing "a trick, a joke/ on Coyote Lady," and they strand Tsuushki by taking their feathers from her. Pondering the problem, Tsuushki is joined on the pinnacle by "Kahmaasquu Dya-ow—/ Spider Grandmother," who is characterized as "always a wonderful helpful person." True to this trait, Spider Grandmother agrees to assist, inviting Tsuushki into a basket at the end of her rope (or web), but adds an injunction: "'While I am letting you down,/ you must not look up, not once,/ not even just a little bit.'" Tsuushki readily agrees. However, as the basket descends, the storyteller says, "Coyote looked up," and the poet inserts another parenthesis, altering the narrative perspective by observing "At this point, the voice telling the story/ is that of the boy," before resuming the account.

Spider Grandmother drops the basket, Coyote goes "crashing down," and the narrator notes that the story has ended but adds, crucially, "as you know, it also goes on." In the continuation, Shuuwimuu Guiguikuutchah ("Skeleton Fixer") arrives, reassembles the bones, dances around them while delivering an invocation—"Skeleton skeleton join together"—twice, and is not entirely pleased to discover "Oh, it's just you Coyote." Tsuushki runs off, followed by Skeleton Fixer's dismissive comment, "Go ahead and go, may you get crushed/ by a falling rock somewhere!" The somewhat inconclusive ending is an appropriate stopping point for a story that is a part of a larger story, the characters appearing at one moment in the extensive, ongoing saga of their existence in communal memory.

Forms and Devices

Ortiz discussed his goals concerning the poems in *A Good Journey* in a preface to the collection, asserting his intention to show "that the narrative style and technique of the oral tradition could be expressed as written narrative." Recognizing that "the spoken word is so immediate and intimate," Ortiz felt that it was important for the reader to be a participant in the process of transmission, and to this end, he inserts in the course of the poem reflective comments by what appear to be different narrators picking up the thread of the story and altering its perspective. This prevents the audience from becoming involved completely with any of the characters, or from identifying with the position of any single narrative consciousness. From the introductory musings of the poet about the fivefold pattern of transmission; to the corrective comment about appropriate form by his daughter, the next generation as participant and listener; to the story unfolding within the control of an omniscient narrator; to the informative but not interruptive comment that "At this point, the voice telling the story/ is that of the boy who said. . . ."; to the unidentified translator who takes the Acoma Pueblo language into English ("which is to say"); the story mingles individual voices with those of the characters to create a verbal collage that, as Ortiz puts it, will "show the energy that language is."

The intricate narrative structure that Ortiz develops does not interfere with the immediate effect of the action because of the clarity of the imagery that the poem offers. The landscape of the southwestern desert is evoked in direct terms—"The water was in a little cistern/ at the top of a tall rock pinnacle/ which stands southeast of Aacqu"— while the remains of the shattered skeleton convey the harsh terrain: "The bones/ were drying white in the sun, lying around." The specific actions of the characters are also presented in spare but evocative language, as at the moment when Coyote defies the injunction, "But Tsuushki/ looked up and saw her butt," or when Skeleton Fixer performs the reorganizing ritual, "And he joined the bones together,/ very carefully,/ and when he had finished doing that,/ he danced around them while he sang."

To further individualize the characters, and to connect the Laguna community with the reader, Ortiz mingles Acoma language with standard English, using both the Native American tribal name and its English equivalent for the characters, as well as introducing other objects ("u-uuhshtyah—juniper berries;") and at key moments putting an entire phrase in the Acoma tongue. "Nahkeh-eh,/ bah aihatih eyownih trudrai-nah!," Skeleton Fixer says at the poem's end, before repeating—for additional emphasis—the words in English. For those who do not hear the poem spoken, these linguistic variants are an inducement to speak the sounds of the unfamiliar language, contributing to the participatory element that Ortiz regards as an important aspect of the oral tradition. The occasional interpolation of conversational devices—"Well, at this point" and "But, pretty soon"—also helps to suggest a storyteller in action before a group of listening faces.

Themes and Meanings

Ortiz has accepted as one of his responsibilities as an artist the preservation of a cultural identity threatened by social and political forces. When asked in an interview why he writes, he replied, "Because Indians always tell a story" and explained that for an endangered community, "The only way to continue is to tell a story." His concept of "continuance" is based on the wisdom of Native American elders who said, "We must always remember" and is informed by a need to keep the stories of the past alive "in the new language" so that they are never lost or forgotten. In this way, each generation is "present in the here and now. . . . Continuance, in this sense, is life itself."

One of the wisdom-figures of Native American life is the mythic entity known as Coyote, whose presence in different forms occurs across tribal divisions and historical epochs. Ortiz acknowledges this mystical power by recognizing "that's what Coyote says" when he refers to the storytelling trait as fundamental for American Indians, and in the poem, Coyote plays a prominent part as a source of almost instinctive emotional responses that are the product of a previous history of unsettling activity. While the poem does not explain these responses, they would be familiar to an audience used to the oral tradition, and Ortiz frequently brings Coyote into stories and poems in his collected writing to widen the scope for other readers and listeners. In this poem, it is Coyote Lady who is present among the Quail Women, the correspondence in gender suggesting both the protean, shape-changing properties of the trickster and the fact that perhaps Coyote can also exist within the mind as a projection of a psychological impulse.

Recognizing the needs of a kindred spirit, a "beloved comadre" (with the word "Comadre" implying both "comrade" and "mother"), the Quail Women share their powers of flight with Coyote so they can all reach life-sustaining water, but then in the spirit of Coyote's legendary, perverse, prank-playing dark mischief, they strand her on the pinnacle. As if from a beneficient cosmos, one of the most powerful natural forces, Spider Grandmother, a revered goddess, appears and offers to help, with the qualification that the recipient acknowledge the higher power by accepting a limit to desire. Coyote, characteristically, agrees but, also characteristically, challenges the goddess in a Promethean gesture of individual will and defiance. Naturally, this leads to the wrath of the deity, and Coyote falls to her destruction.

However, within the theological realm that the poem presupposes, existence is not terminated by the end of the corporeal body. Thus, the arrival of another beneficient force, Skeleton Fixer—a character without or beyond gender—leads to the reconstruction or resurrection of Coyote. In another shift, this displeases Skeleton Fixer, whose good deed was predicated on the expectation of saving a valuable and honored spirit, not this notorious troublemaker. Skeleton Fixer's concluding invocation, "may you get crushed/ by a falling rock somewhere!," is an exasperated tribute to the survival of an aspect of human/animal nature that is probably necessary for the continuance of the species in a precarious and perplexing universe.

Leon Lewis

ANDREA DEL SARTO

Author: Robert Browning (1812-1889)
Type of poem: Dramatic monologue
First published: 1855, in *Men and Women*

The Poem

"Andrea del Sarto" is a meandering poem of 267 lines in blank verse, broken un-evenly into three stanzas of 243, 23, and 1 line(s). The title identifies the subject of the poem, Andrea del Sarto, a distinguished artist of the Florentine School of painting. The poem is written in the first person, the speaker being Andrea, not Robert Browning. Andrea, conversing with his silent wife, Lucrezia, reflects on his life and art, thereby dramatically revealing his moral and aesthetic failure.

The poem begins with Andrea's placative request to Lucrezia to sit with him and not "quarrel any more." The failure of the marriage quickly becomes evident as Andrea acknowledges that her physical presence affords no guarantee of intimacy or rapport. His wife's consent to sit is rewarded with a promise that he will accede to her wishes, permitting Lucrezia's friends to dictate the circumference and price of his art. His most persuasive ploy for the pleasure of her company—even for a few evening hours—is his pledge to "shut the money" from his work in her hand.

As Andrea muses over the state of his life and his art, detailing his experiences and implying his dreams, he becomes an unconscious study in the complexity of failure: an artist possessing an uncommon aptitude for perfection in execution, but lacking the personal character traits to achieve success. Andrea views in all that he has touched—his life, his marriage, and his paintings—a "common greyness." He gropes desultorily for the cause of this diminution of his promise.

He first speculates that his failure is attributable to determinism; an authoritative, controlling god predestines individual accomplishments. Such rationale, however, is too simplistic for the sensitive, intelligent artist. He reflects on his potential. Self-confident, he affirms his innate genius: Unlike others, he does not have to struggle for perfection in line and color; for him, process is facile. Michelangelo has even identi-fied him as a serious Renaissance contender—that is, he would be if he were as moti-vated and dedicated as the masters are.

Momentarily elated at his recollection and seeking to demonstrate this ability to his wife, Andrea almost presumes to correct a flawed line of a copy of a master painting; belatedly, however, withdrawing his brush from the surface of the painting, he sur-mises that technique is not the critical factor determining greatness. More significant is the soul of the artist. Andrea ponders over Lucrezia's influence on his work: If she "had a mind," if she were spiritual rather than carnal, he might have triumphed. He concludes, however, that incentive is not an external, but an internal phenomenon.

Nostalgically, Andrea reflects on his year of prominence, basking in the favor of King Francis I and his royal court. Those golden years had ended abruptly at his decision to return to Italy and Lucrezia (at her request) and his embezzlement of money intrusted to him by the king for art purchases. Now, alienated from that glory, cuckolded—and aware of it—he prostitutes his art to delight Lucrezia and even to pay the debts of her lover.

The dispassionate Andrea seems resigned to the diminished state of his life and art as the second stanza begins. Experiencing guilt over his neglect of his aged, impoverished parents and his betrayal of the king, he purports consolation at "having" Lucrezia. His sense of frustration, however, continues; in one last effort at consolation, he speculates on the afterlife. He will compete successfully with Raphael, Leonardo da Vinci, and Michelangelo in the New Jerusalem. His obsession with Lucrezia and his resignation, however, surface once more: Even in heaven—at his choice—his wife will take precedence, negating any change in his performance.

The extent of Andrea's decadence is further emphasized in the concluding, one-line stanza: The effete husband, with seeming nonchalance, releases his wife to her lover at his casual whistle.

Forms and Devices

The dramatic monologue has become synonymous with Robert Browning's genius, and in "Andrea del Sarto" the poet probes the nature of one human failure. Form follows content, the language being informal as is natural in conversation. In harmony with the dwindling quality of Andrea's life, the tone is subdued, reflecting the passive resignation that feeds Andrea's impotence. In meter, also, the rhythm yields to the emotional tenor of the speaker's reverie, moving from the placid acceptance of the present through a lively reflection on his Fontainebleau years to the wistful contemplation of eternity. His low-pulsed "quietly, quietly the evening through" is interrupted by brief spurts of broken rhythm and faster-paced patterns: "Dream? strive to do, and agonize to do,/ And fail in doing."

The diction is sometimes oblique and indirect, conveying the ambiguity of Andrea's perception of truth. Browning also employs a rhetorical technique of questions and answers to advance the reader through time and provide details of the speaker's past. The questions are not directly responded to, but answers emerge through roundabout discourse: Andrea's "you turn your face, but does it bring your heart" arouses doubt concerning Lucrezia's affection for her husband, but his subsequent bribe—an offer to prostitute his art for her greed—turns the skepticism into a certainty that she is indifferent not only to Andrea but also to art in general.

Browning relies heavily on irony in "Andrea del Sarto." Overall there is a pervasive cosmic irony that Andrea, rarely gifted, lacks the ardor and capability to animate his paintings. Fate, too, seems to deny any personal or professional fulfillment; whatever the extent of his desire or the magnitude of his sacrifice, he falls short. Ironically, too, Andrea's introspection and his matter-of-fact observations about Lucrezia convey truths to the reader that he cannot even surmise. Incongruously, his words are often denied by the reality of his reverie: An assertion of "peace" initiates a return to the inner turmoil attendant to failure.

"A common greyness silvers everything," muses Andrea, thereby opening the monologue to the juxtaposition of two color images, "grey" and "golden," to symbolize mediocrity and transcendence, respectively. The concept of "grey" is expanded metaphorically in "toned down," "autumn in everything," "a twilight piece," and "a settled dusk now," becoming synonymous with Andrea himself. In marked contrast is "golden." Andrea's halcyon days in France were "golden." There he basked in the "golden looks" and wore "golden chains." Lucrezia, too, is included among these transcendent moments, Andrea making reference to her "hair's gold."

Themes and Meanings

"Andrea del Sarto" is a poem about success and failure in life and art, as expressed through the unconscious self-analysis of a sensitive, intelligent artist.

Andrea's mediocrity stresses the truth of a common Browning motif: "A man's reach should exceed his grasp." Unfortunately, such a premise negates success for Andrea (known in history as the "faultless painter"), for he possesses an ability for technique that others "agonize" to reach. Significantly, this excellence comes facilely: "I can do with my pencil what I know,/ What I see, . . ./ Do easily, too . . . perfectly." Yet, as Andrea theorizes, "In this world, who can do a thing will not;/ And who would do it, cannot, I perceive." Therefore, since Andrea is one who "can," he is ineffective.

His plaintive observation that others whose works lack precision "reach many a time a heaven" denied him reveals frustration; however, his very expertise, according to Browning's credo, signifies baseness and superficiality. Andrea's cognizance of his own ennui as, amoebalike, he is indifferent to criticism or praise, is indicative of a paralysis precluding an essential motivation, which would empower transcendence. Andrea should be "reaching that heaven might so replenish him/ Above and through his art."

Inextricably intertwined with the preceding theme is another, focusing on the balance between mind (art) and heart (love). For Andrea, love takes preeminence, and he evaluates all experience by the light in Lucrezia's eyes. In his art, Andrea's efforts are not determined by his own imagination, they are subjugated to the whims of his wife, as he commercializes his art to buy her a "ruff" or pay her lover's gambling debts. Even in France, his ultimate concern was not for self-realization or for meeting the king's expectations, it was for meriting Lucrezia's approval. At Lucrezia's request, he returned to Italy, forfeiting his promising career in France. Even Michelangelo's generous words of recognition serve only to impress his wife rather than arouse joy in his soul. His obsession has corrupted his values and destroyed his reputation. For love he became an embezzler and failed his parents.

Sacrificed, too, for love is Andrea's dignity. Servile, Andrea begs to hold his wife's hand; humiliated, he condones his wife's infidelity. His "moon" has become "everybody's." The epitomy of shamed manhood, he exercises an annoying forbearance as he releases his wife temporarily to the arms of her lover. The extent of Andrea's demoralization is infinitely destructive, as shown by his final sacrifice: He forgoes his final opportunity for excellence. Even in eternity, he will "choose" Lucrezia and, therefore, deny his soul again. Andrea's unhealthy skewing of his life toward love has upset an essential balance between art and life, resulting in the betrayal of self and extinguishing the light of his soul.

Phyllis J. Scherle

ANECDOTE OF THE JAR

Author: Wallace Stevens (1879-1955)
Type of poem: Lyric
First published: 1919; collected in *Harmonium*, 1923

The Poem

Wallace Stevens's "Anecdote of the Jar" is a short lyric poem of three four-line stanzas that explore certain aspects of the relationship between art and the natural world. Although the lines have no definite, formal meter they are generally iambic with four stresses per line. With few exceptions, the words used in the poem are all commonplace and monosyllabic, allowing Stevens to employ at key points a variety of hammer-stroke rhythms for emphasis. The appearance at intervals of those words that are more than one syllable ("slovenly," "wilderness," and "dominion," for example) help emphasize the poem's dominant theme, the gulf between art and nature in the contrast between the short and "natural" words and the longer and "artistic" words. While there is no formal rhyming scheme to the poem, Stevens's characteristic skill with sounds, in particular consonants in the middle of words and the repetition of key words, helps link the piece together as well as further emphasizes the difference between "nature" and "art" or "artifice."

Ostensibly, "Anecdote of the Jar" is a straightforward, even simple, account of a commonplace action by the unnamed speaker, presumably Stevens himself. The speaker of the poem places a glass jar on the side of a hill in Tennessee. No reason is given for this action (as one shall see, the action of placing the jar is symbolic of artistic creation, which has no "reason" in the natural sense). Furthermore, this action takes place in the first line of "Anecdote of the Jar"; the rest of the poem is a reflection on what it means to have set the jar in the middle of the woods and what the jar's presence means for the poet, his readers, and the entire natural world.

In the first stanza, Stevens uses the verb "placed" to describe his action with the jar. What the speaker does with the jar is not an idle, unreflective deed but rather a conscious act; indeed, it is symbolic of artistic creation, and in a sense it is itself an artistic action. By the fact that it has so been placed, the jar, an artificial object, immediately affects the "slovenly wilderness," first by causing the wilderness to "surround that hill" and then, in the second stanza, forcing that wilderness to become "no longer wild." By the third and final stanza the jar has assumed control of the entire natural landscape ("It took dominion everywhere") and has in fact supplanted the natural landscape, the artificial world imposing its ideals of order and aesthetics on nature itself. Significantly, the jar "surrounds" and "takes dominion everywhere" without visible motion or activity but simply by the fact of its presence, its mere existence as counterpart and counterpoint to the natural world.

Forms and Devices

Known for the originality and individuality of his syntax and vocabulary, Stevens frequently teases his readers with a lexicon that seems commonplace but that, upon closer inspection, refuses to yield a single unambiguous meaning. At the same time, he often places these placidly baffling word choices within lines of deceptively straightforward narrative. In "Anecdote of the Jar" he presents the reader with a series of simple, declarative sentences whose individual words and overall meaning, while generally clear, can be difficult to unravel.

As previously noted, the action of the poem is deceptively simple: The poet places a glass jar on the side of a Tennessee hill. Then, however, the poem calmly informs readers that the jar assumes some sort of control over the wilderness, paradoxically taming it. Apparently the jar can accomplish this because it was "round upon the ground/ And tall and of a port in air." The internal rhyme of "round" and "ground" reinforces the concept of the jar (or a poem) as a conscious work of human artistry, an artificial creation that draws attention to its nature by the almost doggerel nature of the rhymes. As an artifact the poem is linked to the jar, which is also a creation of human beings.

Each created object is in some way capable of at least some control over nature. So much is clear: Art is a way of imposing order and meaning to a natural world that otherwise lies outside one's powers. However, Stevens's full meaning in the phrase "tall and of a port in air" is suggestive but tantalizingly unclear. Is the "port" here that similar to a harbor where ships (artificially constructed objects) and human beings can find refuge against nature's storms and tides? Or is the jar, made of glass and open at one end, being compared to a portal (such as the "port hole" of a ship) that allows passage from one world to another? Here, as elsewhere, Stevens's poem initially states what seems to be a plain fact, which upon closer reflection sees its meanings dissolve into a puzzle of contradictions.

By the final stanza these deceptively simple statements have elevated the jar's status to that far beyond what is realistically possible. It "took dominion everywhere" paradoxically because it was dull ("The jar was gray and bare") and lifeless ("It did not give of bird or bush"). These attributes, which would seem to weaken and diffuse the jar's mysterious power, actually are the source of its strength and order-imposing capability.

Themes and Meanings

As is often the case with Stevens's poetry, the underlying theme of "Anecdote of the Jar" is the division between the natural and artistic realms, a study in the conflict between outer and inner worlds, and, above all, the often conflicting relationship between the actual and the ideal. As Stevens himself once phrased it, the theme here is, yet again, the disparity between "imagination and reality." This division, Stevens maintained, could be resolved only through art and, in particular, through the medium of poetry, which he termed "the supreme fiction." "Anecdote of the Jar" is a symbolic representation of and reflection on how art controls, shapes, and ultimately determines the so-called real world.

To begin with, the jar is decidedly not natural but artificial. It is of human origin, deliberately manufactured and consciously placed on the hillside, thus doubly removing it from the natural order of things. It is further removed by the fact that the jar is not placed on the hillside to fulfill its original purpose (to hold or store items, generally foodstuffs). It is there as an artificial item, pure and simple—to fulfill an aesthetic rather than utilitarian purpose.

In contrast to the sleek, smooth sides of the fabricated jar as an object, the natural wilderness is "slovenly" and, to some degree, therefore inferior. In the poem, when the wilderness finally "rose up" to the jar (with a deliberate punning meaning clearly intended by Stevens in those words) that wilderness is "no longer wild" even though, paradoxically, it still "sprawled around." Poetry, and by extension all arts that are represented by the symbolic jar, thus have a dual capacity to tame and order nature while at the same time emphasizing nature's fundamental characteristics. The Tennessee wilderness is tamed twice: first by being literally contrasted to the glass jar, and second and more important by being described in the poem titled "Anecdote of the Jar."

However, there is a paradox inherent in art's ability to tame and control nature, for art is, in one sense, sterile. It can impose order but ultimately is not capable of true creation itself. The jar on the hill is "gray and bare" and alone in Tennessee "did not give of bird or bush." While it may be symbolically active, literally the jar (like art) is not alive. Cold, impersonal, and unnatural, the jar has undeniable value but questionable value: What does the jar do that is important to the poet, the reader, or the world? Essentially, the jar is important because of what it is not: It is not the natural world, it is not the hill, and it does not give indiscriminately and randomly "of bird or bush"— therefore it is unlike anything else in Tennessee or elsewhere.

What the jar does and what art accomplishes are to impose a sense of order and reality beyond the immediate sense of the natural world. They do this by becoming the "supreme fiction" that replaces the older, now lost fictions of religion, philosophy, and materialistic science. The order that the jar (or art) imposes is a mysterious one that, in the end, Stevens can assert but not fully explain. "The Anecdote of the Jar" gives readers a brief and highly memorable glimpse of "the supreme fiction" whose ultimate truth remains just beyond the meaning of the poet's words but whose importance is clearly felt.

Michael Witkoski

ANGEL

Author: James Merrill (1926-1995)
Type of poem: Lyric
First published: 1962, in *Water Street*

The Poem

This short, unrhymed exercise in free verse has the intimacy of a bit of private conversation about it. The poet, seated at his desk at a moment of creative frustration, his poem "thus far clotted, unconnected," notices a tiny angel hovering above his desk. Whether this is a figment of his imagination or a real spiritual intrusion is never made clear, and there are aspects of the description that possess intimations of the natural and the artistic worlds about them. The "whirring" sound leads directly to an association with the hummingbird, and its robes remind one of the colorful plumage of the tiny bird—robes which are described in terms of art, since Jan van Eyck is a fifteenth century Flemish painter whose work was bright and highly colored. There is, however, another association which may come to mind, getting its strength from the pointing finger; it may remind some readers of those small hanging mobiles, usually made of thin metal, painted gold, in which a figure, often an angel, cut out in profile and with arms outstretched, swings around in a circle, responding to air currents.

The tiny figure is pointing out the window with one hand. It is winter, and seemingly a particularly cold day, as evidenced by the smoke from the houses showing sharply in the crystal air and the haste with which people hurry by. The window seems to be in a house by the sea, since the speaker can see the sun's cold rays bouncing on the waves. With the other hand, the angel is pointing at the piano inside the room, upon which lies a copy of Erik Satie's Sarabande No. 1, a work that the speaker has never been able to learn to play well.

The angel's mouth is open, and the speaker imagines that he is poised either to speak or sing. The angel does not do either, but the writer thinks that if the angel were speaking, he would be chiding the writer for wasting his time trying to write when the obvious artistic successes of God and Satie are at hand to be admired. Defensively, the speaker thinks that it was wise of the angel not to have said anything of the kind, since there are arguments that could be made to suggest that neither God nor Satie created perfect works of art. In his chagrin, he also wonders at the presumption of the angel in admiring Satie. What is an angel doing admiring the works of an ordinary man? The angel has said nothing, but the speaker imagines his attitude toward the poem he is trying to write and is determined to show that he is not affected by the angel's presence. He gets back to the work of attempting to clean up the poem and give it some kind of artistic form. The angel, seemingly unimpressed by this show of busyness, unsmilingly shakes its head, making it clear that it does not approve even of the poem as it is printed.

Forms and Devices

Lurking behind this slender, witty lyric is a form that is usually developed into something rather more substantial, but which James Merrill has managed to keep small in this work. It is, in a sense, a "dramatic monologue" in the tradition of Robert Browning, but also reminiscent of the short, problem poems of John Donne. It starts *in medias res*, clearly in the middle of a situation which has developed to a point at which the poem begins. This gives the poem a kind of dramatic immediacy, a feeling of having inadvertently broken into a conversation which has been going on for some time. The reader is not sure of what has gone before, but the poem itself provides sufficient clues to the fact that somehow the speaker, who is a writer, has reached some kind of impediment, and his work is not going well. The angel provides him with the excuse for giving up, with the seemingly unassailable argument that the writer is striving beyond himself, presumptuous in assuming that he can make art; indeed, the argument is made more convincing by the admission by the writer that however much he desires to play the Satie composition, he cannot master it. The formidable counters of creative success used to discourage him are a sophisticated mix of the divine, the natural, and the artistic. God creates all, including the world, even in winter an object of awe. He also creates the angel, who is splendidly dressed in colors that connect him to the angels in the world of art, in the paintings of van Eyck. The angel sets the beauty and power of the spiritual, the natural, and the world of human artistic creation in the works of van Eyck and Satie against the seeming failure of the speaker's text, thus far turgid and aimless compared with the angel's examples, "whole/ Radiant and willed."

As is the way of the "dramatic monologue," the problem is seemingly impossible of solution, but in the very act of contemplating its difficulties the character in trouble not only faces the difficulties, but learns to understand and confront them, and ultimately to move back into action. In this poem the writer asks himself why he should bother, given the example of past greatness, both spiritual and human. How can he hope to compete? Asking the question helps him to see that creative art is not all done, that both God and Satie have limitations in their respective creations. The poem is a process of understanding, of movement from modest despair through serious confrontation with the problem of choosing between being a cowed consumer of others' creative gifts and deciding to try once more, even in the face of the seeming disdain of the spiritual world. In the end, the writer gets his confidence back and is determined to try again, partly to annoy, if genially, the angel, who clearly thinks the writer incapable of reaching his goal, and partly to reestablish his place as a creator.

Much of the success of this poem depends upon its "smartness," its sophistication, which is not an uncommon element in Merrill's work. He is a writer whose work commonly shows up in the first instance in the pages of *The New Yorker* magazine, which has a reputation for appealing to educated, intelligent, worldly-wise readers. Merrill has wider and deeper ambitions than simply pleasing the intelligentsia, but this poem has a strong aura of cleverness, albeit tenderly expressed. It could be read without recognizing its "dramatic monologue" form, but it is much more effective, intellectually and aesthetically, when that is seen. Certainly the choice of Satie and van Eyck suggests a kind of fastidious aestheticism. Ludwig van Beethoven and Rembrandt van Rijn would have been too obvious, and one suspects too important, too powerful, to conform to Merrill's idea of himself as a second-line artist such as van Eyck and Satie: tasteful, circumscribed and not inclined to grand gestures.

Themes and Meanings

"Angel" is a poem about the artistic process and the relation of the artist to the world of art, on the one hand, and the wonders of God's creation, on the other. Lighthearted and wry, it imagines the moment when the work of art is not going well, that moment when the artist is most likely to lose heart and give up, particularly if the overwhelming beauty and power of nature, even in its severest winter garb, is brought to the artist's attention. The temptation to quit is even more powerful when an example of the admired, finished, discrete art form (in this case, the charming Satie Sarabande No. 1) is thrust upon him, particularly since he cannot even play it. Not only is he being mocked as a producer of art, but also as an interpreter thereof.

The angel is an appropriate commentator on the writer's ability to make art, given the theological belief that one of the functions of angels is to sing the praises of God, the greatest Creator and, as such, the first and greatest artist. How can the poet sit there, fussing with his literary chaos, when he is surrounded by the power of God's example of making form out of confusion, and when the angel has pointed out to him the success of Satie, one of God's creatures who has proved his Godlike talents by producing the composition which the artist obviously much admired? If the poet cannot make art, he should give up trying and be content to adore those who can.

Merrill seems to be accepting the not uncommon idea that there is something divine about the artistic act. The angel seems to be denying the writer in the poem this gift, at least for the moment. The poem might be read, if not too exclusively or dogmatically, as a metaphor for the split personality of the artist, part human, part spiritual; the angel might stand for the artistic part of his own personality, discouraged by the failure to get the lines of poetry right, urging the writer to give up the attempt as presumptuous in the face of God's obvious creative force, on the one hand, and Satie's creative success on the human level, on the other. It is perhaps helpful to remember that this poem was originally called "Another Angel," which seems to suggest that this is not the first time the author has had this experience of artistic failure.

The poet, however, has the last laugh. The poem may be about not being able to write a poem, and how the artist's failure is deepened by lost confidence and by confrontation with creations, artistic, human, and spiritual, that suggest his efforts are not only futile, as in his attempt at piano playing, but inconsistent with his real role as a consumer of art rather than a producer. He rejects that argument, however. What is more to the point is the "fact" of the poem on the page. In the very act of rejecting the angel's hints and getting back to work on his inchoate lines, confused and aimless as they are, he creates the poem "Angel," which is, cheekily, about the very experience of being assailed by the suggestion of his unworthiness as an artist. He proves the contrary in making the aesthetic object, the poem, in the very act of fighting for the right to do so.

Charles Pullen

THE ANGEL OF HISTORY

Author: Carolyn Forché (1950-   )
Type of poem: Meditation
First published: 1988; revised and collected in *The Angel of History*, 1994

The Poem

Many of the eighteen sections of "The Angel of History" recount recollections of World War II, particularly horrors of persecution, dislocation, and loss. The memories belong primarily to a war victim named Ellie, a deported Jew whom the speaker befriended and has known for a number of years. Ellie is the poem's magnetic center, attracting a variety of associations, some of which are clarified in notes. While the poem does not proceed chronologically, images and repeated phrases link the sections, some analytical, others narrative.

Indeed, the mental and emotional work of comprehending shapes the poem. The first section portrays the shock of knowledge upon the speaker, and the next three sections elaborate. When children are destroyed in concentration camps, windows seem blank, games become ominous, sleep is impossible, and "the silence of God is God." The speaker's descent into the poem takes the form of disconnected fragments, but images of sea, light, vigilance, sleeplessness, fire, and memory create a matrix of emotion.

The next seven sections develop Ellie's experience—the loss of sons, her husband's death from cholera, her affliction with St. Anthony's Fire, the memory of her wedding dress, prompted by news of a plane crash. The events range from the war to her confinement much later in a French sanatorium. Her suffering and hatred of France have made her bitterly defiant. Homeless, sure that no country is safe, she believes that God is "insane," and she wants "to leave *life*." The speaker devotes herself to caring for Ellie, missing events of her own son's childhood. She laments that Ellie's predicament "is worse than memory, the open country of death."

Whereas many poems move toward resolution, the last seven sections of "The Angel of History" emphasize disturbance. The speaker is haunted by an undefinable presence ("as if someone not alive were watching"). An unidentified voice in section 12 recounts a nightmare of nonexistence, in the process referring to sites of atrocities in El Salvador. The process of empathizing, recounted in the thirteenth section, affects the speaker to the extent that it seems "As if it were possible to go on living for someone else." The next two sections depict her disorientation. A letter from Ellie describes changes over eight years, but in the speaker's memory, Ellie does not change: "Here you live in an atelier."

The sixteenth section opens with a bitter definition—"Surely all art is the result of one's having been in danger, of having gone through an experience all the way to the end"—and recounts the terrifying evacuation of Beirut, Lebanon, where the women first meet and the speaker first tried to comfort Ellie. The repeated phrase "And it went on" suggests not only the rigors of the evacuation but also their lasting impact upon the speaker. Just as her recollection of Ellie seems more vital than the more recent events Ellie describes in her letter, the speaker's mind has associated (her word is "confuse") Ellie and the entirety of wartime horror. Logic and language both falter, as difficulties in translation illustrate. Initially a polite inquiry, Ellie's "Est-ce que je vous dérange?" ("Am I disturbing you?") sounds here and in the final section like a bell tolling and assumes ironic resonance. The final section serves as a musical coda, reiterating emptiness and irreparability. The poem ends not with any final pronouncement but with the voice of Ellie, or perhaps a nameless victim, inquiring of the reader what the speaker has said.

One understands that the poem, while cohesive, cannot resolve. The horrors that Ellie (and countless others) have endured radically alter the world and the way one speaks of it. Like writers who endured the horrors of Naziism—Nobel Laureate Elie Wiesel, critic George Steiner, and poet Paul Celan, to name a few—the speaker becomes a witness even as she questions the adequacy of language to carry out her task.

Forms and Devices

"The Angel of History" looks unconventional. Its lines are sentences—one or more. Never enjambed, they cross the page like prose. Often the sections have divisions, but they have more to do with content than with stanza structure. On the other hand, "The Angel of History" *sounds* like a poem. The lines are lyrical and emotional, the limpid images a consistent synthesis of the beautiful and the ruined. Repeated phrases (repetends) create powerful rhythms, and a sense of recurring dream.

That the subject is distant, even exotic, contributes to the mystique. That the poem is not continuous or linear may also contribute, at least at first. Forché is employing montage—the technique of combining disparate elements into a unified whole. In Forché's hands, montage means composing without violating essential qualities of the vision she describes in her notes on the poem as "polyphonic, broken, haunted, and in ruins, with no possibility of restoration." Individual images may not be surreal, but the world about which she writes and her discontinuous presentation of it may seem to be. Thus, montage permits one to share in comprehending and feeling.

Themes and Meanings

Few American poets of the last hundred years have dedicated themselves to witnessing great human rights catastrophes. From Forché's early interest in people's vibrancy and suffering has grown a poetry that applies a persuasive lyricism to some of the worst horrors of the age. In portraying what she observes (and what she feels while observing), Forché imparts immediacy and emotional intensity to vignettes of political significance. After observing the grisly prelude to El Salvador's civil war in the 1970's, she vowed, "I will live/ and living cry out until my voice is gone/ to its hollow of earth." The power and desperation of this declaration must be understood against the background of two realizations that Forché made at that time. First, language lacked the means to describe horrors she was seeing; in fact, the shock might well render one speechless. Second, among the societies and nations of the world, Americans were anomalous—protected yet confined in relative calm "like netted fish." Witnessing events in various parts of the world severed Forché from the complacency of her country and from hope of comfort and rest.

The travel—geographical and spiritual—that led to "The Angel of History" might be seen as fulfilling the legacy of Anna, the Slovak grandmother Forché mentions throughout her poetry, who had firsthand experience of World War II and became, in "What It Cost," the first other voice to speak an entire Forché poem. Forché's program, explicit by the end of the 1970's, has included intensive study of languages, translations of poets such as Salvadoran Claribel Alegría, and the production of the 1993 anthology *Against Forgetting: Twentieth-Century Poetry of Witness*. Thirteen years separate the publication of her second and third books of poems, a period that she calls "the muffling and silence of a decade." When the "wound" of her accumulated experiences opened, "The Angel of History" took her beyond the limits of the "first-person, free-verse, lyric-narrative of my earlier years."

Another valuable context for appreciating the poem is its epigraph, the German Jewish Marxist philosopher and critic Walter Benjamin's description of the angel of history's helplessness amid ruin. To the angel, history is "one single catastrophe which keeps piling wreckage." He would like to "make whole what has been smashed," but he is propelled "irresistibly . . . into the future." The storm blows from Paradise, indicating both the origin of the angel and the standard against which he views history. Moreover, the storm, carrying him backward, blows so hard that the angel cannot close his wings. That such a figure, longing to repair the infinite ruins, cannot free himself from the catastrophe suggests the immensity against which Forché's characters struggle.

When the Modernist poet T. S. Eliot wrote of the horrors and disillusionment of World War I in his famous poem *The Waste Land* (1922), he chose urban European settings and pitted imagery of illness and dissipation against the vulnerable beauty of the month of April. Seven decades later, when Carolyn Forché wrote of the horrors of World War II in "The Angel of History," April was the time that "The tubercular man offers his cigarette and the snow falls, patiently, across the spring flowers." Eliot composed, from fragments of the world's cultures, allusions to traditions that he and many of his contemporaries believed had been destroyed by World War I. Forché, too, composes from fragments, but "The Angel of History" consists of individuals' memories. Her main character has survived the horrors of persecution, grief, dislocation, and continuing trauma, while the speaker herself has lived through the evacuation of Beirut.

The speaker's carrying and giving birth to her boy emphasize one of the great causes of Ellie's suffering—the loss of two sons. Forché also makes gestation and birth her metaphor for the immense importance of "The Angel of History" and the other poems published with it, referring to it as "a work which has desired its own bodying forth." In the language of the poem's opening, the speaker's time of "intimacy and sleep" has given way to a "vigilance" of the irreparable damages that the rest of the poem—as well as the book it initiates—reveals.

Jay Paul

THE ANGELS

Author: Rainer Maria Rilke (1875-1926)
Type of poem: Lyric
First published: 1906, as "Die Engel," in *Das Buch der Bilder,* second edition; English
    translation collected in *Translations from the Poetry of Rainer Maria Rilke,* 1962

The Poem

"The Angels" is a three-stanza poem of thirteen lines. In the original German ver-
sion, the rhyme scheme, *abab, cdcd, efeef,* nearly resembles that of an irregular son-
net. The English translation does not seek to reproduce that rhyme scheme (with the
exception of the "seam" and "dream" rhyme at the end of lines 2 and 4), but it does ac-
curately reproduce Rainer Maria Rilke's use of alliteration in the second line of each
stanza, a use of alliteration that underlines poetically strategic images of the nature
and function of angels as Rilke conceives them to be. The poem is a reflection on the
nature of angels. One might well expect an emphasis on visual representation and de-
tail in a collection of poems whose German title translates into English as the book of
images or the book of pictures. In the poem "The Angels," the emphasis is not on a vi-
sual image but rather on a mode of feeling and perceiving: Rilke's meditation here is
on that which has not been seen.

Rilke's lyricism has resonance with European Romantic poetry—that of John Keats,
Friedrich Hölderlin, William Wordsworth, and Novalis in particular. Unlike in the typi-
cal Romantic lyric poem, however, where the poet speaking in the first person focuses
upon nature to present or resolve a problem, in Rilke's poem the Romantic "I" of the
poet gives way to the disembodied third-person speaker whose observations on angels
are filtered through his own modern and wounded sensitivity. The details the speaking
voice of the poet provides are unsettling because they suggest that angels with their
"weary mouths" and their "yearning (as toward sin)" participate in the same cosmic
melodrama as humankind, even if their existence is on a higher plane of reality.

In the poem, the angels do no heroic deeds. They are silent statues or decorations
"in God's gardens," monuments without monumentality. There is little suggestion of
power, authority, or joy on the part of these creatures who are traditionally depicted as
superior to man and next to God in the hierarchy of being. Indeed, these twentieth cen-
tury angels are lacking in the grandeur usually encountered in literature and the visual
arts when angels are represented. Rilke's presentation will not allow any traditional
exaltation of their unique individual status, since he tells us that they "Almost . . . are
all alike."

Rather than denying the existence of God, angels, or spiritual reality, Rilke reinter-
prets these concepts for his own age and that devastating reinterpretation reveals the
spiritual desolation of the individual in the modern age, in which the sensitive human
being seeks to make relevant received structures of value and belief. The angels and,
by implication, man, have been created by divinity as carefully wrought works of art,

but that creation appears to be surrounded in mystery. There is in Rilke's poem no hint of transcendence, of a special fate or bliss for God's creations.

Forms and Devices

There is an extraordinary tension in Rilke's poetry arising from the nature of the charged imagery that he employs. In his representation of the angels, he alternates between what appear to be realistic details and metaphysical details. The first line of the poem attributes physicality, "mouths," to angels, and their souls are declared to be "without seam." The utilization of the words "mouths" and "seam" with their respective suggestions of the human and a physical division or demarcation contrasts with the word "soul," which, by definition, is nonmaterial. These angelic beings reveal themselves to be the poet's attempt at interpretation of a dimly perceived spiritual concept rather than direct physical description. In this poem, *Sehnsucht* or "yearning" implies a passionate and unquiet desire on the part of the angels, and the defective nature of this desire is confirmed by the fact that it is directed toward "sin." This desire arises in the dreams of the angels as if to intimate that perfect beings (even God the Creator seems strangely cold and distant from his creations, the angels) do not exist in any sphere. In spite of the notion of otherness that angelic beings ordinarily suggest, these flawed creatures constitute a link with another creation, the flawed, spiritual/physical human species.

In representing and informing his own concept of angels, Rilke appears to be speaking about them, but in reality his discourse points to the complexity of his own interior life; he is actually revealing more about the quality of spiritual energies and anxieties that animate the poem. The poem provides few specific details about the angels' appearance. One might venture to say that these are not physical, but symbolic details.

The silent angels, compared to "intervals" in God's "might and melody," raise more questions than they answer. How are they like intervals? Intervals are the spaces that mark off one thing from another or that differentiate one segment from another of the same entity. The interval, as such, has no substance and can only be conceptualized and recognized in view of its relation to what it differentiates. The "bright souls" and "wings" point to a sphere associated with divinity, with God, yet the angels' "weary mouths" and "yearning" point back to the finite, physical world. One sees that structurally the angels differentiate the realms of the divine and the human. If they are intervals, gaps that mark off while they indicate God's power and harmony ("might and melody"), then in the poem they ultimately have no substance, and one might say that within this poetic frame of reference their position between God and man in no way enables them to function as intermediaries. In this poetic universe, God does not speak to or with his creations.

Themes and Meanings

In the twentieth century, such diverse poets as Wallace Stevens in America, Diego Valeri in Italy, and Dannie Abse in England, to name only a few, utilized the figure of the angel in their poetry as a way of drawing together into one symbol their concerns about the nature and quality of the spiritual dimension of human life. In Rilke's "The Angels," this concern with the spiritual should not be seen as the conventionally religious concern of the orthodox believer, as Rilke had rejected, largely in reaction to his mother's superficial and narrow Catholicism, Christianity and its belief system. Precisely because Rilke's poetry is so committed to the sensuous aspects of nature, precisely because in much of his major poetry Rilke reveals the painter's eye for the contours and depths of physical reality, one comes to understand the spiritual as not opposed to or beyond the real, but as the usually unperceived extension of the real. "The Angels" seeks to explore, even illuminate, the basic texture of the spiritual dimension of human existence as the poet's vision of the angels tells of what the impoverished, post-Romantic imagination can still see even after the historical loss of traditional religious belief. These Rilkean angels are not the angels of Judeo-Christian tradition, but instead, complex symbols of the difficult relationships of the human to the divine when divinity itself is conceived of by the poet as an essentially aesthetic and moral ideal of power and harmony ("might and melody").

It is to this ideal of divinity that the poet implicitly compares himself in "The Angels." God is presented as an artist, a sculptor who through his own dispensations and actions gives life and meaning (though that meaning is difficult to discern, since it is hidden in the mystery of "the pages/ in the dark book of first beginning") to his creations. The poet as creator brings into existence his own poem; like God's control over his angels to the point of reducing them to mute and static figures in his garden, the poet's control of the figures of his poem seems all but absolute. It is for the poet to decide whether the poem will come into being—that is to say, whether he will exercise his power to create and impose unity and harmony on his creation. This notion of the absolute quality of the power of God and of the poet is called into question by the poem itself. Just as the angels, in spite of their "bright souls," manifest their inclination for "sin," thus revealing their defective or flawed nature, so does the poem reveal its technically flawed nature through the highly irregular structure of the last stanza, a five-line stanza that destroys any hope of structural symmetry or harmony. The five lines disrupt the symmetry of the previous two four-line stanzas; by the choice of five rather than six lines the technical or formal perfection of the fourteen-line sonnet is forbidden.

Ray Fleming

THE ANGER THAT BREAKS THE MAN INTO CHILDREN

Author: César Vallejo (1892-1938)
Type of poem: Lyric
First published: 1937, as "La colera que quiebra al hombre en niños"; collected in
Poemas humanos, 1939; English translation collected in *Human Poems,* 1968

The Poem

The anger in César Vallejo's "The Anger That Breaks the Man into Children" is a force that shatters and divides so that it may reach a point of unification, the point of origin. The poem presents a reversal of Darwinian evolution as each stanza fragments its subject into increasingly numerous portions. The anger, specifically, as Vallejo reiterates in each stanza, "the anger of the poor," works to break down human constructions and social orders. Four different directions this anger takes are described in four five-line stanzas of a similar, almost cyclical, structure, each stanza beginning with the anger and ending with the power—now honed and concentrated—that remains in that anger and that must be returned to if revolution, whether political or spiritual, is to be achieved.

While each stanza completes its own cycle, a progression in the poem as a whole can be seen in the decreasing levels of consciousness of the objects of each stanza's anger. The first of the anger's objects, for instance, is "the man," the pinnacle of evolutionary development thus far. The man, however, with his constructs of experience and strength, must be broken into "children"—reminiscent of Jesus' decree in Matthew 18:3 that "unless you change and become like little children, you will never enter the kingdom of heaven" (Vallejo, who rejected Catholicism, is known for his Christian references). The division continues as the child is broken into birds, then eggs. Each stanza ends by describing what the anger "has," which is always the origin opposed to the derivative; in the first stanza "one oil against two vinegars."

In the second stanza the anger breaks the "tree"—a step lower in the chain of consciousness from animal to vegetal matter—into leaves, then into buds, then into "telescopic grooves," finally indicating the extinction of consciousness. The stanza ends with the anger that has "two rivers against many seas." Not only are rivers obviously the origins of seas, but also their water nourishes the tree, thus indicating the regenerative potential of the origin.

In the third stanza the subject being destroyed by the anger moves further from consciousness and from individuality. Here the object is no longer an individual creature or natural object but an abstraction: "the good." Representing a human construction, especially, an idea traditionally considered a source of human strength and ideals, "the good" is broken into doubts: the human ideal crushed to vulnerability. The fragmentation continues, ending in this stanza in death, furthest yet from consciousness. The stanza concludes with the anger possessing "one steel" against the less powerful "two daggers."

In the final stanza the soul is the object of fragmentation. The placement of the soul here, in the context of the decreasing consciousness of each stanza's objects, suggests Vallejo's position that the soul—perhaps not all souls but the ill, modern soul deluded by its false notions of progress—is furthest yet from pure, or original, consciousness. The soul is broken into bodies, then into the body's contents; first "organs," then "thoughts." The stanza and the poem end by returning to the most powerful image of origin and unification yet, the "central fire."

Forms and Devices

The central motif of "The Anger That Breaks the Man into Children," with its repetition eight times in a twenty-line poem, is "anger," yet Vallejo's is an unusual kind of anger in that it is not destructive, but rather productive. The anger divides its objects into images of regeneration and fertility. In the first stanza the division of the man moves from children, suggesting innocence and potential, to birds, suggesting flight, to the final image of "little eggs," clearly symbolic of birth.

The second stanza follows the division of a tree into leaves, then buds, again suggesting birth. Vallejo's poetry is never predictable, however, and the third stanza presents a more ironic symbol of birth or origin. Here the good is broken into "unforeseeable tombs," from which, unlike "foreseeable" graves, will rise something different from the usual outcome of death: decay, stagnation. Instead, the opposite will occur: resurrection. The message is that one must die, returning to the point of origin, to be reborn. Other images show fragmentation resulting in a scientific or mathematical view of the object; the tree, for instance, is finally seen as no more than (or no less than) "telescopic grooves." The "good" is divided into "three similar arcs" (perhaps a reference to the Christian Trinity), and the soul into "dissimilar organs," then "octave thoughts."

On the other hand, the images presented as qualities of "the anger of the poor"— oil, rivers, steel, and fire—are earthy and elemental, implying that the anger is also of the earth, primal and fundamental. The final image, "one central fire," a symbol of passion and unity, is set against "two craters," which while greater in number are actually less powerful for their separateness, thus the strength in unity and origin.

The poem's formal structure seems to contradict its central concern, the breaking down of structures. Each stanza begins with the phrase "The anger that breaks," and line 4 of each stanza is always the refrain, "the anger of the poor," set apart to emphasize to what the anger is referring. Besides the cyclical structure of each stanza and the steady descent in degrees of consciousness and individuality of the anger's objects, another structure, noticeably symmetrical, appears in the first and third stanzas, where the results of division are "equal" and "similar," while in the second and fourth stanzas they are "unequal" and "dissimilar." Moreover, the structures and regular progressions that run through the poem create a chantlike effect, perhaps like a battle chant. The battle is against the injustices of social reality for the poor and, more broadly, the delusions of human constructions.

The irony of the formal structure the poet uses to create a poem that tears down structures invokes the question of the role of the poet, always a preoccupation of Vallejo's. Does the poet, speaking from the source, that "central fire," have the vision necessary to transcend the illusions of structure and to use it creatively and productively? The answer does not seem clear; perhaps it lies in its own ambiguity, like the truth in the division of the good into "doubts" in the third stanza.

Themes and Meanings

Considered in the context of the outbreak of the Spanish Civil War in 1936, Vallejo's Peruvian nationality, and his Marxist beliefs, the poem's political implications should not be overlooked. Mention of "the poor" politicizes the poem and focuses on the failure of the social order; however, more important than this failure is the qualitative superiority of the anger of the poor, the only anger strong enough to be revolutionary.

In a more personal reading of the poem, however, "the poor" may be interpreted to refer to the poor in spirit—another Christian reference. The poem then becomes about the human struggle to cast off the limitations of individuality and relocate in a collective energy, the central problem in a number of other poems in *Poemas humanos*. However, in "The Anger That Breaks the Man into Children," the poet does not disown feelings, which are repercussions of one's individuality, but, with the emphasis on the anger the poem continually returns to, insists on them. This anger will be the destructive force necessary to break through the artificial constructs of individuality and social order to reach the origin of the individual, in other words, the point at which the individual ceases to be and becomes part of the whole.

There is debate among critics of Vallejo's place as a modernist poet, but his distrust in this poem in the myth of progress is markedly modern. Here Vallejo depicts evolution, biological and cultural, as a movement away from origins and toward falsehood, the particular falsehood of poverty. Vallejo's antidote is anger, but the anger is located in that fire fueled only by faith.

Vallejo's four volumes of poetry may be ordered by the evolution of faith they demonstrate. His first two collections, *Los heraldos negros* (1918; *The Black Heralds*, 1990) and *Trilce* (1922; Eng. trans., 1973), reveal a poet uncertain about almost everything: his national and political sympathies, the power of language, the possibility of faith and connection. Yet in this third volume, there is a shift toward solidarity, faith, and passion. Interestingly, the real efficacy of these on the future is not of central concern. Rather, in "The Anger That Breaks the Man into Children," it is the anger itself that matters. It is staying in this anger, at the very center of it, burning, that matters. It may or may not allow transcendence—Vallejo stops short of this question or finds it irrelevant—but it does return one to the origin, the only place where deepest regeneration—revolution, in every sense of the word—can ever begin.

Tasha C. Haas

ANGLE OF GEESE

Author: N. Scott Momaday (1934-   )
Type of poem: Elegy
First published: 1968; collected in *Angle of Geese and Other Poems*, 1974

The Poem

"Angle of Geese" is an elegy in six four-line stanzas. The poem presents an initial obscurity to the reader, for the subject and occasion are not immediately clear. The author evidently recognized the reader's potential difficulty; according to Matthias Schubnell, N. Scott Momaday wrote to his friend and mentor, Yvor Winters, that he proposed adding an epigraph to the poem: "For a friend on the death of his child."

In fact, the poem alludes to two separate incidents in the author's life. The first three stanzas express a plural "we": The occasion is the death of a child, and the speaker defines an intimate sympathy with the grieving parents in voicing the impossibility of finding words that "we" may find adequate to this moment. Words are not adequate; they are only superficial decoration for such a profound and inexplicable event as the death of a firstborn child. Custom and manners provide both a means and a barrier to the expression of feelings. The speaker feels almost able to comprehend the parents' grief; he attempts to sound the depth of their loss but is hard put to achieve any reconciliation to it.

The last three stanzas move to an earlier event in Momaday's life, the recollection of a hunt for wild geese. On that occasion, as the poet wrote about it elsewhere, he witnessed the calm but alert wariness of geese resting on water, then the rushing chaos as, at the first gunshot, they ascended from the water, and then the sudden, astonishing beauty of their flying formation. One goose had been hit, and the young man held it as it died. It is this event that is recollected in the elegy for his friend's child. The ancestral goose recalls the clan emblems that related the tribal peoples of America to their history and to the natural world; the great size of the goose also indicates that it is both real physical animal and spiritual ancestor from the early days of creation. The wedge formation of geese in the sky represents visually the intersection of time and eternity that is death. The speaker remembers that the goose fell awkwardly out of the sky, disrupting the perfect symmetry of the flying wedge of vibrantly alive animals. The animal died calmly, perturbed by neither expectation nor emotion; it was a full participant in its own being even in the act of dying. Its gaze lay fixed on the distant flock with neither longing nor regret until its end.

Forms and Devices

"Angle of Geese" is written in syllabic meter: The first and third lines of each stanza are each of five syllables, the second and fourth of seven syllables; there is no fixed pattern of accent (in contrast to metrical verse, in which a pattern of feet composed of stressed and unstressed syllables prevails). Syllabic verse is a favorite form of the author, and it is one that subdues the verse of a poem to a more proselike uncertainty of rhythm.

Further deemphasizing the verse form is the subtlety of the rhyme. The first and third lines of each stanza rhyme, but the second and fourth do not, reversing the more common pattern of the four-line stanza in English verse. The third stanza does suggest an off-rhyme in the second and fourth lines ending with "loss" and "repose," respectively, which is echoed in turn by the ending of the fourth line of the next stanza with "goose." The use of such near rhyme is characteristic of the poetry of Emily Dickinson, whom Momaday greatly admires, and who also wrote very movingly on the subject of the fundamental enigma of death. These suggestions of closing rhyme, however, remain tenuous and extremely subtle. The lack of rhyme to end each stanza correlates with the acknowledged inability of the speaker to come to any definitive statement of the meaning of so profound an event as death. The rhyme scheme supports the lack of closure, the ambiguity, that the speaker feels.

Other sound qualities in the poem are also extremely subtle. An example is the judicious use of alliteration. The device is notable in the first three stanzas. Stanza 2 contains six words that alliterate on the letter m, including "more" at the end of the second line, which is repeated immediately at the beginning of the third; the sound echoes again in the following stanza in "almost" and "mind," bridging the transition from the plural "we" to singular "I" as the speaker gropes for the "mere margin" of rest or acceptance of the event. One could speculate on the effect of this nasal consonant as a humming or murmuring sound appropriate to the muted emotions and desire to comfort that is expressed in the poem. The second half of the poem does not show sustained repetition of consonant alliteration, but subtle paired words: "so" and "symmetry" in the fifth stanza; in the sixth, "hope" and "hurt" in the first line, followed by "held" in the second; and "dark" and "distant" in the last line.

"Angle of Geese" is an example of the plain style identified in the work of Renaissance poets such as Ben Jonson and continuing through the tradition of English poetry down to twentieth century exemplars such as Louise Bogan and Thom Gunn. The style is characterized by controlled emotion—which may nevertheless be extremely intense—by precision of diction, and by little or no rhetorical ornamentation. Momaday even announces plain style as most appropriate to his subject in the first lines of the poem, which question the propriety or adequacy of language to "adorn" an event so profound as death. In keeping with this philosophy, the poet uses precise but measured language: Indeed, the term "measure" appears, as the speaker acknowledges the impossibility of determining the extent of such a loss. There is one brief exclamation, but that refers to the precisely ordered formation, the "symmetry," of the flying wedge of geese. The poem's only outright metaphor is the brief simile comparing the angle of the geese in flight as they disappear into the sky with the meeting of time and eternity that is death.

Themes and Meanings

In developing its themes relating to death, grief, and loss, "Angle of Geese" departs

in significant ways from some traditional aspects of the elegy. In general, elegiac po-
ems express the movement of a speaker through a process of grieving that comprises
several phases. A typical formal elegy, including such famous examples as John Mil-
ton's "Lycidas" or Ben Jonson's "On My First Son," contains certain elements: an ex-
position of the loss, explaining who has died, and an expression of deep feeling—
sorrow often mixed with outrage at the injustice and inexplicability of the particular
loss. The elegist then typically introduces some philosophical statement regarding
death: a universal principle that rationalizes death or endows it with some positive
quality. Finally, the elegist will apply the universal principle to his or her individual
situation and come to some reconciliation or at least resignation by placing the indi-
vidual loss in a context of larger meaning. Sometimes hope or resolve for the future is
expressed. Not all elegies contain all these steps, but at least some of them are charac-
teristic of elegiac poetry.

Momaday, rather than moving discursively through the elegiac form, depends on
the juxtaposition of the two events—the death of the child, and the remembered goose
hunt—to imply by association the relationship of the individual death to the universal
fact of death. The child's death remains beyond rational thought and language, an
enigma and profoundly disturbing thought for which any attempt at explanation
would be an impertinence. The death of the goose, on the other hand, is accepted as
part of life (the hunt which killed the goose is suppressed in the poem, and the goose
seems to fall spontaneously from the sky before the awed gaze of uninvolved watch-
ers); the animal struggles neither for life nor against death, but remains a detached yet
fully conscious participant in the cycle of nature.

Yet the poet makes no explicit connection between the natural cycle of life and
death, as recognized in the memory of the animal's death, and the specific loss of the
child. The two events are juxtaposed, and any connection between them must be left
for the reader to infer. Such an inference might be made following the characteriza-
tion of the goose as the "ancestral" goose. The term suggests the continuity between
the human and natural world that Momaday finds is characteristic of Native American
philosophies, in which man is part of nature, indivisible from its processes and kin to
all its creatures. Such a philosophy finds usable wisdom in nature, transcending the
enigma of death and the discontinuity between time and eternity. The suggestion of
this continuity as relevant to the occasion of the child's death remains a suggestion,
however; the meaning of death remains elusive, undecidable, and open. Hence, "An-
gle of Geese" lacks the closure of explicit reconciliation to the death being mourned
and the addition of a promise or resolution for the future. Death, particular or abstract,
remains a profound enigma, though sorrow may be tempered with friendship and
sympathy.

Helen Jaskoski

ANIMALS ARE PASSING FROM OUR LIVES

Author: Philip Levine (1928-   )
Type of poem: Dramatic monologue
First published: 1968, in *Not This Pig*

The Poem

Philip Levine's often anthologized "Animals Are Passing from Our Lives" consists of six stanzas of four lines each. The first stanza is a discrete statement of self-description, followed by five stanzas that express the thoughts of the speaker in anticipation of the termination of the speaker's existence. A mood of mordant irony is established from the start as the reader learns from the speaker's self-portrait that the poem is an expression of the flow of consciousness in the mind of a pig destined for slaughter. "It's wonderful how I jog/ on four honed-down ivory toes," the pig proclaims, both contradicting the common perception of a pig as merely gross and clumsy, while introducing an element of reflective awareness that challenges the concept of animals as dumb beasts that lack, as William Shakespeare called it, "discourse of reason." The tension between the standard image of a pig and the sensitive, socially attuned speaker creates an intense kind of energy that illuminates the pig's predicament and introduces a strain of poignancy that evokes a degree of sympathy beyond the natural sadness of an animal's death.

After the personal introduction, the pig tersely asserts its situation in a blunt factual statement—"I'm to market"—and then anticipates a fateful inevitability by projecting with a sensory vividness the smell of the "sour, grooved block," the "blade" and the "pudgy white fingers" that constitute the instruments of death. This vision is expanded by a recollection of dreams in which the pig has a horrifying and recurring experience of "snouts" drooling on a marble slab, somehow still aware and "suffering" after death the uneasy gaze of consumers "who won't meet their steady eyes/ for fear they could see."

Then the poem shifts back to the immediate present as the pig describes "the boy" who is responsible for conveying the animal to the place of slaughter. The boy is oblivious to the pig's appealing qualities—the "massive buttocks slipping/ like oiled parts with each light step"—and expects the pig to succumb to panic and collapse into a hysterical tremor of terror, to "fall/ on my side and drum my toes/ like a typewriter." The boy, who is a generic representation of ignorance and received information, can see nothing beyond the clichéd, standard dismissal of a subspecies bereft of any attributes that correspond to appealing human traits.

The unforgettable conclusion of the poem expresses the pig's resolute refusal in the face of death to completely give in to the desperate fear engendered by the terrible circumstances of the situation. Instead of reverting totally to an instinctive, animalistic physicality in which the pig will "turn like a beast,/ cleverly to hook his teeth/ with my teeth," the last line is a powerful declaration of dignity. With nothing left in the way of resistance other than the will to maintain some vestige of self-respect, the pig summons a kind of innate strength to proclaim, in the face of familiar social expectations that smugly assume a feeble compliance, "No. Not this pig."

Forms and Devices

During an interview in 1999, Levine commented that "if you're going to say something difficult or hard about the nature of our experience, the reader will resist, and so you have to involve the reader shrewdly." Levine said that one of the techniques he used to do this was to "catch readers off balance, entangle them." In "Animals Are Passing from Our Lives," by placing the poem literally and directly within the perceptual and reflective consciousness of a pig—albeit one whose capacity to feel and speak corresponds to that of a human being—Levine has devised a method that is extremely effective in entangling the reader so that resistance to the unconventional can be overcome.

The confessional address to the reader that starts the poem, with its self-mocking reference to the pig's means of motion, not only establishes a recognizable and appealing voice but also offers the first in a series of vivid images that leave an indelible impression on the reader's mind. As the poem proceeds, these images continue to accumulate, alternating between the senses of sight and smell in terms of the pig's appearance prior to and after its arrival at the market. Levine draws the reader further into the action of the poem here as the pig envisions the uneasy interaction between product (pig) and consumer (reader) in terms of a reciprocal avoidance and baleful confrontation.

Levine also mentioned in an interview how important it is for him to carry "throughout the whole poem" that voice "that is most alive in the poem." The pig speaks first in an informally conversational mode, then shifts abruptly to a graphically devastating description of the processes of slaughter, then extends this unsettling vision further in the depiction of the marketplace, where the word "suffering" occurs three times to concentrate the psychological mood. Following this section, the vocal perspective shifts again toward the final assertion of the poem.

In the last stanzas, the pig seems to step back from the immediacy of the moment, or to begin to develop a kind of double consciousness in which the events of the present are seen as if from the consequences of their occurrence. This tends to make the pig's final act of defiance more plausible. The separation between the pig and "The boy/ who drives me along" suggests that there is a kind of courage inherent in the choice to defy the limited expectations of the mundane. The exuberant anger of the pig's contemptuous dismissal of a dumb beast's mindless hysteria—expressed as the boy's belief that the pig will "fall/ on my side and drum my toes/ like a typewriter or squeal" and conveyed by the image of instinctive retribution where the pig turns "like a beast/ cleverly to hook his teeth/ with my teeth"—leads to the radical change in tone of the pig's claim for individual identity. The word "No," standing alone, has the force of a gavel struck on the bar of justice. This is an echo of Herman Melville's insistence, in a letter to Nathaniel Hawthorne, that the artist must say "No! in thunder" when a so-

ciety asks for easy affirmation. The final statement, "Not this pig," comes as an ulti-
mate proclamation of singularity against the pressures of mindless conformity.

Themes and Meanings

Levine published "Animals Are Passing from Our Lives" in his first collection of
poetry in 1968, choosing the last words of the poem as the book's title. In that year, the
United States was in the midst of the Vietnam War, four students were killed in a polit-
ical demonstration at Kent State University, activists Robert F. Kennedy and Martin
Luther King, Jr., were assassinated, and throughout Europe revolutionary activities
rocked an established social order. By this time, Levine was teaching in California,
but he had worked at what he called "a succession of stupid jobs" while he was in high
school and Wayne State University and had a deep feeling for blue-collar workers
who were not highly valued or acknowledged by a corporate state.

In addition, as the child of recent immigrants from Europe, Levine grew up in a
neighborhood with a strong international flavor, and he recalled that "a great many
young men from my neighborhood went" as volunteers in the Spanish Civil War. The
anarchists who fought for a democratic state impressed him as idealists willing "to
take everything the world could dish out and still keep coming back." This is the spirit
he celebrates in "Animals Are Passing from Our Lives," a poem that accepts the real-
ity of sacrifice and failure in a struggle, but which honors the strength and courage of
those who did not let a hopeless position diminish their will to continue. The events of
the late 1960's were discouraging for many Americans, and Levine felt that the persis-
tence of individuals of conscience and character could eventually lead toward a more
humane condition of government.

One of the poets he admires is Antonio Machado, who had the ability "to take what
we've marginalized and pull it into the center." As a crucial poetic precept, Levine has
focused on the imagination as a means to see beyond the self. "Imagine yourself being
something other than what you are," he has counseled. For centuries, swine have sym-
bolized a variety of disreputable traits in Western society, and through an act of imagi-
native empathy, Levine has forcefully challenged a generally accepted version of be-
ing. In this way, he has tried to jolt the reader out of a lazy habit of receiving an official
presentation of reality and placed a marginalized creature at a center of social con-
sciousness. By implication, if this most denigrated animal is capable of such a noble
and admirable act of resistance to conscienceless power, than how can the human ani-
mal resign itself to anything less?

Leon Lewis

ANIMULA

Author: T. S. Eliot (1888-1965)
Type of poem: Lyric
First published: 1929; collected in *Collected Poems, 1909-1962*, 1963

The Poem

"Animula" is written in irregularly rhyming iambic pentameter, with only one stanza break that separates the last six lines of the piece from the rest—almost as a brief litany. The title may have been suggested by a prayer of Hadrian to his soul, but T. S. Eliot began with his own adaptation of a line in Dante's *Purgatario* XVI, "There comes from his hand, like a wayfarer . . . the simple soul." Dante's "anima" is compared to a seeker of God who is deflected by daily trifles and follies.

Almost like the questing hero described by mythology scholar Joseph Campbell, the anima—or, here, the animula—moves in a world of wonders, now faring forward boldly, now retreating to some safe haven. It enjoys the Christmas tree, the natural world, and stags on a tray—it cannot tell fact from fantasy. The early venturesome innocence of the animula becomes daily more confused by the world of adult control, by perplexity between what "is" and what "seems." Awake and in pain caused by a conflict between desire and control, it seeks escape in dreams, in hiding behind books in a secret spot.

It grows; becoming selfish and misshapen as it learns, it is torn between desire, "the importunity of the blood," and the propriety of "may and may not." It is caught by its shadows and an awareness of death, and its end is in fragments of papers, dust, silence, and last rites.

In the major part of the poem, Eliot has a recollection that is somewhat similar to the one in William Wordsworth's "Ode: Intimations of Immortality" (in which "shades of the prison house surround the growing boy"). Eliot's vision, however, is much more terse and intense in its few words.

The second stanza, a pastiche of images, reflects on certain souls—the unknown Guiterriez and Boudin—symbols of those who "represent different types of cancer, the successful men in technology, the unknown killed in war" (Eliot, quoted in Ethel M. Stephenson's *T. S. Eliot and the Lay Reader*, 1974). No one has identified—probably Eliot intended it thus—the one who made a great fortune or the one who went his own way. Floret may be a symbol of Adonis or Actaeon, slain fertility gods. The two yew trees symbolize both death and resurrection.

The final line, a variation on the Hail Mary, "pray for us sinners now and at the hour of our death," may be seen as a statement of resurrection. "Death is life and life is death" pontificates Sweeney in *Sweeney Agonistes* (1932). The life in death in life imagery appears in many of Eliot's works: *The Waste Land* (1922), "The Hollow Men," and two other Ariel poems, "Journey of the Magi" and "A Song for Simeon."

Forms and Devices

Eliot presents the reader with images of physical things—table legs, toys, playing cards—mingled with feelings—chill, warmth, pleasure, and fear. All figure in the complex world of the small, growing soul.

The opening quoted line is echoed in line 24: "Issues from the hand of time the simple soul." Although God has sent the animula forth, time has perplexed and offended it. Where it was first bold, eager, rejoicing in wind or sunlight, it is now irresolute, selfish, and unable to move forward on its quest or backward to the innocence of fairies and fancy.

Eliot makes effective use of internal, oblique rhymes that are based on the concept of the poem's opening phrase. In the first seven lines, one finds "moving," "rising," and "advancing." These words are balanced, in the long stanza's last five lines, by "fearing," "denying," "leaving," and "living." The result is a sound pattern that suggests the continuity of life. Punctuation also creates emphasis on the movement of the soul. The first period, after "what the servants say," makes the break between childhood and the change of pace, the "heavy burden" which drives the soul to take refuge in second-hand learning. The soul, changed, hesitant amid shadow and specters, lives again only in the silence after "last rites."

The sudden change of tone in the last six lines is startling. One could well ask whether these lines have any connection with the preceding part of the poem. No single interpretation is possible, but the relationship between "living . . . after the viaticum" and "pray for us . . . at the hour of our birth" can be seen as implying continuity.

Eliot's poetry often includes such puzzling, apparently irrelevant references to unidentifiable persons and events; "A Cooking Egg," "Gerontion," and "Sweeney Agonistes," for example, have such inserts. One assumes good reason, yet one cannot find an entirely acceptable explanation. For those who enjoy Eliot, this is one of the persistent delights the poet offers.

Themes and Meanings

It is difficult to pin down exactly what "Animula" is about. It may concern the life quest of a soul, with no impressive ending or glorious triumph. It may be a reminder that life implies death and death, life. Grover Smith declared it to be "Eliot's most pessimistic poem," but it may be a promise of help for the helpless human condition.

The world of this "Animula" is not one of rare excitement, adventure, and challenge. It is the world in which most people live, with moments of joy (a Christmas tree, pleasure in the wind) and much pain and frustration—fear mingled with desire. Eliot may, indeed, be suggesting that peace only comes after death and that the strongest prayers are made "at the hour of our birth." Yet the promise of rebirth (if this is indeed his message) is a promise of something else, of another voyage through life that may be very unlike the one completed.

Taken in company with the other Ariel poems—"Journey of the Magi," "A Song for Simeon," and "Marina"—"Animula" fits into a pattern. The first two reflect on the meaning of Christ's birth, and both end on a note of death in this birth. "Marina" is a triumphant affirmation of life rising out of death. "Animula" may be seen as the bridge from the biblical events to the assurance of a life fully realized in "Marina."

Anne K. LeCroy

ANNABEL LEE

Author: Edgar Allan Poe (1809-1849)
Type of poem: Narrative
First published: 1849; collected in *The Works of the Late Edgar Allan Poe*, 1850

The Poem

"Annabel Lee" is in some ways a simple ballad—that is, a narrative poem intended to be recited or sung. The first four lines of the six-line first stanza are written in the traditional ballad stanza form. The rhyme scheme is *abab,* the first and third lines have four metrical feet, and the second and fourth lines have three feet. The language, too, is conventional for a ballad. The poem begins: "It was many and many a year ago,/ In a kingdom by the sea." This is the language of fairy tales, of beautiful princesses and their admirers, of great deeds and tragic consequences.

The poem is written in the first person, spoken by a man who was once the lover of "the beautiful Annabel Lee." The story, as it unfolds through six stanzas of six to eight lines each, is a simple one.

When the speaker and Annabel Lee were young ("I was a child and she was a child"), they loved each other passionately "in a kingdom by the sea." There is some evidence that the couple were actually married; at one point the speaker refers to Annabel Lee as his "bride." So great was their love that even the angels, who were "not half so happy in heaven," were envious of it. In their jealousy, the angels sent a chilling wind and killed Annabel Lee.

There are hints that it was not only the angels who disapproved of this courtship. The narrator reveals resentment of Annabel Lee's "highborn kinsmen" who take her away after death. He also takes pains to point out that those who were "older" and "far wiser" than the young couple did not understand the strength of their love. The clear implication is that the speaker was not the social equal of Annabel Lee and that the families did not bless their union.

It seems that the speaker's primary reason for telling his story is not to reminisce and enjoy again for a moment the pleasures of that great love. Instead, his purpose is to accuse those who tried to separate him from his Annabel Lee and to tell them defiantly that their machinations did not work. Although her death occurred "many and many a year ago," their love has not ended. The narrator is still devoted to her, still dreams of her, still feels that their souls are united. He has remained true to her; in fact, he has literally never left her side. He says in the poem's last lines that he spends every night lying next to her in her sepulchre by the sea.

The entire story is told in the words of Annabel Lee's lover, with no omniscient narrator to offer guidance. The reader must decide, then, how to interpret that story. Edgar Allan Poe may have intended this as a romantic tale of young lovers who could not be parted even in death. Perhaps, however, "Annabel Lee" is the demented reflection of a madman.

Forms and Devices

If "Annabel Lee" has become one of Poe's most popular poems, its popularity is probably attributable to its haunting rhythm, its lulling repetition. Like many of Poe's poems—and this is no slight to them—the sound is more significant than the thematic content. The story takes place "in a kingdom by the sea," and Poe takes great pains to capture the sound of the sea in his poem. A wavelike cadence is suggested by the rhymes on the three-foot lines; all the shorter lines in the poem end with the same *e* sound.

The echoing of "sea," "Lee," and "me" throughout the poem is hypnotic. Like the sound of waves in the background, the reader gradually stops being aware of the repetitive sound but is stirred by it on a subconscious level. Internal rhyme also contributes to this wavelike rhythm. In phrases such as "can never dissever" and "chilling and killing," the stressed syllables seem to receive a bit of additional stress because of the rhyme, and the effect is of regular, lulling pulses.

The poet uses the power of his rhythm to particular effect in stanza 5, where he breaks out of the established pattern of alternating three- and four-foot lines. In this stanza, he adds an extra three-foot line: "Of those who were older than we—/ Of many far wiser than we—." The unexpected change in rhythm jars the reader out of a lulled, dreamlike state for a moment, so that the irony of these two lines is not missed.

The hypnotic rhythm operates on another level through the repetition of entire words and phrases. Variations of "in a kingdom by the sea" occur five times in this forty-one-line poem, and the name "Annabel Lee" occurs seven times. Key words appear a surprising number of times in such a short poem; for example, "love" occurs six times in the first two stanzas.

Within individual lines, the repetition is even more striking. Lines such as "But we loved with a love that was more than love" are almost numbing; the reader is not expected to pause over such a line and analyze its logical sense, but simply to experience the accumulation of "love" after "love" and derive meaning (perhaps "sensation" would be more accurate) that way.

The dreamlike feeling of this poem is further enhanced by the poet's use of consonants that do not jar or explode, but rather glide smoothly. The poem is full of *m, n, l,* and *s* sounds, with very few harsh consonants. The only stressed word beginning with *t*, for example (excluding words beginning with *th*), is the dramatic "tomb" in the last line. The sound of the poem, then, is quiet, rhythmic, hypnotic. It is this haunting sound, not the story itself, that causes most readers to remember "Annabel Lee."

Themes and Meanings

The central question to be faced in interpreting "Annabel Lee" is what the reader is to think of the speaker's enduring love for Annabel Lee. Is he the model of a devoted lover, or is he mentally unbalanced? Based only on the words on the page, it is possible to make a good case for either view, but within the context of Poe's entire body of work, it would seem likely that the reader is dealing with the chilling story of a madman.

As already noted, the poem begins in the traditional form of a ballad. The speaker is calm, his language is straightforward, and his poetic form is tightly controlled. As the first stanza moves into its fifth line, however, the control begins to slip.

Instead of adhering to his ballad stanza form, the poet tacks on two more lines. The content of those lines is surprising, especially on a second reading of the poem. One might expect the speaker to announce his love for the maiden early in the poem as he sets the scene and introduces characters; instead, this speaker tells the reader—rather insistently—that "this maiden she lived with no other thought/ Than to love and be loved by me."

The exaggeration of "no other thought" could be taken merely as conventional rhetoric if the speaker were talking about his own feelings, but to declare that another person adored oneself so fiercely sounds wishful, even desperately so. The paranoia in the second through fifth stanzas is clear. The speaker feels that angels, demons, and kinsmen are all deliberately attempting to keep him from his love. The angels kill her out of malice, and "all men" know it. When Annabel Lee's "highborn kinsmen" come to entomb her dead body—a natural thing to do—all he can see is that they are taking her "away from me."

All this could perhaps be attributed to normal grief at the death of a loved one, were the death a recent one, the wounds fresh. Annabel Lee, however, died "many and many a year ago." One might wonder whether the speaker should be getting over the loss. Again, this instability on the part of the speaker is noticeable only on a second reading. Nothing he says in the first five stanzas is wrong enough to prepare the reader for the gruesome revelation in the sixth: that he in fact spends his nights lying beside Annabel Lee's dead body. Years after her death, she is still his "darling," his "life."

Cynthia A. Bily

ANTHEM FOR DOOMED YOUTH

Author: Wilfred Owen (1893-1918)
Type of poem: Sonnet
First published: 1920, in *Poems by Wilfred Owen*

The Poem

Wilfred Owen's "Anthem for Doomed Youth" asks what burial rites will be offered for the soldiers who die on the battlefields of World War I (1914-1918) and argues that, in place of a normal funeral, these men "who die as cattle" will receive, initially, a parody of funeral rites, enacted by the noise of guns, rifles, and "wailing shells," and later the more authentic rites of mourning supplied by the enduring grief of family and friends at home. The poem thus begins in a mood of bitterness and irony, but as the focus shifts from the battlefield to the home front, from the immediate setting of mechanized warfare to the distant calm of civilian life, the mood shifts toward poignant sadness and regret.

The poem, a Petrarchian sonnet—an octave followed by a sestet—draws a sharp, satiric contrast between the peaceful sounds associated with the formal Anglo-Catholic burial rite and the "monstrous" and "demented" noises of modern warfare. The "anger" of the guns (the big guns used on the western front were so deafening they could frequently be heard and even felt in England) is the only "passing-bell" for these dead soldiers, the rapid fire of rifles the only "orisons" (prayers), the wail of shells the only choir music. The octave's last line, however, mentions another "voice of mourning": the bugles that call to them from "sad shires," from the towns and villages of the English countryside.

This thought effects a transition to the theme of the sestet. There, the contrast is between the visible (rather than aural) aspects of the burial rite and the various signs of quiet grieving among the dead soldiers' relations at home. Tears will glimmer in the eyes of boys instead of the flames of candles that, as altar boys, they would normally carry during a burial service; paleness on the brows of girls will stand in place of a white pall over a casket; and finally, private sorrowing—"tenderness" of mind, the "drawing-down of blinds" at dusk—will replace flowers in a church or on a grave.

By ending with a striking image of long, interior grieving, Owen completes the movement from satire to elegy. Whereas the octave expresses bitterness that these soldiers would pass from life "as cattle," accorded only a terrible parody of the rites owed to human beings, the sestet expresses the realization that each dead soldier was an individual man, and each would be mourned for years by those who love him. These observances are more genuine and meaningful than the merely formal rites of burial and requiem.

Forms and Devices

The poem's effect relies on the contrast between the actual scene on the war front described in the present tense in the first seven lines and the imagined scene on the home front described in the future tense in the last six lines, with line 8 effecting the transition. Unlike poets who wrote "patriotic" verses aiming to disguise the horrors of trench warfare, Owen insisted on telling the truth as he saw it in order to voice a protest against the war. The poem opens with the shocking image of the battlefield as a slaughterhouse where men die "as cattle"—the mention of "passing-bells" may even hint at cowbells, as though these men were stumbling as innocently to their deaths as were cows.

The scene might become simply gruesome and ugly, but Owen prevents this by focusing on the sounds of warfare (rather than the sights) in order to draw parallels between the rites of burial and the conditions of the front lines. Complicated patterns of sound in these first seven lines represent the noise and chaos of the front: lines 1 and 3 add an extra short syllable to the usual iambic pentameter, so that these lines end haltingly, stumbling to a close. The repetition of a stressed open vowel followed by the sound of the letter *n* in line 2 ("only," "monstrous," "anger," "guns") mimics the steady, regular thundering of the heavy guns, while the repetition of a vowel followed by the sound of the letter *t* in lines 3 and 4 ("stuttering," "rattle," "patter") combined with the alliteration of "rifles' rapid rattle" mimics the crack of gunfire.

The fact that the iambic pentameter of line 3 is violated by both the dactyl of "Only the" and the trochee of "stutter-," along with the aforementioned extra syllable that ends the line, means that the line literally stutters, imitating the irregular staccato of rifle fire up and down the trenches. However, there is more to these lines than straightforward onomatopoeia: Owen personifies the weapons as ministers in a grotesque parody of the rites of burial, who bring "monstrous anger" to the rite, who "patter out" prayers, and who choir in "shrill, demented" wails. These satiric images express a kind of scornful disdain for the instruments of death, however, and the scene as a whole is one of chaos and horror in which the poet finds only the absence of dignity and solace, an absence underscored by the repetition of the words "no" and "nor" in lines 5 and 6.

The thought of "bugles" (line 8), associated with both the battlefield and the village green, brings about a dramatic change in tone and setting. The poet shifts his perspective here from the immediate present scene ("now") to an imagined future set in England. The violence of the octave is replaced in the sestet by tranquillity: gentle images of quiet grieving framed in strictly regular meter and masculine rhymes. The word "held" in line 9 does double duty, meaning both "considered" and, literally, "held in hand," the pun taking effect in the following line, which places the candles' glimmers "not in the hands of boys, but in their eyes" (as tears).

Further wordplay occurs in line 12, which identifies "the pallor of girls' brows" (pallor deriving from a Latin verb meaning "to pale") with the coffin's "pall" (deriving from the Latin for "cloak"). The mood throughout these lines is elegaic, their solemn lyricism enhanced by the effective use of conventional devices such as alliteration, assonance and internal rhyme (the repeated "sh" and hard *g* in line 11; the stressed plosives of "pallor," "brows," "be," and "pall" in line 12; the repeated "er" of "their flowers" and "tender-" in line 13; and finally, the repeated stressed *d* of line 14).

While the sonnet is basically Petrarchan in form (divided into octave and sestet),

Owen also incorporates the strong closure of the Shakespearean form of the sonnet by working rhyming couplets into the sestet. The final line brings the poem to an extraordinarily effective close: The long vowel in "slow" in place of a short syllable produces a series of stressed monosyllables—"each slow dusk"—that enact the slowness they describe. The hyphenated "drawing-down" momentarily restores the iambic rhythm and, by alliterating with "dusk," inexorably carries the reader into the long, drawn-out vowel and palatal diphthong of the closing word "blinds" with a finality that underscores the hopelessness of death and grief.

The syntax of this final couplet implies that this closing of blinds, along with the "tenderness of patient minds," stands in place of the flowers that would adorn a funeral or a grave, and flowers, like blinds, close as night falls. This private, patient, silent grieving stands in stark contrast to the noise and violence of the battlefield not only in mood but also in meaning: Instead of representing a poor parody of the rites of burial, this grieving transcends mere outward observance, replacing ritual with a deeply felt and lasting interior observance.

Themes and Meanings

In the preface that Owen sketched out for a planned volume of poems, he stated that he was not concerned with "Poetry": "My subject is War, and the pity of war." "Pity" is for Owen never condescending or detached: It suggests, rather, a deep feeling and love for the soldiers with whom he fought. "Anthem for Doomed Youth" reminds readers that each one of the millions who died in World War I was an individual, and though on the fields of France and Belgium they were slaughtered "like cattle," each separate death brought with it immeasurable sadness and loss.

The poem has been read as a reply to Rupert Brooke's *1914* sonnets, especially the two entitled "The Dead," in which death in war is presented as something to be celebrated and even desired. Some readers have found sentimentality in Owen's poem also, a retreat from the ugly truth of war to the piquant pleasures of mourning. However, the poem combines satire and elegy with remarkable economy and power and brings home to the reader the enormity of a tragedy that dragged on year after year. Owen, who had once planned to be a clergyman, represents the burial rites of the established Church as "mockeries" and imagines instead a private, nonconformist ritual of the heart and mind.

Owen worked on the poem while convalescing at Craiglockhart War Hospital in Scotland, and in September, 1917, he showed the poem to his fellow patient, the poet Siegfried Sassoon, who recognized at once its exceptional merit. Sassoon, Owen wrote, suggested the title, and made other suggestions, such as the word "patient" in line 13 to replace "silent." Whereas Sassoon's poems (which Owen greatly admired) tended to be sharply satiric, Owen's achieve a more complicated effect, one that utilizes satire but also foregrounds the suffering and sorrow of soldiers, the tragedy of the endless murder and suffering they helplessly inflicted on either side.

Matthew Parfitt

THE ANTI-LAZARUS

Author: Nicanor Parra (1914-　　)
Type of poem: Lyric
First published: 1982, as "El anti-Lázaro"; collected in *Poemas Inéditos*, 1984; English translation collected in *Antipoems: New and Selected*, 1985

The Poem

"The Anti-Lazarus" is an "antipoem" composed of forty-seven free-verse lines divided nonsystematically into eleven stanzas. Its title is a compound word that encloses references both to the Western cultural heritage and to Nicanor Parra's own innovative artistic ideals. It points, on the one hand, to the biblical figure of Lazarus, the brother of Mary and Martha who was raised from the dead at Jesus' command (John 11:1-44). In this sense, it refers to the miracle of resurrection, one of the most important miracles within the Christian tradition. On the other hand, the use of the prefix "anti" refers to the concept of the antipoem, implying a conscious attempt at breaking with traditional lyric forms and constituting Parra's most significant contribution to contemporary poetics.

The speaker of the poem is addressing an absent interlocutor. Under the guise of an impossible and thwarting telephone call, the poetic voice speaks to an anonymous deceased poet, trying to dissuade him from rising from the dead. The poet reminds his addressee of the many negative aspects of earthly life—the daily routine, human needs and anxieties, the increasing loss of tolerance when facing setbacks, and the vacuity of literature. As a counterweight to all of these, he notes the many positive aspects that the dead man's present condition has to offer: the happiness of being a corpse, which assures absolute independence and peace, and the perfect communion of the body and the land in which it was buried.

The topic of resurrection occupies the center of the first stanza. In it, anecdotal information is reduced to a minimum, so the reader seems to witness a lyrical monologue in which one human being addresses another in order to impart his wisdom: To resuscitate oneself would be a real deed, but instead of leading to a glorious future, it would evolve into unvarying routine. The next two stanzas enumerate and unfold different aspects of that routine, both at the level of direct vital experience and at the level of philosophical concerns. Three other stanzas retrieve personal recollections from the dead poet's past, and it is in the last stanza of this group that he is characterized as a poet. In this sense, the seventh stanza becomes a central point in the poem, since it defines poetry, emblematized by Dante Alighieri's *Inferno*, as a mirage—more than an ostentatious amusement but inadequate to the task of making sense out of the effort of living.

A change of perspective is shown in the last four stanzas of the poem. Rather than continuing and advancing the skeptical depiction of life, the poetic voice discusses the beneficial elements of being dead, particularly the fact that, unlike life, death is eternal. With all of these, the name "Lazarus" acquires a new significance, and the concept of resurrection, losing its liberating potential as a tool for providing hope beyond the natural limits of human life, is reduced to a senseless effort.

Forms and Devices

The first example of Parra's innovative approach to poetry may be found in his book *Poemas y antipoemas* (1954; *Poems and Antipoems*, 1967), which gained international recognition for the author. Although "The Anti-Lazarus" does not belong to this early collection, it marks a continuation of all the formal and thematic characteristics of the antipoem. Essentially, an antipoem aims to surpass the traditional language of poetry through the recovery of the language and topics of everyday life. The search for this voice implies a new treatment of linguistic resources and the inclusion of colloquialism.

"The Anti-Lazarus" challenges and subverts literary conventions in various ways. Reviving some of the innovations introduced in modern poetry by avant-garde and post-avant-garde writers, Parra puts aside the norms of punctuation and uses only occasional quotation and exclamation marks. He also abandons the principles of regular capitalization and mixes numerals and letters. In addition, the use of formulas typical of a telephone conversation ("hello-hello"), of colloquial and affectionate expressions commonly used to attract someone's attention, and of the grammatical second person as well as several clichés taken from oral language ("my foot") contributes to the creation of an atmosphere of informality.

Another characteristic that helps to strengthen the sensation of colloquial communication is the absence of stylized imagery, of conventionally poetic vocabulary and tropes. This does not mean that the poem lacks metaphorical elements—in fact, Parra uses some metaphors from everyday speech ("you used to explode/ in insults right and left")—or other dominantly poetic devices such as chaotic enumeration ("pride blood greed"). The poet is looking for a way of generating a communication in which rhetorical and literary resources do not interfere in the fluency of the act of reading. The goal of all these expressive searches is to revive language, restoring to it a lost effectiveness.

As Naín Nómez remarks in *Poesía chilena contemporánea* (1992; contemporary Chilean poetry), "the antipoem is an inverted image of a poem, but it is not governed by the total principle of symmetry. Instead, it is governed by a particularly intense asymmetric force." This distorting force, essential to the antipoem, is satire, conceived as the center of many literary resources such as duplication, inversion, and deformation. In "The Anti-Lazarus," the satirical impulse intends to destroy the distinctive aureole that tradition has assigned to the poetic word through the ages.

Themes and Meanings

Together with love, death has been one of the major themes throughout literary history. Its presence in poetry has been a constant from the beginnings of humankind, and death has prompted various poetic forms, from elegies to epitaphs and funeral chanting. Parra believes that poets have lost their capacity for redemption if they are concerned either with the recovery of an original harmony or with access to the absolute. Since Parra's attitude as a poet is intentionally antiromantic and antisacralizing, his concept of the "antipoem" is a reaction against the metaphysical function of language.

"The Anti-Lazarus" is a perfect example of this stance. In the poem, Parra inverts the semantic values ordinarily associated with the idea of death. He is interested neither in the pain it provokes among the survivors nor in the possibilities of life after death. On the contrary, the poet understands death as a natural phenomenon, deprived of any sacred connotation. Death is simply a state of being that is superior to all others insofar as it frees human beings from suffering while giving them endless permanence. Because of this conceptual shift, death is not completely emptied of meaning but is reconfigured with a new and unusual semantic value.

A second aspect present in the poem, through the characterization of the dead person being addressed as a poet, is the questioning of literature's effectiveness. Parra chooses the first section of *The Divine Comedy* as a quintessential example of literary tradition. In the *Inferno*, Dante descends through nine internal circles of Hell in a purifying journey that will finally lead him to Heaven. There he will meet Beatrice, his true love, in celestial form. Contrary to this idea of the spiritual quest, Parra seems to suggest that the real Inferno is earthly life and that, in spite of all hardships and sufferings, life is not the doorway to a better and more fulfilling state of being. Thus, the poet rejects any metaphysical way out and implies, further, that the many efforts, both religious and poetic, to sacralize death are useless.

Adopting literary historian Harold Bloom's terminology, it may be said that Parra developed his notion of antipoetry as a reaction to the modern imperative to become a strong poet. In fact, three Chilean poets figure prominently in twentieth century Latin American literature: promoter of the avant-garde Vicente Huidobro and two Nobel Prize winners, Gabriela Mistral and Pablo Neruda. In an interview with the writer Mario Benedetti, published in the Uruguayan journal *Marcha* in 1969, Parra defined his poetic project as "an anti-Neruda poetry, also anti-Vallejo, anti-Mistral, a poetry against everything, but at the same time . . . a poetry where all those echoes still resound." Ultimately, in "The Anti-Lazarus," Parra states that literary processes and the creative forces behind them are incapable of renovating the meaning of death beyond its natural condition as an everyday phenomenon. Nevertheless, Parra's negation is only partial: He does not affirm the complete fruitlessness of literary communication. Through his poetry, he expresses his faith in poetic experimentation as a way of permanent renovation.

Daniel Altamiranda

ANYONE LIVED IN A PRETTY HOW TOWN

Author: E. E. Cummings (1894-1962)
Type of poem: Narrative
First published: 1940, in *Fifty Poems*

The Poem

The poem "anyone lived in a pretty how town" is basically a narrative with a strong lyric component—that is to say, it is a ballad. Written in nine variably rhyming quatrain stanzas, it does not show a normative or "running" verse foot, such as the iamb; therefore, the poem is written in podic prosody, a system of accentual verse that is sometimes called "folk meters." It is the prosody in which most nursery rhymes and folk ballads are written, which accounts for its strongly rhythmical quality. Specifically, the lines have four stresses, or are "tetrapodic."

E. E. Cummings was in many ways a sentimental poet, although he hid this sentimentality with all sorts of typographical, grammatic, syntactic, and rhetorical tricks and, sometimes, with a slangy and "wise-guy" level of diction, though that is not the case with this poem. Complicating his essential sentimentality was his rather sarcastic outlook on life: Cummings did not care for what he called "mostpeople," who, it seemed to him, were against culture and art and were too wrapped up in the quotidian—Cummings's "mostpeople" were what H. L. Mencken called the "booboisie." Very often this split-mindedness of Cummings led to what might almost be called a schizoid poetry, and no poem more so than "anyone lived in a pretty how town," which tells the story of a person named "anyone" and his lover, "noone" (that is to say "no one"). Anyone lived in a town where "women and men . . ./ cared for" him "not at all." They "sowed" their seeds of negativism in their dull lives. Some of their children guessed that there was someone in town, the woman named "noone," who loved him, yet even the children forgot this as they grew older. Nevertheless, "noone" loved "anyone" so much that his "any was all to her."

As life went along, the townsfolk lived their ordinary lives, "someones married their everyones," the children grew up, and "anyone" and "noone" grew older; "one day anyone died i guess/ (and noone stooped to kiss his face)." Nobody else paid much attention. Eventually "noone" died as well, and "busy folk buried them side by side." Still, life went on; people continued doing what they do in all seasons, beneath the rising and setting sun, moon, and stars, in all weathers.

That is the basic story, but it can also be read in a diametrically opposite way. Take, for example, line 4 of the third stanza, which can be read either as "noone loved him," or as "no one loved him." Stanza 7 might mean "one day anyone died," or "one day anyone died" (anyone at all); and either "noone stooped to kiss his face" or "no one" did. In what way are these two people, anyone and noone, to be distinguished from mostpeople? Are they to be distinguished at all? Are they, perhaps, representative of "someones" and "everyones"? There is a deliberate ambiguity about the story Cummings is telling.

Forms and Devices

From the very first line, the poem's ambiguity is seen to be a purposeful component of the poem, for Cummings uses the technique of hypallage: rearrangement of syntax—word order—in a sentence. "[A]nyone lived in a pretty how town" can be put back into a more normal form easily: "Anyone lived in how pretty a town," or "How anyone lived in a pretty town." He chose neither of these forms because he intended the poem to be ambiguous, and he chose a syntactic form that would imply both constructions, and perhaps others as well—for example, "How pretty a town anyone lived in." The second line continues and reinforces the double sense of the first; it could just as easily be read, "(with so many bells floating up, down)."

Like many ballads, this one has a refrain; in fact, it has more than one. There is a listing of the seasons which appears as line 3 of the first and second stanzas and line 2 of the last stanza. This is an "incremental" refrain, because it is slightly changed each time it appears—the order of the seasons is switched. A second refrain is "sun moon stars rain," which appears as line 4 of stanza 2, the first line of stanza 6, and the last line of the poem. The second time this refrain appears it is incremental, but the third time it reverts to its original order. A third demi-refrain is "Women and men (both little and small)," which appears incrementally one time as the first line of the last stanza, "Women and men (both dong and ding)," a reference to the sounds of the floating bells. A fourth is line 3 of stanza 2, "they sowed their isn't they reaped their same," which reappears in the penultimate line as "reaped their sowing and went their came."

This last refrain illustrates another rhetorical device that Cummings uses throughout the poem, antithesis in parallel constructions: "he sang his didn't he danced his did"; "and down they forgot as up they grew"; "she laughed his joy she cried his grief." These parallel repetitive schemes are mirrored in other lines that do not repeat but give almost the effect of refrains, as in the first line of the fourth stanza, "when by now and tree by leaf," and the first line of the penultimate stanza, "all by all and deep by deep," which continues into the next line, "and more by more." The rest of this stanza is similarly constructed.

All these sonic devices give the poem an extremely lyrical quality even though the rhyme scheme is not exact and at times, the lines do not rhyme. For example, although the poem begins with a rhyming couplet, the next two lines do not chime at all. The next stanza also begins with couplet rhyme, but the following two lines consonate (they off-rhyme). Consonance is often a feature of the anonymous folk ballad; here, it appears in a literary ballad.

The third stanza does the same thing, but the fourth goes back to the pattern of the first—though if one looks closely, one will see that the last line ends with the word "her," which light-rhymes with line 3 of stanza 1, "winter." An examination of the poem will disclose many other effects on the sonic level, including assonance ("how town"); alliteration ("spring," "summer," "sang"); consonantal echo (the *m* sounds of stanza 2); cross-rhyme ("stir" and "her"); and internal consonance ("bird" and "stir").

Themes and Meanings

The two major themes of "anyone lived in a pretty how town" are to be found in the first line or, rather, in the implications of the first line. One implication is, "how can anyone live in a pretty town" where nothing much goes on, where people are completely caught up in their everyday lives—where, though everyone is involved with everyone else, mostpeople do not really know or, in fact, care what their neighbors are really like? It is a rhetorical question because, in fact, most people do live in such a town—they are anyone and no one, of no particular significance except to one another on an individual basis. Anyone does mean something to noone, and that is the basic paradox of existence. Human beings—who, after all, are mostpeople—both care and do not care; both love and do not love; are important to one another and are not important at all.

These twin themes comprise thesis and antithesis; they make up a paradox. One theme appears to cancel out the other, but in fact does not: Both themes continue to exist and remain true. Thus, "anyone lived in a pretty how town" encompasses within its brief lyric tale two truths, not one, and these truths exist in tension with each other, each pulling and pushing against the other but remaining in a state of impossible equilibrium, which is the human condition. Humankind simultaneously treats itself with indifference and compassion, with cruelty and kindness, with trust and suspicion, and with many other antitheses one might list, all of which will, paradoxically, be true. E. E. Cummings, in this poem, managed to invent a poetic vehicle which exemplifies and illustrates these opposites, telling a story about mostpeople and individuals that is simultaneously a joyous and a sorrowful song.

Lewis Turco

APOLLO AND MARSYAS

Author: Zbigniew Herbert (1924-1998)
Type of poem: Meditation
First published: 1961, as "Apollo: Marsjasz," in *Studium przedmiotu*; English transla-
tion collected in *Selected Poems*, 1968

The Poem

"Apollo and Marsyas" is a meditation or reflection on the meaning of an ancient
Greek myth. According to the legendary story, Marsyas, a satyr—part man, part ani-
mal—challenges the god Apollo to a musical contest. For a mortal to challenge a deity
is always dangerous. Not only will the god or goddess almost invariably win but, in
victory, the deity often takes vengeance on the opponent as well. Apollo does win the
competition, and he punishes Marsyas by hanging him from a tree and stripping off
his skin.

Risking a contest with Apollo was foolhardy for Marsyas: As a satyr, he ranked far
below the gods. Satyrs, imagined as having a human body and the tail, ears, and some-
times legs of an animal, were associated with revelry, lechery, and the god of wine and
excess, Dionysus. At the opposite extreme would be Apollo, god of the sun, poetry,
music, medicine, and prophecy. Because of Apollo's link with reason, order, balance,
and harmony, he would be a natural foe of Marsyas.

Zbigniew Herbert's poem describes the aftermath rather than the contest. In the
first stanza, the contest has been decided. In the second stanza, Herbert describes the
howling sound that Marsyas, tied to a tree, makes after losing his skin. Herbert inter-
prets the howling as Marsyas's real music. In this poem, the contest has not ended but
has only begun.

In the third stanza, Apollo is disgusted by the sound, which he hears while cleaning
his musical instrument. Always self-controlled, Apollo has not been carried away
emotionally by his victory but takes time to prepare his instrument for its next use. Re-
moved from the painful aspects of life, Apollo's response is an involuntary "shudder."

The following stanza shows that Apollo's reaction is not the proper one. Apollo
wrongly thinks that the howl of Marsyas is "monotonous," consisting only of one
note, the vowel "Aaa." By challenging Apollo's judgment, Herbert is being not only
audacious but also ironic. In the contest, Apollo's music represents "absolute ear,"
perfect pitch, but this is overruled by the poet: What seems to be true turns out to be
otherwise. In the sixth stanza, the howl expresses the different parts of Marsyas's
body. Herbert describes them as elements of nature: "mountains," "ravines," "for-
ests," and "hillocks." The bones have become "wintry wind." Joining this "chorus" is
Marsyas's "backbone," suspended in mid-air, deepening the sound and adding "rust."

In the ninth stanza, Apollo leaves, walking along the path of a formal garden. Per-
haps sarcastically, he imagines that the sounds emitted by Marsyas may some day be-
come a "new kind/ of art," perhaps "concrete." Apollo's smug departure is interrupted

suddenly when a dead nightingale lands "at his feet." Startled, Apollo looks again at his defeated rival. To Apollo's surprise, the "hair" of the tree from which Marsyas is hanging has been transformed and is now "white/ completely."

Forms and Devices

Herbert's poem is based on allusion, an abbreviated reference to a historical or literary person, place, or event. The title and first two stanzas of the poem allude to the famous musical contest and to the loser's punishment. The poet assumes that the myth is sufficiently familiar so that the reader can supply the missing details. Herbert also assumes that the reader will know the qualities with which Apollo is associated. Apollo's link with reason, order, and harmony explains his "shudder" of disgust at the howl. Herbert also merely suggests Marsyas's identity as a satyr. Other than the detail of Marsyas's "tall ears" in the second stanza, Herbert treats Marsyas as a person.

"Apollo and Marsyas" does not have the formal appearance of a traditional poem. As in the original Polish, the stanzas of the poem vary considerably in length and the number of words in each line varies from one to several. In addition, only the first word of the poem, the two proper names, and the letter A are capitalized. Adding to the untraditional look of the poem is the almost complete absence of punctuation. The form and style of the poem announce that Herbert's treatment of the legend will be modern.

Until the sixth stanza, Herbert is sparing in his use of poetic devices. For example, few metaphors are used early in the poem. In the fifth stanza, however, Herbert departs from this straightforward style. Highly original metaphors describe the inner body of Marsyas as natural terrain. "Aliment," the alimentary system of organs for digesting food, such as the intestines, is transformed into "ravines," narrow valleys worn by running water. Lungs are compared to "rustling forests," as they are shaped like an inverted tree and the intake of air can make a "rustling" sound.

In the next stanza, the "backbone" of the satyr, the main support of Marsyas's body, is added to the sound. Metaphorically, the backbone represents Marsyas's strength of will. Despite his horrendous punishment, Marsyas remains true to his convictions: He has lost the contest but he has kept his principles.

In the tenth stanza, the nightingale falls at Apollo's feet. Because of the beauty of its song, the nightingale symbolizes romantic love, lyrical poetry, and intense emotion. The bird's death, therefore, is ominous. The blame is the god's for punishing Marsyas, as Apollo's victory has dealt a mortal blow to passion and lyrical poetry.

In the last stanza, the poem ends on a disturbing note. Shaken by the bird's fall, Apollo looks again at Marsyas. The tree's growth has turned white and, like the bird, it is dead. Although Marsyas lives and howls, two natural beings have perished as if in sympathy with the satyr's pain. The poem concludes with this ghastly image, and Apollo must be unsettled in his triumph.

Themes and Meanings

In "Apollo and Marsyas," Herbert departs far from the Greek myth. The poet restates the nature of the competition as one of "absolute ear" (Apollo) versus "immense range" (Marsyas). This parenthetical comment lets the reader know that Herbert sees the rivalry in terms of contrasting views of poetry. Apollo's strength, "absolute ear," indicates that his goals are purity, distance from life, and flawless form. To achieve formal perfection, a poet must restrict the subject matter. In contrast, Marsyas seeks "immense range," scope being more important in his music than purity, as he tries to encompass the wide variety of life. Herbert's sympathy with Marsyas's approach is revealed by the absence of formal symmetry in his poem.

Beginning with the fourth stanza, "Apollo and Marsyas" focuses on Marsyas's pain. The superficial interpretation of the howl is that the sound consists only of one vowel, *a*. As the letter *a* is the first letter of the alphabet, Herbert suggests, great pain may be the basis of human experience. The connection of the letter *a* with Marsyas's backbone supports the idea that pain is fundamental to language and poetry. The reference to "rust" implies the passage of time and links this cry to history. Poetry is one way that humans vent their pain throughout time.

An ambiguity present in the treatment of the vowel is its conflicting association with pleasure. Although Marsyas is in great pain, his sound expresses his body's "inexhaustible wealth." The description of his body includes pleasurable aspects, for example, the "sweet hillocks of muscle." As a satyr, Marsyas is identified with bodily pleasure, especially drinking and sex, in contrast to Apollo, a god distanced from ordinary human pleasures.

Instead of lamenting his skinned body, Marsyas is defiant. Perhaps influenced by Apollo's disgust, Marsyas celebrates the joys of the body at a moment when he suffers enormously. Preparing to depart, Apollo indeed may wonder who is the victor.

The god may also hesitate because of the effect of Marsyas's howl on nature. Herbert describes the deaths of the bird and the tree as brought about by fear. The nightingale lies "petrified" and the tree's "hair" has turned white. According to the Greeks, Apollo was capable of inflicting such terror that even the gods feared him. In punishing Marsyas, Apollo has created dreadful consequences: The bird of poetry and romance has died and a tree has ceased to grow.

Herbert's unusual use of the word "hair" to describe the growing part of the tree links human and natural life. By maiming the satyr, Apollo strikes a blow at the heart of nature itself. Marsyas's association with sensuality and the pleasures of the body indicates that punishing that side of life is not only wrong but also a crime. Sensual life is impure and is associated with animals, but the description of Marsyas's insides shows that the human body is an integral part of the earth. The god of reason and harmony recoils in disgust at the cry of a creature who indulges in pleasure, but Herbert sides with Marsyas, affirming a poetry which is all-inclusive. Herbert argues that the poet should accept and articulate all aspects of human existence, both great joy and rending pain. If the type of poetry represented by Marsyas loses—poetry filled with the impure essences of sensual life—then the consequences will be serious. To Herbert, poetry cannot be separated from the earth.

Samuel B. Garren

APOLOGY OF GENIUS

Author: Mina Loy (1882-1966)
Type of poem: Lyric
First published: 1922; collected in *Lunar Baedeker,* 1923

The Poem

The title "Apology of Genius" invokes the classical meaning of "apology" as *apologia*: a vigorous explanation and defense of the subject. In the poem the speaker will defend "genius," or inborn talents and capacities beyond the normal or ordinary. In particular, the poem refers to an artistic avant-garde that creates new kinds of beauty unrecognized by the philistine masses. The voice in the poem speaks for this group, explaining that "we are with God" and "we come among you." "We" appears to be those infused with genius, who are radically different from the audience being addressed. The audience within the poem is an indeterminate "you" representing those who are ignorant, insensitive, unreceptive, or otherwise incapable of comprehending the innovators and their productions.

At the outset the speaker, on behalf of all who embody genius, describes these artistic souls as superior and alienated: "Ostracized as we are with God." The sentence is truncated, as the speaker abruptly turns to the guardians of convention, "watchers of the civilized wastes," who "reverse their signals" in attempts to thwart the forward movement of the avant-garde. The theme of alienation recurs in the second stanza, when the geniuses are further characterized as "lepers" and "magically diseased." The geniuses are unaware of how deeply they disturb the masses until suddenly they confront the "smooth fools' faces" of a mocking, ignorant audience.

The next two stanzas emphasize again the separateness of geniuses from ordinary people: Geniuses are a special priesthood, "sacerdotal clowns" who can "feed on" the beauty of nature although they are materially poor. They are essentially different from ordinary people, for their inner life is structured by "curious disciplines" that are "beyond your laws," not subject to commonplace rules of art or society.

The speaker then goes on to explain that, although geniuses may be related by birth or marriage to ordinary people, they are not bound by the same rules. The avant-garde acts without reference to the constraints of convention. In another fragmentary aside the speaker characterizes genius as an armor of the soul that "still shines" in spite of ignorant people who try to suppress such inspiration. The speaker then returns to the relationship of the inspired individual with a conformist family, stating that the geniuses simply pay no attention to the attempted possessiveness of relatives (or anyone understood under the general "you").

The poem's last two stanzas describe the artistic avant-garde as creative workers set apart from everyday people and at work in mysterious hidden places hammering out beautiful objects from the raw materials of indifferent matter. Although geniuses exert monumental labor in creating great and stunning works of art, their works are misunderstood and attacked by the ignorant. The speaker again castigates the "you" who do not see the beauty being created but who regard the birth of new, original art as a crime that must be controlled or even killed by censorship.

Forms and Devices

In keeping with its subject, the defense of avant-garde art, "Apology of Genius" employs unconventional grammatical and poetic features. The only punctuation is four dashes; capital letters signal initial words of sentences as well as terms set off as abstract universals, and they mark other terms as ironic. Stanza divisions do not correspond with sentence endings, and indented lines occur in unexpected places. The first line is extended beyond the left margin, suggesting that the entire poem hinges on the initial statement of alienation and superiority. The metrical structure is thirty-eight short lines of "free verse" with a basic pattern of two-stressed lines.

"Apology of Genius" contains virtually no rhyme, with the possible exception of reverse rhymes on "wills" and "laws" in the fifth stanza and "eyes" and "scythe" in the last. However, subtle effects of vowel assonance recur, as in "moon" and "among" in the first stanza, "passion" and "man" in the second, and "corrosion with possession" in the seventh; the echoing of "Beautiful" and "immortelles" at the end is another hint of rhyme. In contrast to the absence of rhyme, the poem's rhythm is heavily marked by alliteration, with reinforcement from consonantal echoes. The second line introduces alliteration as a device with the repetition of *w* in "watchers of the civilized wastes." In the second stanza the alliterative repetition is suspended from "Lepers" at the beginning of the sentence to "luminous" five lines later, but the liquid sound pattern is sustained in "all" and "magically" and continues into the following stanza (still within the same sentence) in "lights," "until," and "fool's." Within the alliteration on the liquid *l* in the first stanza the poet introduces a nasal pattern on *m* and *n* with "moon" and "magically," echoed in "among," "innocent," and "luminous" and continuing with "unknowing," "passion," "Man," "until," "turn," and "smooth." The delicate intricacy of these patterns contrasts with the harsh plosives that abruptly end the sentence by characterizing the poem's audience as having "fools' faces" resembling "buttocks bared." The voiced plosive *b* then continues three lines down with unvoiced plosives in "pulverous pastures of poverty," bringing the alliterative emphasis almost to the point of parody. Alliteration in the last three stanzas turns on the hard *c* of "cuirass" repeated in "confuse," "corrosion," "caverns," and "Chaos."

Metaphor is the predominant figure of speech. An implicit metaphor introduces the notion of the avant-garde: "Avant-garde" is a military term denoting soldiers who lead a charge into battle and was adopted by the modernists to describe artistic innovators. The speaker of "Apology of Genius" states that guardians of conformity "reverse their signals on our track," suggesting an attempt to derail the forward progress of a group whom the poem goes on to characterize as innovative artists. The speaker returns to the metaphorical domain of the military in referring to an armor of the soul. Other metaphors are drawn from the realm of medicine and disease, as artists are called "Lepers" with "luminous sores," and from religion in references to "spirit" and the "passion of Man," to geniuses as "sacerdotal clowns" and to works of art as "mystic." In the last stanzas the speaker suggests a mythological allusion in a vision of artists as blacksmiths or jewelers working in "raw caverns" to "forge" a kind of "imperious jewelry." Finally, the speaker asserts that ignorant people construe new art in an organic metaphor as a "delicate crop" of "immortelles," flowers preserved by drying.

Themes and Meanings

In "Apology of Genius" Mina Loy draws on the romantic vision of the artist as a uniquely gifted and inspired individual set apart from and incomprehensible to ordinary people. In Western culture the idea is as old as Plato, who regarded poets as visited by a kind of divine madness and therefore unsuitable citizens of a totally rational society. "Apology of Genius" emphasizes the ostracism of the innovative or avantgarde artist through metaphors and images calculated to shock anyone who subscribes to the philistine values that the poem deplores. The initial characterization of artistic genius as a "disease" and artists as "lepers" initiates the series of outré images, but the most startling is the poem's single simile, which likens the uncomprehending gaze of the ignorant audience's "fools' faces" to "buttocks bared" in primitive rituals of mockery. A yoking together of disparate concepts, as in the figure of "sacerdotal clowns," linking buffoon performers and priests in a single image, may call to mind the extreme conceits of seventeenth century metaphysical poems. However, Mina Loy was more immediately inspired by the Italian futurist poets who were her friends, mentors, and lovers during the years when her poetic style was being formed. Violent joining together of images drawn from the most diverse and contradictory sources is an explicit strategy of futurists, according to the manifestos of Italian futurist F. T. Marinetti. Another fusion of contrary images occurs in the final image of a field of "criminal mystic immortelles," which links the themes of antisocialism and marginalization (criminal), religious ecstasy (mystic), and organic beauty (immortelles) in a metaphor for works of art.

"Apology of Genius" also belongs to the tradition of writing that defends art and artists; examples go back to Ovid and Sir Philip Sidney. Unlike earlier writers, however, who offered arguments intended to persuade their audiences of the beauty and virtue of poetry, Loy frames this strong, even savage harangue attacking ignorance and misunderstanding as a sermonlike speech that purports to affront the ignorant reader. The poem can evoke highly charged, emotional responses, depending on whether the reader identifies with the poem's internal audience (the "you" that the speaker castigates) or with the "we" for whom the persona speaks. The choice of "cuirass" is indicative of the highly charged emotional tone of the poem; the image refers to armor protecting the soul of the genius from the casual damages of the ignorant, but a cuirass is specifically armor for the torso, suggesting that protection of the heart and other internal organs, traditional seats of the emotions, is paramount.

Helen Jaskoski

APPRAISAL

Author: Sara Teasdale (1884-1933)
Type of poem: Lyric
First published: 1926, in *Dark of the Moon*

The Poem

Sara Teasdale's "Appraisal," a metrical lyric poem, displays remarkable complexity despite the surface clarity of its nineteen lines. The poem falls within the tradition of love lyrics that celebrate rather than critique, probe, or explore. As a consequence, it creates poetic dissonance from its first line: "Never think she loves him wholly." Simultaneously the reader learns that the loved one of the poem, a man, is under critical scrutiny and that the lover, a woman, is the scrutinizer. The reader also immediately understands that the poet is distancing herself from her subjects: She presents her third-person lovers as if under a bright light, without coyness or deception. Even though the literary vehicle is a lyric poem, her intent to make a statement is clear. "Appraisal," the poet seems to say, will not be another simple evocation of a notoriously elusive emotional state. The worldly and possibly cynical connotations of the title itself reinforce this.

The blanket statements of the first two lines, "Never think she loves him wholly,/ Never believe her love is blind," could stand as universal declarations. The "she" could be any woman and the "him" any man. From these generalizations, which suggest the existence of shortcomings in the loved one, the poem moves swiftly to particulars. The shortcomings are defined and placed in context: "All his faults are locked securely/ In a closet of her mind," the poet says first. She then specifies two such faults: indecisiveness and cautiousness. She couches them in familiar terms. The indecisions appear "folded/ Like old flags that time has faded,/ Limp and streaked with rain." Similarly, the poet characterizes cautiousness as being like old clothes, "frayed and thin, with many a stain."

The middle line of the poem provides a pivot point on which the poem's focus turns. "Let them be, oh let them be," the poet says, less to the woman in the loving relationship than to the reader. The poet then makes her central statement: "There is treasure to outweigh them." The reader thus learns how the poem will circle back into the proper realm of the love lyric. The faults of the loved one may be serious, they may be of consequence, yet the man has strengths, too. From this second general statement, the poet proceeds to particulars, first by identifying a trait conventionally masculine, "proud will," followed by virtues that are more domestic: gentleness, humor, and tenderness.

Forms and Devices

Teasdale achieves part of her effect by playing against expectations, beginning with her choice of the anacreontic for a lyric form. Conventionally, anacreontics speak of the pleasures of wine, women, and song. In tone, the lyrics rarely move beyond the celebratory and joyous to the critical or even realistic. While Teasdale does address the matter of love, she chooses realism as her mode. Moreover, she delays any sense of celebration until the latter half of the poem. Anacreontics are usually in trochaic tetrameter, which refers to the poem having lines of four two-syllable feet with stresses falling on the first syllables. In "Appraisal," the poet uses this meter, although not rigidly. Teasdale, one of the most consciously musical of twentieth century poets, employs several devices to achieve rhythmic variety, including the measured substitution of iambs for trochees. Many of the lines are varied by catalexis (the dropping of the final, unaccented syllable). Strikingly, the seventh line, "Limp and streaked with rain," has only three feet, perhaps as a means of underlining the inadequacy or insufficiency being discussed.

Teasdale supports the two halves of the poem with different sets of imagery. In the first listing of shortcomings, she uses metaphors that are anything but romantic: She speaks of faded cloth and old clothing and of a closet that conceals the unwanted. The subsequent list of strengths then adopts terms of the natural world, reclaiming the romantic territory of the love poem. The shift in types of imagery provides a means of creating movement within the lyric, which otherwise lacks narrative flow. Teasdale similarly shifts poetic gears in the lyric "Those Who Love." The short poem's first stanza states its contention that "Those who love the most,/ Do not talk of their love" and supports it with such elevated examples from myth and literature as Iseult, Heloise, and Guinevere. The second stanza, in contrast, descends to the everyday, referring to "a woman I used to know." Teasdale's poem "Wisdom" similarly uses a shift of imagery to create a sense of progression. The word "spring" occurs in a literal sense, or nearly so, in the first two stanzas, then recurs in the third in a new and figurative sense, symbolizing love that was never realized.

Like these two poems, the shifting imagery in "Appraisal" includes a change from the tangible or accessible to the intangible and unreachable. "Those Who Love" turns its focus to one of those "who love the most," whose love was never requited. Similarly in "Wisdom," the "spring" that never arrived seems now forever out of reach. The shift of imagery in "Appraisal" moves the poem from the controlled realm of the domestic world to the uncontrollable realm of nature. The loved one's will is compared to the ocean's tide. He exhibits gentleness not to people but "to beast and bird." In the most beautiful evocation of his elusiveness, the poet describes him as possessing "Humor flickering hushed and wide/ As the moon on moving water." Even his tenderness escapes the lover's grasp, for it is "too deep/ To be gathered in a word." Ironically, these strengths are typically considered domestic virtues.

Also like "Those Who Love" and "Wisdom," "Appraisal" strikes a tonal balance characteristic of Teasdale's mature works. In this balance, the romantic and practical coexist. Romance never becomes sentimental just as the poet's sense of practical limits never becomes too coldly conclusive. The title "Appraisal" is thus entirely appropriate. The poem describes a judgment of value, a weighing of pluses and minuses. In the end, the balance weighs toward the heart. Teasdale stretches but does not break the anacreontic form.

Themes and Meanings

Outwardly, "Appraisal" appears to be a mature variation on a theme introduced in one of Teasdale's earliest poems. "Faults" begins with the line "They came to tell your faults to me" and ends with these lines: "Oh, they were blind, too blind to see/ Your faults had made me love you more." "Appraisal" seems to reflect the similar but more mature viewpoint of long-married lovers who have grown to know each other's weaknesses without losing sight of their strengths.

While none of Teasdale's poems depends on knowledge of her life for their understanding, such knowledge gives added dimension to many. "Appraisal" ranks among these. In her youth, Teasdale had the habit of speaking about herself in the third person. While it is common enough for poets to write of themselves from behind the guise of the third person, with Teasdale the practice was apparently a commonplace. Readers acquainted with this fact might tend to read her line in "Those Who Love" about "a woman I used to know," for instance, as referring to herself. One might approach "Appraisal" in much the same way.

The poem itself appeared in Teasdale's 1926 collection *Dark of the Moon* in a section entitled "Portraits." Alongside "Appraisal" are "Those Who Love," which portrays an unrequited but intensely felt love, and "The Wise Woman," which paints a similar picture of a woman contemplating an affair that never occurred. In "The Wise Woman," the poet wonders about a woman "who can forego/ An hour so jewelled with delight." She suggests that "She must have treasuries of joy/ That she can draw on day and night." The poem concludes with rational reconciliation: "Or is it only that she feels/ How much more safe it is to lack/ A thing that time so often steals." The collection also includes the poem "Wisdom," which speaks most pointedly and poignantly of a mutually felt love that has existed for years without physical realization. It also expresses the lover's reconciliation with the state of affairs: "It was as spring that never came,/ But we have lived enough to know/ What we have never had, remains;/ It is the things we have that go."

According to biographer Margaret Haley Carpenter, many of Teasdale's poems, especially later works, were written with poet John Hall Wheelock in mind. Among others, she points to "Appraisal" as being written specifically about Wheelock. Seen in this light, the imagery of the poem takes on a new aspect. The shift from domestic imagery to images drawn from uncontrollable nature in itself becomes part of the portrait: The man under discussion, who was never a part of Teasdale's domestic life, was as elusive to her as "the moon on moving water."

Mark Rich

APRIL FOOL BIRTHDAY POEM FOR GRANDPA

Author: Diane di Prima (1934-   )
Type of poem: Elegy
First published: 1971, in *Revolutionary Letters*

The Poem

"April Fool Birthday Poem for Grandpa" is occasioned by the day of poet Diane di Prima's grandfather's birth, and though the reference to April Fool's Day in the title might seem to suggest a prank or joke, the poem is a serious tribute. The author apologizes for her previous unsuccessful efforts to write this tribute, but "the gathering madness" of the moment at hand makes her recognize the urgency of paying homage to her grandfather, and she sets to the task.

The second section of the poem is devoted to expressions of thanks to the grandfather, who was a model of honesty, integrity, and compassion for di Prima. The grandfather told di Prima "what to expect," and "back there in that scrubbed Bronx parlor" he always was straightforward, "pulling/ no punches." He was a lover of Italian operas, and he listened to them regularly, not weeping in an obligatory way, but "honestly weeping in time to/ innumerable heartbreaking/ italian operas," revealing his sensitivity and sincerity. The grandfather's delicate outlook and his capability to teach effectively are shown by his lesson about children who pull leaves from trees. The grandfather pulled the hair of di Prima herself so that she could know the pain the tree must feel when its leaves are pulled.

The poem progresses into di Prima's own declaration that she, like her grandfather, is a revolutionary. Her struggle in the present drives her mind into recollection of the past, when her grandfather spoke publicly "in that Bronx park," insisting that love "had to come or we/ die." The memory has an ethereal quality, as di Prima refers to "spring Bronx dusk" and recalls her grandfather's "fierce/ blue eyes" and "white hair." Her grandfather was a source of pride because people listened to him. Di Prima esteems her grandfather as a loving intellectual.

The final portion of the poem is a vow that di Prima and her fellow revolutionaries will dedicate their pursuit of their revolutionary goals to di Prima's grandfather and other anarchists and revolutionaries of the past. The poem lists various anarchists, socialists, and artists, creating a sort of hall of fame for people who took social action and made sacrifices to foster love and fairness. The "stars over the Bronx . . . look on earth," see di Prima and her cohorts following great models from the past, and have no reason for shame.

Forms and Devices

"April Fool Birthday Poem for Grandpa" breaks from tradition because the poem assumes an open form, with no rhyme scheme, no fixed metrical pattern, and no stanzaic arrangement. In fact, the separation between units of thought is slightly obscured by enjambment: Line breaks occur in the middle of sentences, with thoughts running over from one line to the next. No white space is exploited to denote a division or succession of main points.

The poem begins with an apostrophe—di Prima addresses her grandfather, even though he cannot literally hear her words or respond to what she says. This poetic address is carried out in the tradition of the occasional poem—the poem written for a particular day or event—in this case di Prima's grandfather's birthday. This arrangement incorporates drama in the poem because the reader, like a member of an audience in a theater, is not directly addressed but is positioned to overhear the words that pass from di Prima to her grandfather.

"April Fool Birthday Poem for Grandpa" follows the convention of the elegy to honor the dead as the poem lists the characteristics of the grandfather that are worthy of admiration. Furthermore, the elegiac convention of providing comfort for the bereaved is observed because the poem asserts that the grandfather's ideals live on because di Prima and her friends keep the spirit of revolution alive.

A shift in tense from past to present is pivotal as di Prima establishes a link between the revolutionary activity with her grandfather and the similar activities in the present. In the past, di Prima "stood/ a ways off, looking up at" her grandfather; now she stands "a ways off listening," still hearing her grandfather's words in her mind as she proudly serves soup to "young men with light in their faces." Di Prima is confident that her grandfather would love the scene at her table, where people are "talking love, talking revolution." He would forcefully deliver "anarchist wisdom" informed by his reading of Dante and Giordano Bruno.

The closing section of the poem makes extensive use of allusions, both literary and historical, as di Prima includes the names of famous and noteworthy people who, in her view, have lovingly fought for justice and made great sacrifices in the process. Some of the allusions are easy to recognize: Most readers have some knowledge of Dante (1265-1321), Oscar Wilde (1854-1900), and Percy Bysshe Shelley (1792-1822), all great authors dedicated to love and truth. Others may be familiar with the Italian philosopher Giordano Bruno (1548-1600), who was burned at the stake for his refusal to revise his views on transubstantiation and the Immaculate Conception. Nicola Sacco (1891-1927) and Bartolomeo Vanzetti (1888-1927) were executed in Massachusetts for robbery and murder, even though their guilt was questionable and their "crime" may have been simply their anarchist political viewpoint. Carlo Tresca (1879-1943), a newspaper publisher, defended Sacco and Vanzetti in his radical publications.

Those with a background in Russian history, especially the revolutions of 1917, may know about filmmaker Sergei Eisenstein (1898-1948), whose film *Stachka* (1925; *Strike*) immortalized the struggle of workers; these readers may also recall Peter Kropotkin (1842-1921), the exiled author, philosopher, and anarchist, or may be aware of Leon Trotsky (1879-1940), the spellbinding revolutionary speaker who endured imprisonment in Siberia. Readers with a background in art may recall Aubrey Beardsley (1872-1898), whose shocking illustrations of books challenged mainstream views, and Jean Cocteau (1889-1963), the daring French author, dramatist, and filmmaker whom many established artists and critics refused to take seriously.

The poem ends with a final connection between the past and present, between heaven and earth. When di Prima's grandfather was active in his anarchist endeavors, his magical energy made di Prima feel as if she were "breathing stars." Now that the grandfather is gone, his star and the stars of other great champions of anarchy are above in heaven. As they look down on earth to see today's revolutionaries, they can know that the cause of revolution is not forgotten.

Themes and Meanings

At the center of "April Fool Birthday Poem for Grandpa" is family pride. Di Prima loves and admires her grandfather, pays tribute to him, and takes inspiration from him. She recalls his personal attention and love for her and is thankful for all the things she learned from him. In addition, a strong sense of national pride is developed as memories of the grandfather call attention to the glorious tradition of Italy, including immortal artists and philosophers such as Dante and Bruno as well as dedicated contemporary Italian reformers such as Tresca, Sacco, and Vanzetti. Finally, the revolutionary cause is honored as a timeless, worldwide effort, with noble figures such as Beardsley, Wilde, Trotsky, Shelley, Kropotkin, Eisenstein, and Cocteau taking part. Today, di Prima and her revolutionary associates carry on a great tradition.

A further significance in di Prima's poem is her clarification of the spirit of anarchism. For some, anarchy suggests disorder and violence. While some anarchists are guilty of violent crimes, the anarchists that di Prima honors represent an emphasis on general human well-being and love. Thus, di Prima's poem contradicts an erroneous generalization about the proponents of anarchy and the meaning of their philosophy. Today, di Prima's partners in revolution are not assassins and agents of chaos, but "young men with light in their faces"; di Prima herself finds that she must "embrace strangers on the street" as part of her effort to create a society free from oppressive authority. In addition, the poet calls attention to the sacrifices and injustices that reformers must endure. For a belief in love and freedom, one may be scorned, ridiculed, arrested, imprisoned, exiled, or even executed.

Finally, "April Fool Birthday Poem for Grandpa" is a comment on what a poem can be. While the poem observes the conventions of the elegy and incorporates familiar methods, such as apostrophe and allusion, the poem abandons rhyme, meter, and, for the most part, figurative language. Lines may have as many as ten words or may be a single word. This combination of standard methods with unconventional methods underscores the central theme of the poem. Just as revolution, the process for establishing a new and better world, has a long-standing tradition, so di Prima's poem, which honors the pursuit of a new and better world, is based on the old and the new in poetic design.

William T. Lawlor

APRIL INVENTORY

Author: W. D. Snodgrass (1926-   )
Type of poem: Lyric
First published: 1959, in *Heart's Needle*

The Poem

The sixty lines of "April Inventory" comprise ten stanzas of six lines each. The stanzas consist of a quatrain followed by a couplet, rhyming *ababcc*. Though W. D. Snodgrass varies the metric foot in many of his lines, the basic structure is iambic tetrameter. Many of the structural features create an interplay between fluidity and disconnection, between pause and flow. All the stanzas are closed, for example, and within all but two of them the concluding couplet is set off from the quatrain by punctuation. These minor divisions create distinct units of thought, while other features—such as the repetition of words, enjambment, and rhyme—sustain the poem's continuity.

The focus of the speaker's subjectivity is established from the beginning. The blooming of the trees reminds him of his own failure to blossom, both academically and personally. They will lose their flowers and leaves, and he will lose his teeth and hair, not to be replenished by another spring as the flowers and leaves will be. In the fourth stanza, as the speaker turns from the spring blossoms and their symbolic meaning to the academic world, the natural and the human elements merge. The girls he teaches have the pinkness of the cherry blossom, and they "Bloom gradually out of reach," as the cherry tree does. His attention broadens to include his friends, parents, and psychoanalyst—all those who expect him to flower—as he reviews his failure in academic pursuits: He has not read "one book about a book," memorized a plot, remembered the one date he learned, or found a mind he did not doubt. As a consequence, his colleagues, and not he, have advanced.

Midway through his inventory, his introspection takes another turn, and the mood shifts from the negative to the positive—from his academic failures to the modest successes in his private life. If he has fallen short in the world of books, he can name some accomplishments in personal relationships. Implicit in his assessment is that human contact and love offer more promise to him than academic competition and career obligations. He taught his classes "Whitehead's notions," taught a young woman "a song of Mahler's," and taught a child "the colors of/ A luna moth and how to love." He has learned to be tender, nurturing, caring. What he has, and has not, learned has brought important understanding and the ability to see better how he still can grow. He has not learned the old lie, that love "shall be blonder, slimmer, younger"; that he loves by his "body's hunger"; or "that the lovely world is real." Yet he has achieved a better perspective on himself and his academic shortcomings: As scholars develop ulcers and the seasons pass, he is left with the knowledge of his own worth. His inventory has brought him self-understanding and self-assurance, and the poem ends on triumphant acceptance of his own limitations and eventual decline, for he now knows that he has the strength to endure, as well as gentleness. He now can see beyond the narrow world of academics, can see that in the world at large "a loveliness exists,/ Preserves us." Ironically, he has had to fail in one respect to succeed in another, more important one, and in the expression of this ultimate insight he includes his readers.

Forms and Devices

Despite the freshness of its highly personal voice, the poem is grounded in tradition. By using the same stanzaic structure William Wordsworth used in his famous lyric "I Wandered Lonely as a Cloud," Snodgrass gives notice that the ancestry of his poem is Romantic. This tradition is evident also in the speaker's affinity for natural objects and in his seeing his own condition mirrored in seasonal changes in the landscape, particularly the trees. The fact that the speaker is introspective, solitary, contemplative, even melancholy, is reminiscent of the Romantic spirit.

The use of conventional devices is a constant reminder throughout the poem that the speaker is a scholar struggling to come to terms with his academic obligations. Convention offers the advantages of structure, organization, and direction; at the same time, it limits the speaker to pursuits that are unsuitable to his intellectual and emotional interests and gifts. The poem's structural features and language reflect the speaker's dual loyalties. The poem's vocabulary, for example, is for the most part modern, but it includes echoes of Snodgrass's literary forebears. In the first stanza, "The blossoms snow down in my hair," recalls the well-known line in the poem "Song" by Metaphysical poet John Donne, "Till age snow white haires on thee." In the third stanza, "they smile and mind me how" recalls a similar usage by Walt Whitman in "Song of Myself": "I mind how once we lay."

These elements, together with the use of rhyme, meter, simile, and stanzaic structure, play off the poem's departure from convention as the poet conducts his self-examination in a mode that is thoroughly modern. Readers see him, as it were, on the analyst's couch confessing his innermost feelings and very private concerns, including self-doubt, a sense of failure, and moral errancy, evident in his "equivocating eye" that loves only by his "body's hunger." He is conscious of his falling teeth and hair; the "dandruff on a tabletop" is probably his own; he cannot remember plots, names, dates. The six iambic tetrameter lines set within closed stanzaic units offer a secure framework well suited to the confessor's self-doubts, vocal rhythms, and need for guidance as he takes stock of his life. The revelations are delivered in measured units of thought that can be seen as distinct stages in the speaker's growing awareness of his own worth.

Themes and Meanings

Snodgrass surveys the landscape of his life with the same equipoise and solitary grace with which Wordsworth regards the golden daffodils in his poem. There the resemblance ends, however, for Snodgrass's subject is pointedly himself—his failures and modest accomplishments. The catalpa tree, green with white blossoms, symbolizes the speaker's fundamental ambivalence toward himself. The April of the title represents early spring, when the natural landscape is festooned with blossoms. Yet April also reminds one of T. S. Eliot's pronouncement in *The Waste Land* (1922) that "April is the cruellest month, breeding Lilacs out of the dead land." This sentiment underlies what the poet says of his own landscape: Though it is spring and the natural world is blossoming, and his colleagues in the academic world are prospering, his own efforts have not borne fruit; moreover, he is all too aware of his own physical decline. This April inventory is a cruel revelation that he has fallen far short of his early promise and that his time is short.

Despite the speaker's emphasis on his own failings, he conducts his inventory with a detachment that keeps the poem from slipping into maudlin self-pity and self-abasement. One of the ways he maintains control is to keep the reader's attention on the manner of his speaking and on the poetic conventions he is employing. While being deeply sincere and personal, he is also showing wit and dexterity in the use of rhyme, meter, and language. "I taught myself to name my name," for example, momentarily diverts one's attention from the speaker's feelings to his skill with language, and the couplets concluding every stanza reiterate the fact that the speaker is practicing poetic skill as much as he is confessing. He confesses to having made "a little list" for the tenth time of all that he ought to know, and he has told others he would be "substantial, presently." That final qualifier, "presently," has the wry irony of one who knows the futility of promising what is not in his heart to do. He is sincere enough to admit that in some ways he is not entirely sincere.

The antithesis of the speaker's personal vision is the narrowness of scholarship, which blinds one to the loveliness of the world beyond academic ambition and isolates one from the gentleness and nurturing aspect of personal relationships. The "authority" of the scornful scholars in their "starchy collars" causes ulcers and, presumably, speaks in the rhythms of conventional rhyme and meter. This authority is offset by the speaker's "equivocating eye," which in academic circles is a deficit but in "the lovely world" can see the human worth beneath appearances. Throughout the poem, the academic world is seen to be at odds with the human. The mind that lapses from the strict discipline of scholarship and falls short of its demands cannot prosper in that world, but, ironically, it is through doubt, equivocation, and human imperfection that the speaker has acquired knowledge of his real worth and the "lovely world" outside. Discovery of what is in the heart is at the heart of this poem. In the end, the poem reaches beyond the personal to include all of humanity in its plea to discover where the loveliness lies, to get in touch with the worth beneath the outer trappings of life, and to feel the gentleness.

Bernard E. Morris

ARCHAIC TORSO OF APOLLO

Author: Rainer Maria Rilke (1875-1926)
Type of poem: Sonnet
First published: 1908, as "Archaïscher Torso Apollos," in *Der neuen Gedichte anderer Teil*; English translation collected in *New Poems (1908): The Other Part,* 1987

The Poem

"Archaic Torso of Apollo" is a sonnet divided into four stanzas, the first two stanzas containing four lines each, the last two containing three each. In the original German, the first two stanzas follow an *abba, cddc* rhyme scheme, while the last two stanzas together follow an *eef, gfg* scheme. In the German version, each line averages ten syllables in length. As is characteristic of the work of Rainer Maria Rilke throughout the two volumes of *New Poems*, the title unambiguously states the poem's subject matter, much as the title of a painted still life might refer the viewer directly to an object depicted therein.

In "Archaic Torso of Apollo," the poet depicts an ancient fragment of a statue of Apollo, the Greek god of the sun, of music, and of poetry. As one finds so often with the classical statuary now confined to museums, only the torso remains—the statue's legs, arms, and head have long been missing, leaving the poet to conjecture how the whole statue once must have looked. In the first line of the poem, the poet begins to describe the torso before him by calling attention to what is now missing. Once the statue had a head from which Apollo's eyes gazed forth brightly, "fabled eyes" about whose power the poet can now only wonder.

Yet the gaze that once must have been present in the statue's eyes, Rilke suggests, still seems to shine from the surface of the torso. This now-absent gaze, in fact, will haunt the entire poem. Its light, "turned down low," shines forth from the torso's breast and turns the curve of the upper thigh into a "smile." Although the statue is only a battered fragment, the now-absent light from the statue's eyes invests the remaining torso with a startling potency. Paradoxically, the very loss of those features which gave the statue of the god a recognizably human form has turned it into something more than human and truly mysterious. Battered by time, the torso has shed its human qualities and come to seem almost godlike, as though it were indeed an expression of natural force. This sense of the torso as something extra-human leads the poet in the third stanza to make what on the surface seems a contradictory comparison between the smooth stone of the statue and a "wild beast's fur."

The poet's perception undergoes its most radical transformation in the final stanza. There the vitality inside the statue seems to burst forth from its battered edges "like a star," and the gaze that the poet had directed toward the statue now seems to return to him from the torso itself. The final line enacts an even more dramatic shift, as the poem moves from description to declaration. The concluding statement, "You must change your life," is as forceful and uncompromising in the original German as it is in the English translation.

Forms and Devices

"Archaic Torso of Apollo" opens the second of the two volumes *New Poems (1907)* and *New Poems (1908): The Other Part*; a sonnet on the same theme, "Früher Apollo" ("Early Apollo"), opens the first. At this stage of his long and complex poetic career, Rilke was concentrating on writing short, intense poems that tended to focus almost exclusively on some particular object. While sometimes the poet focuses on an animal, a place, or, as in this case, an object of art, his aim is always to apprehend the object on its own terms, as something that stands apart fundamentally from his own nature. Often the subjects of the poems seem almost banal (a ball, a sundial, a panther in the zoo, and an apple orchard are some other examples), yet inevitably the poet moves from what might seem an unpromising beginning into increasingly resonant and mysterious depths.

"Archaic Torso of Apollo" contains three instances of metaphor, but much of the real force of the poem comes from Rilke's employment of the rhetorical device known as metonymy. Whereas in metaphor the poet's thought jumps from one level of meaning to another, in metonymy the poet focuses his attention on a small part of an object as a means of communicating his sense of the object as a whole. In this poem the poet's attention moves from the torso's breast to its thigh and genitals to the "shoulder's invisible plunge," yet there is little attempt to forge these perceptions into a rationally coherent unity. The effect resembles that of a cubist painting, in which the painter forces the viewer's perception to shift from one disparate glimpse to the next.

One might even argue that Rilke's use of metonymy is of more than merely technical interest, since fragmentation and the complex interplay between the part and the whole are among the principle themes of the poem. Just as the torso is fragmented, the poet is driven to describe it in a language of fragmented perceptions.

Significantly, too, Rilke begins the poem in the first-person plural ("We") and shifts to the second-person "you" in the course of the poem. By employing "We" in the opening line, Rilke creates a sense of identification between his sensibility and the reader's: Both are regarding the statue together. With both poet and reader standing in common awe of the torso, the shift to "you" in the course of the poem creates the sense that the command imparted at its close comes not from poet to reader but from torso to both. This pronoun shift creates the illusion of directing the reader's attention away from Rilke's response and toward the torso itself, so that the final declaration seems almost completely impersonal.

Themes and Meanings

Apollo was the god of the sun, of music, and of poetry; consequently, he came to be associated with principles of order, rationality, and harmony. Certainly Rilke would have expected his readers to be familiar with these associations, yet, while nothing in the poem explicitly denies them, it is interesting to note that his presentation of the god comes wholly in terms of the torso's immediate visual impact. Other than the "fabled eyes" mentioned in the second line, the poet apparently brings no preconceptions of Apollo to the torso. The message "imparted" by the torso seems to spring solely from the poet's sensuous apprehension of it, and the degree to which Rilke's presentation of Apollo coincides with the attributes traditionally assigned to the god is worth some consideration.

Rilke dedicated *New Poems (1908): The Other Part* "To my great friend August Rodin." In the years preceding the publication of the book, Rilke had served as a secretary at the sculptor's studio in Paris. Before meeting Rodin, Rilke had been chiefly a lyrical poet, writing poems focused primarily on his own inner moods. Unlike a poet, however, a sculptor cannot make his art solely from subjective feelings but must pay close attention to the materials with which he works. Being exposed to Rodin caused Rilke to consider a kind of poetry that dealt with the substantial qualities of things in much the way sculpture does. It follows, then, that in some of these poems Rilke would choose an actual sculpture for a subject.

Sculptors, carpenters, or others whose work involves actively making something recognize the importance of respecting and understanding their materials. For Rilke to explore this principle as a poet, however, especially to the profound degree he explores it in the two volumes of the *New Poems*, was a highly original conception. By making the simple yet fundamental shift of his attention outward to things, Rilke began to realize that the world outside human beings is every bit as interesting and meaningful as the world inside them.

For the sculptor or the carpenter, such attention might be a simple everyday habit, but for the poet of "Archaic Torso of Apollo," such attention leads to the startling and mysterious conclusion that, in looking closely at things, the things one looks at somehow seem able to look back. This realization leads to what might be taken as the torso's own concluding command, open-ended yet definite, for the reader alone to decipher.

Vance Crummett

ARCHER IN THE MARROW
The Applewood Cycles, 1967-1987

Author: Peter Viereck (1916-   )
Type of poem: Epic/lyric
First published: 1987

The Poem

   Archer in the Marrow, subtitled *The Applewood Cycles, 1967-1987*, is an epic lyric poem composed of eighteen cycles, a preface, an epilogue, and notes. The preface identifies the speakers, establishes the poem's motifs, and presents an initial "Showdown on Land's End" to establish the conflict or war of contraries that is played out in dramatic fashion throughout the book. The epilogue provides both resolution and direction, a blank canvas that serves as prologue to a new spiral, and there is a lengthy "Appendix: Form in Poetry" that discusses the biology of verse and likens the rhythm of iambic pentameter to the throbbing of the human heart. Strict form in poetry, according to Peter Viereck, is the holy essence of human nature. The section of notes and the "Glossary of Names, Foreign Phrases, Classical, Biblical, and Historical References" were added at the publisher's request.

   Peter Viereck's book-length poem serves as a rite of passage into a harmonious world of spheres that includes a rebirth of rhyme. Poetry is likened to human physiology, and this analogy links the matter of the appendix to the cycles of the poem.

   The three main speakers of the poem (identified in lowercase letters) are the father, the son, and "you"—the human of today who imagines the voices of the father and the son; the son is both Jesus and Dionysus (the annually hacked mythical vine god is presented as the son's lost half). In addition, there is Eve, who is Mary Magdalene in the first cycle of the poem and Aphrodite in the last. A system of delineation helps determine who is speaking throughout. When the father speaks, the text is set at the left margin; his voice is additionally indicated by the use of Roman numerals. The son's words are indented and represented by arabic numbers. The words of "you" are set in italics and quotation marks.

   The text circles around the choice of whether to make a cross or a liberating arrow from the wood of the tree of knowledge in the Garden of Eden. If man should become more than a thing, determined by things, he must be "self-surpassing" (Viereck's term). According to medieval legend, the wood of the apple tree was used to make the cross upon which Jesus was crucified. The "archer" in the bone marrow symbolizes Viereck's idea that man should use applewood to make a liberating arrow rather than a cross.

   The second section of the preface is entitled "Motifs," and Viereck begins it by stating that "Eden's forbidden appletree of knowledge lit man's eyes with consciousness" (page 15). This awakening causes a conflict between man, who wants to be "more than a thing, to expand from dot into circle" and his Father-god, who wants to keep the human toy blank-eyed and robotized. Thus a duel takes place at Land's End—the beach on which a mutant "rogue" gene, the lungfish, man's forebear, first breathed air—and sets into play the motif of self-surpassing.

The discovery of lungs enables man to invade another realm—the sky—with the weapon known as human song or lyric poetry. The acquisition of this "formcraft" (Viereck's term) is an additional motif. It involves the biology of poetry that is discussed at length in the book's appendix. The blood of the poet is "Rh positive," Viereck says, and in *Archer in the Marrow*, the *Rh* is the twofold *Rh* of rhyme and rhythm. These two factors form the poet's rhapsody—the *rhaps* plus the *ody*—the "ode-stitching" of Viereck's crisscross pattern of verse. The swords of the book's dueling voices, then, are rhythms, not creeds, and the fight is for a living, body-rooted poetic form, instead of dead formalism or contemporary free verse.

The setting, or backdrop motif, of Viereck's drama—though he warns that *Archer in the Marrow* is a poem, not a tract or a play—has a ceiling meat hook and two big canvases set up by father and son. The artwork, like poetry's unparaphrasable uniqueness, is organic and nonverbal. Its pulse can be felt, and Rembrandt van Rijn's *Slaughtered Ox* and Jan and Hubert van Eyck's *Adoration of the Lamb* (one panel of the *Ghent Altarpiece*) set up a series of opposites: Hellenic and Hebraic, Dionysus and Jesus, Aphrodite and Eve, dust and loam, goatfoot and lamb. Only by means of free choice can man effect the reconciliation of these opposites. He must free himself from "the script writer in the sky" and by means of formcraft poach "creativity from its Creator" (page 16).

The final section of the preface begins the "Showdown on Land's End." The wine god, Dionysus, watches, and as modern man, or "you," is about to lose the duel, he is cast into timeless Part Zero.

Part Zero, a frozen realm outside time and space, begins the circling or "cycles." It is composed of Cycle One, "Up"; Cycle Two, "Hacked"; and Cycle Three, "Round"; in which "you" encounters the deaths of Jesus, the nailed son, and Dionysus. Cycle Three humorously juxtaposes Los Angeles and ancient Tarsus as east-west landmarks sway and are reversed in a "smog mirage" (page 40).

Two transitions follow. In the first, the father addresses an offstage "you" and claims that "it's not been easy being God." In the second, Dionysus comments that he is a "word-juggler, shape-juggler, world-juggling god, and quack" (page 54). He explains: "I'm Dionysus (or a wino pretending to be);/ Pan's one of my selves; on the Nile, Osiris another" (page 54). Part Zero dissolves, and man's various cycles follow. "Waltz," a section in a waltzlike 1-2-3 rhythm, measures the imprisoning birth-spawn-death—"dumped, dunked, done"—cycle of man. It contains an amusing counterpoint of dialogue between "you" and the son that makes reference to modern technology and poetry: "The devil was never the snake in the tree," the son says. "He's the snake in computers named 'Apple' " (page 64). Alluding to Emily Dickinson, "you" answers: "*A narrow fellow programmed me/ With gene tapes, Xerox at the bone*" (page 64).

In Cycle Five, the "Bread" cycle, a series of sestets, "you" asks the son as Dionysus to "Help us know deeper meanings," but the time for self-surpassing has not come; man's knowledge of applewood is incomplete. This cycle is set against a backdrop of "gas lights, high hats, and such incongruous pairs as Queen Victoria chatting with Freud and Andrew Carnegie with Marx" (page 71). The time is the late nineteenth century, which gives way to the late twentieth century backdrop in the "Epilogue to the Bread Cycle."

Cycle Six, "Rogue," is cast in the Devonian period of the Paleozoic Era. "You" becomes the lungfish and addresses future selves of 1987. Cycles Seven through Nine—"Salt," "Bells," and "Stain"—continue "you's" quest toward self-surpassing as alternate dialogues with father and son and varying poetic forms punctuate the plight of the human toy's attempt to be more than a toy.

Part Two contains a prologue and four additional cycles: Cycle Ten, "Pish"; Eleven, "Eyes"; Twelve, "Book"; and Cycle Thirteen, "Auschwitz." In this latter cycle, "you" and the son argue about Nietzsche, the son's adopted brother, who predicted the slaughter of Jews. Part Three also begins with a prologue to cycles fourteen through eighteen: "Mek," "Core," an epilogue to "Core," "Choose," "Toward," and "Threads." *Mek* is the Hittite word for "power," and in this cycle, modern technology has surpassed Christianity as a significant and meaningful force. The result divides the outdated self and post-modern mechanics; the speaker is a male laboratory boss. In Parts Two and Three, Viereck explains that the father keeps his toys' apple-knowledge blinkered "by luring them to soar beyond that human frailty which is their true strength" (page 16).

"Part Zero Replayed" ends the poem. Opposites are united. The conflicts between the son and his pagan double, Dionysus, between Eve and Aphrodite, and between goatfoot and the lamb are resolved. The son tells "you" at the end of "Part Zero Replayed" that "God only fears one arrow: God's image, made human by Eve./ Now, archer in the marrow, stretch your own birth-cord's bow" (page 196). Wildness is freed. "You" concludes by saying: "Pierced hands . . . bending cross into cross-bow./ Look: goatfoot Jesus on the village green" (page 211).

Forms and Devices

Archer in the Marrow embodies Peter Viereck's contention that poetry is inseparable from biology. Functional form is alive and liberating; mechanical or decorative formalism is dead.

The appendix of the book, subtitled "Form in Poetry: Would Jacob Wrestle with a Flabby Angel?" provides an assessment of Viereck's theory of poetic "formcraft." He asks if modern poetry is alive and has a structure, and points out that a metronome cannot feel; it is a mechanical tic. The rhythms of a lyric, however, are "the onomatopoeia of the flesh" (page 215). Life and poetry are organic recurrent vibrations. Viereck asserts that the formal poet marshals words "the way the body organizes its nervous system" (page 216). Enjambments are "synapses," and the thump-THUMP of the heart is the iambic pentameter of rhyme. Such anatomical functions as the "inhale and exhale of breath, systole and diastole of heart, pound and pause of pulse, in and out of coition, ebb and flow of tide" are all iambics (pages 219-220). Trochees, according to Viereck, are iambics in reverse; dactyls and anapests are iambics with stutter. The Greek word for foot is iamb, the name of the scansion unit. Anatomy, then, is one of the arts, and biology forms a synthesis with poetry. Viereck maintains that rhyme should be extended into new areas of metrical and biological sensation. Poetry should be a rhythm message as well as a word message. While a word message is partly conscious and corresponds to the indicative or imperative in grammar, a rhythm message is partially unaware and is conditional or subjunctive. Poetry needs to concentrate on the nonverbal language of rhythm, which is the noncorporeal origin of form. "Strict form, in the broadest sense of 'form,' " Viereck claims, "may be both creator and product of the entire immortal macrocosm (as well as the microcosmic mortal poem)" (page 223).

Viereck's new form, "crisscross," rhymes the first two syllables of each line with the last syllables of other lines or of the same line. Its intent is to counter a "sloppy neglect of opening syllables and the pompous exaggeration of closing ones" (page 224).

Crisscross rhymes form the prosodic basis of *Archer in the Marrow*, and as poetry is freed from the deadwood, dead-end, formless wildness that is free verse, so is man led to self-surpassing, to a strict wildness in verse that Viereck sees as emancipating and earth-rooted. In the May/June, 1988, issue of *Poets & Writers*, he explains:

> This is why, in our post-modern era, we are witnessing a return, not to the dead mechanical "formalism," which free verse justifiably junked, but to a living, biological, content-expressing form. For if a definition of artistic creativity be demanded . . . then let us define it as expressive form: form for the sake of expressing an imperfection known as humanity.

Form, then, is neither artificial nor outdated. It is holy, a part of human nature. Although many poetic forms are used throughout the book, it is crisscross that liberates. When "you" asks at the end of the poem, "What makes two rival god-lies true for us?" the answer is crisscross—the poem's formcraft and the final appearance of "goatfoot Jesus on the village green" (page 211).

Themes and Meanings

The central theme of Peter Viereck's *Archer in the Marrow* is a crisscross. The first stroke of the crisscross is the biological nature of poetry as heartbeat and pulse, poetic formcraft, and strict wildness. It is the archer in the marrow of human bone who is liberated into making an emancipating arrow of applewood (the symbol of human self-surpassing). The battle fought by and among the father, the son, and the "you" of the poem is the other stroke of the crisscross, which is espoused by Viereck in the book's appendix: the split between form and ethics that resulted when the distinguished literary jury at the Library of Congress awarded Ezra Pound, in 1949, America's highest literary honor—the Bollingen Prize—for his, according to Viereck, Fascist and racist *The Pisan Cantos* (1948).

Although Poundians claim that *The Pisan Cantos* are meaningless and that their symbolism is obscure, Viereck agrees with Charles Tomlinson's claim in *Poetry and Metamorphosis* (1983) that the main message of *The Pisan Cantos* was "to mourn the fall of Troy, "the Troy of the Axis powers," and to compare to the unheeded warnings of Cassandra his own Radio Rome warnings against "Jewish" Roosevelt's "Jew-Nited States" (*Archer in the Marrow*, page 235).

According to Viereck, in an article entitled "Pound at 100: Weighing the Art and the Evil," published on December 19, 1985, in *The New York Times Book Review*:

> One should never judge art by its politics. But Nazism was not a matter of politics or economics. It was a matter of ethics and of a metaphysics of evil—contagious evil. . . . Unlike politics, evil does fall within the purview of esthetic criticism, for it parches empathy and hence parches the artist's creative imagination.

The "Auschwitz" cycle of the book quotes Frau Cosima Wagner's diary note of 1881 about a theater fire that killed four hundred Jews: "*Richard Wagner makes a drastic joke to the effect that all Jews should be burned at a performance of* Nathan the Wise." The parallels between the Pound controversy and the *Archer in the Marrow* issue of "self-surpassing" are striking.

Pound had been an ardent follower of Benito Mussolini since 1920, and Viereck remembers one broadcast in particular in which Pound approved the massacre of the Eastern European Jews and warned the American Jews that their turn was coming (*The New York Times Book Review*, December 19, 1985). Viereck, a soldier in Italy in 1943, heard the broadcasts and believes that Pound lost, in those radio appeals, his human empathy and creativity. Pound's opinions were evil, but his sinister message became focused on literary politics rather than on the malevolent advocacy of slaughter. This resulted in the revival of propaganda poetry, which works neither as poetry nor as propaganda.

When Viereck publicly disagreed with the Bollingen Prize judges and with those who viewed Pound as a persecuted martyr rather than a Fascist who advocated death and torture, he was told by one critic "not to criticize the Pound-Eliot-Tate establishment, or he would no longer be publishable." Decades after the Bollingen controversy, Viereck continued to affirm that "energy should be mustered on the side of fallible yet self-surpassing humanity—not on the side of inhuman abstractions, bloodily inflicted on human beings for their own good" (page 237). Art should be saved from meddling politicians. Peter Viereck, then, is an archer in the marrow who liberates poetry from formless wildness by means of the invention of crisscross, a biology of rhyme, and who frees art from politics by fashioning an applewood arrow instead of a cross.

Sue B. Walker

AN ARGUMENT: ON 1942

Author: David Mura (1952-   )
Type of poem: Meditation
First published: 1989, in *After We Lost Our Way*

The Poem

David Mura's "An Argument: On 1942" is a relatively brief, understated poem of twenty-one lines, but it implies an extended long-standing and angry exposition on two highly charged themes significant to all Asian Americans: first, parent-child miscommunication and conflict and, second, ethnic assimilation and betrayal. The poem's subject matter is one particular crime perpetrated against an ethnic Japanese minority in the United States and the ways in which the offended culture deals with or suppresses such violation.

The subtitle of the poem, "For My Mother," indicates that Mura is writing a tribute, offering his mother, Teruko Mura, a gift. It more subtly suggests that he is making a statement to her with his art that would be difficult for her to process in direct conversation. In this statement he is responding in the best way that he can to a long-held position of hers, one that baffles and confuses and hurts him: He writes her a poem. She has been silent for years in the face of past adversity. He, on the other hand, is insistent that she tell the story; he is eager to listen, to know the truth and to disseminate it. The poem is, then, highly autobiographical both personally and culturally; it is a real story from Mura's own past and a more wide-ranging statement about survivors of the Japanese internment and their descendents.

Some brief history is necessary to understand the poem. After Japanese forces attacked Pearl Harbor on December 7, 1941, the U.S. government forcibly evacuated more than 110,000 Japanese Americans without due process of law, approximately 70 percent of them native-born U.S. citizens, from their homes along the West Coast to one of sixteen makeshift relocation centers inland for the duration of the war. Living behind barbed wire among armed guards, the internees suffered severe financial loss, disruption of education, loss of employment and property, and extraordinary humiliation.

The narrative line of the poem is uncomplicated: It is a probing conversation between a mother and her adult son. An italicized first stanza sets the scene and the context; the speaker is refreshing the mother's memory. The poet re-creates a moment some forty years ago when the relocation began personally for his family: His father was fired from his job. In stanza 2 the mother resists having such an unpleasant chapter of her life brought back. She has no desire to relive the past and says: "No, no, no. . . ./ The camps are over."

In stanza 3 she reluctantly and very briefly talks about daily life in the camps, prefacing this by saying that everyone was, mostly, bored: "Women cooked and sewed,/ men played blackjack, dug gardens, a *benjo* [bathroom facilities]." Because she was a child, she did what children anywhere would do, "[hunt] stones, birds, wild flowers." In stanza 4 the speaker is the poet's father, who contributes a small but significant detail the mother leaves out, that she hides Japanese foods under the bed, "tins of *utskemono* and eel," seeking some small ethnic comfort in a hostile and alien place. At the same time that the poet's father seems to appreciate the poet's quest for knowledge—"it's all/ part of your job, your way"—he does not, finally, really understand. The poem ends with the father's disapproval and trails off: "David, it was so long ago—how useless it seems . . ."

Forms and Devices

"An Argument: On 1942" has a semitraditional poetic form, which seems to want to break rules but not entirely. It consists of five four-line stanzas in roughly free verse. That is, while the poem exhibits no consistent pattern of meter, despite its relative regularity in line length, the stanzas have unpredictable occurrences of pure rhyme (stanza 1: "inspired," "fired"; stanza 3: "towers," "flowers"; stanza 5: "Paul," "all," "recall"), slant or oblique rhyme (stanza 1: "grocery," "mercy"), assonance (stanza 4: "eel," "peeled"), and consonance (stanza 2: "back," "dramatic"). The poet uses enjambment, a device in which the grammatical, logical, and syntactical sense of one poetic line continues into the next. This occurs in the first, fourth, and fifth stanzas, at places where the continued line signals that the emotion is more complex and is striving not to be contained.

By titling his poem an "argument," Mura implies that a thesis will be clearly presented; that there is effort to convince a reluctant party with logic or, in this case, emotion; and that there is deep-seated disagreement that has not been resolved. The poem accomplishes these three things within a family context that renders the disharmony particularly poignant. The final stanza, given heightened emotional impact with its single line and its placement at the end, has, furthermore, an open ending. Lack of terminal final cadence suggests that this argument between older parents and adult son will not easily, if ever, be resolved.

"An Argument: On 1942" appears in Mura's first poetry collection, *After We Lost Our Way*, one of five winners published in the National Poetry Series for 1989. Mura uses, as an epigraph to the book's opening section, a series of poems about his Japanese ancestors, a sentiment from Walter Benjamin: "Nothing that has ever happened should be regarded as lost for history." The title of the book, the epigraph, and its cover art all characterize Mura's difficult dealings with his ethnic heritage. His embrace of his ethnicity as an adult is symbolized by the cover illustration, a colored Japanese patchwork coat dating from 1560, from the Uesugi Shrine. The book's title and epigraph, as well as the rift between parents and son on which "An Argument: On 1942" is based, hint at the alienation from his ethnic heritage that Mura experienced growing up, at the destructive ways in which he acted out that denial and suppression, and at his final resolution and embrace of his culture.

Themes and Meanings

A third-generation Japanese American, a Sansei, Mura grew up on baseball and apple pie in a Chicago suburb, where he heard more Yiddish than Japanese. He cultivated a Eurocentric worldview, avidly reading books by white male authors, cheering for American GIs fighting the Japanese in war movies, and identifying with European traditions. Mura's conflicts with his parents, which is at the heart of "An Argument: On 1942," stem from many things. Politically, his father was a Republican; Mura was a conscientious objector during the Vietnam War and wore his hair long. His father wanted him to become a lawyer; Mura wanted to be a poet. His parents sensed that assimilation, obliterating their ethnicity, was the way to claim the American Dream for themselves and their son. They never mentioned their years in the relocation camps. They seldom spoke of their roots, de-emphasized their skin color, and even modified their surname, which had been Uyemura, to sound less exotic.

The penultimate line of the poem is seeringly telling in its apposition; the poet's father asks, agonizingly, why his son cannot just accept "how far we've come, how much I can't recall." The first clause asks for validation, for gratitude on the son's part for what the parents have attained in fitting into American society and thereby achieving success for the family. The second clause begs respect for their silence, asks their son to back off from subjects they have worked for years to erase and bury. The father wants both acceptance and denial from his son, wants him to value and revere what he does. Yet the very problem is in that juxtaposition: Mura's parents want him to forget the past, and he knows he needs to reclaim it.

Only in adulthood did Mura come to realize that such ethnic repression was personally catastrophic. He began an addictive cycle of drug abuse and sexual promiscuity that led to self-interrogation, to awareness, and finally to self-esteem as he smashed long-held stereotypes and became able to claim his Japanese identity. The books that follow *After We Lost Our Way* trace this trajectory and show how Japanese imagery and concerns become increasingly a significant part of Mura's artistic consciousness..

"An Argument: On 1942" is a significant poem to think about, to teach, and to learn from. Its language and easy diction make it accessible to high schoolers and adults alike. Its generational conflict is an issue that parents and children of all cultures can identify with. It illuminates the cruelties and ironies of history in ways that bear constant investigation and vigilance.

Jill B. Gidmark

ARIEL

Author: Sylvia Plath (1932-1963)
Type of poem: Lyric
First published: 1965, in *Ariel*

The Poem

On first reading, much of Sylvia Plath's poetry seems chaotic, and there is a sense of demoniacal negativity. Some critics have wondered whether her later poetry did not represent a surrender of reason to the turbulence of the emotions and a distraught, hypersensitive mentality. "Ariel," however, shows clearly the sense of control, order, and choice that characterizes her most mature lyrics. It describes in fragmentary, passionate, and almost hallucinogenic vividness an event in Sylvia Plath's life that occurred when she lost control of her horse, Ariel, and, losing the stirrups, clung to its neck while it ran for two miles at full gallop across an English pastoral landscape.

"Stasis in darkness," the first line, describes the moment when she is mounted on the horse but has not yet emerged from the stables into daylight beneath "substanceless blue" skies. A "tor" is a craggy hill, and together with the berry bushes and furrows of a ploughed field, it depicts the English landscape through which she rides at breakneck speed. The exultation of oneness with the raw power and dynamism of the horse hurtling forward produces the words "God's lioness." Is the lioness the rider, the horse, or—as the next line suggests—both, united in a "Pivot of heels and knees"? Actually, "god's lioness" is a literal translation of the Hebrew word "Ariel" which in Isaiah 29:1-3 and 5-7 is an admiring epithet for Jerusalem, a city both favored and cursed by God.

The third three-line stanza compares the plowed furrows of the fields through which they ride with the sloping curve of the horse's neck, which the rider must try to grasp or she will fall. Details of the land blur at this speed, leading to quick images that are allusive and suggestive. Each rises for a moment in her vision and experience and disappears as the horse continues on. They pass bushes full of berries; the bushes seem to grab at the flanks of her horse or at her attention with their "hooks." In the next stanza, they are sensed as "black sweet blood mouthfuls."

She is no longer aware of the horse as a separate being but as a pure force that "Hauls me through air." She has become Lady Godiva, a heroine riding naked but for her long hair. Then, characteristic of Plath's style, in the midst of this frenzy of description comes a coldly intellectual observation as she considers her own body from a strange distance: "Dead hands, dead stringencies."

The separation of subject and object that is usual to acts of observation has disappeared by this point in her ride, and she becomes one even with the landscape: "And now I/ Foam to wheat, a glitter of seas." As the pace of the poem and the galloping of the horse pick up speed, wheat fields appear in her field of vision like waves of sea welling up into view. The cry of a child is heard, then the vision becomes a final pure experience of self uniting with sensation as she feels that she and the horse are a single arrow shot into the eye of the sun, dissolving there, as dew dissolves in the morning light.

Forms and Devices

The structure of "Ariel" is strict: ten three-line stanzas and a final single line for closure. The connections between the stanzas are strange, however, and they make it difficult to tell where one image or subject breaks off and another begins. For example, "God's lioness," which begins the second stanza, seems to refer by apposition to the "pour of tor and distances," the end of the first stanza. In the same way, there is frequently a sort of enjambment or connection between the last line of one stanza and the first of the next.

Ordinary similes and metaphors occur, but they are indicated by the slightest signs. "The furrow" is likened to the "brown arc/ Of the neck I cannot catch" by the words "sister to." The berries are compared to mouthfuls of blood by mere juxtaposition. "God's lioness" is both a metaphor and a complex allusion; the single word "Godiva" is yet another simile. The poem is rich with the resonances and figures of speech of traditional lyric. The poetic innovation here is in the supreme brevity with which these poetic figures are invoked. The meter is so brief that a complex image must be communicated in a few telegraphic words.

There is a general sense of rejection, dissolution, and emptiness in "Ariel": "substanceless blue," "Nigger-eye/ Berries," "hooks," "Flakes from my heels," "Dead hands," the verb "Melts." The sun is seen not as a sign of hope and power but as a red eye and a "cauldron."

The rhythm of "Ariel" has been called sexual, because its pace gradually quickens and crescendos to an orgasmic finish. Yet beneath this constant rise of energies is a sense of immense control—Plath's mastery of the changing energies of selfhood in lyric experience. The poet mentions herself again and again, tracking step-by-step the stages of her disappearance into pure sensation. The first-person pronoun establishes a rhythm for this progress in the second half of the poem: "I unpeel," "And now I/ Foam," "And I/ Am the arrow." One could almost say that the first six stanzas are the cause and the last four the effect. In the first six stanzas, she is propelled through a landscape; in the last four, the attention is drawn to the literal "I" of the poem.

"Dead hands, dead stringencies" creates a sudden pause in the headlong movement, and the reader must stop to think what this intellectual expression could mean. Then the beat is taken up again in a new key with the words "And now I/ Foam." In the end one can see that, despite the apparently overwrought intensity of the poem, a balance has been carefully crafted between feeling and observation, creating what Helen Vendler called "the coordination of intelligence and feeling."

Themes and Meanings

"Ariel" in many ways encapsulates the essence of the lyric form—a sense of nowness, of immediate experience which, because it is unconnected with any domestic narrative, captures the sublimity possible in pure sensation. At the same time, it contains the negativity that is an integral part of Sylvia Plath's vision. This sense of darkness, of fatality, was considered by her early critics to be inseparable from the theme of suicide that was explored in her novel *The Bell Jar* (1963) and that attracted her in life as well. Perhaps a more objective way of putting it would be to say that Plath attempted to see the world in a more honest and direct way; stripping sensation of its conventional meanings, she produced a new, dark vision of transcendence. This she expressed in a personal language with its own systems of classical allusions and correspondences. As she said in her 1956 journal: "[I]t is suddenly either all or nothing; either you break the surface shell into the whistling void or you don't. . . . The horror is the sudden folding up and away of the phenomenal world, leaving nothing. Just rags. Human rooks which say: Fraud."

In "Ariel" one can see this folding up of the phenomenal world and the abandoning in stages of conventional meaning; through tribulation, there is a movement to a new transcendence. This idea is expressed in the Hebrew meaning of the name she gave to her horse, "Ariel." This is the word used for Jerusalem when the prophet Isaiah predicts its tribulation—the period when the holy city will be invaded and the temple destroyed. After the time of its terrible trials, it will be purified and will achieve "deliverance in the apocalypse," as Caroline King Barnard has noted.

In the same way, the poet persona clinging to the fleeing horse gradually journeys through tribulation to a triumphant dissolving of the self. She lets fall the clothes of her conventional self-identity: "I unpeel—/ Dead hands, dead stringencies." This strikes a note of feminine rebellion, for that is the most familiar meaning of the Godiva story—the story of a woman who rides naked through a town as an act of protest. Judith Kroll has also pointed out a second meaning for Lady Godiva, which is her identification with the White Goddess, a female lunar deity discussed by Robert Graves in his exploration of Celtic goddesses.

Freed from external views of the feminine, the persona becomes the androgynous elfin essence of freedom, the Shakespearean Ariel from *The Tempest* (1611). That Ariel undergoes trials and then finds freedom, serving the magician Prospero for a period in order to gain final untrammeled liberation. At the same time, this liberation is a death to the old self, which dissolves like dew or disappears, flying like an arrow into the target, the red eye of the sun.

Robin Kornman

ARIOSTO

Author: Osip Mandelstam (1891-1938)
Type of poem: Lyric
First published: 1964, as "Ariost," in *Sobranie sochinenii*; English translation collected in *Selected Poems*, 1974

The Poem

"Ariosto" is one of many poems by Osip Mandelstam published posthumously. Written on May 4-6, 1933, during a difficult time for the poet (he was arrested only one year later by the Soviet authorities for writing a poem criticizing Joseph Stalin's cruelty), the poem expresses Mandelstam's long-standing interest in, and infatuation with, the Italian culture. The poem was written while Mandelstam was in the Crimea, in the south of Russia, where he also wrote an essay about another Italian poet, "Conversation with Dante." There are two variants of "Ariosto," but the one discussed here is considered to be more authentic. According to Nadezhda Mandelstam, his widow, his poems were confiscated upon his arrest, and he wrote the second version during his house confinement in Voronezh in 1934; the original version was found later.

Mandelstam opens the poem with the name of Ludovico Ariosto (1474-1533), thus establishing at the outset the focal point of the poem. Mandelstam considers Ariosto to be one of Italy's most delightful and wisest poets, but lately Ariosto "has a frog in his throat" and "amuses himself with the names of fish," spilling "nonsense into the seas." This mixture of profound respect and lighthearted familiarity is typical of Mandelstam's treatment of great poets he admired. In his poetry, Ariosto is playing like a musician "with ten cymbals," lost somewhat in "the maze of chivalric scandals"—a reference to the problems he faced as a diplomat at the Italian courts of his time.

In the third stanza, Mandelstam likens Ariosto to the greatest Russian poet, Alexander Pushkin, calling him "a Pushkin in the language of cicadas," who combines "Mediterranean haughtiness" with the Russian's melancholy. Ariosto plays wanton tricks with his hero Orlando in *Orlando furioso* (1516, 1521, 1532; English translation, 1591), undergoing his own metamorphosis in the process. His playfulness is further exemplified by his command to the sea, "roar but don't think!" and to the maiden on the rock, "lie there without bedclothes!" which are taken directly from the tenth song of *Orlando furioso* and indirectly from Pushkin. Indeed, Mandelstam claims, humankind has not had enough of such powerful voices, who can tell wonderful stories again and again that make one's blood run quicker and cause one's ears to roar—an allusion to an artist's power to inspire and make life more vibrant. Mandelstam calls Ariosto's native city, Ferrara, a "lizard city with a crust for a heart, and no soul," voicing his disdain for the intrigues, cloak-and-dagger atmosphere, and disregard for the well-being of the common person. He calls on Ferrara to produce more men like Ariosto and fewer men like the ruthless rulers and courtiers with whom Ariosto had to contend.

In the next stanza, Mandelstam turns to the present, saying that it is cold in Europe and dark in Italy. Both adjectives, cold and dark, are the opposites of what the south and Italy, indeed all Europe, should stand for. He bemoans the fact that raw power has taken over in the 1930's. Despite all of this, Ariosto continues to improve on his act, looking blissfully on the "lamb on the hill" (peasant in the field), at a "monk on his donkey" (Ariosto himself had a desire at one time to become a monk), and at "Duke's men-at-arms" carrying out the silly orders of their masters, drunk and bloated with drink and food, while the common people are living in blight (a baby "dozing under a net of flies"). Mandelstam continues to admire Ariosto in the eighth stanza. He loves "his desperate leisure,/ his babble, the salt and sugar of his words,/ the sounds happily conspiring in twos and threes." Ariosto's works are beautiful as they are and should be accepted as such rather than be subjected to detailed analysis. By asking, "Why should I want to split the pearl?" Mandelstam leaves well enough alone, as if afraid to succumb to the lure of Italian loquaciousness and thereby betray his own language.

In the last stanza, Mandelstam wishes to unite Ariosto's azure sea and the Black Sea "into one wide fraternal blue." He assures Ariosto that this difficult age will eventually pass. The line "We too know it well" resembles a formulaic phrase from a Russian fairy tale as well as from Pushkin's *Ruslan i Lyudmila* (1820; English translation, 1936). By using the pronoun "we," Mandelstam acknowledges that the Russians have feasted on the poetry of their Italian colleagues, assuring the great Italian poet of their fraternal bond because they have drunk wine from the same source—the shores of the Mediterranean.

Forms and Devices

"Ariosto" consists of nine quatrains of twelve-syllabic lines regularly rhymed *abba*. It is replete with images and metaphors. Speaking of Ariosto's poetry, the poet mentions the frog in Ariosto's throat, his preoccupation with the names of the fish, and his raining of nonsense into the seas as a sign of diminution of his poetic power, despite calling him a "musician with ten cymbals." While averring that his greatest love in Italian culture is Dante, while Ariosto and Torquato Tasso, for example, are not without reproach, Mandelstam cannot deny the mellifluousness of Ariosto's language as being "the language of cicadas." He points out again the musicality of Ariosto's language, referring to it as "the salt and sugar of his words" and to its sounds as "happily conspiring in twos and threes," clearly having in mind the highly rhythmical and uncomplicated interchange of vowels and consonants that lend the Italian language its sonorous quality.

Mandelstam reserves his harshest criticism for the circumstances of Ariosto's surrounding, calling Ferrara a "lizard city" teeming with crawling, slimy creatures, its collective heart encrusted and cold, without a soul. With the image "swallowing a barber's hand," however, Mandelstam refers to Ferrara, Peter the Great (who was in the habit of shaving beards, pulling teeth, and chopping heads off of his recalcitrant subjects), and, in a roundabout way, Joseph Stalin. These references are contrasted by peaceful and charming figures, a lamb on the hill and a monk on a donkey, from Ariosto's artistic milieu.

Other striking images are "the maze of chivalric scandals," which underscores the underground atmosphere of the authorities in Ariosto's surroundings; "the maiden on the rock," which is borrowed from both Ariosto and Pushkin's poem "Storm," thus binding the two poets; the cold of Europe and darkness of Italy as befitting the climate in Europe of the 1930's; and the soldiers of Ariosto's rulers, "silly with wine and the plague and garlic," as creatures unworthy of a high artist such as Ariosto.

Themes and Meanings

The basic theme of the poem is encapsulated in Mandelstam's repeated declaration, through the invocation of Ariosto, of his physical and spiritual longing for Italy and Europe. He visited Italy only twice in his life, but he always manifested a kinship with this country and its culture. However, it is not so much the love for Italy's beauty and pleasant climate, although that too is often acknowledged, as it is the love for its spirit as a focal point of an entire culture to which Mandelstam subscribes. The fact that Italy lies in the south of Europe enhances Mandelstam's admiration for it, for he always had a soft spot in his heart for southern regions, be it in Russia or in Europe. Mandelstam goes a step further and declares his love for the entire Mediterranean, calling it a "holy land" and thinking of it as the cradle of Western civilization.

That Mandelstam thought highly of this civilization at its peak can best be seen when he contrasts it with the "cold" and "darkness" of the present, in both Italy and the poet's own land. Yet, noblesse of the spirit and art will survive and triumph over the brute force of evil and darkness, as he assures Ariosto at the end of the poem. At the same time, Mandelstam declares a fraternity of poets ("we've drunk mead on its [Mediterranean] shores") by uniting Ariosto's "azure and our Black Sea together" as a manifestation of a universal brotherhood of spirit and art.

Another theme, appearing in many of Mandelstam's poems in the last decade of his life, is the spirit of the time and a poet's role and fate within it. He finds a parallel between Ariosto's Ferrara and his own Russia in that they are both in the throes of tyranny. In his troubles with the Soviet regime, Mandelstam finds kinship with Ariosto and his time. Even when he is critical of Ariosto's disregard for the plight of his fellow citizens and his avoidance of the wrath of the powers-that-be, Mandelstam only wishes he himself could do the same. By blaming the dictatorial conditions in Ferrara for the diminution of Ariosto's art, Mandelstam alludes to similar phenomena in his own land. Ariosto was frequently at loggerheads with the authorities but managed to survive and even to flourish—something Mandelstam wished to do but of which he was incapable. By extolling the achievements of Ariosto under such circumstances, he is expressing his faith in the survival of poets and the arts.

Vasa D. Mihailovich

THE ARMADILLO

Author: Elizabeth Bishop (1911-1979)
Type of poem: Lyric
First published: 1965, in *Questions of Travel*

The Poem

Elizabeth Bishop's "The Armadillo" consists of ten rhymed quatrains in which the speaker describes the fire balloons that some devout persons release at night to celebrate a local saint, presumably in Brazil. The poem begins by describing the balloons; they are illegal, probably because they are dangerous, but they are also seductively beautiful as they rise into the night sky. Indeed, they often resemble planets as they float into the distance on air currents. The pulse of their emitted light resembles a heart's beating. Nevertheless, the speaker asserts, they can become "suddenly . . . dangerous" if the currents lead them in the wrong direction, and the second half of the poem describes the dangers the balloons can cause.

The speaker describes what happens when a fire balloon crashes into a cliff behind the house and spatters fire like an egg down the cliff side, disrupting the animal life there. The pair of owls which roost in the cliff fly away shrieking, their bodies colored by the flames. Next an armadillo scuttles off, and at last a baby rabbit emerges, looking soft and defenseless and almost as if it has been ignited.

Concrete imagery and a sense of immediacy are common characteristics of Bishop's poetry; they suggest that she herself experienced the things she describes. The result of this groundedness is to give an authenticity to the significance Bishop attaches to her subjects. It also allows her to indicate that significance obliquely instead of relying on direct editorial statement. In her well-known poem "The Fish," Bishop spends almost all the poem offering details that document the heroic weight carried by the old fish that the speaker has caught, so that at the poem's end the reader knows why the speaker can claim that victory fills the rowboat and why the speaker releases the fish although he or she never explains these things directly.

Similarly in "The Armadillo," Bishop devotes most of the poem to describing first the fire balloons, then the results of balloon accidents, and last the creatures routed by the falling fire. Only in the last quatrain does she directly tie together the beauty and terror the balloons inspire and the contrast between their dangerous appeal and the disrupted lives of creatures who cannot possibly understand the balloons' significance. The "dreamlike mimicry" of the balloons, she says, is "too pretty," leading the reader to consider what exactly the balloons mimic. Are they suggestive of candles lit in the saint's honor, or do they evoke martyrdom, perhaps the suffering of the saint being honored or of the innocent animals whose lives are suddenly threatened by fire? In "The Fish," the language allows the reader to conclude that the victory that fills the boat may belong either to the fish or to the speaker, or, more likely, to both. Here too, the picture of the fire in the night sky is linked to beauty, sentimentality ("too pretty"), and terror.

Forms and Devices

Much of Bishop's work demonstrates her fondness for form, but although she often uses forms she rarely uses them strictly. She does not favor precise metrical patterns (such as highly regular iambic pentameter), and her rhyme is often muted. In "The Armadillo," stanzas are composed of four lines each, most of them rhyming *abcb*. Rarely, the first and third lines use an off-rhyme (*wind/between, saint/light*). The lines are roughly iambic tetrameter but there are several exceptions, particularly in the form of short lines of five or six syllables. The stanzas that describe the armadillo and rabbit have several lines of more than eight syllables. Moreover, at several key points in the poem Bishop works directly against the subtle iambic pattern of unstressed syllable followed by stressed. The description of the armadillo—"rose-flecked, head down, tail down"—illustrates that variation, as does the description of the rabbit: "So soft!— a handful of intangible ash."

Typical of Bishop, the persona speaks as an observer of the events that form the poem's substance, beginning with the authoritative "this is the time of year" in which one may see the fire balloons, commenting on their illegality and their appearance in the sky, and moving at last from these general observations to the more specific recording of the events that occurred on the previous night. Only in the last stanza (significantly, it is italicized) does the poem move from what seems to be specific recollections to a commentary on their meaning.

Much of Bishop's language describing the balloons moves carefully between objective detail and language that suggests the details' metaphoric significance. The balloons seem to be impermanent; they are "frail" but "illegal"; the light they contain is intermittent and "comes and goes, like hearts," as if hearts themselves are not to be trusted to carry on their beat. Aloft in the night sky, the balloons resemble planets; Bishop names Mars (the Roman god of war) and Venus (the Roman goddess of love). The planet that Bishop calls "the pale green one" seems to be Jupiter, the largest of the planets, named for Jove, the head of all the Roman gods. The three planets are suggestive of the balloons' ambiguous meanings of love, violence, and power. In any event, when all is well, the balloons seem to steer into the Southern Cross, the guiding constellation in the Southern Hemisphere; from that course they are "steadily forsaking us."

The balloons become dangerous only when downdrafts cause them to crash. Bishop's description of one crash leads to the second simile in the poem—the balloon "spattered like an egg of fire" against a cliff; a stream of flame ran down the cliff, burning an owl's nest and frightening an armadillo and a baby rabbit. Bishop's imagery for these animals suggests their anguish in the blaze. The owls are "stained bright pink underneath" from the color of the flames below, and they shriek as they fly away. The armadillo, too, has taken on rose colored flecks, either of actual fire coals or of their color; it scuttles away in a defensive, head-down posture. The baby rabbit's soft fur seems to be "a handful of intangible ash," and the rabbit has "fixed, ignited eyes" either from its terror or from its actually being burned. The fiery language attached to each of these victims leaves their state ambiguous. Have they actually been burned, or are they merely reflecting the fire's glare?

Themes and Meanings

Two images dominate "The Armadillo": the fire balloons and animals that have been brushed by the fire. Together they create a tension that is brought into harmony, if not exactly resolved, in the last quatrain. Despite the beauty of the balloons, in the end the speaker calls them (or perhaps her description of them) "too pretty" and their mimicry "dreamlike" as if rejecting the poem's initial images. Instead the poem concludes with references to the owls' "piercing cry," the rabbit's panic, and the armadillo itself, weak in its armor, like a "weak mailed fist/ clenched ignorant against the sky!" The impulse to romanticize the picture is revealed in its falsity in the face of the animals' fright.

The rejection of romantic gloss in favor of the hard data of concrete reality is a common theme in Bishop's work, as one can see in "The Fish" or "First Death in Nova Scotia." It is not surprising that Bishop has chosen the armadillo as the title image for the poem. Unlike the innately appealing baby rabbit or the owl with its freight of myth (it is traditionally an emblem of wisdom connected with the goddess Athena), the armadillo is simply an ungainly animal in fallible armor, neither wise nor cuddly. As a "mailed fist" it is nevertheless weak and ignorant in the face of the sky that has so unexpectedly attacked it.

The last quatrain invites the reader to reconsider the opening images of the poem. The very saint in whose devotion the balloons are launched seems remote; "still honored in these parts" suggests that the saint is no longer honored in most places. Nor do the balloons, frail chambers that "flare and falter, wobble and toss" offer any clear honor to the saint as they forsake us. Instead they are linked to unsteady hearts and to planets associated not only with love but also with warfare and the rather unsaintly power of Jove. Better, the poem suggests, to fix one's attention on the owl, the rabbit, and the armadillo, to reject the dreamlike mimicry and see them as they flee the burning cliff, soft now like ashes, with eyes ignited like coals.

Ann D. Garbett

ARMS AND THE BOY

Author: Wilfred Owen (1893-1918)
Type of poem: Lyric
First published: 1920, in *Poems by Wilfred Owen*

The Poem

The poetry of Wilfred Owen must be discussed in its historical context. Owen was one of a generation of British poets of World War I, an educated class of soldier-poets whose poetry can be divided into two distinct periods. The first period is roughly from 1914 to the Battle of the Somme in 1916. In this period, the poetic voice of the generation was generally patriotic and heroic. However, as the war dragged on, the carnage and suffering seemed ceaseless and pointless, since the front lines changed by only a few miles from year to year. The second period of British war poetry is the period to which Owen's important work belongs.

While the officer-poets were becoming deeply disillusioned by the war, a gap was growing between the men fighting and the civilians at home in Britain: Soldiers home on leave found it impossible for their families to understand the realities of trench warfare. Owen wrote, in a preface to a volume of poems planned but not published in his lifetime, "My subject is War, and the pity of War. The Poetry is in the pity." Owen's purpose in "Arms and the Boy" is to communicate some of his view of the "pity of War" to British civilians.

"Arms and the Boy" is a twelve-line meditation on the unnaturalness of weapons. In the first two stanzas, the poet presents a method of training a young boy to know, use, and appreciate a bayonet blade, bullets, and a cartridge. The instructions are heavy with irony. The poem begins: "Let the boy try along this bayonet-blade/ How cold steel is." The first four lines describe, in harsh detail, the "madman's flash" of that blade, "Blue with all malice."

The second four lines speak of the "blind, blunt bullet-heads" and the sharp "cartridges of fine zinc teeth." It is clear that the boy is not familiar with these weapons; this is a first acquaintance with the implements of death. While the first stanza emphasizes the cold malice of the blade, the second stanza moves on to the "sharpness of grief and death."

In the final four lines, the poet makes his point. This child's teeth "seem for laughing round an apple." He hides no claws, nor talons, nor antlers for fighting. God has not made this boy for war, but he will be carefully taught and groomed in the implements of death by the elder generation that Owen condemns as responsible for the war.

In this poem Owen has written of a general situation rather than a specific war. He creates a picture that any English citizen at home can imagine, of boys playing soldier. This is Owen's voice in 1918, saying that war is cruel and that its greatest cruelty is in the destruction of youth and beauty. In the context of 1918 and a generation of young men killed in the trenches, this innocent youth is doomed. The universality of the statement does not weaken its bitterness, for the boy and the "blind, blunt" bullets are not mere generalities after all.

Forms and Devices

Owen was not merely a poet of protest. He was also a poet of technical accomplishment, originality, and assurance. He was greatly influenced by classical models, particularly the nineteenth century British poets John Keats and Alfred, Lord Tennyson. He was accomplished in the art and beauty of the form and language of poetry.

The title of the poem is literary, calling to mind Bernard Shaw's *Arms and the Man* (1894), as well as the opening of Vergil's *Aeneid* (30-19 B.C.E.): "Of arms I sing, and of the man." Such is Owen's control of his material, that by the simple contrast of the heroic man of Vergil's Greek epic with the British schoolboy of his poem, he manages to set a tone of ironic contrast at once.

"Arms and the Boy" is similar in feeling to an elegy, a meditative poem of lamentation for the dead. By the use of this classic form, he is able to indicate a complex progression of feeling, from protest against the futile carnage of the war, to anger at the waste of young life, to a turning inward toward sadness and grief. He mourns an entire generation of innocent youth.

Throughout the poem, Owen uses sensuous, beautiful language and the languid *l* sounds in "Let," "Lend," and "blind, blunt bullet-heads" to heighten the contrast with his harsh message, the cold ugliness of his subject: guns, bullets, implements of carnage, suffering, and death. Thus the rich, musical language of the poem is carefully chosen for its dissonance. The sensuous *l* contrasts with the alliteration of the cold, hard *c* and *k* of the "cold steel," which is "keen with hunger or blood," and the "cartridges of fine zinc." Owen's skill as a poet is evident not only in this use of alliteration but also in his rhyme scheme. He uses inexact or slant rhymes: blade/blood, flash/flesh, heads/lads, teeth/death, apple/supple, heels/curls.

Owen makes no attempt to conceal his homosexual orientation. The homoerotic elements in the poem reflect an intermingling of feelings. Owen presents the relationship of war to the young soldier in the terms of sexual experimentation: "long to nuzzle" and "try" and "stroke" and "famishing for flesh." His imagery is strongly physical, with emphasis on parts of the body: teeth, fingers, heels, and hair. This language reflects the deep feelings that developed between the fighting men and the young officers in the heightened atmosphere of imminent death found in the trenches.

The camaraderie of the trenches is intensified into a love that is, in Owen's case, homosexual but also expresses his deep sorrow at the waste of tender young lives. Even in the works of heterosexual poets of 1918, the image of a beautiful young man dying in the arms of fellow soldiers aroused feelings of love. This homoerotic motif in Great War writings is an expression of a very literary war, reflecting the classical education of the generation, raised on the Greek and Latin of the *Iliad* and the *Aeneid*, and the love of heroes like Achilles and Patroclus.

Themes and Meanings

"Arms and the Boy" is a poem written for a specific purpose: to convey a message about the horror of World War I, from the experience of a soldier who has witnessed the catastrophe of trench warfare to a public composed of patriotic civilians at home in Britain. The poem is an expression of the alienation between the separate worlds. The poet sees the life at home as make-believe, like boys playing soldier, while the world of bombardment and slaughter, the world of malice and madmen, is the real world for the duration of the war. The reality for an entire generation of young men was that they were not likely to survive the horror of the "blind, blunt bullet-heads."

Owen was strongly moved by the waste of young life, of children whose laughter and play would be cut off by bullets which would "nuzzle in the hearts of lads." His poem is a protest against the exploitation of the younger generation for a political purpose that he sees as increasingly futile. By deliberately using images of childhood and the school yard, of "the boy" and "lads" playing at soldiers, he conveys the theme that war and weapons must be taught, that they are not natural to the innocent young of the species but are a tool of the older generation of government and military decision makers. This is one of the meanings Owen seeks to reveal to the civilian population.

There is, however, a sense of the inevitableness of death for these boys in the poem. They are no match for the bullets and cartridges, and the final end is sure to be "grief and death." There is a sense of endurance, an acceptance that there is no fate but violent death, a state that Owen reached only after a period of inward contemplation during his own convalescence in the hospital. He would go back to join the boys at the front, in a war that civilians could never understand and poets could never explain. Owen died in action only a few days before the armistice. He could not save the innocent child, the boy with supple fingers and thick curls. He could not save himself. All that the true war poet could do was warn the next generation.

"Arms and the Boy," for all its graphic description of malicious weaponry, has a musing quality. While Owen's aim is to communicate the horror, futility, and unnatural state of war to civilians and future generations, the poem is his personal meditation on the "pity of War." He reveals his own political protest, his homosexual love for the beauty of young men, and his mastery of classical poetic devices.

Susan Butterworth

THE ARREST OF OSCAR WILDE
AT THE CADOGAN HOTEL

Author: John Betjeman (1906-1984)
Type of poem: Ballad
First published: 1937, in *Continual Dew: A Little Book of Bourgeois Verse*

The Poem

"The Arrest of Oscar Wilde at the Cadogan Hotel" is a mock ballad of nine quatrains. As the title indicates, the narrative recounts the arrest of the Irish writer and aesthete Oscar Wilde on April 6, 1895, on various charges of indecency. Wilde was convicted and jailed for two years.

John Betjeman had developed an early interest in Wilde, his lifestyle, and his theories of art. At Marlborough school, as a teenager, Betjeman had read of the Wildean theme that there can be no morality in art. Wilde, as spokesman for the aesthetic school (he was the so-called apostle of beauty), voiced views compatible with those of Betjeman, who flaunted his own dilettantism and anti-athletics position while at the University of Oxford.

The circumstances of Wilde's arrest were, for the most part, as Betjeman depicts them in the poem. Betjeman's account echoes particulars from the news accounts of the event. The first two stanzas describe Wilde as he awaits the pending arrest, although he has been forewarned by friends, who had urged him to flee the country. Here at the Cadogan, a place of highest respectability in Sloane Street, Wilde faces the ignominy of arrest, sipping Rhine wine and gazing through lace curtains at the "London skies."

The next four stanzas, reproducing Wilde's dialogue, reveal his immediate needs and concerns and, more important, his mental state. He requests additional wine from his close friend Robert Ross, pleads with Robbie for some understanding of the situation, and acknowledges Robbie's gift of the latest issue of *The Yellow Book*, the periodical of the aesthetic movement.

Furthermore, he voices his displeasure with what he perceives to be cretinlike service by the hotel personnel. He laments that neither of two lambskin coats is here, and orders that his leather suitcase be brought around later. In the seventh stanza, a thumping at the door, accompanied by a murmuring of voices, causes Wilde to complain of such din. Two plainclothes policemen enter. In the next quatrain, one of the policemen asks Wilde to accompany them quietly as they leave the Cadogan for the police station. The poem closes as Wilde rises, puts down *The Yellow Book*, staggers to the staircase, and is helped to the horse-drawn cab outside. He is described as being "terrible-eyed."

Forms and Devices

Typical of the ballad form, much of the action is developed through dialogue. Four stanzas plus one additional line (in parentheses) re-create Wilde's conversation. One stanza reproduces the policeman's statement of arrest—rendered in a dialect clearly less cultured than Wilde's. The speech of each—in content and manner—is antithetical to that of the other. Wilde exudes social status; the policeman acknowledges and bends to that status as he asks Wilde "tew leave with us quoietly/ For this *is* the Cadogan Hotel."

The effect is reminiscent of Robert Browning's dialectics. Wilde's dialogue reveals a "soul in action" that is at least suggestive of those in Browning's dramatic monologues. Betjeman's poem also calls to mind the sixteenth century broadside ballads. Betjeman demonstrates here, as in so many of his poems, his fascination with particulars—details that capture the essence of a person or the atmosphere of a place. Betjeman's poem, in one sense, is a "period" piece—with its fastidious cataloging of turn-of-the-century details: hock and seltzer, Nottingham lace, *The Yellow Book*, the astrakhan coat, the morocco portmanteau, and a hansom.

Most of these period phrases are voiced by Wilde, however, so the effect may be more to characterize Wilde and his mind-set than to create a period piece. The same holds for the Wildean epigram in the fourth stanza: "Approval of what is approved of/ Is as false as a well-kept vow." Then, too, the subtitle of the collection in which this poem first appeared is "A Little Book of Bourgeois Verse." Its typography was highly stylized, and it had an ornate cover with imitation gilt-clasps.

Two striking details—especially in their stark contrast—are those describing Wilde's eyes. In the opening stanza, Wilde gazes "Through the Nottingham lace of the curtains/ Or was it his bees-winged eyes?" "Bees-winged" refers to the gauzy film that forms on old wine. It is as if his vision is hindered by his consumption of hock and seltzer, or perhaps his awareness is blurred by (or filtered through) aesthetics-tempered lenses. In the closing stanza, as Wilde staggers to the hansom cab, assisted by others, he is described as "terrible-eyed." Is he beginning to see through the haze of his temporal mind-set? Perhaps the description is an implicit answer to the question Wilde addressed to his friend Robert Ross in the third stanza: "Is this the end or beginning?/ How can I understand?"

Betjeman, who was interested in the typography of both the landscape and printing, employs a striking typographical design to heighten the dramatic and abrupt arrival of the police. Wilde's response to the pounding at the door is set in parentheses: "('Oh why must they make such a din?')." The intrusion of the police is boldly stated: "And Two Plain Clothes POLICEMEN came in." In its excess the technique is farcical.

Themes and Meanings

With its mixture of melodrama, farce, and tragedy, the poem projects an ambiguity that implies a moral neutrality. On the one hand, the piece is pure artistic self-indulgence—the work of a clever craftsman parading that cleverness. On the other hand, the poem evokes a sense of poignancy with its carefully crafted realistic detail and vivid depiction of what in all likelihood happened when Wilde was arrested.

That same kind of ambiguity prevails in terms of Betjeman's own attitudes about the aesthetic movement of which Wilde was so central a part. Betjeman wrote the poem while he was at Oxford, where he deliberately and openly cultivated a public profile laden with aestheticism. The poem, however, seems to run counter to that image. Much of his portrait of Wilde in the ballad is ironically negative—basically comic with hints of the absurd. In addition, the portrayals of both Wilde and the policeman border on the stereotypical.

The duality in Betjeman's recounting of Wilde's arrest is reflective of the emotional state of the central figure in the ballad. Warned of the pending arrest, Wilde seems Hamlet-like, torn between flight and standing his ground—fortified both by aesthetic precepts and, maybe, a vision of himself making one more, perhaps final, grand gesture befitting the "apostle of beauty."

The poem in its dialectical playoff between Wilde and the policeman matches two forces: the voice of individuality, even eccentricity, against the voice of civil authority—communal conformity. In another sense, it is the clash of art and the law, the artist and society. Betjeman's use of the palms image in the closing stanza makes a nod toward this point. As Wilde leaves the Cadogan Hotel, he brushes "past the palms on the staircase." The palms are emblematic of the world Wilde is leaving—the artist is being extracted from his aesthetic domain—assisted, indeed, marshalled from it on the arm of societal order.

For all of its farcical, absurd surface, the poem's undercurrent carries within it something hauntingly autobiographical. Betjeman was born into a wealthy family headed by a strong-willed father who wanted his son, an only child, to follow in his footsteps. Betjeman, who heard the call of the muse early in his life, struggled long and determinedly to practice his vocation against the paternally voiced pressures of the commercial world. Among Betjeman's best poems are those defending individuality against the crushing power of conformity.

Glenn Grever

ARS POETICA

Author: Archibald MacLeish (1892-1982)
Type of poem: Lyric
First published: 1926, in *Streets in the Moon*

The Poem

"Ars Poetica" is a short poem in free verse, its twenty-four lines divided into three stanzas of four couplets each. The Latin title may be translated as "art of poetry," "art of poetics," or "poetic art." Using the poetic form, the author attempts to portray his concept of the "art of poetry." For this reason, "Ars Poetica" is often used as an example of what (and how) a poem "should be."

The poem uses loosely rhymed couplets to project the author's powerful images. A dash follows every third couplet, emphasizing the importance of the fourth couplet in summing up the stanza. In the beginning, MacLeish draws the reader in with three couplets that compare a poem to various physical objects and which seem perfect in both word and cadence. These similes appear to illustrate the author's belief that a poem must be silent in its clarity, transcending words themselves. In the final couplet of the first stanza, he repeats the phrase "A poem should be." While the first six lines describe objects in repose, the last couplet both ties together and climaxes the building images by sending the reader upward in the rush of birds taking to the sky.

In the second stanza, the poem becomes more specific, using the stark image of branches silhouetted against a moon to denote the eternal quality of a poem. MacLeish repeats the first couplet in the last two lines: "A poem should be motionless in time/ As the moon climbs." Though the juxtaposition of a climbing moon with the assertion of motionlessness seems contradictory, the middle two couplets explain his thinking. The second couplet likens the hypothetical poem to the twigs that, once impressed on the mind in their vision of black "night-entangled trees" against the bright moon, remain fixed there as the moon moves. In the third couplet MacLeish becomes even more specific, asking the reader to recall the memories brought to mind by such an image and to compare them to a poem that is as firmly anchored in time as those memories.

The poem's third stanza departs from the previous two in its tone as MacLeish becomes bolder in his assertion of what a poem "should be." In the middle two couplets, he takes the reader on a journey through all of humankind's strife and love with only a few strokes of his metaphorical pen. Yet in his first and last couplets, he abandons image and states precisely his feelings about the art of poetry. The final two lines, "A poem should not mean/ But be," are brief and to the point, having an almost Zenlike quality to them. The words bring the reader to a place of simple rest after an emotive passage through the more esoteric images of the poem. These last two lines of "Ars Poetica" are famous and are often quoted in books on poetry.

Forms and Devices

In a sense, "Ars Poetica" must be in its entirety a metaphor for poetry itself; when it is pulled apart piece by piece, one can see the clever construction that pushes the reader along to an inevitable conclusion. As MacLeish wrote in his *Poetry and Experience* (1960), "If the fragments of experience are in truth parts of a whole, and if the relation of the parts to each other and thus to the whole can in truth be *seen, sensed, felt* in the fragments themselves, then there is meaning in that seeing, in that sensing, in that feeling—extraordinary meaning."

The best poetry needs only a few words to engage readers' imaginations and to make them participants in the poem's creation. In "Ars Poetica" MacLeish employs similes to evoke the reader's senses. The couplet "A poem should be palpable and mute/ As a globed fruit" allows the reader to imagine the fruit—perhaps an apple lying on a bench in the late afternoon sun. It is beautiful yet silent. The next two lines employ the sense of touch. It is easy to conjure up the feeling of rubbing a metal medallion, noting its worn ridges and wondering about its history. Again, in the third couplet, the reader relates to the person suggested by "the sleeve-worn stone." Someone (or perhaps generations of people) has leaned for long hours on the window ledge, waiting, perhaps hoping for a lover or watching anxiously for a child. With similes such as this, the reader is able to fill in the spaces, to embroider the words with his or her own experiences, thus creating a poem unique with each reading.

Note, too, the careful placing of words to make rolling, alliterative sounds: "palpable," "mute," "globed," "fruit." In the second couplet, the words "dumb," "old," "medallions," and "thumb" carry the reader along, as do the phrases in the third couplet. In the second stanza, the similes employ repetitive sounds. The first and last couplets seem almost to murmur with their preponderance of soft words using the letter *m*. In the second couplet, the line "Twig by twig the night-entangled trees" uses the harsher *t* sound to portray a certain amount of conflict.

In the last stanza metaphor takes center stage. An empty doorway and a maple leaf symbolize "all the history of grief." More obscure, perhaps, is the line "The leaning grasses and two lights above the sea," denoting love. Again, the reader must fill in his or her own experience. As Robert Frost said, "Poetry begins in metaphor, in trivial metaphors, and goes on to the profoundest thinking that we have."

Themes and Meanings

Although MacLeish was originally strongly influenced by Ezra Pound and T. S. Eliot, he later came to believe their scholastic poetry was not relevant to society. He turned to the poets of the past, such as Geoffrey Chaucer, William Shakespeare, and John Milton, as examples of how modern poets should make it their duty to participate in the social and political issues of the day.

"Ars Poetica," however, seems more clearly influenced by MacLeish's reverence for Chinese poetry. In *Poetry and Experience*, he quotes extensively from the third century Chinese poet Lu Chi and his famous poem, the *Wên Fu* (*Essay on Literature*). He asserts that "Far more than either Aristotle or Horace, Lu Chi speaks to our condition as contemporary men." In Chinese poetry, relationship is left to be inferred from the context, from the logic of the situation. MacLeish believed that the skill of the Chinese as imagemakers in paint, ink, or words has never been equaled.

In "Ars Poetica" he tries to capture an uncomplicated and direct path to the heart. Each of the couplets can almost be seen as a separate Chinese painting, drawn quickly and masterfully with the sparest of strokes. In particular, the quirky fourth couplet stands out. Its arrhythmic, atonal lines ("A poem should be wordless/ As the flight of birds") not only shows MacLeish's belief that a poem transcends the words of which it is composed but also includes the image of birds in flight, one that is seen repeatedly in Chinese art and poetry. It is a strong archetypal symbol for freedom, including freedom from the common words and meanings that bind all of humankind. The fourth couplet's break in rhythm from the previous three seems to echo this freedom.

In every word of this poem, MacLeish strives for such simplicity and passion, almost as if he were creating an extended haiku. Lu Chi writes "We poets struggle with Non-being to force it to yield Being;/ We knock upon silence for an answering music." MacLeish elaborates on this in the following passage: "The poet's labor is to struggle with the meaningless and silence of the world until he can force it to mean: until he can make the silence answer and the non-Being BE. It is a labor which undertakes to know the world not by exegesis or demonstration or proofs but directly, as a man knows apple in the mouth."

It is futile to spend too much time attempting to extract meaning from a poem which has as its basic tenet the idea that a poem does *not* mean, but simply exists. MacLeish maintains that the art of poetry is a magic one and that the poet is a magician who extracts substance from nonsubstance. He cites often Lu Chi's belief that the poet is one who "traps Heaven and Earth in the cage form."

Sue Storm

THE ARSENAL AT SPRINGFIELD

Author: Henry Wadsworth Longfellow (1807-1882)
Type of poem: Lyric
First published: 1844; collected in *The Belfry of Bruges and Other Poems*, 1845

The Poem

Henry Wadsworth Longfellow's "The Arsenal at Springfield" is a pacifistic, antiwar poem made up of twelve quatrains of loosely iambic pentameter lines, centering on the horrors of war and foreseeing an epoch in which peace replaces the need for arms. Longfellow uses the initial "organ-like" appearance of the "pipes" of the stashed arms as a basis to contrast the music of war to the music of peace throughout the rest of the poem.

The first and second stanzas briefly describe the munitions stored in the Massachusetts armory and point out how their present disuse contrasts with what happens during war when "the death-angel" commands weaponry, resulting in "cries of agony" and "loud lament." Stanzas 3-8 summarize the history and the misery of wars "through the ages" around the world—"the Saxon hammer" in Germany and England, the "roars" of "the Norseman's song" in Scandinavia, "the Tartar gong" in Asia, the Florentine and "his battle-bell" in Italy, and the "Aztec priests" beating "wild war-drums" in Mexico. Stanza 6 includes a striking summary of the devastation of war: the "sacked and burning" towns, the disregarded pleas "for mercy," and the cry of the hungry. Stanza 8 contrasts the "discordant noises" of war with "Nature's sweet and kindly voices," thus emphasizing the unnaturalness of fighting and killing, which conflict with the peaceful existence of the heavens.

The last four stanzas of the poem describe what a peaceful future might be like. Stanzas 9 and 10 note that if only human beings would use "half the power" and "half the wealth" devoted to arms "to redeem the human mind from error," the future could be free of slaughter and wars. In such a peaceful age, were any nation to start a war, it would be cursed. In stanzas 11 and 12, the poet continues to foresee such an age in biblical terms, with Christ saying "'Peace!'" and the hoped-for future described as being as "beautiful" as the heavenly "songs of the immortals" pictured in the Book of Revelation.

Forms and Devices

"The Arsenal at Springfield" is structured in three parts. The first part, stanzas 1 and 2, describes the stored arms at the arsenal in terms of "a huge organ," thus creating an image related to music that the rest of the poem develops, and it provides a generalized statement regarding the agony of war. Stanzas 3-8, the second part of the poem, briefly summarize the horrors of war throughout the world and the ages by citing races and geographical areas noted for legendary warlike behavior. The final part of the poem, stanzas 9-12, looks forward to a time of peace, when war will no longer be a blight on human experience.

In order to emphasize the contrast between the music of war and the music of peace, Longfellow employs aural images throughout the poem, building on the idea of the organ from the first stanza. In stanza 2, the "death-angel" who "touches those swift keys" creates "wild and dreary" music and "awful symphonies." In stanzas 4 and 5, even the references to warlike races and geographical areas is relayed through discordant and loud sounds: a hammer, a gong, a "battle-bell," and war drums. The reader can imagine the sounds of actual fighting in stanzas 7 and 8: "The bursting shell, the gateway wrenched asunder,/ The rattling musketry, the clashing blade." These harsh sounds coming from "accursed instruments" contrast with "Nature's sweet and kindly voices" and "the celestial harmonies" of peace.

Stanzas 9-12 display images of peaceful music in a hoped-for future. In the eleventh stanza, as wars fade from human experience, Christ's voice is heard "with solemn, sweet vibrations." The poem ends with peace described in terms of the "beautiful . . . songs of the immortals" and their "holy melodies of love."

The poem features many metaphors and similes, the most important of which is that found in stanza 1, which forms the foundation of the poem. The arms stacked "From floor to ceiling" are said to be "Like a huge organ." In stanza 11, Christ's voice of peace is in a simile likened to a "bell." Finally, stanza 7 ends with a particularly well-chosen musical metaphor appropriate to organ stops, as Longfellow describes battle sounds as "The diapason of cannonade."

Longfellow's usual virtuosity at handling versification is evident here as well. Each quatrain contains lines that rhyme on the first and third lines as well as on the second and fourth lines, in an *abab* rhyme scheme. Yet Longfellow varies rhyme and the basic iambic pentameter lines effectively by adding an extra unaccented syllable at the end of the first and third lines of each stanza, thus creating a falling rhythm for the rhymes ("ceiling" with "pealing" in stanza 1, for example), resulting in the lines echoing a musical or lilting quality appropriate to the poem's musical images.

Longfellow also varies the metrical system in order to reinforce the meanings of particular lines. In two stanzas (11 and 12), he begins the first lines by reversing the iambic expectations with the use of trochaic feet. In stanza 11, the initial trochaic accentual movement of "Down the" nicely mirrors the falling direction of the meaning of the words. Similarly, the trochaic "Peace! and," which begins the first line of stanza 12, vividly highlights the poem's content and resolution, which emphasizes peace as an alternative to war.

Themes and Meanings

As is the case with most of Longfellow's poems, "The Arsenal at Springfield" is rather explicit in its meaning. This antiwar poem centers on a contrast between the ravages of war and a hoped-for tranquil future of peace. Longfellow was not typically a poet who spoke out about contemporary social or political issues. He did not, for example, become a highly vocal critic of slavery, even though he was a close friend of Charles Sumner, a leading abolitionist, and although he did write a few antislavery poems. Similarly, he did not address the Civil War at length in his poetry, although this national conflict was the most significant disruption of American experience during Longfellow's lifetime. He generally did not comment about the religious ferment of his times either.

"The Arsenal at Springfield" was written as a result of Longfellow's visit with his wife to the Springfield arsenal in 1843, soon after his second marriage. It was this new wife, the former Francis Appleton (his first wife had died some years earlier as a result of a miscarriage), who first noted the similarity of the way the arms were stored to the pipes of an organ. Yet Longfellow, true to his tendency to use history and literature, rather than contemporary issues, as sources for poems, does not comment in the poem on recent wars or disruptions. There is no mention of the Napoleonic conflicts in Europe and their aftermaths, nor reference to American conflicts for independence or with the Native Americans, subject matter of some of his other poetry. Instead, he relies on legendary specifics from more ancient history and literature to develop his antiwar stance: "the Saxon" from Germanic areas and England, the Scandinavian echos in "the Norseman's song," "the Tartar" from Asia, "the Florentine" from Italy, and the "Aztec priests" from Mexico.

It would be a mistake, however, to assume that Longfellow writes insincerely in "The Arsenal at Springfield." It is probably true that his second wife was more pacifistic than Longfellow. Still, throughout his life, Longfellow attempted to live without conflict in a peaceful and comfortable environment. Even his two best-known, long narrative poems, *Evangeline* (1847) and *The Song of Hiawatha* (1855), exhibit a desire for peace and order. Both certainly include references to the difficulties of war and life, but both move their central characters through such traumas in search of a better, more peaceful future. Evangeline, a part of the Acadian displacement from Nova Scotia as a result of the new British regime after being victorious in the French and Indian War (1754-1763), searches many years for her husband, from whom she was separated as a result of the relocation policies. This search for peace and fulfillment is resolved by poem's end.

Similarly, the Native American chief Hiawatha (c. 1525-c. 1575) in *The Song of Hiawatha* takes his people through trials and wars but eventually counsels them to work out a peaceful relationship with the encroaching white settlers and to learn "better" ways from them. In spite of the tragic deaths of both wives (Francis Appleton died in a home fire just prior to the Civil War), Longfellow seemingly never became enraged by life's difficulties but continued to search for the peace and comfortable security that he valued so highly in his own life. "The Arsenal at Springfield," although not a pacifistic poem linked to any contemporary events, does reveal one of Longfellow's central preoccupations throughout his life.

Delmer Davis

THE ART OF POETRY

Author: Charles Tomlinson (1927-   )
Type of poem: Meditation
First published: 1955, in *The Necklace*

The Poem

Formally, this short poem is free verse, divided into five uneven stanzas. On the surface it seems obscure, a mixture of statements and images without much connection. There is no identifiable speaker, even though there is a mention of "we." The poem begins, not with any statement of subject, but with an assertion that "the mind" "feels bruised."

This sentence mixing abstraction and image, "mind" and "bruised," is followed by an image of light making white holes through black "foliage," succeeded in turn by a line that is both abstraction and image: "Or mist hides everything that is not itself." If the poem seems obscure, however, it nevertheless has a precise meaning. All the assertions and images are Charles Tomlinson's way of talking about poetry, by demonstration rather than mere precept. Even the apparently vague "we" becomes, clearly, "we poets."

The alternation of abstraction and image in these first two lines echoes the structure of the rest of the poem, for the second and third stanzas are a series of statements (one should especially note the statement almost in the center that "Proportions/ Matter"), whereas the last two stanzas are almost purely visual imagery. Still, these images require the reader's mind, as well as the poet's mind, to work. In those last stanzas, "green twilight" has "violet borders," a seemingly meaningless image until one thinks of the actualities of colors as evening comes down. The last four lines, describing butterflies, emphasize their "yellow" and then the colors—"scarlet" and "bronze"—of the flowers they are on. The poem is concerned with the effect of a process as well as with presenting static images.

The title of the poem, "The Art of Poetry," announces its subject matter and, by implication, offers an illustration of that subject matter. That title fits the poem into a long tradition of poems that take poetry itself as their subject, beginning with the *Ars poetica* (c. 17 B.C.E.; *The Art of Poetry*) of the Roman poet Horace and continuing through innumerable treatments by later poets, often using the same title. Tomlinson's poem, despite its brevity, is a development of, as well as a reaction to, Horace and all the followers of Horace.

Horace wrote a long, discursive poem on poetic techniques and subjects; basically, he argues that a poem should be a unity, allowing variety in order to avoid simple uniformity. Horace was much concerned with the practical effect of the poem, holding that a poem should either teach or delight. Indeed, he suggested that it should do both ("he who mixes the useful with the sweet gets every vote"); the poem's pleasing qualities exist, essentially, so that the reader will accept the teaching. At the same moment, he attempted to illustrate his own precepts on how to write a poem. Tomlinson, in a much shorter space and using a different technique, is doing the same.

Forms and Devices

Tomlinson has called himself a phenomenologist; what this means to his poetry is that the concrete actuality of the world is primary. Moreover, he was trained as a painter; one would therefore expect visual images in Tomlinson's poetry, and they are there. He was also greatly influenced by certain modernist American poets such as William Carlos Williams and Wallace Stevens.

Those poets were, in their own right, influenced by the Imagist movement of the first part of the twentieth century, a movement that insisted upon the primacy of the image, especially the visual image. Neither Williams nor Stevens ever held that the image existed only for itself, however; it suggests, always, an intellectual element. As with the late poems of Wallace Stevens, Tomlinson's poems are not static images: His images suggest motion: "the light makes white holes," and "butterflies/ [are] Nervously transferring themselves." Motion is the very sign of the modern world, the world with which the poet must deal.

Tomlinson's lines, as well as whole stanzas, are discursive, not merely imagistic. Even in the discursive statements, however, there is either an image or an implied image. If "the mind feels bruised," the mind itself is somehow material, capable of being hurt. The following two lines, very imagistic, are designed to show what "bruises" the mind—the things of this world that are excessive or unclear. The second and third stanzas of the poem are nearly pure statement, but the following two stanzas of visual imagery respond to those two just as the last two lines of the first stanza respond to its first line. They illustrate the abstraction, giving it body.

, The fact that the poem is in free verse is also an illustration of its abstractions; metrical poetry asserts uniformity, but not necessarily unity. Tomlinson's free verse suggests variety, but variety in a whole, emphasizing connections. The poem makes some use of run-on lines, even between the stanzas, as well as employing sentence parallelism, so that the ideas are connected by sound as well as by logic.

The poem's change from a mixture of statement and image through statements to images seems to reject any attempt at unity, but that change actually demonstrates unity. The images of twilight and of yellow butterflies moving from flower to flower are an illustration of how to see the world in order to find the proper proportions.

Moreover, in a traditional poem, the authority of an "I," the poet directly speaking about the craft on which he is an expert, clarifies and reinforces the teaching by identifying the source of the morality. The speaker of Tomlinson's poem, however, is simply an "authorial" voice; the voice speaks of "the mind" and then uses the impersonal "one" and finally "we," but even the "we" is a generalization for poets. Still, and paradoxically, that "authorial" voice, with its almost abstract tone, offers a kind of authority for the poem's implications simply because it is abstract and distant, not limited to some fallible individual.

Themes and Meanings

Every statement and every image in this poem functions directly with all the others. Together they are, despite the appearance to the contrary, a unity as well as a variety, a demonstration of the poem's "teaching" about what a poem should be. The poem is a demonstration that making poetry is a complex, difficult task.

It is not odd that poets should write about poetry itself. Of necessity, they must be concerned with the particulars of their craft. Yet poetry is not only a craft; it is also a way of knowing the world, so the poet is caught up in the questions of how one knows. Tomlinson has said that a poem "is a rite of passage through a terrain which, when we look back over it, has been flashed up into consciousness in a way we should scarcely have foreseen." That is, the poet gains an insight by writing a poem; the reader gains insight by reading the poem. The poem is not static, simply an object to be observed or contemplated with aesthetic delight. It does have an effect upon its audience; Tomlinson here agrees with Horace.

Yet the poem also orders the world around it. Tomlinson connects himself with the Romantic aesthetic, "with roots in Wordsworth and Ruskin," although his Romanticism is much modified by his modernism. The Romantics were concerned with the shaping power of the imagination. The image by itself is nothing "if it is merely that"; that attitude is at the very center of this poem. The poem is not only about what poetry should be, about its function in the world, but is also a poem about the process of creating poetry.

The "mind" that is "bruised" is the creative mind, acted upon by the external world, but also shaping the world. This "mind," in facing the actualities of the world, faces the problems of how to treat those actualities. The question, "how shall one say so," opening the second stanza, is really a question on what the creative process is—how, that is, the poet writes a poem that is true. The answer is given in the two-word sentence that connects the second and third stanzas: "Proportions/ Matter." The mind of the poet must find the balances in the world, but finding those balances is not easy— "It is difficult to get them right." The last two stanzas, then, seemingly pure images, are not only about nature; they also show what the creative mind can and must do with the realities.

L. L. Lee

THE ART OF POETRY

Author: Paul Verlaine (1844-1896)
Type of poem: Lyric
First published: 1882, as "Art poétique"; in *Jadis et naguère*, 1884; English translation collected in *Selected Poems*, 1948

The Poem

"The Art of Poetry" is divided into nine quatrains with a rhyme scheme of *abba* (the French *rime embrassée*), though the C. F. MacIntyre translation of the poem has a rhyme scheme of *abab*. Each verse has nine syllables. The title suggests an addition to the venerable tradition begun by the *Ars poetica* (c. 17 B.C.E.), in which the Latin poet Horace established rules for the writing of poetry. He inspired countless others, notably the English poets of the Renaissance and the seventeenth century Frenchman Nicolas Boileau, to write their own treatises. Paul Verlaine's title is intended both seriously (the poem is, in fact, a guide to poetic composition) and ironically (the poem incites aspiring poets to break the rules).

The poet addresses the reader not as a distant critic does his audience, but as a mentor would address his pupil: In line 5, the reader is addressed as *tu*—the familiar form of "you" in French. In the poem's first stanza, the speaker stresses the importance of music, which is best achieved through uneven rhythm. Verlaine has chosen his own unusual meter well, for the nine-syllable line is uneven or odd (in French, it is "impair," meaning any number not divisible by two), and this gives Verlaine's poetry a light, elusive quality.

In the poem's second stanza, the reader is exhorted to choose his or her words freely, unafraid of mistakes; nothing is better than that "tipsy song/ where the Undefined and Exact combine." "Tipsy" implies the visionary euphoria of unrestrained poetry.

The third stanza extends this vision into a description of the truly poetic, represented by a series of objects, all of which underscore what the fourth stanza calls the shades of colors—never the primary, well-defined colors themselves. Like the music of the poem's beginning, these images suggest a twilight world of free-floating poetry, unfettered by rules: a veiled eye, a bright day "quivering with light," a "confusion of stars."

Stanza 5 marks a return to prescription, with a warning against epigram, harsh wit and laughter, and "all that garlic of vulgar dishes." This gastronomical metaphor reflects the fact that the most refined *haute cuisine* uses bold spices sparingly, if at all. The analogy is clear: Heavy-handed moralizing or content destroys the poetic subtlety of form, that vague, "soluble" quality mentioned in the poem's third line.

Thus far, Verlaine has used all of the senses but the sense of touch, to which he turns with violence in the sixth stanza: "Take Eloquence and wring his neck!" Even rhyme should be kept under watchful eye. Perpetrator of innumerable wrongs, rhyme is the invention of a crazy person or a "deaf child," a worthless bauble.

The poem ends (in stanzas 8 and 9) with an exhortation that returns to the first line: The poet should create music first, and the verse should wing like an amorous soul in flight, or run carefree in the morning wind, smelling of wild herbs. The final verse of the poem is abruptly ironic: "and all the rest is literature." "Literature" is intended pejoratively, to mean stiflingly traditional or academically acceptable poetry, in sharp contrast to the unshackled verse championed by Verlaine.

Forms and Devices

Verlaine's poetry was part of a larger movement in French poetry that occurred in the mid to late nineteenth century. Simply stated, poets increasingly favored oblique, suggestive poetry over the direct expression of events or emotions through clear metaphorical imagery. Musicality became as important as any message the poet might wish to impart, and this emphasis on form became known as "art for art's sake." Thus in "The Art of Poetry," Verlaine concentrates on the poem as an object in itself, not a vessel of meaning imposed from without.

The poem's metaphors continually remind the reader that a poem should be experienced on its own terms. Verlaine suggests such experience with the five senses: hearing ("music," "rhythm," "song," "flute and horn," "laughter"); sight ("the veiled and lovely eye," "Color," "shade"); taste ("garlic of vulgar dishes"); smell ("smelling of wild mint, smelling of thyme"); and touch ("Take Eloquence and wring his neck," "hold Rhyme in check").

Verlaine's poem, however, is not a random series of images. He has his own messages to communicate, and perhaps the most important is his insistence that poetry be suggestive. To avoid being the slave or victim of something else ("Epigram's an assassin! Keep/ away from him, fierce Wit, and vicious/ laughter"), the poem must never state directly, but should instead inhabit an elusive and allusive twilight region; it must have the fleeting beauty of music, or a "veiled and lovely eye." Poetry must never be too clear or well-defined. Verlaine describes his ideal verse variously as "vague in the air and soluble," "quivering," "confusion," "nuance," "dream," "a quick-wing'd thing and light," "a soul in flight," "Happy-go-lucky," running "disheveled . . . where the dawn winds lure."

Although the poet bemoans the "wrongs of Rhyme," his own "The Art of Poetry" is extremely regular in structure. While somewhat rare, the nine-syllable line has a long history in France, and the quatrain is the most common stanza form in French poetry. It is important, then, to note that Verlaine does not condemn rhyme outright, but qualifies that it sounds "hollow and false when filed." Verlaine simply condemns a regularity that, at its worst, approaches the mechanical.

The choice of nine stanzas further underscores the poet's ambivalence toward poetic structure. On the one hand, it reinforces the unevenness of his own verses recommended in the poem's second line: "a rhythm uneven is best." On the other hand, a certain typically French symmetry is sustained by the nine stanzas of nine-syllable verses.

The poem's final words do not resolve its paradoxical treatment of poetic form, but instead seal it permanently in irony: "and all the rest is literature." "Literature" here means the great tradition of French poetry, and Verlaine no doubt had in mind the predictable cadences of the twelve-syllable Alexandrine that dominated this literature from the seventeenth century to his day.

Themes and Meanings

Verlaine contends that poetry should be musically suggestive, "vague and soluble," not something the reader can separate neatly into formal or thematic topics. As its title suggests, however, the poem remains a manifesto, and has practical advice for the apprentice poet. Yet this is advice that Verlaine himself does not always follow, and both his ambivalence and the poem's imagery reveal him to be a transitional figure in the history of nineteenth century French poetics.

The young Verlaine was associated with the Parnassiens (c. the 1860's), a group of poets who celebrated art for art's sake but who also insisted upon an impassive or objective precision they often compared to sculpture or painting. Clearly, in "The Art of Poetry," Verlaine has abandoned such rigor for the fluidity of the Symbolists (c. the 1880's), of whom he is considered both an influence and an early member. For him there is "nothing more dear than the tipsy song/ where the Undefined and Exact combine." The poem's first line—"De la musique avant toute chose" ("You must have music first of all")—can be translated "music above all," for music displaces the sculptural metaphor so dear to the Parnassiens, to whom Verlaine perhaps alludes in calling rhyme a "trinket for a dime,/ sounding hollow and false when filed." The poet repudiates *la lime* ("the file"), a favorite image of the Parnassiens.

Two poetic tendencies are criticized in "The Art of Poetry": form that is too regular, even monotonous; and a preponderance of content, or moral messages, at the expense of poetic qualities. Although form is given priority over meaning, by form Verlaine means a vague, uneven poetry that suggests "Never the color, always the Shade,/ always the nuance." Traditional form and content are both rejected, for together they create the classical French clarity in which verse is considered the mere garment of an idea that already exists. The clear preference in "The Art of Poetry" for music, shades, nuance, dream, flight, wind, and odor—as opposed to color, epigram, wit, eloquence, rhyme, and literature—indicates why the older Verlaine inspired a generation of French Symbolists to attempt an intangible, ineffable poetry of suggestion. With his consistent use of rhyme, line length, and stanza, however, the poet stops far short of poetic nihilism.

Finally, "The Art of Poetry" teaches a lesson—in spite of itself—that transcends French literary history. It both reveals the difficulty of simultaneously prescribing and following rules for poetic composition. For Verlaine, the task is particularly vexing, for his practical recommendations are all negative. Yet in his very failure to make specific suggestions, the poet has brilliantly made his point, that "Only by shade is the trothal made/ between flute and horn, of dream with dream!" With fleeting images of liberation expressed in traditional poetic structure, Verlaine creates his own "tipsy song/ where the Undefined and Exact combine."

Dean de la Motte

THE ARTILLERYMAN'S VISION

Author: Walt Whitman (1819-1892)
Type of poem: Narrative
First published: 1865, in *Drum-Taps*, 1865

The Poem

Walt Whitman's "The Artilleryman's Vision" records the nighttime apparitions of a Civil War veteran after the war has ended. Although "the wars are over long" and this former artilleryman is lying in the safety of his own bedroom, with wife and infant nearby, the memories of fierce battles remain with him, surfacing after midnight in a nightmarish mental picture. "There in the room as I wake from sleep this vision presses upon me," Whitman's speaker, the artilleryman, informs us.

The vision presents the commencement of a Civil War battle in which the artilleryman has participated. The details of the battle are still sharp and precise in this former soldier's mind. The artilleryman, whom Whitman does not identify as either a Union or a Confederate soldier, again sees the skirmishers "crawl cautiously ahead" and then hears the "*t-h-t! t-h-t!* of the rifle-balls." He catches sight of "the shells exploding leaving small white clouds," and he hears "the great shells shrieking as they pass" and the grapeshot "like the hum and whirr of wind through the trees." The "scenes at the batteries rise in detail," "the pride of the men in their pieces," the careful work of the chief gunner who aims his cannon. After the cannon fires, the artilleryman "lean[s] aside and look[s] eagerly off to note the effect."

The entire sweep of the battle appears to the insomniac artilleryman. He hears the cries of the infantry units as they charge into battle and sees a colonel brandishing his sword at the head of the column. He observes the "gaps cut by the enemy's volleys" as men fall wounded and dead on the field. He breathes "the suffocating smoke" that descends upon the battlefield, obscuring the action. After a momentary lull, the activity on the battlefield resumes with greater intensity, a "chaos louder than ever." Infantry units shift positions, and cavalry and artillery batteries move "hither and thither." The artilleryman again experiences the "Grime, heat, rush" of battle as aides-de-camp gallop by amid the "patter of small arms, the warning *s-s-t* of the rifles."

Though this nighttime battle vision seems troubling, the artilleryman reveals that war still holds for him some perverse appeal. This veteran confesses that the sound of the cannons is now "rousing even in dreams a devilish exultation and all the old mad joy in the depths of [his] soul." In this battle in his imagination, Whitman's artilleryman tries to suppress some of the more frightening aspects of war: "The falling, dying, I heed not, the wounded dripping and red I heed not, some to the rear are hobbling." Hence, this war veteran holds in his memory both the horrors of battle and the "old mad joy" of combat. These memories remain persistently alive long after the battles have ended. The poem concludes not with the artilleryman's return to peaceful slumber but with the battle still raging, with "bombs bursting in air, and at night the vari-color'd rockets."

Forms and Devices

Like Whitman's earlier poems, most of those included in the *Drum-Taps* collection, including "The Artilleryman's Vision," are written in free verse. In his preface to the 1855 edition of *Leaves of Grass*, Whitman had described America as "a teeming nation of nations," saying, "Here is action untied from strings necessarily blind to particulars and details magnificently moving in vast masses. . . . Here are the roughs and beards and space and ruggedness and nonchalance that the soul loves." To capture in poetry the spirit of America, Whitman developed a rambling free-verse style that broke with established poetic conventions. Whitman's poems generally eschew traditional rhyme and meter, presenting instead a burst of detail and emotion in free verse—"barbaric yawps," as he once called them.

The poems published before *Drum-Taps* generally concern Whitman's own experiences and emotions as he grows from childhood to adulthood, takes in his teeming nation, and develops his poetic voice. Poems such as "Song of Myself" (1855), "Out of the Cradle Endlessly Rocking" (1859), and "As I Ebb'd with the Ocean of Life" (1860) comprise long emotional outbursts that celebrate the self, placing Whitman squarely within the traditions of American Romanticism. With *Drum-Taps*, however, Whitman moves in a new direction. The *Drum-Taps* poems, like "The Artilleryman's Vision," are generally shorter than those contained in earlier editions of *Leaves of Grass*. Whitman often removes his own personal voice from the poem. In some *Drum-Taps* poems, his speakers are soldiers, nurses, and other participants in the war; other poems are presented from an objective point of view. In "The Artilleryman's Vision," Whitman wisely allows the artilleryman to tell his own story.

The Civil War is partly responsible for ushering realism into American literature, and Whitman's Civil War poems are marked by realistic detail. In "The Artilleryman's Vision," the speaker attempts to record the sights, sounds, and even smells of the battlefield. The artillery shells explode "leaving small white clouds." The chief gunner "sights his piece and selects a fuse of the right time." The rifles fire with a "*t-h-t! t-h-t!*" sound, the shells shriek as they pass, and the grapeshot flies "like the hum and whirr of wind through the trees." The artilleryman breathes "the suffocating smoke" of the battlefield. Whitman presents these details randomly, in a rambling prosaic style that conveys the chaos of battle.

The poem's dramatic intensity hinges on the juxtaposition of details. The poem opens with the artilleryman resting peacefully in his bed. His head "on the pillow rests," and in the darkness he "hear[s], just hear[s], the breath of [his] infant." These details, depicting domestic safety and tranquility, contrast sharply with the details of war presented later in the poem. The infant's quiet breathing gives way to the "irregular snap! snap!" of the skirmishers' rifles and the shrieks and whirr of the ordnance from the artillery pieces fired during the battle. The peaceful opening scene of man, wife, and child asleep gives way to the battlefield scenes depicting the chaos of war.

Themes and Meanings

During the Civil War, Whitman served as a nurse in hospitals for wounded soldiers in Washington, D.C. He never experienced combat on the battlefield, but he heard from the veterans whom he treated tales of the horrors of combat. Whitman puts to use the soldiers' stories in "The Artilleryman's Vision" and other *Drum-Taps* poems. The *Drum-Taps* collection comprises forty-three poems that take the reader from the war's beginnings in 1861, through the conflict, and toward its conclusion four years later. Some of the final poems of the collection present the hope of reconciliation between the warring sides in the bloody conflict that resulted in the loss of more than 600,000 lives.

In "The Artilleryman's Vision," however, Whitman suggests that the war will not be forgotten quickly. The memories of battle remain with Whitman's speaker long after the conflict has ended. They interrupt the artilleryman's attempt to resume a normal life after he has been mustered out of the armed service. He has a wife, an infant child, and a home, but the memories of war intrude upon the peace that he has attempted to create in his postwar life. Perhaps these nighttime visions will continue to break the artilleryman's peaceful sleep for the rest of his life.

In this poem, Whitman shows that he was aware that wartime memories can continue to haunt a veteran long after the fighting has stopped. Twentieth century psychologists used terms such as shellshock and post-traumatic stress syndrome to identify the postwar experiences of men like Whitman's Civil War veteran. Ernest Hemingway and other twentieth century writers who attempted to portray realistically the psychology of men at war created soldiers and veterans like the artilleryman of Whitman's poem, men who continued to experience the shocks of combat during their postwar lives.

Whitman's artilleryman is a universal soldier. Readers acquainted with Whitman's life will realize that the poet is depicting the disturbing nighttime visions of a man who has fought in the American Civil War, but Whitman's veteran lacks a specific identity—he is neither Yankee nor Confederate—and Whitman's description of his battle contains no specific details to indicate his war's time and place. In "The Artilleryman's Vision," Whitman has depicted with psychological verisimilitude the state of mind of many individuals who have participated in armed combat.

James Tackach

AS I WALKED OUT ONE EVENING

Author: W. H. Auden (1907-1973)
Type of poem: Narrative
First published: 1940, in *Another Time*

The Poem

"As I walked out one evening" contains fifteen four-line stanzas rhyming *abcb*. The rhymes are masculine; the meter is a flexible iambic trimeter with all the unrhymed lines ending with an additional unstressed syllable. The language of this poem, which has no title but is usually designated by its first line, is relatively simple, but the poem presents three voices, one of which conveys a relatively short but beautiful love lyric, embedded in a more elaborate structure that complicates the reader's response.

The first voice, not that of a lover but of an observer who is walking on an urban street toward a river, occupies the first stanza and three lines of the second. The walker is in a mood to characterize the passing crowds of people as "fields of harvest wheat." Nearing the "brimming river," this person hears a voice brimming with the rapture of love.

The lovers are embracing under a railroad bridge. One of them, the poem's second voice, is first heard in the last line of the second stanza, "Love has no ending," an assertion that may serve as a title of the song that follows and certainly expressive of its theme. In the next three stanzas the lover pledges undying love in a series of extravagant assertions reminiscent of Robert Burns's "A Red, Red Rose" (1796), in which the speaker vows to love his lady "till a' the seas gang dry." In this poem the couple's love will continue "till the ocean/ Is folded and hung up to dry."

Whereas with Burns the love lyric is the whole poem, however, here there is not only the human observer but also, beginning in the sixth stanza, "all the clocks in the city." The third voice, which proceeds from the mention of the clocks, occupies thirty-four of the poem's sixty lines and ominously contradicts the lover's vow in a series of stark images which have the effect of darkly telescoping the lovers' real, finite time— a time that "leaks away" to its inevitable end. Auden encloses these lines within single quotation marks. The images pile up: snow, glaciers, deserts, tears, and agonized looks in mirrors, as well as perverse variations of nursery rhymes in which, for instance, Jill does not simply tumble down a hill after Jack but, in a context that suggests sexual violence, "goes down on her back." This voice does not deny love, but insists, in the poem's penultimate stanza, that human love is not only finite but "crooked."

The observer's voice returns in the last stanza. The hour is now late, the lovers are no longer there, the clocks are no longer chiming, and the river continues to flow.

Forms and Devices

"As I walked out one evening" reflects Auden's interest in the ballad, a form which he often practiced in the late 1930's, when this poem was composed. The stanza is a slight variation of the ballad stanza of alternate tetrameter and trimeter lines, while the rhyme scheme is typical of the ballad. Several characteristics of the venerable English and Scottish folk ballad tradition are found here: plain diction, carefully calculated repetitions of words and phrases, a tendency toward dialogue, abrupt transitions, and a pervasive sense of irony.

Only four words in the poem have more than two syllables, and a number of lines are entirely monosyllabic. The repetitions include the lover's "I'll love you"; the third voice's iteration of imperative verbs such as "plunge," "look," and "stand"; and the adjectival repetition at the beginning of the last stanza: "It was late, late in the evening." The simplicity of the language heightens the emotional complexity of the poem. The lover's vows are packed with images of vitality, but the stark imagery that follows suggests a world whose corruption threatens to infect lovers no matter how sincere their intentions.

The irony exists on two levels. It is ironic that the lovers can hardly imagine the difficulties involved in maintaining their devotion through the ordinary vicissitudes of life. This poem, however, envelops not only the characters but also its audience in the irony. The faithless, nightmarish world depicted beginning in the sixth stanza has the effect of defying the common hopes and aspirations not only of young lovers but of all who believe in the effectuality of human love.

The voices of the poem do not engage in dialogue in the ordinary sense. Only one of the lovers is heard; the reader can only wonder about the reaction of the other. However, the third voice of the poem, representing time, is in effect "talking back" to the lover, although it seems unlikely that the latter is listening. The voice of time dismisses the lover's promises bluntly but ambiguously: "Life remains a blessing/ Although you cannot bless." Love exists in the world, but the young lover, busy with his own affirmations, has no inkling of its obstacles and contrarieties.

The first transition is the abrupt interposition of the voice of time in the sixth stanza, which is not the voice of author or observer-narrator, neither of whom offers any overt comment on its ominous message. The transition from that message to "late, late in the evening" in the last stanza renders interpretation problematic. The lovers have gone away, whether together or individually the reader does not know. The fact that the clocks are no longer chiming but that the "deep river" flows on might be read as a repudiation of a society given to technological measurement of time and a reaffirmation of the natural order of which young love is a universal component—but the river is its own symbol of the passing time that bids to challenge the lover's vows.

Themes and Meanings

An almost obsessive concentration on time—particularly its clash with the aspirations of young love—dominates the poem. It is not, however, a *carpe diem* ("seize the day") poem of the type that became popular in the seventeenth century and has found many echoes in the twentieth. In the *carpe diem* tradition the lover's intent is often seductive, or can be easily so interpreted. Typically he reminds his beloved that her youthful beauty will soon fade, that she cannot long expect such appreciation as he is now bestowing on her. If he has a certain measure of tact, he may even concede that he too is subject to the ravages of time, but in any event he urges consummation of their love.

"As I walked out one evening," like Burns's "A Red, Red Rose," works quite otherwise. Here is a speaker whose evident sincerity—and naïveté—leads to exaggerated pledges which any observer but a thoroughgoing cynic might applaud. It seems fitting, after all, that true love should generate such vows. A failure to utter them would be somehow disappointing.

The love lyric of Auden's poem, however, is framed not only by the observer, who may well approve, but by the stern and uncompromising voice associated with the city clocks. A future the lover can scarcely imagine will test him with a succession of buffets while life "leaks away." Do the lovers under the railroad bridge sense this truth in the chiming of the town's clocks? Auden's poem does not answer such a question, but surely if the two do not hear the message now, they will soon enough.

This voice which occupies the major portion of the poem strikes a tone that suggests not only time, however, but a particularly harsh and forbidding time. "As I walked out one evening" deviates from the usual ballad in its tendency toward interpretative comment in this third voice, not so much the voice of *time* as the voice of *the times*. Auden composed the poem in 1937, when forces were gathering for a world war, the second of the poet's lifetime. While no explicit references to the era mark this poem, its insistence on the "crookedness" of humans in the face of cataclysmic disorders and vague horrors represents a challenge to the lovers beyond the ordinary power of time considered as an agent of the natural order.

Nature, however, reasserts itself in the consciousness of the observer in the last stanza. Although the clocks will strike again, they are quiet at least for now. The lovers are gone but will presumably meet again and confirm their love in these most difficult of times. The final image of the river, which flows on as time does in the most tumultuous epochs, may signify time according to nature. If so, the last line of the poem affirms an order in which human love has a chance to prevail—an order that persists through the most disorderly of times.

Robert P. Ellis

AS KINGFISHERS CATCH FIRE

Author: Gerard Manley Hopkins (1844-1889)
Type of poem: Sonnet
First published: 1918, in *Poems of Gerard Manley Hopkins, Now First Published, with Notes by Robert Bridges*

The Poem

"As Kingfishers Catch Fire" conveys Gerard Manley Hopkins's sacramental vision that each creature and even each object in the world constantly announces its individuality, and that in so doing, in its own active and perceptible way it proclaims God's grace. As a young man preparing for a career in art, Hopkins had been a close and penetrating observer of his surroundings. After his conversion to Roman Catholicism, this interest in the nature of things took the more spiritual cast that is reflected in this poem.

The poem is a Petrarchan sonnet in which the octave is devoted to the physical world, and the sestet to humanity. The poem begins by noting the play of light on kingfishers (a type of bright-colored bird) and dragonflies and continues with a series of aural images: the sound of a stone striking off the walls of a well, the sound of a plucked string (Hopkins uses the dialectal verb "tucked" rather than "plucked"), the sound of a large bell hung from a bow (as church bells are). In the second half of the octave, Hopkins explains the significance of these images. Ordinary though they are, each of these creatures and each of these objects makes itself, its particular character, known by its tangible, perceptible action. If attended to, the most mundane things are fraught with meaning.

Hopkins begins the sestet by boldly asserting that human beings also express their essential nature in what they do, although this nature is not physical but spiritual and moral. So, for instance, a just person does justice. In doing what he or she *is*, the person is actualizing God's purpose in the world, becoming the word of God incarnate—becoming, in fact, the body of Christ. God the Father, contemplating the beauty of each of these embodiments of Christ, is pleased, just as people are pleased by the beauty of kingfishers, dragonflies, and all the world around them.

The composition of this poem is hard to date. After his religious conversion, Hopkins became a Jesuit, and although he was ambitious as a poet he did not allow poetry to distract him from his vocation and did not publish his poems. This poem was found with Hopkins's papers after his death. Its ideas and wording can be linked to entries in Hopkins's journal as early as 1880 or as late as 1882. "As Kingfishers Catch Fire" was published with Hopkins's other poems in 1918, when his friend and literary executor, Robert Bridges, thought the time propitious for their appreciation.

Forms and Devices

Essentially a private poet, Hopkins developed quite distinctive characteristics of style, some of which are evident in "As Kingfishers Catch Fire." As a Petrarchan sonnet, the poem is quite conventional in its fourteen five-beat lines and its *abba abba cdc dcd* rhyme scheme. It is, however, quite unconventional in its rhythm. Hopkins developed what he called "sprung rhythm," in which a foot consisted of one stressed syllable and any number of unstressed syllables: one, two, three, even four—or none at all. The result can be a perfectly conventional line, such as "Bow swung finds tongue to fling out broad its name;" (stress on the second, fourth, sixth, eighth, and tenth syllables), or a more radical line, such as "Keeps grace: that keeps all his goings graces" (stress on the first, second, third, seventh, and ninth syllables). Hopkins felt that sprung rhythm approximated the rhythms of normal speech more closely than do the strictly patterned rhythms of conventional poetry, allowing for the fluidity of line and the precise placement of emphasis that readily strike the ear throughout "As Kingfishers Catch Fire."

The poem makes use of other sound qualities as well. Hopkins uses consonance and alliteration to reinforce the poem's forward impulsion and to emphasize, albeit unobtrusively, relationships in the poem. In the first line subjects and verbs alliterate, helping to establish the connection between creatures and what they do. In the third line "stones" and "string" alliterate, emphasizing the parallel between them. The alliteration of "Father," "features," and "faces" in the last line similarly underscores the connection that the poem establishes between God and his people.

Hopkins's repeated but unobtrusive use of internal rhymes in lines 3-5 ("ring," "string," "fling," and "thing"; "hung," "swung," and "tongue") also serves to move the poem forward and to unify its content. The internal rhyme of "to" and "through" in the last line underscores the relationship of end and means developed in the poem. The poem employs only four end rhymes. These end rhymes are normally used for emphasis and to establish the sonnet's clearly distinguishable pattern, appropriate to a poem exploring God's design in the world.

Hopkins was interested in onomatopoeia. The stops in "tucked string tells" imitate the sound of a plucked string, as the nasals of "ring," "hung," "swung," "tongue," "fling," and "name" all imitate the resonance of ringing bells—or of stones dropped into wells. The pulses of alliteration and internal rhyme in lines 3-5 also create an onomatopoetic effect suggestive of a ringing bell.

"As Kingfishers Catch Fire" makes striking use of synesthesia (a feeling of a sense other than the one being stimulated) also. Hopkins perceived a similarity between the sound of ringing bells and the sight of sparks or fire. The similarity between the abrupt strokes of a bell and the sudden bright flashes of kingfishers and dragonflies underlies the first quatrain and indeed the whole octave of this poem.

In this poem and in others, Hopkins's diction is sometimes distinctive, even idiosyncratic. The adjective "roundy" is chosen not for metrical reasons (given Hopkins's sprung rhythm) but to fit the childlike action of dropping stones into open wells. The unexpected verb "tucked" is chosen instead of the more usual "plucked" for its greater onomatopoetic value. "Spells" is chosen for its alliterative value and perhaps also for its ambiguity—it surely denotes signification, and it may also suggest an almost magical action. Most striking are the words Hopkins coins from other parts of speech—"indoors," "selves," and "justices."

Themes and Meanings

Not only as a poet but also as a nature writer, Hopkins anticipated writers who followed him. He was interested in the distinctive qualities of things and the relationship of the creatures and objects in the environment to human observers. For the focused and patterned essence of things Hopkins coined the term "inscape," analogous to the word "landscape." As the critical dimension of landscape is breadth, so the critical dimension of inscape is depth. The perception of inscape, Hopkins found, requires concentration and imaginative sensitivity. It is aided by the active energy of the object perceived—an energy that maintains the inscape and projects it to observers. Hopkins called this force and action "instress."

In his journals and in his poems, Hopkins often described inscapes figuratively, as he does in the opening quatrain of "As Kingfishers Catch Fire." The opening line seems unremarkable at first, merely two pretty descriptions cast in terms of flashes of light and color, but given what follows, this line may convey more. If the fire of the kingfishers and the flame of the dragonflies are seen to recall the fire of Moses's burning bush in the third chapter of Exodus and the coming of the Holy Spirit like tongues of flame on Pentecost, kingfishers and dragonflies are in essence touched with divinity. The following lines underscore the individuality of inscapes. The later characterization of God by his eye stresses God's fundamental attentiveness, and the characterization of men by their faces stresses humanity's inherent expectation. The verb in "Christ plays" is especially interesting for the complex of qualities in Christ's inscape and instress that it suggests: both constant activity (as a fountain plays) and rapidly shifting activity (as firelight plays), both easy and enjoyable activity (as a child plays) and competent activity (as a musician plays).

Hopkins made his poetry a part of his vocation as a priest. In "As Kingfishers Catch Fire" as in several other poems, he responded to the religious crisis of the Victorian era—the perceived conflict between science and faith—not by retreating into Romantic medievalism or art-for-art's-sake aestheticism or by falling into agnostic or atheistic despair, but by looking closely at the world around him and finding in it evidences of God's presence and God's grace.

The poem inscapes more than it describes explicitly. As kingfishers catch fire, as dragonflies draw flame, as bells and stones ring out their names, as the Holy Spirit, God's presence and God's grace, manifests itself in the action of mortal things, and as Christ, God's grace and God's person, manifests himself in the living and the doing of humankind, so do poets compose and readers read.

David W. Cole

AS THE DEAD PREY UPON US

Author: Charles Olson (1910-1970)
Type of poem: Elegy
First published: 1957; collected in *The Distances*, 1960

The Poem

As with other poems Charles Olson wrote in the 1950's, "As the Dead Prey Upon Us" is composed in open form using a variety of stanza patterns, from long strophe-like paragraphs to short, lumpy passages dense with imagery. Olson's "Projective Verse" essay, published in 1950, sets forth his strategies for writing poetry, which include the use of the typewriter as an instrument for designing how a poem is to be read as well as for picturing the precise patterns in which a poet's ideas form and fuse together into lyric language. Thus, a "projective" poem should be read as an arrangement of language in which the mental processes of conceiving and composing poetry are reenacted. "Closed form," Olson argued in his essay, smoothed away the precise details of thinking in poetry and manufactured a generalizing, abstract mode in which all the details of imaginative articulation are lumped together and given an overriding and uniform rhythm of speech.

"As the Dead Prey Upon Us" begins with the perception that the ghosts who haunt humans represent those parts of people that have not had the chance to live fully. The ghost may signify a repressed or constrained part of someone's personality or an unresolved conflict nagging at the back of the mind. Hence, when the speaker complains that his mother's death continues to haunt him, he begins by observing that the dead are unacknowledged facts of self. One is free of them only when one has confronted each of them and given them their freedom, that is, allowed them to enter consciousness and to find their relation within the rest of one's awareness. These repressed events or memories are "the sleeping ones," and the speaker bids them to awake and thus to "disentangle from the nets of being!"

The poem is divided into two sprawling sequences of unnumbered stanzas, although only the second section bears a Roman numeral, II. Usually, Olson will mark off the segments of discourse in a poem according to a simple pattern. Part 1 of a long lyric sequence sets up the conditions in which a thinking process will ensue, in which a variety of isolated elements taken from different sources in experience, including dreams, are carefully sifted and their internal relations worked out. Once this operation is complete, a second section or part begins with a richer, more figurative proposition that sets out to interpret what the first part has "assembled." The second discourse thus synthesizes, imagines, and philosophically investigates the "formal" construct, a process in which the new form is woven into the context of other knowledge possessed by the poet. An Olson poem is thus the carefully staged reenactment of how the mind works to understand itself when seized by creative activity, such as dreaming.

In this instance, the speaker is aroused by the irritating insistence of a dream he has had of his dead mother. Olson's mother had died five years before, on Christmas day, 1950. Other poems on her death (such as "In Cold Hell, in Thicket") attest both the closeness of his relationship to her and his need to understand her loss. The speaker has awakened and now recounts his dream to himself (and to the reader) in an effort to decipher its twisted plot.

The progression of stanzas introduces the reader to the other features of the dream: a visit to a tire store, where he may have observed the mechanic working under his car while replacing the tires; a vision of his mother surrounded by other dead souls in the living room of his house, where a film projector is showing a film against one of the walls; and in another room, an American Indian woman walks a blue deer around in circles, a deer that speaks in an African American dialect or like an old woman as it looks for socks or shoes to wear, "now that it was acquiring/ human possibilities." This latter image of the evolving deer generates the discussion on the "nets of being," the laws that govern human identity and set it apart from other orders of nature, animals, and angels. To be human, the speaker notes, is to be limited to the "five hindrances," the five senses of the body from which awareness derives.

Human awareness is a niche in reality that dreaming expands and contradicts. The speaker must try to resolve the differences between what he has dreamed from his unconscious and what he understands as waking awareness, the world perceived by sense and logic. To Olson, the continuum of real human thought should begin with sense and reason and extend into myth and visionary insight. The speaker's dilemma is that he is of two minds that do not connect except here, in this poem, where the reader finds him puzzling out the meaning of a dream in his waking state. The situation is ironic, the perfect representation of the problem of divided nature Olson wishes to resolve.

The self-analysis of the speaker moves quickly through a cascading procession of different stanza shapes; the deeply indented ones are in counterpoint to the stanzas arranged along the left margin. Each time the thought darts inward, the speaker is seized by a new fact taken from memory, or that has flashed from the psychic depths. The passions of the speaker rise as he grapples with his theme of inner division, the spirit-haunted psyche that plagues his dreams and troubles his waking life.

In part 2, the dream state is likened to an underworld of souls lying at the bottom of the mind; hell is interior, a psychological cave within the mind's recesses where spiritual events occur out of the range of conscious attention. This dimension of the dream mind transforms the world of sense into a magic realm of distorted, quick-changing, mysterious properties, most of them made from what was once daily, routine experience, as when the automobile comes alive and mounts the speaker in his dream and then becomes a white chair. The speaker talks freely with the spirits who mill around in his house, a scene reminiscent of Odysseus's descent into the underworld in the *Odyssey* (c. 800 B.C.E.). The blue deer is an animal soul "becoming" human. Yet, the poem ends as things return to their original identities as mother, son, and a blue deer that "need not trouble either of us."

Forms and Devices

Perhaps the most intriguing device in the poem is the use of the dream itself, both as a second reality and as a level of figurative language whose meanings are not merely fantasy but a dimension of hidden meanings, repressed by some function of consciousness. The poem operates as a vehicle in which this second language of the dream is interpreted into lyric speech. The poem draws language from one side of the intellect into the other, as if from an exotic corner of mental space into that of conscious life. The poem reproduces how lyric language is made: Items from the peripheral, shadowy voices of the unconscious are drawn into an argument in which their significance is revealed and incorporated into the rational structure of the poem.

The elegiac form of the poem uses a string of narrative fragments as the links to be joined, in which the mother's appearance in the dream will be understood. All elegies work by remembering the deceased, but Olson's poem considers the remembering process a therapeutic necessity of the griever. As is often the case with Olson's speakers, his persona here has an investigative attitude toward his situation; he remembers events as if they were clues to a mystery, the solution to which will relieve him of a psychological burden. Things that make no sense at first begin to unfold another world within, as cars turn into beasts, animals talk as they approach human stature, and magical transformations occur at any moment. In essence, everything in the poem has a "soul" and is alive and sentient, capable of expressing its true nature in the dream state.

Themes and Meanings

Although "As the Dead Prey Upon Us" is, on the surface, an elegy in which a son mourns the memory of his deceased mother, it is essentially a poem about the mythological imagination that comes awake in dreams and springs forth in fits of inspiration. The poet who recalls his dream is involved in the act of composing language derived from the mythological depths of his unconscious. Olson spent much of his life defending myth as primal vision, but modern culture has rejected the function of myth and looks now to empirical analysis as the means for grasping the truth of events. Olson's speaker longs to decode the narrative of his dream but gropes blindly among its shimmering clues. His struggle to understand his dream is a portrait of the artist attempting to express his imagination: both face the unconscious with perplexed ignorance of its language.

The difference between what one sees with the "five hindrances" and what one dreams is that in waking, things are separate, scattered, inert, but in dreams, one thing becomes another, each connected by invisible threads that together make up the "nets of being" that is the central image of the poem. The speaker demands that this "sleep" state of mind, the dreaming function, awake and become an active part of his intelligence. His demand is to himself, and by addressing the "souls" directly he attempts to close the gap between the two faculties of his awareness. Happiness is that state in which the dream has entered consciousness and enjoys complete understanding. Hell is the limbo of unlived ideas, the ghosts that long to become part of the living self.

Olson's deep interest in Mayan hieroglyphs—the stylized characters and symbols that adorn their stone pillars, or stelae, and ziggurat-like temples—may also figure in this poem. His interest in Mayan language and art arose from his conviction that their art combined both sides of human intelligence, the mythological and the factual. The great bas-reliefs found at Chichén Itzá, Uxmal, and Palenque depict a human figure surrounded by natural objects, including plants, animals, numbers, and astronomical computations. Such was the richness of the intellectual life of a people who had not divided their mental functions into fantasy and reality, as Western culture had done. The totality of mind included both figurative, imaginative products and sensory experiences, the one nurturing the meaning of the other.

"As the Dead Prey Upon Us" attempts to restore a way of thinking in which the dream communicates to reason, uttering an insightful message about the self through its mythic figures and its magic landscape. That is what the detective persona in the poem attempts to penetrate, as if he were an archaeologist at the site of his own intellect, with its buried treasures and its mystical inscriptions. Olson describes the fullness of Mayan intellectual life in his essay "Human Universe," in which he talks eloquently about the dual role of mind in expressing mythological or dreamlike narratives as well as mathematical and scientific facts about nature. Both are valid acts of thought—each approaches the world from its own perspective—but in the end together they define a "heaven" of continuous vitality underlying nature.

Paul Christensen

AS WE FORGIVE THOSE

Author: Eric Pankey (1959-   )
Type of poem: Lyric
First published: 1987; collected in *Heartwood*, 1988

The Poem

"As We Forgive Those," a relatively short poem in free verse, is divided into four stanzas of unequal length and makes use of a natural, almost colloquial, tone to examine rather weighty theological issues. The poem's title is drawn from the Lord's Prayer, widely used in Protestant Christianity, and suggests the struggle of the poet to reconcile his understanding of that prayer, especially its admonitions concerning forgiveness, with his own family experience.

The bulk of Pankey's verse—collected in *For the New Year* (1984), *Heartwood* (1988), *Apocrypha* (1991), and *The Late Romances* (1997)—suggests both a deep fascination with and strong commitment to Christianity, as well as an uneasiness concerning its many permutations and manifestations. While Pankey's discomfort with Christian dogmatism and facile fundamentalism is evident, it is equally clear that such discomfort leads him to examine carefully his own faith and its relationship to his childhood growing up in the United States during the 1960's and early 1970's.

In various poems, particularly those collected in *Heartwood* (where "As We Forgive Those" appears), no clear line exists between the speaker's voice in the poem and that of the poet. While such conflation is common in contemporary poetry, in Pankey's case it is used to dramatic effect to speak about religious experience. Like the poet Andrew Hudgins in his *The Glass Hammer* (1994), Pankey explores his family's history, demonstrating how it shapes his way of seeing the world and his understanding of God's ways in that world.

"As We Forgive Those" begins with the most ordinary of domestic rituals: a father excusing his son from the dinner table. This ritual, however, resonates in the poem because it clearly helps determine the speaker's notion of forgiveness. By demonstrating the power of his father who "excuses" him from the dinner table, a most desirable pardon for any young boy, Pankey intimates that his earthly existence offers him his only clues for coming to terms with his faith.

Although the speaker in the poem says that "All my life I was a child," the poem itself presents the action as part of the past. Thus, Pankey writes from an adult perspective about the innocence of childhood faith and the youthful tendency toward a literal understanding of the language of faith. Instead of a child's thoughts, the poem displays a grown man mulling over his boyhood memories, an activity through which he gains mature insights. Moreover, the poem hinges upon the speaker's explication or close reading of the Lord's Prayer—an intellectual activity that demands reflective distance and allows the poet to understand better how his boyhood activities shaped his use of the prayer—while suggesting the universal power of both earthly and heavenly forgiveness.

Forms and Devices

"As We Forgive Those" finds much of its power in Pankey's use of juxtaposition and allusion. A kind of prayer itself, the poem's clear reference to the Lord's Prayer establishes a pattern of comparison for the poet that allows him to move back and forth between philosophical meditation and the remembered actions of his past.

Derived from the Latin, the word "allusion" literally means "to play with or touch upon," and it remains one of the most effective means of compression in poetry. Merely by mentioning certain names, places, events, or, in this case, specific lines from a spiritual text, the poet creates powerful associations for the reader. Clearly the historic significance of the Lord's Prayer in Christianity and the profound effect of this religion upon the Western world determines the power and resonance of this particular allusion. However, at several points in the poem, Pankey's use of allusion shifts from a universal human history, as reflected in Christendom, to the individual history of Pankey's own American boyhood—a pattern that keeps the poem from becoming mired in theological conundrums of interpretation that ultimately cannot be resolved.

Thus, in the poem's first stanza, Pankey establishes, through juxtaposition, that his own boyhood experience will serve as a metaphor for forgiveness. He remembers that as a boy he learned "to forgive from those who forgave." This is a slight alteration of the Lord's Prayer, which entreats God to "forgive us our trespasses as we forgive those who trespass against us." Yet not all Christian churches translate the word "trespass" in the same manner, and the mature Pankey struggles to remember whether he "was supposed/ to forgive those who trespassed, or my debtors."

Therefore, Pankey not only uses juxtaposition as a tool for organizing the poem's shifts from boyhood experience to theological meditation but also uses it to contrast the significant differences between the words "trespass" and "debt." These levels of juxtaposition, skillfully connected so that they cannot be completely separated, suggest the complexity of forgiveness and its direct relationship to one's own cultural context.

As the poem reveals, because Pankey's family "always owed someone or someone owed" them, he cannot remember a time when they used the word "debtor" while praying the Lord's Prayer. Instead, the poet says they concentrated on the lines, "Give us this day," a prayerful request that seemed odd to the young Pankey because he believed the day already was theirs. His parents, nevertheless, fashion the young boy's understanding of the prayer and, ultimately, his understanding of forgiveness, so that as he grows he too will pray for "this day." The poet also recalls that as a boy, when his parents argued, yelling at each other, he was told not to worry, that such fights did not concern him. From this example, he came to think of forgiveness as a condition in which one was excused from the unknown.

As the poem concludes, the poet juxtaposes the ignorance of his youth against his growing desire for knowledge. This final comparison leads Pankey closer to the mature insight toward which the poem struggles: Forgiveness demands knowledge. Fittingly, the poem culminates with the image of a shadow sweeping across all that the family owns, all for which they are in debt, and it is at this moment that the poet finally comes to a true knowledge of his condition and his need for forgiveness.

Themes and Meanings

In much of his writing, Pankey grapples with the idea of redemption in the contemporary world, a condition that, for him, is intimately linked to the Christian concept of forgiveness. The word "grapples" is appropriately used in this context because of the intellectual honesty that characterizes his struggle with faith. Pankey demands that faith be described as that which is unknown, yet believed. He contests the notion that the knowledge one finds in faith is somehow rational and provable.

In the poem "If You Can," which follows "As We Forgive Those" in *Heartwood* and may be considered a companion piece, Pankey addresses his daughter, describing his own mystical understanding of forgiveness and redemption to her. While he is perplexed by this encounter, he does indeed believe that he has been "saved." However, it is nothing he fully understands. He says, somewhat bewildered, "But saved by whom or for what/ I don't know." "If You Can" turns on a father's loving appeal to his daughter: "If you can, please, believe," the poet says, but he makes no promise that with such belief the world will miraculously become an easier place in which to live. Rather, he tells her that the rocks that will bruise her heel will be no less hard; belief will merely give her the knowledge of forgiveness and show others "where the pain is."

This faith and the hope that faithfulness may touch others seem to hover near the center of "As We Forgive Those," linked to "the maple that ruled/ [Pankey's] house half the day in sunlight, half in shade," an image that the poet uses to great effect to conclude his meditation on forgiveness. In the poem's final lines, Pankey tells of the day he walked out beneath the formidable maple and finally understood the weight of its shadow, how it "swept every inch of what we owned." He realizes that such immature pranks as his trespassing for apples, his stealing of green tomatoes to drop from trees on unsuspecting pedestrians, and his hiding behind juniper bushes to spy upon others were insignificant compared to the knowledge of his family's and his own precarious position in the world.

While the poet tells readers that during that year he learned the word "omniscient" in school, as a boy his knowledge of what the word meant was woefully inadequate. Only after his prayer for knowledge is answered does he come to know that to be forgiven is to be covered in the darkness of this world while seeing to the light that lies beyond, or, as Pankey explains while looking backward, "When it covered me I knew I was forgiven."

Todd Davis

THE ASH

Author: William Heyen (1940-   )
Type of poem: Lyric
First published: 1977; collected in *The Ash*, 1978

The Poem

"The Ash" is a lyric poem in eleven stanzas of four lines each. It is written in controlled free verse, with two to four stresses per line. The title refers to a tree—the mountain ash—which becomes a central symbol in the poem (and in the sequence with which it was published). As well as designating flowering nature, however, the name of the tree inevitably carries with it connotations of decay and death.

The poem opens with direct quotation—the complaining voice of the poet's sick friend, whom he is visiting in the hospital. The poem is composed of two interwoven voices, but it is not an actual dialogue. The friend's voice is present tense, immediate. Until the final stanza, the poet's response is past tense, reflective. He is narrating this encounter as if after the fact. The reader never learns what, if anything, he said in response to the ill man's bitterness. Instead, in traditional lyric fashion, the reader overhears the poet's thoughts. In the second stanza, the poet relates how a nurse gave the ill friend "lithium and thorazine"—medication used to fight depression. The third stanza gives a vivid picture of the friend in the hospital bed. Once again, the reader hears the friend's voice, which runs into the fourth stanza, denouncing the doctors, hospital, and staff.

Repelled, the poet closes his eyes and thinks of "my mountain ash," the tree of the title, which is now (in May) "in white bloom." The poet's reverie of "home" becomes the center of the poem, running through the next four stanzas. The thought of the tree awakens his senses; in a series of intensely physical images, he remembers its "perfume-menstrual smell," and pictures (and seems to hear) the bees "maddened" for its blossoms. This leads him to thoughts of natural decay.

In stanza 9, the poet awakens from his reverie. His attention returns to his immediate surroundings—the hospital room. For the third time, the reader hears directly the voice of the friend, who is now recognizably seriously ill, in spirit as well as body. The poet refers to his friend's remarks as "hate-vapors"; they are a litany of things the friend "hates": books, seasons, children, the dead.

In stanza 11, for the first time, the poet also speaks in present tense (although not aloud—again one "overhears" him). He describes his friend being moved from ward to ward, seemingly without cure, ever closer, it seems, to death. The poem ends neither with the voice of the friend nor with the poet's past-tense narration. Instead of escaping from the scene before him, the poet asks a question: "Where will this end?" What "this" implies is ambiguous: Does he mean the friend's illness, the friend's bitterness, or his own responsibility to confront both of these? The poet's last, tentative statement is one that again removes him from the hospital and returns him in imagination to the outside world, to nature, to the tree.

Forms and Devices

"The Ash" depends for its effect on sharp, sensuous imagery that allows the reader to see the contrasting pictures of the sick friend—"eyes glazed,/ but fists clenched"— and the mountain ash, "in white bloom." There are many images that appeal vividly to the other senses as well: smell, sound, touch, and taste. The sound of the bees is reproduced through the device of onomatopoeia: "humming their hymns of blue flame" actually sounds like bees swarming. This is not an especially "musical" poem in the traditional sense of identifiable rhythmic patterns, but there is a strong controlling voice—the poet's—which occupies the center of the poem with a single grammatical unit running through seven complete stanzas. This long sentence is richly alive with the sounds of the natural world, the "music" of Nature's bloom and decay.

Juxtaposition is the main structuring technique. The probably dying man contrasts with the tree's springtime blooming. The poet's complex voice is opposed to his friend's flat declarations of antipathy, expressed in a diction and syntax as simple as a child's. The poet's intense reverie is set against the ill man's half-conscious state; the shrunken perspective of the hospital room, its "sick-room odors" and "twisted smiles," is balanced by the larger world outside.

The poem works to create the remembered ash as its central symbol, one that somehow combines life and death, flowering and decay, and thereby offers solace to the poet confronted by his friend's illness and negativity. The repeated final image of the circle echoes the description of the ash as "my oval" and seems to symbolize some larger connection to all things in nature, perhaps the hope of another life beyond the body's decay—one that will never end.

Themes and Meanings

"The Ash" is a poem of spiritual affirmation in the face of death. Its underlying theme is the search for transcendence. It presents two points of view on death. The sick friend exemplifies Dylan Thomas's famous injunction to "Rage, rage against the dying of the light." The poet, however, finds balm for the physical and spiritual decay of man not in any specific religious beliefs, but in a vision of the teeming life of nature, which itself is filled with decay and dying. The poem suggests that if, in nature, beauty and decay are inextricable ("blossoms of white filth"), then, for man, despair need not be the only perspective on death. Unlike the friend, the poet refuses to allow the fact of mortality to turn him against life. Against the friend's "hate-vapors," the poet embraces "my own oval of flowering ash." The pain of consciousness, the consciousness of death, is answered by the body's capacity for natural experience. There is at least a hint of possible transcendence in the poet's vision of a larger beauty: "the rainbow glaze of mucous,/ the milky beauty of pond-scum." Such images suggest that physical decay may not be absolute. By imaginatively opening his senses, by immersing himself in the natural rhythms—rather than mentally holding out against them— the poet embraces an identity larger than individual consciousness and seems to discover a body beyond the "sick-room odors." His is, however, a vision that does not deny death. Finally, the image of the circle suggests unity, wholeness, connecting him to his friend's dying—from which, at first, he turned away. Both of them are "circling," but the friend's circle is "lower," closer to the earth. The poet is "outside" this final circling—but, crucially, only "for now." Somehow, he is able, at the end of the poem, to accept even his friend's impoverished spirit, to merge the friend's death with an intimation of his own. The tree becomes the comforting symbol of a realm that includes both of them, containing life and death in a larger whole, the way the friend's bitter resistance is contained within the poet's larger affirmation.

The theme of transcendence intimated in "The Ash" is more fully developed in the sequence of six poems that William Heyen subsequently published under that title. The second poem is "The Ash: Its End," which takes place in June, when the tree has lost its blossoms and is perceived as "almost pure spirit at its end." The next poem, "The Eternal Ash," is set in August, when the tree's "berry clusters/ already tinged orange" are "bending its body/ almost to breaking." Yet the ash is seen as somehow eternal, "its changes mine, delusion," a matter of limited human perception. The fourth poem, "The Flowering Mountain Ash Berry," is a single four-line sentence that takes the cycle further, into the phase of regeneration, by describing the tree's "sperm floating in the air," impregnating earth, the earth itself becoming "one luminous oval seed." The fifth poem, "The Zenith Ash," is a September prayer. The poet explicitly addresses a divine power to which the tree's luminous presence has somehow given access. The tone is urgent: "If I, in human error, lose her,/ even You, my Lord, will curse me." Acknowledging "the slanting cancerous rays/ of autumn sunlight" as divine, the poet sees the ash as a token of divinity, "my ash of praise." The sixth and final poem completes the circle. "The Friend" takes place in winter. We hear again the dying man's bitterness as the poet heard it: "I hate the chairs, the words,/ the winds, the bastards." This time, however, the poet, returning home from a visit to the hospital, has an experience of transcendence: "I stepped/ from my car onto the shocked bone/ of my body, and walked// into the snow-sheathed tree." At the end, he is able to say good-bye to his "dead friend" and even "to love the dead."

Stan Sanvel Rubin

ASHES

Author: Philip Levine (1928-   )
Type of poem: Lyric
First published: 1979, in *Ashes: Poems New and Old*

The Poem

"Ashes" is a free-verse, single-stanza poem that is forty-one lines long. The title points to what a life comes to upon death, and it immediately establishes a mood of fatalism. Ashes are the result of fire, and fire in this poem is a metaphor for life's toil and labor. The poem is written in the first person, and the poet addresses the reader as early as the fourteenth line, telling the reader that "You can howl your name," but the wind will turn it to dust. The direct address links the poet to his reader.

"Ashes" begins at dusk with the poet musing, the classic pose for lyric poetry. Philip Levine sees smoke rising from a field of cotton, from which the workers have already returned several hours earlier. The image of the smoke is the point of departure in the poem—and will become the point of closure as well—as is the bus that passes by the poet and carries the blue-collar laborers home.

While the poet watches the bus pass, he wonders about the workers' fate, the fate of the poor who make their living in the only back-breaking jobs they can get. He wonders about the children who die every day, about the women who curse the very hours of their lives, and about the men who "bow/ to earn our scraps." By saying "our," Levine links himself to the men, suggesting that he, too, in writing the poem, is a laborer, a recorder of their experience, and thus, vicariously at least, experiences their suffering. Yet he only wonders about these people, and in that pose he exposes the differences between the poet and those who inspire him. The answer he provides about their life, which provides the poem's title, is cryptic only in the sense that it is metaphoric: "with fire there is smoke, and after, ashes." That, Levine suggests, is the fate of all people.

Next the poem imagines the darkness coming down for the night, but it is a night representative of all nights. The people go to sleep tired, and when they sleep they dream "of sleep/ without end." That state is fleeting, however, as morning comes in the next line like a blood stain on the sky; the workers are up dressing in clothes that are still warm, though damp, from the day before.

Meanwhile, as the workers head back to the fields, the poet is sleeping. This is a more dramatic difference between them, causing Levine to ask of the reader, "Do you want the earth to be heaven?" The answer given is a call to pray for "all you'll/ never be." Here the poem returns to the imagery of its beginning. In a list of options of what one may never be—"a drop of sea water" or a "small hurtling flame"—is the poem's final image of a "fine flake of dust that moves/ at evening like smoke at great height/ above the earth and sees it all." The image of smoke here represents the vision of the poet as well as the inspiration for poetic vision.

Forms and Devices

Levine has always been attracted to images of fire and smoke, and this poem typifies that interest. His concern, ultimately, is a consideration of living and dying, with which poetry finally must deal. In this sense, the poem's imagery is imbued with an elegiac tone as well as a defiant one.

Levine connects these tones by linking violent and tranquil images—that is to say, he finds an image's internal sense of paradox. For example, fields of cotton are often thought of as a quiet, almost pastoral image. Cotton-picking is hard, back-breaking work, but here the work is made harder because the fields are burning, an image that signifies the life of the laborer. Second, the earth is often thought of as Mother Earth, but it is anything but motherly in this poem. The poet is affected by this contrast. He questions why the earth would let children die and women curse and why it will eat lives the way people "eat/ an apple, meat, skin, core, seeds." He questions why people must tear a living "from the silent earth." The traditional image of the earth as benign and generous has been transformed into an image of affliction and distress.

In addition, Levine finds a paradox in the light. Traditionally, first light is a romantic image, going back to the Greek poet Homer's epithet of "rosy-fingered dawn." Dawn is a beginning, a new start. Yet in "Ashes," the first light "bloodies the sky," and beneath it the cotton-pickers are "bruised by the first hours" of that new sun. These paradoxes have a dramatic effect as they build throughout the poem. Building that kind of energy is a characteristic of Levine's poetry. He gives his images an urgency they might not otherwise have by endowing them with an emotional life: The bus creaks like a tired body; the earth is silent while the people suffer; answers hurt as much as questions; the sun bleeds the way people bleed.

Another device that is effective in this poem is the poet's direct address to the reader. By implication, Levine is suggesting that his readers are like the laborers and like him. All suffer and see suffering. One can "howl" one's name, call attention to oneself in a great burst of sound, but the wind will "blow it into dust." He tells readers that a person could "pledge" a "single life," but the earth "will eat it all."

By addressing readers, he pulls them deeper into his experience. One feels what the poet feels. This is the device for the poem's final movement, the prayer. The poet advises: "go down on your knees/ as though a king stood before you,/ and pray to become all you'll/ never be." One often thinks of hard work as the proper path to take to improve one's lot. Typically, however, Levine suggests that prayer will do as well, because—as the cotton-pickers demonstrate—hard work only begets more hard work.

Themes and Meanings

Readers familiar with Levine's work, his poetry of social protest, will recognize in this poem one of his familiar themes: the endurance and courage of men and women. It is their tenacity that lets them wake from the "dream of sleep/ without end" and return to the fields. It is their tenacity that brings them to his attention and makes him write about their lives.

One of the primary concerns in this poem is that the worker's fate is a life of what could be called "tired bodies"—one is caught in an endless cycle, like riding a bus to and from work, where everyone's face is "wide-eyed with hunger." In this sense, this lyric is not concentrated on an interior vision or revelation, as many lyric poems since the Romantic era have been. Instead, it is a public outcry, a loud "No!" shouted at the sky and at the earth. It presents the poet as someone who may best be described as a seer-activist. Levine is angry. He is angry at the earth in particular, because it burns lives into ashes, and even these ashes are blown away in the wind. He does not express sorrow, however; in another poem, "Red Dust," he writes that he does not "believe in sorrow;/ it is not American." What is American, "Ashes" implies, is work, and the work is never done.

The work of the poet is to see the "meat, skin, core, [and] seeds" of other lives and other suffering. By not feeling sorrowful about the cotton-pickers' lives—though feeling pain for them, empathizing with their general hardship—Levine allows room in his emotional response for something positive. Ironically, he finds in the ashes, at the poem's end, hope. Levine's habit has always been to celebrate the possible. The prayer motif at the end of the poem suggests that prayer cannot hurt. In the least, if the prayer is fulfilled and one does become a "fine flake of dust that moves/ at evening like smoke at great height/ above the earth and sees it all," one will be able to unite with the workers' suffering by also becoming a part of the visionary sky. A more knowing and sensitive aura will perhaps permeate the earth.

Thus, finally, "Ashes" is a poem about burial, but a burial in the sky. The prayer for empathy and vision that concludes the poem circles back to its beginning, to the "last winds of afternoon" that blow the smoke of hardship across the lives of those working on a hostile earth.

David Biespiel

AT GRASS

Author: Philip Larkin (1922-1985)
Type of poem: Lyric
First published: 1951, in *XX Poems*

The Poem

This lyric poem, written in formal verse, presents a meditation that is triggered by a pastoral scene of two horses "at grass." The speaker first observes the horses as an unspecified "them" whose identity must be pieced together, since they are hardly noticeable against the landscape of "cold shade" in which they are comfortably at grass. They "shelter" in it and are noticeable only when the wind brushes across their tails and manes. They are not outstanding but anonymous, simple horses pasturing peacefully.

So far the speaker has only pointed out what an uninformed passerby might notice, but he knows something more about these horses: They have had their moments of fame. The reader learns that fifteen years ago they were at the center of attention at the races, surrounded by excited concern, trophies, crowds, and the colors of the "silk" worn by the jockeys. There was much at stake, as evidenced by "numbers," "distances," and "stop-press columns on the street."

This recollection leads the speaker to wonder (in a phrase with echoes from William Shakespeare), "Do memories plague their ears like flies?" That is, do memories of busier, more glorious and exciting days nag at them and stir regret? The speaker recognizes in the simple shaking of the horses' heads that regret and nostalgia are human experiences and that, on the contrary, the horses seem content to be where they are. The fact that their glory days are gone goes hand-in-hand with their aging, and they are now surrounded by shadows at dusk rather than the sunny-day "parasols" and bright silks. "Summer by summer all stole away," the speaker reflects, musing in a melancholy tone on the passage of time and the inevitable evening of life. On the other hand, the meadows are "unmolesting," in contrast with their demanding days of distinction.

These horses' names are "almanacked" and will be remembered for some time to come. However, the fact that they have "slipped" their names implies that their fame was restricting, like halters, bridles, bits, and all the other paraphernalia of racing. They "stand at ease," and the speaker notices joy and well-being in their present state. They are not measured by "fieldglass" or "stop-watch," and the only ones who see them home are their caretakers, the groom and his boy at evening, in a touching domestic relationship that is lacking in sparkle and acclaim but is caring and durable.

Forms and Devices

A scene that at first seems insignificant yields a story and an understanding of these simple horses and, by extension, given the poet's musings, of human life. The speaker reconstructs the scene of the pasturing horses and the sport of horseracing—a competitive, lucrative undertaking—in a way that can be easily understood as a metaphor for human activity. What starts off as a seemingly simple descriptive lyric raises issues that make the reader reflect more deeply.

Using sport as a metaphor for life is not a novel idea, but seldom is this metaphor presented in calmly, evenly paced metrical language. Formally this poem is quite traditional, with an involved rhyme scheme (*abcabc*) in stanzas of six metered lines that consist of four fairly regular iambic feet; with few exceptions, there are eight syllables per line. Remarkably, these conventional features are not constricting; the poet manages flexibility in his phrasing and works with rhymes whose subtle musicality provides one of the age-old pleasures of poetry. Larkin often complained that modern verse, with its formal experiments and semantic subversions, leaves out the reader. Here Larkin involves the reader not only by means of the comforting, recognizable rhythms and look of the verse but also by presenting an absorbing scene that leads the reader to ponder the issues the poet raises.

In his accurate yet colloquial phrasing, the poet evokes details of the races ("Cups and Stakes and Handicaps," "Silks," "Numbers and parasols," "fieldglass," and "stop-watch"). The crowded excitement of glory days is suggested in words and phrases such as "heat," "littered grass," "the long cry/ Hanging unhushed," words that also connote discomfort and strain. They provide a semantic echo of the opening scene, in which the wind is said to "distress tail and mane." Saying that the horses have "slipped their names," while literally referring to the fact that the horses have outlived their celebrity, also points to the freedom of quiet anonymity.

Finally, "dusk," "shadows," and "evening" alert the reader to the symbolic suggestiveness underlying the whole poem. In his diction Larkin subtly raises metaphysical issues that are dealt with in an accessible manner. The ideas come from a particular situation. They are not superimposed, nor is the scene manufactured merely to illustrate an idea. The reality takes center stage.

Themes and Meanings

Larkin sees in these horses an enviable equilibrium; they finally "stand at ease." With evening comes a world of darkness, but the horses are in the "unmolesting meadows" where only the wind "distresses" them now. One cannot help but conclude that anonymity is something Larkin treasures; the spectacle of competition and risk—vital affairs of the world though these may be—is merely momentary glitter and show. Most living occurs in the quiet and nameless moments when stability and true caring flourish. The groom and his son care for the horses, whereas the "stop-watch" crowds at "starting gates" are interested in the vagaries of worldly fortune. The racetrack and other such arenas may have their appealing features, but once these are stripped away, a more stable reality emerges. As critic Alan Brownjohn noted in his book *Philip Larkin* (1975), "Life, for Larkin and, implicitly, for all of us, is something lived mundanely, with a gradually accumulating certainty that its golden prizes are sheer illusion." Brownjohn also remarks that in Larkin's poetry "the recognized rewards and goals in life are deceptions."

Larkin sees something relieving, even joyful in the anonymous decline of the horses. Furthermore, there is something undignified about the past's "starting-gates, the crowds and cries," in contrast to the present's "unmolesting meadows." Measuring life in terms of performance violates the dignity of the spirit. Perhaps, like racehorses who are valued for three or four years of their prime, human lives are also measured and valued for a brief time but continue for some time after. "At Grass" subtly poses a number of questions. Is public acclaim the only measure of value? Can one live anonymously and be happy? Does acclaim bring happiness? Horses, unlike humans, do not invest in worldly activities; it is all the same to them whether their names are "artificed" or "faded." That seems to be Larkin's view as well.

One might wonder why the poem ends with "the groom's boy" as well as with the groom himself. The poem posits no grand reward of life as "Dusk brims the shadows." The ease that comes at evening is apparently its own reward. The way that the horses at grass fit into the overall pattern of life is that there will always be another generation of horses. Human continuity and involvement are suggested by the inclusion of the groom and his boy. The fact that Larkin mentions the boy suggests that the groom shares in the horses' fate and their rising and "faded" glory. A. E. Housman, in his 1896 poem "To an Athlete Dying Young," celebrated the early death of a record-breaking athlete because it served to assure his lasting glory. Larkin's poem, by contrast, suggests that the fading of the glory brings fulfillment of a larger life plan. Everyone must fade and be sheltered in the "cold shade" and will be met at evening by caretakers, be they nurses and orderlies or, ultimately, the undertaker with the "bridles" of his trade.

Paul Serralheiro

AT LUCA SIGNORELLI'S RESURRECTION OF THE BODY

Author: Jorie Graham (1951-   )
Type of poem: Meditation
First published: 1983, in *Erosion*

The Poem

"At Luca Signorelli's Resurrection of the Body" is a long, free-verse poem of 106 lines divided into eighteen stanzas; the first seventeen stanzas have 6 lines and the final stanza contains 4 lines. The lines of this poem are mostly short and vary from two to six syllables per line, although some lines have as many as eight or nine syllables. The title immediately locates the poem's speaker in front of a fresco by Luca Signorelli, an Umbrian painter known for depicting muscular bodies in violent action, capturing them in a wide variety of poses and foreshortenings. *Resurrection of the Body* is in the San Brizo Chapel in Orvieto Cathedral, where, between 1499 and 1502, Signorelli painted a series of scenes depicting the end of the world.

Jorie Graham's persona speaks in the first person in a voice that is likely analogous to, if not wholly imitative of, the voice of the poet. With the speaker's voice so similar to Graham's, one is encouraged to read the tone of this poem as serious and philosophical. It appears that Graham will attempt to pose an answer to the introductory question, "Is it better, flesh/ that they/ should hurry so?" The poem is organized into three unannounced sections that show the speaker's meditation progressing from one subject to another. The first section comprises the first thirty-three lines, in which Graham gazes at the details of the fresco. She notices the violence of the bodies and points out how the subjects of the painting "hurry/ to enter/ their bodies." There is a bombastic and cacophonous quality to these images. Angels "blare down/ trumpets and light." Graham questions whether the spirits entering these bodies truly desire perfection because the precision of Signorelli's work, evident in the detailed muscles of the subjects in the painting, suggests that only the painter desires such perfection.

In the second section, Graham looks outside the cathedral. When she states that "Outside/ it is 1500," she brings together the time of the fresco's composition with the lyric moment of the poem. This suggests that Signorelli's frescoes have powerfully altered her perceptions of the world. Graham also juxtaposes thoughts about the figures on the wall, which remain ignorant of their experience, with a recognition that she, as a viewer of this fresco, is unable to tell them that there will be no fulfillment of their dreams of "wanting names,/ wanting/ happiness." In the third movement of the poem, Graham's thoughts lead her away from the fresco and the cathedral to a narrative about how Signorelli dissected the body of his young son who died in an accident. Graham portrays this action as a loving search for truth, emphasizing words such as "beauty," "care," and "caress." In order to understand his grief and loss, Signorelli, a master of depicting the muscles of the body, must explore what is unknown to him: the inside of his son's body.

Forms and Devices

The experience of standing in front of a painting and contemplating its meaning is an experience that is likely familiar to most readers. Poems written about this type of experience are part of a genre called ekphrastic poetry. Ekphrastic poems often show a speaker attempting to find meaning or feeling by looking intently and deeply at a painting, sculpture, or photograph. The images of the art object often become a part of the imagery of the poem. Two familiar examples of ekphrastic poetry are John Keats's "Ode on a Grecian Urn" and William Carlos Williams's "Pictures from Brueghel." There are several other ekphrastic poems in Graham's *Erosion* collection. Paintings by Signorelli, Piero della Francesca, Masaccio, Francisco de Goya, and Gustav Klimt allow Graham to interact with visual art in a way that makes art objects part of a living, breathing tradition of attempting to make philosophical sense of the world. Signorelli's painting is as real and as vivid as any image in twentieth century poetry. Just as Williams's "The Red Wheelbarrow" is about the visual importance of a commonplace object because of the mental connections that it can stimulate in one who sees it, Graham's poem focuses upon the value of art's ability to focus her thought. Art allows Graham to understand how one can make sense of the relationship between body and mind. This specific fresco is not only valuable for its intellectual and historical importance, but it is also of value because of the thoughts and responses that it continues to trigger in its viewers.

One of the most obvious aspects of this poem's form is Graham's use of a short line that approximates Williams's trimeter line. These lines, barely long enough to contain more than three or four words, require the reader to move down the page quickly. Instead of reading each line as a freestanding unit of thought or imagery, Graham's short line encourages the reader to recognize the dependence of each line upon the lines that precede and follow it. In the first stanza, an associative logic becomes apparent as Graham's thinking leads her from her command to notice the fresco to a questioning of whether such action is good and back to a recognition of the image of the angels in the fresco.

While there is a sequential, orderly logic that leads Graham from a contemplation in front of the painting into a meditation about the relationship between the body and mind, this logic may not be obvious to the reader. Graham's poem does not proceed line by line as much as it proceeds step by step. There is a movement between discursive commentary and imagistic detail that organizes the poem thought by thought. These thoughts are then broken down into lines that reflect the complications of tonal change that occur. Graham's philosophical poem does not offer a coherent argument with thesis, proof, and conclusion; it is more analogous to a private moment that the reader has been privileged to overhear, a moment in which an engaged and intelligent speaker attempts to sort something out.

Themes and Meanings

"At Luca Signorelli's Resurrection of the Body" is a poem that contemplates the relationship between body and mind. At what point, the poem asks of its readers, subject, and speaker, can the work of the mind transcend the body, or is the mind permanently fixed to the body? There is a paradox in this relationship in Graham's poem. Signorelli, who painted bodies of exquisite precision and beauty, who understood the physical nature of the body as well as anyone of his time, found himself plagued by doubt upon the death of his son and could not understand his son's death until he explored every cavern of his corpse.

Graham's attempt to understand how Signorelli graduates from the "symbolic/ to the beautiful" causes her to ask, "How far is true?" Her poem does not answer this question definitively. For Signorelli, truth was found by an exploration deep inside the body. For Graham, truth is less easily defined. The present-tense lyric moment of this poem is permanently altered by the experience of viewing the frescoes when she looks out and finds Orvieto of 1500. After this experience, Graham is unable to recognize Orvieto in the present; she can only understand it through the artifice of the past. As for the question of truth, there is no definitive truth, only a multiplicity of particulars that swirl around in the poet's mind like leaves rising in the wind. The beauty of such experience is unlike the confident assertion at the end of Keats's "Ode on a Grecian Urn": "Beauty is truth, truth beauty,—that is all/ ye know on earth, and all ye need to know." Unlike Keats's assurance that truth is beauty, Graham is unable to offer a definitive answer. Graham's truth is unstable and mutable; it is difficult to understand because it is constantly shaped by experience.

In an interview, Graham speaks of her poems as "exploded instants," moments in which sequential and lyrical moments in time move the poem along. This method allows her to capture the immediacy and timing of sequential instants in a way that mirrors the processes of thought. Instead of using narrative progression, Graham's poems are organized more impressionistically. They are composed of haikulike moments that accumulate musically instead of logically. This strategy allows Graham to incorporate moments of doubt, questioning, and uncertainty into her work. These moments, because they allow readers to understand the processes of thought in their full complexity, are the distinct achievement of Graham's poetry.

Jeffrey Greer

AT MELVILLE'S TOMB

Author: Hart Crane (1899-1932)
Type of poem: Lyric
First published: 1926, in *White Buildings*

The Poem

"At Melville's Tomb" is written in four four-line stanzas that follow an irregular rhyme scheme. The reader is placed at the gravesite of the noted nineteenth century American novelist, Herman Melville, whose tales of the sea—most notably *Moby Dick* (1851)—are generally regarded as commentaries on humans coping with one another and nature in a vast, often inimical, and ultimately destructive universe. The speaker, while he may be inspired by Melville, shares with the reader his own personal feelings and observations as he stands "at Melville's tomb."

There is not the expected use of the first person. Rather, one is told what Melville, identified only by the third-person pronoun "he," must have felt and observed when he had stood apparently at the same spot where he is now buried—"wide from this ledge"—and, considering the flotsam and jetsam washing up onto the Atlantic shore, had reflected on the relationship not only between man and the sea but also between man and eternity.

The images are difficult, but not impenetrable. The reader is told that amid the wreckage, and hence the apparent waste, that the sea washes up exist records of human passings, "The dice of drowned men's bones bequeath[ing]/ An embassy"—that is, imparting some message from the past. What are ostensibly tokens of destruction and loss can in fact be constructive elements if one can read them effectively.

Melville, too, is a messenger from the past, known now only in his works; the poem, except for the final stanza, is written in the past tense. Any record is only a remnant of some greater and more actual whole, after all, so the "numbers" (not simply the dice, but those messages and meaning the past might hold) are "obscured." In the middle two stanzas, one is thrust from the safety of the shore into a confused and nightmarish world wherein the sea becomes a whirlpool, the whirlpool a seashell, and the seashell "one vast coil," until in a turmoil of language and image one's vision is swept downward into an incredible sinkhole of misguided or mistaken information— "A scattered chapter, livid hieroglyphs,/ . . . portent"—and in desperation one raises "Frosted eyes" to see on "lifted altars . . . silent answers [creep] across the stars."

This movement from tumult to silence, from a barrage of sensations to a single, quiescent image, may be welcome, but it is less than rewarding. Unlike the certain, but obscured messages that the sea offers, whatever is revealed by the stars comes without the benefit of words or images and therefore perhaps comes without meaning.

Instead, in the fourth and final stanza, which has the poem's only present-tense verb, "contrive," the reader is told that all human knowing is in a sense a contrivance. Human instruments are limited in their ability to discern the actual meaning that the sea or the universe holds. This is true not only of those instruments that nature provided, but also of the instruments that humans make. Thus, "Compass, quadrant and sextant [can] contrive/ No farther tides," simply because they are man-made measures only of what one needs to know in practical terms, not of what is there to be known.

When it comes to that vision found "High in the azure steeps," from which one would hope for more timeless messages, one is left, if not confused, at least asleep—"Monody shall not wake the mariner." The sea to which Melville, for one, had looked for an answer to the ageless human dilemmas of sorrow and death can offer only the "fabulous shadow," or distant reflection, of that higher and more enduring truth that the stars hold.

Forms and Devices

An examination of something as simple as Hart Crane's rhyme scheme gives insight into the complex technical virtuosities for which he is both renowned and criticized. The four-line stanzas combine blank verse and rhymed couplets virtually at will, with no attempt at creating a pattern, let alone repeating it from one stanza to the next.

This creation of anticipations that are then either discarded or confounded is in keeping both with Crane's poetry and with the period in which he wrote. The ultimate modernist poet, Crane worked with words the way a painter works with pigments, combining them into larger and larger blends of imagery and detail until even the most trivial subject-verb combinations—"he saw . . . he watched"—become entangled in complexities: "The dice of drowned men's bones he saw bequeath/ An embassy. Their numbers as he watched,/ Beat on the dusty shore and were obscured."

In a famous exchange of letters, Harriet Monroe, then editor of *Poetry* magazine, challenged Crane to clarify the apparent obscurity of this particular imagery. He was easily able to do so precisely because every word and its associations had been chosen and then constructed with great care toward both lexical and figurative meaning.

By using ambiguous syntactical elements as well, such as verbs that could be nouns—"portent wound," for example—Crane is able to make each image cluster serve double and often triple duty. Similarly, "this ledge" can be an actual point on an actual shoreline above the actual sea, or it could be a figurative description of a human plane of reference, making the sea the figurative emblem of eternity.

Meaning in a Crane poem often floats freely between all literal and figurative potentialities. What is difficult in his poetry can become easier to unravel and reconstruct once one understands that Crane never obscures merely for the sake of obscuring. Rather, if and when Crane does obscure normal meaning and syntax, it is done in order to arrive at a wider and therefore richer range of associations and connections.

Finally, Crane's poetry is steeped in both the English and American literary traditions. Besides the overt allusions to Melville's body of work, one might be reminded of Pip, who in *Moby Dick* survives a drowning only at the expense of his sanity; of the whirlpool in Edgar Allan Poe's *The Narrative of Arthur Gordon Pym* (1838); or of Samuel Taylor Coleridge's beleaguered Ancient Mariner—yet another nightmarish vision of the sea as a metaphor both for the destructiveness of nature and for the human spiritual condition. Such literary associations add to the richness and scope of Crane's own intentions.

Themes and Meanings

If there is a single theme to a poetic experience as rich and complex as the one "At Melville's Tomb" provides, it is that there are limits to human knowledge, yet that does not mean that there are limits to human vision. The poet warns one not to expect the typical from his poetry while nevertheless allowing one to imagine that there is some overriding and predictable formal order to the poem. To some degree, that is the message of the poem as well.

The more deeply one looks into things, the more obscure and confused one's vision becomes; however, the instant one casts one's eyes into the most expansive of vistas, one recognizes some overriding structure to time and space and eternity—even if one finds it impossible to say or to measure what that structure may be.

By avoiding the present tense, Crane pushes the reader into an epistemological quagmire. What one knows and how one knows it are revealed to be worthless pieces of information in comparison with the ultimate mystery: the momentary existence of the universe itself. In the process of resurrecting Melville and his vision, for example, the poet nevertheless keeps his reader mindful of the pastness of the present that Melville occupied, just as the "he" of the poem is examining information whose living, or useful, significance lies in the past.

The danger is in thinking that Crane is saying that one must therefore "know" nothing. By poem's end, Crane allows one to imagine only some future epiphany that may not even wake one. What is clearly absent is a knowable present, and that, for the living, feeling mind, is the biggest problem. If we can realize, however, as the poem suggests, that all one's so-called knowledge is in fact berthed in one's very unknowing—that it is, in very real terms, one's confusions and uncertainties that cause one to raise eyes and lift altars—then one can understand why the stars, even in their silence, offer something "fabulous." Their very silence tells a far more profound tale than the worldly detritus on the shores of human knowledge can ever repeat.

Russell Elliott Murphy

AT THE BALL GAME

Author: William Carlos Williams (1883-1963)
Type of poem: Lyric
First published: 1923, in *Spring and All*

The Poem

"At the Ball Game" is a short poem in free verse, its thirty-six lines divided into eighteen stanzas of two lines apiece. The title suggests events occurring at a traditional American pastime, a baseball game; its function, however, is darker, as what actually happens at the ball game shows a side of the American character that most people would prefer to keep hidden.

The poem is written in a third-person dramatic style, with the narrator commenting on the mood of the crowd as it watches the game and observes individuals in its midst. One never enters directly into the mind of anyone in the crowd, but one sees from this more objective perspective how quickly normal spectators can be transformed into a snarling pack.

"At the Ball Game" begins with a scene that most Americans will recognize: a crowd at a game existing for one purpose only—to delight in the beauty of "the exciting detail/ of the chase/ and the escape" (lines 5-7). The crowd, described with the personal third-person plural "they" and "them," may be witnessing a runner racing to first base; it may be witnessing an "error/ flash of genius" (lines 7-8) that either helps the runner reach base safely or sees him put out in the nick of time. It is of no real consequence to the crowd or poet whether the runner is "out" or "safe" ultimately; they simply want to see athletic prowess—the skill and grace of players enjoying and excelling in their sport.

The crowd, which was "moved uniformly" in the first two lines of the poem, is still described as being "beautiful . . . in detail" in lines 11 and 12. Immediately afterward, still within the same sentence, William Carlos Williams darkens the scene. The "beautiful" crowd is now "to be warned against/ saluted, and defied." The crowd is a potent force that can do more than appreciate the beauty of the game. What might it do in a lull in the action, or between innings, for example? What reverence or allegiance might it demand of those in its midst? Thus the crowd goes from being the protagonist of the piece to being the force of opposition.

In line 16, Williams changes his use of personal pronouns to the neuter "it": "It is alive, venomous/ it smiles grimly." "Its" force, moreover, is directed against those who traditionally stand out in the crowd: "The flashy female" and "the Jew" (lines 19 and 21). They are discussed, verbally abused with gossip or open jibes; they "get it straight," and what they get from the crowd is reminiscent of "the Inquisition" and of a "Revolution" (lines 23 and 24) in which those who are different are swept away, put out of sight.

The poem ends by reminding the reader of the potential beauty still residing in the crowd, living "day by day in them/ idly" (lines 27 and 28). While the "power of their faces" (line 30) harbors great beauty, it also contains and is most willing to emit horrible abuse in the form of the stares they have given earlier to those they do not like. This is Williams's final irony. In the summer solstice, at a normal gathering of fans at a ball game, people laugh and cheer "permanently, seriously" (line 35) at the same time that they ridicule and mentally attack others near them who simply want to enjoy the game and the summer day.

Forms and Devices

Since the poem is in free verse, it avoids many obvious devices. The two most obvious literary devices used in "At the Ball Game" are the images of the crowd and game—suggested by the way Williams phrases what are rather ordinary, colorless words—and the extended metaphor of the crowd itself representing any group of people that can shift its temper suddenly and drastically.

Though one must read to the end of the poem to determine exactly the sport being played (baseball being the dominant American sport played during the summer solstice), one can from the beginning imagine the scene of an enthusiastic crowd at a sporting event, sitting in a large stadium, thanks to Williams's suggestive diction. Although Williams never names the sport, his brief mentioning of the "chase," "escape," "error," and "flash of genius" helps one imagine various scenarios: a base runner caught in a run-down; a runner from third base trying to beat the throw from the outfield home; an error made as the outfielder bobbles the ball, or as the short-stop allows a ground ball to pass between his legs; or the "genius" of the runner eluding the tag from the catcher. These are a few of the possibilities regarding baseball that a few well-chosen words might cause one to imagine.

Just as one imagines these scenes and the crowd's exclamations of joy and delight, so might one imagine the ugly stares or verbal swipes of the crowd toward the overdressed young woman and the dark-skinned Jew who pass by, perhaps on their way to the restroom or concession stand, simply by the repetition of the otherwise vague phrase "they get it." By contrast, though, Williams's precise language enables the reader to see and hear the crowd turn into an unruly and crude mob through the use of the words "Inquisition" and "Revolution"—words that conjure more violent and threatening images of people being caught up in a mass frenzy.

The crowd as metaphor works equally as well to engender feelings of uneasiness within the reader—to keep the reader off-guard as to how he or she should feel about the crowd. Since most people have attended sporting contests, one knows how crowds can quickly go from being delighted to being ugly. Ideally, everyone is at the event for the same reason: to appreciate the skill of the athletes. Yet people not only turn on them if they err, they also turn on one another if they root for opposite teams, or if in their anxiety or boredom they need an outlet, a scapegoat. The beautiful crowd of people who seem harmless, innocuous, and only interested in apprehending beauty at one moment turn into a poisonous "It" capable of any sort of abuse in the next.

When one thinks of what sorts of mobs a few groups of people have changed into—

lynch mobs, the Ku Klux Klan, or Nazis—one cannot miss the potential of Williams's metaphorical implications.

Themes and Meanings

"At the Ball Game" is a perfect example of Williams's desire to create a new kind of poetry. In keeping with other writers of the modernist period (roughly from the 1890's to the 1940's), Williams equates style with meaning: The way he structures the poem is integral to what he wants to say through the poem.

For example, just as the crowd changes with no warning from delighting in beauty to jeering at its own members, so the poem, with its lack of punctuation and refusal to end a thought at the end of a line, keeps the reader from reaching a full stop until the very last line. The reader thereby witnesses the abrupt transformations as they occur; he or she sees the crowd go from a "uniform beauty" to a deadly and terrifying "Inquisition" in a matter of seconds.

In this way, "At the Ball Game" strongly resembles Williams's well-known poem "The Red Wheelbarrow." The theme and style of "At the Ball Game" are dependent on the crowd, and what seems so simple at first becomes complicated by the end. For example, in reading the lines "So in detail they, the crowd,/ are beautiful/ for this/ to be warned against" (lines 11-14), one sees the continuation from line to line of a thought that instead of simply completing itself, transforms itself into something unexpected, challenging, and quite the opposite of where the thought started. The crowd's momentary beauty lulls one into perceiving what is only partially true; the reader is "warned" that the beauty of the crowd may be one's undoing—then, before one fully digests the warning, one discovers how transitory that beauty really is.

This transformation of seemingly continuous thoughts should then cause the reader to ask the central question: How can such an appreciation of skill and beauty coexist with such an abusive intolerance? Given America's internal conflicts and contradictions, however, Williams might ask, Why be so startled? It is perfectly normal, like a day at the ball game. The crowd, then, is simply like the whole of the American people. It is also like a poem: It may seem easy to read, but it may be quite difficult and even dangerous to comprehend.

Terry Barr

AT THE EXECUTED MURDERER'S GRAVE

Author: James Wright (1927-1980)
Type of poem: Meditation
First published: 1958, revised and collected in *Saint Judas*, 1959

The Poem

"At the Executed Murderer's Grave" is composed of seventy-seven lines of freely rhymed iambic pentameter. The title expresses the subject. The poet is meditating on the grave of the convicted murderer George Doty, a taxi driver from Belaire, Ohio. Doty drove a girl out of town, made a pass at her, and, when she resisted, killed her. In an interview with Dave Smith (in *The Pure Clear Word: Essays on the Poetry of James Wright*, 1982, edited by Smith), Wright explains, "Many people in that community thought [Doty] was terribly wicked, but he did not seem to be wicked. He was just a dumb guy who was suddenly thrust into the middle of the problem of evil." Doty was executed in the electric chair.

Like many of Wright's poems, this one is about the outcast. Part of his concern is the incapacity of some members of society to understand other members. The severing of communications between the living and the dead becomes, for him, the ultimate barrier to human connectedness. Kindness and vengeance, pity and loathing, empathy and fear are important contrasts in the poem.

The poem begins by showing Wright's position to the killer: "I was born/ Twenty-five miles from this infected grave." He says that his father "tried to teach me kindness," that he once went to the grave ("I made my loud display"), that he is "Now sick of lies," and that he will "add my easy grievance to the rest."

It is no easy grievance, however, as the rest of the poem will show. In fact, Wright identifies himself with the insane, "Pleased to be playing guilty." In an early version of the poem, he wrote, "I killed this man,/ This man who killed another," for "Man's wild blood has no heart to overcome/ Vengeance." In the final version, he says truly, though still ironically, "I croon my tears at fifty cents per line."

In stanza 3, after a list of Doty's crimes, the poet's disgust is expressed in the image of Doty as a dog, "Fitter for vomit than a kind man's grief." He also confesses no love for "the crying/ Drunks of Belaire," brutalized by the police. "I do not pity the dead," he says, "I pity the dying," of which he is one.

In stanza 4, Wright focuses on three key issues: "If Belmont County killed him, what of me?/ His victims never loved him. Why should we?/ And yet, nobody had to kill him either." In answer: "I kick the clods away."

Stanza 5 is a key section. According to John 8:7, Jesus told the one among the accusers "without sin to throw the stone first." Here the poet acknowledges "My sneaking crimes" and believes "the earth/ And its dead" shall be judged by "the princes of the sea." In the short stanza that follows, he concludes that none will "mark my face/ From any murderer's," since "We are nothing but a man."

In stanza 7, the final one, Wright realizes that "God knows, not I," when "suicides will stop." Doty "Sleeps in a ditch of fire," like one of Dante's souls, and Wright feels "fear, not grief." He bids the ground to open, knowing Doty, "Dirt of my flesh," is "defeated, underground."

Forms and Devices

Despite iambic pentameter and end rhyme, the lines are not always dulcet, unlike many of Wright's earlier efforts. The poet and his commentators, including Smith and poet and critic Donald Hall, see "At the Executed Murderer's Grave" as a "watershed poem," dividing his earlier style from his more mature work.

Wright's first book, *The Green Wall* (1957), contains "A Poem About George Doty in the Death House." This precursor poem has six stanzas in trimeter verse with regular rhyme scheme and unobtrusive diction. Though scorned by community members for caring more about Doty than the murdered girl ("I mourn no soul but his"), his language is passionless, guarded, and devoid of commitment. The later poem, with its harsh colloquial language and candid utterance, is another case entirely.

What changed? Hall, in his introduction to *Above the River* (1990), quotes Wright describing himself as "a literary operator (and one of the slickest, cleverest, most charming' concoctors of the do-it-yourself . . . verse)." Hall says Wright was thinking of quitting poetry altogether because it was not real to him anymore. Then he began this poem.

Though still producing a metric line, Wright's use of diction creates a different kind of poetry. For one thing, proper nouns appear in abundance. By using his and Doty's names and the place-names of his region, the poet acquires a direct voice. As a consequence, he stops using persona (speaking as though he were someone else, as in "Sappho," for example, where he speaks as a barren woman). What is more, frank admissions ("To hell with them") and strong language ("giggling muckers") present a sharper, more nonliterary surface.

At times, the iambic pentameter is roughened up. The aforementioned last line of stanza 3 has an extra foot, and two lines of stanza 6 have an extra syllable. The eleventh line of stanza 7 requires an elision ("th' Ohio grass"), setting off the imagery of sea and stars with near rhyme, "a tide of gray disastrousness." In themselves, these are only mild aberrations. In stanza 7 alone, however, eleven of fifteen lines begin with a noniambic foot and the tenth line (the only line in the poem using parentheses and exclamation marks) begins in trochaic measure, to stark effect.

The greatest deviation from iambic pentameter occurs in stanza 5, the only part of the poem that speaks of the future otherworld. These ten lines are a study in metrical contrast and meaning. They contain two sentences, one very short and one very long. More interestingly, the perfect iambic pentameter sixth line ("To lay away their robes, to judge the earth") is embedded in four irregular lines; and these, in turn, along with the sixth, are embedded in regular lines. The effect is to highlight the imagery of Judgment Day against "bodies" in Ohio—Wright's, his father's, Doty's—which "Ridiculously kneel" under "God's unpitying stars."

Themes and Meanings

The first two versions of the poem appeared in *Botteghe Oscure* (a quote from which appeared above) and *Poetry*, respectively. Wright was unsatisfied with both versions and asked James Dickey (the J. L. D. to whom the final version is dedicated), the poet who would later write "The Fiend" and other psychological poems, for help. While aboard a train, without a copy of the earlier versions and with only the memory of Dickey's verbal comments, Wright wrote the final version.

Topical poems such as this are difficult. No matter which insights the poet brings to bear, opinions precede him. With controversial subjects like capital punishment and sympathy for criminals, he knew he could not avoid treading on zealously held beliefs of the 1950's. As a result, he and the poem were vulnerable to attack. Commendably, Wright allowed his beliefs and feelings to shine forth, and the subsequent development of not only his own poems but also of modern poetry in general is better for this painstaking exhibition.

The epigraph of the poem is from Sigmund Freud's *Das Unbehagen in der Kultur* (1930; *Civilization and Its Discontents*, 1961), a work that shows that civilization is possible only by the individual's renunciation of deep-seated pleasures and aggressions. The puzzling quote is about the biblical admonition "Love thy neighbor as thyself," a topic that leads Freud to declare subsequently, "[Civilization] hopes to prevent the crudest excesses of brutal violence by itself assuming the right to use violence against criminals."

A poet who was to grow with each of his books, Wright's first poems glittered with promise. This is true because he possessed a fine ear for meter and rhyme early in his career. Later, when he abandoned these devices, his ear held fast to near-perfect rhythms and economies of emotive phrase. His ability to turn personal experience into poetry was his finest asset.

"To a Fugitive" and "American Twilights, 1957" are also about slain prisoners. The latter is about Caryl Chessman, the Red-Light Bandit, who smuggled his writings out of death row before being executed in California for murder and rape. "The Fugitive" is a sonnet advising a man in flight from the law to "break the last law" and "race between the stars." The title poem, "Saint Judas," is a sonnet about one who knew "The kiss that ate my flesh." Ostensibly from the Gospel, this poem reveals the betrayal of man by man.

The theme of the grave occurs throughout Wright's writings. "A Dream of Burial," in *The Branch Will Not Break* (1963), is a vision about his own decomposition. The poem preceding "At the Executed Murderer's Grave," entitled "Devotions," tells how "I must find/ A grave to prod my wrath/ Back to its just devotions." Wrath seems a doubtful quality to turn into devotion, yet Wright is able to assume the "dual role" (as Edward Butscher says in Smith's book) "of outcast and savior." This spiritual stance, not unlike that of poet Sylvia Plath, produces an "inward voice" capable of turning death into art. Even so, Wright is one who affirmed the goodness of life.

John Young

AN ATLAS OF THE DIFFICULT WORLD

Author: Adrienne Rich (1929-　　)
Type of poem: Poetic sequence
First published: 1991, in *An Atlas of the Difficult World: Poems, 1988-1991*

The Poem

"An Atlas of the Difficult World" is a long poem divided into thirteen sections or short poems that relate experiences and observations. The sections are of varying length and are identified only by roman numerals, except for the seventh and the final ones, parenthetically titled "(The Dream-Site)" and "(Dedications)," respectively. Although in the poem the persona, or poetic voice, is often an assumed identity, Adrienne Rich's poetic journey is enriched by personal images and observations. In this, her thirteenth volume of poetry, Rich provides readers with a mural that does not begin or end with this poem but connects with previous works dating back to 1951, when her first collection, *A Change of World*, was published.

As denoted by the term "atlas," the series of poems describes a collection of American scenes that are bound together. Starting in California's Salinas Valley, "THE SALAD BOWL OF THE WORLD," Rich characterizes the place not only by location but also by the people who live and work in the "agribusiness empires."

Throughout the poem, the people she describes are not famous but are always recognizable. They are, in a sense, the landscape of the American journey, which, as the title implies, is part of a difficult world. In the second section Rich addresses the central focus of the poem, looking at "our country" as a whole and alluding to social and economic conditions in the United States. The section ends with an imagined dialogue with a reader: "I promised to show you a map you say but this is a mural." Rich responds to the hypothetical comment by replying that such distinctions are not important: "where do we see it from is the question."

In section III Rich relates experiences and memories in the East as she sits "at this table in Vermont." She describes past summers with her husband and children, which then connect with her own childhood. The image of her father, a Jew whose motto was "Without labor, no sweetness," illustrates the continuity of existence that the poet conveys in every section of the poem; it also allows Rich to comment that she now knows that "not all labor ends in sweetness." Next, in section IV, she mentions the girasole plant (a type of sunflower), which "laces the roadsides from Vermont to California," the implied cross-country trip providing a desperate view of a countryside in decay, in need of repair. In California (section V) she takes the reader to San Francisco and its contrasting images of splendor and human waste—from views of the Palace of Fine Arts to San Quentin, Alcatraz, and "places where life is cheap poor quick unmonumented." From the start she is the reader's tour guide, deciding the itinerary and providing the background needed to appreciate the scenes. In section VI, set in nineteenth century Ireland and America, poetry becomes the necessary tool for expressing the nature of the human condition: "poetry of cursing and silence," "of I.R.A.-talk, kitchen-talk, dream-talk." Section VII, "(The Dream-Site)," is about New York City, where Rich once lived, and it conveys a sense of why she had to leave the East.

Sections IX and X depict scenes of loneliness and isolation. Citing the Mohave Desert and the Grand Canyon, the poems describe human loneliness as immense and infertile. In section X she includes excerpts from a book entitled *Soledad Brother: The Prison Letters of George Jackson* (1970). Soledad, a California prison located near Monterey, is an artificial structure, unlike the Mohave Desert and Grand Canyon, but it still signifies through its cavelike structure the loneliness that the poet sees carved into the human landscape of the country.

In section XI the people of Monterey have gone through several natural disasters, including earthquakes and a devastating drought. Analogous to these natural holocausts is war. Rich meditates on what it means to love one's country, to be a citizen, to be a patriot. Some march for peace, some contemplate "the shapes of/ powerlessness and power." The poet attempts to define the word "patriot"—an emotionally charged word that has been used on all sides of the political spectrum—and comes to a series of conclusions, including the concepts that a patriot "wrestles for the soul of her country" and is "a citizen trying to wake/ from the burnt-out dream of innocence."

In section XII Rich as tour guide takes the reader to New Mexico, with its "Indian distance, Indian presence." She had driven through it with her companion a month ago, she writes; at the time she did not speak of her companion's beauty, her spirit's gaze, or her hands, but, she says, "I speak of them now." Section XIII, "(Dedication)," captures the connection between reader and poet. Like Walt Whitman, she reaches out to the reader with empathy and simple yet universal images. Repeatedly beginning lines with "I know you are reading this poem," Rich presents descriptions of her imagined readers. They range from an office worker on her way home to an elderly reader with "failing sight" to a young mother warming milk for a crying child. Each figure, despite difficulties, is reading the poem, "listening for something, torn between bitterness and hope."

Forms and Devices

"An Atlas of the Difficult World" is a mural of the American landscape—emotional, economic, social, political—painted through imagery and metaphor. Images of ordinary people, especially women, are highlighted in each of the thirteen segments. The scenes, although specific and detailed, represent the universality of women's experiences. Rich's metaphoric language adds richness to the vignettes, and she appeals to the senses with such phrases as "strawberry blood on the wrist." However, it is her use of the atlas as the extended metaphor that synthesizes the discrete scenes, unifying them into a comprehensive whole.

In section V each image describes "your country's moment"; each is a significantly historical event that has left devastation, from the Battle of Wounded Knee to the last airlift from Saigon to a more recent event: Rich records a heinous attack on two lesbians who were camping along the Appalachian Trail in 1988. One was killed, and the other managed to drag herself back to town to notify the authorities. The attacker, in defending himself, states that they had "teased his loathing." The image of death, literal and powerful, sparks a universal connection as Rich realizes, "A crosshair against the pupil of an eye/ could blow my life from hers."

Reaching out to those who are disfranchised from the politics of the American landscape, Rich cites excerpts from *Soledad Brother* in section X. Soledad Prison is aptly named; Rich introduces the section with the dictionary meanings of the Spanish word *soledad:* "Solitude, loneliness, homesickness; lonely retreat." The passages from the prison letters not only provide a glimpse into prison life but also allow the reader to comprehend the impact that imprisonment has on a human being: "a man's thoughts/ become completely disorganized." The desperate man understands that this "college of force," as Rich calls it, has made him bitter, angry, and full of self-hatred. All these feelings are comprehended by women, Rich implies, because they also are oppressed. In the poem's final section, the images of women are patterned after imagined readers, struggling in various situations to read the poem. They read it because "there is nothing else left to read."

In Rich's poetry, metaphors involve thriving, ongoing processes that are linked together by memories or imagination. For example, in section VI, the potato exploding in the oven alludes to the potato famine that brought many Irish immigrants to the United States at the turn of the twentieth century. The famine and immigration are linked metaphorically to the poetry that is not taken seriously as such, the colloquialisms of workers and common people: "Poetry/ in the workhouse," "poetry of cursing and silence." In section XI, natural disasters become metaphors for both internal and universal devastation: "Earthquake and drought followed by freezing followed by war." Every person, Rich contends, is in crisis. Extending the metaphor, the poet focuses on the poet as patriot: "A patriot is one who wrestles for the soul of her country/ as she wrestles for her own being." Rich guides the reader to a redefinition of "patriot" as one remembering "her true country."

Rich's atlas, her collection of maps, becomes a human mural that stretches from coast to coast. Like Dante's Vergil in the *Inferno*, Rich as a guide possesses the vision and the wisdom needed to make the poetic journey. With the ultimate goal of reconstructing society, Rich must represent contemporary failings and atrocities to the reader. The tone is urgent as Rich escorts the reader across the American landscape, commingling past and present, personal and universal events. She provides a view of a "familiar globe," as she described it in a 1984 essay entitled "Notes Toward a Politics of Location" (collected in *Blood, Bread, and Poetry,* 1986). Continuing, she states that only by repairing the "toxic rivers, the cancerous wells, the strangled valleys" can humankind move to a better place.

Themes and Meanings

"An Atlas of the Difficult World" is a poetic pilgrimage to a place where change is possible. As Adrienne Rich states in "Notes Toward a Politics of Location," "*I am the woman who asks the questions.*" Advocating social and political change is not new for

Rich, who since the 1960's has been prominent in the women's and the feminist-lesbian movements. The theme of inclusion rather than separatism permeates this poem as it identifies and reaffirms the poet's connection with the common woman and even the common man. Unlike *The Dream of a Common Language* (1978), written for and about women, this poetic sequence embraces all who are disfranchised, disenchanted, and conscious of the oppression and decay of Western society. Rich sees hope resting in her readers, notably her female readers, as envisioned in the final section. The questions she reiterates in two earlier sections (V and XI) resonate with her purpose:

> Where are we moored?
> What are the bindings?
> What behooves us?

Both challenging and embracing the reader by using the pronoun "we," she bridges the gap between herself, a self-described white, Jewish, middle-class woman, and others who are very different. This tone of inclusiveness provides a sense of community in the struggle and dramatizes the poet's recognition that she is not alone, that there are others "torn between bitterness and hope."

Ultimately, the text of feminism is too confining to construct the foundation necessary to build a better world. Therefore, the philosophical framework for her vision of the transformation of women, depicted in earlier works including *Diving into the Wreck* (1973) and *The Dream of a Common Language*, must be expanded. It must include both men and women in order to create the changes necessary for emerging from "the death-freeze of the century." Rich calls to those who have marched before and are homesick for their "true country" and to those who have the moral courage to ask difficult questions.

A formidable poet, Rich is unwilling to let her poetic voice for change be silenced because of political expediency or immobilizing apathy. As she explained in *On Lies, Secrets, and Silence* (1979), a collection of prose written between 1966 and 1978, she feels compelled to speak for those who "are less conscious of what they are living through." In "An Atlas of the Difficult World" she is not only speaking for other women but also describing them and internalizing their lives in an attempt to enlist them in the struggle for change. They, she believes, are the hope for the future. As she states in "Final Notations," the last poem of the collection *An Atlas of the Difficult World*, the struggle "will take all your heart, it will take all your breath."

Cynthia S. Becerra

ATOMIC PANTOUM

Author: Peter Meinke (1932-   )
Type of poem: Meditation
First published: 1987, in *Night Watch on the Chesapeake*

The Poem

"Atomic Pantoum" angrily reflects on the human fascination with destruction, specifically the terrible power of nuclear weapons. The first two stanzas describe the chain reaction that generates the energy for such a weapon: The force of individual neutrons splitting splits the centers of others, releasing energy to split still more in a rapidly enlarging progression impossible to stop. By the third and fourth stanzas, the factual, even colloquial, language ("start this all over") of the opening turns strongly emotional. Let the process continue, Peter Meinke warns, and destruction will expand as wildly as the splitting of the atoms. Churches will collapse and people and creatures of the sea will incinerate in the terrific, irresistible inferno. Meinke thus extends the term "chain reaction" to the uncontrollably expanding effects of the colossal weapon.

The fifth and sixth stanzas involve and implicate human beings. Whereas in the first two stanzas Meinke limits his description to a physical process, he now reminds readers that humanity is responsible for this process. The model of the sun's energy, also generated by nuclear fission, has imprinted itself in people's minds, he suggests. By using the word "blazed," he implies that the imprinting is a sort of blinding. The sixth stanza clarifies the connection: The sun has provided the model for the "plutonium trigger," a small initial explosion that supplies the energy to detonate the main weapon. Humans have learned to create nuclear weapons from the sun's model, and, he adds, punning grimly, "we are dying to use it." That is, humans are both eager to exert their immense power and destined to be the victims.

The next two stanzas complete the meaning implicit throughout the poem. Humans control the trigger. Describing the trigger as "curled and tightened" may be intended to evoke the more familiar image of the trigger finger (an analogy that would be visually misleading). The word "torching" in the seventh stanza reveals the sheer sadistic delight of striking out in hatred. The phrase "blind to the end" in the eighth stanza makes explicit the irrationality of such hatred, and this is followed by a heartbreaking self-delusion—the human inclination to dedicate even warfare to the greatness of a god. The ninth and final stanza adds no new lines but makes the central analogy of the poem explicit. The concept of a "chain reaction" characterizes both the process by which nuclear weapons generate force and the situation in which humans find themselves, having devised ways to use nuclear fission in weapons. Blinded by a fascination with the potential to destroy their enemies, humans are "split up like nuclei," and even their worship is part of—and consumed in—the chain reaction.

Forms and Devices

The repetition of lines is perhaps the poem's most important device. When repeated, a phrase may accrue additional meanings or assume entirely new ones. Repetition is a type of rhythm, and it also establishes predictability or a sense of expectancy. Because the final stanza includes two lines from the first stanza, the poem seems rounded off or circular. The form Meinke employs is the pantoum, in which the second and fourth lines of each four-line stanza (or quatrain), moving as a pair, become the first and third lines of the next stanza. These repeated lines are sometimes called repetons. In the final stanza, the first and third lines of the opening stanza appear, in inverted order, as the second and fourth lines; thus, the poem opens and closes with the same line. Conventionally, the quatrains rhyme *abab*.

Meinke employs all these devices except the rhyming. After becoming familiar with the sense of the poem, one should linger over individual stanzas to appreciate the effects. In the second stanza, the repeton "blow open some others" states the effect of the released neutrons during the chain reaction. However, in the third stanza, Meinke turns "blow" into an imperative as the chain of cause and effect becomes destructive. Similarly, in the third stanza the phrase "with eyes burned to ashes" pertains to humanity, but when the line recurs it refers to the destroyed fish. Finally, "curled and tightened," which appears first in the seventh stanza, applies to the plutonium trigger, the small explosion that starts the chain reaction. Repeated, however, the phrase describes the human psyche in its irrationality. The return of the poem's first and third lines to shape the final stanza imparts finality and completeness. Like previous repetons, the reused lines are themselves affected. In fact, Meinke alters "split other nuclei" to read "split up like nuclei" as he likens humanity to—and implicates it in—the process of chain reaction. In regard to the final line, "in a chain reaction," it is worth noting that its earlier recurrence—in stanzas 4 and 5, where it helpfully reminds readers of the poem's focus—is not obligatory and may in fact diminish the line's impact at the end of the poem.

Another device is the lack of punctuation. Far from unique in modern poetry, this device nonetheless contributes an appropriate sense of inconstancy or randomness. One is tempted to entertain alternative ways to connect the parts of a sentence. For example, the phrase "eyes burned to ashes" in the third stanza may characterize victims of nuclear holocaust or suggest the fallibility of the perpetrators of the destruction, or both.

Themes and Meanings

"Atomic Pantoum" does not try to conceal its meaning. It might be possible to imagine Meinke, teeth clenched in anger, stabbing his words into paper with the point of his pen. However, meaning and significance accumulate from many contexts, connections that radiate outward from the poem like rings on water or, more appropriately, shock waves from an explosion.

The effects of the pantoum form become meaningful as they conspire with the subject. Like a chain reaction, repetition, as described earlier, is generative. Some pantoums emphasize circularity, but "Atomic Pantoum" gains complexity as it extends the meanings of the chain reaction. The first stanzas state the theme, while later iterations vary the theme, always focusing on it, until the poem ends in the slamming together of meanings that have been implicit in the images all along. Like the chain reaction itself, the form lets details split and release more energy and meaning. Also, the form establishes a kind of inevitability, the lines necessarily repeating and obligating the poet to devise applications for them, a process that continues as long as the poem requires. By writing a poem about the fission of nuclear weapons, Meinke has kept the pantoum alive, redefined it in relation to this subject, and shown that it can apply to what might seem to be a very unpoetic facet of the contemporary world.

The imagery of "Atomic Pantoum" draws on the poetry of others. The word "choirs," for instance, recalls William Shakespeare's "bare ruined choirs" in his famous sonnet (73) about aging and mortality. The phrase "fish catch on fire" might remind one of Gerard Manley Hopkins's famous sonnet that starts with the line "As kingfishers catch fire," a poem about the immanence of Christ in all things. Meinke has declared an interest in the "formal problems of sounding contemporary in traditional forms," and *Night Watch on the Chesapeake* contains many poems with some or all of the features of several traditional forms, particularly sonnets. Therefore, "Atomic Pantoum" might be regarded as part of a conversation between poets, centuries old, on subjects essential to the human experience; moreover, this poem seems to subsume some famous predecessors.

Finally, one can consider "Atomic Pantoum" in relation to Meinke's other work, particularly selections grouped under the heading "Night Watch" in *Night Watch on the Chesapeake*. When one considers the horrible effects of nuclear weapons, devices that can quickly exceed human capacity to control them, one begins to understand the moral agenda behind "Atomic Pantoum." Like the poem "Hermann Ludwig Ferdinand von Helmholtz," "Atomic Pantoum" is concerned with the fact that, for the poet and the scientist, "there is always another layer/ above, beyond, below/ the last answer." As Meinke says in "Rage," another poem from this part of the book, "rage, too, will never go away, never." Some of the "Night Watch" poems, which tend to be darker than others in the book, refer to sites notorious for violence and atrocities. There is a sinister quality in his work as he deals, from an adult perspective, with matters such as the need for alertness and responsibility.

Meinke, however, is not a poet of despair. He does not dismiss humanity as hopeless. A single one of his poems can contain both delight and doom. "Atomic Pantoum" is an unusually outraged poem for Meinke, but one should not miss the inspired playfulness in his use of the pantoum form. As one reads more of his work, one may appreciate the pervasiveness not only of humor but also of a great and unwavering passion for people and for life. Rage, then, is part of something bigger and more diverse, something with moral legitimacy, part of the moral imperatives by which one tries to fashion a life.

Jay Paul

AUBADE

Author: William Empson (1906-1984)
Type of poem: Lyric
First published: 1940, in *The Gathering Storm*

The Poem

An aubade is a poem of love, usually sung by lovers at dawn after a night together. There is no fixed form for an aubade, and William Empson has chosen to use four sets of alternating five- and three-line stanzas, followed by two five-line stanzas with which the poem concludes.

Empson spent the 1930's as a university lecturer in Japan and China, and the poem seems to be set in the Far East. At some time in the middle of the night an earthquake is felt; the lovers are shaken awake by the first tremor, which is followed by a stronger quake. They decide to get up and part. There is some suggestion that the male lover would like harm to come to some others through the quake, and there is the first appearance of the ambiguous line, "The heart of standing is you cannot fly."

The woman dresses, and the male lover, the writer or voice of the poem, who sees himself as apprehensively insecure (a "guarded tourist"), suggests that she might want to leave through the garden, obviously to avoid being seen. This amuses the woman, who is clearly more secure; she will take a taxi, and he will go back to bed. Before she leaves they discuss as well as they can, since they seem to have a bit of a language problem, how she will deal with her husband. It is now obvious that the relationship is adulterous and that they are of different races. She makes it clear that she is not worried about the earthquake and the deaths it might have caused, but that her husband, who might also have been disturbed and might be calling for her, might discover that she is missing. The lover goes back to sleep, hoping that while he sleeps all their problems will be solved.

Guilty but defensive, he imagines that he is being chided for his selfishness in carrying on an illicit love affair when politics in Europe are so dangerous (it is the 1930's, the time of the spread of Fascism). He goes on rhetorically to reject the political, personal, and natural troubles of both East and West, seeing in the Japanese intrusions into Manchuria only another version of the same things that are happening in Europe. He does not care; what matters is his love affair.

The rejection of imagined advice and criticism is brought to a personal level as he imagines the criticism naturally arising from an affair between lovers of different races. He admits that, as in the case of the earthquake, the wisest thing would be to get out of the affair before the matter gets out of hand, but the poem ends with a repetition of the "heart of standing" line, which by now clearly suggests that he will remain and continue the relationship. What begins, then, as a description of incidents occurring as a result of a middle-of-the-night earthquake and the parting of two lovers to avoid possible discovery, develops, in the last four stanzas of the poem, into a monologue in

which the male lover—guilty, apprehensive, and defensive—rationalizes their con-
duct set against the wider problems of the world; he refuses either to abandon his love
or to allow its importance to him to be debased.

Forms and Devices

The aubade has a long history in European poetry; it can be found in France, and
particularly in Provence, by the end of the twelfth century, and has always had a touch
of impropriety about it in its suggestion of secret assignation and regret as the lovers
must part as the light of day comes on. Sometimes there is a husband to be deceived;
sometimes it is simply a matter of sexual congress outside wedlock. It can use a wide
tonal range and often ranges from celebration, through chagrin, to torment. Empson
chooses to mix the form with two other interests which often appear in his poetry. The
second half of the poem is strongly indebted to his admiration for the problem poems
of John Donne, in which the enthusiasm of the male lover is rhetorically attacked by
an outside voice and provides the lover with the opportunity to "argufy" in poetry, as
Empson put it. This poem makes use of the disastrous nature of natural calamities,
such as earthquake and flood, to diminish the importance of the love affair, but also
makes use of the serious political and military adventures of the 1930's (which were
to lead eventually to World War II in 1939)—not without some pertinence, since this
is an affair between a Caucasian and an Oriental.

Another element in the poem, for which Empson is also strongly indebted to John
Donne and the Metaphysical poets in general, is the ambiguity of the language.
Empson's main reputation is as a critic, and in his most famous book, appropriately
named *Seven Types of Ambiguity* (1930), he explores the way in which literary artists
use words and phrases which have, quite deliberately, more than one meaning, and
may sometimes have several. There is, as a result, an uneasy sense that things are be-
ing said in the poem which are not quite clear and often may be taken in more than one
way. The poem is a peculiar combination of straightforward narrative and confusing
repetitions which seem to mean not quite the same thing as they reappear throughout
the poem. "It seemed the best thing to be up and go" and "The heart of standing is you
cannot fly" are used in this manner, but they are also used in the aesthetic structure of
the poem as alternating endings for the five- and three-line stanzas as a kind of choral
repetition and a show of technical prowess.

Part of the problem of uncertainty about what is being said in the poem can be
solved when it is recognized that the first three sets of double stanzas are in the past
tense, a "telling" of the incident, perhaps to the person addressed rhetorically at the
beginning of the seventh stanza. That narration, however, is mixed with comments on
the incident made by the speaker, often unclear in meaning, and with snatches of con-
versation between the lovers which are sometimes hard to understand since they are
conversing in a kind of shorthand not uncommon for people who know each other
well. There is, as a result, a vivacity and immediacy, but also a sense of the reader be-
ing an outsider, not entirely sure of what is happening. For example, two sentences, al-
though not consecutive, make sense if thought about for a moment. "Some solid

ground for lying could she show? . . . None of these deaths were her point at all." If somewhat perversely confusing, they probably are part of the conversation about her reason for leaving. The seriousness of the earthquake and the possible deaths that might have occurred are not the reason she feels she must go; the reason is simply that her husband might have been calling for her. If he finds that she is not at home, what can she say to keep him from uncovering her infidelity? Perhaps she can lie and say that she was out looking about. The lover lamely suggests "saying Half an Hour to pay this call." Clearly this would seem suspicious in the middle of the night, and he immediately concedes that "it seemed the best thing to be up and go."

The second half of the poem is in the present tense as the lover defends himself against the good advice that he has no intention of taking. It is somewhat more straightforward but occasionally lapses into a kind of conversational shorthand, which is so common in John Donne's poems of romantic enthusiasm confronted by common sense; like Donne's lover, this man has a quick, sophisticated way with language and a tendency to say things ambiguously.

Themes and Meanings

It has been said of Empson's poetry that it provides the reader with the sensation of feeling sure that the poem is good, both aesthetically and intellectually, without the reader quite knowing what it means. This is not so severely the case with "Aubade," which could be described as being only occasionally, only seemingly, meaningless. At the most obvious level, it is what it says it is: an aubade, a love song on the necessity of the loved one to steal home, not because the night is over, but because everyone's sleep has been disturbed by an earthquake which may also have disturbed the unsuspecting husband who may notice the absence of his wife. Lovers in aubades usually complain about the intrusion of the light; in this case, a much more unusual and more destructive aspect of nature has intruded on the bliss of the lovers.

As is always the case, the lovers are reluctant to part; they are made aware of the facts of life, however, and are sufficiently cautious not to flaunt them. If they are to continue their affair, they must be careful—and that is one of the meanings of the "heart of standing" line. They must not do anything too romantic, which seems to be the meaning of the first use of the line and, perhaps, the second one, where the necessity of providing a solid lie is recognized. The third time the line appears, it may suggest something of a variation on that idea: that they can do no more than keep still until they know the consequences of their conduct. When it appears in the criticism of their conduct, it may be a repudiation of more serious worldwide matters, which proves how deeply they love—real lovers are proven to be so by their refusal to be distracted by the troubles of the outside world. Its last use is a rejection of the idea that their racial differences make it necessary for them to part and for the lover to leave and end the affair. Empson indulges in a very subtle manipulation of the idea of rising that any Metaphysical poet would immediately understand. The statement in itself has an obvious meaning: It would be the wisest thing for the two lovers to part. Yet that must be seen in the light of the other statement about the "heart of standing," precluding flight.

It, too, is at first sight, simple. Obviously, one who stands cannot fly, but it can also mean that the heart (the lover) of standing (integrity) would not desert the loved one. Getting up to go, therefore, is not possible in the long run, though it may be necessary once in a while to protect the lovers from detection. "Standing" is character in action.

In the last stanza, however, it assumes the complicated, tricky reasoning of the Metaphysicals. One might get "up" to go, but there is another kind of "rising" which contradicts that retreat: the "rising" of erotic desire, where "up" is related to the heart, not the mind, and confirms the determination not to fly, but to remain with the loved one whatever the consequences. "Standing" now has a sexual implication.

This is not necessarily the only reading of the poem; it is a reading that attempts to make sense of the ambiguities in a way that is consistent with the more obviously factual elements in the work. It is possible to read this poem as a simple aubade and rationalization of an affair without worrying too fastidiously about what some of the more gnomic lines mean. The poem will work as poetry with a reasonable amount of "sense" even if the lines of ambiguity are taken as found, as bits of anarchic musing, tonally supporting the situation of ardor, uncertainty, and insecurity.

Charles Pullen

AUBADE

Author: Philip Larkin (1922-1985)
Type of poem: Lyric
First published: 1977; collected in *Collected Poems*, 1988

The Poem

An aubade, deriving from the medieval French word for dawn, is a lyric poem with no prescribed form in which the poet typically celebrates the beauty of his mistress as the sun rises and he must leave her bed: John Donne's "The Sun Rising" is a well-known example. Philip Larkin's "Aubade" is an ironic variation on the themes traditionally associated with this kind of lyric. In this, Larkin's last major poem, the first-person speaker, who is closely identified with the poet himself, describes a typical early morning when, waking alone in the darkness before the dawn, he contemplates the terrifying inevitability of his own absolute extinction.

The speaker states that he is in the habit of working all day, getting "half-drunk at night," and then waking involuntarily in early morning darkness to contemplate the horror of his death, which is always one day nearer. He then clarifies the source of his dread. He is not in despair at having wasted his life, because he has accepted that it was his innate destiny to always have to struggle against difficult odds. He is simply in existential terror of certain personal extinction.

He contemptuously dismisses as potential consolations for his mortality both religious faith in the afterlife and the rationalist assurance that one cannot be hurt by what one cannot feel. Religion is simply a worn-out charade, while rationalism fails to take into account that the idea of the total loss of sensation is precisely what is so terrifying about death. He notes how his fear of death stands most of the time at the edge of his awareness, kept at bay by human relationships or by the numbing effect of alcohol. However, when he wakes alone in darkness, there is nothing to insulate him from the full ferocity of his terror. Even courage seems useless, for however bravely one faces the end of one's life, one still ends up dead.

In the final stanza, the light of dawn begins to give form to the speaker's surroundings, and one might expect that this would console him. However, as objects emerge from the gloom he sees only more clearly the truth of death. Outside, the urban world prepares to return to life after the night, but to the speaker, existence seems indifferent and temporary, and he sees through its routines to the cruel emptiness beneath.

Forms and Devices

Like many of Larkin's best poems, "Aubade" is elaborately wrought in a traditional manner yet reads almost as clearly as good prose. It opens strikingly with a metrical tour de force: Each of the first three lines is a complete sentence. The effect is to warn the reader that prosaic bluntness will here replace the traditional aubade's tendency to the rhapsodic. The poem is strongly unified by a series of perceptual tropes that reflect the movement from darkness to dawn. It begins with the speaker in "soundless dark" seeing "what's really always there" and culminates in the simile of death seen "plain as a wardrobe" as the dawn light conjures form out of darkness.

Each of the poem's five ten-line stanzas has an *ababccdeed* rhyme scheme. An open quatrain is succeeded by a couplet and then by a closed quatrain, allowing for considerable variation of movement within each stanza and giving each stanza a self-contained quality. The dominant meter is iambic pentameter, except for the pen-ultimate line of each stanza, which is—usually—a trimeter. There are many subtle rhythmic variations to reduce monotony: For example, some significant first feet are reversed (trochaic) for emphasis, and may even rhyme internally, as in "Making" and "Waking" (lines 2 and 6); some of the couplets have feminine rhymes; and the short lines sometimes indicate a dactylic contrapuntal rhythm.

"An only life" exhibits Larkin's ability to coin striking phrases that have a rightness and inevitability yet do not disrupt the informality of the poem's diction. The phrase, constructed on the analogy of "an only child," suggests that the speaker's isolation and loneliness are innate, the result of his "wrong beginnings." One thinks of a personal, secularized, post-Freudian version of Original Sin. At the same time the phrase stresses the high value of life to the speaker: There is "only life," and only one life, separating him from annihilation. Indeed, the speaker's "only life" replaces the beloved in the traditional aubade. The narcissistic implications are part of the poem's grim and astringent humor, which also leads the speaker to describe death as "the anaesthetic from which none come round."

The line "Death is no different whined at than withstood" is a good example of both the traditionalism and subtlety of Larkin's prosody. The alliterative pairs, "death"/"different" and "whined"/"withstood," are divided by a caesura, and at least three of the alliterated syllables bear stresses, so that the line conforms fairly closely to the ancient pattern of Old English alliterative verse.

There is at the end of "Aubade" an expansion of vision that suddenly and almost painfully involves the reader, who up to this point has perhaps merely sympathized from a distance with the speaker's private terror. On the word "meanwhile," the focus shifts from self to society, just as the fifth stanza moves from an open to a closed form. The phrase "telephones crouch, getting ready to ring" (one expects this last word to be "spring") suggests a fatal menace about to thwart hopes of connection with others.

The sky is "white as clay," as if blanched with horror at what daylight discloses, and though the poem is an aubade, there will be, the spondee emphatically insists, "no sun." Then the trimeter announces bluntly, "Work has to be done," and the poem concludes with the image of postmen "like doctors" going about their work. Weak substitutes for physicians or priests, they seem to be paying brief and indifferent house calls to a whole world that is terminally ill.

Themes and Meanings

"Aubade" articulates an ancient poetic theme, one expressed by the Latin tag *timor mortis conturbat me* ("the fear of death confounds me"). This tag appears as a refrain in a number of medieval poems, such as the lyric by William Dunbar known as "Lament for the Makars" (1508). The tag alludes to the brevity of life in the Middle Ages and to the hope in an eternal afterlife in heaven that will console humanity for the harshness of the mortal world.

However, the terror of death as expressed in "Aubade" has quite a different origin. The speaker's emotional predicament is not the result of the threats of disease, war, or social collapse, those constants of medieval life. It is the result of the unprecedented conditions of individual existence in the late twentieth century, relatively secure in the physical sense but assailed mentally and spiritually by a profound sense of loneliness and desolation.

The title "Aubade" points ironically to the speaker's predicament. He awakes alone, having no beloved to share his existence. When the sun eventually rises to dispel the literal darkness, it casts no warmth or enlightenment. "An only life" is all he has. When parted from it, as he must be by "unresting death," he will be nothing, nowhere, erased forever. Secular, scientific skepticism has produced an "intricate rented world" that people inhabit temporarily, which is typically urban and technologically developed. It keeps one safe from physical harm and usually pacified by its routine demands. Yet under this life is a vacancy that sometimes leaks menacingly through. All this busyness then seems merely another drug to keep the nothingness in abeyance. The speaker's personal anguish is merely an intensified version of the existential isolation faced by everyone in the modern world.

Is there any comfort to be taken from this very dark poem, or does it suggest that the only valid responses to life in the modern world are nihilism, despair, and suicide? "Aubade" can be viewed as a guardedly affirmative statement, or at least as an artistic performance that is, perhaps in spite of itself, on the side of life. The poem is painfully honest: Its confession of weakness and cowardice paradoxically required great courage to make. Moreover, it challenges readers to identify with the speaker and confront in themselves what they share with him: the essential isolation of the modern self. It offers none of the traditional consolations of philosophy; yet the terror that it movingly articulates comes from the very high value that the modern world attributes by default to life itself. People love it with instinctual passion and cannot bear the thought of being parted from it, for they know that it is all they have.

At once grimly humorous and deadly serious, Larkin's "Aubade" is one of the classic articulations of the twentieth century existential predicament. It is also a masterly verbal construct, drawing a deep strength from and implying great faith in the poetic tradition.

Nicholas Ruddick

AN AUBADE

Author: Timothy Steele (1948-   )
Type of poem: Lyric
First published: 1986, in *Sapphics Against Anger and Other Poems*

The Poem

Timothy Steele's "An Aubade" uses and renews an ancient poetic form, the aubade. In a traditional aubade, the dawn comes to announce the separation of two lovers. In Steele's poem, the lovers are already separated in the first stanza: She is in the shower and he is waking in the bed. In addition, there is no dawn announced or described in this stanza; there is, however, the "shine of earrings on the bedside stand." There is also a light that comes from a "yellow sheet" covering him like a false dawn. Its "folds" are metaphorically described as a painting "from some fine old master's hand."

The lovers are brought more closely together in the second stanza, although they are not united. He embraces the "pillow" that "Retains the salty sweetness of her skin." The image is an interesting mixture of tastes, and it connects the lovers through imagery and memory although they are still physically separated. From this image, he can "sense her smooth back, buttocks, belly, waist." One image of her body triggers other images that bring her closer to him. In addition, he retains the memory of their lovemaking and her "leggy warmth" which "laced/ Around my legs and loins, and drew me in."

The lovers are connected by a sound image in the third stanza as he hears her "Singing among the water's hiss and race." Then the dawn comes, as "early light" reveals a scene of "perfume bottles" and a "silver flashlight" on the dresser. Significantly, this dawn does not separate the lovers but brings them closer. The flashlight and the bottles are other shining objects that substitute for the real presence of the beloved who has not yet arrived; these images seem to fill the room, although she is still in the shower.

In the fourth stanza, the male lover speaks not of his coming separation as the poetic tradition demands but of his "content." He is so content that he can "forgive/ Pleasure for being brief and fugitive." The male lover also suspends rising from the bed until the woman comes out of the shower and dries herself. This contrasts sharply with the enforced rising of the lovers that is a part of a traditional aubade.

The last stanza is one of description as the female lover finally comes forth. The speaker describes her delicately drying "this and now that foot placed on a chair." This is followed by a detailed and loving inventory of her and her beauty: "Her fine-boned ankles, and her calves and thighs,/ The pink full nipples of her breasts, and ties/ Her towel up, turban-style, about her hair." With this final revealing of her true self, she has asserted her body and her presence. This is the opposite of a traditional aubade.

Forms and Devices

"An Aubade" is written in a regular iambic pentameter throughout the poem. Steele uses a five-line stanza in this poem with an intricate *abaab* rhyme scheme. The lines, for the most part, run on and support the ongoing observation of the male lover who narrates the poem. This is especially so as the poem, and the view of the speaker, spills from line to line and object to object until the speaker lights upon the naked woman. The rhymes seem natural and are never forced. Steele wittily rhymes "hear her" and "clearer" in the third stanza. In the fourth stanza, there is a break in the rhyme scheme as "with" does not rhyme with "forgive" or "fugitive." It does not seem to have any expressive purpose.

There is one simile in the poem, although it does not contribute as much as other elements to the overall effect of the poem. In the first stanza, the covers over the male lover are described in "folds as intricate as drapery/ In paintings from some fine old master's hand." This is another object that is precisely described in the poem, and it is a male image, contrasting with the feminine objects that dominate the poem.

The principal poetic element in the poem is the imagery. There are images of light, such as the "shine of earrings" and the "silver flashlight," which take the place of the dawn in the usual aubade. There are images of other objects, such as the "perfume bottles" and the "shiny flashlight," that define the place and its context. However, the images of the body seem to be most important in the poem. The first images are those of taste; the female lover is absent, but her presence can be felt in "the salty sweetness of her skin." This leads to the tactile images of her "smooth back, buttocks, belly, waist." Her legs are connected to a beautiful image of "leggy warmth."

An image of "early light" clarifies the scene, but it is curiously less important in this aubade than the images of the body. In the last stanza, there is a long list of erotic and precise images of the body of the beloved, which announces her coming out and joining the male lover: "Her fine-boned ankles, and her calves and thighs,/ The pink full nipples of her breast." The last image is an exotic and an erotic one in which the beloved is seen with a "towel up, turban-style, about her hair."

Themes and Meanings

Steele is usually identified as one of the New Formalists. His poetry is nearly always in regular accentual meters and rhyme. He makes good uses of these formal devices in "An Aubade" to show the wit and sensuous detail that is the mark of his poetry. In addition, he uses an ancient poetic form: the aubade. He is not content to merely reproduce the form but rather renews it in the context of his own time; it is not a completely modern aubade. The poem does reveal much irony, however. The male lover is awakened not by the dawn but by the sound of the woman "showering." In addition, he "postpones" arising until she gets out of the shower. He never gets out of bed to join the beloved, in an amusing revision of a traditional aubade.

Another feature of the poem is its appeal to the senses. The images comprise nearly all the senses. There are visual, auditory, olfactory images first of objects and then of the female; significantly there are no tactile images, since the lovers do not touch. The meaning of the poem is contained in the loving descriptions of things associated with her and the final revelation and description of her beauty and her overwhelming presence. This description, in the present tense, is both imagined and a real description of her drying her body and revealing it.

The themes of "An Aubade" are focused on the attitude of the male speaker, which is somewhat distant as he is content to remain only an observer. He can remain in bed and be perfectly content about his closeness to her despite her physical absence. For example, he speaks of being so "content" that he is willing to forgive "Pleasure for being brief and fugitive." He acknowledges the fading of sexual pleasure and is still willing to accept it rather than demand its immediate renewal. This focus on observation rather than sexual desire is also found in his reaction to the beauty of the woman as she comes forth to announce and reveal herself. It is an admiring and loving description of her being and presence after a curiously long delay before her arrival.

James Sullivan

AUDUBON
A Vision

Author: Robert Penn Warren (1905-1989)
Type of poem: Poetic sequence
First published: 1969; collected in *Selected Poems, 1923-1975,* 1976

The Poem

Robert Penn Warren once said that he had started *Audubon: A Vision,* about the American naturalist and painter of native birds John James Audubon, in 1946-1947, when he was reading Audubon's and other subhistories of early nineteenth century America. He was dissatisfied with it then and threw away what he had written. Twenty years later he suddenly remembered one line of his poem and immediately knew what he must do with it. The line he remembered is the only remnant of the original poem: "Was not the lost dauphin," which begins the first poem in this seven-part meditation on the mystery of identity.

This odd disclaimer derives from a legend which arose after Audubon's death that he was the lost Dauphin of France, son of Louis XVI and Marie Antoinette. He was, in fact, the son of a sea captain and his mistress. The obvious contrast between the fanta-sized origin and his humble beginnings provides the first irony in the question of his identity.

That the poem is called a vision suggests that the insight it provides is only partly derived from the known facts of Audubon's life. The first stanza ends with the asser-tion that he (Audubon) was only himself "and his passion—what/ Is man but his pas-sion?" This suggests that the poem will inquire into the nature of Audubon's obses-sion with wild nature, which was the wellspring of his art.

The rest of this first poem imagines the painter's rapt attention to color, form, and the effects of light: how the great white heron looks black against a blood-red sunset, how the overflowing juice of blueberries that drool from a bear's yawn highlights the surprising whiteness of its teeth, and how the bee's wings glint like mica in the sun-light.

The second poem, entitled "The Dream He Never Knew the End Of," is a narrative about Audubon asking for shelter in an isolated forest cabin and then being rescued, at the last moment, from the old woman, his host, and her rascally sons who intended to murder him in his sleep. The three would-be killers are hanged in the morning— frontier justice as speedy and merciless as the crone's impulse to murder for the gold watch he had shown her the night before. Although this story may have some factual basis, it is told for its archetypal mythic nature—the recurring nightmare of a person drawn to the wilderness, recognizing that brute nature, especially unfettered human nature, can be dangerous.

Yet even here, when the persona's paralyzing terror evaporates, he sees something beautiful and dignified in the old woman. Though her sons snivel and beg, she remains calm and defiant, indifferent to fate. The persona, with spontaneous empathy, realizes that the gold watch was an emblem of a civilized, ordered world which had been denied her. With this understanding, he felt compassion, even love, rather than revulsion for his assailant.

The poems continue exploring Audubon's emotional bond to the timeless world of the wilderness, sometimes in philosophical terms, sometimes lyrical, sometimes simply factual. Unlike the old woman in the forest, Audubon had clear alternatives available. He had a wife and apparently loved her—but usually from a distance, communing with "dear Lucy" by letter and playing his flute alone in the forest after sunset. He could have been a successful trader on the frontier; he could have slept in a bed at home—but did not. Neither comfort nor money could lure him. He declined Daniel Webster's kindness when, Audubon himself wrote, he "would give me a fat place was I willing to/ have one; but I love indepenn and piece more/ than humbug and money [sic]."

Yet he did eventually succumb in some measure to fame and honor, even traveling to Europe, where he entertained his hosts by whistling bird calls of his distant forest. He wrote that he continually dreamt of birds. He even came back and lived at home with his wife, but clearly the wellsprings of his art were failing—"the mouthpiece/ Of his flute was dry, and his brushes."

Audubon died in bed, and the poet suggests that with him faded the timeless wilderness world of America: "For everything there is a season." Yet the last poem of the sequence, in which the poet speaks as his own persona, remembering his own fascination with nature from childhood, suggests that the dream of the timeless world never dies. It continues to inspire the artist, whether painter or poet, and offers a secret well of joy for those who both know and love the world. Warren's special affinity for Audubon's passion is understandable, since he himself aspired to be a painter of wildlife when he was a child.

Forms and Devices

The diction and the metaphors in this free-verse poem maintain a certain tension that prevents it from lapsing into either the purely sentimental or the purely Gothic treatment of nature. Although sometimes lyrical, as befits Audubon's passion for the wilderness, metaphors are sometimes startling, even unpleasant. The color of the dawn against which the great heron rises is "redder than meat." Later in the same stanza, it is the "color of God's blood spilt." The heron rises slowly as though "pulled by a string." The first of these curious metaphors may suggest a conventional attitude toward nature as savage, "red in tooth and claw." The second seems to introduce a religious element, perhaps redemption (or at least the need for it), while the third gives a peculiarly mechanical impression, as though all were part of some kind of elaborate stage setting.

Audubon, however, with the sensitivity of the painter, both marvels at the stage setting and mentally "corrects" the reality of the creatures he observes. Although the bird looks black against the red sky, Audubon names the genus and species and knows exactly the heron's true color. The undertone of potential savagery is caught again in the brilliance of a yawning bear's teeth, even though this particular bear is only eating berries and about to hibernate peacefully for the winter.

In the nightmare sequence, the images and metaphors suggest not the relatively innocent potential for violence in nature but a truly ominous quality, the degeneration possible in humans who know neither the natural curbs of instinct nor the social deterrence of law. Even the smoke rising, or rather sinking, from the chimney is described in disgusting terms: It "ravels,/ White, thin, down the shakes, like sputum." The words describing the old woman who opens the door are suspiciously like a child's version of a wicked witch: She is "strong-beaked, the haired mole/ Near the nose." One side of her face is in deep shadow, the other glows in the firelight. Later the woman spits on a knife as she sharpens it on a stone, and the reader remembers the slimey smoke like sputum.

The action becomes more surreal as it blends with remembered childhood nightmares. Although the uneasy visitor lying by the fire keeps his rifle loaded and cocked beside him, he becomes immobilized by a strange lassitude, as though helpless to defend himself. His rescue when three strong men burst in the door seems equally unreal, since no clue is given as to who they are or why they came.

Nevertheless, the later part of that section is surprisingly rational, relentlessly realistic in some details, as though to clear away all illusions. "The affair was not tidy," and later, "The affair was not quick: both sons long jerking and farting." The old woman, however, is "without motion, frozen/ In a rage of will, an ecstasy of iron, as though/ This was the dream that, lifelong, she had dreamed toward." In this usage, "dream" is almost synonymous with "fate," which casts another light upon the ambiguity of experience and choice.

After this dark night of the soul, the diction and metaphors are lighter, more informed with joy. The persona becomes more human and more comfortable with his life decisions. The section filled with quotes from Audubon's diaries or letters provides intimate glimpses of a varied personality. Sometimes he affirms the attitudes of the romantic naturalist, with his devotion to the noble savage view of the Native American: "He saw the Indian, and felt the splendor of God." Audubon wrote that he saw "the Man Naked from his/ hand and yet free from acquired Sorrow." In other words, the wilderness had the innocence of the world before the Fall of Man.

Other vignettes show Audubon as being as vulnerable to wounded pride as anyone, as when a pretty girl passed him by without so much as a nod, not remembering "how beautiful/ I had rendered her face once by Painting it/ at her Request with Pastelles [sic]."

The poem makes effective use of symbols. The most important of these is the gold watch that fascinates the old woman of the forest. It is the quintessential emblem of the man-made ordered world that humankind has superimposed upon nature, which knows only the ordering of the seasons and the pulses of instinct. The action of the heron, which seemed mechanical in its motion across the sky—but was not—is countered close to the end of the poem by a symbolic image of the truly mechanical contrivance.

"The Northwest Orient plane, New York to Seattle, has passed, winking westward." This is one of the triumphs of the modern clock-oriented time—to keep the world on schedule; there is no more wandering around at will in a trackless wilderness.

Themes and Meanings

Audubon: A Vision develops three related themes that Warren used over and over in his fiction and poetry: the quest for identity, the loss of innocence, and reconciliation to the changes brought by time. The last two might be expressed in religious terms as the Fall and the Redemption. Warren was well acquainted with and skillful in the use of traditional Christian imagery, but he was more likely to consider these issues as psychological conditions or rites of passage than as religious doctrine. The psychological journey unfolds from an inner necessity.

Each of these themes has a double, or perhaps even a triple, layer of meaning in the poem. Each applies personally to Audubon, the naturalist and painter, and his quest for identity and validation for his life's work. Each applies as well to America as a whole, which was living through radical changes at the same time, losing its wild, free heritage of wilderness. Was the white man bringing "civilization" or simply corrupting an order more finely tuned to the needs of living things than anything men have invented since?

One cannot turn back the clock, however, or regain the original paradise (if, indeed, it ever existed—either in childhood or in the primeval forest). Warren does insist that the vision does not die, admitting that "For everything there is a season./ But there is a dream/ Of a season past all seasons." Some might call this sentimental, but Warren probably considered it an archetypal idea necessary to maintain one's moral equilibrium in a fallen world. It may also be the primary source of art: Audubon would probably not have painted pictures, nor would Warren have written poetry, without that dream.

This suggests the hidden third layer of meaning that may be assumed, given some knowledge of Warren's life. As suggested above, Warren himself aspired to being a painter of wildlife. He took lessons for a while as a child but learned that he was not especially talented in that field. Perhaps all stories are, in some measure, autobiographical. At least, the subject or plot of the tale introduces some compulsion upon the teller, because it rings true to his own experience. When the title calls this poem a vision, therefore, that may refer to Audubon's vision of the wilderness, to America's vision of itself, or to Warren's vision of Audubon living the life Warren coveted as a boy. He hints as much in the last section, called "Tell Me a Story," which begins:

> Long ago, in Kentucky, I, a boy, stood
> By a dirt road, in first dark, and heard
> The great geese hoot northward.

Moreover, there is at least one curious detail of the poem that seems to serve no significant function in the story except, perhaps, as a secret talisman of the author. That infamous cabin in the forest had one other visitor for the night, who warns the protagonist in sign language of their hosts' evil intent and alerts the three men who burst in upon the group. This second, somewhat superfluous character, is an Indian who has a badly injured eye. The old woman laughs at the Indian, calling him a "durn fool" for accidentally putting out his own eye.

Oddly enough, a serious eye injury had a curious relevance to Warren's decision to become a poet rather than, say, an admiral of the Pacific Fleet—his dream at age sixteen. His father had been getting him an appointment at Annapolis, when a stone tossed carelessly in the air by a child struck Warren in the eye as he lay in the grass. Warren lost that eye, which prevented him from going into the Navy. He went to Vanderbilt University instead, where John Crowe Ransom and others discovered his ability to write and turned his attention to poetry. His career as a writer seemed, therefore, to have resulted from a fluke of fate. That accident was perhaps his own dark night of the soul, from which he emerged as a better man, or at least a different man, even as Audubon ironically learned a new compassion and understanding from the old woman of the forest.

The poet may speak for himself as well as for Audubon when he says, "His life, at the end, seemed—even the anguish—simple,/ Simple, at least, in that it had to be,/ Simply what it was." Perhaps this impression of one's fate as somehow predestined, even when it is partly instinctive, partly accidental, and partly consciously chosen, is simply another illusion of perspective:

> To wake in some dawn and see,
> As though down a rifle barrel, lined up
> Like sights, the self that was, the self that is, and there,
> Far off but in range, completing that alignment, your fate.

Katherine Snipes

AUGURIES OF INNOCENCE

Author: William Blake (1757-1827)
Type of poem: Poetic sequence
First published: 1863, in *Life of William Blake*, by Alexander Gilchrist

The Poem

Except for the first four lines, "Auguries of Innocence" (written in 1803 but unpublished until 1863) consists of a long series of couplets, each of which contains a proverb. Although William Blake may have intended to reorganize the couplets, the poem as he left it in manuscript has no clear order. For this reason, some editors of the poem have rearranged "Auguries of Innocence" by grouping the couplets according to theme.

"Auguries" means omens or divinations, and "Innocence," according to the subtitle of Blake's *Songs of Innocence and of Experience* (1794), is one of the two contrary states of the human soul. In Blake's poetry, innocence is related to existence in Paradise (what Blake calls Beulah) and is associated with the joy and spontaneity of childhood. Thus the title of "Auguries of Innocence" suggests that the poem will present omens from an innocent perspective, in which "the Infants Faith," not the cynic's mockery, is valid.

"Auguries of Innocence" begins with four alternately rhymed lines questioning the absolute nature of space and time. According to these opening lines, one can "see a World in a Grain of Sand," and Eternity can be contained "in an hour." This quatrain asserts that something infinitesimal can expand into immensity, an idea that prepares the reader for the rest of the poem, in which small proverbs are used to comment on such immensities as heaven, hell, and "endless Night."

At least some of these proverbs can be grouped roughly according to subject, but the poem as a whole is difficult to paraphrase. Most of the couplets in the first fifty lines of "Auguries of Innocence" mention animals, relating them to moral error, humans, heaven, hell, and the last judgment. As in the first four lines of the poem, there is a frequent movement from microcosm to macrocosm, from a caged robin to the rage of heaven, from a starving dog to "the ruin of the State." Several proverbs claim that animal abusers will be punished—for example, a man who angers an ox will never be loved by a woman.

Moreover, "Auguries of Innocence" attacks some favorite targets of Blake: those who are corrupted by power or money, and doubters. The poet declares that the armed soldier strikes the sun with palsy, the laborer is worth more than the miser, and the "Infants faith" is far greater than the mocker's doubt. "If the Sun and Moon should Doubt," one proverb claims, "Theyd immediately Go out." The last four lines of the poem contrast "those poor Souls who dwell in night" and perceive God as light to "those who Dwell in Realms of day" and know God in "Human Form." Like many of the preceding couplets, these last lines serve to challenge the beliefs of the literal minded.

Forms and Devices

The essential formlessness of "Auguries of Innocence" recalls Blake's "Proverbs of Hell" (a section of *The Marriage of Heaven and Hell*, 1790)—in both, Blake lists a series of provocative aphorisms that, collectively, represent a vision of reality. Thus "Auguries of Innocence" begins with the act of seeing "a World in a Grain of Sand" and ends with the assertion that God displays his human form to those who can correctly perceive Him. Even though the proverbs are haphazardly listed, they share a common vision. Moreover, each reading of the poem can be seen as a collaboration between Blake and the reader: Blake supplies the couplets, but it is up to the reader to see the connection between them, to learn to read them in a visionary way.

The model for a series of proverbs is the Bible, and in "Auguries of Innocence" Blake's proverbs often predict the future in true biblical fashion. For example, the poem contains prophecies of moral turpitude leading to disaster, such as "The Harlots cry from Street to Street/ Shall weave Old Englands winding Sheet." It is the nature of proverbs to be cryptic and suggestive, and several of the couplets are, like the poem itself, riddles in need of explication. Other aphorisms, however, are visionary, and some simply call for kindness to all living things—in "Auguries of Innocence," Blake strings contrasting proverbs together in a bewildering succession, perhaps suggesting the spontaneity and freedom from rules that characterize his vision of innocence. An advantage of these proverbs is that any one of them can be removed from the context of the rest of the poem and examined as a separate unit. Even readers who dislike the poem as a whole may find some proverb that interests them. Moreover, the use of the proverb gives the poem a biblical quality—these proverb-couplets seem appropriate as vehicles for the work's moral and visionary judgments. Clearly, an aphorism such as "Kill not the Moth nor Butterfly/ For the Last Judgment draweth nigh" is strengthened by its biblical echo.

Many of Blake's proverbs emphasize points by asserting startling cause-and-effect relationships. Thus the wounding of a skylark is said to stop cherubim from singing, and a gamecock prepared for combat frightens the rising sun. These hyperbolic declarations are clearly forceful—the message of many of the proverbs, that cruelty has consequences that reach far beyond the initial act, is powerfully made. Some readers will dismiss such wildly incongruous aphorisms as palpably absurd. How, some might ask, can the cry of a hunted hare tear a fiber from a brain? The poem has an aphorism for a reader who would make such an objection: "The Questioner who sits so sly/ Shall never know how to Reply." One should also remember that these are auguries of *innocence*. From the perspective of experience, it may seem ludicrous to suggest that someone who would hurt a wren will never be loved, but from an innocent point of view, harming a small bird must necessarily meet with universal disgust. These aphorisms have more in common with an "Infants faith" than with the logic of experience.

Themes and Meanings

In his prophetic works, Blake describes four types of vision: fourfold vision, the highest visionary state; threefold vision, identified with Beulah (Paradise) and innocence; twofold vision, which is the realm of experience; and the single vision of Newtonian physics and abstract reasoning. "Auguries of Innocence" deals primarily with threefold vision, the mental state closest to the true enlightenment of fourfold vision, and one should not, therefore, expect the poem to reflect either the realism of experience or the formal consistency of abstract logic. For example, the couplet that asserts that "Each outcry of the hunted Hare/ A fibre from the Brain does tear" does not seem accurate in terms of experience or logic, but, from a more visionary perspective, such a statement can have much validity. It describes the consequences of the physical act of rabbit hunting on the visionary ability of the hunter, who through his cruelty falls from innocence to the less imaginative state of experience. Many of the poem's couplets are, in fact, warnings about loss of vision as a result of acts of cruelty, and the poem as a whole attests the fragility of innocence. Since innocence is prized in the poem as the gateway to fourfold vision, the doubter who would mock an infant's faith is seen as particularly criminal: "He who shall teach the Child to Doubt/ The rotting Grave shall neer get out." The doubter's total lack of imagination will ultimately trap him in the "rotting Grave" of the physical universe.

Thus the couplets of the poem, through a series of paradoxes and riddles, seek to challenge and expand the reader's vision of reality. Those who are cruel, or who become obsessed with rank, wealth, or power, can never see beyond the twofold vision of experience to the threefold vision of innocence or the fourfold vision of eternity. Moreover, those who put their faith in the visible universe are doomed from the start: "He who Doubts from what he sees/ Will neer Believe do what you Please."

The poem's last six lines describe two ways of seeing: *with* the eyes and *through* the eyes. Seeing with the eyes leads the percipient to a mistaken faith in the visible universe, but by seeing through the eyes, with imaginative vision rather than physical sight, the percipient can break through the physical world and escape its "Night." To those who dwell in this night of visible perception, "God appears & God is Light," but to the visionaries "who Dwell in Realms of day," God "does a Human Form Display." As in the opening quatrain of the poem, the infinite is represented by the particular: God can be visualized in human form just as the world can be seen in a grain of sand or heaven in a wildflower. In essence, "Auguries of Innocence" reveals the illusory nature of the physical universe in order to develop the reader's ability to see the infinite in everything. This perceptual cleansing, Blake suggests, will ultimately lead to fourfold vision.

William D. Brewer

AUGUST MOON

Author: Robert Penn Warren (1905-1989)
Type of poem: Lyric
First published: 1979; collected in *Being Here: Poetry, 1977-1980,* 1980

The Poem

"August Moon" is a poem of forty-seven lines dispersed among thirteen stanzas varying in length: The shortest stanza has only one line; the longest has eight. It is written entirely in free verse and is, therefore, typical of most of Robert Penn Warren's poetry in that imagery and metaphor are always the dominant vehicle of expression.

The title, though ostensibly a simple one, is highly suggestive both as a metaphor and as an image in itself. Literally, it is readily discoverable that the moon is bright and half-full, shining on a clear August night when literal heat and the clearness of the sky are at their zeniths. Metaphorically, such a moon represents the emotional intensity the poet feels for his beloved. As an image, it is indicative of the intellectual passion the poet experiences, not in the heat of the moment, but in the heat of his life.

The poem is written in the first person, both singular and plural. The use of "we" is not as a plural voice; rather, "we" is undoubtedly intended as a way to personalize the experience and to involve the poem's readers. Warren uses the second-person "you" in three instances. He does so not to suggest that he is addressing a second person, even the lover or the reader, but to talk to some component of his self.

The first stanza of the poem contains two metaphorical images: The August moon of the title is "Gold like a half-slice of orange/ Fished from a stiff Old-Fashioned." Similarly, it is "like a real brass button" on "an expensive seagoing blue blazer." The shining moon is the focus of all that it is near simply because of its overwhelming powers.

The third stanza is one of three in the poem to be emphasized by being set apart in a singular line. This line indicates the topic of the poem in the form of a question that the poet will answer as he proceeds: "What kind of world is this we walk in?" The preceding stanza had aroused the question through showing the poet's recognition of the stars surrounding the August moon, themselves contained in an "Eczema of glory."

In the next stanza, Warren gives the first part of this answer, though indirectly; it is the kind of world where people must die. He writes that "It makes no sense except/ . . . the body's old business" and lists three occurrences that typify death: "Your father's cancer, or/ Mother's stroke, or/ The cat's fifth pregnancy."

The plural "we" is used in the following two stanzas as the poet continues to answer the question of the poem. The reader is instructed that "we" walk in a world where communication is possible, although it is a "darkling susurration" that must be deciphered. It is also a world where time, though never directly mentioned, is counted by children at birthday parties.

In the eighth stanza, Warren tells the reader exactly the answer to this earlier question: "the point" is that one lives in a world in which the "counting of years" goes on for adults as well as for children, although in different ways. Toward the end of the poem, the poet compares life to a "pale path between treetops." Finally, he instructs the reader that the world is one in which travelers on life's journey should communicate by holding hands and not talking at all.

Forms and Devices

As is typical of Warren's poetry, imagery and metaphor dominate; the poem is devoid of standard poetic devices such as rhyme or alliteration. He conveys his message through a series of images, many of which are embedded in metaphors. The August moon itself is used to establish a mood of contemplation and a setting of quiet emotional intensity. The moon is set in the universe among the stars in the same way that the poet as an individual, his lover as another separate individual, and readers as yet another entity of individuals are set in the world to walk their respective paths through pale moonlight among darkened treetops. It is hopeless, the poet realizes, for these stars to attempt communication; so it is with all humans who "walk down the woods-lane." The stars attempt no communication, and neither should the individuals who are the "we" of the poem; the difference is that the individuals of this "we" can hold hands.

Initially, the moon is compared to the gold "half-slice of orange" in a drink and to a brass button on a blue blazer. It is a part of the physical universe, the most prominent, visible feature in the heavens (the "Eczema of glory"); yet it is entirely personalized in something so common, even mundane, as a button. The moon provides the setting both for the universe and for the people on earth who walk under it; the moon itself is set in the universe in time "By the tick of the watch." Children most successfully escape this concern with time. Adults cannot do so, for they are thrust into its reality "At random, like/ A half-wit pulling both triggers/ Of a ten-gauge with no target, then/ Wondering what made the noise."

Two other images are mysteriously embedded in questions in separate short stanzas near the end of the poem. The first of these is "Do you hear the great owl in distance?" Animals perhaps know the significance of the August moon and would attempt their own forms of communication. If the poet and his cotraveler(s) can hear the owl, they, too, can achieve a similar understanding. Then the poet asks, "Do you remember a childhood prayer—/ A hand on your head?" This particular childhood prayer would be one prayed by another—by the adult who has, in the Protestant style of Warren's own youth, placed hands of anointment or ordination upon a child's head. Again, the impetus for such action is the communication of something important about the order and nature of a universal truth.

The last two metaphors are simple, even simplistic: "The track of white gravel leads forward into darkness." Life is, for those who would walk a gravel road, unpaved, yet white. It leads into darkness, the totality of which the travelers are spared only because of the light shed from the August moon. The darkness is and will remain all-encompassing, so the travelers are told to hold hands, walk on, and "speak not a word." Nothing that could be said is of importance, for only the moon will control the journey.

Themes and Meanings

Warren's purpose in "August Moon" is to explain some of the significant concerns of a traveler through life. These include one's station in and relation to the universe; one's place in the world in which one lives; the function and effects of time; and the proper perspective one should have as one proceeds into the inexplicable, cosmic darkness of the woods. Answers to all these questions relate to the August moon.

The walker through life is initially alone. One will remain that way if one steps out of line with nature by expressing oneself. (Ironically, this is exactly the function of the poet.) Individuals are like stars in that both possess (and are possessed by) a physical existence. In the face of the August moon, however, individuals can walk on in silence in order to maintain at least a semblance of companionship. One does so under the auspices of omnipotent time; here, the importance of time is simply that it makes one old.

At one point in the poem, Warren asks the question "who/ Wants to live anyway/ Except to be of use to/ Somebody loved?" The question is followed by a single-line stanza that questions the premise of that question: "At least, that's what they say." For the poet to suggest that others ("they") say this shows that he may not fully accept the idea himself. One can best be of service to someone one loves through companionship down the gravel road. A simple act such as holding hands in the pale moonlight under the treetops is what counts—not the counting of years. Older persons, perhaps, have little reason to count years, which already exist as an accomplishment. Rather, they count the importance of a single companion.

The world of words, as the poet shows, will not permit the deciphering of the night of one's life as it "Hardens into its infinite being." In this regard, finally, the poem is about how an older person prepares for an approaching death. Under the August moon, birthdays will no longer be counted because the counters will be gone, willfully having walked through life and on into the silence of the universe at some point on the white gravel path. The moon will become "lost in tree-darkness"; only stars will be visible. The poet will take his place in a universe of stars after walking through the life of this world governed by the moon. In making this passage, hand-holding and silence are the best for which he can hope.

Carl Singleton

THE AURORAS OF AUTUMN

Author: Wallace Stevens (1879-1955)
Type of poem: Meditation
First published: 1948; collected in *The Auroras of Autumn*, 1950

The Poem

"The Auroras of Autumn" contains 240 lines, divided into ten sections with 24 lines each. The title refers to the northern lights in autumn. The speaker first sees them as a serpent winding upwards, hungry to find a form for itself. The scene changes in the next section to a deserted, white beach cabin. Its whiteness is a memory, like clouds in winter. Autumn is a time for change, warning of winter. A man "turns blankly" as the sky makes change seem larger. The speaker feels utterly alone.

Section 3 begins, like section 2, with a farewell. Memory is focused on "mother's face," filling a room at evening. The aurora's lights are reflected from the windows, and the wind knocks at the door, "like a rifle-butt." The "farewell" continues, now focusing on the father, who is agreeable to everything. He enjoys change. He hears things that are not there, and he sees drama everywhere.

Section 5 examines the father's talent for imagining: He could fetch "pageants out of air"; and he made poems, though they were works "of barbarous tongue." These poems were the work of a man like Chatillon, an obscure sixteenth century writer who also said "yes" to everything. In the real world, the speaker objects, there is "no play" apart from mere existence.

In the next section, the poet, like his father, imagines nature's lights as a "theatre floating through the clouds": They become birds, volcanic smoke, floating in the sky's corridor. The "denouement" of this theatrical spectacle, however, cannot be completed because it has no inherent solution. The poet is defiant: Natural phenomena do not mean anything, or they mean whatever human beings allow them to mean. He boldly opens his door, but he is frightened. He is a puny "scholar" who sees by "one candle," when nature flashes out to overwhelm him, threatening "everything he is."

Section 7 reacts to this fear. The poet identifies the auroras with imagination, which leaps into the north, where it reigns supreme over all reality, displaying its energies in a proud burst of beauty. This imagination gets its energies from devouring reality: It is "the white creator of black," absorbing the planets to turn matter into energy. The speaker asserts that the aurora does not control its own destiny. It is an inscription on the blank of the heavens ("stele"), written there by the force that can both make and unmake it.

There is, the poet says in section 8, an innocence of time. Its existence is visible, as in "these lights" of the auroras in autumn. The poet reclines beneath them, "like children" secure "in the quiet of sleep," while mother sings. The next section continues this mood: The poet and his brothers lived each day as an adventure in the "outlandish." Each slept easily, fed on the honey of experience. In that innocent time, "fate" brought "freedom." Now, grown up and recalling innocence, the poet reconsiders the auroras: They are his mother soothing him for his fate. The autumn winds are sharp with the imminence of disaster. The auroras, however, are a shelter for imagination, cloaking darkness with a "flash" of innocence, so that the poet accepts death, which "may come tomorrow."

The concluding section is a tailpiece. The serpentlike auroras of autumn have been transformed into an imagination of "innocent earth." The auroras had been described in Section 7 as a regal figure crowned by a "diamond cabala." The conclusion asks a rabbi to explicate that text of gnostic wisdom. The poet imagines himself in "all lives" so he can know the world is noisy and hag-ridden, not a quiet Eden. The auroras join the winds of autumn to announce destruction; they are the "blaze of summer straw" seen "in winter's nick."

Forms and Devices

"The Auroras of Autumn" follows the rhythm of the meditation, from landscape observation, to focused detail from the natural scene, to personal associations from memory, to interpretation, and finally to a form of imaginative transcendence, signaled in the concluding section as "fulfilling his meditations."

This rhythm is made through eight (mainly) unrhymed tercets (three-line stanzas) in each of the poem's ten sections. While there is no standard rhyme scheme to the tercets, occasionally rhymes will occur to emphasize images and themes, as in the transition from the sixth to the seventh tercets of section 2: "fall" yields to "wall." More often, the sections contain "identical" rhymes (repetitions of the same word), as in "white" (section 2), "innocence" (section 8), and "world" (section 10). A form of rhyming occurs between sections, as certain words are repeated to form motifs of the theme throughout the poem as a whole: These include "wind," "changes," and "innocence."

The poem creates uncertainty and tentativeness with its interrogative mode of questioning the significance of what the senses report. It also makes difficult a certain identification of referents for pronouns (both demonstrative and personal). The title itself, however, hovers over all to suggest that the auroras of autumn will often serve as referents.

Images of light and wind, derived from the situation described by the title, dominate the figurative devices of "The Auroras of Autumn." While these images allude, sometimes subtly and sometimes obviously, to other poems by other poets (such as Percy Bysshe Shelley's *Mont Blanc* and "Ode to the West Wind," as well as to William Wordsworth's "Ode: Intimations of Immortality"), light as a figure for imagination and wind as a figure for communication do not need larger contexts to function clearly in Wallace Stevens's poem. The light of the auroras is transformed, though, to create a complication of its meaning: It is a "bodiless form" in section 1, "frigid brilliances" of color at the conclusion of section 2, "Boreal night" in section 3, an "ever-brightening origin" in section 4, an "Arctic effulgence flaring" in section 6, and a "blaze of summer straw" at the end of section 10. Similarly, the wind of autumn goes through several transformations: from the "cold wind" that "chills the beach" in section 2, to "windy grandeurs" knocking "like a rifle-butt against the door" of section 3, "the naked wind" that ends section 4, "a wind as sharp as salt" in section 9, and finally the "haggling wind" of section 10.

Themes and Meanings

While the light and wind imagery in "The Auroras of Autumn" may allude to poetry by Wordsworth, Shelley, and others (such as Walt Whitman), the more interesting indebtedness of the poem is to some of Stevens's own earlier poems. In particular, the refrain "Farewell to an idea" opening sections 2, 3, and 4 alludes to the poems Stevens published under the title *Ideas of Order* (1935), which included "Farewell to Florida" and "The Idea of Order at Key West." "Farewell to an idea," then, evokes an attitude of transformation in the poet's own life, poetic style and theme, or philosophical orientation. This marks Stevens's poem as a "hail and farewell" experience, in which he meets an object (or person) in passing on his way elsewhere. "The Auroras of Autumn" is a greeting to the spectacle of the northern lights at a time of transition (autumn) for the poet, who is looking for death (winter) in the flash of illumination provided by the auroras as his (innocent) imagination.

This theme of farewell allows the poem to be a vehicle for some private experiences from Stevens's life, such as those associated with his mother (her necklace and her hands in section 3, her singing in section 8) and his father (his eyes in section 4, his poems in section 5). Perhaps he refers to his brothers in section 5, as well as in section 9, where he may also refer to his wife as one whose "coming became a freedom" for himself and her. These personal, family "ideas" are sources of warmth but also obstacles to imaginative freedom; to them he must also bid farewell. Everything dissolves and disappears, everything is transformed, as both the light of the auroras and the wind of autumn signal.

The meaning of the poem is that everything changes, including the poet and his imagination. The power of change may be innocent or malicious, grimly benevolent, both just and unjust. The auroras of autumn are nothing in themselves without the innocent imagination; they are the inscriptions on a heavenly tablet, and they are the occasion for insight—not the insight itself. They do, however, as imagination's own power, illuminate ever so briefly the nature of a reality usually concealed by darkness, and what they reveal is a "harridan" world haggled "by wind and weather." This revelation, however frightening, is welcomed in the "nick" of time because it comes before winter and death overtake the poet or overwhelm "unhappy people" who think they exist in "a happy world."

Richard D. McGhee

AUSPICE OF JEWELS

Author: Laura Riding (1901-1991)
Type of poem: Meditation
First published: 1938, in *Collected Poems*

The Poem

"Auspice of Jewels" is a poem in free verse that is divided into eight sections of ir-regular length. Although the title alludes to jewelry, the poem actually concerns the source of power, of luminescence, for women. In fact, the language of the poem is charged by the metaphor of light.

There are two groups of personae in the poem: "us" and "them," women and men. Laura Riding contrasts the two. Men believe they give significance to women by giv-ing them objects of value. Actually, the significance of women is repressed or ob-scured by the gifts. In abandoning gifts, women become active rather than passive: "We have passed from plaintive visibility/ Into total rareness."

The poem begins with the assertion that men have weakened women through subter-fuge: "They have connived at those jewelled fascinations." With constant shifting from "they" to "us," the poem leads the reader to realize that the speaker of the poem assumes an adversarial role as she comes to realize the extent to which she, as representative of women, has been repressed, compromised by the attention of men. This attitude is simi-lar to that of Virginia Woolf, who classified a type of woman as "the angel in the house" in her essay "A Room of One's Own." Both writers contend that men, probably con-sciously, have belittled women by treating them as decorative objects rather than as hu-man beings who, in their own right, possess intelligence and genius.

One can understand why Robert Graves so admired Laura Riding, his companion from 1926 to 1940. Throughout most of his writing, Robert Graves asserted the supe-riority of women to men and devoted much of his writing to correcting what he re-garded as patriarchal corruptions of the literature of the matriarchy. Riding appears in the poem as a writer and a person who would elicit such a response.

The first three sections of the poem present women as compromised in a male-dominated society. Sections 4 and 5 begin with the words "Until now," signaling that a change has occurred. The luminescence of women in the present of the poem is no longer merely reflected; it comes from within the women. Section 7 begins: "For we are now otherwise luminous," indicating that the source of luminosity has moved from without to within. The poem ends with section 8, a parenthetical comment on the "Gemmed ladies" who are still attended by those whose light they reflect. Riding did not expect the dominance of male history and tradition to change because women had seen the light, but she did expect change to occur in women (and men) who chose to live according to what she regarded as honest attention to life and truth. She thought of such people as living on the "inside," not simply on the outside. Such insiders, she be-lieved, had the power to cause change.

Forms and Devices

References to jewels, the women who wear them, and the men who give them create the central metaphor of the poem. The metaphor causes the reader to consider whether women, like jewels, have significance only because of their assigned value, or whether their innate significance is no less valuable than that of those men who regard them as decorative.

The metaphor shifts in the fourth section to the unreflected luminosity of women, leading the reader to see that jewels have distracted women from their own power and worth. By using light as a metaphor, Riding evokes resonances that go far back into history and myth. In the Bible, God says: "Let there be light." In Greek mythology, Prometheus was punished for giving fire (light) to human beings, and Artemis was the Greek goddess of the moon. Light has been generally associated in religion with power and creativity; for example, Apollo, the god of poetry, drives his chariot, the sun, across the heavens.

In her light metaphor, Riding contests the idea that women have only reflected light (power). She uses words such as "brilliance," "obscure," "twinkling," "gloom," "luminous," and "snuffed lanterns" to give the poem light, and to make the reader aware of the metaphor. The poem ends with a dreamlike stanza that tells the reader one last time that the language is figurative, not literal.

The contrast between "them" and "us" increases the metaphoric force of the poem by showing the recipients of the jewels to be passive. Those who are not bejeweled have their own power. This difference illustrates that the poem is concerned with the possession of power, not with the giving of gifts.

Themes and Meanings

The title "Auspice of Jewels" prepares the reader for a prophecy, since auspice actually means prophecy. The prophecy is that significance is inner for those women who know that they are human beings of significance and genius. In her life and writing, Riding never questioned either her significance or her genius.

In contrasting inner and outer reality, "Auspice of Jewels" adheres to a basic concern of Modernism. As Virginia Woolf noted in her essay "Modern Fiction," the popular writers at the beginning of the twentieth century adhered to a view that limited reality to physical characteristics. Since those characteristics were often of dress and accoutrements, social and economic class were presented as the major determinants of identity. The jewels in this poem illustrate that view. The inner value of a person is the proper concern of the artist.

Such a tendency to look inward was prevalent in the generation that emerged after World War I, since so many artists of that time, Riding among them, had viewed the horrors of that war and come to reject the ideals that were used to justify it. In *Goodbye to All That* (1929), Robert Graves wrote of his rejection of the society and culture that he viewed as responsible for the war.

Though Riding was certainly aware of such views as those held by Woolf and Graves, her views are her own. They are part of the awareness of the inner world that had been brought about by the writings of Sigmund Freud. They are also a response to the political activity of women at the time, whose efforts had earned for women the right to vote.

Riding believed, as have many others, that her poems spoke with power of a truth that is greater than the historical moment. "Auspice of Jewels" is a poem that ends with a reference to medieval times, when there were knights and ladies. With this reference, Laura Riding clearly moves her concern with significance and value from the momentary to the universal.

Frank L. Kersnowski

AUTO WRECK

Author: Karl Shapiro (1913-2000)
Type of poem: Lyric
First published: 1941, in *Five Young American Poets*; collected in *Person, Place, and Thing*, 1942

The Poem

"Auto Wreck" is an impressionistic poem of three stanzas and thirty-nine lines that takes a hard look at the spectacle of injury and accident in a crassly technological world. The title, in trademark Karl Shapiro style, focuses attention on the unadorned, literalist description of a common event or experience.

In the first stanza, which comprises the first fourteen lines, the reader is situated, as it were, in front of an ambulance that is speeding toward the scene of an automobile accident; the reader is kept informed by an omniscient voice, which scrupulously provides both sensual and metaphorical detail that brings the reader uncomfortably close to both the horrifying event and his or her own matter-of-fact response to its horror.

The ambulance's red light pulses "like an artery," confronting the reader early with an image of blood, anticipating the arrival at the accident scene and preparing the reader for the sight of "stretchers . . . laid out, the mangled lifted/ And stowed into the little hospital." As the ambulance and its "terrible cargo" move away, the reader is left to contemplate the waiting physicians who will attempt to restore seeping life to the victims.

In the second stanza, the point of view shifts and the narrative voice becomes an introspective "we," implicating the reader as one of the "deranged, walking among the cops/ Who sweep glass and are large and uncomposed." These police officers, who are depicted as anonymous civil servants dutifully performing the tasks assigned them, are identified hauntingly by the impersonal singular pronoun "one": "One is still making notes," "One with a bucket douches ponds of blood/ Into the street and gutter," "One hangs lanterns on the wrecks that cling . . . to iron poles." The corps of officials and the spectators are united in their cold and predictable routine, beyond grief, beyond sympathy for the injured.

The third and longest stanza moves away from the accident scene to reflect on what the accident means. The poet punishes the reader with a series of hospital metaphors that puncture the reader's smug and complacent attitude toward the victims of technological disaster, which is mirrored in the inevitable carnage that high-speed, piston-driven vehicles precipitate. Throats as tight as "tourniquets," feet "bound with splints," this poem's readers try to speak through "sickly smiles" like "convalescents" attempting to make the best of a bad situation.

The auto wreck that occurred offstage in the poem's landscape has given way to the mental "wreck" that pushes one further toward one's "richest horror": The question "Who shall die?" turns into "Who is innocent?" While one contemplates the answers to these rhetorical questions, the poem takes a sudden turn toward a climax, surveying the more "natural" deaths of war, suicide, and cancer—each of which has its own logic and order.

Death by machine, by negligence, "invites the occult mind,/ Cancels our physics with a sneer," and disorients human beings' sensibilities and capacity to respond with compassion. One is left with a "denouement" splattered "across the expedient and wicked stones" of pavement and traffic lanes—whose silence speaks volumes about the increasing difficulty of discerning humane and human values in a world made alien by the presence of "empty husks of locusts," the wheels, motors, and steel bodies of the quintessential twentieth century innovation: the automobile.

Forms and Devices

To say that "Auto Wreck" takes its place among other "gut response to the world" poems that are characteristic of Shapiro's early craft is to say that his poems feature such subject matter as social injustice, the planned obsolescence and decay of man-made machines, and the alienation of modern humans from a world that barely resembles the one that was handed to them by their parents. "Auto Wreck," like similar Shapiro poems of the 1940's ("Hospital," "Washington Cathedral," and "University"), features obsessive, naturalistic treatment of the commonplace. It is the poet's intention to exaggerate the ordinariness of the mundane—or that which has become mundane by virtue of its perpetual presence or repetition—in modern culture in order to "defamiliarize" it and to enable one to see it as if for the first time.

In so doing, he is performing the function of art that was described by Soviet literary theorist Viktor Shklovsky, who believed that such defamiliarization works through poignant, graphic description of the real, a technique that borders on the surreal but stays safely this side of it by virtue of its intense view of the literal. In "Auto Wreck," this literalness is coupled with a metaphoric complement that combines the factual with the imaged; for example, in lines 9 and 10, "Stretchers are laid out, the mangled lifted/ And stowed into the little hospital." At first, the reader is meant to see a vehicle in which medical supplies are stored; next, to visualize a hospital on wheels. Shapiro thus achieves a marriage of the sensual and the analogous that forces the reader simultaneously both to look and to reflect on what has been seen.

As a result, many of Shapiro's stanzas feel as if they are being spoken in the first-person plural to fellow bystanders who are nodding silently in agreement. Although few explicit moral judgments are expressed in Shapiro's poetry, they linger, as they do in "Auto Wreck," on the edge of consciousness: "Already old, the question Who shall die?/ Becomes unspoken Who is innocent?" Such questions are raised only peripherally, however, never centrally.

Shapiro is adamant in embracing the view shared by the Southern "Fugitive" school of poets he admired that poetry with a "message" is mere propaganda. Shapiro's impressionistic poetics exalts immediacy, concreteness, and individuality. The crowd, the mob, is held at arm's distance, for it inevitably obscures the one, the individual life and its worth that the poet is at pains to make the reader see.

Shapiro has therefore always preferred a "low" or "common" English as the language of poetic life—a bridge or a concession to readers and poets who have tired of complex or contrived patterns or rhyme schemes. "Auto Wreck" exemplifies a poetic stance that is clearly opposed to that of the postmodernist poets, whom Shapiro has caricatured as propounding "apologies for the personal, the narcissistic, and the solipsistic, as well as for the tribal, antifamilial, and antinational ethos, drawn from both primitive and esoteric lore."

Themes and Meanings

"Auto Wreck" reveals what its author considers to be the terrible secret of modern life: the creeping indifference toward technological determinism, the simple violence of machine against human being in which everyone participates by failing to be troubled or moved by such disasters as automobile wrecks. Humanity sees but does not see; what is inherently unnatural or antihuman—traveling at high speeds in mechanical monsters that threaten both drivers and pedestrians—becomes the commonplace, the expected, and the normal.

One witnesses horrors and quickly dismisses them as part of the world one inhabits, a world that no one can control or understand fully: "We speak through sickly smiles and warn/ With the stubborn saw of common sense." Were one to understand it, the poet surmises, one would be even more horrified; hence, the better alternative is to register the horrific as the "official version" of an otherwise unbroken line of human catastrophes. It is not evil that should surprise one, but good; not failure, but success; not ugliness, but beauty; not revenge, but mercy; not despair, but hope.

The world of "Auto Wreck" is thus a sinister realm of everydayness. The details of horror are intensified by the images the poet chooses to portray his readers' response to that horror. Their "throats are tourniquets," their feet, "bound with splint," the badge of initiation into the labyrinth of stunned adulthood.

Whatever one chooses as tools for understanding become tools of ignorance, invitations to the deferral of meaning, preludes to the renunciation of "sense." One trusts one's senses but betrays one's mind; the longing for redemption or release from the mundane is but cruel illusion—a mocking and macabre invitation to either intellectual suicide or mad self-deception.

The "large and composed" cops in line 15 indifferently make "notes under the light" or "douche" "ponds of blood/ Into the street and gutter." Thus the threatened end of human life is transmogrified into the simple custodial task of sweeping the life source into the bowels of the city.

This thematic underscoring of a recurrent trait in Shapiro's poetry catches even the casual reader by surprise: Diction, image, metaphor—these must all be calculated to evince the proposition that in the modern world everything is arbitrary. Although things might have been otherwise, they are, in fact, not—indeed, they cannot be in a world run by machines. "Auto Wreck" thus becomes Shapiro's prototypical accusation against a world that is bereft of the transcendent values that give human life meaning and purpose.

Bruce L. Edwards

AUTOBIOGRAPHY

Author: Dan Pagis (1930-1986)
Type of poem: Lyric
First published: 1975, as "Ōtōbiyōgrafyah," in *Moah*; English translation collected in
Points of Departure, 1981

The Poem

"Autobiography," a poem of twenty-six lines divided into six stanzas of four or five lines apiece, requires some knowledge of Dan Pagis's biography. Pagis, a leading Israeli poet of his generation, was born in Radautz, in Romanian Bukovina (now Russia). A Jew, he was incarcerated for three years of his early adolescence in a Nazi concentration camp. At the age of sixteen, in 1946, Pagis, like many Jewish survivors of the Holocaust, emigrated to Palestine. (The nation of Israel was officially established by the United Nations as a homeland for Jews in 1948.) His native tongue was German, and he learned Hebrew in order to assimilate into Israeli society. He began writing poetry in Hebrew in about four years; it is remarkable that he later became a preeminent poet—not to mention a respected scholar of the literature—in a language not native to him.

The first line of the poem establishes that the speaker is dead. Clearly, the poem cannot be an "autobiography" in a literal sense. When the reader considers the author's biography, it begins to seem possible that the "I" who "died with the first blow" is collective rather than individual. The "I" in this poem symbolizes Jews murdered by the Third Reich's diabolical "final solution" or perhaps, in a larger sense, all Jewish people who have endured persecution. The identification of the "I" with victimized Jews becomes stronger in the next stanza, in which the speaker reveals that he was murdered by a brother who "invented murder." This brother is Cain, the slain speaker Abel, and the parents who "invented grief" Adam and Eve. The story of the first murder, from Genesis 4, here represents the brutal persecution of Jews, especially those murdered during the Holocaust.

If Abel is the world's first murder victim, many others followed. The third stanza seems to make a leap forward in history to the twentieth century, when "the well-known events took place" and "our inventions"—presumably the elaborate death machinery systematically and efficiently employed by the Nazis—"were perfected."

Abel continues reflecting on his death in the final three stanzas. He declines, in stanza 4, to "mention names," the names of generations murdered after him; such "details," he says, horrifying at first, are finally "a bore." The suggestion is that human beings, the poem's readers included, have a limited capacity for details of horror. Stanza 5 develops this idea further: "you can die once, twice, even seven times,/ but you can't die a thousand times." The narrator, however, does claim the power to die a thousand deaths, and his "underground cells reach everywhere."

Neither of the brothers is mentioned by name until the sixth stanza, in which Cain's name appears in the first line. Cain, the murderer, has multiplied "on the face of the earth," while Abel, his victim, "began to multiply in the belly of the earth." Victimizers proliferate and live; their victims' bodies pile up in graves. Nevertheless, the speaker claims that his strength "has long been greater than" Cain's. The poem concludes with an explanation and emotional assessment of why this is and how it feels: "His legions desert him and go over to me,/ and even this is only half a revenge."

Forms and Devices

Pagis uses allusions to Old Testament myth in much of his work and alludes to the story of Cain and Abel, archetypes in the Judeo-Christian tradition for the victimizer and victim, in at least two of his best-known poems, "Brothers" and "Written in Pencil in the Sealed Railway Car." Clearly, Pagis is using imagery from this archetypal murder metaphorically, and the most immediate comparison is to the Nazis' murder of millions of Jews during the Holocaust.

The reader may well ask just how this is so clear. No details in the poem refer specifically to the Holocaust, or even World War II. Lines from stanza 3, "Our inventions were perfected. One thing led to another,/ orders were given," contain the most direct references in the poem, and even these are oblique. Again, knowing the poet's personal history is helpful, as is a passing familiarity with Pagis's other work, in which the Holocaust is a persistent, although hardly omnipresent concern.

The very fact that Pagis refers to the Holocaust only indirectly—there are no swastikas, no images of crematoria—is in itself of interest. Pagis is a master of understatement, which is a form of irony; and irony is perhaps the dominant mode for serious literature written after the horrors of World War II. It is almost as if mere language were incapable of rising to the occasion of describing or paying appropriate homage to human suffering on a scale as vast as the Holocaust deserved. The German philosopher and critic Theodor Adorno wrote, "After Auschwitz, to write poetry is barbaric." Pagis wrote poetry, but the mask he wears as a poet is of one unable or possibly unwilling to give full voice to the incomprehensible suffering of millions.

This poem was originally written in Hebrew, a language richer than English in sound devices such as assonance and consonance. Although it would not have been possible for Stephen Mitchell's translations of Pagis's poetry to approximate the poet's sense of sound play, Mitchell's translations have been praised for their "resourcefulness and sensitivity," and readers of Hebrew have admired how Mitchell captures Pagis's sparse, elusive qualities in English.

One of Pagis's poetic devices which Mitchell is able to incorporate is repetition. Lines such as "My brother invented murder,/ my parents invented grief,/ I invented silence" and "There were those who murdered in their own way,/ grieved in their own way" use repetition and, in the first example, parallel structure to give the poem an Old Testament flavor. If the Old Testament is the principal book of myth for Jews, this poem, alluding to the Old Testament both in its use of metaphor and through stylistic devices like repetition and parallel structure, serves as a fragment in the Jewish people's continuing, modern saga—a story with the Holocaust persistently looming in the background.

Themes and Meanings

Perhaps the first question the reader confronts is why Pagis uses Cain's murder of Abel as a metaphor for the Nazi persecution of the Jews. It may seem a startling choice: Cain murdered his brother out of jealousy because God delighted in the sacrifices of Abel but was displeased with those of Cain. Enraged, Cain killed Abel. As punishment for the first murder, God placed a mark on Cain and made him forever, in the language of the King James Old Testament, a "fugitive and vagabond."

Pagis's choice of metaphor becomes especially interesting when the reader considers Cain and Abel as brothers. If Cain represents the Nazis and Abel the Jews, the implication is that the Nazis and the Jews are also, at least on a metaphorical level, brothers. What Cain is not, from Abel's point of view, is an animal, a monster, one completely alien or "other." It is easy, perhaps, for readers to think of Nazis as inhuman, completely incomprehensible, not true human beings at all. Abel, as the speaker of this poem, does not seem to share that perspective.

It is tempting to think of the categories Jew and victim, and Nazi and victimizer, as falling at opposite ends of the spectrum of human experience; one surprise in this poem is that Pagis, himself having suffered at the hands of the Nazis, resists that impulse. The notion of a thread of commonality between the Jew and the Nazi is strengthened when the reader considers that it is Cain, in the Old Testament story, whom God makes the eternal wanderer. The Jews have historically been a people who wandered, always searching for a place where they might be free from persecution. In this sense, Pagis adds another layer of irony to his poem.

Nazi and European Jew share a European heritage and, more specifically, in Pagis's case, the German language. German was Pagis's native tongue, and he was raised in a family without an especially strong connection to Jewish traditions or the Hebrew language. Although genocide is horrific in any circumstance, it may at least be comprehensible when it is carried out against a people very foreign, very different from the perpetrators. The attempt to eradicate a group of people whose differences from the perpetrators are minimal, however, is so absurd as to be nearly beyond comprehension.

The reader should not conclude, however, that this sense of shared identity between victimizer and victim means that neither the poet nor the speaker feels anger. The last stanza, the concluding lines in particular, makes clear that Cain desires and to an extent has achieved a certain revenge: "His [Cain's] legions desert him and go over to me/ and this is only half a revenge." These enigmatic lines suggest a continuing and perhaps eternal conflict between the brutal and the brutalized—a conflict only partially relieved by the fact that death, that great common denominator, comes eventually to even the cruelest person.

Douglas Branch

THE AUTOPSY

Author: Odysseus Elytis (Odysseus Alepoudhélis, 1911-1996)
Type of poem: Lyric
First published: 1960, as "E autopsia," in *Exi ke mia tipsis yia ton ourano*; English
translation collected in *The Sovereign Sun: Selected Poems*, 1974

The Poem

"The Autopsy" is a short free-verse poem consisting of ten lines, the majority of which are long and flowing as well as rich and evocative. The remainder—the fifth, seventh, and tenth lines—are economic, almost laconic, and comment on or serve as links to the lines that precede or follow them.

The poem is written in the third person; this not only amplifies the objective, detached perspective that the title implies but also contributes to the analytical tone of the poem. The nostalgic, evocative language which the poet uses to describe the "findings" of the autopsy, however, belies this objectivity, thus creating the tension of the poem; this tension is sustained until the final line, which signals completion and fulfillment.

The poet permits only certain parts of the body to be dissected. Specifically, those parts are related to the senses through which he perceives the sources in the physical world which awaken and aid him in expressing his inner, poetic world.

First, the heart, the seat of all emotions, is examined and found to be permeated with the "gold of the olive root." The olive traditionally symbolizes peace, immortality, and the Golden Age. For Odysseus Elytis, however, it is emblematic of Greek culture, its fruit having sustained the Greeks, physically as well as economically, through the olive oil trade. It is the quintessential Greek commodity, the "golden" gift of the gods. In the second line, the entrails are seized by "a strange heat," the result, apparently, of the poet's quest for light—whether in the candle's flame or in the coming of dawn. The entrails represent the physical self but also signify intuition, and Elytis typically intuits in light the presence of pure spirit.

In the third line, the tactile sense is recalled, as the veins beneath the skin are likened to the "blue line of the horizon." This image occurs frequently in Elytis, who, from the onset of his career, has elevated the landscape—and particularly the sea, sun, and sky—of his native land. The "cries of birds" in the fourth line also represent an element of this landscape, the divine realm of nature filtered through the subjectivity of the senses, which the poet has attempted to distill and express through poetry. If, in these attempts, he has been led astray or fallen short of the mark, "Probably the intention sufficed for the evil."

If the poet has succumbed to this evil in any way, the reader is told in the sixth line, it was the result of his own ingenuousness, his openness toward and his desire to participate fully in life, as evidenced by the vision of the "whole forest moving still on the unblemished retina." The forest symbolizes, on the one hand, society, and on the other, the realm of the psyche. In the seventh line, the brain, the reliquary of memory, is left empty. Only an echo of the poet's former ideal—the clear, inviolate sky—remains.

The auditory sense is summoned once again in the eighth line, which recalls more sea imagery; the sounds of the wind and the waves are, as is so often the case in Elytis's work, almost palpable. In the ninth line, the poet cites the power of erotic love as one of the sources which have inspired his poetic voice. The tenth and final line acts as a coda, commenting on all that has preceded. It suggests that the poet has succeeded in entering and confronting life with purpose and courage and that his virtue will be rewarded with the promised renewal: "We shall have early fruit this year."

Forms and Devices

The most impressive device employed in the poem is the analogy of the autopsy, which the poet develops through a series of extremely effective, related metaphors, all of which reinforce the image of a surgeon performing this act. The analogy of the autopsy reinforces, in turn, the image of ritual sacrifice—the poet as an Adonis figure whose life has been dedicated to the quest for truth and beauty—which is implied in the regeneration indicated in the final line of the poem.

The imagery in this poem is typical of Elytis's work in two respects: First, it evinces his roots in his native Greek tradition, and second, it reflects his fundamentally surrealist orientation. The Greek heritage, for Elytis, is not merely that of classical Greece. Rather, it encompasses a number of indigenous sources, including pagan mysticism, animism, and nature worship, as well as the Byzantine, Eastern Orthodox, folkloric, epic, and demotic traditions. The Greek tradition is most frequently expressed in Elytis's poetry, however, through the imagery of the sea. This sea imagery so dominated his early collections that, early in his career, he became known as the "poet of the Aegean."

For Elytis, the seascape is not only the quintessential icon of Greece but also the only one that can convey the holistic worldview which he embraces, which constantly seeks to reunite man's physical and spiritual natures. In his poetry, the essence of things resides in the divine natural realm, which he perceives as a point of contact, a link between man's physical self and his divine inner world, the fusion of which Elytis seeks to attain through the poetic act.

Surrealism enabled Elytis to succeed in this effort to a great degree, as the images in "The Autopsy" attest. In the poem, the spiritual is constantly juxtaposed with the physical, and man and nature undergo a metamorphosis which renders the one indistinguishable from the other. The olive root becomes the human heart, the core of being; the blue line of the vein is transmuted into the horizon, and all that the body retains are the melancholic cries of birds and a few grains of fine sand. These incongruous juxtapositions are standard in the work of French surrealist poets such as Paul Éluard, to whom Elytis is frequently compared. In Elytis's work, however, they are always grounded in his native Greek environment. Moreover, Elytis rejects the "automatic," unordered flow of thoughts, which the French surrealists admired; his poetry consistently reflects a clear, preconceived aim, subject unity, and the carefully controlled ordering of images.

Themes and Meanings

"The Autopsy" reflects the mature Elytis, the poet who has acknowledged and reconciled himself to the presence of the tragic, but who, despite this acceptance, mourns the loss of the clear blue sky of his youth in these "remorses." He is no longer innocent; the once azure vault is now cloudy and polluted by the forces of chaos and destruction, and only a "dead echo" of it remains. His aim in the poem is to determine whether he has combated those malign forces fully and courageously.

The poem examines the poet's performance not only as an artist but as a human being as well. He assesses all the sources which have inspired his artistic life and evaluates, in addition, the events of his personal life. He finds that he has participated fully and served valiantly—"His eyes open, proud." He has lived with dignity as well as passion.

The poem is also about nature, specifically as a vehicle for penetrating the inner, spiritual realm of human existence. In Elytis's terms, that means the world evoked by the interplay of water and light, which dominates the Greek landscape—hence the prevalence of sea imagery in his work. Yet the prevalence of nature in the poem reflects, as well, the particular affinity of the Greek for the landscape which has nourished him for so many centuries. The lull of the Aegean, the dazzling light of the sun on the sparkling water cast blue in the sky's reflection, wild birds crying above the edge of the horizon, and the omnipresent olive trees all permeate the Greek's entire being to a degree to which he himself is not fully aware, and it is this specific meaning which motivates Elytis.

Finally, while the subject of the poem is the body of the poet, on a second level of meaning it is the body of Greece as well; in Elytis's poetry, the poet and the country often seem inseparable. With tenderness and pride, the poet examines the timeless features of his country which constitute its unique essence, its Greekness. Taken from this perspective, the poem acquires a mythical dimension, which culminates in the reference to the resurrected Adonis in the enigmatic final line. Hence, it is not only the worthiness of the poet that is in question but also that of Greece itself. The final line, then, serves as an affirmation in both cases. Just as the poet has faced the forces of chaos and tragedy and emerged renewed, so too has his native land been strengthened by the centuries-long struggle against foreign domination and oppression. "The Autopsy" testifies to the worthiness of these sacrifices and celebrates the triumph of the human spirit.

Maria Budisavljević-Oparnica

AUTUMN BEGINS IN MARTINS FERRY, OHIO

Author: James Wright (1927-1980)
Type of poem: Lyric
First published: 1963, in *The Branch Will Not Break*

The Poem

"Autumn Begins in Martins Ferry, Ohio" is a short poem in free verse, its one-dozen lines divided into three unequal stanzas, forming an argument with two premises and an inescapable conclusion. The title of the poem both identifies the poem's locale and suggests the cyclical, seasonal, almost ritual quality of the football game which is the poem's central focus. In the bleak industrial Midwest of James Wright's poetry, the stylized violence of the gridiron takes the place of the traditional harvest festival celebrated by more peaceful, agrarian folk.

Wright wrote "Autumn Begins in Martins Ferry, Ohio" in the first person, and it is typical of many poems that he wrote, not behind the mask of a fictional persona, but in his own passionate voice. Wright was an advocate for both the confessional style and the poetry of personality, which were in vogue in the 1960's. It is quite logical, therefore, to identify the speaker of this poem with Wright himself, especially since Wright was born in Martins Ferry, Ohio, and grew up in that working-class community watching his father and others being brutalized by grueling factory work.

The first stanza of "Autumn Begins in Martins Ferry, Ohio" takes place in the Shreve High football stadium, where the first game of the season teases Wright "out of thought," much as John Keats is put into a reverie by his famous Grecian urn. As he sits in the stadium and observes the men around him, he cannot help but think of their lives outside the event, and he presents the reader with a grim picture of men whose work is physically and emotionally draining as well as ultimately unsatisfying. It is these broken men, these "Polacks" and "Negroes," who sit in the stadium "Dreaming of heroes." The poem strongly suggests that these men are both reminiscing about their own former greatness and reveling in the present victories of their sons.

In stanza 2, Wright extends his imagination to encompass the women of the community who, equally affected by the squalor of their lives, are "Dying for love." In a very short stanza of only eighteen words, Wright is able to characterize the family life of the spectators and the players of the game. These thwarted, needy women are one of the reasons "All the proud fathers are ashamed to go home."

Stanza 3 is a direct result of what the reader now understands was the argument of the first two stanzas. Men such as these, with wives such as these, mired in a situation such as this, are responsible for the spectacle of football, where all the combined frustrations of the parents are acted out in the beautiful and terrifying bodies of their sons, who are doomed to repeat the cycle of flowering and death as surely as the seasons perennially repeat themselves.

Forms and Devices

In his first two books, *The Green Wall* (1957) and *Saint Judas* (1959), Wright was composing clearly under the influence of Robert Frost and Edwin Arlington Robinson. In *The Branch Will Not Break*, where "Autumn Begins in Martins Ferry, Ohio" first appeared, Wright was turning away from the traditional verse forms represented by these mentors and embracing the poetic doctrines of Robert Bly and such foreign poets as Pablo Neruda, César Vallejo, and Georg Trakl, all of whom Wright had been reading and translating. What he borrowed from these widely varied sources, as well as from a number of Chinese poets, was a more spontaneous and visionary approach to poetry and a firm commitment to William Carlos Williams's famous dictum, "No ideas but in things."

It is not surprising, then, that the two most important poetic strategies in "Autumn Begins in Martins Ferry, Ohio" are diction and imagery. The brevity of the poem is only possible because of the haiku-like precision of the language and details. While the poem is not without figurative language—for example, the moving simile, "Their women cluck like starved pullets"—it relies more heavily on the freshness of its simple, powerful, and precise diction. This spare language becomes nearly apocalyptic in the last stanza of the poem, where the sons "grow suicidally beautiful" and "gallop terribly against each other's bodies." The choice of a word such as "gallop," more usually attributed to horses than men, helps the reader to see these young athletes as the powerful, graceful animals that they are, and makes the reader even more sensible of the degrading forces against which they must ultimately struggle. Wright is also addicted to the plain words of traditional Romantic poetry, and the word "beautiful" and "terrible" appear in this poem as well as throughout his work, as a kind of touchstone for his thoughts.

There is a strong pattern of animal imagery in "Autumn Begins in Martins Ferry, Ohio" which emphasizes the dehumanizing influence of the mines and the steel mills in these people's lives—it is no accident that the women are seen as chickens and the young boys as horses. While Wright's images are always strongly visual, they also appeal to the reader's other senses, as in the "gray faces of Negroes in the blast furnace at Benwood." Here the reader can not only see the ashen workers but can also feel the heat of the smoldering furnace.

Wright's great skill is his ability to turn three short images into an indictment of a whole way of life. If the game of poetry is one of compression, of saying the most about a subject in the least number of words, then Wright shows himself a consummate player in "Autumn Begins in Martins Ferry, Ohio."

Themes and Meanings

Sitting at the fulcrum of Wright's poetic career, "Autumn Begins in Martins Ferry, Ohio" is in many ways a compendium of Wright's major themes and concerns. Many of his poems are an attempt, by a mature and contemplative adult, to come to terms with the perceived horror of his American Gothic upbringing in a small Midwestern steel town. The "Polacks," the "Negroes," and the "ruptured night watchman of

Wheeling Steel" who appear in "Autumn Begins in Martins Ferry, Ohio" are typical of the characters that populate Wright's industrial wasteland. His poems are littered with drunks, hobos, and murderers; his concern with the suffering of the derelict, the dispossessed, and the victim is clear. Also clear are Wright's feelings of guilt for not staying to suffer with them, his essential alienation from these characters and the environment in which they continue to live. While the men of "Autumn Begins in Martins Ferry, Ohio" are "Dreaming of heroes" and the women are "Dying for love," the poet sits in the football stadium and says, "I think." It is his penchant for thinking, and then writing poetry about what he thinks, which both isolates Wright from his background and ties him to it. Wright is one of the most regional of American poets, and this has contributed to both the strength and the narrowness of his poetic vision.

Wright certainly is not the first writer to mine this particular thematic vein: investigation of the predicament of society's outcasts, the outlaws and the orphans, the lepers and the debtors. Charles Dickens did it with more anger; Walt Whitman did it with more gusto; D. H. Lawrence did it with more sensuality; Thomas Hardy did it with more irony—but certainly no modern author has done it with more authenticity and sincerity than James Wright.

Cynthia Lee Katona

AUTUMN DAY

Author: Rainer Maria Rilke (1875-1926)
Type of poem: Lyric
First published: 1906, as "Herbsttag," in *Das Buch der Bilder*, second edition; English
  translation collected in *Translations from the Poetry of Rainer Maria Rilke*, 1938

The Poem

"Autumn Day" is a short poem of twelve lines broken into three stanzas of three, four, and five lines. The original poem is predominantly in iambic pentameter (with the frequent substitution of stressed syllables to begin lines) and rhymes *aba, cddc, effef.*

The title of the poem recalls a familiar literary motif—autumn as the season of moving toward the end of a natural cycle. Autumn often calls up the melancholy feeling of things drawing to their close and reminds one of death. In this poem, the poet brings the reader to consider autumn's various aspects and what they might symbolize for man on a broader level.

The first stanza emphasizes autumn's association with endings, and so with death, by pointing out that the warm and nurturing days of summer have been great and full, and that now the creator who controls the seasons must curtail summertime in order to move on to autumn. The shadow being cast on the sundials symbolizes this act of divine curtailment. The almost biblical rhetoric with which the poet addresses the "Lord" in the first phrase adds a serious and spiritual tone to the poet's meditation. This same biblical tone returns in the last stanza of the poem.

Rainer Maria Rilke, however, also suggests the fullness of autumn as the time of ripe maturity and abundant harvest in stanza 2. The imminence of winter and death from stanza 1 is thus tempered by the ripening fruit and the "southern days" which bring life to its final perfection and fulfillment. Autumn becomes a time of full harvest and almost superabundance. Both the melancholy and the positive sides of the autumn day are embodied in these two stanzas.

The urgency of time running out, exemplified by the shadowed sundials of the first stanza, returns in the last stanza's first two lines as the poet echoes a biblical cadence and uses the repetition common in biblical passages. These lines admonish man that it is now too late to undertake life's primary tasks of building one's house or finding one's mate. Autumn—and the passing time it symbolizes—sweeps relentlessly forward. Like the leaves blown by the autumn wind, man too is driven along by time toward his own end. If he has not already attended to the important aspects of life and of love, he will not have time to do so as the year, and his life, draw to their close.

This last stanza also introduces the process of reading and writing into this natural cycle. Almost as in preparation for death, man will read and write long letters to leave behind. Writing thus becomes a link to some more permanent state. This poem itself is such a document of poetic permanence that outlasts the seasonal changes. The last phrase of the German text, "wenn die Blätter treiben"—translated as "when the leaves are blowing"—has a dual meaning; "Blätter" can also mean the pages of a letter or a text. The term "leaves" also carries this dual meaning in English, although it is less commonly used. The word "leaves" thus connects the natural cycle (blowing autumn leaves) to the act of writing (the pages of a text being ruffled by wind) and unifies the natural and the human realms.

Forms and Devices

Among many minor poetic touches, Rilke employs two main devices in this poem. The first is the use of nature and its temporal cycle as a metaphor for man as he approaches the end of his life. This use of a strong central image is common to many of the poems in Rilke's collection *Das Buch der Bilder* (the book of pictures) in which this poem appears. The second characteristic is the biblical tone of the poem, which adds a spiritual seriousness to the poet's ruminations.

The references to nature and to the natural cycle begin with the poem's first line. Summer and its growth are at an end; the shadows lengthen as night and the end of the year draw closer; the autumn winds begin to blow. In stanza 2, the references to nature continue as the fruits reach final ripeness in the warm late-summer days and the grapes achieve their final sweet fullness. While all of these images are familiar tropes for the end of the natural cycle, they also serve as metaphors for the end of man's life as well. As a part of nature, man too is subject to the winding down of time, to the end of abundance and the approach of winter and death.

This implied comparison is made explicit in the final stanza of the poem in which the poet's focus shifts from nature to man himself. It is man now who must realize that no time remains to him. He can no longer build or be fruitful. If he is alone as the end of his life approaches, he will remain alone. As the leaves in his path are blown by the autumn winds let loose in the first stanza, man too is driven restlessly forward toward his own end. Thus nature serves as the model for man's own progression in life.

To provide an even more serious mood for his meditations, the poet couches his thoughts in a tone reminiscent of biblical language. Not only does he address the "Lord" in the opening phrase, but he also echoes biblical rhythms and repetitions in the last stanza. This return to a biblical tone helps to bring the poem to full circle and to unify its natural and human components as well as adding the weight of biblical tradition to the poet's aesthetic contemplation.

Finally, Rilke uses stress and rhyme to emphasize his points. The unusual number of stressed syllables that open his lines (Lord, lay, bid, who, who) interrupt the more familiar iambic rhythm to call attention to the urgency and gravity of the situation. In the final stanza, the stresses pile up to create urgency in the phrases "Who has no house now will not build him one. Who is alone now will be long alone." The poem itself is propelled forward toward its end just as both the leaves and man are compelled to go on by the movement of time. This driving force is nicely preserved in the translations of the poem.

A formal characteristic of Rilke's German poem not easily carried over to the English translations is its rhyme scheme. Particularly in stanzas 2 and 3, Rilke uses rhyme to reinforce his message. For example, he rhymes *Tage* (days) and *jage* (pursue, chase, hunt) at the ends of lines 2 and 3 in stanza 2. He thus links the idea of time (days) with the idea of pursuit to produce the concept of time running out for nature and for man. In the final stanza, Rilke rhymes the second, third and fifth lines to similar effect. *Bleiben* (to remain), *schreiben* (to write), and *treiben* (to drive or push) rhyme and create a structure in which writing forms the bridge between remaining or enduring and being pushed or propelled by time. In the rhyme itself, Rilke indicates that even though we are driven unavoidably by time, writing may provide some form of human duration. The written word, the letter or the poem, helps us to endure beyond our own autumn and winter.

Themes and Meanings

"Autumn Day" is a poem about time running out. Nature is approaching winter and must employ all of its force to produce the final fullness of fruit and vine before winter sets in. Similarly, man approaches the twilight of his own life. He feels compelled to produce all the perfection of which he is capable before his time runs out in death.

The theme is not a new one. Many poets (William Shakespeare, for one) have used the impending end of a cycle of nature to symbolize human life. Such thoughts often trigger a sense of urgency and of intensification in human activity. Shakespeare in Sonnet 73, for example, cajoles his lover to love more intensely because of the thought of imminent departure: "This thou perceiv'st, which makes thy love more strong,/ To love that well which thou must leave ere long." Rilke's poetic persona does not have the comfort of a beloved, however; he is alone with his reading and writing, but his writing itself may offer him some means of enduring. Being alone may provide a melancholy tinge to Rilke's considerations, but his poem also focuses on nature's and life's fullness and sweetness. As in Shakespeare's case, the thought of losing that moment of fulfillment and perfection makes it all the more poignant.

Rilke's poem also reveals a persona ready to face autumn and the end of a temporal cycle. This is somewhat surprising, since Rilke was a young man of twenty-six when he wrote the poem in Paris in September, 1902. Poetic resignation or maturity of thought, however, does not necessarily depend on age. In this case, the poet is using his observations of nature and its seasons to think about his own future end as well as to intensify his present moment.

Kathleen L. Komar

AUTUMN LEAVES

Author: Jacques Prévert (1900-1977)
Type of poem: Lyric
First published: 1947, as "Les Feuilles mortes"; in *Soleil de nuit*, 1980; English translation collected in *Our Huckleberry Friend: The Life, Times, and Lyrics of Johnny Mercer*, 1982

The Poem

"Autumn Leaves" is a short poem in free verse. Its forty-six lines are divided into four stanzas. The first and third stanzas contain twelve lines each, and the second and fourth stanzas have the same eleven-line refrain. The only punctuation in the entire poem is a period placed at the end of the last line. This almost complete lack of punctuation permits diverse interpretations of many lines because it is not at all clear exactly how one should interpret them. In many cases, two or three different explanations are grammatically possible.

The poem is written in the first person. The unnamed speaker is a man who is addressing a woman whom he used to love. Although their love for each other has now ended, he still feels an emotional bond with her. He addresses her with the intimate *tu* (for "you"), not with the formal *vous*. It is clear that these are two decent people "whom life has separated."

In the first stanza, the speaker calls upon his former lover to "remember the happy days" that now exist only in their memories. When re-creating these days of happiness, Jacques Prévert utilizes the imperfect tense in French. This is entirely appropriate because the imperfect tense refers to habitual past actions or to past actions that lasted for an extended period of time. These were wonderful days for them because "they were then friends." Their love is described as platonic and pure.

The title, "Autumn Leaves," occurs twice in the first stanza and once in the third stanza. Prévert states that "Autumn leaves are gathered together in a shovel" for disposal; similarly "memories" and "regrets" are carried away by the "north wind" "into the night of forgetfulness." These images of "wind" and "night" are richly connotative, suggesting the powerful and almost unconscious human need to remember pleasant experiences from the past. The speaker ends the first stanza by recalling a love song that she used to sing to him.

The identical eleven-line refrain that follows the first and third stanzas is written in a deceptively simple but very evocative style. The speaker imagines that this love song "resembles" them, and he tells her twice within five lines: "You used to love me/ I used to love you." The loss of love occurs slowly, in an almost imperceptible manner that Prévert compares to the "sea," which "erases on the sand/ the steps of disunited lovers."

In the third stanza, Prévert suggests once again that "autumn leaves, memories, and regrets" are all "gathered together in a shovel" for disposal, but the lovers choose to preserve their memories. Although they no longer love each other, he is thankful because she enriched his life and was his "dearest friend." He regrets nothing because he will always hear in his mind the love song that she used to sing to him. The emotional power of their love still influences their lives although they both realize that they can no longer live together.

Forms and Devices

"Autumn Leaves" illustrates very effectively the refined art of Prévert, who wrote in an apparently straightforward style and yet expressed deep feelings with which all readers can identify. The use of verb tenses in this poem does not seem to be complicated. Prévert, in fact, uses those verb tenses (specifically, the present indicative, the imperfect, and the compound past) that are most frequently used in spoken French. He avoids an overtly literary style, which would have created a barrier between his poem and certain readers. Prévert strove to attract readers who were alienated from extremely esoteric poetry. His poems deal directly with such basic human emotions as love, loss of love, grief, and despair.

The apparent simplicity of style and vocabulary in this poem should not cause one to overlook the subtle art of Prévert. He skillfully contrasts the present with several different periods in the speaker's past. Prévert's use of verb tenses is very effective in "Autumn Leaves." In this forty-six-line poem, there is only one verb in the present conditional and one verb in the future tense, yet each is used extremely effectively. Prévert begins this poem with a wish: "Oh! I would like you to remember/ the happy days when we were friends." If she still remembers their love, this will bring him much satisfaction, but he realizes that he may no longer be part of her memories. Only one future tense is used in this poem, and even then Prévert links it not with the present but with the past. The speaker tells his former lover: "And the song that you used to sing/ always always I will hear it." In "Autumn Leaves," Prévert evokes past feelings by using verbs in the imperfect tense; this is entirely appropriate because lovers cannot link the gradual development and fading of their love to specific events. In French, the compound past tense is used to describe single past actions that may still have a slight effect on the present. Prévert uses only one compound past tense in this poem. The speaker tells his former lover twice in the first stanza: "You see that I have not forgotten." Through the very effective repetition of these words, which he evokes in the third stanza with the question "How do you believe that I could forget you," Prévert suggests subtly that he has not forgotten her because he cannot bring himself to forget her. The repetition of both entire sentences and similar expressions also serves to reinforce the fact that this speaker once experienced a pure happiness that he can no longer recapture.

In the first and third stanzas, Prévert included the elegant lines: "At that time life was more beautiful/ and the sun was hotter than it is today." A warm summer sun brings one much pleasure, but it pales in comparison to the ecstasy that love alone enables one to experience, even if it is only for fleeting moments. Jacques Prévert's extremely effective use of French verb tenses allows his readers to appreciate more thoroughly the simple but profound psychological insights in this poem, whose eloquence and musicality have been recognized by several famous French singers, including Yves Montand, who have performed and recorded "Autumn Leaves."

Themes and Meanings

"Autumn Leaves" is a poem about the power of memory. "Les Feuilles mortes" literally means "Dead Leaves," suggesting the paradoxical coexistence of the past and the present. Although one may delude oneself into believing that one has completely recovered from the loss of love, modern psychology has shown that it is never possible to suppress completely painful experiences from the past. One may not, however, fully appreciate the degree to which the past has formed one's perceptions of reality and one's personality. The "leaves" of the past are never completely "dead." Seeing a certain thing may somehow remind one of experiences in the distant past. This process is called involuntary memory because one has made no conscious effort to recall these events. When the speaker sees someone collecting "autumn leaves" with a shovel before the wind can blow them away, this commonplace occurrence reminds him that it is also possible to collect things that are infinitely more significant: "memories" and "regrets." Recapturing his memories is bittersweet for the speaker because he recalls simultaneously moments of happiness and his loss of love. He realizes that regret cannot diminish his present sadness; he prefers to think of the fleeting moments of joy that he and his beloved experienced together. Although they no longer live together, he still appreciates the importance of their love in his life. He expresses the essence of his love with these two exquisite lines: "But my silent and faithful love/ still smiles and thanks life."

In "Autumn Leaves," Jacques Prévert wrote in a deceptively simple style that hides the subtle and profound psychological power of this poem. The vocabulary used in "Autumn Leaves" can be understood even by intermediate students of French. Prévert clearly wanted his poetry to be accessible to as many readers as possible. A poem such as "Autumn Leaves" can be interpreted at several different levels, and each interpretation reveals the refined artistry and sensitivity of Jacques Prévert.

Edmund J. Campion

AUTUMN SONG

Author: Paul Verlaine (1844-1896)
Type of poem: Lyric
First published: 1866, as "Chanson d'automne," in *Poèmes saturniens*; English trans-
  lation collected in *French Symbolist Poetry*, 1971

The Poem

"Autumn Song" is the most famous poem from the collection of verse known as
Poèmes saturniens (Saturnian poems), published when Paul Verlaine was only twenty-
two years old. Like most of the French Symbolist poets of his day, Verlaine was enor-
mously focused on the art of poetry for its own sake and often presented the soul of the
artist and the creation of art as the only topics worthy of consideration.

Verlaine was singled out among his colleagues for his insistence on the notion that
the poem must be musical. His often quoted theory, "De la musique avant toute
chose" ("Music first and foremost"), is amply demonstrated in "Autumn Song." For
this reason, many of his alliterations, phrasings, rhymes, and the poem's rhythm are
untranslatable, leaving much of the powerful impact of "Autumn Song" diluted when
the poem is not read in the original French.

Verlaine's genius was appreciated by many around the globe, and his influence on
the Hispanic "Generation of '98" is widely documented. "Autumn Song" is one of the
most quoted and most imitated poems of the late nineteenth century. The ennui ex-
pressed by the poet is a posture that was to be characteristic of his work for years to
come, and the title, "Autumn Song," immediately marks this poem as one whose time
and place do not celebrate vitality. The "song" is a lament of the process of withering.
Decay was of great interest to the Symbolist poet, and here, Paul Verlaine begins his
career as a young man who sees the parallels between an exhausted universe and the
soul's fatigue. For the artist, it is a time to comment on his own frustration with his in-
ability to experience exaltation through art whose meaning or message has dulled.

"Autumn Song" is a short poem of only eighteen lines, yet it is a complete composi-
tion. Composed mainly of rhyming couplets, it has been constructed like a musical
score, with crescendo and decrescendo communicating in the classical lyric tradition.
The intense feelings of the narrator are expressed through a first-person voice in de-
liberately plodding rhythm quite pronounced in the original French, formed with
short meters that demonstrate a somber and disturbed tonality.

The first stanza begins with an image of a violin sobbing out a monotonous and lan-
guorous song that pierces the poet's heart. The personification of this musical instru-
ment is a metaphor for the poet: He is the vessel through which the sadness of human-
ity is expressed.

Another sound is heard in the second stanza as the orchestration becomes more
complicated. The clock strikes. As the hours proceed, time ticks onward. In contrast,
the poet's memory returns to the past. The intrusion of this regression creates a coun-

terpoint. Two melodies, as in a fugue, lend dimension to this stanza, and their simultaneous activities give the poem its tension. As his mind "strays," the poet weeps. Therefore, both the sobs of the autumn song and the tears of the poet create a groundswell of emotion at the end of the second stanza.

The poem is resolved in the third stanza by the annihilation of these feelings as he is left parched like a "dead leaf," transported "now here, now there," blown about by "ill winds" that leave him a passive object tossed about by unfavorable circumstance. The monotony of the autumn song is transposed to randomness and inconstancy.

Forms and Devices

The content of "Autumn Song" works brilliantly with its musicality, although its forcefulness has been affected by translation. For example, the first two lines of the first stanza have been translated as "With long sobs/ the violin throbs." Although rhyme and rhythm are evident, the intended onomatopoeic device of the long, nasal *o* sound in "Les sanglots longs/ Des violons," which accurately bring to life the sound of a violin, is obliterated.

The "languor" of the poet's soul is mirrored in the sluggish rhythm of the poem. Although the use of imagery like autumn to express decay and a sadly playing violin to reveal a disquiet heart are devices that, to the poet of Verlaine's generation, would have seemed to be hackneyed Romantic clichés (certainly they would have elicited a bored reaction), Verlaine's use of meter elevates the poem from the banal to a thing of consummate beauty. Verlaine is exhibiting his skill as a technician here in order to show that even an "autumn song"—a timeworn theme or topic for the artist—can be treated in a new way if the poet pays attention to his craft. In contrast to the effusive and melodramatic Romantic poetic presentation, Verlaine's short meter demonstrates, through its gasping cadence, that nostalgia is not always comforting.

Irony is another poetic device prevalent in "Autumn Song." The irony of naming the poem "Autumn Song" while attempting to rejuvenate a frequently used theme is Verlaine's artistically self-conscious method of calling attention to his own purpose. He uses paradox, as well; for example, the soul is bathed in tears (life-sustaining water) at the same time it is dry "as a dead leaf." The title of this early collection of work, *Poèmes saturniens*, was chosen by Verlaine to provide an ironic message of his intent. "Saturnian" is a word that is associated equally with abundance, feasting, and merriment as it is with the astrological sign of sadness and the description of a gloomy temperament. Although the reader might think, at first glance, that the collection is a celebration of plenty, most of the works contained within are about the paucity of the poet's soul as a result of an unnamed pain and unlocated depression. The reader experiences these sensations not solely through visual imagery and metaphor, but through the rhythm of the music, which has, in effect, made the reader become the narrator through its psychological impact.

Themes and Meanings

"Autumn Song" is a poem whose intent is to create a literary atmosphere. Verlaine chooses familiar concerns—melancholia, nostalgia, and so on—and attempts to show his contemporaries how these themes can be treated in a fresh way. This emphasis is present not only in this first collection of poetry but throughout his later works as he presents poetry not for the sake of social or moral commentary but as paradigms of technical accomplishment. The structure and the harmony, the forms and sounds are of consummate importance to Verlaine. The poem must embody the sensation that the poet wishes to express and not function as merely a picture of it.

The Symbolist poets were sometimes known as "decadents." The label of "dandyism" or "decadent" was applied to some for their lifestyles, but it was mostly a term used to characterize the poetry of artists such as Verlaine, Arthur Rimbaud, and Stéphane Mallarmé for a particular vision and aesthetic accord. The point of view in most of the poetry penned by Verlaine and his group expresses the world as seen through the eyes of a somewhat jaded and bored individual. Bored with conventional representation, Verlaine makes a strong argument in "Autumn Song" supporting the artistic credo of his fellow Symbolists in their attempt to revitalize poetry. He is "wounded" by the monotonous sounds of irritating music just as his sensibilities are offended by much of the clumsy and awkward poetry that was being written at the time. The Symbolists despised the kind of poetry that had little regard for innovation and instead preached morality to a wide, middle-class audience. The Symbolist poets, with their unexpected associations and hermetic symbols, addressed a more intellectual and cultivated audience. Hence, the subtle allusions to Charles Baudelaire's *Les Fleurs du mal* (1857; *Flowers of Evil*, 1909) in "Autumn Song" that pay tribute to Charles Baudelaire (who called his own collection "Saturnian") would have been known to only a select few despite the poem's seeming simplicity of subject.

Although the poet has control over his creation, he has no control over the state of sadness that envelops him. His poetry, measured and chiseled, fastidiously fashioned, contrasts with his own haphazard wanderings "now here, now there," and the care with which he creates the poem is out of keeping with his own personal "harried and sped" feelings, over which he exercised no composure. "Look to the poem," Verlaine is telling his reader, "not to the poet. For you will surely be deceived." The passivity expressed by the Symbolist narrator is a veil that thinly and exquisitely hides the aggressive, enthusiastic, and arduous honing of such radical poetry.

Susan Nagel

AVAILABLE LIGHT

Author: Marge Piercy (1936-   )
Type of poem: Meditation
First published: 1988, in *Available Light*

The Poem

"Available Light" is an autobiographical meditation in free verse. It consists of eleven six-line stanzas. Each of the first five of these stanzas has a definitive ending. However, the last six stanzas are paired: In each case, the first stanza ends in mid-sentence, unpunctuated, and the thought moves without a pause into the second. The final stanza ends with two lines that sum up all that has gone before. Though the title is a term taken from photography, it is meant to be a play on words: It is not visualized reality but the development of her own inner vision that Marge Piercy will be describing. A mature woman, she is looking back over her life in order to understand the person she has become.

"Available Light" begins in the present. In middle age, the poet asserts, sexual appetites are both "rampant" and "allowed," and she is as filled with desire as nature itself. In the second stanza, the poet moves to another favorite activity, her four-mile morning walks. However, in this stanza she also introduces the theme of self-knowledge: "I know myself," she begins the stanza, but she later modifies this statement by explaining that she also knows that her knowledge is imperfect. The poem, then, will shed some light on her past and on herself, but only the light that is "available."

In the third stanza, Piercy moves into the past, recalling scenes from four different times in her life, the last when she was twenty-four. As she points out in the fourth stanza, there seems to be no logical connection between these memories. The past is a medium in which, like a person under water, she has difficulty breathing. She is assaulted with details; she is confused as she keeps finding "new beings" in herself, unlike the friends mentioned in the fifth stanza, each of whom is committed to a single cause or faith. For someone who is Jewish, she explains, it is not so easy. Her God expects believers to remake themselves continually, while at the same time God refuses to intervene between cause and effect.

The two-stanza segment that follows begins with this problem of "consequences." Though the poet yearns to see "the larger picture," she knows that she cannot change nature, with its "million deaths" per inch, or, brought down to more comprehensible terms, its grounded "pilot whales," which human beings are struggling so desperately but perhaps so hopelessly to save. Appropriately, the next two-stanza segment is set in winter, the darkest time of year. The fifty-year-old poet's effort to learn Hebrew is somehow connected with the need to forgive her parents, who she now realizes, like the poet herself, were hampered by having only "scanty light." Finally, the poet once more ventures out into the night. Tranquil at last, she can now see even the distant stars, and she can also see all the creatures around her. Though this is called the "dead of winter," she concludes, it contains more life than she can ever "live to name and speak." Thus, surrounded by the profusion of nature, she seems to accept the limitations of her own understanding and of her own life.

Forms and Devices

In a generally enthusiastic review of the book *Available Light* for the *Women's Review of Books*, Diane Wakoski raised questions about the book title, pointing out that Piercy's poetry depends much less on visual perception than on the other senses. It may be relevant that by the time this collection appeared, Piercy had developed such serious problems with her eyes that she had difficulty reading and even traveling. A decade later, despite eighteen operations, she had only one eye that was of much use. Given this personal history, the title *Available Light* seems more than appropriate. However, there is not necessarily any connection between Piercy's physical problems and her imagery; it may be that she is simply more attuned than other writers to input from the other four senses.

Images are certainly of major importance in the title poem of the collection, and it is true that they are perceived in various ways. Many are visual: The poet sees the sky, the airplanes, the tracks in the snow, the skunk, and the weasel. Naturally, before the use of television became common, she would hear about the president on the radio instead of viewing him. However, she also mentions a "p.a. system" and the hooting of the owl, while she imagines smelling "Leviathan" (a whale). As for touch or feeling, the poet describes the frozen ground beneath her feet, the cold air against her skin, sexual experiences, the sensation of trying to breathe under water, and even the imagined penetration of the blood by "glowing isotopes." By depending on so many different modes of perception for her imagery, Piercy creates a texture that is strikingly vivid and rich. However, she also utilizes patterns of imagery as a device for suggesting her own conflicts and her abiding concerns. Piercy's images fall naturally into such dichotomies as light and darkness, sky and earth, indoors and outdoors, past and present, and life and death. As "Available Light" progresses, specific images appear and disappear, but these conflicting elements are evident throughout. For example, the poem begins with the "solstice moon" and the dark places of the female genitalia, proceeds to a winter day when "the light is red and short," and ends with a starlit night. In the third stanza, the procreative impulse is followed immediately by a friend's death, and, in the final lines, the "dead" time of the year is more alive than the poet "can ever live to name and speak." It is these contrasting images that dramatize Piercy's stated theme.

Themes and Meanings

The dichotomies in imagery are so important in "Available Light" because the real subject of the poem is the search for a harmonious life. At fifty, Piercy is learning how to accept the past, the present, the future, and her own limitations. Admittedly, much of what she remembers from the past is a jumble of impressions such as the clipper ship and the radio broadcast. However, there are also old conflicts that Piercy now has the courage and the wisdom to resolve. Since she now knows that she will never know or understand everything, she can forgive her dead parents for living by "their own squinty light," much as she realizes she must do.

Piercy has suggested to interviewers that one of her parents' omissions actually worked to her benefit. Probably because only her mother was Jewish, as a child Piercy was exposed to Judaism just enough to capture her interest but not enough to make her rebellious. The fact that she is learning Hebrew of her own volition indicates the degree to which the poet has accepted her Jewish heritage. Judaism also saved Piercy from building her expectations of life on a simplistic faith such as those that her friends have chosen. As a person who feels strongly about right and wrong, Piercy could have become committed to an easy answer with which she would have become disillusioned in time. Fortunately, she has a God who, rather than promising miracles, promises only that life is hard and that morality, though expected, will go unrewarded.

If learning about life, like learning Hebrew, demands great patience, it can also bring unexpected joy, such as the fact that sex is just as pleasurable in one's mature years as it is when one is young. Piercy has also found new fulfillment in living close to nature. She often speaks of the difference between her early years in New York, which, along with her excessive smoking, almost killed her, and her present contentment in a pleasant little town on Cape Cod in Massachusetts. Like Judaism, nature has taught Piercy acceptance of that which cannot be changed, cold, darkness, old age, even death. However, nature has also taught her to look for beauty everywhere: in those long morning walks in the winter, for instance, or when, venturing out into the winter night, Piercy realizes that almost total darkness makes it possible for one to see the distant stars.

The dichotomies in "Available Light," then, must not be perceived in terms of good or evil. The years have brought to Piercy a deeper knowledge of herself and of the world around her so that now she sees such opposites as past and present, life and death as more apparent than real. Now she understands that though the past cannot be changed, it can be newly understood in the present and thus, in a sense, redeemed. Similarly, the very fact that she will not "live to name and speak" all that she sees around her makes her own poem, produced in the "dead of winter," just that much more a celebration of life.

Rosemary M. Canfield Reisman

THE AVENUE BEARING THE INITIAL OF
CHRIST INTO THE NEW WORLD

Author: Galway Kinnell (1927-   )
Type of poem: Poetic sequence
First published: 1960, in *What a Kingdom It Was*

The Poem

"The Avenue Bearing the Initial of Christ into the New World," a long poem in free verse, is divided into fourteen sections of varying lengths. The title suggests the setting for the poem, Avenue C in New York City's Lower East Side.

Although a first-person narrator does appear in section 9, essentially, the poem's concern is larger than a single consciousness: Galway Kinnell is more interested in revealing the complexities of urban life in twentieth century America than he is in telling secrets about his own personal life.

Kinnell begins the poem with sounds: "pcheek pcheek pcheek pcheek pcheek." These are the sounds of recently hatched birds demanding their due; their mothers then "thieve the air/ To appease them." The first section continues to provide a variety of sounds not necessarily specific to the area of Avenue C: A tug on the East River "Blasts the bass-note of its passage"; a broom "Swishes over the sidewalk"; a pushcart moves "clack/ clack/ clack/ On a broken wheelrim"; and a man leaves a doorway, and the sounds he makes walking enter the poem and bring the notion of time with them: "tic toc tic toc tic." The section concludes without any pontificating by the poet; he is there, and he watches and records. Time passes, "the babybirds pipe down," and the poem's overture concludes.

Section 2 introduces two characters: an unnamed Orthodox or Hasidic Jew "near burial" and a Catholic, Bunko, who is a certified embalmer. The Jew has twelve sons, eleven of whom are named: They bear the names of eleven of the twelve tribes of ancient Israel. The old man, however, mourns his one lost son, probably Ephraim or Manasseh, and his wives "who bore him sons/ And are past bearing, mourn for the son/ And for the father." Kinnell pairs the Jew and the embalmer Bunko because the "sad-faced" Jew is close to death, but the funeral parlor near him is not for Jews. In the new world, the Jew and the Catholic live side by side, but there is no link between them; in fact, the Jew's final words in the section are: "Bury me not Bunko damned Catholic I pray you in Egypt."

There is one moment of happiness in this second section. The Jew "Confronts the sun" that was introduced in section 1, and he nearly has a religious experience staring at it: "he does not understand/ Fruits and vegetables live by the sun" because he is no mere lover of nature, but "he sees/ A blinding signal in the sky" and smiles. The new world does not prevent the old world values from surviving; his faith in Judaism and God sustains him.

Section 3 begins with a list similar to the epic catalogs in the poems by Homer or Vergil, but instead of naming families on a journey or warriors preparing for battle, Kinnell lists the signs along the avenue that the "Jews, Negroes, Puerto Ricans" might see as they "Walk in the spring sunlight": everything from "Nathan Kugler Chicken Store Fresh Killed Daily" to an advertisement in Spanish promising death to the most poison-resistant cockroaches. Kinnell then, interestingly, moves to the old women living "in the cockroached rooms" above the stores, and he has them consuming nearly all the products and services the previous lines named; the Avenue is a closed circle. Even when a small boy is introduced watching the pigeons' flight from a rooftop, the pigeons and boy transmogrify into chickens hanging "In Kugler's glass headdown dangling by yellow legs."

The poem moves oddly in section 4 from the first "Sun Day of the year" to the future tense and the nighttime when "The crone who sells the *News* and the *Mirror*" will appear. She has forgotten her dead husband and her children, she has no idea what the papers are reporting, and she is "sure only of the look of a nickel/ And that there is a Lord in the sky overhead." Yahweh lives in the firmament and in the streetlights of the avenue or in the "feeble bulb/ That lights her face"; in her dementia, she is able to see God clearly.

Section 5 returns to the birds whose "pcheek" sounds opened the poem. Now Kinnell wonders if they have matured enough to take up flight, and whether the mother birds are now dead. The mystery of life and death, the cycles of nature, are referred to here. The pushcart market on a Sunday is the focus of section 6. Here Kinnell glories, momentarily, in the beauty of the fruits and vegetables in the sun, but he also realizes they too have been "uprooted,/ Maimed, lopped, shucked, and misaimed," perhaps like the inhabitants of the Lower East Side.

The poet, in section 7, wonders why "Of all places on earth inhabited by men," he finds himself on Avenue C among all the people with "wiped-out lives." The poet is obviously not trapped in the city the way others must be; he has memories of the beauty of nature in New Hampshire and in France. He moves away from these personal memories and returns to the street and an "ancient Negro . . ./ Outside the Happy Days Bar & Grill." The man starts to sing but then is silenced as he "Stares into the polaroid Wilderness" of "Villages,/ . . . on the far side of the river" because the towns are sites of World War II concentration camps: Bergen-Belsen, Treblinka, Buchenwald, Auschwitz.

Section 8 brings to a close the pushcart market as the "merchants infold their stores." More importantly, Kinnell comments on the lives of the people on the avenue. The Jews who survived the Holocaust live in this neighborhood where they survive like "cedars on a cliff, roots/ Hooked in any crevice they can find."

In section 9, Kinnell appears in the first person in perhaps the angriest section of the poem. The biblical story of Abraham and Isaac is transformed: God turns away while Isaac burns in the flames. Walt Whitman appears as a believer in a harmonious cosmos, but Kinnell's friend Isaac, the week before he dies, reads Whitman and can only say, "Oi!/ What shit!"

Gold's junkhouse goes up in flames in section 10, and no one mourns as it burns. In the evening, however, after the conflagration has gone out, the people appear to witness the destruction: After each person sees the power of the past—the "Carriages we were babies in,/ Springs that used to resist love"—reduced to rubble, "Nobody knows for sure what is left of him."

In section 11, the fish market is described horribly. The varieties of fish for sale are listed, but they are described with such tenderness that the carnage becomes awful. The fish lose their spirit and become flesh only when the store owner "lops off the heads" and "Shakes out the guts as if they did not belong in the first place." The inclusion of a form letter from a concentration camp is incongruously placed in this section. Is the reader somehow to equate the fish deaths with the Holocaust?

Night officially arrives in section 12, and the poet can only imagine what is taking place outside by the sounds he hears from his bedroom; this brings the reader back to the sounds of morning from section 1. In the sentence framing the section, Kinnell hears the "Carols of the Caribbean, plinkings of guitars" outside the Bodega Hispano, but inside the parenthesis there are uncomfortable images: A child cries, "wailing/ As if it could foresee everything"; a hook and ladder truck moves "with an explosion of mufflers"; and a cat caterwauls a "hair-raising shriek." The joy of morning is gone.

The noises of the trash truck arrive in section 13 as it "sucks in garbage in the place/ Where other animals evacuate it." Again, the poet only hears sounds in the darkness. He says, bleakly, "If it is raining outside/ . . . It would be the spring rain." There really is no spring in this poem, however: Death lives too close to life.

The concluding section is as dismal as the previous ones. The street bearing the initial of Christ is a "God-forsaken Avenue," and in the entire neighborhood of the poem, "instants of transcendence/ Drift in oceans of loathing and fear." There is a hint of nostalgia in the last few lines of the poem, as if a paradise has been lost. The people say, "what a kingdom it was!" as if, at some point, life was good. The Yiddish expression of grief is an appropriate place for the poem to end: "oi weih, oi weih."

Forms and Devices

The principal device employed by Kinnell to create meaning through form is the poem's movement from the possibilities of morning to the hopelessness of night. He also transforms traditionally positive stories, such as the biblical tale of Abraham and Isaac, by allowing the innocent Isaac to burn while a useless God turns away and washes his hands like "a common housefly." The avenue that bears the initial of Christ as its name offers a sign to the denizens of the Lower East Side, but the signs are only advertisements for roach killers or a Happy Days Bar. These twists allow the reader to see what has happened to the pure, new world: It has been corrupted.

Humans are not the only ones who are forced to endure in this world. Through metaphor, Kinnell allows the animal and vegetable worlds to also participate in the suffering. Porgies on sale have their "jaws hinged apart/ In a grimace of dejection"; onions sit in the sun "with their shirts ripped"; and cabbages lie about "like sea-green brains/ The skulls have been shucked from." Through personification, the reader is able to sense the suffering of all living things on earth.

In a poem that from the beginning is filled with sounds of birds and brooms and carts, Kinnell accentuates the absence of sound when, in section 12, he lies in bed "Expecting a visitation" of some sort, but hears nothing at all. In addition, the final image of God in section 14 is not one of an immanent deity or a concerned parent figure; instead, "God is a held breath," an absence of sound, a zero in the world.

Themes and Meanings

"The Avenue Bearing the Initial of Christ into the New World" is a large poem that addresses large themes. Kinnell is attempting to do for twentieth century New York what T. S. Eliot did for London in *The Waste Land* (1922), what Guillaume Apollinaire did for Paris in "Zone," and what Walt Whitman accomplished for nineteenth century America in *Leaves of Grass* (1855). By concentrating on a small area of a single city, Kinnell is trying to make a statement about the new world as a whole, and perhaps all of creation.

All of the characters in the poem seem to be suffering from one malady or another. They are all transplants, either from Africa, Puerto Rico, or Jewish ghettos in Europe, and they are not surviving terribly well in this new world. Fathers are removed from sons, and old men and women are headed toward death. The creative power of sex is not felt anywhere in the poem; Whitman's "procreant urge" has been replaced by the sounds of despair, the "oi weih" of the poem's close. Although in the early part of the poem God's presence alleviated some suffering, especially in sections 2 and 4 in which the old Jewish man and woman see God in the sky, by the end of the poem, God is only a "held breath," the Avenue bearing the initial of Christ is "God-forsaken," and a fishmonger who lops off fish heads and nails the fish to wood "stands like Christ" in the new world.

The fault does not lie in America only. The immigrants from Europe, for example, carry the memories of the Holocaust with them. The natural laws that force humans to kill in order to survive operate in Damascus, where twelve goatheads "were lined up for sale," as well as in New York. Kinnell is suggesting that something is wrong with the divine plan; or perhaps, there is no plan or no God. The poem catalogs all the varieties of loss a human can endure, but it offers few possibilities for redemption. The old crone who sells newspapers in section 4 offers some hope. Even though she has forgotten her husband and her children's whereabouts and "She can't tell one newspaper from another," she accepts the mystery of life, and she believes "there is a Lord in the sky overhead." After ten more sections of misery and despair, however, the reader has almost forgotten the old woman's hopeful senility. In the end, the "brain turns and rattles/ In its own black axlegrease" trying to make some sense of the mystery of life.

Kevin Boyle

AWAKENING

Author: Lucien Stryk (1924-   )
Type of poem: Meditation
First published: 1973, in *Awakening*

The Poem

"Awakening" is an unrhymed poem in numbered sections that run I through VII. The title suggests an epiphany, referred to in Zen as *satori*. The dedication reads, *Homage to Hakuin, Zen Master, 1685-1768.*

In section I Shoichi, a sixteenth century Japanese painter and calligrapher, has drawn a black circle. Above the circle he has composed a poem, a haiku. Having been penned in the traditional Japanese fashion, with the lines and individual symbols running up and down the page, the poem and circle take on the appearance of budding flowers growing from a bowl. Shoichi tells the reader that the bowl has, "Since the moment of my/ pointing," held "nothing but the dawn."

In section II Lucien Stryk presents a winter scene, frost on a window that looks like "laced ice flowers" and a meadow covered with ice and frost that looks as if it drifted off the side of a glacier. The scene reminds the poet of a description by Hakuin in which Hakuin was alone, "Freezing in an icefield," so cold he "could not move." The poet realizes that, even though his legs have cramped and he cannot see beyond the frost, his mind is still "pointing/ like a torch." He does not move. In section III it is spring. The poet examines a stone as he holds it in the palm of his hand and turns it "full circle/ slowly, in the late sun." He feels a sting in his hand, like the pressure of a "troubled head." The stone falls from his hand, and "A small dust rises."

In section IV the poet describes the air that moves westward, "Beyond the sycamore," as something nameless and dark, like smoke or a cloud. He traces "a simple word" in the condensation that his breath has left on a window. In section V the poet presents a scene in which he and his daughter are on a beach where the poet, thirty years before this time, had played with shells. His daughter gathers shells and directs him in making a model of the universe. They watch the "planets whirling in the sand" till sundown.

In section VI the poet presents the reader with a series of elusive though generic sensations, mostly of touch, and abstractions such as "Time. Place. Thing." In section VII Stryk presents a setting that is very much like a mirror image of section I. Instead of an ancient artist drawing and composing a poem in the light of dawn, the poet is writing a poem himself and using a watercolor image to describe what the fading light of evening is doing to the trees. He ends the poem by saying that dusk is the time of day that always makes him happy and ready for death if it should come.

Forms and Devices

The first device this poem uses is a dedication. Presenting the poem as homage to a great (perhaps the greatest) Zen master, Stryk prepares the reader for what most Western writers try to lay before their readers whenever they write about Zen—paradox.

Stryk uses a set of framing elements that give the poem a sense of unity and a feeling of formality. Whenever a poem is presented to the reader in numbered units it is natural for the reader to expect that each unit will have both an independent sense of its own and a modular function within the larger framework of the poem. In classic Zen fashion, the author opens the poem at dawn and closes with dusk. Along with reinforcing the unity of the poem and all its elements, this adds a sense of completeness. Typical of Zen thinking, the five sections between I (dawn) and VII (dusk) do not have to carry a sense of having equal importance or of occurring at specific or evenly spaced points within the progression. It is sufficient that they all occur between dawn and dusk.

By dividing most of the poem (all but the first section) into tercets, the poet creates a visual resonance with a large body of Japanese poetry. This is especially true of haiku—and of the work of Hakuin in particular because of his fame not only as a composer of haiku but also as an artist who enhanced his paintings with haiku. Beginning the poem with a reference to another classic Japanese artist who enhanced his paintings with haiku, and ending the poem with a modern poet who describes the world from the perspective of a painter is another framing device that further unifies all elements of the poem.

Metaphor is important to almost all Western poetry and plays a large role in Asian poetry as well; however, the role of metaphor within cultures heavily influenced by Zen can be very confusing to people of Judeo-Christian-Islamic cultures. Although Zen poetry is full of objects found in nature, these objects will rarely be metaphors for individual aspects; however, any physical object found in nature can represent the nature and workings of all existence. With Zen it is all or nothing.

Stryk has used the most basic of Zen symbols. Dawn symbolizes beginning and ending, and dusk ending and beginning. The circle, much like the figure-eight symbol for infinity, represents the endless cycle of life.

Themes and Meanings

One of the prominent themes of the poem, perhaps the most prominent, concerns Zen, the form of Buddhism that holds meditation as the primary key to all knowledge, and how Zen compares to Western philosophies, especially those that rely on more analytical approaches to understanding the universe. The circle that Shoichi paints in the first section of the poem is a mystic circle, a Zen symbol for a personal awakening—a sudden awareness or epiphany that bypasses the rational part of the human mind. Such epiphanies often come after meditation.

In section II the poet's meditation on the "laced ice flowers" leads to a vision, a sudden transformation to a meadow, born from the side of a glacier, and the near-death experience of Hakuin "Freezing in an icefield." These associations lead to an identification with Hakuin that is so strong that the poet vicariously experiences leg cramps and such an overpowering feeling of cold that he cannot move. He has been transformed into a state of understanding that is unattainable through simple logic.

In section III the poet presents another conflict between Zen and Western patterns of thought, especially in regard to the physical world. At first the poet tries to make too much of the stone. As he turns it in his hand he searches the stone for metaphorical meanings, perhaps something relating to the sun and the changing of the seasons. To the practitioner of Zen, the stone is itself, a stone, a part of the whole of existence that needs no further justification. Its true nature and purpose are found when the poet drops it. "It falls. A small dust rises." What seems so paradoxical to Westerners is that, although an object is not used as a metaphor for some other object, the object can be representative of the whole of existence, the entire universe, physically, mentally, spiritually. The stone cannot hold just the seasons or just the sun; it holds everything at once, and everything holds the stone.

Section IV, one of the more elusive sections, deals with naming and with uncertainty, a principle that makes most Westerners uncomfortable. Westerners depend heavily on analytical thinking and on attributing names to things so that they can pin them down or compartmentalize them. When one's understanding of things expands them beyond one's expectations, one often finds the names inadequate. In Zen the name simply expands and contracts with the object named. The poet has, through his meditations, learned from the objects about the nature of the world.

In section V the poet's daughter amazes the poet with her sudden desire to understand the shape and nature of the entire universe and by her intuitive knowledge that the only devices she needs are pieces of the universe, each of which carries within it the nature of the whole. There is at least an implication here that Zen or Zenlike understanding is sometimes possible without the tutelage of a mentor or master. It may even be possible for the uninitiated to function as mentor. Children may be more receptive to Zen because their experiences have not yet encouraged them to prioritize and categorize.

In section VI the poet provides the reader with a taste of the universe and its total lack of discrimination. It is "Softness everywhere,/ snow a smear,/ air a gray sack." The final section of the poem is like a summary of everything presented in the six preceding sections. The meditations of the poet have brought the poet full circle. By understanding the inevitability and the beauty of his beginning, he is now prepared for the necessity and the beauty of his death.

Edmund August

AXE HANDLES

Author: Gary Snyder (1930-   )
Type of poem: Narrative lyric
First published: 1983, in *Axe Handles: Poems*

The Poem

Gary Snyder's "Axe Handles," a thirty-six-line poem, tells a small domestic story that widens into a meditation on parenting, the transmission of cultural heritage, and the relevance of ancient wisdom to ordinary, everyday life. The poet (who speaks the poem), tells about teaching his son Kai, on an April afternoon, how to throw a hatchet so deftly that it will lodge into a stump. Kai remembers having seen a hatchet-head stored in "the shop" and goes to get it. He "wants it for his own."

The father uses the hatchet they had been throwing to shape an old broken axe handle into a handle for Kai's rescued hatchet-head. As he works, the speaker suddenly recalls a phrase from his reading of modern American poet Ezra Pound, who did free translations of Chinese literature: "'When making an axe handle/ the pattern is not far off.'" He paraphrases the quotation to his son, relating it to their own task of using a hatchet to make a handle for a hatchet.

The speaker, meditating again, associates the wisdom of the phrase first with Lu Ji, a Chinese poet and essayist who died early in the fourth century C.E., and then with a former teacher of his own who translated Lu Ji's work. Then the speaker has a revelation that leads him to compare Lu Ji; Pound; his teacher, Shih-hsiang Chen; and himself to axes, simultaneously models and tools in the ongoing handing-down of cultural patterns, particularly poetry, from generation to generation. The speaker predicts that Kai, as yet just a "handle," is also slated "soon/ To be shaping again" for generations yet unborn. The poem ends with a simple understated phrase expressing the speaker's awe at the continuity of human culture expressed by people in tools as well as in books: "How we go on."

Forms and Devices

Snyder is known for the plainness of his diction and the accessibility of his style. "Axe Handles" is written in unrhymed free-verse lines of from three to ten syllables, resulting in a long and narrow shape on the page and a forward propulsion. Words at the beginning of phrases echo one another in randomly placed half rhymes and with alliteration, giving supple shape and musicality to the poem: "show," "how," "throw"; "sticks," "stump," "shop"; "gets it," "wants it," "hatchet," "cut it," "take it"; "long," "length." These sonic pleasures add to the genial tone of the poem, the sense that the speaker and his son enjoy each other's company, that the atmosphere is bright and relaxed, and that what one initiates, the other will follow.

The first half of the poem is laced with verbs as two male members of one family work and play during an afternoon in early spring. There is something mimetic of the arch and thudding fall of a flying hatchet in the consonant clusters and rhythm of "One-half turn and it sticks in a stump." All the lines are phrase-length, ending cleanly without disconcerting enjambments; the verse proceeds with balance and grace, with an almost kind, storytelling tone of voice.

Snyder emphasizes the surprise and serendipity of "the phrase/ First learned from Ezra Pound" occurring to him right on cue by cutting the poem in half with it. He marks it off with quotation marks and indents its second line dramatically from the left-hand margin. He does not say that he remembers, or calls to mind, Pound's phrase, but instead, he seems to hear it, clear as a clarion: It "Rings in [his] ears!"—a stunning use of the only exclamation mark in the poem. The sudden route that opens up to him between the real and the literary is not an abstraction but a sensuous experience; not a conscious thought but an unbidden spoken sound. So should his reading function in his life, Snyder seems to imply, as coterminous with his work and play with tools, as a seamless part of his afternoons with his growing son, a "natural" bolstering of everything he does.

"Axe Handles" is a poem of many and varied repetitions, loving its own vocabulary for its usefulness in the here and now, and over long, long centuries. In a poem that stresses how much of language and culture is inherited, it is appropriate that Snyder does not strain for synonyms but instead lovingly repeats again and again the same words: the word "hatchet" six times in the first thirteen lines, the word "axe" seven times in the last half of the poem, the word "handle" eight times, weaving through the lines from beginning to end. These words, and the tools they refer to, belong to the Snyders and are used casually by them, but they have been handed down over centuries, burnished by use, and remade according to pattern.

The wisdom first quoted in the poem as derived from Ezra Pound is repeated in the poem twice again, once in his own words, as if the speaker could not relish it enough. What was taught to him by Pound, by Lu, and by Shih-hsiang, he seizes to teach to Kai in this providential moment. He is a disciple of archaic wisdom, a practitioner of it, and a teacher in his own right, using the tools in his hands to demonstrate how "we'll shape the handle/ by checking the handle/ Of the axe we cut with." This is a lesson at once in tool-making, in philosophy, and in aesthetics.

It is part of the casual anecdotal feel of the poem that it is held together by "ands," each development in its small drama introduced by this humble conjunction. Although this is a rudimentary method of plot advancement, the word "and" can be read as profoundly connective, as well as casually so. When Snyder turns, in the middle of the poem, to paraphrase Pound's phrase to his son, he begins with an "And" that teaches the reader the connection between the two halves of the poem, between action and contemplation, between the past and the present, between the external order of things and the imaginative order of things, between parenting and poetry.

Also, the word "and" is followed twice by epiphany, by an expansion of the horizon of understanding. In line 22 the poet says, "And he sees" and in line 31, "And I see." That Kai "sees" so swiftly the elegance and comedy of using a tool to make a tool of the same kind justifies the speaker's understated pride in him.

Snyder himself takes the second epiphany, expressed in terms of metaphor, casting himself simultaneously as late learner and mature teacher among teachers: "And I see: Pound was an axe,/ Chen was an axe, I am an axe/ And my son a handle." Part of what Snyder "sees" here is that he has earned his space among the masters, those who actively craft the culture, by receiving it, using it, and passing it on. It is typical of Snyder that he should announce this profound connection with mingled confidence and humility, in language without a hint of grandiosity: "How we go on." Without ado, the "we" of that phrase acknowledges a familial lineage of makers from the fourth century C.E. to the present, from Lu Ji to Kai, and beyond.

Themes and Meanings

A recurring theme in Snyder's poetry is his love for tools, which he presents as providing ways to interact with the physical environment, ways of negotiating human life. Often the tools of physical labor are seen as analogous to the poet's tools of the trade. In "Axe Handles," the handle itself is very important: literally, the part of the tool that is designed to be held or operated by the hand. The poem also demonstrates how immersion in the world, either by manual or by scholarly labor, gives people a kind of metaphorical "handle" as well, a sense of competence, achievement, or understanding. When, in the poem, Snyder's experience in the everyday world of working and playing outdoors with his son coincides with wisdom gleaned from literature, he is deeply gratified. The fact that the piece of wisdom is precisely about the method and value of cultural transmission deepens and justifies his love for intensely lived daily experience and for poetic tradition, particularly Asian poetic traditions.

The poem reveals Snyder's way out of finding the past burdensome, as some twentieth century American poets find it. Instead he "hears" his forebears' words spoken as if into his ear and knows them to be of immediate and absolute pertinence. He finds his embeddedness in history not a trap, but rather a secure path, a repeating pattern in which "we go on." The sweet companionability of his relationship with Kai is contiguous with his filial relationships with teachers and with poets he has read and emulated. They pass down to him not only their poetry but also their poetics, bound together as in Lu Ji's *Wen Fu* (c. 302; *Essay on Literature*, 1948), which both describes and demonstrates the art of poetry.

The "tool" of poetry is forever both a model artifact and a device for making more poetry, just as the axe is itself a model and a tool. So the poem "Axe Handles" is a new poem (a brand-new, finely hewn axe), made out of Snyder's living experience yet also modeled on and constructed by using those venerable "axes," Ezra Pound, Lu Ji, and the translator Shih-hsiang Chen.

Sara Lundquist

THE AZURE

Author: Stéphane Mallarmé (1842-1898)
Type of poem: Lyric
First published: 1886, as "L'Azur"; in *Les Poésies de Stéphane Mallarmé*, 1887; English translation collected in *An Anthology of French Poetry from Nerval to Valéry in English Translation with French Originals*, 1958

The Poem

"The Azure," a dramatic lyric poem that consists of nine quatrains and contains thirty-six lines in the original French, utilizes a melodic rhyme scheme that is characteristic of the French Symbolist school of poetry.

The poem reflects on the blue sky, a typically Symbolist aspect of nature, which the poet interfuses with his creative personality; thus art, nature, and the poet merge, and what transpires is a state of poetic meditation of thought, mood, and creativity.

The poem merges the idea of the infinite azure with creativity to develop an artistic and poetic aesthetic. Creativity is blended with the poet's empty soul, the ephemeral fog (an image that appears in the works of Charles Baudelaire, a Symbolist, and T. S. Eliot), and ennui (vexation—a condition of the poetic spirit that also appears in the works of Baudelaire) to represent a poetic state.

The poem presents the nineteenth century in negative terms, in images such as those of "the sad chimneys," chimneys filled with smoke—which reminds one of Charles Dickens's prison of soot. For Stéphane Mallarmé, however, smoke and soot are not related to social or economic oppression; they may represent instead a stifling of poetic creativity. Instead of inspiring the artist, as nature did for the Romantics, the sun in "The Azure" is "dying yellowish on the horizon"—an image that reflects the poet's own mood and soul. There is a sense of stasis in the poem; the poet's stasis is expressed in the stanza that compares his brain to an empty pot of paint: He has no muse to inspire him to create. Sleep and death replace activity and life.

Ambivalence appears in the poem in the images of the azure (infinity) and ennui, and the poem's imagery also expresses the isolation of the poet in society. Essentially, however, the poet's concern is with beauty or perhaps with an unattainable ideal. The poem expresses the desire to achieve perfection and the struggle, apparently unsuccessful, to achieve it. Certainly, the conflict and struggle of the act of creation are apparent in the images of the azure and the ennui. The artist who strives to attain the artistic ideal of the azure must contend with his own fears and inadequacies—the ennui.

The azure triumphs, instilling fear in the poet; instead of the beauty of a peaceful, serene, blue sky, the azure evokes an agony—the poet is "obsessed." The poem ends with a repetition: "The Azure! The Azure! The Azure!" The poem's emphasis is on symbolic meanings, dimensions, and transformations: "The Azure" creates a mood and presents a creative challenge, but it provides no resolution of the conflict it has presented.

Forms and Devices

"The Azure" utilizes the techniques and devices of Symbolism, a nineteenth century poetic movement in France, whose exponents included Charles Baudelaire, Arthur Rimbaud, and Paul Verlaine as well as Mallarmé.

The Symbolist poetic doctrine advocated using language to suggest rather than to explain. The Symbolists used words to evoke moods and feelings, not to name things or describe them in precise terms. Their approach to poetic language was magical and transformational; Rimbaud endorsed what he called "verbal alchemy" (*l'alchimie du verbe*), and Baudelaire described his approach as "an evocative sorcery" (*une sorcellerie évocatoire*). Mallarmé himself believed that a poem was a mystery whose key must be sought by its readers.

The blue of the sky and the ennui that figure so prominently in the poem are symbols that are used frequently in the poetry of the Symbolists. The blue sky, which represents the eternal, the ideal, is particularly important to Mallarmé, who used it as a symbol in his poem "The Windows" (Les Fenêtres) as well as in "The Azure." A mood of ennui, which in "The Azure" represents the fears, indolence, and artistic impotence that the artist must overcome in order to create, is evoked by many poems in the Symbolist tradition.

Among the many stylistic devices that Mallarmé uses in "The Azure" are condensed syntax, difficult grammar, esoteric vocabulary, and enigmatic poetic concepts, which are well suited to Mallarmé's purpose. His intention is to depict the feelings that objects evoke, the effects that they have, rather than the objects themselves. Mallarmé's evocative language, with its use of innovative syntax and complex metaphors, sometimes makes it difficult to determine his meaning.

The opening stanza of "The Azure" is written in the third person, thus setting up an omniscient point of view and casting the poet as the narrator of the poem. The second stanza introduces the pronoun "I," and the first-person point of view is used throughout the rest of the poem.

Themes and Meanings

Mallarmé, a hermetic poet who held poetic gatherings at his home on Tuesday evenings at which poets espoused the cause of art for art's sake, writes a poetry of complex imagery and condensed syntax. His frustration at not finding the right words with which to express an idea is presented in his poetry in the symbol of a white swan whose wings are imprisoned in a frozen lake—the idea of an impasse.

The theme of the impasse that is contained in "The Azure" concerns the difficulty of expressing the artistic ideal in words, not merely the sterility or lack of creativity that hampers the act of creation. The poem's theme is the challenge of writing, the challenge of creativity, the challenge of finding the right words and the right medium in which to express the poetic sensibility. The challenge also lies in finding the right way to connect thoughts, to create a coherent artistic form.

The azure represents the infinite and the eternal, the ideal that the poet can never hope to attain; its very existence mocks the poet, smites him "in serene irony." The poet must struggle to come as close as possible to the artistic ideal; poems and poetic symbols may not be eternal, but they may endure beyond one's own lifetime.

The ennui in the poem represents lamentation or boredom, a recurrent theme in Symbolist works. The death that is referred to is an artistic death; the poet's soul is confined to a state of oblivion, emptiness, and desolation. The bells in which the poet hears the azure singing are poetic bells that awaken him from his torpor, but there is no release for him, and the concluding line of the poem focuses on his obsession with the azure. The blue sky seduces the poet, and he is caught in an inescapable trance.

The poem contains a metaphysical theme that relates to the possibility (or impossibility) of transcending reality and reaching a mysterious world of pure art that exists in the mind and can be expressed in language. Mallarmé focuses on the blue sky not in order to describe it, but in order to relate it to the artist's creative role and to the very essence of creativity itself, thus producing a unique poetic effect. The poem expresses Symbolist critic Arthur Symons's idea that every word is a jewel and every image is a symbol.

Stéphane Mallarmé's "The Azure" embodies the Symbolist idea that to name an object in a poem is to suppress most of the joy of reading poetry, which is derived from divining meaning little by little. The poet who suggests is the poet who creates true poetry.

Clarence McClanahan

BABII YAR

Author: Yevgeny Yevtushenko (1933-   )
Type of poem: Dramatic monologue
First published: 1961, as "Babiy Yar"; English translation collected in *The Poetry of Yevgeny Yevtushenko, 1953 to 1965*, 1965

The Poem
    "Babii Yar" is a poem in free verse consisting of ninety-two lines. The title, roughly translated as "Women's Cliff," refers to a ravine near Kiev where thousands of Jews were massacred during the Nazi occupation of the Ukraine in the Soviet Union. The name of the place in itself has no symbolic connotation in the poem, even though Babii Yar has become one of the most recognizable symbols of the Nazi crimes perpetrated against the Jews. The Holocaust is not the main focus of the poem. The very first line, "No monument stands over Babii Yar," reveals Yevgeny Yevtushenko's main concern. The original crime was bad enough, he seems to say, but it has been compounded by a lack of visible recognition and respect for its victims. The poet immediately identifies with the Jewish people. He goes back to ancient Egypt and the agony of crucifixion, then leaps across the centuries to Alfred Dreyfus, who was the subject of a celebrated case of prejudice and persecution in nineteenth century France. The poet then turns to a boy in Byelostok, a town in Byelorussia near the Polish border, which has a large Jewish population that has been decimated—first in the pogroms in Tsarist Russia, then during the Holocaust. Finally, the poet identifies with Anne Frank's feelings of fear and needs for love and kindness.
    In the final verses, the poet identifies with the victims buried in Babii Yar; this is his most powerful declaration of solidarity. As the trees stand as judges and "all things scream silently," he sees himself transformed into one massive, soundless scream, thus becoming the voice of each old man, each child who was murdered and buried there. He vows never to forget the tragic fate of these innocent victims, which brings him to his last point. He believes that there is no monument at Babii Yar because of the forgetfulness of the non-Jewish survivors and, more ominously, because of the anti-Semitism that existed before the advent of the Nazis and remains latent in the Russian people. This is illustrated by the shout of the pogrom bullies: "Beat the Yids, Save Russia!" By invoking the name of the "Internationale," the battle cry of the Russian revolution, the poet declares that he will fight against the anti-Semites until the last of them is defeated. He is not concerned that the anti-Semites hate him as a Jew even though there is no Jewish blood in his veins. On the contrary, it is because of their hatred that he sees himself as a true Russian, since the Russians are "international to the core."

Forms and Devices
    "Babii Yar" is a simple, unambiguous, declarative poem, told in the first person and replete with straightforward rhetorical statements such as "O my Russian people!" "I

am behind bars," "I am afraid," "I know the goodness of my land," "And I love." Such direct, terse statements fit a particular style of verse making that was popularized in Russia by Vladimir Mayakovsky and in America by William Carlos Williams. Such verses often consist of only one or two words lined in a cascading fashion. They are used primarily for emphasis, but they also add a dramatic flair, which Yevgeny Yevtushenko, a gifted actor and skillful reader of poetry, inherited from Mayakovsky, who was also a powerful declamator.

The main device used by Yevtushenko in this poem is metaphor. In a series of identification metaphors already mentioned, he not only drives his points home but also makes his references in an interesting way. When he says that he is an old Jew plodding through ancient Egypt, he immediately establishes a link between a history-laden people and himself as a present-day observer of history. When he sees himself crucified, he subtly reminds the reader or listener of the common origin of Christ and the Jewish people. A very brief mention of Alfred Dreyfus (only six words) is sufficient to evoke the terrible injustice done to him and all Jews. The metaphor of a young boy in Byelostok being kicked while lying in the blood that is spilling over the floors brings into stark relief the bestial cruelty of crimes among whose victims are the innocent young.

The poet reserves the most powerful metaphor for Anne Frank, to whom he devotes one-fourth of the poem. During his "conversations" with her, her innocence and tenderness evoke the noblest feelings in him. Even the love he professes for her is ethereal, just as she is "transparent as a branch in April." By emphasizing the innocence of a young girl on a threshold of life, the poet underscores the depth of the injustice perpetrated against her and all young people like her. The images employed here tend to highlight the interplay of innocence and injustice. In addition to the visual image of a branch in April, the poet uses auditory images such as the steps of the police Anne hears and the smashing down of the door; to soothe Anne's fears, he tells her they are the booming sounds of spring and the ice breaking, respectively. The love that his encounter with her brings forth is unreal, desperate, and painfully tender, used to raise hope in a hopeless situation and to confirm the existence of humaneness in an inhumane world. Yevtushenko is at his best in creating metaphors and images that flesh out and animate his references.

Themes and Meanings

It is clear that "Babii Yar" is a poem with a thesis. The thesis is that anti-Semitism exists in the Soviet Union, the official disclaimers notwithstanding. Yevtushenko protests against it by using perhaps the most suitable symbol—Babii Yar. The fact that the atrocities were committed by the hated enemy, the Nazis, amplifies the unforgivability of anti-Semitic attitudes, let alone actions. The fact that this anti-Semitism is camouflaged makes the original crime even more heinous.

Throughout his career, Yevtushenko has been known as a fiery dissident. He has used many of his poems to express his dissatisfaction with, and disapproval of, things that have happened in his country (next to "Babii Yar," "The Heirs of Stalin" is perhaps the best example). His protests have met with varying degrees of success, and his animosity toward the system has had its ebb and flow, but he has never been reluctant to speak his mind. In "Babii Yar," as a member of a post-Holocaust generation of Soviet citizens, Yevtushenko makes a strong statement on behalf of his peers.

"Babii Yar" is, however, more than a political statement about a problem in the Soviet Union. It is a declaration of solidarity with the oppressed, no matter who they may be, no matter where and when the oppression may be practiced. This solidarity with all humankind gives the poem a universal appeal, raising it above local politics and ideology. That is why the poet identifies with ancient figures as well as modern ones such as Dreyfus, Anne Frank, and the boy from Byelostok. It is evident, therefore, that Yevtushenko is warning not only the Soviet authorities and his compatriots but also the entire world against the pernicious effects of anti-Semitism and, in fact, of all injustice. While it is true that he has written other poems to this end, "Babii Yar" can be considered Yevtushenko's main protest against injustice, and a plea for a better world.

The ultimate merits of this poem lie in its aesthetics, however, and in the poet's ability to dress his basically nonliterary aim in a formidable artistic garb that transcends all mundane concerns. The best proof of the effect of the poem is its use by Dmitri Shostakovich in the opening movement of his Thirteenth Symphony.

Vasa D. Mihailovich

BADGER

Author: John Clare (1793-1864)
Type of poem: Lyric
First published: 1920, in *John Clare: Poems Chiefly from Manuscript*

The Poem

"Badger" is written in heroic couplets, its sixty-eight lines divided into five sonnet-length stanzas. Since the copy-text of "Badger" is untitled, some editors have chosen to call it "Badger" and others "[The Badger]"; it has been anthologized in both five- and three-stanza versions. The following description of the poem refers to the five-stanza "Badger."

The first stanza of the poem gives the reader a general sense of the badger's appearance and activities. An awkward and unattractive animal, the badger does not live in harmony with humans and domestic animals: "The shepherds dog will run him to his den/ Followed and hooted by the dogs and men." When the woodman goes hunting for foxes, he does not see the badger's many holes and often tumbles into them.

In the second stanza, the men and their dogs trap the badger and bring him to town to be baited. The noise of the hunt frightens an old fox and a poacher, who misfires, wounding a hare. Although the badger is reputed to be an aggressive animal, much of the violence in the poem seems to come from men, who take a sadistic delight in tormenting the beast.

The badger fights heroically in the third stanza, turning on the crowds and the packs of dogs, beating them all, even the "heavy mastiff savage in the fray" and the bulldog. Despite being relatively diminutive in size, the badger fights for hours against impossible odds, and John Clare describes the beast as grinning throughout the battle. In contrast, the only human mentioned in this stanza is a drunkard who "swears and reels."

The contrast between the valiant badger and the ignoble townspeople is further developed in the fourth stanza, where the badger is finally "kicked and torn and beaten out." His attackers are larger and more numerous; they use sticks and clubs and kick the badger when he is down. The badger plays dead and then, grinning, chases the crowd away, but at last he "leaves his hold and cackles groans and dies." The poem emphasizes the badger's courage and the cowardly bullying of the village mob—although the badger dies, one might say that he wins a moral victory.

Some versions of the poem end with the fourth stanza, which certainly provides the poem with a climax, but Clare wrote a final, concluding stanza, describing a tame badger. This section of the poem presents the badger in another light—rather than a wild animal struggling for survival, the domesticated badger fights dogs when so commanded by his master, but it also "licks the patting hand and trys to play." The last lines of the poem describe the tame badger's essential timidity, as he "runs away from noise in hollow trees[s]/ Burnt by the boys to get a swarm of bees." Given the chance, the badger seems capable of living with people in an affectionate and harmonious manner.

Forms and Devices

Clare's poems are often loose in structure, catalogs of observations about nature that begin and end arbitrarily. Thus some of Clare's editors have felt free to drop the last stanza of "Badger," which seems to take away from the dramatic power of the three middle stanzas. "Badger" is unpunctuated, and this lack of punctuation makes it a fast-paced poem to read, with scarcely a stop (except for the line breaks) for the reader to take a breath. The fact that most lines are end-stopped allows Clare to dispense with punctuation, but he is not able to indicate midline pauses. This lack of punctuation gives the poem a spontaneous quality, as if it were being recited by the poet as he made it up, without much regard to grammar or organization. Unfortunately, many editors have chosen to punctuate Clare's poems for him, and the editorially corrected poems seem less natural and more "literary" than the originals.

"Badger" contains relatively few dialect-words, and thus readers do not need to consult glossaries as much with this poem as they would with many of Clare's other works. Some of the local terms Clare uses in "Badger" are "scrowed" (marked), "clapt the dogs" (set the dogs on), "dimute" (diminished), and "lapt" (wrapped or folded). Although Charles Lamb discouraged Clare from writing in dialect, Clare used Northamptonshire words and phrases in much of his verse. A word such as "scrowed" gives his poetry a regional flavor and distinguishes his verse from the more formally correct writings of his Romantic contemporaries.

In "Badger," Clare piles up verbs in order to show the chaotic violence of the badger's baiting through the streets of the town. In stanzas 3 and 4 the verb "drives" is used six times, as the badger aggressively drives away the sheeplike mob of people and dogs. One gets a sense of the power of the diminutive badger and the mindless cowardice of his tormentors. The violence of the badger-biting section of the poem reaches a crescendo in stanza 4, with the piling on of the verbs "drives," "beats," "falls," "kicked," "torn," and "dies." The badger, grinning and cackling to the end, is nevertheless the victim of a terrific display of communal violence—the animal is not simply killed, it is beaten to the point of dismemberment. The last stanza, although not without its share of violent verbs, seems almost idyllic in comparison with stanzas 2 through 4, and it ends with the image of a timid, tame badger running away from a noise.

In general, the language of the poem is concrete and unsentimental—some would even say harsh. Clare avoids the literary diction of other poets—he once criticized John Keats for using classical imagery in verse dealing with nature—and renders his descriptions of rural life as realistically as possible. Rather than philosophizing or examining his emotional reactions, Clare describes how the badger is killed in a noncommittal way and allows the reader to come to his or her own conclusions.

Themes and Meanings

The main subject of "Badger" is the relationship of the wild animal to the humans who bait and tame it. What is the reader to make of the townspeople's cruelty to the badger? One response to the poem would be to condemn the badger-baiters as ignorant sadists, but Clare's avoidance of moral judgment suggests that he would not necessarily agree with this view. Although Clare would not have been aware of Charles Darwin's theory of natural selection, he understood the concept of survival of the fittest from observing animal behavior in the fields near Helpston. For example, in his natural history notes, Clare carefully describes how green beetles will attack a large moth, devour part of it, and drag the moth's corpse to their hole. There is the same sense of detachment in "Badger"; Clare never expresses pity for the badger nor outrage against the townspeople. In fact, the townspeople and the badger resemble each other in their ferocity—one might even say that in the poem the animal and his tormentors become indistinguishable.

Despite Clare's detachment, the poem does seem to imply that the badger is being cruelly mistreated—certainly the odds, one small badger versus a whole town of dogs and rock-throwing and cudgel-wielding people, do not seem even remotely fair. Thus some readers of the poem consider the baited badger as a victim of the townspeople's capricious exercise of power over a vulnerable creature and, by extension, a reflection of Clare's own feelings about tyranny. As an agricultural laborer, Clare was well aware of abuses of power—his satire *The Parish* is a bitter attack on the tyrants of a country parish—the greedy farmers, constables, overseers, judges, and bailiffs who could make a poor man's life miserable. Clare also considered the acts of enclosure, which destroyed cherished landmarks and drove peasants off the land, as examples of political oppression. Put in the context of Clare's sincere hatred of tyranny and slavery in any form, "Badger" could be seen as a protest against the unfair use of power against a weaker adversary. When the badger runs toward the woods and freedom, the townspeople turn him back with clubs; when the badger is beaten and helpless, he is kicked and torn by the savage mob. Moreover, the last stanza about the tame badger, which must fight at his master's bidding, is yet another example of human tyranny over less fortunate creatures. Examined in this light, "Badger" is more than the description of cruelty against badgers—it is a blanket indictment of the abuses visited upon the powerless by the powerful.

Much of the power of "Badger" comes, however, from its harsh realism: One can tell by reading the poem that this poet-naturalist has carefully studied nature and country life. Clare's main task in "Badger" is to present the reader with a vivid portrait of this misunderstood animal and its sometimes violent relationship with the inhabitants of a rural community, and he succeeds brilliantly.

William D. Brewer

THE BAIT

Author: John Donne (1572-1631)
Type of poem: Lyric
First published: 1633, in *Poems, by J. D.: With Elegies on the Authors Death*

The Poem

"The Bait," a seven-stanza, twenty-eight-line invitatory, reveals its indebtedness to Christopher Marlowe in its first line, which imitates the opening of Marlowe's "Passionate shepherd to his love." Moreover, the general construction of John Donne's poem—four lines of two pairs of rhymed couplets, or quatrains, with the exception of an added stanza—is not, at first glance, unlike that of the earlier poem, in which a would-be lover entices his beloved by calling up scenes of exquisite bliss. Before and after Donne, this type of poem found a wide audience. Before Donne, there was a unity between purpose and technique, and the voice of the importunate lover combined flattery with pleading. Donne, however, broke with this pattern; one has only to listen to "The Bait" (a title whose meaning deliberately contains ominous overtones) to hear a lover's voice by turns wily, suggestive, flattering, almost threatening, and ultimately rueful. Further, the abrupt changes in mood and tone coalesce to impart a characteristically rough sense of urgency found in much of Donne's work.

The poem begins conventionally enough, with pretty images and compliments. The sands, brooks, river, and sun, the lovely eyes of the beloved, are familiar territory. The mood shift in the third quatrain catches the reader unprepared; the beautiful beloved is now (apparently unclothed) swimming in "live" water, sought eagerly, even passionately, by the hitherto quiescent fish. Should this intimacy intimidate the lover, she is reminded that her own brilliance outshines both sun and moon and that thus neither gives its light to the proceedings. Significantly, the lover is at home in the darkness. In the fourth and fifth stanzas, the lover ostensibly establishes the superiority of his own type of "fishing" to the methods of his colleagues or competition, whose techniques vary from brute force, "the bedded fish in banks out-wrest," to the false and fatal promises held out by the "sleavesilk flies." This introduction of the specters of violence and treachery is only partially dissipated by the return to amorousness in the concluding verse, in which the speaker acknowledges that, ironically, it is he who has surrendered to the attractions of his purported prey.

The reader is challenged to discern who is fish, who is fishing, and who catches whom, all of which is bound to cause some confusion. Furthermore, the manifold sudden changes of emotional gear, all the more startling for being so economically presented, form an integral part of Donne's technique and account for, at least in part, the fascination with which he is regarded by readers more than 350 years after his death.

Forms and Devices

The Marlowe poem consisted of six quatrains; by adding a seventh, Donne brings the line total to twenty-eight, or twice fourteen (the length of a sonnet). Donne, in the interests of parodying Marlowe, chooses not to utilize sonnet form, but he has demonstrated to his contemporaries that the choice is his, and in choosing he has established a distinction between speaker and poet. The speaker is the captive of his desires; the poet weighs every word and leaves a bread-crumb trail through the poem so that the discerning reader might appreciate the subtleties of technique.

The element that most stands out in Donne's poetry is his intelligence—not even his passion or his wit can equal it. His dazzling manipulations of syntax, his juxtapositions of unlikely images, are as calculated as they are effective. Tracing Donne's intent in his poetry is a bit like watching a hunting cheetah spin and seemingly reverse direction. It takes some concentration to pursue "Begging themselves [the fish] they may betray" to achieve Donne's meaning, that the fish seek to be caught. The reader's deepening involvement with the text is further challenged by the pivotal third quatrain, which couples the languor of the bath with the eroticism of underwater pursuit and capture. Soon Donne moves from flattery to a hint of indirect but threatening force. Images such as "cut legs," "coarse bold hands," "slimy nest," and "curious traitors" would be jangling and discordant in a conventional love poem, but they work well here to establish Donne's emotional detachment from and, to some degree, cynicism about the process in which he is engaged. Even when the body is most needy and the passions most persuasive, the speaker wants his audience to admire his intellectual sophistication and his innovative mastery of form.

A reader in Donne's own times would have marked the many "conceits" that operate in the poem. These images and manifestations of design would conspire to create a bond between poet and reader. This becomes clear as one recalls the lack of complexity in Marlowe's poem; by loading his poem with ironic ambiguities, Donne assumes the willingness of his reader to be challenged and stimulated. The reader who correctly decodes Donne is intrigued and flattered, ready to draw inferences from every departure from the norm.

Donne certainly did not invent the love lyric; in this poem, for example, Donne assumes that the reader is familiar with Marlowe's earlier work. Donne's genius lies in his ability to take what was current and transcend it, changing its form while he ostensibly conforms to it. One can trace this pattern in his satires, his sermons, and his invocations to lovers.

In fact, the speaker never uses the word "love." If the hearer, or for that matter, the reader, thinks that the poem is about love, the speaker—and the poet—are not to be held accountable, even when the last stanza ruefully, even reluctantly, returns to the conventional image of the enthralled suitor. Very few poets have been as able as Donne to calibrate the differences between love and lust; here he and his speaker are as one. Both know perfectly well that the driving force in "The Bait" has to do with a hoped for physical union in which the absence of spiritual commitment is clear and not without meaning.

Themes and Meaning

Very few of Donne's poems were published in his lifetime, although hand-written copies enjoyed a wide readership. What appealed to his contemporaries was his open treatment of seduction, expressed typically through the voice of a would-be seducer. One can conjecture at length, and many critics have, as to how much his poetry mirrors Donne's direct experience and how much of it is an exaggeration of both his prowess and his stamina. Donne studied the ways of the court, the intricacies of the law, the controversies of religious disputation, and he uses and refers to them all in his poetry. Yet it would be a mistake to try to infer specifics about his self from the poetry; readers can see the connections that Donne allows them to see.

"The Bait," like the well-known "The Flea," is directed toward one end, the capitulation of a woman listener. She is the one who is to be overcome "with silken lines, and silver hooks." She is bombarded with language, and if she should have modest, if perhaps unlikely, second thoughts, she is assured that the lover who sees her surrender has already testified to the strength of his feelings, such as they are, for her. She is played, like a fish; dangling before her are all the protestations of the speaker, in which the reader may choose to place limited faith.

The speaker, in the last stanza, claims that it is he who has been unable to resist the pull of her allure; she is fisher, he fish. This may express Donne's considered opinion on the sport—that one should not engage in it if one is not willing to be caught. On the other hand, the reader may well dismiss this as another of the speaker's gambits; the speaker is certainly clever enough to manipulate his lover's feelings by appealing to her pity. The end result in either case, however, is a constant: She is to yield, he to triumph.

That this is the work of a man who later became known for his sermons as well as for his poetry, and that his poetry itself later underwent a radical reconfiguration of theme, seems unlikely if not preposterous as one reads "The Bait." Both the frank sensuality and the tour de force technique catch and hold the attention of the reader. To admirers of Donne's religious poetry and prose, "The Bait" may seem like a prodigal wasting of talent—but Donne, as his later life proved, always knew about prodigals.

Judith N. Mitchell

BALAKIREV'S DREAM

Author: Tomas Tranströmer (1931-   )
Type of poem: Narrative/lyric
First published: 1958, as "Balakirevs dröm (1905)," in *Hemligheter på vågen*; English translation collected in *Windows and Stones: Selected Poems*, 1972, and in *Tomas Tranströmer: Selected Poems: 1954-1986*, 1987

The Poem

Written almost entirely in the third person, "Balakirev's Dream (1905)" is really a lyric poem masquerading as a narrative. The poem consists of nineteen unrhymed couplets, all but three of which are self-contained syntactical units. As the title indicates, the poem purports to recount the dream of Mily Balakirev (1837-1910), a famous Russian conductor and composer. Both the date in the title and the reference to the warship *Sevastopol* carefully situate the poem in time: during or just after the *Sevastopol* mutiny, which broke out spontaneously on November 11, 1905, and which, despite the support of other groups of insurgents, was soon crushed. Like the much more famous mutiny aboard the battleship *Potemkin*, the *Sevastopol* mutiny was but a single episode in the ill-fated Russian Revolution of 1905-1907, which was ruthlessly suppressed by czarist forces.

The poem begins at a piano recital. Outside the concert hall, the streets are darkened by a strike; inside the hall, a pianist has begun to conjure up a dream world in which real stones (the brutal outside world?) become as light as dewdrops. The poet likens the black grand piano to a large spider trembling in its net of music. Listening to this music, the aging composer dozes off and dreams about a journey he is taking in the czar's carriage (*droshky*), which is rumbling over cobblestones in a "crow-cawing" world that is both dark and threatening.

As frequently occurs in dream situations, the dreamer imagines that he is in two places at the same time: inside the carriage and running along beside it. Moreover, his sense of time is distorted: His clock shows that the trip has taken not hours, but years. He finds himself in a field in which a plow is lying idle; then the plow becomes a fallen bird that is transformed, in turn, into a darkened, icebound ship with people on its deck. As the carriage approaches the icebound vessel, the grating and clattering sounds it makes subside, and the wheels spin over the ice with a sound that is as soft as silk, recalling perhaps the activity of the grand piano-spider, weaving its delicate net.

Next, Balakirev finds himself the prisoner of the mutineers on board the *Sevastopol*. Handing him a curious "instrument," which is "like a tuba or a phonograph/ or part of some unknown engine," the hostile sailors tell him that only by playing this instrument can he save his life. Paralyzed with fear, Balakirev realizes that this instrument is the piston that runs the ship. He tries to defend himself by turning to the nearest sailor and begging him to cross himself. The symbolic gesture he urges upon the sailor becomes a reality when the man turns his sad eyes on Balakirev and—"as if nailed in the air"—is crucified. Just as the dreamer is about to witness the execution of the mutineers, the drumrolls that often accompany executions become a round of applause. The pianist has finished weaving his net of music, and Balakirev awakens with the impression that wings of applause are flapping in the hall as the pianist takes a bow. Though the fallen bird from the dream may once again have taken wing, the continued agitation in the street outside suggests that Balakirev's anxiety dream is prophetic.

Forms and Devices

As was mentioned above, the poem consists of nineteen unrhymed, strongly rhythmical couplets. All but three of these couplets are self-contained syntactical units. Tomas Tranströmer uses this structural device, which enables sudden displacements in time and space, to create a realistically presented dream pattern. As each indeterminate dream image recedes, it is replaced by another. The succession of images appears to mobilize the dreamer's repressed fears, finally bringing him to a confrontation with the hostile mutineers aboard the *Sevastopol* who threaten his life at the climax of the dream—that is, in the three couplets that are syntactically connected, from "He turned and faced the nearest sailor" to "as if nailed in the air." This climactic scene—and, indeed, the cinematic presentation of the whole dream sequence—is reminiscent of Sergei Eisenstein's famous film about the revolutionary events of 1905, *Potemkin* (1925). Tranströmer has in fact admitted that memories of this film are associated with the composition of "Balakirev's Dream (1905)."

This poem is partly based on one of Tranströmer's own dreams, which he originally intended to attribute to Anatoly Lyadov, one of Balakirev's colleagues. This leads one to wonder why Tranströmer has chosen to enter the world of political tyranny through a dream that he attributes to Balakirev. As is frequently the case (especially in his earlier poems), he apparently wished both to avoid personal involvement and to gain objectivity by transferring this confrontation between the artist and political reality to a Russian composer who was alive at the time of the Revolution of 1905.

A professional psychologist, Tranströmer has both a deep interest in dreams and a detailed technical knowledge of their function in people's psychic lives. He believes that in dreams—or on the threshold of the dream state—the experiencing self penetrates more deeply into itself and into life's secrets than it can in the waking state. Many of his poems describe dreams, which he sees as mediating between the inner world and the outer world of social life. The vivid dream images in "Balakirev's Dream (1905)" become a series of graphic metaphors that enable the reader to share the emotional reactions of the dreamer, even if the reader is ultimately unable to interpret the dream.

The opening line of the poem transforms the grand piano into a large black spider, trembling in its net of music. The primary aim of this poetic equation is to show that just as the spider makes a net strong enough to support drops of dew, so the music creates an alternative world in which stones (the cares and worries of the outer world) are as light as dewdrops. Yet it is difficult to overlook the fact that the spider's insubstantial net is not only its home, but also a trap for its victims.

Itself a metaphor, the Swedish word for grand piano (*flygel*) means "wing." Thus, besides establishing the setting of the poem, it also subtly introduces the idea of flight and birds that figures so prominently in the dream: for example, the "crow-cawing dark," the "fallen bird," and the "wings of applause" (the "fallen bird" resuscitated?) that flap in the hall when the pianist finishes playing. Near the end of his dream journey, Balakirev sees an abandoned plow (representing the nurturing activities of peace) and then an icebound warship (representing the powerlessness of the insurgents to resist tyranny). These images of disuse, impotence, and death reinforce the dreamer's inability to remedy a desperate situation.

Themes and Meanings

"Balakirev's Dream (1905)" is a poem about the relationship between art and reality. It tests the value of "escapist" art and asks if poetry must inevitably be politically engaged. Written in 1957—one year after the ill-fated revolt of the Hungarian freedom fighters—this appears to be a poem in which Tranströmer asks his readers to consider what is to be gained and what is to be lost if the artist takes a firm stand on political issues and uses his talent primarily as a means of goading others to action. By casting his poem in the form of Balakirev's fictive dream, he not only depersonalizes and objectifies his own strong feelings about the disastrous consequences of the Hungarian revolt of 1956 but also indicates that he believes that this impersonal, quasi-historical approach will be more effective than a first-person lyrical outcry might have been.

The artist he has chosen to play the central role in this poem, Mily Balakirev, is certainly not known to have harbored any deep sympathies for the insurgents—around 1905 he was, in fact, chiefly devoted to preparing a new edition of the works of Mikhail Glinka (1804-1857). Between 1883 and 1895, Balakirev had served as director of the court chapel, which provided music for the imperial family. His divided loyalties seem to be reflected in the fact that in his dream he is both riding in the czar's carriage and running alongside it. Why does he try to defend himself by turning to the nearest sailor and begging him to cross himself? According to Nikolay Rimsky-Korsakov, Balakirev, who had become fanatically religious in the early 1870's, often pressed his friends to cross themselves because he believed that this symbolic gesture might help bring them to religion. His superstitious reaction to the hostile sailor is one of fear, not sympathy, and by urging the rebel to make the sign of the cross—the only thing in the poem that really corresponds to what is known about Balakirev's personal habits—he appears to cause his death. (The leaders of the *Sevastopol* mutiny were shot on March 6, 1906.) In other words, the artist's empty gesture of spiritual aid (or moral support) has only made things worse. Perhaps Tranströmer wants to suggest that highly politicized poetry does more harm than good.

The crisis in Balakirev's dream (that is, the drumrolls betokening execution) coincides with the round of applause that greets the performing artist and wakes the dreamer. Balakirev awakens to applause that is likened to a bird flapping about the hall. The bird (a phoenix?) completes one series of images that bind the poem together. This soaring bird may suggest the idea that art can—at least temporarily—triumph over life. Outside, however, in the streets darkened by the strike, the agitated motion of the droshkies shows that the political situation cannot be ignored. (In the original Swedish, the generally rising meter of the first eighteen couplets changes abruptly and dramatically to a heavily falling meter in the last couplet. This metrical change seems to underscore the fact that Balakirev's dream has alerted him to political reality and to suggest that perhaps the shortest way to political awareness lies within.)

One gains considerable perspective on Tranströmer's position on the question of the proper relation of art to reality by reading "Balakirev's Dream (1905)" in close conjunction with "Allegro," a short poem that appeared in *Den halvfärdiga himlen* (1962, the half-finished heaven), his next verse collection. In "Allegro," the poet sits down at the piano after a bad day and plays a spirited piece by Franz Josef Haydn. The music he makes becomes a house of glass that is assailed by a shower of stones—stones that are by no means as light as dewdrops. Yet though these stones roll right through the glass walls, they cannot shatter them. Tranströmer seems to believe that, far from being a paradise for escapists, the world that artistic experience can provide is a place where freedom exists and persists, despite the brutal assaults of external existence.

Barry Jacobs

THE BALCONY

Author: Charles Baudelaire (1821-1867)
Type of poem: Lyric
First published: 1857, as "Le Balcon," in *Les Fleurs du mal*; English translation collected in *The Flowers of Evil*, 1993

The Poem

"The Balcony" first appeared as number 34 in the "Spleen and Ideal" section of the first, banned edition of *Les Fleurs du mal* (*Flowers of Evil*, first translated in 1931) and as poem number 36 in the second, definitive edition (1861). The poem consists of six five-line stanzas in the "enveloped strophe" form—that is, the first line of each stanza reappears as its last line. The first, third, and fifth line of each stanza rhyme, as do the second and fourth.

In "The Balcony" a first-person voice, closely associated with the poet himself, speaks to a beloved woman using the familiar form of address, reserved in nineteenth century French for the most intimate relationships. The first stanza apostrophizes the beloved as "Mother of memories, Mistress of mistresses" and invites her to remember an earlier period of shared love. These memories are located in the home, or hearth; their time is evening, and the tone of the stanza, as of the poem in general, is elegiac and directs the reader's attention to a lost past of beauty, caresses, sweetness, and charm.

The second stanza is written in the imperfect tense, indicating habitual action in the past. The scene is set in early evening, either by the glow of a coal fire or of sunset on the balcony of the title. In an atmosphere of warmth and enclosure, the breast and heart of the beloved are offered to the poet; they say "imperishable" things.

The third stanza opens in the present tense; it evokes the eternal beauty of evening skies, the depth of space, and the power of the heart. The beloved is addressed as a queen. The poet remembers physical closeness so intense that he used to breathe the scent of her blood. This stanza is remarkable in its simultaneous evocation of light, warmth, and scent.

The fourth stanza, in the imperfect tense, moves from sunset to nightfall, when darkness deepens to form a wall about the balcony. The poet divines, rather than sees, the eyes of the beloved. Within this wall of darkness, intimacy is absolute. The poet "drinks" the breath of the beloved, which is both sweet and poisonous, and holds her slumbering feet in "brotherly" hands. The fifth stanza returns to the present tense and declares the poet's power to evoke past happiness; he relives the past paradise in the present embrace of the beloved. It is her "languorous beauties" which defined the past and provide the key to recalling it.

In stanzas 1 through 5, each first line is repeated word-for-word in the fifth line. In the sixth stanza, the first and fifth lines, although similar in their wording, are not identical. The first line refers to "These vows, these sweet perfumes, these kisses" as objects, the fifth line apostrophizes them. This strophe turns wistfully to the future and asks if past delights can be born again as setting suns are reborn.

Forms and Devices

Charles Baudelaire chose the enveloped strophe form for several poems in *Les Fleurs du mal.* In "Reversibility" (number 44), a beloved woman is addressed as an angel and implored for her prayers. The repeated formulas shape the poem as an incantation, a way of controlling the powers of beauty, joy, and health attributed to the angelic woman. In "Moesta et errabunda" (Latin for "sorrowful and wandering woman"), number 62, the poet invites the beloved to escape with him from the monstrous city to the purity of the ocean, a return to the innocent "green paradise" of childhood.

In these poems, and particularly in "The Balcony," the repetitive stanza structure establishes a powerful echo, musically evocative and strongly nostalgic. Each stanza looks backward and forward simultaneously. The returning note of the last line changes subtly by progression through the rest of the strophe. In "The Balcony," where the central theme of the poem is a wish to re-create a happy past, coupled with the image of rebirth in the setting sun, this formal feature is especially important.

Within the polished, formal universe of the poem, the dominant images are the glowing hearth and the setting sun. The hearth, necessarily, is enclosed within walls, but the balcony also is defined as an enclosed space, since first the "pink veils" of sunset light, then the wall of descending night cut it off from the world, the profound space which lies outside the circle of warmth. The body of the beloved is an intimate part of this circle. "Mother of memories," she is breast, heart, blood, eyes, breath, feet, knees, the "dear body" to which the poet must have recourse to relive these happy moments.

The setting sun offers a final redemptive image in "The Balcony." As the ultimate source of light and warmth, descending each evening into the sea, it is a universal symbol of age and death. However, each day it returns "rejuvenated" to repeat its cycle of life. The past is a "gulf we cannot sound," deep as space beyond the walls of the balcony, deep as the seas, yet the daily return of the sun in its rising and setting allows the rebirth of hope.

Themes and Meanings

Baudelaire's poetry returns often to the moment of sunset, the poignant melting of light into darkness, and the evocation of erotic pleasures in the half light. However, this sunset moment is also a little death; it brings a heightened consciousness of mortality and the passage of time. Love is the most delicious at that moment when it most resembles death.

Many of Baudelaire's love lyrics, including the notorious "A Carcass" (number 29), identify the loved woman with suffering in some way. Sometimes she is threatened with injury, sometimes accused of injuring the poet or reminded of impending death. His idealized goddess of Beauty is "a stone-fashioned dream" whose essence is paralysis, a mineral fascination in which all movement ceases (number 17, "Beauty"). "The Balcony" offers no overt violence to the beloved woman. Indeed it seems exceptionally gentle in its evocation of sweet memories.

The beloved woman is presented immediately as a powerful figure, the mother of memory in a poem devoted to memory, the "mistress of mistresses" in a poem devoted to love. These incantations are introduced and echoed in the repetition of the first stanza. Her physical presence is felt through all the senses; sight that persists through darkness, the voice that speaks "imperishable things," touch of her breast and hand, scent of her blood, taste of her breath. She is, indeed, the human hearth, the glowing sun, source of warmth and light.

Yet the reader must remember that all these charms and all this happiness are expressed in the past tense. The beloved must recall them as memories and must lend her body to the poet for him to relive them. Although she is still physically present and available to his caress, the paradise of the balcony is gone. In every way that the beloved is physically real, warm, and living, thus capable of inspiring and rewarding love, she is also mortal, aging, and herself moving into darkness. In the recollection of their moments of greatest intimacy, the poet evokes the scent of her blood in the darkness, the taste of her breath, both delight and poison. Her breath is poisonous because it is not only proof of physical life but also a measure of mortality.

When the fifth stanza proclaims knowledge of an "art" as a means of reliving happiness, the poet is not speaking of his verse. Rather, this "art" consists of burying himself in the knees of the beloved, returning to her physical presence, which paradoxically must eventually fail him. The exceptional changes in the repeating fifth line of the stanza subtly acknowledge the futility of the poet's attempt to return to past experience. The profound gulf of past time is too deep to sound, and the beloved, in whose physical beauty the past happiness is personified, will not transcend time to rise "rejuvenated" like the sun.

The poem itself, however, remains as incantation and invocation. Without the physical presence of the beloved—indeed, long after the death of both poet and loved woman—"The Balcony" continues to present the polished form, the glowing warmth of memory. The true art of the poet, his true evocation, lies in the verse he created to preserve the magic of happy memory.

Anne W. Sienkewicz

BALLAD OF AN OLD CYPRESS

Author: Du Fu (712-770)
Type of poem: Ballad
First published: Written after 766; collected as "Gǔ bó xíng," in *Jiu-jia ji-zhu Du shi,* 1181; English translation collected in *A Little Primer of Tu Fu,* 1967

The Poem

"Ballad of an Old Cypress" is a short poem written by a talented Confucian scholar in his old age, who had tried repeatedly but failed, in the end, to realize his dream of serving a noble ruler in order to build a just and harmonious society. The poem addresses scholars who have "grand aims" as well as men who "live hidden away." It explores the issue of how to cope with the ironic situation that great talents often lack the opportunity to meet rulers eager for their services. The advice it offers to its readers is that they should accept the irony without a "sigh."

The poem can be divided into three eight-line sections. In the first section, the poet first depicts an aging cypress planted in Kuizhou in front of the shrine of Zhuge Liang (181-234 C.E.), a scholar, statesman, military strategist, and tactician who was fortunate to meet Liu Bei, the ruler of Shu, who anxiously sought Zhuge Liang's advice. The depiction is characterized by realistic details about the tree's boughs and bark fused with romantic hyperbole about its height of two thousand feet. The poet then reflects on the significance of the tree in history, saying that it is a treasured reminder of the meeting between a talented scholar and an ideal ruler. Finally, Du Fu assesses its effect on the meteorological condition of the Three Gorges and the Mountains of Snow.

In the second section, the poet first carries his audience, through his memory, to the Brocade Pavilion in Chengdu, the site of the adjacent shrines dedicated, respectively, to Zhuge Liang and his lord (in most English translations of the poem, the two are said to share one shrine). There were cypresses looming "high there,/ ancient upon the meadows"; however, the poet felt a sense of loss when he caught sight of "paintings dark and hidden away/ through the empty doors and windows." Du Fu had reasons for his sense of loss: Zhuge Liang died in a military campaign before he had time to carry out his political program, and the story of Zhuge Liang was considered to be a very rare instance in history of a gifted scholar serving a high-minded ruler. The poet then refers to the tree in Kuizhou, saying that, unlike the trees in Chengdu that cluster together, it stands "firm," "high and alone in the black of sky" in defiance of "many violent storms." These qualities of the tree, according to the poet, are attributed to the creative power of nature itself.

The last section opens with the poet's reflection on the troubled political condition of his time and similar situations in the past. He compares the Tang Dynasty to "some great mansion" about to collapse and compares talented scholars with the giant cypress in Kuizhou, which can serve as the "beams and rafters" needed to save the mansion. Unfortunately, there is no way to move the tree to the mansion; even ten thousand oxen would not be able to accomplish the mission. The implication is that a ruler with Liu Bei's temperament is what is really needed, but there is simply no such ruler in sight. Du Fu ends his poem by urging his fellow scholars not to lament over their own fate, for "it has always been true that the greatest timber/ is hardest to put to use."

Forms and Devices

"Ballad of an Old Cypress" is written in *qigu* (*chiku*), an old poetic form in which each line consists of seven words. This form was an effective vehicle for Du Fu's impassioned poem on the issue concerning great talents. As an ancient, popular ballad form, it allowed him to convey his own views and emotions directly to his audience— aspiring Confucian scholars or disappointed talents in seclusion.

Among the most important technical aspects of the poem that have survived the translation into English is Du Fu's skillfully orchestrated presentation of the cypress as the central image in the poem. He presents the tree from various perspectives and distances. A close-up of its "frosted bark" is accompanied by a distant shot of it standing on the northern bank of the Yangtze River with the Snow Mountains looming in the distance. A vertical view of the tree of "forty armspans" is followed by an angle shot of it reaching the sky "two thousand feet" above the ground. A mystic vision of the tree "vapor-linking" to the Wu Gorge is placed beside a heroic image of it standing "high and alone" braving "many violent storms." Finally, a current view of the tree against the background of a tottering "great mansion" is complemented by a historical survey of it in light of the tumultuous years of the Three Kingdoms.

The poet's artistic manipulation of the central image in the poem endows the tree with metaphorical, symbolic, and allegorical meanings. The cypress stands for Zhuge Liang as well as other gifted scholars, including the poet himself; it embodies their "upright straightness" and their aloofness; it manifests their potential to shape the destiny of their country; and it reflects their aspirations and frustrations. The cypress also stands as a symbol of the ideal that Confucian scholars pursue, that of bringing their talents and skills into full play in the service of a noble ruler. However, as the meeting of Zhuge Liang and Liu Bei is considered to be a rare event in history, the lone cypress also points to the tremendous odds against a "man of grand aims."

Stylistic diversity is another important aspect that remains somewhat visible in the English translation of the poem. Objective depictions of the cypress in Kuizhou are juxtaposed with extravagant statements about its mystic role on the grand landscape. As shown at the very beginning of the poem, use of prose coexists with indulgence in poetic elevation, as indicated in lines depicting the "vapors" of the tree touching "the full length of Wu Gorge" and its "chill" reaching "the white of the Mountains of Snow." Finally, an optimistic voice calling for persistent participation in politics is intermingled with a somewhat pessimistic voice endorsing resignation. Hence, one finds incorporated into the poem such diverse elements as authentic details and romantic visions, prosaic narrative and euphoric exaltation, the language of Confucian political activism and the rhetoric of Daoist passivism.

Themes and Meanings

"Ballad of an Old Cypress" is, among other things, Du Fu's reflection on a paradox with which he and his fellow Confucian scholars have to cope, namely, that their great talents are "hard to put to use." It ends with the poet urging his audience not to "sigh." Since Du Fu's audience consists of aspiring scholars and disappointed talents in seclusion, his appeal has different implications for them. It encourages the former to strive for active participation in politics but, at the same time, warns them of the difficulty ahead. It consoles the latter in their Taoist seclusion but reminds them of the possibility of a return to active service. This thematic multiplicity is informed and reinforced by many of the devices in the poem. Among these devices are the historical allusion to Zhuge Liang and Liu Bei and the poet's symbolic depiction of the cypresses.

A genius in political and military affairs, Zhuge Liang chose to live under a thatched roof in a remote place called Longzhong; however, he closely watched the political development in the Three Kingdoms that divided China, and he cherished a secret desire to help achieve the reunification of his country. Liu Bei, ruler of Kingdom of Shu, visited him three times in order to seek his advice on effective strategies against the other two kingdoms. It was Liu Bei's visits that "sent" the "cypress" or the "timber" to the "great mansion." Zhuge Liang was named prime minister and devoted himself to the cause of ending the wars among the Three Kingdoms.

Du Fu's reference to Zhuge Liang provides his audience with a shared context. Regardless of their own situations, the two groups of scholars will see the meeting of Zhuge Liang and Liu Bei as a Confucian scholar's dream come true. To the men of "grand aims" among the audience, the historical event is encouraging: There was a high-minded ruler in the past, and what happened in the past may very well repeat itself in the future. To the disappointed scholars in seclusion, the event is comforting. It at least makes them wonder whether it is possible that some day a royal visitor will come to knock at the door of a thatched hut again. However, the story of Zhuge Liang is also a story of dreams unfulfilled. The prime minister was completely exhausted by the very mission that he worked arduously to accomplish. Like the cypress with "its bitter core" unable to "keep out/ intrusions of termites," he fell seriously ill during a prolonged military campaign. He died in Wuzhangyuan at the age of fifty-three before he was able to complete his magnificent political and social programs.

Chenliang Sheng

BALLAD OF BIRMINGHAM

Author: Dudley Randall (1914-   )
Type of poem: Ballad
First published: 1965, as a broadside; collected in *The Black Poets,* 1971

The Poem

September 15, 1963, was not a typical Sunday in Birmingham, Alabama; it was a day of devastation. Sunday school had just ended at the Seventeenth Street Baptist Church when nineteen sticks of dynamite, stashed under a stairwell, exploded. Twenty-two of the black congregation's adults and children, although injured, survived the bombing. Four little girls, Addie Mae Collins, Denise McNair, Carole Robertson, and Cynthia Wesley, did not. The bombing was a horrific reminder of the dangers of the Civil Rights movement of the 1960's as well as of the even greater danger and murderous power of unchecked racism. Americans were shocked as they watched televised accounts of the explosion. It was unfathomable that four little girls would be murdered in church.

Dudley Randall's poem about the event, "Ballad of Birmingham," was set to music and recorded prior to its 1965 publication as a broadside. The poem of thirty-two lines is divided into eight four-line stanzas; in each stanza, the second and fourth lines rhyme. In the first stanza, Randall begins a dialogue between a daughter and her mother and presents the child's unusual request to forsake play in order to participate in one of the civil rights demonstrations that were prevalent in the South during the 1950's and 1960's. In the second stanza, the mother denies her daughter's request because she fears for her daughter's safety amid the clubs, police dogs, firehoses, and guns; she also worries that her child could be jailed. Hearing her mother's fears, the daughter appears unafraid and determined to participate in the freedom demonstration. The child responds in stanza 3 that she will not be alone, because "Other children will go with me,/ and march the streets of Birmingham/ to make our country free." In the fourth stanza, the mother, worrying about gunfire, continues to tell her young daughter no. The mother then gives her permission to go to church instead and "sing in the children's choir," and the dialogue between child and mother ends.

Randall writes the remainder of "Ballad of Birmingham" in the third person. In the fifth stanza, the girl's preparations for church are described: combing and brushing her hair, bathing, and putting on white gloves and white shoes. In stanza 6 the mother, no longer fearful for her child's safety, smiles because her daughter is in church, "the sacred place"; then, in stanza 7, she hears the explosion. Her peace of mind is abruptly shattered, and with eyes "wet and wild" she runs toward the church "calling for her child." The mother arrives at the church, the site of the bombing, in the final stanza. Amid the "bits of glass and brick," she finds a shoe. "Ballad of Birmingham" ends with the distraught mother's extremely brief monologue: "O, here's the shoe my baby wore,/ but, baby, where are you?" The little girl does not respond. Never again can the daughter and mother engage in conversation. The child who eagerly wanted to raise her small voice in protest of social injustice has been silenced.

Forms and Devices

Typical of a ballad, Randall's poem presents a brief narrative that includes a dramatic event—the bombing of the church and the loss of lives. Imagery is an important device in "Ballad of Birmingham." Imagery is the use of a word or a group of words to elicit various sensory experiences. From the first to the last stanzas, readers of "Ballad of Birmingham" encounter multiple images that are primarily visual and associated with the dialogue, the girl's preparation for church, and the explosion. Randall invites readers to visualize and hear a mother-daughter conversation in stanzas 1 through 4. Their dialogue evokes visual images of the many civil rights demonstrators marching through the streets of Birmingham and elsewhere. In stanza 2 are the dogs, clubs, firehoses, guns, and jails used to control the primarily black protesters; in stanza 3 are children marching the Birmingham streets; in stanza 4 are "guns [that] will fire." The mother sends the child to church "to sing in the children's choir," and auditory images of young voices singing are called forth.

The next group of images is centered on the little girl's preparations for church in stanza 5; readers see her combing and brushing "her nightdark hair," bathing "rose petal sweet" (which also evokes a fragrant image), and putting "white gloves on her small brown hands" and "white shoes on her feet." The last group of images focuses on the explosion in stanza 7. Readers visualize and hear the explosion, see the mother's wet, wild eyes, see her frantically racing through the streets of Birmingham, and hear her calling for her daughter in vain. Then, in stanza 8, readers visualize the mother clawing through "bits of glass and brick" and ultimately lifting her daughter's shoe from the bombing debris.

A second major device is irony. The central irony in the poem involves the fact that the mother, in trying to keep her daughter safe, wishes her to go to church rather than to a demonstration, and the girl is killed in church. Subsumed within this irony are lesser ironies: The daughter's preparations for church become her preparations for death; knowing that her child is "safe" in church causes the mother to smile before the explosion occurs; a church is expected to be a sanctuary, not a place of death.

Themes and Meanings

"Ballad of Birmingham" is a tribute to Addie Mae Collins, Denise McNair, Carole Robertson, and Cynthia Wesley, the bombing's four fatalities, as well as their mothers. Randall's presentation of a nameless daughter and mother is significant. Although he focuses on one daughter, he honors all four deceased girls. His omission of names also allows him to represent and remember the anonymous multitude of victims of racism and the civil rights struggle and to remember the families left behind to mourn their dead. Thus "Ballad of Birmingham" is their tribute as well.

Randall's nameless daughter and mother also represent the bonds that exist between daughters and mothers everywhere. An important message of the poem is that a mother's love cannot protect her offspring from racism; nothing can. The most powerful aspect of this message is that as recently as 1963 in the United States there was no place safe from the destructive power of racism. The church is sacred ground, yet it proves to be no sanctuary.

"Ballad of Birmingham" concisely interprets a tragic event in American history and recalls the intense racial tensions and strong emotions of the civil rights era. Although there were many other important civil rights events, including the freedom rides, sit-ins, school desegregation attempts, bombings, fires, and racially motivated murders, the September 15, 1963, bombing of the Seventeenth Street Baptist Church remains among the most poignant moments in black Americans' collective quest for equality, liberty, and identity. Dudley Randall's "Ballad of Birmingham" is one of the most dramatic and memorable of the many works of literature that document the African American struggle for equality.

In 1977, fourteen years after the bombing, Robert Chambliss, a member of the Ku Klux Klan, was finally convicted of first-degree murder and sentenced to life in prison. Federal authorities, continuing to believe that Chambliss had accomplices, reopened the case in 1980, 1988, and 1997—the last also being the year that filmmaker Spike Lee's documentary film on the bombing, *4 Little Girls*, debuted.

Linda M. Carter

THE BALLAD OF READING GAOL

Author: Oscar Wilde (1854-1900)
Type of poem: Ballad
First published: 1898

The Poem

The Ballad of Reading Gaol is not a typical ballad in that commentary ranges beyond the narrative. While Oscar Wilde is focusing on the story of the execution of Royal House Guards trooper Charles Thomas Wooldridge for the brutal murder of his wife, he is also meditating on injustice, betrayal, and the need for prison reform. The poem is divided, rather unevenly, into six "cantos," as Wilde labeled them; each division is further subdivided into groupings usually separated by asterisks.

The first canto (sixteen stanzas: six and ten) concentrates on the condemned man, whom the persona (the voice speaking in the poem) never meets but observes during exercise period, eyeing the sky wistfully. Wilde quickly shifts to presenting the impact on the persona, who reacts to the news that the convict is to be executed. He then meditates on the wider implications of guilt: "each man" is guilty of a crime—killing the thing he loves—but is not held accountable. The persona then resumes his account of the plight of the condemned man, execution (a fate withheld from all the guilty, bonded as they are to the condemned man). The description is remarkable in that while Wilde never actually witnessed an execution, he used his creative imagination to help his readers share the agony of the experience.

In the second canto, Wilde reiterates the convicted man's pathos as he enjoys the last delights of the earth: the sun and the morning air. The speaker and his fellow convicts regard the condemned man with awe, and they regret the debt the prisoner must pay. At this point, Wilde unites himself and the condemned man in a strange bond: Both are outcasts caught in a trap of sin and punishment.

Canto 3 is the longest (at thirty-seven stanzas), describing the period of the pre-execution ritual. Cool, unfeeling administrators play their roles: the governor, the doctor, and the chaplain, who seem callously indifferent to the man's plight. The condemned man wishes that the day of execution would come, perhaps to end the unbearable waiting. Guards may wonder about his motives in welcoming death but cannot express any sympathy, or their positions would be intolerable. Wilde empathizes with the warders here, perhaps recalling his own kind treatment by guard Thomas Martin at Reading Gaol. The major emphasis in this section is on the shared feeling of the convicts, who serve almost as a Greek chorus and as fellow victims as the day of execution approaches. The men are shocked to see the open grave readied for the condemned man and spend the night tortured by terror and mad phantoms. Their identification with the condemned man is complete. They dread the dawn, and its arrival is described in a brilliant stanza as the shadows of the window bars move across the persona's cell. Hope for a reprieve dies as the morning progresses. The men do not actually witness the execution, but their imaginations draw a more horrible view than the actual event. When the appointed hour strikes on the prison clock, the execution is signaled by a "wail/ Of impotent despair." The speaker and his fellow convicts share the agony.

Wilde continues to describe the day of execution in canto 4, with the prisoners confined to their cells until noon, when they are released for exercise. Now the impact of the execution is evident as each man avoids the other's eye. They suffer in their shared guilt, stalked by horror and fear. The watchful guards seem insensitive in this section as the speaker remarks on the discrepancy between their fresh uniforms and their quicklime-splattered boots. The executed man has been buried in quicklime to speed the decaying process; unfortunately, the sterile ground over his grave will never yield any growth. The persona wishes for a sign of redemption, roses blooming in the yard or a cross to mark the location. While the executed man may now be at peace, he was allowed no funeral rites; although Christ came to save sinners, the dead man is not allowed any indication of salvation. His only mourners are his fellow outcasts, the convicts. At this point, the poem might have concluded, if Wilde had not chosen to continue with two more cantos, deploring injustice and cruelty. The last four lines of the canto serve as Wilde's epitaph.

Canto 5 is the controversial canto that is often excised by editors to "improve" the poem. Wilde is at his most emotional as he excoriates injustice and the inadequacies of the prison system. Prisons are built with "bricks of shame" (canto 5, line 3), kept from the sight of society. He adds his own indignation at the imprisonment of children (which shocked Wilde in Reading; he offered to pay the children's fine). Food, water, and sanitary facilities are vile and scanty, degrading to the prisoners; the worst torture is isolation. These combine to break men's spirits. Wilde contributes a brief sermon on repentance: "How else but through a broken heart/ May Lord Christ enter in?" (canto 5, line 14). These sorrowing souls have suffered enough punishment to merit salvation.

The shortest of the cantos is the sixth, with only three stanzas. It seems impersonal and objective after the passion of the previous stanzas. It offers a précis of the narrative, reiterating the message of killing the thing beloved, and restating Wilde's theme of universal guilt.

Forms and Devices

The poem represents a break with Wilde's previous poetic style, lush verse heavily indebted to Romantic poets such as Samuel Taylor Coleridge and John Keats, and to Victorian poets Algernon Swinburne and Alfred, Lord Tennyson. Wilde, instead, chooses a more direct, less flamboyant style and often concentrates on detail: "We sewed the sacks, we broke the stones/ We turned the dusty drill" (canto 3, line 9).

Some of the weaker passages depend upon cold abstractions (Death, Dread, Doom), but the strain in poetic technique is eased with vivid personifications: "Sleep walks wild-eyed and cries to Time" (canto 5, line 8); "crooked shapes of Terror crouched" (canto 3, line 19). The grim narrative is brightened by images such as "the little tent of blue" and "clouds with sails of silver." These personifications are often supported by similes: "Like a casque of scorching steel" (canto 1, line 5).

It is not surprising, in a poem about sin and redemption, that Wilde alludes to biblical sources, as in the description of sacrificial victims, "The bitter wine upon a sponge"; in "the holy hands that took/ The thief to Paradise" (canto 5, line 15), suggesting Christ as redeemer; and in the description of the first murder (the story of Cain and Abel). Another powerful allusion is to the legend found in Wagner's *Tannhauser* (canto 4, line 4) when a pilgrim's staff blossoms to signify the redemption of a sinner. These allusions brighten the grim narrative and enhance Wilde's message.

Although the poem is labeled a "ballad," Wilde did not adhere to the traditional, four-line ballad stanza (with the second and fourth lines rhyming) but adopted the six-line stanza used occasionally in Samuel Taylor Coleridge's *The Rime of the Ancient Mariner* (1798) and in Thomas Hood's "The Dream of Eugene Aram" to provide commentary. Wilde also borrowed iambic tetrameter (four repetitions of the iambic pattern of stress on the second syllable) rather than the five repetitions popular in English poetry. Frequently, this pattern has been used in humorous verse (by Lewis Carroll, for example), but Wilde managed it creditably. The metrical form and internal rhyme (a word in midline rhyming with a word at the end), as in "To dance to flutes to dance to lutes," are effective in those passages describing the puppetlike jerking of the phantoms terrifying the convicts, but the general effect can be monotonous.

Indeed, Wilde borrowed more than the stanza form from Coleridge. Like Wilde's phantoms, Coleridge's "death fires" dance "About, about in reel and rout." Early reviewers recognized Wilde's debt to Coleridge and to Hood. They rated Wilde as more realistic in the trenchant narrative of the execution and burial of the convicted murderer, but more mannered and self-conscious in the total presentation.

Themes and Meanings

Writing the poem within months of his release from prison proved cathartic to Wilde and restored his confidence in his creative powers. Wilde had been imprisoned for two years at hard labor after his conviction in May, 1895, for homosexual offenses. The legal proceedings and imprisonment were humiliating; he remarked that he was inspired to write the poem while "in the dock." The poem was originally published with the author's name given simply as "C.3.3," his prison number at Reading, providing the poem with a grim souvenir of his prison life.

He found the opportunity to attack the penal system in the case of trooper Charles Wooldridge, who had slit his wife's throat with a razor and was hanged at Reading. The incident appealed to Wilde on several levels: his pity for the condemned man, his identification with the trooper, and his conviction that humanity shares in guilt. While Wooldridge's crime was vicious, his execution was inhumane. In recognizing that his own punishment exceeded his crime, Wilde accepted a bond with the condemned man, trapped in the same snare (canto 2, line 13).

He extends this identification to the reader; following Charles Baudelaire's taunt "*hypocrite lecteur* [reader]," Wilde embroils the reader in his accusation of guilt: "For each man kills the thing he loves/ Yet each man does not die" (canto 1, line 9). Convicts were punished by the brutal prison system, by insensitive guards, and often by fellow convicts—all unpunished crimes. Furthermore, Wilde boldly convicts humanity of sins of commission and omission, particularly through indifference or betrayal. If his poetic technique changed in this poem, Wilde's themes did not: Betrayal as a theme can be detected in most of his works, including the comedies. Appropriately, his last celebrated work emphasized this same theme.

The betrayed protagonist thus becomes a sacrificial hero, a penitent martyr (illustrated in the poem by the reference to the redeemed Parsifal's staff blooming after his death). Had he been content to restrict himself to this theme, Wilde's poem might have been his masterpiece. Wilde was passionate about the need to expose the brutality of the prison system, however, and wrote to his friend Robert Ross (who had suggested the poem's title) that while he agreed that the poem should end at the lines "outcasts always mourn" (end of canto 5), he insisted that the rest of the poem be included as "propaganda." The reference was to Wilde's exposure of the harsh prison conditions he experienced. He suffered from the poor food, isolation, and inadequate sanitary provision and medical treatment, and used the poem to reveal these deprivations to the public in the hope of initiating reform. He risked ruining the poem, realizing that it suffered from a division in intention, but while he regretted the loss of art, he chose altruism. Ironically, although he consistently used betrayal as a theme, he betrayed his own artistic instincts for propaganda and won a small victory when his poem brought prison conditions to the attention of legislators.

The propagandizing sections, especially canto 5, received the harshest criticism. Most critics agree that exclusion of these sections strengthens the poem; William Butler Yeats printed an abbreviated version in his *Oxford Book of Modern Verse* (1936). In whatever form it is encountered, most readers would agree with Wilde's biographer Richard Ellman: "[O]nce read, it is never forgotten."

Elizabeth Nelson

THE BALLAD OF RUDOLPH REED

Author: Gwendolyn Brooks (1917-2000)
Type of poem: Ballad
First published: 1950; collected in *The Bean Eaters*, 1960

The Poem

"The Ballad of Rudolph Reed" employs a traditional verse form to tell a heroic and finally tragic story of human struggle against the contemporary forces of discrimination and hate. Gwendolyn Brooks's poem is powerful and unrelenting in its cry for social justice, and it holds only a small hope for redemption for its characters. The story is told in sixteen ballad stanzas of regular structure, broken roughly into three sections. The first five stanzas describe the players in the drama and their dreams. In the first stanza, readers are introduced to the central character, Rudolph Reed, and his wife, two daughters, and son. The only thing Rudolph wants, readers learn in the second stanza, is a house, a house, stanzas 3 and 4 continue, that is not in a slum where "a man in bed" may "hear the roaches" but rather one that is "full of room." Rudolph warns readers in stanza 5 that he will "fight" for such a house when he finds it.

In stanzas 6 through 10, Rudolph finds his dream dwelling and moves in "With his dark little wife,/ And his dark little children three." The house is on a "street of bitter white" residents, but the Reeds are "too joyous to notice" the reactions ("a yawning eye/ That squeezed into a slit") of their bigoted neighbors. In the final six stanzas, the tragedy waiting to befall the Reeds is acted out. Rocks are thrown through their windows, presumably by their white neighbors trying to force them to move, but Rudolph does not act until his daughter Mabel's blood is "staining her gaze so pure":

> Then up did rise our Rudolph Reed
> And pressed the hand of his wife,
> And went to the door with a thirty-four
> And a beastly butcher knife.

The conclusion is tragically predictable: Rudolph kills four white men before he himself is killed. The gathered neighbors kick "his corpse" and call him "Nigger." The final stanza leaves readers without poetic resolution or catharsis:

> Small Mabel whimpered all night long,
> For calling herself the cause.
> Her oak-eyed mother did no thing
> But change the bloody gauze.

Rudolph's revenge has only resulted in his own death; his surviving family exists in a tableau of guilt and blood. There is no redemption here for any of the characters—and yet the "oak-eyed" mother gives readers at least a small hope that the violence is finished and the Reeds will be able to stay in the house they have now earned with their own blood.

Forms and Devices

There are a number of important poetic devices in this poem. Most noteworthy is the ballad form itself, which Brooks has taken from an ancient and popular tradition and which she uses in a fairly traditional way. The rhyme scheme in every stanza (*abcb*) is that of the ballad form, and the meter is also fairly regular; while line length varies, there are either three or four accented syllables to each line, usually in the typical ballad stanza of four beats to the first and third lines and three beats to the second and fourth lines. Variations on this pattern (as in the first line of stanza 1) are made for emphasis. In stanza 7, the irregularly accented third line captures the natural rhythms of the real estate agent's voice, but the regularity of the surrounding three lines contains that variation to its one line:

> The agent's steep and steady stare
> Corroded to a grin
> *Why, you black old, tough old hell of a man,*
> *Move your family in!*

Echoes of the older ballad form are also found in the archaic syntax or word arrangement ("her gaze so pure," "Then up did rise"). Brooks occasionally uses alliteration ("steep and steady stare," "beastly butcher knife") to help hold the various poetic elements together.

If the ballad form is fairly traditional, however, Brooks's poetic diction is contemporary. While her language is quite simple and accessible—which is true to the narrative tradition of the ballad form, which often exhibits an almost childlike or fairy-tale quality—Brooks allows herself a number of figurative phrases ("yawning eye," "silvery ring," "fat rain," "oak-eyed mother"). The most interesting metaphorical figure in the poem is the use of "oak" as a descriptive word. Rudolph, readers learn in the very first line, "was oaken./ His wife was oaken too./ And his two good girls and his good little man./ Oakened as they grew." Several other times in the poem Brooks reminds readers that Rudolph is "oaken"; he is, in fact, as line 23 tells readers, "oakener/ Than others in the nation." The word conveys not only a sense of color but also a feeling of strength and toughness, and Rudolph lives out that figurative description. Whatever hope readers have at the end of the poem comes from the fact that, in the penultimate line, Rudolph's wife is now the "oak-eyed mother," which implies that she has the strength to live through this tragedy. If Rudolph was "oakener" than others, perhaps his family has inherited that strength as part of his legacy to them.

Themes and Meanings

The meaning of "The Ballad of Rudolph Reed" is as accessible as its language. Brooks's poem dramatizes the blatant discrimination, especially in housing, that characterized American society until the Civil Rights movement of the late 1950's and the 1960's. In this sense, Brooks's poem was ahead of its time, but a number of African American writers dramatized the problem of discrimination in this country shortly after World War II; for example, Lorraine Hansberry's powerful and popular play *A Rai-*

sin in the Sun (1959) dealt with the same issue of housing discrimination in Chicago. Brooks had experienced that discrimination personally when she was unable to find adequate housing in Chicago for her family as city officials continued to confine black residents to restricted areas at the same time that the population was rapidly increasing (particularly because of northward migration from rural Southern regions of the country).

As in most ballads, Brooks's poem traces the heroic struggles of a set of characters as they act out their tragedy. They have a home of their own, the dream of many American families; their own blindness and the implicit greed of their real estate agent combine to make them "block-busters"—the first family of color to move into an all-white neighborhood—and the tragedy spirals out of control after this move. The Reeds even ignore the first signs of trouble; it is only when Mabel's blood is spilled that Rudolph acts. In the heroic language of the inherited ballad form, Brooks tells readers "Then up did rise our Rudolph Reed." His instinctual protection of his family turns into revenge upon the white neighbors who are trying to drive the Reeds from their home. Even in his death, the hatred continues as the neighbors kick and insult his corpse.

Brooks leaves the issue hanging in the last stanza: The family survives, but will they have the strength to carry on Rudolph's fight? Will they continue to be "oaken"? Will they move or will they stay? In certain ways, "The Ballad of Rudolph Reed" has the feel of classical Greek drama, with characters playing out their fated and tragic roles. The main difference is that in Brooks's poem there is no *deus ex machina* at the end to resolve the conflicts, no sense of resolution to provide catharsis for the audience. Readers, Brooks insists, must provide that for themselves. The civil rights struggles of the 1950's and 1960's were composed of hundreds, perhaps thousands, of tragic battles and sacrifices such as this one. Brooks's Pulitzer Prize in poetry in 1950, like her many awards since then, was in part a tribute to her poetic efforts to point out and eradicate some of the worst inequities in her society.

David Peck

BALLAD OF THE LANDLORD

Author: Langston Hughes (1902-1967)
Type of poem: Ballad
First published: 1940; collected in *Montage of a Dream Deferred*, 1951

The Poem

In "Ballad of the Landlord," Langston Hughes appropriates the traditional ballad form but uses it in a contemporary urban setting to relate a current and crushing social problem. This conjunction of traditional form and contemporary content lends further power to the poem's cry for social justice. The poem contains nine ballad stanzas (although the strict stanzaic structure is abandoned in the last three) that, in traditional use of the form, would narrate a tale of a dramatic or romantic adventure. The story here, however, tells of protest and jail. In the opening five stanzas, the first-person narrator/tenant is talking to and complaining about a landlord who has not done the repairs that would justify paying the rent on his house. In the remaining four stanzas, readers are told of the terrible consequences of the narrator's protest.

In the first stanza, the persona of the poem complains to the landlord (in direct address) about the leak in the roof that he first mentioned to him "Way last week." The complaint in the second stanza is about the stairs that have not been fixed; the narrator is surprised that the landlord (who has apparently come by the narrator's house to collect the rent) has not injured himself: "It's a wonder you don't fall down." In the third stanza, the tenant refuses to pay the ten dollars the landlord is demanding until the landlord fixes "this house up new." In the fourth stanza, the tenant repeats the multiple threats of the landlord—to get an eviction notice, to cut off the heat, and to throw the tenant's furniture into the street—and, in the fifth stanza, the tenant replies by threatening to "land [his] fist" on the landlord.

The remaining four stanzas undergo a radical shift in point of view and tone and move further and further away from the tenant's perspective and pleas. The sixth stanza is italicized in order to convey the hysterical and exaggerated words of the landlord: "*Police! Police!/ Come and get this man!/ He's trying to ruin the government/ And overturn the land!*" The last three stanzas, in machine-gun fashion, contain society's responses to those unfair charges: The police arrest the tenant (stanza 7) and throw him in jail (stanza 8); the newspaper headlines proclaim "MAN THREATENS LANDLORD/ TENANT HELD NO BAIL/ JUDGE GIVES NEGRO 90 DAYS IN COUNTY JAIL" (stanza 9).

The poem, therefore, breaks into two uneven parts. In the first five stanzas, the tenant gives his story to a landlord who ignores the cries for adequate housing and fair treatment. In the last four stanzas, the point of view shifts to the landlord, then to the society as a whole, and finally to the newspaper headlines about the incident in the final stanza. It is significant that the word "Negro" is only used in the last stanza when the point of view shifts and the society that now has control wants to identify those it labels as criminals. The social justice the tenant demands in the first two-thirds of the poem becomes the jail this society imposes on its victims in the final third.

Forms and Devices

The most important device in "Ballad of the Landlord" is the ballad form itself. Meant to recount a story, the popular ballad form often includes dialogue (as here) and employs a simple four-line stanza rhyming *abcb*. Readers must wonder why Hughes would use such a traditional form for such an untraditional topic and employ it for only two-thirds of the poem. Actually, the ballad form has been used for centuries, as it is here, as a vehicle of social protest, and it is significant that a number of other twentieth century African American poets have employed the form in a similar way: Gwendolyn Brooks, for example, in "The Ballad of Rudolph Reed" (1960), Robert Hayden in "A Ballad of Remembrance" (1966), and Dudley Randall in "Ballad of Birmingham" (1966). African American poets, in short, have often utilized the ballad form as a convenient way to convey their multiple messages of social protest.

Again, however, Hughes only uses the form for two-thirds of the poem and then violates it with two three-line stanzas of a harsh, fragmentary third-person description of what happens to the protesting tenant followed by the concluding three lines of newspaper headlines. (Notice that a continuing rhyme helps to tie these three short, final stanzas together: bell/cell, bail/jail.) The simple ballad form of the first six stanzas, which conveys the struggles of the tenant against his landlord, gives way to the staccato response of the tenant's society: eviction, arrest, and, finally, jail. Hughes has used the ballad form to build a poetic structure of contrasts that works well to his purposes.

Beyond the ballad form, the poem uses several other devices that define Hughes as among the most prominent African American poets of the middle decades of the twentieth century. The poetic diction of the tenant's narration, like the meter, is conversational and colloquial ("Don't you 'member . . . ?" and "You gonna cut off my heat?") and works well in contrast to the more objective vocabulary of the concluding stanzas (like the staccato rhythm), especially the supposedly "neutral" language of the newspaper headlines ("MAN THREATENS LANDLORD"). The language of Hughes's poetry, in "Ballad of the Landlord" and elsewhere, helps make it perfectly accessible in both form and content and is meant to convey an obvious, if ironic, message. Hughes, like many of his fellow African American poets in the 1920's and 1930's, wanted nothing to do with the difficulty and obfuscation that characterized so much of the high modernist verse of those decades.

Themes and Meanings

The themes of "Ballad of the Landlord" come out of a vital American literary tradition: The poem taps the energy and meaning of much of the social protest literature of the 1930's. Poems, stories, and essays about tenant evictions, rent protests, and similar activities were common fare in the social realist American literature of the 1930's. In that tradition, Hughes represents the unfair advantage of society in this struggle:

The landlord has only to call the tenant a communist (*"He's trying to ruin the government/ And overturn the land!"*) for the police to throw the tenant in jail. Another example of the influence of radical 1930's literary roots is the abrupt form of the last three stanzas and, particularly, the capitalized words of the last stanza, which may remind readers of the "newsreels" in John Dos Passos's trilogy of novels, *U.S.A.* (1930-1936), in which he creates montages of newspaper headlines to construct a realistic background for his fictional narratives. Nowhere was this 1930's social realism stronger than in the African American literary tradition, which goes back to the Harlem Renaissance (1920-1929), a literary, musical, and artistic movement that included Hughes as one of its major practitioners: His first collection of poetry, *The Weary Blues* (1926), is one of the landmarks of the movement.

What makes "Ballad of the Landlord" unique is Hughes's own special treatment of this incident. In the early stanzas, he establishes the justice of the tenant's claims against his landlord but closes realistically with American society's typical response to protests similar to the tenant's, especially in the 1930's: eviction and jail. There is no justice in this society, Hughes complains, particularly for African Americans. The landlord has all the weight of the police and the judicial system on his side; the tenant has only truth and moral rightness. Like many traditional ballads about folk heroes fighting for justice (Robin Hood, for example), Hughes's "Ballad of the Landlord" honors the struggle of the poor and disenfranchised. However, the title of the poem ultimately and ironically tells readers who the hero of the poem in this society really is and who will finally win this struggle.

David Peck

THE BANQUET

Author: George Herbert (1593-1633)
Type of poem: Meditation
First published: 1633, in *The Temple*

The Poem

"The Banquet" first appeared in a posthumous collection of George Herbert's work published as *The Temple*. Divided into three parts (the church porch, the church, and the church militant), *The Temple* was designed by Herbert to reflect the structure of the Old Testament tabernacle (the outer porch, the Holy Room, and the Holy of Holies). This tripartite division also yields numerical significance as the symbol of the triune God.

As a religious meditation, "The Banquet" appears in the section labeled "The Church" as a method of preparation for Holy Communion, in which earthly and heavenly elements are combined into a whole that is greater than the sum of its parts. The poem can be roughly divided into two parts. Stanzas 1 through 5 focus on the present, in this case the immediate joys of celebrating the sacrament. In keeping with this pattern, the initial verse contains an allusion to Solomon's *Song of Songs* and welcomes the spiritual cheer provided by the Holy Supper in the way one might welcome a lover. In stanza 2, Herbert goes on to compare the divine sweetness of the wine to a sugared liquor; specifically, he envisions a star melted in the liquid, a combination of heaven and the fruit of earth. This metaphor involves sight as well as taste, perhaps suggesting that in the sacrament an earthly sense (taste) is transformed into a heavenly vision (sight).

Stanzas 3 and 4 shift the emphasis to a sense of smell as the sweetness of the bread is compared with flowers, gums, powders, and perfumes. This smell goes beyond physical sweetness, however, and can "subdue the smell of sin." Verse 4 then assures the reader that by assuming flesh, the Godhead has joined the physical and the spiritual and continues to impart them to believers through a heavenly meal.

Stanza 5 serves as both the climax of the first section and the transition to the second. Herbert argues that just as wood gives off a sweeter scent when the tree is cut than when it is standing whole, so God's love is made sweeter through the sacrifice of His broken body.

The second section (stanzas 6 through 9) provides both a flashback and a projection of the future. Here Herbert explains why the sacrifice of a broken body is necessary and then rejoices in the unity of God and man that is brought about by such a sacrifice. Stanza 6 mirrors verse 5 by dealing with another type of "sweet breaking." Herbert must break with earthly ways and reacquaint himself with his heavenly heritage. This movement from the corporeal to the ethereal can only be accomplished by breaking his willful human spirit, which, by its nature, opposes God. Thus the symbolic "breaking" of worldly desires for Herbert coincides with God's willingness to be "broken" for humankind's sins.

Following the biblical precedent, "whoever humbles himself will be exalted" (Matthew 23:12), stanzas 7 and 8 comprise the movement of sinful man back to his God. The persona gradually moves from the ground to the sky, now viewing God in shared glory rather than in a state of humiliation. The final stanza appropriately returns the reader to earth, where Herbert must continue to serve his Lord. Herbert has learned during his journey, however, and concludes the poem with a paradox resolved. Having experienced Christ's sacrifice as well as His glory, he is unified with the Godhead and can continue "to strive in this" (life) and simultaneously "to love the strife."

Forms and Devices

Perhaps more than other poets of his time, Herbert is known for building the meanings of his poems into the external structure of the work. Although "The Banquet" does not reveal its meaning directly through shape, Herbert has experimented with both rhyme and meter to emphasize religious symbolism. The rhyme pattern is *aabccb*, which suggests the idea of the Trinity (three persons, one God). Moreover, the syllabic structure of the verses is 7-3-7-7-3-7. Once again, the three is Trinitarian, while the seven, another holy number, has often been seen as an archetypal image for the joining of God (three) and man (four for the four corners of the earth). Together they form ten, the number of completeness, while the nine stanzas that compose the poem represent a perfect square of three.

In addition to numeric devices, "The Banquet" relies heavily on metaphor, drawing direct comparisons of two dissimilar things. The metaphysical technique of "conceit" climaxes in verse 5 as Herbert unites several spiritual ideas with the physical concept of sweetness. Earthly taste (sugar) melts into a heavenly vision (star). The metaphors of stanzas 2 and 3 continue this theme of unification as the sweetness of the Host (bread) is compared to the fragrance of "flowers, and gums, and powders." Both star and flower suggest the image of Christ (the star of Bethlehem and the Rose of Sharon) and imply the spiritual and physical oneness created by God putting on human flesh. Thus the God/man (Christ) is the real power and sweetness in communion, in which He gives Himself to redeem sinful man. Like "pomanders and wood," whose scents are better when they are bruised, God's love takes on a sweeter aroma, since he was "bruised for our transgressions" (Isaiah 53).

Thus Christ's sacrifice on the cross is translated into the symbolic breaking of the bread and the blessing of the wine. The body and blood received through the Holy Supper is efficacious in restoring fallen man momentarily to his former glory at the right hand of God. Herbert realizes that the ecstasy provided by the feast is only temporary, yet it is necessary for man's spiritual health, his resurrection to new life on earth. Herbert ends the poem with yet another technique associated with the Metaphysicals: a pun. Utilizing the words "strive" and "strife," he reminds his readers that the Christian life requires struggle, but as Christ overcame the strife of both death and the grave, the believer can "love the strife." For through it, as through Holy Communion, he attains unity with the Savior and both experiences a partial resurrection now and awaits an eternal resurrection after death and the Last Judgment.

Themes and Meanings

Although the first section of "The Banquet" is rich in poetic devices, the second section speaks more personally of the theme of the poem. Section 1 provides a succession of metaphors that build toward a parable of life that emphasizes the unity of flesh and spirit found both in the sacrament and in the God/man, Christ Jesus. This building pattern is also significant because it relates to the title of the collection, *The Temple*. This image suggests not only a physical building but also human beings themselves, who as God's temples constantly desire their bodies to be built up in the Spirit. Thus the abstract combinations of sweetness and wine, fragrance and bread, and the associations of wood and star suddenly become a more personalized parable of the unity of God and man.

This unity is attainable only through bruised wood, an image that recalls not only the cross but also the battered body of Christ, dying for the sins of the world. To emphasize the importance of this event, Herbert flashes back to a time before he was redeemed. Here he pictures himself "drowned" in the delights of the earth. Oddly enough, he is saved from drowning (the punishment for wickedness during the Flood) by another liquid, the blood of Christ. God in His Son comes down to the author and is "spilt with me." Christ joins Himself to human suffering and then adds His victory and resurrection so that man can be restored.

A movement upward, culminating in a heavenly vision, results when man puts on Christ. Literally, Herbert is doing this through the reception of Holy Communion. "Wine becomes a wing," and Herbert beholds a revelation or epiphany as he observes Christ in the fullness of His heavenly glory (the Transfiguration). This vision enables Herbert to make sense even of the insensible. He understands that since he has been lifted up through the sacrament, he must return to earth, and he does so with a greater vision. With "wonder" and awe, he takes up his ditty and returns to his "lines" [poetry] and life. In the last stanza, by joining the senses of touch (hands) and hearing (hearken) to the senses of taste and smell, Herbert seems to suggest that only through receiving the Lord's Supper can one be wholly complete.

Such a completeness overcomes all earthly desires, even those of success and renown. Since it is known that Herbert had aspirations in the court of England, one line from the poem stands out in relationship to his own life. Lines 40 to 42 read as follows: "But still being low and short,/ far from court/ wine becomes wing at last." Whether his hopes were crushed by political disasters in his family or whether he shunned his aspirations for grandeur in favor of the priesthood, Herbert seems to have recognized that the calling of God's kingdom (His court) exceeds the appeals of earthly monarchs and their power. The journey of the soul to its Lord supersedes the finery offered by the world, and "the Banquet" of Holy Communion overshadows and supersedes any physical feast or celebration that might invite individuals to glory in their own abilities and accomplishments rather than in those of their Savior.

Michael J. Meyer

BARBARA FRIETCHIE

Author: John Greenleaf Whittier (1807-1892)
Type of poem: Ballad
First published: 1863, in *In War Time*

The Poem

John Greenleaf Whittier's patriotic ballad "Barbara Frietchie" is one of the most popular poems ever published in American literature. Whittier first heard about the incident described in the poem in Frederick, Maryland, more than a year after the fact. Historical investigations have made problematic any claim the poem might have to authenticity; Whittier freely embellished the story of a courageous ninety-year-old woman who dared to wave the Union flag from her second-story window in the face of Confederate general Stonewall Jackson as his troops marched through the small Maryland town. The poem, which passionately validated the importance of the Union, was widely embraced as inspiration for a North weary of the long, bloody war.

Thus, along with Julia Ward Howe's "The Battle Hymn of the Republic" and Walt Whitman's "O Captain, My Captain," "Barbara Frietchie" affirms that poetry, occasioned by a specific event, can arouse strong public sentiment. After the war, a generation of schoolchildren memorized Whittier's dramatic poem, its relative brevity (thirty couplets), its irresistible staccato rhythm, and its heavy masculine rhyme scheme making it ideal for recitation.

The poem can be divided into three sections: prologue/exposition (stanzas 1-8), complication/resolution (stanzas 9-25), and peroration (stanzas 26-30). The poem begins quietly. Whittier creates with spare but vivid details the countryside surrounding Frederick. It is the morning of September 10, 1862. Amid the ravages of war, the Maryland countryside itself is bountiful with its fall harvest, the trees "fruited deep" and as fair as "the garden of the Lord." Whittier abruptly introduces into this edenic setting the rebel soldiers heading into Frederick. Fresh from taking the federal garrison at Harpers Ferry, West Virginia, as part of general Robert E. Lee's master strategy to take the war into the North, Stonewall Jackson's division is on its way to rejoin Lee near Sharpsburg, Maryland. As the rebel "horde" marches through Frederick, they haul down whatever Union flags they see.

In the long second section Whittier recounts with tense economy the two central dramatic acts: Frietchie's defiance and Jackson's response. As the rebel troops approach, the elderly Frietchie sets her flag outside her attic window. When Jackson sees the flag, he orders his troops to bring it down in a volley of fire. When Frietchie instinctively snatches the falling flag and waves it "with royal will," she enjoins them to shoot her but to spare the flag. Jackson, his "nobler nature" stirred, commands his troops not to disturb either the woman or the flag. For the rest of the day, the torn flag waves defiantly above the marching troops.

In a somber peroration Whittier provides the confrontation's moral perspective. In keeping with the ballad genre he employs, Whittier does not indulge excessive emotionalism or didactic sermonizing. Rather, he ends with an eloquent image. In the year between the poem's events and the poem's publication, both Frietchie and Jackson have died, Frietchie presumably from old age and Jackson from friendly fire at Chancellorsville, Virginia. Although he permits a tear for Jackson, Whittier closes the poem with the stirring image of the Union flag, representing "light and law," still flying proudly, albeit now over Frietchie's humble grave.

Forms and Devices

"Barbara Frietchie" is styled as a traditional folk ballad, a compact, rhythmic verse narrative, told impersonally by an omniscient voice, which recounts the courage of common people in a crisis. Whittier, who mastered the form by reading the poetry of Robert Burns and Sir Walter Scott, self-consciously draws on that style to give this contemporary event importance and historic largeness. Because ballads were originally composed as songs intended for public performance for (at best) a semi-literate audience, the conventions are deliberately accessible: The setting is recognizable and realistic, the characters act without complex psychological depth, the centering tension is unambiguously drawn between right and wrong, the dialogue is theatrical and heightens the suspense, and the lines are uncluttered by elevated diction or suggestive symbols. The story is related primarily for its dramatic appeal and its inspirational impact. Its steady four-beat-per-line rhythm, suggesting the heavy cadence of the marching soldiers, creates an unrelenting, irresistible forward movement.

Whittier draws heavily on established, largely British poetic conventions to create his ballad's sonic effects. Hence, the poem has a clear respect for the rules of composition. It provides expected rhythms and anticipated beats (iambic tetrameter) and maintains a patterned rhyme scheme. It further deploys traditional language devices for manipulating the poem's aural impact, including assonance, consonance, alliteration, the repetition of critical phrasing, inverted syntactical sequencing to create dramatic emphasis (particularly displacing prepositional phrases to enhance suspense), and synecdoche (using part of an image to represent the whole—for instance, the phrase "horse and foot" to represent the soldiers or Frietchie's telling the soldiers to shoot "this old gray head"). Apart from such traditional devices, the poetic line is uncluttered by figurative language and is deliberately straightforward, reflecting both the ballad genre and Whittier's own preference, drawn from his Quaker background, for unadorned diction.

Themes and Meanings

It is tempting to pigeonhole "Barbara Frietchie" as a dated historical piece, its labored rhythm and insistent rhyming distracting to the modern ear, its sentimentality and unabashed defense of the Union non-involving to a contemporary audience. Clearly, the poem does not demand sophisticated analysis as much as public recitation. It further presumes a public role for the poet that in the contemporary era poets seldom perform. Yet "Barbara Frietchie" is more than recitable propaganda. For a contemporary reader the poem is a passionate assertion of the conservative virtue of order that dominated British neoclassical thought in the eighteenth century—indeed, Frietchie's formidable age grounds her in the earlier century.

To make its point the poem juxtaposes three emblems. Unlike symbols, which invite interpretive, often creative analysis, emblems are vivid pictorial images that directly correspond to a clear abstract principle and are intended for instruction. Here Whittier deploys the natural world itself, emblem of the universal principle of order; the flag, emblem not only of the social and political construct called the Union but also of the same universal principle of order as expressed by human endeavor; and the guns of the rebel army, the emblem of disorder, the dangerous assertion of anarchy that, in neoclassical thought, has represented since Lucifer's rebellion a dire threat to order. The Civil War then is not merely a political, military, economic, or cultural act—it is also a moral act, specifically a violation of a universal principle of order.

Thus, in the temerity of Frietchie's action, Whittier, a Quaker and a pacifist, is not sanctioning the Union fight. He was deeply disturbed by the violence of the war. This poem is no stirring call to arms and is strikingly nonviolent, centering as it does on shots that are not fired. Rather, Whittier sanctions the Union cause: the restoration of order. The invading rebel troops are clearly out of place not only in the Northern state of Maryland but also in the natural world itself. They are "famished" and "dust-brown" amid the vibrant autumnal abundance. Further, amid such fertility, they destroy. They haul down flags and riddle Frietchie's flag with a terrific blast. Those violations are in Whittier's moral vision far graver offenses than any battle casualty, directed as they are against the visible emblem of order.

The turning point comes in Frietchie's often-quoted couplet: "Shoot, if you must, this old gray head/ But spare your country's flag." The key is the second-person possessive pronoun. In this lexical gesture, in its way far more defiant than waving the flag, the old woman reminds the rebels that their treasonous assertion of separation from the Union is a violation of form. More to the point, their rebellion is seen as a temporary disruption that the moral universe, itself governed by a principle of order, will never sanction. Jackson orders his men to hold fire not because Frietchie is an unarmed civilian but because she is right. Barbara Frietchie and Stonewall Jackson thus move dramatically to the same moral position against the Confederacy's unnatural assertion of extremism, revolution, and rebellion. Frietchie's assertion of the rightness of form is emblematically represented by the Union flag. Its return to a position of prominence, unchallenged by the passive rebel horde, represents Whittier's affirmation of an ordered universe restored—the very winds that hold the flag aloft are "loyal" to its cause.

As the backdrop, nature itself provides the reassuring model of order in the emblem of the rich Maryland countryside that rings, "green-walled," around the town. Its stately, orderly progressions are indicated by the poem's movement from morning to evening; by the poem's evocation of the seasons, specifically the movement into harvesting; and ultimately by the movement of both the main characters from life to death. Indeed, the order of the natural world is decidedly undisturbed by the ongoing war. It is sunny morning of a "pleasant" autumn day, the orchards bursting with life. That rightness of nature reassures that even amid the terrible chaos of war the universe will ultimately reassert order. In the closing stanzas the universe itself validates the flag and the order that it represents: The stars in the night sky correspond to the stars on the flag over Frietchie's grave. Barbara Frietchie's gesture, then, is not merely a political or military statement bound to its moment in history but rather a timeless moral judgment, an unambiguous assertion that the universe embraces order and will triumph over the threat implicit in chaos.

Joseph Dewey

BARBIE DOLL

Author: Marge Piercy (1936-   )
Type of poem: Narrative
First published: 1973, in *To Be of Use*

The Poem

Contemporary poet Marge Piercy published a twenty-five line, open-form narrative poem titled "Barbie Doll." Four stanzas provide the reader with a brief tale of a nameless "girlchild" whose life, markedly influenced by others' opinions, comes to a sad and premature end.

"This girlchild was born as usual," the poem begins. The little girl receives ostensibly appropriate gifts: dolls, miniature home appliances, some makeup. Later, "in the magic of puberty," a schoolmate comments unflatteringly on her appearance, noting her "great big nose and fat legs."

From the second stanza the reader learns about the young adolescent's intelligence, physical prowess, and sexual drive. She appears to be healthy, strong, and capable, but she ignores these attributes, instead going "to and fro apologizing." "Everyone" sees her as only "a fat nose on thick legs."

As she matures, she receives counsel from others. The third stanza lists behaviors aimed at promoting her happiness and success. In time, her natural goodness breaks down like a worn-out automobile part. Finally, as an adult, she permanently rids herself of her perceived inadequacies by means of a sacrificial offering.

In the final stanza, the reader discovers the now-deceased woman displayed in her casket. She has been artificially fabricated by an undertaker, with a "turned-up putty nose,/ dressed in a pink and white nightie." Onlookers find her "pretty." The final two lines of the poem resolve the narrative: "Consummation at last./ To every woman a happy ending."

Forms and Devices

No direct mention of a Barbie doll is made in the poem. However, the reader may connect the title with the piece as a key to subsequent interpretation, perhaps noting also the urinating doll described in the first stanza and the corpse in the last.

Each of the free-verse stanzas contains relatively short lines and conversational diction. End rhyme is absent, but the reader can locate internal assonance and alliteration with relative ease. Iambs and anapests sustain a melodic rhythm throughout the poem. Not only relevant to poetic form, these "upbeat" accents provide ironic contrast to the poem's serious content.

Uses and omissions of traditional punctuation marks and capitalization are commonplace in modern poetry. "Barbie Doll" is no exception. Reading the poem aloud demonstrates how these devices, along with the enjambed lines, support emphases and ironies.

Repetition of words, such as the initial "and" in lines 2,3, and 4, suggests a childlike voice or perhaps boredom. In later stanzas, certain morphological structures (past participle endings throughout the poem: "presented," "tested," "possessed," "advised," "exhorted," "offered," "displayed") convey a tone of formality and detachment, as though one were reading a case history or clinical report.

Piercy's diction also highlights relative degrees of significance. For example, "dolls that did pee-pee" and "wee lipsticks" sound less important than "the magic of puberty" and the list of qualities that follow in stanza 2. The deceased appears in the final stanza with "turned-up putty nose,/dressed in a pink and white nightie" and looking "pretty." These descriptors—"putty," "pink," "pretty"—markedly contrast in both sound and sense with the penultimate line, "Consummation at last."

At least three more poetic devices help readers derive meaning from the experience of "Barbie Doll." First, the simile in stanza 3 compares the individual's "good nature," something that is a part of human development and useful to one's self, with a "fan belt," something that is mechanical and useful to—also used by—others. Second, "nose and legs," a synecdoche for the whole body if not the whole person, develops from an initial observation of a trait in stanza 1, to an image of diminished identity in stanza 2, and finally to a symbol of total inadequacy in stanza 3. Third, the last line of the poem constitutes a striking irony as the "happy ending" brings this bitter fairy tale to a close not only for the hapless subject of the poem but also for "every woman."

Themes and Meanings

Piercy has regarded the activity of making poetry as such an admixture of the personal and impersonal that it becomes "addictive." In an essay, "Writers on Writing," appearing on December 20, 1999, in *The New York Times*, she stated that her state of mind usually leads her to translate whatever subject she is working on into "molten ore." She once said that anything can be subject matter for a poem as long as the poet is willing to focus on it intensely enough.

If Piercy is direct and accessible as human being and artist, her work is similarly so to readers. Her themes span a wide range, including civil rights, ecology, feminism, relationships, and religion (particularly her Jewish heritage). Although some critics find influences of Walt Whitman and Denise Levertov in her work, Piercy's opus and style seem rather uniquely her own.

In the introduction to *Circles on the Water: Selected Poems of Marge Piercy* (1982), the anthology that includes "Barbie Doll," Piercy claims that she wants her poetry to be useful, "simply that readers will find poems that speak to and for them . . . to give voice to something in the experience of a life. . . ." Somewhat ironically, "Barbie Doll" originally appeared in a volume of poems titled *To Be of Use*. Written in 1970, many of the poems reflect ideas having to do with feminist consciousness: sexual, political, and professional. Within that context, "Barbie Doll" emerges as terse commentary about society's stereotypical expectations for females, and what happens if the authentic self is bypassed.

It is possible for the reader to discover a dual movement in each stanza of "Barbie

Doll," the first section describing situational circumstances, the final two lines indicating their consequences. Hence, in stanza 1, "this girlchild" comes into a world where things exist "as usual" for female children. However, later, when "a classmate" observes her unattractive nose and legs, the "magic" of pubescence is under attack.

Stanza 2 develops the girl's positive qualities. However, while she is apologetic, those around her see her presumably physical flaws as who she is, not just something she has. In lines 10 and 11 ("She went to and fro apologizing./ Everyone saw a fat nose on thick legs"), the reader notes the use of functional ambiguity, almost simultaneously allowing more than a single interpretation of the lines. Line 9 closes the preceding statement with a period. Lines 10 and 11 are each one-line declarations also closing with a period. Without the presence of transitional words or even comma breaks, the reader may ask whether the young girl is apologizing for her talents or for her large nose and legs? Is her anatomy truly offensive or only perceived by her as such?

In stanza 3, the maturing female acquires advice that seems to combine useful behaviors (exercise, diet) with those more typical of what society expects from women, at least in 1970. Unfortunately, the poem's subject finds difficulty keeping up the pace. Human beings wear out when they cannot discover or be themselves. Thus the last two lines of the stanza record the nameless girl's final decision. Unable to cope, she chooses suicide, expressed in a metaphoric amputation of nose and legs, and makes a final oblation of her inadequacies.

With her death (stanza 4), "everyone" is finally satisfied. Sadly, it is too late for the woman to enjoy their praise; equally sad is the onlookers' response since it is not for the loss of an authentic human being but rather for a stunted life ultimately fulfilled: "Consummation at last." "This girlchild" has paid a high price to achieve cosmetic, doll-like attractiveness, but at last she has a name. It is "Barbie Doll." If this tragic ending were not enough, the poet suggests that the "happy ending" is available to "every woman" willing to travel a similar path.

Piercy offers the reader, in minimalist, almost clinical third-person narration, what may happen to women who accept or fail to transcend their objectification by society. In other poems Piercy revisits this theme using even more powerful images, greater length, and personal voice. "Barbie Doll" constitutes a useful doorway to Piercy's work and to women's issues expressed in twentieth century poetry. In case readers imagine that this issue has become obsolete, they may visit any toy store to find Barbie dolls still occupying shelf space. Dressed for the third millennium, their presence still poses this question: Is business for women still "as usual"?

Louise A. DeSantis Deutsch

A BAROQUE WALL-FOUNTAIN IN THE VILLA SCIARRA

Author: Richard Wilbur (1921-   )
Type of poem: Lyric
First published: 1956, in *Things of This World*

The Poem

Richard Wilbur's poem "A Baroque Wall-Fountain in the Villa Sciarra" consists of a long meditation that springs from a careful examination of two types of fountains in Rome, the first constructed in a large public park, the second, the fountains placed at Saint Peter's Basilica. The rhyme scheme used throughout fifteen stanzas is *abba*, with new rhymes occurring in each stanza.

The poem opens with a description of the fountain, greatly elaborating on the high degree of decoration, the qualities that make the fountain's decor Baroque. The poet advances a mixture of Roman and Christian allusions, blending angels and fauns throughout. This combination produces a line of thought that the poet follows to the conclusion of the poem. The three stone cockles that collect and disburse the water from shell to shell establish the basic structure of the baroque fountain, not only physically but also thematically. A snake has begun to eat the feet of a cherub who acts as guardian of the first shell, from which water spills into the next shell. The water creates a tent of spray for a family of fauns, whose father holds the third shell.

At this point, the poet chooses words that forecast the thematic shift that transpires in the next several stanzas. Water covers the flesh of the fauness "In a saecular ecstasy," a reference to the sheer physicality of a faun's worldly concern. Half goat and half human, associated with merrymaking, fauns traditionally guarded crops and woods as part of the Roman pantheon. Wilbur then refers to the "trefoil" pool, its three-part structure, a reference to the Christian notion of the trinity. Wilbur makes double use of this image, in that the serpent bothering the angel in the first stanza alludes to the Garden of Eden and the Fall of Man.

Frequently in his poetry Wilbur poses rhetorical questions after having thoroughly developed one idea, in order to venture into areas of thought that perhaps contradict or complicate the rather easy conclusions reached earlier in the poem. After an elaborate description of the fountain, with its fauns, cherubs, and serpents, the poet asks his first question, wondering if "pleasure, flash, and waterfall" cannot adequately account for the longing of the human spirit. Human beings are too complex in nature to be easily classified as belonging solely to the world of the spirit or the world of the physical.

Consequently, the poet then considers the plainer fountains erected outside Saint Peter's Basilica in Rome. The poet asks his second question, speculating about the idea that these fountains more fittingly represent the struggle that inheres in human experience. While fauns and cherubs can dance and play under the water's cooling spray, in spite of the serpent at the heel, humans cannot. The water in these fountains rises as if it reaches self-fulfillment, finding rest "in the act of rising," as if the human goal to achieve peace occurs within the struggle to live a meaningful life.

Yet, Wilbur is not willing to cast a negative judgment on the fauns' way of being in the world. Instead, asking "What of these showered fauns," he concludes that they reach fulfillment as well, finding rest "in fulness of desire" for the things of this world. The poem takes an ironic twist at this point. The poet compares the satisfaction with the things of this world that the fauns celebrate with the attitude of acceptance that Saint Francis brought to bear in praise of creation, discovering in the natural order a beautiful reflection, albeit pale, of heaven.

Forms and Devices

Each of the fifteen stanzas contains end rhymes that do not continue into the next stanza. As none of these stanzas use interlocking rhymes, the poet makes use of other devices rhetorically to draw the meaning through the lines. Most of the stanzas, for example, use enjambment, pulling images through several lines or stanzas before concluding. Only one stanza comes to a full stop, having asked the second question. Such a varied rhyme allows the reader to avoid premature conclusions about where the poet is proceeding with his thought. The discontinuous rhyme seems speculative in nature, as if even the structure of the poem itself is ripe for probing, as if the poet remains open to the possibilities of new discovery.

Although the poem does use end rhyme to strengthen the melody, the musicality of the lines does not completely depend upon that structure. Within each stanza, the repetition of vowel or consonant sounds echoes the rhyme, formulating the sense of the poem even deeper within the structure. For example, in the first stanza, whose second and third lines end with "feet" and "eat," the fourth line begins with "Sweet." In the second stanza, the short "i" sound in "tipped" in the second line repeats in "fills" and "spills," which end the second and third lines. The eighth stanza concludes each line with "e" sounds, as if stylistically acknowledging the turn that occurred in the previous stanza. Wilbur's use of a highly developed sound structure mirrors the play in dualities that becomes the center of thematic speculation within the poem.

Sometimes the words themselves sound like what they represent, adding another layer of melodic patterning, onomatopoeia. The seventh stanza ushers in liquid "l" sounds, ending the third line with "waterfall." Yet in the ninth stanza, "The very wish of water is reversed." The use of "s" and "i" sounds seems to suggest the sound of water flowing in an opposite direction from the previous stanza.

Wilbur sets up an extended comparison between two worldviews, using the two different fountains as the specific images upon which to build his argument. He establishes the first fountain in six stanzas, followed by his first rhetorical turn in which he questions his own conclusions. The second fountain requires only three stanzas for discussion, being less ornate. Thus, even the space that Wilbur devotes to each image reflects the nature of the ideas discussed. The second twist comes toward the end of the poem, when he compares the ideas represented by the first fountain with the ideas that Saint Francis came to embody. Therefore, while avoiding labeling his comparisons, Wilbur achieves a higher, denser use of the metaphor.

Themes and Meanings

Many of Wilbur's poems reflect his having spent time in Italy during World War II. This poem describes fountains constructed in Rome, with classical and Christian allusions as it contrasts two different ways of approaching life. The highly decorated first fountain represents the more physical, earthbound connection that the speaker feels as one way of being in the world. This fountain, set in a public park, illustrates an easier, more accessible path to take. The plainer second fountain, set outside a church, exemplifies a more challenging path. Wilbur, however, does not completely dismiss either idea, seeing in both the possibilities for fulfillment, ironically by referring to Saint Francis and his relationship to nature.

The use of flowing water adds to the spiritual-physical dialectic inherent in Wilbur's comparison. As a symbol at the heart of many religions, water represents baptism into a given way of thought. Certainly ancient peoples saw water as a primary source of life itself, ascribing various gods and goddesses as protectors of rivers and streams upon which the people relied. This poem is consistent thematically with other poems in this collection, in which Wilbur celebrates the physical world while longing for the clarity of vision that meditation on the sacred can provide.

While not overtly religious or sectarian, this poem addresses the nature of the human spirit when confronted with what seems to be a choice between the sacred and the profane, each perceived as being mutually incompatible. The waters spewing forth from the plain fountains are "water-saints," teaching humans how to struggle against a tendency to fall. The fauns, however, represent the need to celebrate the world in all its complexity. Wilbur suggests that people should look beyond the simplicity of such a dichotomy in order to discover and experience the world in all its fullness.

Martha Modena Vertreace-Doody

THE BASKET-MAKER

Author: Padraic Colum (1881-1972)
Type of poem: Lyric
First published: 1957, in *Ten Poems*

The Poem

"The Basket-Maker," by the Irish poet Padraic Colum, is a lyric poem that considers the role of the anonymous artisan in connecting the present with the historical past. The speaker calls attention to the specific roles and uses of baskets in rural Irish life, the solitary role of the itinerant basket-maker, and, ultimately, the importance of the nameless laborers who produce the stuff of civilization.

The basket-maker serves an important practical function in Irish society, illustrated in the poem through the discussion of the functionality of the baskets he produces, but his deeper importance pertains to his position, as a member of the working class and also as an artist, within the larger context of Irish cultural identity. When the basket-maker asserts, toward the end of the poem, "'I travel Ireland's length and breadth,'" his tone reveals a unity with his country, even a sense of ownership or propriety: "There was dominion in the way he said it." The apparent humility of the basket-maker's station in life is transformed into a pride both in his craft and in his very anonymity.

The poem opens by highlighting connections between ancient and modern, as the speaker, while watching the basket-maker at his craft in the marketplace, is approached by a friend who is versed in "the lore of ancient fields and houses." The friend bears recently excavated Bronze Age relics, including golden arm-rings, such as would have been given by princes as rewards in Anglo-Saxon times; a quern, a primitive device, consisting of two circular stones, used for grinding grain; and "woven hazel twigs," the presence of which underscores the antiquity of the basket-maker's craft: He uses the same methods, and creates the same product, as did basket-makers of a thousand years ago.

The speaker's stake in the basket-maker's craftsmanship rests in his identification with his fellow artisan. The speaker is a poet, and he calls attention to his own craft even as he describes the basket-maker's. Both crafts, poetry and basket-making, are ancient, and both are practiced in relative silence with only simple tools. Further, the speaker's description of the basket-maker's youthful apprenticeship "when hazel-nuts were green" connects that craft (and, by extension, poetry) to the work of the natural world. The wren's "bulky nest" is woven by the same means, using the same materials, as the different varieties of basket—wicker round, creel, and kish—produced by the basket-maker.

As the speaker dwells on the basket-maker's craft, he also calls attention to his own art, simultaneously watching the craftsman "weave/ Rod over rod" and thinking about the "woven hazel twigs/ Laid down in summer, since the hazel nuts/ were not then filled [ripe]." Observing the weaver's repetitive motion, the poet-speaker mimics it by repeating and reconsidering the phrase he has just used. This affinity between the basket-maker and the speaker stops short of reducing the basket-maker's craft to allegorical representation of the process of poetic creation; instead, the comparison allows the speaker to share in the basket-maker's "dominion" over the Ireland whose "length and breadth" he travels.

Forms and Devices

The predominant style of "The Basket-Maker" is blank verse—unrhymed iambic pentameter—though Colum uses several shorter lines throughout for variation and emphasis. Blank verse, the most natural and least obtrusive regular meter in English language poetry, is entirely appropriate to the poet's theme and purpose; in a poem about unpretentious natural craftsmanship and tradition both in basket-making and poet craft, the use of blank verse subtly reinforces the poet's message, and the parallel between the speaker and the basket-maker, "two of [them] only in the market-place," is emphasized. The basket-maker uses "No tool . . . but his own hands, a knife/ That he had used since his apprenticeship," while the poet-speaker uses unrhymed iambic pentameter, one of the most common and natural tools in English prosody, to depict the craftsman and describe his relationship to his craft and his native land.

Just as the poem's meter emphasizes its theme, Colum's careful choice of unfamiliar words serves to highlight the poem's main ideas. His description of the basket he is purchasing as a "withied shape," for example, calls attention to the archaic and potentially foreign nature of his subject matter. The word "withied" pertains to willows (the long, supple twigs of which are frequently used in basket-making) or to something tied with twigs. Like several of the more unfamiliar words the speaker uses, the origin of "withied," in this case, Old English, is just as significant as the literal meaning of the word itself. Its use relates to and prefigures the artifacts introduced by the friend several lines later, for the word itself is an artifact of sorts. Similarly, the speaker's use of it identifies him as someone who, like his friend, is similarly versed in "the lore of ancient fields and houses."

The "quern" mentioned several lines later also stresses the speaker's familiarity with this ancient lore. Again, the word comes from the Old English and denotes a primitive hand-held mill, composed of two round stones, used for grinding grain. Both the word and the object to which it refers would probably be foreign to most of the speaker's contemporaries, but the poet-speaker knows the raw materials of his trade in the same way that the basket-maker's "supple hands" know the "woven hazel twigs" with which he works. Thus, Colum's choice of words, his decision to use archaic words of Old English origin rather than their more familiar modern counterparts, functions in direct support of the poem's themes and subject matter.

Though the nominal subject of the poem is the basket-maker, the basket he weaves does not bear particular symbolic weight in the poem; the process of its creation is described in detail, but the basket itself is only a "withied shape." However, the ring the basket-maker shows the speaker is of particular symbolic significance: The Claddagh ring is a traditional Irish wedding ring, formed of "two hands clasped" holding a heart with a crown above it. Though it was presented to him as payment for his wares and not as a token of love, the ring represents faith and a connection, not specifically between the basket-maker and his customer but between him and his region and its traditions.

Themes and Meanings

"The Basket-Maker," like many other poems about artistic creation, makes a significant statement about its narrator's attitude toward his own craft. The speaker's self-conscious allusion to his own creative process as he repeats and mulls over a phrase from earlier in the poem draws the reader's attention to the parallels between the speaker and the basket-weaver. The craftsman's skill is ancient in origin, like the Bronze Age artifacts revealed by the receding lake waters, but it requires the poet's skill to find the poem in the experience. The friend of the poet, with his knowledge of historical lore, is able to appreciate the arm-rings, the quern, the boar-tusk pendants, and the piece of amber, but only the poet recognizes the treasure on which these other treasures rest: the "woven hazel twigs," which provide historical validation of the basket-maker's craft. The poet's ability to appreciate the basket-maker's art, past and present, is precisely what makes him an artist in his own right.

While the themes of artistic creation and the link between the past and the present are universal, the setting of "The Basket-Maker" is quite specific, and consideration of the poem in that context provides insight into another layer of meaning. The poem is explicitly set in a marketplace, and it can be gathered from the reference to Counties Kerry and Galway that the marketplace is located in the rural west of Ireland. As the poem progresses and the setting becomes more identifiable, the basket-maker's pride takes on a more patriotic character, and his description of people who use his wares is also clearly intended to present a specifically Irish rural culture: The "old woman out for marketing" suggests the Poor Old Woman, a traditional personification of Ireland; the reference to "potatoes from the pot" alludes to a dietary staple of the region; the harvesting of turf to burn as fuel is likewise a specifically Irish occupation; and the word "kish," used to denote the woven basket for carrying this turf, comes from the Irish language.

In the penultimate stanza the basket-maker mentions the "Kerry glens" and the arbutus trees that grow there. Significantly, the word "arbutus" is Latin in origin, a later addition to the local language. The tree to which the word refers is an ornamental evergreen, useless for basket-making. The "reeks" the basket-maker traverses are the stacked hills found in Kerry. These topographical references, along with the other specific geographical details, serve to locate the action of the poem in a specific place and to underscore the theme of pride in tradition that the final stanza stresses. They define an Ireland the "length and breadth" of which the basket-maker travels, and over which he feels the sense of "dominion" evident in his voice at the poem's close.

James S. Brown

BATTER MY HEART, THREE-PERSONED GOD

Author: John Donne (1572-1631)
Type of poem: Sonnet
First published: 1633, in *Poems, by J.D.: With Elegies on the Authors Death*

The Poem

"Batter my heart, three-personed God" is a sonnet, a short lyric poem of fourteen lines. In the Renaissance, two kinds of sonnets were popular. The Shakespearean, or English, sonnet has three quatrains, rhyming *abab*, *cdcd*, *efef*, and a final couplet, rhyming *gg*, which usually contains a short statement of the theme. The Petrarchan, or Italian, sonnet is divided into an octave rhyming *abbaabba*, and a sestet rhyming *cdecde*; the sestet moves from the questions, causes, or complaints presented in the octave to answers, effects, or resolutions.

John Donne combines both forms in his Holy Sonnet sequence; his octave uses the *abbaabba* rhyme scheme of the Italian sonnet, while his sestet rhymes *cdcdee*, the rhyme scheme of the English sonnet. The couplet usually contains a thematic affirmation of man's sinfulness and God's love for humanity.

The poem uses a first-person narrator. This speaker (not necessarily Donne) is a Christian man trying to come to terms with his own unworthiness in the face of God's never-ending love. In the first four lines, the anguished speaker begs God to make him a new man. He calls God a "three-personed God" and uses a parallel series of verbs to reflect the three persons of the Trinity. "Knock" and "break" belong to God the Father (representing power); "breathe" and "blow" belong to the Holy Spirit (the Latin root of "spirit" literally means "breathe"; the words also allude to God's spirit breathing over the waters in Genesis); "shine" and "burn" belong to God the Son (incorporating a pun: Christ is both Son and sun). Each subsequent verb used in the verb pairs likewise adds an urgency to the speaker's pleas. It is not enough for God to mend the sinner; the sinner needs the more violent approach of total annihilation and remaking.

The next four lines focus on the depraved state of the speaker, who has been taken over by the Devil (the "another" in line 5). Even reason, the manifestation of God's wisdom in man, is captured by the enemy and unable to lead the sinner back to God.

In lines 9 through 12, the speaker admits his love for God but confesses that he has espoused sin (Satan, God's enemy). Repeating the trinity of supplicating verbs, "Divorce," "untie," and "break," he begs God to divorce him from his relation with sin and to release him from his pact with the Devil.

The couplet brings his petitions to a violent close; the speaker demands that God rape him so that he can be pure.

Forms and Devices

This sonnet employs metaphor and simile, the figurative language of comparison, to illustrate the anguished state of the speaker and his desire to free soul, mind, and

Masterplots II

body from the captivity of sin. The force of the comparison lies in its power to surprise and instruct by yoking distinctly different ideas or images together.

Donne's power to startle by pairing disparate ideas and images in his metaphors and similes is one of the hallmarks of his strong poetic voice; his figurative language asks from the reader a bold leap in imagination and involves a mental translation that often brings a deeper understanding of the theme of the particular lines. The metaphors and similes in "Batter my heart" are no exception.

In the first four lines, the Trinity is metaphorically compared with a tinker, or metalsmith, who, instead of trying to patch the kettle (the sinner), is asked to create a new kettle by completely destroying the old.

The comparison in lines 5 through 8, this time a simile, focuses on the sinner himself. He is like a town that has been unlawfully taken (usurped) by the Devil. The reasoning power of his mind, likened to God's governor, is also captured and unable to break the bonds of captivity. Although God is outside the gate, the sinner is too weak to hear God's knocking: "Behold I stand at the door, and knock: if any man hear my voice, and open the door, I will come in to him, and will sup with him, and he with me" (Revelation 3:20).

Donne switches back to metaphor in lines 9 through 14, and anchors the relationship of Christ as bridegroom and the Christian as bride in a series of comparisons that are both disturbingly violent and openly sexual. The speaker explains his dilemma: He loves Christ but is engaged to the Devil. He (although a feminine speaker is implied) begs for a release from this relationship. In the last two lines, Donne stretches the tenuous link in the comparison to its breaking point when he asks Christ to rape him so that his soul can be free: "Nor ever chaste, except you ravish me."

In addition to metaphor and simile, Donne employs paradox (a seemingly contradictory statement) to add compression and precision to the poem. Donne cannot express the religious truths imbedded in the poem any other way without distorting them. Christianity itself is built upon the paradox that Christ died in order to restore life to those who believe, and that believers need to emulate this death: "For whosoever will save his life shall lose it: and whosoever will lose his life for my sake shall find it" (Matthew 17:25).

Donne echoes this basic paradox, in his own forcible way, when the speaker claims that only by death to sin can he rise with Christ ("That I may rise, and stand, o'erthrow me"), that only through imprisonment by God can the soul be freed of sin and Satan ("for I/ Except you enthral me, never shall be free"), and that only by using the extreme image of a violent rape by Christ can the sinner obtain a virginal soul.

Themes and Meanings

The best way to understand Donne's religious poetry is to consider each poem as part of a series of progressions of a man depraved by sin but relying on the grace of `1 16, in her numbering) can be divided into three meditative sequences. The first group of six has as a theme the end of time; the theme of the next six sonnets is the love of God for his creation; and the last four deal with sin and repentance. Gardner places

"Batter my heart, three-personed God" as number ten of the series, the central sonnet on the love of God toward His creation, no matter how far man has wandered from the true way. (H. J. C. Grierson, the early compiler of Donne's poetry, assigns number fourteen to this sonnet.)

The metaphors and similes in this sonnet present a Christian man unable to overcome his sinfulness by his own powers, thus underscoring the Christian tenets that "all have sinned and come short of the glory of God" (Romans 3:23) and that only God's unlimiting grace suffices to save the sinner: "For by grace are ye saved through faith; and that not of yourselves: it is the gift of God" (Ephesians 2:8).

The paradoxes incorporated in the sonnet not only give an immediacy to the speaker's dilemma but also mirror the paradoxical truths of the Christian faith. All the seeming contradictions testify that true spiritual life is only possible through death with Christ so that the Christian's faith may grow to maturity: "Verily, verily, I say unto you, Except a corn of wheat fall into the ground and die, it abideth alone: but if it die, it bringeth forth much fruit" (John 12:24).

The sonnet is centered on the regeneration process, the "making new" of the soul so that God's image may be restored. The passiveness of the sinner, emphasized by his anguished pleas that God begin the renewal process ("Batter my heart," "o'erthrow me," "Divorce me," "imprison me," "ravish me"), reinforces the Christian tenet that God's grace alone can effect this regeneration.

Donne repeats the theme of regeneration through the violent actions of God on the sinful soul at the close of "Good Friday, 1613. Riding Westward." In the same anguished but demanding voice, the speaker asks God to make him a new man: "Burn off my rusts, and my deformity,/ Restore thine image, so much, by thy grace,/ That thou mayst know me, and I'll turn my face."

Although the speakers in Donne's religious poetry express their depravity and their agony over personal salvation, "Batter my heart, three-personed God" stands as an eloquent and intense witness to the belief that through God's grace the Christian soul can begin its journey of regeneration that will find its ultimate glorification in heaven.

Koos Daley

384

BATTLE-PIECES AND ASPECTS OF THE WAR

Author: Herman Melville (1819-1891)
Type of poem: Book of poems
First published: 1866

The Poems

  Battle-Pieces and Aspects of the War is a collection of seventy-two poems that de-
pict key episodes and individuals of the Civil War as well as the temperament of the
American people during the great conflict. Herman Melville arranges the poems in a
chronological order so that the collection becomes an impressionistic history of the
war delivered in verses rather than in prose. The first poem of the volume, "The Por-
tent," depicts the hanging of John Brown, the abolitionist who, in 1859, failed in his
attempt to start a slave rebellion by capturing the United States military arsenal at
Harpers Ferry, Virginia, and arming the slaves on nearby plantations. Brown's
Harpers Ferry raid is often cited as the first skirmish of the Civil War, and the poem re-
fers to Brown as "The meteor of the war." *Battle-Pieces* concludes with "A Medita-
tion," a poem in which the speaker speculates on whether the United States will be
able to heal its war wounds and reunite itself after a four-year conflict that bitterly di-
vided the nation and took the lives of more than 600,000 Americans.

  Individual poems in *Battle-Pieces* re-create many of the key engagements and inci-
dents of the war—the battles of Manassas, Fort Donelson, Shiloh, Antietam, Stones
River, Gettysburg, Lookout Mountain, Wilderness, Cedar Creek; the fall of Rich-
mond; the assassination of President Abraham Lincoln; General Robert E. Lee's sur-
render at Appomattox court house—and provide portraits of many of the war's impor-
tant individuals, among them General Stonewall Jackson, General Philip Sheridan,
and Colonel John Mosby. Several poems in *Battle-Pieces* depict war waged from sail-
ing vessels. Melville, who spent much time at sea as a young man, had previously
used an ocean setting in many of his best-known fictional works, including *Moby-
Dick* (1851), generally considered Melville's masterwork.

  The poems vary in type and length. *Battle-Pieces* contains narrative poems, bal-
lads, hymns, elegies, meditations, and epitaphs. The shortest poem, "On the Grave,"
an inscription for the gravestone of a cavalry officer killed on a battlefield in Virginia,
comprises only five lines; the longest, "The Scout Toward Aldie," which depicts the
guerrilla tactics of Confederate colonel John Mosby, runs 798 lines.

  The collection's title comes from the world of art. Paintings and sketches depicting
war were generally called battle pieces. Melville had developed an interest in such art
works even before the Civil War began; after the war, when he commenced writing
poems that captured the conflict, Melville attempted to render in verse what he had
seen artists create on canvas and paper. Indeed, a few of the poems in *Battle-Pieces* are
named specifically for famous paintings. In the poem " 'The Coming Storm,'" for ex-
ample, Melville draws an analogy between the wilderness landscape at the start of a

storm, depicted in the 1865 painting by Sandford Robinson Gifford, and the situation in the United States as the Civil War approached. In "Formerly a Slave," Melville also re-creates in verse the woman who is the subject of an 1865 painting by Elihu Vedder.

The poems of *Battle-Pieces* clearly reveal Melville's position on the great conflict. Melville dedicates the volume "to the memory of the three hundred thousand who in the war for the maintenance of the union fell devotedly under the flag of their fathers"; the dedication makes no mention of the three hundred thousand Confederate dead. In "The Fortitude of the North," Melville asserts that the Union soldiers "fight for the Right." In "Dupont's Round Fight," a poem depicting a Union naval victory engineered by Commander Samuel Francis DuPont, Melville states that the Union fleet "Warred for Right,/ And, warring so, prevailed." The South, according to Melville, fought in defense of slavery, described in "Misgivings" as "man's foulest crime." In an essay appended to the collection, Melville condemns the South for supporting a war "whose implied end was the erecting in our advanced century of an Anglo-American empire based upon the systematic degradation of man." Hence, a poem that recognizes the battlefield prowess of Stonewall Jackson also identifies the great Confederate general as a man "who stoutly stood for Wrong."

Nonetheless, Melville shows much sympathy for the defeated South. For example, in a poem titled "Rebel Color-Bearers at Shiloh," and subtitled "A plea against the vindictive cry raised by civilians shortly after the surrender at Appomattox," Melville paints an admirable portrait of Confederate color bearers; he advises readers, "Perish their Cause! but mark the men." In "A Grave near Petersburg, Virginia," Melville describes a Rebel soldier's grave and declares, "May his grave be green, though he/ Was a rebel of iron mould." Melville praises President Lincoln in "The Martyr" for his conciliatory postwar policy, and in "Meditation," the volume's concluding poem, he urges Americans to set aside wartime animosities and engage in the act of reconciliation.

Melville never saw the war first hand. He did not join the Union army; he spent the war years in Pittsfield, Massachusetts, and New York. He did visit a cousin at the front in Virginia in 1864 and heard the war stories of battle-tested troopers. He also read about the war in newspapers, in magazines such as *Harper's Weekly*, and in a postwar publication titled *The Rebellion Record*. Moreover, after the war, he spoke with many veterans of the conflict who supplied him with the details that he used in the poems.

Forms and Devices

No two poems in *Battle-Pieces* look or read alike. Besides varying in length and type, the poems also differ according to rhyme scheme and meter. In some poems Melville employs traditional rhyme schemes, while others read like prose poems. In "A Dirge for McPherson," for example, the four-line stanzas adhere to a traditional *abab* rhyme pattern. "The House-top," on the other hand, reads more like a descriptive paragraph than a poem and is virtually without rhyme.

Weather imagery dominates *Battle-Pieces*. For Melville, the Civil War was a storm that threw the nation into disorder and chaos. For example, "Misgivings," the second poem of the collection, opens with these lines:

> When ocean-clouds over inland hills
>   Sweep storming in late autumn brown,
> And horror the sodden valley fills,
>   And the spire falls crashing in the town,
> I muse upon my country's ills—
> The tempest bursting from the waste of Time
> On the world's fairest hope linked with man's foulest crime.

Likewise, "Apathy and Enthusiasm," another poem set early in the collection, compares the mood of the nation on the eve of war with a "clammy, cold November" day with "the sky a sheet of lead." The events precipitating the war "came resounding/ With the cry that *All was lost,*/ Like the thundercracks of massy ice/ In intensity of frost—/ Bursting one upon another/ Through the horror of the calm."

Melville also sometimes compares the fury of battle with the raging power of a storm. In "Gettysburg," for example, the speaker describes Confederate general George Pickett's fatal charge into the center of the Union line on the third day of the battle as a storm at sea: "Before our lines it seemed a beach/ Which wild September gales have strown/ With havoc on wreck, and dashed therewith/ Pale crews unknown—/ Men, arms, and steeds." In "The College Colonel," Melville describes a regiment of battle-weary soldiers as "castaway sailors . . . stunned/ By the surf's loud roar."

Melville frequently juxtaposes images and moods within individual poems. "Shiloh," for example, features a sharp contrast between the peaceful setting and the fury of the battle that recently took place. In the Old Testament, Shiloh is a place of peace, and the poem opens with swallows flying gently over the "forest-field of Shiloh," where one of the bloodiest battles of the Civil War has just concluded. Rain is falling, but instead of producing new life, it merely provides solace to "the parched ones stretched in pain"—the dying soldiers still lying untreated on the field. The violent battle has taken place on a Sunday, the traditional Christian day of peace, near a church, a place of sanctuary and peace. The noise of battle is now replaced by quiet, as the swallows skim over the dead and dying soldiers, "And all is hushed at Shiloh."

In "The College Colonel," Melville juxtaposes the public celebration of a war hero returning to his hometown with the veteran's private thoughts. As the wounded colonel marches through the streets of his hometown, "There are welcoming shouts, and flags;/ Old men off hat to the Boy,/ Wreaths from gay balconies fall at his feet." However, the colonel's private thoughts are of his terrifying war experiences—frightening episodes during the battles of Seven Days, Wilderness, Petersburg, and his captivity at Libby prison:

> But all through the Seven Days' Fight,
>   And deep in the Wilderness grim,
> And in the field-hospital tent,
>   And Petersburg crater, and dim
> Lean brooding in Libby, there came—
>   Ah heaven!—what *truth* to him.

Throughout *Battle-Pieces* Melville makes frequent allusions to the Bible and to *Paradise Lost* (1667), the epic poem by John Milton that recounts the war between God's heavenly angels and the legions of Lucifer. Like many Northerners, Melville viewed the Civil War as an epic struggle between the forces of good and evil. In several poems he personifies the South as Satan waging a war of disunion against the North, whose troops are identified with God's angels, led by Michael the archangel. In "The Fall of Richmond" Melville equates the capture of the Confederate capital with the fall of Babylon and says that the Northern armies have deterred "the helmed dilated Lucifer." During the conflict, "Hell made loud hurrah," but now, with Richmond in Northern hands, "God is in Heaven, and Grant in the Town." In his novels, Melville makes frequent allusions to the Fall of Man, the sin of Adam and Eve in the Garden of Eden, as recorded in the book of Genesis. In *Battle-Pieces* he depicts the United States as a second Eden, corrupted by the sin of slavery,

Themes and Meanings

The overall thematic movement of *Battle-Pieces* is from the chaos of war to the order of peace and reconciliation, a movement also evident in *Drum-Taps* (1865), Walt Whitman's collection of Civil War poems. Melville's volume's early poems depict a nation torn asunder by a violent storm, but the war's end and the North's victory reestablish order in the American universe. For example, "Aurora-Borealis," a poem commemorating the end of the war, opens with the question, "What power disbands the Northern Lights/ After their steely play?" The northern lights, which appeared vividly in the evening sky after the devastating Union defeat at Fredericksburg, symbolize both the Confederate victory in that battle and the triumph of the forces of night, the forces of disorder and chaos. Yet at the war's end, "The phantom-host has faded quite,/ Splendor and Terror gone," giving way to "pale, meek Dawn." In "Lee in the Capitol," a poem depicting a postwar visit to the Capitol by Robert E. Lee, Melville describes a nation at peace: "Trees and green terraces sleep below" the Capitol building.

A frequent theme in individual poems of *Battle-Pieces* is the loss of innocence, a common theme in the literature of the Civil War. Melville, like other Civil War-era writers, viewed the war as the violent initiation experience that ended American innocence. Melville expresses that theme in "The March into Virginia," a poem marking the Battle of First Manassas (called the Battle of Bull Run by the North), the first major engagement of the Civil War. Melville declares that "All wars are boyish, and are fought by boys," and the young Yankee soldiers depicted in the poem march off to battle as if they were going on a picnic. The youthful troops anticipate the war as an exciting adventure, but many "who this blithe mood present,/ . . . Shall die experienced ere three days are spent."

The same theme is present in "Ball's Bluff." The speaker observes a regiment of soldiers marching past his home on their way to an engagement at Ball's Bluff:

> One noonday, at my window in the town,
>> I saw a sight—saddest that eyes can see—
> Young soldiers marching lustily
>> Unto the wars,
> With fifes, and flags in mottoed pageantry;
>> While all the porches, walks, and doors
> Were rich with ladies cheering royally.

The young men marching off to battle have hearts "fresh as clover in its prime." The speaker, however, sensing the horrors that lie ahead, asks, "How should they dream that Death in a rosy clime/ Would come to thin their shining throng?" Melville articulates a similar lament in "On the Slain Collegians," a poem commemorating the many regiments of college students who took sabbaticals from their studies to join in the war effort:

> Each bloomed and died an unabated Boy;
> Nor dreamed what death was—thought it mere
> Sliding into some vernal sphere.
> They knew the joy, but leaped the grief,
> Like plants that flower ere comes the leaf—
> Which storms lay low in kindly doom,
> And kill them in their flush of bloom.

Another persistent theme is *Battle-Pieces* is the endurance of nature in the face of the affairs of humankind. This theme is evident in "Shiloh" in Melville's description of the swallows swooping over the battlefield to reclaim it after the terrible battle has ended. Melville expresses a similar idea in "Malvern Hill," a poem depicting an engagement during the Seven Days' Battle. The speaker addresses the elm trees that stand on Malvern Hill, asking if they recall the great conflict that took place there. The speaker recounts the bloody battle that occurred, describing "rigid comrades" who lay dead in the forest and soldiers fighting with "haggard beards of blood." The elms respond that they "Remember every thing;/ But sap the twig will fill:/ Wag the world how it will,/ Leaves must be green in Spring." Regardless of the violent battle, regardless of the heroic stand made by the Union soldiers who fought at Malvern Hill, the elms must simply conduct nature's business, filling twigs with saps so that the trees will sprout leaves again.

The themes articulated in *Battle-Pieces* are also present in many of Melville's fictional works. Melville earned his place in American literary history as a fiction writer and is not generally appreciated as a great poet. Nonetheless, *Battle-Pieces* represents an ambitious effort by Melville, an attempt to compose an American *Iliad*, a history of the Civil War in verse.

James Tackach

BAVARIAN GENTIANS

Author: D. H. Lawrence (1885-1930)
Type of poem: Lyric
First published: 1932, in *Last Poems*

The Poem

This short poem in free verse opens with a two-line stanza that implies the speaker has some bavarian gentians (bright blue flowers) growing in his house in September. The poem then turns into an invocation, or prayer written in the imperative mood, in which the speaker calls to the flowers to act as torches to lead him into the dark underworld of Pluto and Persephone's marriage. "Bavarian Gentians" thus becomes an imaginative journey motivated by the contrast between the somber and unexceptional scene evoked in the opening lines and the vividly described phantasmal underworld of Roman mythology.

The poet's allusions to Pluto, Dis, Demeter, and Persephone invoke a particular Roman myth that explains seasonal change. Pluto, the ruler of the underworld, abducts Persephone, the daughter of the goddess of grain and fertility, Demeter. Though Pluto makes Persephone his underworld queen, Demeter exacts a compromise: Persephone can return each April to her mother for six months, after which (in September) she must return to her husband and the underworld. During the time Persephone is away from her mother, Demeter mourns her absence and the ground becomes barren; with Persephone's return in spring, the earth becomes fertile anew.

Thus, the poem's September setting is significant. The speaker longs to follow Persephone back into Pluto's kingdom at the very time when the earth is dormant and barren: "even where Persephone goes, just now, from the frosted September." The twist D. H. Lawrence gives the myth is his surprising association of vitality with the underworld abode of Pluto. Against the sterility of autumn and winter is posed the dark energy of the mystical underworld.

Into this underworld, the speaker of the poem imaginatively leads us. Images of darkness and blueness abound as we seem to descend deeper. The third and final stanza again cites the gentian flower as a guiding light: "let me guide myself with the blue, forked torch of this flower." The descent continues past a Persephone that exists only as "a voice . . . enfolded in the deeper dark/ of the arms Plutonic." The final image of the poem shows the gentian torch paradoxically "shedding darkness on the lost bride and her groom." The speaker seems to desire to enter this forbidden kingdom, and Lawrence seems to celebrate the Plutonic underworld in the poem. Why this underworld deserves celebration and draws the speaker to it becomes a central interpretive question.

Forms and Devices

Lawrence's mythological allusions structure "Bavarian Gentians," and the reader

senses quickly that some knowledge of the myth invoked is necessary for an under-
standing of the poem. The imagery, however, as reinforced through word repetition, is
the poem's most startling technical characteristic. Lawrence repeats references to
darkness and blueness throughout the poem. Forms of the word "dark" appear seven-
teen times in this nineteen-line poem. It seems as if Lawrence is straining the re-
sources of the language to suggest an ultimate darkness, a darkness beyond the power
of visual imagery. He refers to "the darker and darker stairs, where blue is darkened on
blueness"; the world is a blind one, a "sightless realm where darkness is awake upon
the dark." The references to the color blue come from the gentians' natural color, but
the use of blue darkness rather than black allows Lawrence to charge the description
with vitality. This underworld is not a realm of lifelessness, nor is its darkness anti-
thetical to light in the sense of knowledge or awareness. Thus the "torch-like" flowers
offer a "blaze of darkness." The oxymoron of "torches of darkness, shedding dark-
ness" is crucial to the poem: The darkness attains some of the metaphorical properties
of light. The darkness can illuminate, in contrast to "Demeter's pale lamps." All the
intense, even hyperbolic imagery of darkness contrasts with the staid quality of the
opening lines: "in soft September, at slow, sad Michaelmas."

The use of assonance and alliteration is as blatant and forceful as the use of imag-
ery, as the line above suggests. The *d* and *k* sounds of the oft-repeated "dark" initiate a
good deal of alliteration. In one three-line sequence, Lawrence uses "day," "daze,"
"Dis" (another term for Pluto or his underworld), and "darkness." The *oo* assonance
of the "blueness of Pluto's gloom" is similarly prominent, and a link to the words that
end the last two lines: "gloom" and "groom" (in this otherwise unrhyming poem). The
word repetition, blatant imagery of darkness and light, and prominent assonance and
alliteration all create a poem with a potent emotional and poetic charge. Lawrence is
not striving for a natural, speechlike level of diction, though his word choice is also
not elevated in the sense of traditional poetic diction. The reader enters a world of po-
etry and myth, but by descent, not ascent, and the language reflects this new poetic
territory of a celebrated netherworld.

Themes and Meanings

The poem presents several paradoxes: The darkness is illuminating; the dead un-
derworld possesses vitality; the reluctant journey of Persephone becomes the desired
journey of the speaker. These paradoxes are familiar ones for Lawrence, who saw
contemporary European society as overly cerebral and stripped of life-giving, primi-
tive physicality. Throughout his poetry and fiction, Lawrence espouses the virtues of
blood and earth: The spiritual is rooted in the bodily and the natural, not in the intel-
lectual (at least not in contemporary society, which has corrupted the intellectual).
"Bavarian Gentians" is wholly consistent with and expressive of this vision.

The opening lines identify the time of year not only as September but also as
Michaelmas, the Christian celebration of the Archangel Michael held on September
29. Significantly, this Christian reference falls in the lines set above ground in the bar-
ren world of deserted Demeter. Against this lone Christian allusion, Lawrence places

a plethora of pagan images, which he associates with life and sexuality. This contrast identifies the central tension of the poem: between those respectable European and Christian forces of the staid aboveground world and the seething vitality Lawrence locates within the earth and through pagan mythology.

Poet and speaker value the existence of passion in Pluto's kingdom, signified by Pluto's original desire for Persephone and its continued enactment. Enfolded Persephone is "pierced with the passion," and the subterranean world is a place of consummated desire. The sexually charged language of the poem suggests repressed or forbidden pleasures located in the underworld kingdom. Even the "ribbed and torch-like" flowers have phallic connotations (as they clearly do in an earlier version of the poem, in which Lawrence calls them "ribbed hellish flowers erect").

The descent into underground darkness has a psychological quality, as well. The speaker's longing to explore the darkness that lies beneath the somber autumn may well signify a journey into the repressed subconscious. The desires and longings that cannot stand the light of day are here illuminated by the gentians' dark blueness. Lawrence himself resisted Freudian terms, but his project was clearly one of recovery of the repressed. Like Freud, he saw basic human drives and passions distorted by the demands of social propriety. The descent into the underworld as a descent into the subconscious is a distinctively modern theme, and "Bavarian Gentians" is a powerful example of it.

The poem remains ambiguous about what the speaker actually gains from the underworld journey. Indeed, he is a sort of wedding guest at the Plutonic nuptial rites, and he remains an outsider. It is worth remembering that the poem is cast as an invocation: "lead the way," he cries; "let me guide myself." The poem presents the imaginative longing for an entrance into the underworld, an account of rather than the experience itself; however, the very action of the poet's imagination in giving life to the desired experience becomes a kind of experience or journey. That poetry and mythology might point the direction for revivifying humanity is typically Lawrentian. So is the ambiguity, for Lawrence's vision of a world free of the repressions of sterile modernity was never conceived as a wholly literary project. It must, Lawrence believed, be lived.

The poem was written in Lawrence's last year, and, as an imaginative exploration of the afterlife, it could well be read as a study of the poet's own encounter with mortality. Indeed, that theme appears explicitly in other poems written by Lawrence in this period. In "Bavarian Gentians," the celebratory tone and the impassioned vision of underworld vitality suggest an imaginative coming-to-terms with death.

Christopher Ames

THE BEACONS

Author: Charles Baudelaire (1821-1867)
Type of poem: Ode
First published: 1857, as "Les Phares," in *Les Fleurs du mal*; English translation collected in *Baudelaire: His Prose and Poetry*, 1919

The Poem

"The Beacons" uses a catalog of artists to illustrate the relation of the artist to humanity and to God. It is the sixth poem in Charles Baudelaire's principal collection, *Les Fleurs du mal*, set early in "Spleen et idéal" ("Spleen and Ideal"), a section that examines the competing drives of willful degradation and artistic elevation.

In the original French, the poem was written in eleven quatrains using Alexandrines, twelve-syllable lines traditionally chosen for elevated subjects. The rhymes follow a simple, alternating *abab* pattern. The title, which can mean watch fires, as well as beacons, is echoed and explained in the tenth stanza. Each of the eight artists addressed in the first eight stanzas is characterized as a beacon, a warning or guide, in the darkness.

Each of the first eight quatrains addresses and defines the work of a sculptor or painter drawn from periods ranging from the Italian Renaissance through the nineteenth century. The first stanza is dedicated to Flemish artist Peter Paul Rubens, whose work evokes a river of forgetfulness, a garden of indolence, a pillow of flesh, all images of detached opulence. On this pillow of flesh no one can love, although life flows and moves in it.

In the second quatrain, Leonardo da Vinci is a profound, dark mirror where charming, sweetly smiling angels, weighed down with mystery, appear in the shadow of glaciers and pines which enclose their world. Rembrandt is presented as a sad hospital, filled with murmurs, decorated with a great crucifix, where weeping prayer rises from filth, a dark space slashed by a ray of winter light. The fourth quatrain presents the Italian sculptor and painter Michelangelo. His work is a vague place where one sees (pagan) Hercules figures mixed with Christs, where powerful phantoms rise straight up in twilight, tearing their shrouds.

In a break from the general pattern, the fifth stanza names its artist in the last line and addresses him directly. Pierre Puget, French Baroque painter and sculptor, is presented in terms of emotions—boxers' angers and fauns' impudence. A figure of contradictions, he found beauty in the lower classes, had a great heart, yet was swollen with pride, a sickly, yellow man, the melancholy emperor of convicts.

In the sixth quatrain, Antoine Watteau evokes a mad carnival, where hearts wander like butterflies in flames. Fresh and light surroundings are illuminated by lamps that pour madness on spinning dancers. The images are graceful but terrifying, tainted by flame and madness. The seventh stanza, dedicated to Francisco de Goya, presents visions drawn from a witches' Sabbath, a nightmare where fetuses are cooked and old women and naked children tempt demons.

Eugène Delacroix is a lake of blood, haunted by bad angels, shadowed by a wood where strange fanfares pass under a troubled sky. The fanfares are compared to a stifled sigh from the music of Carl Maria von Weber. With these two figures, Baudelaire brings his catalog of immortal artists from the past to his own contemporaries.

The ninth and tenth stanzas join the individual qualities of these artists in their general human character; they are maledictions, blasphemies, complaints, ecstasies, cries, tears, Te Deums. The catalog of terms which takes up the first two lines of the ninth stanza is resumed in the third line as an echo repeated by a thousand labyrinths, multiple, repeated, and confined in the most elaborate of traps. The fourth line calls these voices a divine opium, both a deadener of pain and an agent of dreams. The tenth stanza expands their role to a means of escape or rescue from danger, a sentinel cry repeated a thousandfold, an order sent along by a thousand messengers, a beacon lit on a thousand citadels, a cry of hunters lost in great woods.

The eleventh stanza addresses God directly, qualifying the united witness of the great artists as proof of human dignity in suffering and passion, one sob rolling as a wave to die out on the border of eternity.

Forms and Devices

Charles Baudelaire used verse, couched in traditional form, to express personal anguish and aspirations in a way that made him a model for new generations of poets. In "The Beacons," the poet uses the Alexandrine verse and a regular rhyme scheme. The rhetorical pattern of the poem is regular as well. All but one of the eight first stanzas begin with a proper name. Only one is addressed directly (Puget); the others are treated as objective examples through their works. The parallel construction of these seven stanzas emphasizes the deviation of the fifth stanza. In this one stanza, emotion is emphasized. The poet's own emotions and the emotions expressed in his works are described. Here the reader is invited to pause and contemplate the figure of an unhappy invalid who combines qualities from the highest and lowest strata of human societies ("emperor of convicts").

Although the first eight stanzas are treated independently, none is an independent sentence. They do not end until the ninth stanza, where they are resumed as "these curses, these blasphemies." Baudelaire uses the mechanism of repetition on several levels. The repeated parallel structure of the first eight stanzas is the most obvious example, but in the first two lines of the ninth stanza he uses the repetitive catalog of verbal complaint forms. In the ninth and tenth stanzas the poet employs repeated parallel grammatical constructions and repeats the word "thousand" four times. The cumulative effect of these multiple repetitions on a formal level reinforces the theme of echo and multiplicity, the swelling wave of voices rolling onward toward God's eternity.

Themes and Meanings

Baudelaire constantly scrutinizes the role of the poet and artist in human society. "Benediction," the poem that opens "Spleen and Ideal," shows the poet rejected at birth by his mother, reviled by the world, but sustained by the aid of an angel and his own devout aspirations. "The Beacons" presents a number of artists whose works made them spokesmen for humanity. Among them, Puget stars in the role of unhappy artist; he is clearly presented as joining the sublime and sordid aspects of humanity. Not only does the formal structure of the fifth stanza set Puget apart, but he is treated differently thematically, with the themes and emotions of his work brought to the forefront.

The poet Baudelaire was also a music enthusiast and was as well known for his art criticism as for his verse, particularly for his essays on the Paris salons of 1845, 1846, and 1859. His address to the great masters in "The Beacons" comes from a connoisseur of the fine arts as well as literature. In "The Beacons," Baudelaire associates varied sensual images, speaking of the works of visual artists in terms of scent, sound, light, and form.

Light and shadow are evoked throughout the poem. In the first stanza, both the river and cool flesh are reflective surfaces for a certain kind of light. The second stanza brings the contrast of light and shadow, with a mirror (essentially a reflective surface) qualified as profound and somber. Rembrandt's dark world is cut through by winter light, cold but powerful in its contrast. The third stanza, however, emphasizes smell and hearing, with a sharp contrast of sublime and sordid elements, into which light intrudes abruptly.

In Michelangelo, the quality of the light is attenuated, vague, and dusky. The atmosphere is ambiguous, threatening with its evocation of physical power and suffering (both Hercules and Christ died in horrible torment), its linking of ancient mythology with Christian themes.

In the sixth stanza, Watteau's light is hectic, the light of flaming butterflies or of lamps which pour madness on the dancers below. Here light implies color with the images of a carnival, of butterflies, of fresh and light settings. Goya's world, dark as a Black Sabbath, still has a light-reflective mirror and the naked flesh of children, while Delacroix's lake of blood, with its combination of liquid surface and deep color, is shaded by more color, the evergreen fir wood. The common quality of shade from evergreen woods echoes the light effect of the da Vinci stanza.

The ninth and tenth stanzas unite all these evocations of visual images with scent and sound, including Puget's emotions, in a blend of impressions. They are finally transmuted into vocal expressions, both curses and Te Deums. The poet's accomplishment, to transform the visual arts into words, is made explicit in these stanzas.

Only the third line of the tenth stanza, the image of the beacon light, remains visual, and from this line the poet took his title. As the reader is drawn back to the title, he must acknowledge the unity imposed on apparently episodic or particular material. All these voices (with full consciousness of the synesthetic union of visual and vocal) are gathered into one, just as the poem is gathered into one great cry, and this wave is thrown forward as witness toward God and His eternity.

Art lends a measure of immortality to the individual; Baudelaire recognizes this in his choice of a range of artists readily recognized and venerated by the public. "The Beacons" argues that great artists lend a voice to humanity and plead eternally for human dignity.

Anne W. Sienkewicz

THE BEAR

Author: Galway Kinnell (1927-   )
Type of poem: Lyric
First published: 1968, in *Body Rags*

The Poem

Galway Kinnell's poem "The Bear" consists of seven numbered sections of varying lengths that explore the disquieting relationship between the rational and instinctual selves. In the opening section, the speaker adopts the persona of a hunter seeking to "know" and thus pursue his prey, a bear that figuratively represents the primal self. As it progresses, the poem constructs and develops an elaborate metaphor in which the poet compares the spontaneous and untamed corners of the self to its more rational regions, those which infuse raw experience with order and meaning. The poem's central image, a bear foraging the primeval wilderness for food, represents the unbridled, animalistic self in action. In deliberate contrast, the speaker embodies the rational self, which through the transformative experience of composing a poem seeks to integrate all aspects of consciousness, both reflective and intuitive, into a unified whole.

Despite its markedly introspective subject matter, "The Bear" follows a traditional narrative structure, borrowing as much from the short story as it does from the traditional lyric poem. The opening three sections establish a conflict and its two adversaries—a starving but driven speaker and the elusive wild bear that is for him the source of both physical and emotional sustenance. In section 1 the speaker detects the bear's proximity, recognizing in "some fault in the old snow" its "chilly, enduring odor." By the end of the second section, the speaker is in determined pursuit, "dragging [himself] forward with bear-knives in [his] fists." Despite the extreme challenges he faces in stalking such daunting prey, he remains driven to "rise/ and go on running."

In section 4, the speaker finally encounters his prey. To this point the poem has characterized the animal as strong and vital, a source of energy from which the speaker has gained increasing personal strength and resoluteness as his pursuit has narrowed. Ironically, by the time he actually sees the bear, nothing of its former stature and promise remains except an "upturned carcass"; his voracious pursuit has drained the animal completely of its life force. The speaker describes his once-awesome nemesis as "a scraggled,/ steamy hulk,/ the heavy fur riffling in the wind."

After this narrative climax, the poem takes a distinctively metaphysical turn, abandoning its intense physical immediacy and becoming more abstract and introspective. At the end of section 4, the speaker attempts to fully internalize his prey, "hack[ing]/ a ravine in [the bear's] thigh," into which he climbs for shelter "against the wind." The beast's body is described as a kind of impenetrable sanctuary of comfort and resolution that allows the speaker to fully isolate himself from his own consciousness of himself. Curiously, however, the speaker does not take the ultimate step and fully metamorphose into the bear. Instead, a powerful wind that symbolizes self-awareness, the one characteristic no human being can fully shed, forcefully ejects him from the bear's carcass and "blows off/ the hideous belches of ill-digested bear blood" the speaker has willingly but haplessly allowed to permeate his being. The speaker emerges from the encounter able to "dance," thus embracing the reconciliation between his formerly adversarial selves.

Forms and Devices

"The Bear" is structured cyclically, reflecting a common motif in Kinnell's poetry. Poets who work in free verse often face the challenge of sustaining rhythmical unity in a form that is by its nature more organic and abstract than traditional poetic structures. In "The Bear," however, Kinnell achieves and maintains an exceptional coherence by employing a host of familiar cyclical images, including the seven-day cycle of the biblical Creation story. The poem contains seven sections, in which the speaker's quest for the bear lasts seven days. This echoes the Judeo-Christian account of Creation, in which it takes God seven days to create the world and impose order on primeval chaos. Adopting such a familiar idea suggests that the speaker's quest for inner resolution is not merely a personal one but also one that has more universal, mythic dimensions.

The diction of "The Bear" also stands out as one of its most distinctive technical features. In innovative and insightful fashion, Kinnell uses an ample amount of visceral, even scatological language in a poem that is conversely metaphysical in temper. This unexpected juxtaposition uniquely underscores the conflicts between mind and spirit, between primal and rational selves, around which the poem centers. "The Bear" is permeated with memorable physical imagery, particularly in its opening sections. Images of body excretions, organs, and functions—both animal and human—pervade the first three segments. The speaker is first made aware of the bear's proximity by "lung-colored" steam rising from the earth. To entice the animal into revealing itself, he places "a wolf's rib" frozen in "blubber" into its path. When he at last sees the bear's footprints, punctuated by "splashes/ of blood," he springs into a pursuit as ferocious and instinctual as any of which his adversary might be capable. This fittingly suggests that as the hunter nears his prey, it is he who becomes the animal—summoning within himself the capacity to blindly and instinctively stalk and kill, an absolute requisite for self-preservation. To transport the reader more convincingly into this experience, Kinnell chooses imagery and language that are in themselves both tacit and brutal.

The image that commands perhaps the keenest attention in "The Bear" occurs in section 3, just before the speaker finally sees the animal. Starved, but intensely aware that the climax of his quest is at hand, the speaker bends down "at a turd sopped in blood," picks it up, and "thrust[s] it in [his] mouth," only then rising to "go on running." Many poets might shy away from such unabashed vulgarity, fearing that the sheer baseness of this image might alienate the reader. However, Kinnell employs it here precisely because it is both memorable and unsavory. It is thus even more effective, since the poem's chief concern is the process of shedding everything human, everything decorous, in an attempt to reconnect with that part of the psyche that is preconscious, unfettered, animalistic.

Themes and Meanings

Kinnell's poems are known widely for their attempt to explore conflicts between the human and natural world, a world humans paradoxically feel both part of and separate from. Poems such as "The Bear" acknowledge a significant paradox imbedded in human nature—that humans are simultaneously subject to the contradictory demands of rational and irrational drives. Kinnell chooses a bear, a recognizable and forceful image, to represent the preconscious, instinctual side of the self that the rational mind is charged with keeping in check. How it is able to do this is the focus of the poem.

For centuries, poets have embraced what they see as an inherent physical and perhaps spiritual kinship between humans and animals. In contrast, the Western philosophical tradition has sought to eradicate categorically this intuitive connection, championing "consciousness" as a capacity that separates humans entirely from their animal kin. That humans are able to think, which is evinced by the ability to exchange ideas with other human beings through language, has traditionally suggested that human intuitive affinity with animals is ill-conceived and misguided.

However, poets such as Kinnell have never been satisfied with such a wholesale dismissal of the human being's relationship to the natural world. After all, even if one's mind is immaterial, it must be housed in a physical body, a "scraggled,/ steamy hulk" from which it cannot free itself without annihilating itself. In the logic of "The Bear," it therefore follows that if one seeks to be more human one must embrace the intuitive, irrational dynamics of the self rather than reject them. Kinnell's poem looks to the behavior of that most primeval of animals, the wild bear, as a source of understanding of one's own preconscious dimension—what Carl Jung called the *animus*.

In "The Bear," the speaker figuratively identifies with his own "bear-ness" in the most extreme and meaningful way possible. In a singular act of imaginative transformation, he projects himself into the bear's world by attempting to fully internalize the animal. When merely tracking the beast fails to satisfy him he eats the bear's blood-soaked feces, hoping that through this ritualistic act he may draw some of the animal's life force, its *animus*, into himself. When he actually locates the animal, nothing is left of it but a decaying carcass framed only by "narrow-spaced, petty eyes." Still, the speaker is undeterred—he gains further internal resolution by cutting the bear open and crawling inside to sleep "And dream/ of lumbering flatfooted/ over the tundra," just as the living animal itself would. Through this act he absorbs into his own being the bear's raw, primeval energy.

In its broader context, "The Bear" also comments on the nature of poetry, which is in itself merely a formal manifestation of the transformative capacity and will of the human imagination. In its final couplet, the poem refers to the speaker's encounter with the bear as "that/ poetry, by which I lived," suggesting that it is a poem very much about the process of making and experiencing poems. A poem such as "The Bear" offers both writer and reader an invitation to connect more vitally with their primal, intuitive selves–a process that indeed is the "poetry" by which humans all live.

Gregory D. Horn

BEARDED OAKS

Author: Robert Penn Warren (1905-1989)
Type of poem: Lyric
First published: 1942, in *Eleven Poems on the Same Theme*

The Poem

The title "Bearded Oaks" calls to mind the image of moss-draped stands of trees in the American South. As with many short lyric poems, Robert Penn Warren's poem uses its title to identify the object with which the poet's meditation begins and around which his meaning develops. As objects of immediate perception, the oaks serve as a focal element in the complex of imagery and metaphor that Warren develops. As icons of the idealized past specific to the South, the oaks of the title anticipate the poem's general concern with loss and the claims of history.

The four-line stanzas—quatrains—coupled with a somewhat irregular *abab* rhyme scheme give the poem a visual signature that alerts the reader that the poem is likely to include such traditional formal poetic devices as metaphor and ambiguity. The poetic voice is characteristically lyric: Observations are related in the first person in a manner that implies immediacy of reflection. A second person is present but is not addressed directly until stanza 9: "I do not love you less." Either the reader is overhearing the address or has been implicated in the poem's pronoun "we."

In stanzas 1 to 4, the poet and his companion lie beneath the oaks and hanging moss, through which filter the day's last light. The sensuous surroundings—the "languorous" light and swaying grass—encourage the reader to see the two figures as lovers. A second set of images describes the two lying on the bottom of the darkening sea—"the floor of light and time"—silent and still, similar to coral "atolls" created over "ages" by the work of communities of individual "polyps." Although the lovers are both unmoving and "unmurmuring" and are subjected to a somewhat unflattering comparison with marine invertebrates, there is as yet no reason to see their situation as in any way tragic.

Halfway through the fourth stanza, however, the past ceases to be an orderly unfolding of architectural form. Lines 15 to 24 describe a violent storm at the height of the day, whose effects are still faintly touching the seafloor, where darkness is now spreading. The real objects of the poem's opening scene become secondary, replaced by the metaphoric images of the sea. The sixth stanza further develops the idea that the light above the trees is a storm raging on the ocean surface and provides human terms into which the metaphor can be translated. Intense emotion ("passion") and physical extinction ("slaughter") filter down to the ocean floor, along with their aftereffects—"ruth" (regret) and "decay"—where they are somehow responsible for the silent repose of the lovers. The emotional cause and effect described by these images recalls Emily Dickinson's poem "After great pain, a formal feeling comes—." Mere quiet has become "voicelessness."

Stanza 7 has the effect of concluding the previous six stanzas. The literal setting of the poem and its imaginative elaboration in the metaphor of the sea are both replaced by formal logic that struggles against the paradox of "hope is hopeless" and "fearless is fear" and by the somewhat oracular assertion "And history is undone." The inarticulate and inert state of the poet and his companion has now a larger significance: Quiet bliss seems an absence of vitality uncomfortably akin to death.

Abruptly in stanza 8, the poem restarts itself with another image from the poet's memory. The lines might almost begin another poem, for the poet does not reveal why the moment springs to mind. The scene is an empty street where footsteps echo among darkened windows after the couple's car headlights have frightened away a female deer. Both events recall a period prior to the poet's present impasse and seem somehow connected to it, for the deer, so alive and animate in the flash of light, leaves behind only the "hollow street" with its hints of the "shelf of shade" to come.

In stanza 9, the poet claims love is possible in a state that stills the feelings that normally accompany it. The cryptic final stanza explains how this paradox is possible. There, also, the constellation of silence, stillness, and dark that hints at death is also finally identified explicitly with "eternity." These difficult lines suggest that humans live in mortal time only briefly and that human knowledge of life, including love, is gained with such effort that the duration of an hour can be given over to the easeful anticipation of eternity, even at the expense of human relations. The lines further imply, however, that it is the value of that scarce earthly time that gives meaning to the hour devoted to experiencing eternity.

Forms and Devices

Complex and extended metaphor is typical of Warren's early poetry, as is his use of paradox and fragmented and inverted sentences. These features give his work the flavor of Metaphysical poems such as Andrew Marvell's "To His Coy Mistress" and John Donne's "The Compass." In "Bearded Oaks," the marine metaphor explicitly transforms part of the literal surface of the poem and is then interrupted by the abstract ruminations of the poet on history, love, time, and eternity. These elements work to set up a series of oppositions that describe two states of being.

The literal level of the poem, the physical setting, consists of the poet speaking while gazing toward the light through the oaks and moss above him. The beginning of the translation into metaphor is signaled by "kelp-like" and concludes with the logic and argument of stanza 7. History stops beneath the trees' limbs, where darkness, stillness, voicelessness, and calcified separateness describe the poet and his companion. Above the oaks are light, animation, sound, and emotional vitality. These two states of illumination are tied to the second literal setting of the poem in stanza 8. The remembered images of the startled doe fleeing the car's headlights and of the darkened street reprise the contrast between dark and light.

With the philosophical tone of the last two stanzas, the abstract terms "love" and "eternity" reconceive the problem of what the world of light and the world of dark mean. They are now evaluated according to whether the poet's love is preserved, and the dark, in which light's qualities are revoked, is redeemed by the proposal that immersion in it may be preparation for eternity.

Meaning develops in the poem through the mutual definition of the literal setting and the metaphor of sea and polyps and through their connection to the street and the doe. Although the literal and the metaphoric can be distinguished, that distinction is blurred as the poem evolves, while the emergent realms of light and dark resist being fully explained and interpreted by the abstract passages in the poem. Image, metaphor, and abstraction, then, are not only making meaning in "Bearded Oaks" but also represent meaning itself and the imperfect relations among objects, vision, and intellect.

Themes and Meanings

Warren was concerned in much of his early poetry with the loss of innocence and with the acquisition of self-knowledge in a world of historical contingency where perfect knowledge and an Edenic sense of unity—of oneness between the self and the world—do not exist but are vaguely recalled. He said in "Knowledge and The Image of Man" (1955) that humankind's very process of self-definition is "the discovery of separateness" but that it moves beyond this state: "Man eats of the tree of life and falls. But if he takes another bite, he may get at least a sort of redemption." To "take another bite" is to accept fully humankind's fallen state and to undertake the process of making meaning and knowledge through the perpetual oscillation between the states that Warren calls "doing" and "seeing." Each modifies the other; doing changes what a person is and how he or she sees, thus changing what will be seen, what will be done, and other actions and reactions. To be fixed in the state of seeing or of doing is to suffer the extinction of identity—to become either a chain of acts without the form of identity or an outline of identity lacking acts to give it substance.

In "Bearded Oaks," the poetic self rests in a state of seeing, having withdrawn from the world of light and of making and doing. The suspended state of seeing is not Edenic. The poet, after all, is separate from his love; they are both constructs of history, and neither can ever fully enter the other's heart and mind. For separateness even to be known, however, requires that one have some experience of unity. The fleeting glimpse of the doe—beautiful and unconscious—stands for the momentary inkling of oneness in a world otherwise echoing human beings' own footsteps and isolation back to them. If one pursues a reading of "Bearded Oaks" that acknowledges Warren's views on separateness, identity, and knowledge, then the last stanzas suggest that love is not extinguished in a world that does not allow perfect emotional expression and understanding. Rather than being extinguished, love as human beings know it becomes possible. In "Birches," Robert Frost, too, states that "Earth's the right place for love." Love is identified so strongly with separateness and action in "Bearded Oaks" that the last stanza seems almost an apology for the visionary and reflective state from which the poet writes.

Out of its multiple thematic concerns and its carefully wrought formal tension between objects, metaphor, and intellect, "Bearded Oaks" speaks to the human conviction that the life of the heart and the mind is imperfectly related to the world outside it. The poem urges the reader, nevertheless, to find meaning and redemption in the earthly state.

Peter Lapp

A BEAUTIFUL YOUNG NYMPH GOING TO BED

Author: Jonathan Swift (1667-1745)
Type of poem: Satire
First published: 1734, in *"A Beautiful Young Nymph Going to Bed, Written for the Honour of the Fair Sex"; To Which Are Added, "Strephon and Chloe," and "Cassinus and Peter"*

The Poem

Jonathan Swift's ironically entitled "A Beautiful Young Nymph Going to Bed," composed in 1731 and puckishly subtitled "Written for the Honour of the Fair Sex," reflects the relentless, emphatically unromantic, and savagely satirical vision that marks the later years of Swift's art. This most unpoetic of poems presents the uproarious process by means of which an eighteenth century London prostitute prepares for sleep—a process which involves her divesting herself of those various artifices with which she seeks to disguise both her physical and moral corruption. "Corinna," Swift's broad caricature of a Drury Lane bawd, is here portrayed in the privacy of her shabby bedchamber. The poet etches three separate portraits of Corinna: her preparations for bed (lines 1-38), her fitful dreams (lines 39-59), and her waking to personal disaster (lines 58-64). The "I" of a first-person narrator—Swift himself?—then intrudes (lines 65-74) to provide moral commentary on the composition as a whole.

The detailed description of Corinna's ritualistic undressing is essentially a revelation of the various artful deceptions by means of which she establishes her outward appearance. Indeed, nearly all her dubious charms, it turns out, are factitious: her hair, for example, is a wig; one eye is glass; her eyebrows have been crafted from the skins of mice; the bountiful curves of her figure are supplied by padding and a "Steel-Rib'd Bodice"; and all her teeth are false. More to the point, these deceptive cosmetic devices seek, however imperfectly, to conceal a physical reality that is distinctly repulsive and disgusting; her denuded body is tainted, for example, by "Shankers [cancerous growths], Issues, [and] running Sores"—the results, no doubt, of the "pox" and other venereal diseases, inevitable and disfiguring occupational hazards for this woman of the streets.

These sexually transmitted "pains of love" similarly disturb Corinna's sleep, and her dreams are dominated by horrific images of what, for her, are very real life possibilities, including the terrifying prospect of debtors' prison ("the Compter"), corporal punishment, and forced deportation to distant colonies. She dreams as well of other threats that beset her waking life—the clients who abandon her with tavern bills to pay, the police who pursue her, and the bill collectors who shadow her every step. The harlot finds some consolation, however, in dreaming about members of the clergy (denizens of "Religious Clubs"), with whom she enjoys steady, if illicit, business.

Corinna awakens to a real, not imagined, calamity. Overnight, her elaborate disguise has been defiled by household vermin: her glass eye stolen by a rat, her wig infested with her dog's fleas, and her "Plumpers" soiled by her incontinent cat. Confronting her "mangled Plight," Corinna strives to reassemble the scattered and polluted parts of her artificial self, observed by a first-person narrator, who, while remarking on her "Anguish, Toil, and Pain," nonetheless reminds his audience that Corinna is a kind of walking contagion at loose in the city of London.

Forms and Devices

"A Beautiful Young Nymph Going to Bed" is composed of heroic couplets, a series of rhymed line pairs written in iambic tetrameter. This form is very old and common in English, having been introduced into the language in the Middle Ages by Geoffrey Chaucer (c. 1343-1400) and adopted widely thereafter, notably by Swift's cousin John Dryden (1631-1700) and by his celebrated friend Alexander Pope (1688-1744), the device's absolute master. What is startling and remarkable about Swift's poem, therefore, is not its form but rather its diction (word choice) and tone (the scathing attitude that Swift brings to his subject matter and that he conveys to his audience).

The poem's language is notable, first, for its overt and premeditated ugliness: Corinna's physicality is described in a manner calculated to disgust and even nauseate. (Indeed, Swift's friend Laetitia Pilkington is said to have vomited when she first heard "The Lady's Dressing Room," a companion poem to "A Beautiful Young Nymph," claiming that it had collected "all the dirty ideas in the world in one piece.") Moreover, the poem's diction—even when it seems to strive for beauty—unsettles its audience by flying in the face of a long tradition of lyric poetry writing, such as that practiced in the preceding century by the so-called Cavalier poets, such as Thomas Carew (1594 or 1595-1640) and Robert Herrick (1591-1674). In their poems, women are habitually praised for their (perhaps imaginary) charms. In Swift's poem, conversely, there exists a yawning, deeply ironic discrepancy between occasionally elevated, romanticized language on one hand and a degraded subject matter on the other. For example, when Corinna is referred to as a "lovely Goddess," or when her sty of an apartment is loftily called "her Bow'r," Swift intends his audience to understand the satiric gap he has excavated, for comic effect, between words and realities.

All this is an instance of form following function, or of diction following satiric purpose. Swift's poem is often ugly precisely because, to him, its subject, Corinna, is both morally and physically ugly. It is no accident that the harlot's appliances are soiled by vermin: The animal imagery that pervades this passage makes an implicit connection between the bestial and the bawdy. The unremitting ugliness of Swift's language, in other words, perfectly fits his attitude of outright revulsion toward the poem's protagonist and toward all the human deceptions, vanities, and lusts that she represents.

Themes and Meanings

"A Beautiful Young Nymph Going to Bed" is commonly linked by critics to three other so-called "excremental poems" by Swift—"The Lady's Dressing Room," "Strephon and Chloe," and "Cassinus and Peter"—all produced by the poet during 1730 and 1731. While there exist important thematic differences among these poems, they are certainly similar in their overt physicality and, more important, in their common assault on deception. Swift's mad persona in *A Tale of a Tub* (1704) observes that happiness resides in "a perpetual Possession of being well Deceived," but it is the role of satirists everywhere to compel their audience to look beyond those comfortable constructs by which humans customarily seek to delude themselves into a facile state of contentment. "A Beautiful Young Nymph Going to Bed," accordingly, aims at stripping away such obfuscation by depicting the rank grossness of human flesh when it is divested of all ornament and is operating in its natural state.

Indeed, any temptation to sympathize with the downtrodden, much-victimized Corinna inevitably runs up against Swift's conception of both God and humankind. For Swift, God is a largely unapproachable, unspeakably transcendent being who created the world and left behind certain commandments, laws that establish minimal requirements of human behavior. In Swift's view, Corinna and her clients clearly fall short of those moral standards, to the point that the harlot poses an outright danger to the community.

Further, any sympathetic response to Corinna and her troubles must first be grounded in seeing her as a real human being. However, this particular prostitute's ills are so calamitous—and her prosthetic efforts after beauty are so patently absurd— that she calls forth much more laughter than empathy. While any person might rightly respond sympathetically toward a "beautiful nymph" with, say, a glass eye, that milk becomes distinctly clabbered when the reader learns that the same woman is bald, crafts her eyebrows from mouse skins, has no teeth, props up her breasts with rags, and wears a steel-ribbed corset and artificial hips. In short, her farcical portrayal in the poem is so purposefully and grotesquely overdone as to effectively block any empathetic response.

However, while Corinna may not be "real," the hazards that she poses certainly are; paradoxically, the unreality of the harlot allows Corinna to be betrayed for what she really is—namely, a social menace. After all, her morning-after attempt to restore her mechanical, absurdly artificial body ultimately represents an effort at general contagion: "Corinna in the morning dizen'd,/ Who sees, will spew; who smells, be poison'd."

In short, Swift here presents what critic Nora Crow Jaffe termed a "pure invective against vice" and what Maurice Johnson called "the wages of sin . . . [like] a preacher shouting hell-fire and brimstone, or the photographs in a medical treatise." Indeed, to the degree that Swift succeeds in disgusting his audience through his graphic depiction of Corinna, he succeeds as well in accomplishing his thematic and moral purposes in this disturbing poem.

William Ryland Drennan

BECAUSE I COULD NOT STOP FOR DEATH

Author: Emily Dickinson (1830-1886)
Type of poem: Lyric
First published: 1890, in *Poems*

The Poem

In "Because I could not stop for Death," one of the most celebrated of any poems Emily Dickinson wrote, the deceased narrator reminisces about the day Death came calling on her. In the first stanza, the speaker remarks that she had been too busy to stop for Death, so in his civility, he stopped for her. In his carriage, she was accompanied by Immortality as well as Death. Many readers have wanted to know why Immortality also rides in the carriage, but when thinking of the courting patterns in Dickinson's day, one recalls the necessity of a chaperon. In any event, Dickinson considers Death and Immortality fellow travelers. This interaction with Death shows the complete trust that the speaker had placed in her wooer. It is not until the end of the poem, from the perspective of Eternity, that one is able to see behind the semblance of Death. Far from being the gentlemanly caller that he appears to be, Death is in reality a ghoulish seducer. Perhaps Dickinson, in her familiarity with the Bible, draws upon Satan's visitation of God in similar pose as a country gentleman. In this way, Dickinson's poem resembles the Gothic novel, a popular Romantic genre given to the sinister and supernatural.

In the second stanza, the reader learns that the journey was leisurely and that the speaker did not mind the interruption from her tasks because Death was courteous. Along the way, they passed the children's school at recess time and fields of ripened grain. They even passed the setting sun—or rather, it passed them, so slow was their pace. With the coming of evening, a coolness had fallen for which the speaker found herself unprepared with regard to clothing. They drew near a cemetery, the place where the speaker has been dwelling for centuries. In the realm of Death, time has elapsed into centuries for the speaker, though it seems shorter than her last day of life when she first "surmised" that her journey was toward Eternity.

Forms and Devices

Tone, or the emotional stance of the speaker in the poem, is a central artifice in "Because I could not stop for Death." Though the subject is death, this is not a somber rendering. On the contrary, Death is made analogous to a wooer in what emerges as essentially an allegory, with abstractions consistently personified. Impressed by Death's thoughtfulness and patience, the speaker reciprocates by putting aside her work and free time. Judging by the last stanza, where the speaker talks of having "first surmised" their destination, it can be determined that Death was more seducer than beau. The tone of congeniality here becomes a vehicle for stating the proximity of death even in the thoroughfares of life, though one does not know it. Consequently, one is often caught unprepared. The journey motif is at the core of the poem's stratagem, a common device (as in poem 615, "Our Journey had Advanced") in Dickinson's poetry for depicting human mortality.

Stanza 3 offers an example of Dickinson's substantial capacity for compression, which on occasion can create a challenge for readers. This stanza epitomizes the circle of life, not so much as to life's continuity despite death, but more in fusion with the journey within the poem—life as procession toward conclusion. Thus, "the School, where Children strove" applies to childhood and youth. Dickinson's dictional acuity carries over to "Recess—in the Ring." Early life, with its sheltering from duress and breakdown and death, its distance in experience from the common fate, is but a deceptive lull—its own kind of seduction and, hence, recess from decline. Yet children are said to be in the "Ring." Time is on the move even for them, though its pace seems slow. Ironically, the dictional elements coalesce in the stanza to create a subrendering of the greater theme of the poem: the seduction of the persona by Death. The children are also without surmise, and like the speaker, they are too busy with themselves (as represented in the verb "strove") to know that time is passing.

Dictional nuance is critical to the meaning of the last two lines of the third stanza. The word "passed" sets up verbal irony (the tension of statement and meaning). The carriage occupants are not merely passing a motley collection of scenes, they are passing out of life—reaching the high afternoon of life, or maturity. Maturation, or adulthood, is also represented in the "Fields of Gazing Grain." This line depicts grain in a state of maturity, its stalk replete with head of seed. There is intimation of harvest and perhaps, in its gaze, nature's indifference to a universal process. Appropriately, the next line speaks of "the Setting Sun," meaning the evening of life, or old age.

Reiteration of the word "passed" occurs in stanza 4, emphasizing the idea of life as a procession toward conclusion. Its recurring use as a past-tense verb suggests the continuation of an action in the past, yet the noncontinuance of those actions in the present in keeping with the norms of the imperfect tense. Human generations will collectively engage in the three life stages, dropping out individually, never to engage in them again.

Dictional elements in stanza 5 hint at unpreparedness for death. The persona's gown was but "Gossamer," a light material highly unsuitable for evening chill. For a scarf ("Tippet"), she wore only silk netting ("Tulle").

The poem is written in alternating iambic tetrameter and trimeter lines, with near rhyme occasionally employed in the second and fourth lines. Regular rhyme occurs sporadically and unexpectedly in its spatial distancing. The use of the dash in the stanza's concluding line compels the reader to pause before entering into the monosyllabic prepositional phrase in which there is a heaviness that suggests the grave's finality. The seemingly disheveled rhyme scheme in actuality intimates one of the poem's central themes: unpreparedness.

Themes and Meanings

Death is a frequent concern of Dickinson's poetry. Often as a means to its exploration, she will seek its objectification through a persona who has already died. In other poems, she is quite sensitive to the fact of death and its impoverishment of those who remain. In some poems, she is resentful toward God, who robs people of those they love and is seemingly indifferent to such loss. One cannot explore the catalyst of life events behind Dickinson's marked sensitivity with any certainty because she lived a remarkably private life. For her, death was only one more form of distancing. As she wrote in poem 749: "All but Death can be Adjusted." Perhaps two of her most famous lines express it best: "Parting is all we know of heaven,/ And all we need of hell" (poem 1732).

Emily Dickinson was very familiar with death. Thirty-three of her acquaintances had died between February, 1851, and November, 1854, including her roommate at Holyoke College. Her mother's family seemed predisposed to early deaths. Then the momentous death of her father occurred in 1874. In 1882, eight years after the death of her father, she wrote that "no verse in the Bible has frightened me so much from a Child as 'from him that hath not, shall be taken even that he hath.' Was it because its dark menace deepened our own Door?"

Some may see this poem as conciliatory, even Christian, given that Immortality rides in the carriage and that the persona speaks of Eternity in the end. Death, by this notion, becomes God's emissary taking one into Eternity. For others, however, there is no resurrection, no specifying of an afterlife. Immortality is employed ironically, not to suggest everlasting life, but everlasting death. As a consort of death, one need not be puzzled by Immortality's presence in the carriage. This is the import of the final stanza, when the speaker exclaims, "Since then—'tis Centuries—and yet/ Feels shorter than the Day/ I first surmised the Horses Heads/ Were toward Eternity." There is a sense that the journey has never ended and never will. There is much eternity up ahead, for death is a realm without temporal-spatial parameters.

The truth is that life is short and death is long. Perhaps in this sobering truth one may find that Dickinson's poem is as much about life—about how one ought to redeem it from the banal—as it is about death.

Ralph Robert Joly

A BEDTIME STORY

Author: Mitsuye Yamada (1923-   )
Type of poem: Lyric
First published: 1976, in *Camp Notes and Other Poems*

The Poem

The narrative of Mitsuye Yamada's "A Bedtime Story" tells a story within a story. In the frame story an adult recalls a folktale that had been told as a bedtime story. The main part of the poem consists of that story, a Japanese legend about an elderly woman seeking shelter in rural villages. According to the tale, the old woman is refused entry at every household she approaches. Finally, growing exhausted, she lies down to rest in a clearing on a hilltop. All is dark in the sleeping village below, except for a few scattered lights. As the old woman is catching her breath, the moon appears between parted clouds. Upon seeing it, the woman addresses the sleeping villagers.

The final stanza returns to the frame story, as the speaker recollects the story-telling occasion. The speaker pictures the comfortable family home on a hillside in Seattle and remembers the father pausing right at the point in the story when the old woman thanks the villagers for refusing to give her hospitality, since being forced to stay outdoors has enabled her the privilege of seeing the full moon, a "memorable sight." Finally, the child's incredulous question ends the poem: Was that all there was?

Forms and Devices

The poem fuses lyric and meditative modes. The two stories that the speaker remembers—the frame story of recollection and the inner folktale—carry the statement to the moment of insight characteristic of the meditative mode. In keeping with the folktale at the heart of this poem, the language and form are austere and restrained. In forty-five short lines of free verse the speaker narrates the father's story without ornamentation or explanation. The poem's only figure of speech is the simile at its center comparing the lights of the sleeping village with the stars overhead.

The speaker opens with the traditional English folktale formula "Once upon a time," thus weaving the frame story within the legend. The language is detached, in keeping with the folktale emphasis. The villagers are implied in metonymy: Doors open themselves; the town sleeps. Only in the old woman's speech do "people/ of the village" enter the text. Subtle irony enters the poem at this point. The woman is said to have called out "in supplication"; however, her supplication for shelter was refused earlier, and her actual words are not suppliant but thankful.

More irony surfaces in her characterization of the villagers' rejection as "kindness" and continues with her reference to her "humble" eyes. The polite formula of humble eyes emphasizes that the old woman can see what the villagers cannot see and is therefore superior, both physically on the hilltop and morally in her insight, to the obtuse community. The poem's closing also invokes folklore formula. The English folktale traditionally closes with the formula "The end." In "A Bedtime Story," however, the phrase "the end" that concludes the poem is posed by the child as a question that is not explicitly answered. Thus, in spite of the poem's apparent simplicity and transparency, it is suffused with ambiguity and uncertainty.

Themes and Meanings

The outlines of the Japanese folktale in this poem are familiar in stories from many cultures. The motif of the "outsider" or the "thrown-away person" recurs throughout many oral traditions and frequently involves an elderly person, one who has no physical utility and who might be thought of as a liability to the village economy. As is also characteristic of traditional tales, this story offers rich possibilities for interpretation.

An initial interpretation might see the woman's attitude toward the villagers as merely rationalizing their inhospitable behavior. Instead of demanding humane conduct on their part she accepts their rudeness and then offers them the gift of her gratitude. Can the sight of a full moon really make up for and surpass the physical hunger, cold, and discomfort this old woman is forced to endure? This is one of the questions that the ending of the poem poses.

The question underscores the value of the old woman's wisdom, compared with the creature comforts of the imperceptive villagers. In return for their selfishness the old woman offers the villagers a gift, and indeed her "supplication" may be understood as virtually begging them to accept the gift of her insight. This reading of the poem brings into focus the parallel image contrasts of light and darkness, closeness and openness. The darkness of the village, where only a few lights shine, corresponds with the cramped lives of the villagers, who can open their doors only "a sliver" to respond to the woman's approach. The physical darkness and confinement figure the mental and spiritual narrowness of the self-centered villagers: Their minds are shut as tightly as their houses.

In contrast with this meanness of the valley-dwellers the fable offers the openness of the hilltop, where the old woman finds a "clearing" to rest in: The physical clearing on the earth parallels the parting of the clouds when the heavens clear to reveal the moon, as well as the subsequent physical and spiritual enlightenment she experiences.

Assigning the highest value to the woman's insight and her appreciation of the moon's beauty also subverts the ironic reading of the poem's ending and finds a moral dimension that transcends simple rationalization. The poem is about selfishness and generosity. The self-centered—or fearful—villagers can only admit a "sliver" of the external world. In contrast, the full moon shines "over the town": It is a gift that all the villagers might appreciate as the old woman does; however, the villagers by their own possessiveness deny themselves this generous gift of beauty.

The old woman's characterization of the sight of the full moon as "memorable" suggests another dimension in the story, the association of moral sensitivity and aesthetic appreciation. In the poem the woman's appreciation of the beauty of the moon parallels her sense of the importance of such qualities as gratitude, kindness, humility, and respect. Significantly, she does not call attention to the moon's beauty but rather characterizes the moon's appearance as something important to remember. Beauty may be transitory, but its memory is involved in the formation of character.

The phrase "memorable sight," which closes the father's telling of the story, also introduces the idea of the speaker's memory of the story. Memory is critical to the traditional function of oral tales like this, which are vehicles for the preservation and transmission of all knowledge in a culture without writing. In telling the story, the father becomes, like the old woman, a repository of wisdom engaged in transmitting that insight to an audience that is not entirely appreciative. The speaker, in revealing the story to readers of the poem, in turn takes on the father's role, offering the reader the same insight that the old woman is prepared to give to the villagers.

Because the poem is framed as the meditation of an adult, the childhood memory and memory in general become relevant to its overall meaning. The poem first appeared in a book titled *Camp Notes and Other Poems*. The camp of the title was a concentration camp in Idaho in which the author was imprisoned, with other Japanese residents and American citizens of Japanese descent, during World War II. Within that context, the poem is part of the whole collection's extended critique of injustice and lack of humanity. The experience of the old woman in the folktale, of abandonment, exile, and rejection, recapitulates the experience of internment for the author and her parents. Read in this manner, the poem itself becomes comparable with the old woman's vision of the moon. The poem, like the folktale that constitutes the bedtime story, is a message of enlightenment and the creation of beauty, and the villagers in the story can be seen as surrogates for the poem's readers, for whom the poem presents a similar occasion for either narrow-minded rejection or opening to insight.

The speaker cites no specific interpretation of the folktale but raises the question of how the child's and the adult's understanding of the story may be different. The child's frustration with the story's apparent inconclusiveness may mutate into the adult's sense of its multivalent potential for meaning. Thus the question at the end of the poem both concludes the story with the traditional formula of "the end" and opens it for continued reinterpretation and possibility.

Helen Jaskoski

BEFORE AN OLD PAINTING OF THE CRUCIFIXION

Author: N. Scott Momaday (1934-   )
Type of poem: Lyric
First published: 1965; collected in *Angle of Geese and Other Poems*, 1974

The Poem

"Before an Old Painting of the Crucifixion" by N. Scott Momaday is a poem divided into six stanzas, each with six verses. As a lyric poem, it is a variation of the Italian or Petrarchan sonnet usually defined as fourteen lines of iambic pentameter. Although differing in the number of stanzas and verses, "Before an Old Painting of the Crucifixion" retains the traditional iambic pentameter rhythm of the Italian sonnet and follows the most frequently used rhyme scheme of its second stanza, *abcabc*.

The title informs the reader of the subject of the poem, an old painting of Jesus Christ's Crucifixion. The title's opening word, "before," serves to position the reader with the poet, facing the painting. The subtitle or heading, "The Mission Carmel," defines the setting. Overlooking California's Monterey Bay, the Mission Carmel's landscape enhances the reader's appreciation of the poem.

The poem opens in the first person: "I ponder how He died, despairing once." By using the proper pronoun "He," the poet assumes familiarity with the narrative of Jesus Christ. Christ's despair is the focus of the first stanza. Momaday suggests that the stillness following Christ's anguish offers no comfort.

The second stanza continues the pondering of Christ's Crucifixion and death, using as its subject the "calm" introduced in the first stanza. This quiet following Christ's cry of despair is one where "no peace inheres but solitude." Momaday closes this stanza implying that not only the poet but also the artist(s) of the mural are incapable of comprehending Christ's agony. He writes, "Inscrutably itself, nor misconstrued,/ Nor metaphrased in art or pseudonym."

Momaday has now shifted the focus away from the actual Crucifixion and death to the painting itself, which becomes the subject of stanza 3. Momaday ends the first half of the poem by declaring, "The mural but implies eternity."

The remaining stanzas respond to the first three in a manner not unlike the Petrarchan sonnet (where the second stanza responds to the first). Returning to death in the fourth stanza, the poet joins the reader as he connects Christ's agony and despair with "our sorrow." Stanza 4 closes with Momaday's first criticism of the painting as he writes, "There shines too much a sterile loveliness." He is referring to the brightness of the blue sky in the mural as well as at the mission.

As evening shadows approach the mural in stanza 5, the visual "Passion" (or Crucifixion story) becomes less apparent. Both the approaching darkness and the centuries that have passed since the mural was painted are "of little consequence." In response to stanza 3, the poem closes with a comment on the "eternity" of the mural and the message it has held for centuries.

Forms and Devices

Landscape imagery and storytelling perform important functions within American Indian literature. Although Momaday refers to himself not as an Indian writer but as an Indian and a writer, his poetry is decidedly informed by the importance of landscape and by oral tradition. The subject of "Before an Old Painting of the Crucifixion," while not Indian in nature, is thoroughly informed by landscapes and stories.

Momaday's use of both landscape imagery and storytelling derives from within the mural itself (Christ and the Judean hills) and his immediate surroundings (the mission at Monterey Bay). The reader not only sees the mural but also hears its silence. This is also true of the reader's placement with the author at the Mission Carmel as the reader sees and hears the sea.

In "Before an Old Painting of the Crucifixion," Momaday relies on the reader's knowledge of biblical crucifixion stories that have been handed down for centuries. For instance, the "cry" in stanza 1 is translated in the New Testament Gospels of Matthew (27:26) and Mark (15:34) as, "My God, My God, why hast thou forsaken me?" In his interpretation of the scene depicted in the mural, Momaday contrasts Christ's cry of "despair" with the "calm" following it. Many of Momaday's images combine with others, such as the "calm" of the sea in stanza 2 and the "silence after death" in the Judean hills (stanza 4). Both the mural and the sea are "mute in constancy!" (stanza 3).

The author's use of nautical imagery throughout the poem is both visual and aural. For instance, "calm" can mean lack of sound and lack of movement. In stanza 3, Momaday moves the reader's vision from the old, fading mural to the "fainter sea" that lies beyond the mission. In stanza 5, he applies the imagery of waves swelling and waning in his description of time passing and its effect on the importance of the Passion. The last nautical image lies in the final verse of the poem. The reader can see and hear the surf while reading of "flecks of foam borne landward and destroyed." The eroding surf represents the time that has passed since the Crucifixion. Here Momaday uses imagery from outside the mural (the surf) in response to the internal message of the painting (the Crucifixion).

Just as Momaday's nautical imagery is both visual and aural, the landscape imagery, both inside and outside the mural, has a dual nature as well. For example, the "vacant skies" behind Christ on the cross (stanza 1) are not only silent, as the poem informs readers, but also cloudless, while the background of the actual mural to which Momaday refers in the poem is a sunlit blue. Stanza 4 contains another example of duality in the poem's imagery: The "farther groves and arbors seasonless" of the Judean hills are similar to the area below the mission. Both landscapes have mild climates with year-round vegetation and fruit-bearing trees.

Themes and Meanings

"Before an Old Painting of the Crucifixion" is a poem that goes deep into the meaning of the Crucifixion and explores Christ's despair. The poem questions whether anyone, artist or writer, is capable of comprehending, much less conveying, the purpose of Christ's Passion. Centuries lie between the painting of the mural and the writing of this poem, and yet there seems to be "no peace," only "solitude." Christ is still hanging on the cross in the quiet following his despair: "The mural but implies eternity." The closing verse in stanza 3 emphasizes the major theme of the poem, that of time and timelessness. Again, as with Momaday's imagery, duality is represented in the theme of time. Time stands still within the mural even though it fades. However, it is only the colors that begin to pale, not the agony and despair it depicts.

As evening approaches at the mission and shadows fall upon the mural, "time is stayed" even though it swells like a wave on the sea (stanza 5). Momaday releases the authoritative voice of author at the end of stanza 5 by telling the reader, "time and timelessness confuse, I'm told." It becomes apparent that while this section of the poem is in response to the opening stanzas, Momaday is not offering any definitive answers to his initial pondering. How did He die? Was it for the timelessness of His message?

While never really declaring the actual message of the Crucifixion, Momaday does offer examples of how time and timelessness affect it. "Change" that can occur only in time is "silence after death" (stanza 4). The centuries that have passed since the Crucifixion and the painting of the mural are insignificant. Humanity's attempt to record, in stone, "the void" or feeling of emptiness and loss caused by His death is, according to Momaday, "outrageous" and in "vain" (stanza 6).

The lyricalness of the poem reflects Momaday's love for language and his sense of artistry. He vividly describes not only what the mural looks like but also the feelings it evokes. This poem is as much about art and writing as it is about its subject, an old painting of the Crucifixion. The main message concerns the timelessness of Christ's agony. Final interpretation of His death is left to the individual, as it was at the beginning of the poem. Interpretation is different for the painter, the author, and the reader. It is what ones sees, hears, and feels it to be. Although the message disappears like the "flecks of foam" on the surf, the waves will continue to swell and move forward to the shore.

Susan Dominguez

BEFORE I KNOCKED

Author: Dylan Thomas (1914-1953)
Type of poem: Lyric
First published: 1934, as poem number 4 in *Eighteen Poems*; as "Before I Knocked" in *Collected Poems, 1934-1952*, 1952

The Poem

"Before I Knocked" is a monologue consisting of seven six-line stanzas and a concluding stanza of four lines. The speaker throughout is Christ, who describes his consciousness of his own existence, and the conditions under which that consciousness functions, from the prenatal state to his incarnation in human form.

In the first stanza the speaker describes his essence, before he became a fertilized egg in the womb, as liquid, shapeless as water. This essence might also be understood as the seminal fluid. Christ already possesses, before his growth in the womb, a relationship to the world: He was a brother to "Mnetha's daughter" and sister to the "fathering worm." Mnetha is a character in "Tiriel," a poem by William Blake, whose daughter's brother is named Har. Har is usually seen by commentators as old and senile, which links the unborn Christ in the poem to the tragic world of human process, an interpretation that is supported by the image of the worm, a symbol of death.

Stanza 2 reveals that the unformed, unborn Christ was unaware of the passages of the seasons and had no knowledge, at least by name, of sun and moon. Yet even when the "flesh's armour," his human body, was still in "molten form," he could feel, and he had an awareness of the sexual act that created him in time.

The speaker's relationship to the physical world is the subject of stanza 3. He knew winter, with its hail, snow, and wind, and he knew night and day. The images are largely negative, which prepare the way for stanza 4, which clearly reveals that the speaker is Christ, who describes his capacity to experience suffering, even in the womb, in terms that strongly suggest the crucifixion: "gallow crosses," for example, and "brambles in the wringing brains," which suggest the crown of thorns that was placed on the head of Christ.

The emphasis on suffering continues in the next stanza. Like Christ on the cross, the Christ of the poem knew thirst, but he knew it even before his mouth and throat were formed. He also knew love and hunger and was aware of decay and death and the world of natural process ("I smelt the maggot in my stool").

Christ's birth is described in contradictory terms in stanza 6. In the first two lines he resembles a helpless, passive infant with no control over his destiny. The situation shifts in mid-stanza with the more positive connotations of "salt adventure," and the "tides that never touch the shores" suggest an infinite dimension to Christ's experience. By the end of the stanza, the incarnation has become, for the only time in the poem, a wholly positive event. Already rich in eternity, Christ was made richer by partaking in the temporal world.

The paradoxes of Christ's life, already hinted at, are approached again in stanza 7. He was born of flesh and of spirit ("ghost"), but it is the mortal side that is emphasized here. This emphasis can be seen especially in the lower-case "christ" of the final line, which humanizes him. Stanza 8 is addressed directly to the Christian worshipper. Again it is the mortal figure that speaks (the lower-case "me"), asking the worshipper to pity God ("Him"), who "doublecrossed" his mother's womb by promising a savior but delivering only a man.

Forms and Devices

Each stanza has three feminine (unstressed) endings that all end with the *r* sound. These occur in lines 1, 3, and 5. In stanza 1, for example, the feminine endings are "enter," "water," and "daughter." In stanza 2 they are "summer," "armour," and "hammer," and so on throughout the poem. Masculine (stressed) endings occur in lines 2, 4, and 6 of each stanza. Stanza 1, for example, produces "womb," "home," and "worm." The masculine endings are always monosyllabic and usually have one consonant in common: *m* in the first and second stanzas; *s* in stanzas 4, 6, and 7; *l* in stanza 5.

One of Thomas's most frequent poetic devices is partial rhyme. He employs it extensively in one of his most famous poems, "The Force That Through the Green Fuse Drives the Flower," which was written within a few weeks of "Before I Knocked." Partial rhyme is a noticeable feature of the latter poem, occurring with both vowels and consonants. Examples include enter-water, womb-home, womb-worm (stanza 1); name-dome, winter-suitor, snow-dew, dew-day (stanza 3); suffer-cipher-liver; bones-lines-brains (stanza 4); structure-mixture (stanza 5); creature-adventure (stanza 6); neither-feather (stanza 7).

The language is less dense and more lucid than is usual in Thomas's early style, and the predominant imagery establishes an interplay of the cosmic with the individual and the infinite with the finite; the physical universe is found within the human physiology. In stanza 1, for example, the formless liquid that will become the fetus is compared in a simile to the River Jordan; the "rainy hammer" suggests at once rain in the natural world, the mythological hammer of Vulcan the blacksmith at his forge, and, in anatomical terms, the phallus of the father. The cosmic image of "leaden stars" also suggests—because of its link to "molten form" in the previous line—the drops of the seminal fluid as seen by the as yet unformed fetus. This is an imaginative leap typical of this period of Thomas's work. In stanza 3, the wind that leaps in the still unborn Christ is also, perhaps, the oxygen that reaches him in the womb. His veins flow not with blood but with the "Eastern weather."

Thomas himself commented almost apologetically on the "almost totally anatomical" imagery of a group of five poems that included "Before I Knocked." Yet he continued, "[I]t is impossible for me to raise myself to the altitude of the stars, and . . . I am forced, therefore, to bring down the stars to my own level and to incorporate them in my own physical universe." In this characteristic practice of incorporating the entire universe in the human form, Thomas was following his mentor, Blake.

Themes and Meanings

"Before I Knocked" is a poem about Christ, but what sort of Christ does it portray? In orthodox Christian thought, Christ was both fully man and fully God; he combined two natures within one person. He suffered and died to save fallen man, and he rose from the dead.

It is obvious that "Before I Knocked" is not a pious poem in the traditional sense. Christ is not exalted as God; his death is emphasized without implication that anyone is saved as a result of it, and there is not even a hint of the resurrection. It is by no means clear that Thomas means to impute any divine status to Christ at all. While it is true that his Christ possesses a consciousness prior to his incarnation, there is little about it that could properly be said to be divine. Moreover, it is not uncommon in Thomas's poetry for a fetus, or simply an unborn spirit, to be the speaker, so the fact that in this poem Christ has life, feelings, and thought prior to his birth does not mean that any special status is attributed to him.

From an orthodox point of view, then, "Before I Knocked" might be seen as heretical. It emphasizes the human dimension of Christ while slighting the divine. Even the two lines in which an exalted status is suggested ("I who was rich was made the richer/ By sipping at the vine of days") subverts orthodox thought, in which Christ, even before his incarnation, was fully God and therefore could not be made richer by entering the temporal world. Indeed, traditionally, the incarnation is referred to as an emptying, not an augmentation. It was humanity, not Christ, who was enriched by it.

The Christ of this poem is therefore not transcendent but human, and in that respect he is simply a representative of humanity: All people are Christ. Once again Thomas may have been inspired by Blake, who wrote in "The Everlasting Gospel," "Thou art a Man, God is no more/ Thy own humanity learn to adore."

The bringing down of Christ to human level and the debunking of orthodoxy is implied also in the powerful last line of the poem, with its reference to "doublecrossed." Attempts have been made to interpret this in an orthodox sense: The Holy Spirit first crossed the womb to make Christ's mother pregnant, then crossed it again in the form of the Son of God, whom she bore. The implication of betrayal in "doublecrossed" seems too strong to ignore, however, and might be seen in the context of the annunciation scene in the Gospel of Luke, in which the angel announces that Mary is to give birth to the Son of God who would rule without end over the house of Jacob. Instead, Thomas's Christ is "struck down by death's feather" and asks only that God himself should be pitied.

Bryan Aubrey

BEFORE THE BIRTH OF ONE OF HER CHILDREN

Author: Anne Bradstreet (1612? –1672)
Type of poem: Lyric
First published: 1678, in *Several Poems Compiled with Great Variety of Wit and Learning*

The Poem

In Anne Bradstreet's "Before the Birth of One of Her Children," set in seventeenth century New England, a pregnant woman, fearing death in childbirth, writes a farewell message for her husband. While the speaker emphasizes the reality of the physical separation that death will bring, she also finds the one way to cross over the barrier of death, leaving her manuscript, her words, with him.

The poet's first six lines assert that "death's parting blow" separates one from all bonds with friends and that death is universal, "irrevocable," and "inevitable." The poet, a professed Christian, does not say that such partings end when all are together in heaven, or that the life of the spirit is superior to life of the flesh, as one might expect in a time when religion was a strong force in the world. She faces death's physical separation from all acquaintances without offering consolation.

The poet moves from this general idea of death's reality to a particularly painful situation she faces, the separation from someone who is "dear" to her, someone to whom she is bound by a "knot": her spouse, the one to whom she addresses "these farewell lines." The context now clear, the speaker addresses to her spouse a series of concerns she has about the impending separation.

First, in the only religious reference in the poem, she tells him that she prays that God will grant her husband and children a long life. Next she asks her husband to forget her flaws but to remember her virtues. Moreover, she asks that he continue to love her in memory even after her physical presence is gone. She asks that he heal his loss and grieving by his ongoing care of the children she leaves with him. Assuming that her widowed husband will remarry, she asks that he protect the children from any cruelty their stepmother might practice on them.

Finally, she asks that if he finds her farewell message after she has died he cherish it, touch it, even kiss it, almost as if the manuscript and her words, in remaining after her death, allow her to cross back over that barrier, if only for an instant. One reading the poem so many hundreds of years later can, perhaps, enable the writer to cross the barrier of death one more time.

Forms and Devices

Bradstreet in "Before the Birth of One of Her Children" writes in a formal rhyme and metrical pattern, as was the norm in seventeenth century British poetry. Her iambic pentameter rhymed couplets are exact examples of the "heroic couplets" form, so popular in a time when God's laws regulated human conduct and poetic laws regulated creative writers. Her format is conventional and correct.

Much else about this poem is unconventional, however. First of all, Bradstreet, raised in England and well educated in her family setting, is the first person in the American colonies to have published, albeit without her knowledge or approval, a book of poetry (*The Tenth Muse Lately Sprung Up in America*, 1650). Second, that she is an educated woman and a sophisticated poet in this time period and in the American colonies is unconventional. As a mother of eight children living in a wilderness setting, her accomplishments as poet are even more uncommon.

Yet it is the plain language of this poem that is most unconventional. Much of Bradstreet's work contains the poetic devices popular in her time period. For example, she uses metaphors and similes liberally in her other writing. Such figures come from conventional sources, including classical mythology, other writers, and contemporary science. In one poem she compares her absent husband to the "sun . . . gone so far in's zodiac," and in another poem she calls his love richer than "whole mines of gold." In other writings Bradstreet alludes to such classical mythological figures as the Muses and Calliope. She used such figures in both her early poetry, which was clearly written for a broad public audience, and in her later verse, which turned to material from a wife and mother's experience. In "Before the Birth of One of Her Children" such figures of speech, except one brief personification of "oblivion's grave," are absent.

Another quality of much of Bradstreet's writing, and also common among seventeenth century poets who embraced God and Scripture in their Christian world, was a didactic or teaching purpose supported by biblical allusion. This was particularly true in her early verse, much of which was written as public poetry. Yet even in her later years, when her writings became more personal, her poetry had religious overtones. One example, "Contemplations," is a thirty-three-stanza retelling of Christian mythology with a didactic purpose. In another later poem, "The Flesh and the Spirit," these entities debate. Such debate is a a common seventeenth century literary-religious topic and also didactic in purpose. Thus, "Before the Birth of One of Her Children," with its unadorned style and secular content, seems to stand apart from the other writings of Bradstreet.

Themes and Meanings

The themes of "Before the Birth of One of Her Children" are intensely personal. The title suggests what is commonly a happy event, so perhaps the poem's focus on death in its opening surprises the reader. However, the context of seventeenth century colonial life, where among women death by childbirth was second only to death by open-hearth cooking fires, justifies the link between childbirth and dying. With that explained, a second surprise is that the speaker does not soften death's reality with pious words about an expectation of heaven or by a repentance for sin. The tone of these first six lines is as somber as the feet are even. Death is real; death's separation is real.

At first the images of "death's parting blow" refer to separation from friends in general, but thereafter comes a quick shift to the personal, to the separation that death might cause between the speaker and a "dear" friend, the one she is bound to by a spousal "knot." That such a death comes well before old age adds to its pain. Now the reader has the whole picture: A woman about to give birth knows that her death is possibly imminent; the poem's lines are her early "farewell" to her beloved husband. In this reflection pregnancy and its attending hope become irrelevant. Death's power to separate is the only topic of importance: "I may seem thine, who in effect am none." An image of her husband standing beside an "absent hearse" reiterates this theme in the final lines of the poem.

In the second half of the poem, the poet empties herself of her complicated emotional reaction to this potential separation, even as she sharpens her own awareness of the reality of death. What she asks of her husband on the literal level seems innocent enough: Forget my flaws, remember my virtues. Love me "who long lay in thine arms"; comfort yourself by the presence of our children; do not let your new wife mistreat our children. On the surface, her requests are peaceful-sounding and straightforward. The lack of poetic figures supports this sense of calm.

However, the words in which she makes these ordinary requests have some subtle reminders of the pain of possible separation from her husband that tortures the speaker. Thus she will pray, she says to her husband, for "you and yours," not for "you and ours." She asks that her husband "love thy dead, who long lay in thine arms," an almost ghoulish distortion of their previous physical lovemaking. She calls the babies she leaves behind to be loved in her place "my dear remains," using a word that often refers to the physical decay that death brings. She sees herself physically replaced by her husband's next wife and asks only that her husband protect his children from "step-dame's injury." Is it her own pain at this replacement wife that causes the speaker to impute cruelty to the next wife in her husband's arms? The reader feels the reality of separation that death brings when reading these words.

Whatever words the speaker chooses to convey the reality of physical separation from her husband, from his bed, from his memory, her writing of a farewell message seems to have brought the healing that she did not ask for from her Christian God. The final four lines of the poem contain the "absent hearse" image that is so central to the poem, but around it are images not of acceptance, but of comfort. The speaker sees her husband, after her death, holding and kissing the manuscript "for thy love's dear sake." The manuscript paper and the words on it are more than a "last farewell." The words of the poem connect the speaker and her great love back to her beloved spouse, as they, these many years later, connect the speaker and her reader.

Francine Dempsey

BEHAVING LIKE A JEW

Author: Gerald Stern (1925-   )
Type of poem: Lyric
First published: 1977, in *Lucky Life*

The Poem

Gerald Stern's "Behaving Like a Jew" is a short lyric poem, twenty-eight lines of free verse in one stanza. It might better be called a lyric meditation, or even an elegy. The poem opens with a simple past-tense description of the body of a dead opossum. It looked like "an enormous baby sleeping on the road." However, the wind was blowing through its hair, making it appear lifelike, and the speaker is overcome with an overwhelming feeling of sadness, something he terms his "animal sorrow." This is physical sorrow, expressed by the body, a genuine mourning.

The poem shifts into the present tense ("I am sick of the country") as he laments the ever-present roadkill, the generic deaths that leave bloodstained bumpers and lifeless birds at the edge of the highway. The speaker realizes that he is unwilling to simply note this one small death and go on. He is "sick" of the spirit of Charles Lindbergh, what he calls "that joy in death, that philosophical/ understanding of carnage." In opposition to a predominantly Christian world, he decides that he will, in effect, weep and wail, that he will treat it for what it is—the singular death of a singular living creature—without recourse to a concept of an afterlife. Beginning with the poem's only short sentence, set off with a dash, the poet self-consciously announces what he is going to do:

> —I am going to be unappeased at the opossum's death.
> I am going to behave like a Jew
> and touch his face, and stare into his eyes,
> and pull him off the road.

The poem has shifted to a hypothetical future in which the speaker contemplates how he is "going to" behave like a Jew. He thinks about how he will not stand at the side of the road and "praise the beauty and the balance," how he will refuse to think of this as part of a long, natural progression. He will refuse to give credence to the concept of immortality. Instead, he will touch the body and note its "fingers" and its "whiskers" and its "little dancing feet."

The poet will grieve this particular death, and he will not call on a higher power for sustenance. The poem becomes lamentation. Yet, through its description, the opossum is seen as a Jew, and the speaker has manifested his grief in a traditional Jewish manner. The poet laments the death not only of the opossum but also of millions of victims throughout centuries of oppression. The poet will not be reconciled by doctrine or faith, and yet, almost against his will, the poem reconciles its imagery and associations. The speaker may have refused to praise beauty and balance, but he ends up praising life itself.

Forms and Devices

Stern's poetry is characterized by its idiosyncratic voice—one any reader could recognize instantly as belonging to him alone. Exuberant and celebratory, it is a voice that always seems to come from the most visceral center of the man: To read his books is to accompany the poet on a sort of spiritual autobiography. This voice is not that of a confessional persona pretending to "tell all"; what is most amazing perhaps is that it does not invite or even seem to need the reader. Readers participate fully, but as bystanders. The voice performs, and the reader follows.

Stern's expansive voice is achieved through an associative method of progression. What one sees is the process—a scattering of real moments and personal connections, a twist of synapses, then further observation, odd pairings that lead to new ideas. The effect is that of spontaneous thought. "Behaving Like a Jew" is no exception. There is a complicated mix of tenses so that chronological time becomes somewhat meaningless. The poem begins in the past but soon resorts to the participle, what could be called speculative time: an imagined space in which Stern thinks his way into an imagined action. Stern uses a number of repetitive moves ("I am sick . . . I am sick . . . I am going . . . I am going . . . I am not going") to identify the trajectory of his thought. Thus the poem is able to contain the long past (the past of Lindbergh, the past of the Holocaust) as it spirals inward to where self and history are intimates.

"Behaving Like a Jew" is filled with implicit dualities. The opossum comes from the "animal" world, and yet it is given human characteristics. The image of the baby is reestablished to complete the identification with its "fingers" and "feet." The addition of the adjectives ("round," "curved," "black," "little," "dancing") makes the opossum even more fully human. Stern's choice of the word "dancing"—and the emotions it conveys—breathes life back into what was dead.

There is nothing the speaker can do in the circumstances, and yet he decides on a course of action. However, this action takes place only inside his head. Thought itself is at stake, presenting alternative ways of approaching the subject. So Stern balances fact with idea. He gives readers detail, beginning with the hole in the back of the opossum, the "stiff hairs sticking out of the grilles" of automobiles, the Toyotas and Chevys going sixty miles an hour, all leading inevitably to the fact of those little fingers and feet. He constantly couples these details with abstractions—the "spirit" of Lindbergh, "philosophical" understanding, concepts of beauty and balance, and the "immortal lifestream." The poem wavers between the real and the conceptual, between the here and the hereafter.

The cadence is that of the spoken voice—narrative, sometimes digressive, good-humored, bemused—heightened through the use of poetic devices. Even the alliteration seems easy, almost natural, as the intervals of sound stretch from line to line ("bloodstained bumpers," "stiff . . . sticking," "carnage . . . concentration," "beauty . . . balance," "still . . . stiffness . . . still," "fingers . . . feet"). The reader is never consciously aware of the deliberate choice of words, and yet the choice has the subtle effect of charging the language so that it can accommodate the enlarged meanings of the poem.

Themes and Meanings

"Behaving Like a Jew" acts almost like a direct response to another famous poem, "Travelling Through the Dark" by William Stafford. In Stafford's poem, the speaker relinquishes any personal grief to the larger forces of nature: "Around us all I could hear the wilderness listen." Stafford's response is one of stoicism and practicality. In Stern's poem, there is no "us" and no concept of an autonomous "wilderness." The lone speaker is wailing into the void, flaunting his grief with grandiose impracticality. It is for nothing—and everything—that he stands at the side of the road and moans.

The poem is also reminiscent of another poem by Stern, "The Dancing," in which the speaker remembers his family's raucous celebration at the ending of World War II. That poem follows a process of association to a conjunction of specific time and place that sends the speaker reeling outward in his imagination to the shared experience of millions and, finally, to the unknown (and unknowable) mind of God: "oh God of mercy, oh wild God." The poem is Jewish to its core—especially in its enigmatic closure, which is worthy of whole pages of the Talmud. In "The Dancing," Stern was speaking not *about* his Jewishness but *through* it—speaking out its painful wrestling with the nature of a God who can spare or condemn as part of the same dance.

If "The Dancing" began with celebration and ended with a sudden, sobering empathy, then "Behaving Like a Jew" begins with empathy and ends in celebration. It does this through a circuitous route, described by Stern in an interview with the Brockport Writers Forum in 1982: He was sitting in a hospital waiting room on a plastic chair reading *Reader's Digest*, thinking about life and death and reading Charles Lindbergh's treatise on the glory of death, and he began to think about Lindbergh—"about his embracing Fascism and his flying alone and thinking how a Jew wouldn't go alone over the ocean, unless he was an Israeli"—until the entire experience coalesced into the five sentences that constitute the poem. All pretenses and postures, all of humankind's lofty ideas and concepts, are stripped away in the face of death—any death.

The meaning of the poem can be discerned in its tone. It is at once dark and joyous, sweeping readers along in its urgency. It manages to speak for something larger than itself without pretending to speak for everyone. That it does this with great good humor is Stern's greatest achievement. Contrary to what many critics have suggested, Stern does not seem to be a contemporary version of Walt Whitman. For all his long lines and his inclusive tone, his voice is lonelier, more independent, closer to the bone.

"Behaving Like a Jew" finds its own form of balance and beauty. It does not even mention God; it leaves that to the world that Lindbergh represents. To love life in spite of death is to forgive it. Gerald Stern loves with all the passion of someone who refuses to drown. The cumulative effect is life-affirming; for all its pain and irrationality, life has room for the ecstatic and the redemptive.

Judith Kitchen

BELLS FOR JOHN WHITESIDE'S DAUGHTER

Author: John Crowe Ransom (1888-1974)
Type of poem: Elegy
First published: 1924; collected in *Chills and Fever*, 1924

The Poem

"Bells for John Whiteside's Daughter" is a short funeral poem in five quatrains. Through a series of restrained images, John Crowe Ransom transfixes the grief of the entire community over the inexplicable death of a young girl. He accomplishes this primarily by refusing to admit to the fact of death. The speaker of the poem, representing the community, merely declares perplexity at the little girl's sudden inactivity.

The first stanza uses the past tense to refer to the girl's former busy activity, then leads to contemplation of her current, mystifying "brown study" (an old-fashioned term for rapt daydream). This attitude suggests that her stillness is unnatural, even perverse—as if she were going through one of those childish stages so incomprehensible to the adult world. This fixity contradicts her former habit of action. Yet this is fitting, for the death of children perplexes the standard assumptions of the adult world for the next generation. Faced with that reversal, spectators can only stop and stare, dumbfounded.

The following three stanzas are run together, one leading immediately to the next, to form a unit commemorating the girl's activities. Ransom uses language that elevates the girl's games, giving them public status and the remoteness of romance. In this way, Ransom creates the impression that the townspeople watched this outdoor playing and projected into it their hopes for the future. For example, instead of simply playing war games, she "takes arms against her shadow." Then, those were games of life and death; now, she casts no shadow.

Her major campaigns, however, were waged against the geese that usually inhabited the orchard. These geese occupy the entire third stanza. Ransom paradoxically shows them driven into activity by the girl. Previously the geese possessed the undifferentiated shapelessness of a cloud; now they become a troop of individualists, each reacting in its own way to the driving energy of the girl. She arouses them from their "noon apple-dreams" induced by feeding on windfalls and scatters them in a frenzy of motion.

The engine that drives this activity is the girl's "tireless heart," which ironically has stopped beating. The phrase also suggests the essential innocence of this type of play. It is the kind of thing a good-hearted person does—the kind of play that prepares for and initiates the activities of adulthood.

This leads to the final stanza, which returns to the basic paradox: This girl will never reach adulthood. In language that becomes hard-edged and stark, Ransom returns from reverie about the past to the reality of death. This death stops the breath of the entire community. It seems profoundly wrong. The body lies "primly propped," unnatural in death—forced out of its usual motion, fixed in the brown study it had not known in life. The community is "vexed" at the senseless perversity of this death.

Forms and Devices

The two major techniques used by Ransom in "Bells for John Whiteside's Daughter" are formal diction and understatement, and both work together to reinforce the theme of the poem. Both appear in the title: Instead of "elegy," "lament," or even a more emotive term to announce his subject, Ransom simply uses "bells." This establishes a formal response to an intense emotional situation; it also suggests the futility of any human restitution for this loss. Together, these devices generate the irony that pervades the poem. John Whiteside's daughter is dead, and all one can do is offer the empty gesture of a solemn funeral.

Both devices are used to weave the body of the poem. The first stanza contrasts the former "lightness in her footfall" with her present "brown study," which "astonishes us all." Each of these phrases is either formal or old-fashioned, the language of the older generation left to account for this loss. Again, this generates a fundamental irony: Parents are not supposed to bury their children. The language accentuates this. "Lightness" can suggest emptiness or insubstantiality, reminding readers that those footsteps will never fall again. "Footfall" should refer only to an adult, which this little girl will never become. Further, in life she never would have chosen the rapt, meditative state of brown study. She is in such a state now against her will, and the elders can only stare open-mouthed.

Ransom compounds the ironies in the central section of the poem. The little girl's play activities are described in the terminology of an epic or of a high romance, both old-fashioned conventions. The line "Her wars were bruited in our high window" creates a formal frame about her actions, as if forming a heraldic emblem. The girl's play takes place in an orchard, a region of fertility—no place to memorialize the deeds of the dead before their time. In the orchard, the girl "took arms against her shadow," a phrase that again uses formal terminology inappropriate for one whose combats were innocent, not life-threatening. Nevertheless, these battles seem to have taken her life, and the reader remembers that she now casts no shadow.

The central image within the body of the poem is the girl's driving of the flock of geese, contrasting their pointless somnolence with her directed activity. This interaction is described, as before, in formal, understated terms that generate irony. The geese are an undifferentiated, impersonal mob compared with the girl's intense personality. They are an amorphous "snow cloud," made to cry "in goose" and "scuttle/ Goose-fashion" by the "little body" with the "tireless heart." She is a champion in a war against geese, victor in a trivial mock-epic, made more trivial because that heart has now stopped.

The final stanza announces the bells and ends with a concluding static image of the community "sternly stopped" and "vexed." It is stopped in several ways. The girl's activity—and that of the younger generation—is at a standstill. The routine activities of the town are broken for the funeral. The heart of the community has been taken out.

Ransom uses subtle fractures of rhyme and rhythm patterns throughout the poem to underscore this sense of the expected order being frustrated in the death of a child.

Themes and Meanings

In "Bells for John Whiteside's Daughter," Ransom takes an oblique approach to one of the most difficult human experiences: coping with the death of children. He presents no direct resolution for this ethical dilemma. In fact, he treats it as a cosmic irony, properly placed within a context of ironies. It is almost as if he is suggesting that humans need to use intelligence and wit to insulate themselves against the shocks of experience. Life may be inexplicably painful, but one does not have to be broken by it.

The poem may be considered Ransom's notion of the mourning of an intellectual. For this reason, upon first reading, it is likely to seem guarded, cold, and impersonal—distant and distancing in its very playfulness. In refusing to grieve, it seems to pretend that human emotions are too elementary to provide satisfying and equivalent responses to loss. It suggests that the heart needs to be shielded against reality.

Subsequent readings disclose that Ransom's lament is deep-rooted, genuine, and sincere, although it certainly does not wear its heart on its sleeve. On any account, it does not evade the question. The death of children is cruel and inhumane; it violates expectations of the normal and the proper. Death provokes immediate emotional reactions: tears and, paradoxically, laughter—reactions that are not very far apart. Death also requires long-term adjustment because the survivors have to go on with the business of living. Overindulgence in emotion can interfere with this recovery, but a tempered response can promote it. Ransom provides this kind of response.

There is deep grief at the core of the poem, although it is masked by irony. Ransom's failure to name the girl or to look directly at the body is not merely a technique of avoidance. By depicting the community as astonished at the girl's inexplicable stillness, "vexed" at her contemplative inactivity, and "sternly stopped" for the funeral, Ransom is using understatement to suggest the inexpressible. Far from minimizing feeling, it is intensified, suggesting that the grief is not expressed directly because it cannot be stated in straightforward language.

In fact, Ransom's use of understatement and ironic distancing here is a technique of transcendence. This technique simultaneously suggests the depth of his grief and the way intelligence can help when coping with grief in order to get beyond it. The ironies abounding in the poem develop out of Ransom's sense that the only suitable response to the irony of early death is multiple irony. Grief is powerful, but it must be overcome. Irony begins by establishing a distance from which healing can begin. In "Bells for John Whiteside's Daughter," Ransom presents a poem in which ironic intelligence suggests a way out of the eternal sadness of the death of children.

James Livingston

BENEATH THE SHADOW OF THE FREEWAY

Author: Lorna Dee Cervantes (1954-   )
Type of poem: Lyric
First published: 1977; collected in *Emplumada*, 1981

The Poem

In spite of its title and all its natural imagery, "Beneath the Shadow of the Freeway" is really a celebration of the power of women and a guide to dealing with men. In language that lifts her thoughts to a mythic level, Lorna Dee Cervantes has created a powerful statement of Latina strength—and a reminder about those who so often take it away.

The poem is broken into six numbered parts; all except the first contain verse stanzas themselves. The whole poem is thus made up of six shorter poems. Section 1 is a kind of preface to the entire poem and introduces several of its characters and some of its natural imagery. The freeway across the street from her house, the narrator of the poem declares, is a "blind worm," "unwinding" and "wrapping the valley up." (According to the geography of the poem, the freeway is probably U.S. Route 280, running up the peninsula from San Jose to San Francisco. Cervantes wrote another, shorter poem in 1977 with a similar setting titled "Freeway 280.") Every evening her grandmother waters geraniums as "the shadow of the freeway lengthened." These concluding lines of this section not only pit a natural act (tending flowers) against a human-made structure (the freeway) but also present a premonition (in the freeway's lengthening shadow) of some looming danger or disaster.

In the first line of section 2, the narrator declares one of her main themes—"We were a woman family"—and then describes the three generations of women who live in this house in a royal metaphor, of the grandmother as "Queen" and the mother as "Knight" or "Warrior" (who really wanted to be "Princess instead"). The narrator herself, she declares in the second stanza of this section, "could never decide" her own role and turned instead "to books, those staunch, upright men." She also became a kind of man about the house, not only the "Scribe" reading the mail and paying bills but also the handyman taking care of small repairs.

Sections 3 and 4 tell readers more about the grandmother and her house; "She believes in myths and birds," knows that seagulls predict rain, and that male mockingbirds sing "for their nesting wives" all night—in sharp contrast, apparently, to the generations of drunken husbands now missing from this home. The grandmother "trusts only what she builds/ with her own hands," including this house, which she apparently constructed "after living twenty-five years/ with a man who tried to kill her." The mother in the poem still berates the grandmother for her marriage, but the narrator speaks more gently of "Grandma," and pictures her in the morning, "her hair loose in braids," and as "soft she was soft."

Section 5 breaks the structure and rhythm the poem has built so far by entering a more interior monologue: "in the night I would hear it/ glass bottles shattering the street," possibly thrown from the freeway above, and the speaker would experience "the cold fear" that accompanies such violence in the night. There is an intruder—most likely the mother's or the grandmother's husband returning drunk—and the narrator promises to call the police if he comes again. Inside the house, however, the sounds of a purring gray kitten ("beneath the quilts" made from the intruder's old suits) and the singing of mockingbirds indicate relative safety for the women inhabitants.

In the final section of the poem, the mother warns the narrator to be hard: "Baby, don't count on nobody," particularly men. The narrator disagrees, saying, "if you're good to them/ they'll be good to you back." As if to prove her point, she declares, "Every night I sleep with a gentle man/ to the hymn of mockingbirds," and, in the last stanza of this last section, "tie up my hair into loose braids"—as her grandmother used to do—"and trust only what I have built/ with my own hands." The narrator, in short, celebrates the strength and wisdom of her grandmother and quietly ignores the advice of her own, more bitter mother.

Forms and Devices

Perhaps the most obvious formal quality of the poem is its complex structure of six parts and seventeen separate verse stanzas. In addition, each of the six sections has a different form, a varying number of stanzas, and even a separate tone (especially section 5, with its almost stream-of-consciousness voice). The complexity of the structure is apparent, however, and works to provide pauses between sections. In the end, the ideas of the poem are unified organically by the poem's language and imagery.

What is most effective in the poem is the way that Cervantes finds figurative equivalents for her thoughts and feelings, from the metaphor of the royal family in part 2 and the birds throughout the poem, to the opposition between the concrete freeway and the geraniums in the opening and closing stanzas of the poem. At a certain point, those metaphors become the symbols that carry the meaning of the poem, but they also help to ground Cervantes' experience and ideas, to make her verse concrete, not only like the freeway overshadowing the house but also like the kitten and the faucet and the other actual objects of her world. Incidentally, the imagery does not reduce the ideas of the poem to any simplistic, black and white opposition: Men, for example, can be not only drunken intruders but also mockingbirds and "staunch, upright" books as well.

Cervantes uses a few Spanish words in the poem, such as "borrachando," but probably fewer than she does in some of her other poetry. For a poet like Cervantes, living (like many Latino writers) between two linguistic communities, both English and Spanish are necessary for a full expression of her life in poetry.

Themes and Meanings

"Beneath the Shadow of the Freeway" has several thematic threads running through it. On the most obvious level, the poem is a celebration of three generations of

Latinas, particularly the grandmother who built the house and still lives in it as "Queen." The mother gets credit as well, and her "wisdom," while it is ignored in the end, is an important part of the world the speaker has inherited. The granddaughter has chosen to emulate her grandmother: She dresses like her and, in the end, opts for a life with men. The important difference is that she has developed her own masculine traits along the way and is able to do "light man-work" around the house, for example. She is, in short, a unified person who has both male and female strengths, is both—in the language of the poem—"hard" and "soft." Her grandmother, who built the house after her husband left, is the role model here. The narrator's philosophy, summed up in the simple "if you're good to them/ they'll be good to you back," comes from a position of strength. Women have been the bulwark of the family in the past, Cervantes is saying, and they can achieve a sexual identity and happiness in the present and the future.

The main metaphorical opposition in the poem is between the freeway and the natural imagery of the house with its geraniums, kitten, and birds, and it is easy to see this opposition as a reinforcement of Cervantes' main theme. After all, the freeway in the first stanza is given living qualities itself; it is a "blind worm," among other things. Women have stood in the "shadow" of men for generations (especially "borrachando," or "getting drunk"), but the narrator has found a way to make a man "gentle" and faithful (like the male mockingbird). She has the example of her grandmother's self-reliance and her mother's warnings about men, and she has the balance of male and female qualities in her own person—strength and tenderness, self-reliance, and vulnerability. It is a powerful mix.

In the end, "Beneath the Shadow of the Freeway" is a realistic poem with a strong feminist theme and a number of classical allusions. Cervantes portrays her three generations of women realistically but finds hope in their lives and possibilities in this urban world. The poem rises to a mythic level as Cervantes links both men and women to other worlds: men as faithful mockingbirds, for example, and women as characters in some medieval drama. (Readers can compare a number of classical precursors here, from Ovid's *Metamorphoses* [c. 8 C.E., English trans., 1567] to T. S. Eliot's *The Waste Land* [1922].) In a contemporary society filled with gender conflicts and environmental problems, the poem is no small accomplishment.

David Peck

BENEDICTION

Author: Charles Baudelaire (1821-1867)
Type of poem: Narrative
First published: 1857, "Bénédiction," in *Les Fleurs du mal*; English translation collected in *Baudelaire: Selected Verse*, 1961

The Poem

"Benediction" is composed of nineteen quatrains written in regular Alexandrine, or twelve-syllable, lines with an alternating *abab* rhyme scheme. Charles Baudelaire's choice of this traditional verse form contrasts with his innovative use of imagery that was to inspire a new symbolic form of expression in French poetry.

While the poem uses the third person, the poet it describes clearly represents Baudelaire himself. The autobiographical elements, however, are generalized enough for the poet to represent at the same time the romantic archetype of the poet as an inspired figure misunderstood by society.

The first five quatrains form the most clearly autobiographical section of the poem and emphasize the irony of the title, "Benediction." The idea that a blessing from God is associated with the poet's birth is suggested in the first line, where his appearance is said to be "by a decree of supreme powers." Yet the child is anything but blessed when, immediately after his birth, his mother rejects him.

The mother's rejection echoes Baudelaire's own feeling of abandonment when, after his father died when Baudelaire was only six years old, his mother remarried, choosing a military man with whom the future poet had little in common. As this experience is translated into the poem "Benediction," however, the mother rails against the defects of her child, whom she calls the "damned instrument" of God's persecution of her. This rejection continues in quatrains 8 through 13 as friends and then specific women conspire to torment the poet.

Amid these rejections, quatrains 6 and 7 offer a contrasting hint of the poet's salvation. An angel appears to guide the child amid the perils of the world. These quatrains combine elements of nature and of religion, as the poet "plays with the wind, chats with the cloud/ and becomes drunk while singing the way of the cross." While the angel guides the child in these activities and seems to direct him toward the consoling elements of nature and of religion, the ambiguity of this passage makes it unclear whether the poet will actually achieve a satisfying life.

In the final six quatrains of the poem, the poet experiences a vision of hope. The reader sees him praying and blessing the same God against whom his mother had cried out. These prayers seem to be answered when the poet sees his suffering as a means to salvation: "I know that suffering is the only nobility." The poet then describes a vision of "my mystic crown" that should be the emblem of his redemption. The crown, however, must be described in terms of the objects of the present world. It appears as "pure light" but also as a "diadem" surpassing the brilliance of gems, metals, and pearls. The poet's need to express celestial light in worldly terms prefigures the loss of this vision that will become evident in subsequent poems of *Les Fleurs du mal* (*Flowers of Evil*, 1909).

Forms and Devices

Baudelaire's collection of poems *Flowers of Evil* deals extensively with the elements of good and evil posited in its title. "Benediction" opens the first, and longest, section of the work, "Spleen et idéal" ("Spleen and Ideal"). Baudelaire's concept of "spleen" incorporates the negative elements of fallen nature that contrast with the ideal he envisions at the end of this poem. The poet's tragic fate lies in his consciousness that he is simultaneously drawn to each of these extremes.

Baudelaire created the basis for poetic symbolism by establishing groups of related images that work together to form highly nuanced constructs in his poetry. In "Benediction," both positive and negative references continue the religious theme established in the title. When his friends mock the poet, they sully the "bread and wine" he will consume, thus potentially corrupting a form of Holy Communion. Similarly, the woman, taking advantage of the fact that the poet adores her, assumes the role of "ancient idols," leading him to a pagan form of worship that "usurps" the otherwise Christian devotion of the poem.

The positive vision of the "celestial crown" offers a radiant affirmation of the poet's redemption. That is undercut, however, by certain elements both in this description and in the two quatrains in which the angel seems to protect the poet. Under the angel's care, the child twice "becomes drunk": once from the effects of the sun and once while singing the way of the cross. Drunkenness, as Baudelaire defined it in a prose poem, "Enivrez-vous," was not limited to the action of alcohol, but it does imply a state in which the poet gives up rational control of himself. Thus the angel, even while he permits the child to run this risk, "cries to see him gay as a bird in the wood."

This recognition of the child's vulnerability is based in part on a definition of Baudelaire's language drawn from sources beyond the present poem. This technique exemplifies another source of complexity in Baudelaire's symbolism. The poems of *Flowers of Evil* are clearly meant to be read consecutively, as a whole. When, in the second line of "Benediction," the poet appears in "ce monde ennuyé," this phrase, describing ambiguously a world that is either troubled or bored, draws on the image of Ennui, the monster that Baudelaire described in his preceding poem, "To The Reader."

In the same way, the final lines of "Benediction" undercut the vision of the "celestial crown" with images linked to the poet's moral fall in subsequent poems. The "mortal eyes" seen as "obscure and pitiful mirrors" of celestial light foreshadow the eyes of the woman through whose seduction the poet will be separated from his ideal. Numerous repetitions of the images of both eyes and mirror develop this theme throughout *Les Fleurs du mal*.

The device of linking, through which images are reused from poem to poem, allows Baudelaire to add nuances to his central motifs as they recur in various contexts. The complexity resulting from this multiple redefinition forms the essence of his poetic symbolism.

Themes and Meanings

Baudelaire introduced a number of important themes in "Benediction" that he would develop more fully in subsequent poems. Such themes as the dangerous hostility of women and the painful realities of the poet's life form a part of the negative, and later dominant, dimension of *Flowers of Evil*. The greatest importance of "Benediction" within Baudelaire's work, however, lies in its positive elements. The reader meets the child-poet when he is still naïve enough to believe in the vision of his own salvation. His progressive consciousness of his fall from grace in later poems gains poignancy through its contrast with the vision presented here and never completely regained.

Although Baudelaire's life in the dissipation of nineteenth century Paris could hardly have been further from that of a religious ascetic, he retained a strong sense of traditional Christianity. Religious themes persist even in his most negative descriptions. Thus the poet's mother, turning to God in anger after the poet's birth, says, "Since you chose me from among all women," clearly recalling the similar choice of Mary for the birth of Christ.

The parallelism established between the poet and Christ, both of whom were destined to bring messages of a higher truth to people who would misunderstand them, lends urgency to the poet's desire for salvation. The singing of the way of the cross and the attempt at Communion, when others intercept the bread and wine, prepare the poet for a vision of paradise in which he sees the "splendid throne," implying the presence of God himself.

Interwoven with these images of paradise, however, are suggestions of an earthly paradise. It has already been seen how the celestial crown is related to earthly gems. Similarly, the poet, while accompanied by the angel, finds himself in a seemingly pure natural setting defined by allusions to sun, wind, and cloud. The sun, one source of the poet's drunkenness, takes on more negative connotations later in *Flowers of Evil* until, in "Une Charogne" ("Carrion"), it becomes the source of decay in a corpse.

One need not go beyond "Benediction," however, to find suggestions that paradise cannot be transposed into the context of this world. The angel sees the child as "a bird of the woods," but only six quatrains later, the woman seeks to torment the poet's heart when she finds it as vulnerable as a baby bird. Images such as the sun and the bird, together with the poet's own drunkenness, set the stage for his loss of paradise.

The theme of paradise, both earthly and celestial, persists throughout *Flowers of Evil*, but with increasing indications that the poet is separated from it. His consciousness of this separation gives Baudelaire's protagonist the dimensions of a true tragic hero. Even his most vivid imagining of his own salvation, as he recorded it in "Benediction," contained the seeds of his ultimate failure.

Dorothy M. Betz

BERMUDAS

Author: Andrew Marvell (1621-1678)
Type of poem: Lyric
First published: 1681, in *Miscellaneous Poems*

The Poem

"Bermudas" is a short poem of eight-syllable (octosyllabic) lines arranged in iambic tetrameter couplets. The poem begins with a four-line exordium, or introduction, by a narrator. The next thirty-two lines consist of a song of thanksgiving being sung by people in a boat as they row. The poem then ends with a peroration, or conclusion, of four lines by the narrator, who identifies the people as English.

In the first section, an omniscient narrator—a mysterious persona who is so objective that he seems to be absent from the scene—immediately situates the action of the poem in the Bermudas (a group of more than two hundred islands, also simply called Bermuda). His description of the islands as "remote" and "unespy'd" creates the image of a distant, hidden, and private place. Since there are no human observers to the scene, only "The listning Winds" hear the song of the people in the boat.

The song, which is a hymn of praise and gratitude to God, has four parts. In the first part (lines 5-12), the boatmen praise God for having brought them safely across the Atlantic Ocean ("the watry Maze") to the Bermudas. Although these waters had begun to be charted since the discovery of the New World, ocean voyages were still risky undertakings in Marvell's day. (The islands had been discovered by Europeans only in 1515 and settled in 1609 by Sir George Somers.) The reference to this "Isle" as "far kinder than our own" has at least two levels of meaning. First, the weather in this tropical area is much kinder than the harsh weather, especially winter, in England. Second, these islands, like much of the New World, represent a place of religious freedom, in contrast to their own land, where religious persecution ("Prelat's rage") was occurring. (In the 1630's, William Laud, the archbishop of Canterbury during the reign of Charles I, was persecuting and imprisoning Puritans; many religious refugees fled to the New World at this time, and one of those groups landed on Bermuda.)

The next part of the poem (lines 13-28) describes the islands. The "eternal Spring" weather produces colors everywhere (it "enamells every thing") all year long. Every day God sends fowl through the air as food for the people. There is an abundance of exotic fruit: oranges, pomegranates, figs, melons, and pineapples ("Apples"). The shore is full of ambergris, an expensive waxy substance from sperm whales, used in making perfume. Continuous verdancy, abundant food, and costly ambergris all point to the rich bounty of these islands and to an effortless existence for the inhabitants.

The third part of the song (lines 29-32) focuses on the spiritual significance of the islands as a temple for worship. When the sailors sing, "He cast . . ./ The Gospels Pearl upon our Coast," they imply that the Bermudas are a manifestation of the Kingdom of God and also that the gospel message has been brought here by them.

The fourth part (lines 33-36) is a prayer that the gospel will reach beyond these islands. As their praise reaches heaven, they hope that it will rebound off "Heavens Vault" and produce an echo of praise past the Gulf of Mexico (*"Mexique Bay"*), reaching other parts of the New World. After the song, the narrator provides a descriptive commentary on the cheerful boatmen whose song is dictating the rhythm of the oars, implying that prayer and praise set the pace for their life and work.

Forms and Devices

The sailors' narrative points to God, or Divine Providence, as the main protagonist in the poem. The narrator is unidentified and impersonal; the nameless, faceless boatmen are only indirectly identified through the phrase "the *English* boat." Almost all the action verbs in the song have God as the subject: He is the prime agent, and the boatmen are the passive receivers of God's actions. God is credited with having protected them from the dangerous waters and from persecution; he is the one who has given these refugees this new home. He is the one who "sends" the fowls, "hangs" the oranges in the trees, and "throws the Melons" at their feet. The boatmen's description reflects their belief in the daily action and care of God in all the details of their lives.

Marvell conveys the significance of this island-paradise through a confluence of several archetypes. First, there are parallels with the biblical Garden of Eden. Just as God planted a garden and brought Adam to it, so too he has prepared this new "garden" and brought these people to it. In this place where all is provided—where God "makes the Figs our mouths to meet"—there is no labor, no sweat, no toil.

Second, there are specific reminiscences of the Garden of Hesperides. This classical paradise lay far to the west of known civilization, across a vast body of water, just as the Bermudas do. The oranges in the Bermudas, that are hung "Like golden Lamps in a green Night," function as a parallel image to the famous golden apples of the Hesperides.

Third, these islands bear some similarities to the New Jerusalem in the Book of Revelation. That whole city, like the Bermudas in this poem, is the temple of God and is full of his presence. There is no need for sun and moon, since God is the light of that city (Revelation 21:23); on these islands, there is no darkness or night—only bright colors and the "green Night" of the orange trees whose fruits are like golden lamps. In the heavenly Jerusalem, God will feed his chosen at a banquet that he has prepared (Revelation 19:7-9); on this island, God supplies food for the people. Each of the twelve gates of the New Jerusalem is a huge pearl; the coast, or "gate," to the Bermudas is the place upon which God has "cast . . ./ The Gospels Pearl." For his description of the Bermudas, Marvell draws from classical and biblical archetypes, weaving together details from various paradisiacal garden models in Western tradition, to create a powerful depiction of a land of beauty, abundance, and blessedness.

Themes and Meanings

One of the central elements of the boatmen's song is their description of life in an earthly paradise. Ancient classical writers shared a tradition about a "Golden Age," an idyllic pastoral existence of peace, whose biblical counterpart is Eden. Every civilization and culture have had their dreams of paradise, although there are variations in the details. The human dream of a paradisiacal life can represent a memory of the distant past (human beginnings), can function as an ideal for the future, or can take the shape of a fictive utopia occurring any time.

Marvell's depiction of this age-old dream has a number of distinctive characteristics. As a synthesis of classical, Old Testament, and New Testament elements, it transcends specific nations or cultures and thus has a universal quality. Unlike mythological garden-paradises and utopias whose locations are vague or unknown, Marvell's garden-paradise has a real geographical and historical existence. Finally, Marvell's "Eden" is neither in the distant past nor in the distant future, but in the present, and it functions as a fulfillment of humankind's dream.

However, Marvell's primary theme is not the proclamation that humankind's idyllic dream has finally come to pass. Rather, the paradise theme is subordinated to, and helps support, the chief emphasis of the poem, which is a celebration of a new Exodus, a new deliverance of God's people to a new Promised Land. Marvell establishes the similarity between the boatmen and the Israelites primarily through a situational parallel. Just as the chosen people were led out of Egypt during a period of persecution by the pharaoh, the boatmen were led from their land during their persecution. Just as the Israelites crossed the Red Sea to arrive at the Promised Land, the boatmen crossed a new sea to arrive at a new Promised Land. Just as the Israelites were protected and guided throughout their journey, the boatmen were protected and guided to this new destination.

Marvell strengthens this metaphoric identification of the two groups through structural elements and story details. The poem has forty lines, recalling the forty years it took the Israelites to reach the Promised Land. The boatmen's song is a poetical prayer, sung in unison by the people, recalling Old Testament psalms of thanksgiving for deliverance. The fowls sent through the air by God recall the quail sent to the Israelites during their journey. The cedars of Lebanon, "chosen by his [God's] hand" and transplanted in Bermuda, were the trees used in building Solomon's Temple in the Promised Land.

Marvell, well known for his defense of independence and his championing of civil and religious liberties during the reign of Charles I and under the subsequent rule of Oliver Cromwell, uses the biblical Exodus as a paradigm, a prototype, to make his metaphoric statement about the Puritan refugees of pre-Cromwellian England. Although Marvell never visited the Bermudas himself, the islands presented him with the chance to render poetically an image of a garden paradise while making a political and religious statement concerning an actual historical event.

Marsha Daigle-Williamson

BETWEEN THE WARS

Author: Robert Hass (1941-   )
Type of poem: Lyric
First published: 1989, in *Human Wishes*

The Poem

"Between the Wars" is a lyrical meditation of fifty-one lines. The opening lines place the poet in his setting and report on his activities: He runs in late afternoons, in the midsummer heat and humidity of upstate New York. He is writing, and at the same time reading Polish history; he is also thinking of a woman. He addresses the woman, speaking to her of his desire in the voice of Poland, in the "*'era of the dawn of freedom,' nineteen twenty-two.*" The title, "Between the Wars," and this line inform the reader that he refers to the time between the two world wars, actually between 1918 and 1939. Why he refers to Poland specifically in 1922 is not stated. Poland gained its independence in 1918, but its independent existence was precarious and short-lived, for Adolf Hitler invaded it in 1939. As a country overrun for most of its history by more powerful neighbors, Poland's people have suffered the worst indignities and persecutions of war. Knowing Poland's history in the twentieth century, the reader realizes that the optimism expressed in the phrase "dawn of freedom" will prove naïve.

The poem is not divided into stanzas and may be thought of as consisting of long sentences rather than lines demarcated by end-breaks, as in most shorter lyric or rhymed poems. Though it has no spatial divisions on the page, the opening sentence, "When I ran, it rained," repeats at line 15, introducing a deepening of the poet's preoccupation with the late-afternoon light of this region, which he terms a version of the "American sublime." Late afternoon turns to a fiery sunset, then to night. "Out of nothing/ it boils up," he writes, tracking the setting sun through the color spectrum toward night: "pink flame,/ red flame, vermilion, purple, deeper purple, dark."

At this point, the focus shifts to a personification of night as a god disguised as a beggar and offers two folk legends as cautionary tales that function as the poem's moral center. The first tells what will happen to the populace that turns away the beggar from their door. The second offers a parable of why the leaves of the aspen quiver: "it failed to hide the Virgin and the Child/ when Herod's hunters were abroad." These folk tales call forth a strong peasant tradition, as in a country such as Poland; together with the mention of the children of the "eastern marches," they connect this section of the poem to its opening and to the title.

In the final section of the poem, the poet returns to his tale of night as "the god/ dressed as the beggar drinking the sweet milk." He extends the description of the beggar, comparing him to an alternately suckling and crying infant. Here Hass associates himself with the beggar, saying that he too would like to suckle at that breast, the one which has mysteriously appeared as his tale evolved out of the darkness of night into an image of nurture and desire ("The pink nubbin/ of the nipple glistens"). The reader will be reminded of his desire for the woman, expressed in the first section of the poem.

The mysterious glistening breast is also connected to the fiery colors of sunset: "the muttering illumination/ of the fields before the sun goes down," before the American relief train came to Poland from Prussia bringing medicine and canned goods (this would have to be at the end of World War I, before Prussia ceased to exist). The concluding lines, presumably also drawn from Hass's reading of Polish history, proclaim the end of the war and catalog his ambiguous feelings about this "era of the dawn of freedom"—on the positive side, there is a new day with "skylarks singing," but on the negative side, there are unburied dead and "starved children begging chocolate on the tracks."

Forms and Devices

The reader will quickly notice that imagery of light and dark dominates the first half of the poem. Within a landscape darkened by rain, then lighted by an incendiary sunset, and finally settling into darkness, Hass depicts a world alive in its sensual particularities. Hass is a careful namer of plants and animals, a barometer of the slightest changes in the weather, a recorder of the sounds of birds, insects, and odors rising from the land. With great care he specifies the redwings in the cattails, the blackbirds in the reeds, the blossoms of the wild carrot, the sour odor of the sumac, the sweetness of the fescue, the loud insistence of cicadas, the colors of the sunset.

All of this teeming life—what he terms "the moody, humid/ American sublime"— is organized into a metaphor of encroaching night as death, and presented in quasi-religious terms in the first half of the poem. The redwings and the "massed clouds" perform a "requiem," a Mass for the dead. Possibly the red stripe on the wings of the otherwise black birds is what Hass means when he refers to them as "death's idea of twilight."

The American sublime suggests a nineteenth century view of nature that elevated it to quasi-religious status, assigning it transcendental powers. The description of "the levitating, Congregational, meadow-light-at-twilight/ light" continues the religious connotations by associating the quality of the light with religious experience. The Congregational church is an American denomination of Protestantism founded in colonial New England. Working against the temptation to sacralize nature, however, is the imagery of impending darkness, the heavy air, the sour smells, the "impure" sunset, "maniacal cicadas"—earth itself seems violent, capable of evil.

Hass employs two modes of discourse in the poem. The first is colloquial, as in the opening line, "When I ran, it rained." This is his hook; it is catchy (it almost rhymes), and it invites the reader's commiseration with a familiar situation. This line is also a structural device, since it is repeated midway through the first half of the poem, the point at which Hass wishes to draw attention to the darkening afternoon. He also tends to address the reader directly, informally ("You could wring the sourness of the sumac from the air"; "Think: night is the god dressed as the beggar").

Set against this familiar, colloquial style is Hass's second mode of discourse, the self-consciously poetic, in which he employs several traditional poetic devices. The first, italicized, as if to call attention to it, is the apostrophe to the "*Lady of eyelashes,*" presumably the woman he has been thinking about a few lines earlier. Apostrophe is the love poet's time-honored way of expressing his desire for his lady. This passage eroticizes the already sensual descriptions of "the moody, humid" afternoon by connecting them to the poet's desire.

Readers will also note the personification of night as the god disguised as a beggar, and the development of this personification into an extended metaphor. The rather revolting beggar in his extreme old age turns back into an infant as he sucks the nurturing milk from the breast. Thus his symbolic value becomes apparent. Moreover, this figure appears to serve multiple symbolic functions. Hass makes him represent night turning into day, war giving way to peace, Poland in its new era of independence, as well as the ages of man, or Everyman, an ancient allegorical figure.

Themes and Meanings

If one takes the title, "Between the Wars," as an announcement of the poem's main concerns and considers the ambiguous images of the concluding lines, wherein the "era of the dawn of freedom" brings both the end of war and the specter of starving children and unburied dead, then the poem's theme is the precariousness of peace in this world. Peace is difficult to maintain because people are governed by desire. In this poem, Hass is governed by his desire for a woman, by his running, his reading, and writing—the urges and impulses that make up an individual human life. As a poet, he is governed by his desire to praise the world and its multiple beauties even though the evidence of war's horrors haunts his descriptions of fields and sunset from the outset. It is noteworthy that the voice of unqualified praise goes to the newly independent Poland, cast (appropriately) in the role of passionate and hopeful lover.

Thus the poem is divided between the poet's impulse to praise and his moral imperative to warn and caution. People who turn away the beggar and refuse to shelter the innocent will be punished for their selfishness. War is the ultimate failure of love. If the evidence of his century will not permit him to write the sensual poem of praise that arises out of desire for the world, he will write a parable, a poem of moral instruction. This impulse nearly wins out in the second half of the poem. In the end, however, desire for the beautiful world is the breast that "glistens" with promise, and the poet appears to find its temptation irresistible. Nevertheless, his acceptance of the world is qualified by the closing lines, drawing the reader back to images of war and its aftermath. Optimistic statements about a new "dawn of freedom" can only be read as tragically ironic in the light of history.

Sandra Cookson

BEWARE: DO NOT READ THIS POEM

Author: Ishmael Reed (1938-   )
Type of poem: Satire
First published: 1970; collected in *Conjure: Selected Poems, 1963-1970*, 1972

The Poem

"Beware: do not read this poem" is written in free verse, divided into six unequal stanzas. There are no capital letters, and the poem has many spelling irregularities and abbreviations, with apparently random spacing in many lines. There are very few punctuation marks except for an occasional comma or slash, usually in an odd place. However, a single voice speaks the whole poem, and, although there are no neat markers to indicate divisions, the poem can be divided into three distinct parts. Moreover, despite its appearance on the page, the "grammar" of the poem is straightforward and clear.

A story is told in the first three stanzas. This story, a kind of modern folktale, is related by the speaker as he synopsizes the plot of a television show he has just watched ("tonite, *thriller*"). The episode concerned an old woman who was so vain that she filled her house with mirrors, becoming finally so wrapped up in the mirrors that they became her life and she locked herself indoors. Eventually "the villagers" broke into her house, but she escaped by disappearing into a mirror. Thereafter, she seemed to haunt the house. Everyone who lived there "lost a loved one to/ the ol woman in the mirror."

In the fourth stanza the poem changes; instead of narrative fantasy, the poem becomes more discursive, and the speech pattern becomes more concrete. Now the voice speaks of the poem itself as though it were the mirrors or the old woman, warning the reader that "the hunger of this poem is legendary" and telling the reader to "back off," for the poem swallows people. Thus the poem itself becomes a kind of devourer, not merely a mirror that reflects the external world. There is a significant difference, though, between the poem and the mirrors: The poem is alive—and this is a major point of the poem. The voice goes on to say that "you," the reader, are being swallowed by the poem. The reader is advised to "go w/ this poem," to "relax." Finally, with the reader no longer being directly addressed as "you," poem and reader become one.

Now, disconcertingly, the language changes again. In the last short section there is a flat, bureaucratic statement about the great numbers of people who disappeared without a trace in 1968. Yet at the end the flatness is transformed into a short, abrupt cry of feeling, almost a protest, about the loss felt by the friends of those who have disappeared.

Forms and Devices

The poem is not realistic narrative or even a typical fantasy story. It is, rather, about language and how language makes culture. Three types of language usage appear in the poem. In the first section, although the voice seems to be African American, there is an underlying European style of speech and a European subject. It is written with run-on sentences, the sense going from line to line. The run-on sentences have a different rhythm from the second section, suggesting a cultural difference. The second section is much more rhythmic, more African American. The last section is almost dry, until the final quietly sad statement about there being a "space" in the lives of those left behind.

The sounds in the poem are essential to its meaning. Most European American poetry is umbilically connected to the written word. Even the oral poetry of poets such as Allen Ginsberg is very "literary"; its roots are in the letter. Reed's poem, on the other hand, uses the rhythms and short lines of actual speech—at bottom African American speech—although there are some careful exceptions to the accurate representation of speech. The deliberate misspellings, the lack of standard punctuation, the contractions, are speech, speech with rhythm, reflecting the community that is their base. The poem is, despite or even because of its appearance on the page, the result of a living oral tradition—yet, paradoxically, it uses "literature" as a foil.

In the first part, the run-on sentences do indeed tell the story, which emphasizes time, past, present, and, especially, future, an emphasis that is European American. The second part of the poem, however, is composed of lines that are complete sentences in themselves, even with the expected punctuation left out. There are no run-on lines until the final couplet, where the speaker asserts flatly that "this poem is the reader & the/ reader this poem." This couplet, solidly closing the section, is also a summation of the series of statements above it. However, it also speaks of time as a now, something to be lived in, emphasizing life—a more African American approach.

Reed also rejects the standard grammatical forms and poetic formulas of the past, but he uses those forms for contrast. Like the American poet Ezra Pound, Reed is saying, "Make it new," but to make it new one must show what one is rejecting. Reed himself has pointed out that his earliest poetry was influenced by poets such as William Butler Yeats; by implication, he is both using and refusing such influence here.

Themes and Meanings

Thematically, "beware: do not read this poem" is a complex case. It is about language, about art, about people, and about politics. Language and art are intimately bound to one another, and they are central aspects of culture. Culture, at least in part, makes people. The poem is therefore about how people are made by, and lost to (other), cultures. It is a protest against cultural dominance, and it works by concrete demonstration.

In the immediate sense, the poem's theme is about how the poem itself affects, even creates its reader by involving the reader in the world created by the poem. That concept is an exhibition of the power of poetry, for poetry is an act of speech, showing that language, how one uses language, is vital to one's existence. The poem also shows how a culture can swallow one up, denying one's real existence. It rejects the idea of art as a simple mirror reflecting life; art is, rather, a living experience.

There are some generic conventions in the poem that may seem at first to be merely decorative or entertaining, but they actually represent essential elements of the theme. In the first section, the convention of the European folktale is derived from a literary, European tradition. This folktale is presented as the product of modern technology— a television plot—which makes it very European American, mechanical and hypnotizing in a negative way. Too, the tale, with its "ol woman," essentially a witch, in the house which is attacked by "villagers" uses words and images that are not American ("villagers" is not a term commonly used in the United States). Yet, as has been already noted, the poem's basic language is the language of African America, and there is a deliberate tension between the convention and the language. Indeed, here the language is a protest against the culture implied in the folktale.

The second section is an assertion that the poem, made of language, creates a culture. Although the "ol woman" and her house seem to become the poem, this section really rejects the European American culture of the first part. For the moment, all is African American. Instead of being swallowed by mirrors and disappearing, one is swallowed by the rhythms of the language and is made more alive.

Yet the larger world encompasses, surrounds, this positive one, so the poem must return to the European American world. In the first line of the last section, the speaker speaks of the "us bureau of missing persons," the "us" obviously standing for United States. However, it is also the pronoun "us," and the bald statistic presented is a reference to Americans. People are involved in this world of loss, where words do and do not quite make connections between them. Moreover, there is a contrast between the state, the national apparatus, and the individuals, the "us" of the United States. When the poem turns to the dry official language of this section, the language of the dominant culture that the poem is rejecting, the reader again is shown how that culture has swallowed people. The poem must therefore end with its note of regret, for those who have lost people to that culture have a "space" in their lives.

L. L. Lee

BEYOND THE ALPS

Author: Robert Lowell (1917-1977)
Type of poem: Lyric
First published: 1959, in *Life Studies*

The Poem

"Beyond the Alps" is a lyric poem written in iambic pentameter; each of its three stanzas is a sonnet. The rhyming pattern of each sonnet is irregular and typifies, as do other elements in the poem, Robert Lowell's experiments with convention.

Lowell's career was marked by several dramatic shifts in style, and this poem does not fit snugly into a formal category. The epigraph suggests that the poem is an occasional piece, written as a consequence of Pope Pius XII's pronouncement that made Mary's bodily Assumption church dogma; however, the structure of the poem is primarily personal narrative. In the first and third stanzas, the speaker, who can only be viewed as Lowell himself, is on a train that has left Rome and is bound for Paris. He notes the "Alpine snow," stewards "banging on their gongs," and the "hush hush of the wheels." The second stanza is a meditation about the pope's decree. The poet's mind moves over the landscape as well as historical, religious, and literary issues. In the third stanza, he refers to his "blear-eyed ego kicking in my berth," which illustrates the depth of his personal religious struggle, which is the emotional center of the poem.

"Beyond the Alps" was the first poem in Lowell's third book, *Life Studies*. It serves as an announcement that he no longer can believe in the dogma of the church. The title is an allusion to the religious debate over papal authority; the transalpiners were a group in the Roman Catholic church who opposed the ultramontanes and their belief in the infallibility of the pope. The poet is literally and figuratively crossing over the Alps, leaving both Rome and traditional Catholic doctrine, to arrive in Paris and uncertainty.

Lowell begins the poem very casually by saying that he had read in the newspaper about an expedition of Swiss climbers who had given up trying to scale Mt. Everest. This sets the scene for his own travel and metaphorically suggests that he too has "thrown the sponge/ in once again"—on traditional religion. He says that "Much against my will/ I left the City of God where it belongs." Pius's interpretation of Mary's Assumption, and Lowell's own observations about human nature, have made it impossible for him to reside in his previous convictions. The subsequent lines, "There the skirt-mad Mussolini unfurled/ the eagle of Caesar. He was one of us/ only, pure prose," suggests that the City of God is inhabited by people such as Benito Mussolini. Mussolini was the Fascist dictator of Italy from 1923-1945; he imprisoned, tortured, and murdered people who opposed him. He was also infamous for his mistresses; he and his mistress Clara Petacci were shot and hung by their heels for the public to scorn. Lowell refers to this in the second stanza, when he says, "The Duce's lynched, bare, booted skull still spoke." Lowell implies that all people are potential

Mussolinis if they are given enough power; for Lowell, this dramatizes the imperfection of God's creation.

The second stanza illustrates one cost of Lowell's traveling: his vision and moral integrity. His point of view enlarges to that of an omniscient narrator. He therefore can simultaneously observe the crowd yelling "Papa" outside Saint Peter's Basilica, and Pope Pius himself. The pope is shocked by the crowd's reaction to the announcement about Mary's Assumption, and he drops the mirror he was holding while shaving. This scene subtly suggests that the pope is merely a man—one who has to shave every day, too. He has an electric razor and a pet canary. This humorous scene is further developed in the next sentence, where Lowell playfully combines two clichés to show how unreasonable and ridiculous he thinks this new interpretation of Mary's Assumption is. The "light" of science is not even a "candle" when compared to Mary rising bodily into heaven "angel-wing'd, and gorgeous as a jungle-bird." He cannot imagine any reasonable person believing this or understanding this belief.

Lowell thinks that people tend to confuse the icon with the saint; the pilgrims to the Vatican still kiss Saint Peter's bronze sandal as if that will bring them good luck. They indulge ostentation and neglect their faith. Lowell suggests that people have not learned much from the example of Mussolini and that God himself, by allowing these traits to flourish, "herded this people to the *coup de grâce.* A *coup de grâce* is a stroke that kills someone who is wounded; it literally means a "stroke of mercy." The "stroke" here can either refer to Mussolini's hanging or to the dogma that ended Lowell's faith. The fact that the Vatican's Swiss Guard must guide the pope through the crowd with their pikes to keep the people from crushing him implies that these people have again confused the man with what he represents and that in human nature the light of reason shines rather dimly.

This theme is further developed in the final stanza. The "mountain-climbing train has come to earth," and with it Lowell's aspirations for himself and humankind. Although he had aspired to faith and a more generous view of humanity, his experiences at Saint Peter's and his reading of history have caused disillusionment and despair. Lowell was graduated with a degree in classics from Kenyon College, and in a sense the third stanza can be seen as a yearning for a myth system in which he had once found value. Apollo, the Greek god of the sun, poetry, and music, has had to "plant his heels" on the ground; this questions the value and efficacy of aspiration in general and art in particular. Each disappearing mountain peak becomes a metaphor for some "wasted" and "backward" achievement of the past, such as the Greek Parthenon or Ulysses poking out the eye of the Cyclops. The lack of distinction between historical events, artistic achievements, and mythological feats implies the depth of Lowell's despair. About three thousand years of human history are indicted by this poem— from the "killer" Etruscan kings of the tenth century B.C.E. to Rome of the 1950's. Lowell is as blind or "blear-eyed" as the Cyclops, because he can find no clear access to "that altitude" to which he once aspired, and his reading of history is no help.

Forms and Devices

The poems that Robert Lowell wrote before *Life Studies* were tightly formal, with a restless urgency, a barely containable energy. "Beyond the Alps" begins this book to announce both an intellectual and stylistic deviation from his previously published poems. Lowell's line relaxes; the syntax is clearer, and there is a confident ease in the language. This casualness is evident in the opening line, where he has just finished reading the paper and looks out the window:

> Reading how even the Swiss had thrown the sponge
> in once again and Everest was still
> unscaled, I watched our Paris pullman lunge
> mooning across the fallow Alpine snow.

He enjambs the lines so that the reader reads past the rhymes; one does not linger on "sponge" because one needs to know the preposition that goes with the verb "thrown." In the second line, one reads past "still" to get to the verb "unscaled." By disguising the rhymes, Lowell puts more weight on the narrative.

There is still a rich medley of sounds in his language. If one considers "mooning across the fallow Alpine snow," one can see how complex it is. The assonance (the *a* and *o* sounds), the consonance (the *l* and *s* sounds), and the meter allow the reader to participate in the beauty Lowell observes.

The only formal deviation from typical sonnets is in the stanzas' rhyme schemes. In fact, the rhyme scheme of each succeeding sonnet becomes more and more Shakespearean, which also echoes the intellectual progress of the poem: from chaos to a nostalgic yearning for a classical myth system.

Themes and Meanings

Lowell once remarked that this poem is "about people who go beyond nature, Mussolini or the Pope." Throughout Lowell's work, he was concerned about the way human nature abdicates nature. Although the mountains in the opening stanza are symbolic of man's thwarted ambition and aspiration, they come back in the last stanza to loom over the "mountain-climbing train" that "had come to earth." He is exhausted by his mental traveling and his "blear-eyed ego" that will not allow him any rest. Human ego—whether it is Mussolini's, the pope's, or his own—often causes people to be inhuman. In fact, the occasion for this poem is an example of human ego. Mary must rise bodily into heaven because human vanity does not like to imagine her moldering in the earth like everyone else.

In "Fall 1961" from his subsequent book, *For the Union Dead* (1964), Lowell wrote that "Nature holds up its mirror" to provide a contrast with humans who "have talked our extinction to death." In that poem, his only "point of rest" as he looks out the window of his apartment is an oriole's nest. In both poems, he suggests that humans return to earth, terra firma, and abandon the ego that causes many of humankind's problems.

Joseph Powell

THE BIGHT

Author: Elizabeth Bishop (1911-1979)
Type of poem: Lyric
First published: 1949; collected in *Poems: North and South—A Cold Spring*, 1955

The Poem

"The Bight" is a lyric of thirty-six lines that provides a veritable showcase of Elizabeth Bishop's aesthetic of observation and her metaphoric impulse. The bracketed subtitle—"On my birthday"—suggests both an occasion and, perhaps, a gift. Such an occasion usually implies the assessment that people are prone to on their birthdays, but, in this case, the poet seems to be tallying up the contents of a localized landscape.

A bight is a small bay between two points of land, and here the topography in question is Garrison Bight in Key West, Florida, where Bishop lived during the winter of 1948-1949. The poem draws heavily from a letter Bishop wrote to poet and close friend Robert Lowell in January, 1948. The details of her description of Key West appear in the poem's opening lines, and she tells him that the untidy bay resembles her desk.

One of the problems Bishop faces in this poem is how to infuse what seems like a purely descriptive exercise with some of the impetus of narrative. The poem consists of an apparently random survey of activity, both natural and human, and the detritus left behind by it all. Each focused detail, however, is an invitation to concentrate and see clearly not just what is but also what can be. The speaker seems separate from the scene, distanced, but her imaginative capacity closes the gap. The water, the birds, the "frowsy sponge boats," the ramshackle scenery are eventually taken in by the speaker/observer, a gift on her birthday, one might say, to herself and to the reader. In the following passage, the movement from distance to interiority, from disparate object to meaningful symbol, reflects the overall movement of the poem:

> Some of the little white boats are still piled up
> against each other, or lie on their sides, stove in,
> and not yet salvaged, if they ever will be, from the last bad storm,
> like torn-open, unanswered letters.
> The bight is littered with old correspondences.

Like her early mentor, poet Marianne Moore, Bishop finds a more compelling reality in the imagined scene, the individualized, personalized world. "The Bight" depicts that reality as it comes into being.

Forms and Devices

One of Bishop's aesthetic standards as a poet was accuracy; poet-critic Randall Jarrell noted in one of his reviews that "all her poems have written underneath, *I have seen it*." Yet accuracy for Bishop means something more than objective, literal transcription. She must allow her reader not only to see the object before her but also to experience the whole meditative, discursive act of perception. To re-create this experience, she brings to bear a range of poetic devices, tactics that give her language the expansiveness and elasticity of a mind freed by engagement with the world around her. Thus, the envisioned objects can take on symbolic significance.

The mention of the great French poet Charles Baudelaire seems justified by his own proclivity for searching the material world for analogies to the human soul, as when he writes: "Imagination is an almost divine faculty which perceives immediately and without philosophical methods the inner and secret relations of things, the correspondences and analogies." In her allusion, however, Bishop treats this idea ironically, noting that "if one were Baudelaire/ one could probably hear" the evaporating water in the bay "turning to marimba music." The qualifications in this passage ("*if* one were . . ./ one could *probably* . . . ") suggest that Bishop herself draws back from such fanciful and elaborate flights of invention. Later she confirms a less exalted, more modest intention than Baudelaire: "The bight is littered with old correspondences."

In keeping with this urge for a down-to-earth clarity, Bishop's tropes are designed to link whatever is seen with something that is at least as common or more so. Pelicans crash into the water "like pickaxes"; man-of-war birds open their tails "like scissors" or tense them "like wishbones"; shark tails are hung on a fence, "glinting like little plowshares." All such similes envelop the reader in Bishop's own conception of the interconnectedness of things. Readers are meant to delight in their sheer appropriateness.

The poet's presence is also registered in the masterful but subtle control she exerts over the form of the poem. She constructs sentences that sprawl over the course of several lines, seemingly casual but pulling the reader from phrase to phrase by means of their accumulated detail and sporadic enjambment. Note the momentum in the following passage and the way in which Bishop herself slips into the description, less to qualify it than to endorse it:

> The birds are outsize. Pelicans crash
> into this peculiar gas unnecessarily hard,
> it seems to me, like pickaxes,
> rarely coming up with anything to show for it,
> and going off with humorous elbowings.

Bishop also links the various images of the poem by her use of sound, employing feminine rhymes ("jawful"/"awful") and assonance ("plays"/"claves"; "jawful of marl"). In the passage cited first, near the end of the poem, she quietly puns on Baudelaire's "correspondences," aligning them with "torn-open, unanswered letters." As "untidy" as the poem itself might appear, she reminds the reader, it has been carefully arranged, and such rhymes and word-play are there as inconspicuous evidence. However, it is just such allusion and figurative language that establishes Bishop's claim upon the scene.

Themes and Meanings

The theme of poetic intervention and invention is fairly clear. Early in the poem, Bishop alludes to another poet and gently mocks his kind of intervention in the observed world; she then sets about producing her own. A few characteristics of that vision are important to note since they contribute to whatever meaning might be drawn.

First, there is a suggestion of violence about the scene—the remnants of previous upheaval and the potential for some explosive instant to come. The water is "the color of the gas flame turned as low as possible" and is turning to gas, while the pilings are "dry as matches." Pelicans "crash" into the surface of the bay, while above them soar "man-of-war birds." Sharks have been harvested along with the sponges, and their tails hang on a fence, drying, *memento mori* from the sea beyond. The dredge itself brings up a "dripping jawful of marl," personifying the mechanism with the traits of some carnivorous beast. The little boats have been piled up or stove in by the last hurricane. This impression of violence is countered with the simultaneous, ongoing actions of exposure. The water absorbs, but low tide has left much of the content of the bight revealed, and the work of the dredge is the "untidy activity" of bringing to light what is yet beneath the surface. Even the pelicans and the "frowsy sponge boats" are engaged in bringing something up. What is one to make of these impressions when one considers as well the work of the poet in presenting them, and her pronouncement upon the whole scene as "awful but cheerful"? Should one of these adjectives be stressed more than the other?

The reader must keep in mind that Bishop's "accuracy" is not a matter of photojournalism, of absolute fidelity to fact. Instead, she recognizes that the poetic vision— even of a negligible panorama like Garrison Bight—involves a certain wrenching on her part. (The word *trope*, in its Greek origin, means "to turn or twist.") Poetry wreaks a kind of violence on the real world in order to reveal the imaginative potential of what lies before one. On one hand, this poem reveals some anxiety on Bishop's part about this; on the other hand, one can see that she is committed to it nonetheless. She knows that this activity is paramount to possess the world more fully and dispel whatever isolation she may feel as a human being.

Bishop's resistance to Baudelaire's exotic analogies, her rootedness in the physicality of the witnessed scene, her embrace of the whole range of activity—"awful but cheerful"—all suggest an allegiance to the world of objects. "The Bight" insists not on grand design and poetry as statement but upon the power of the ordinary to inspire a kind of loving attention. The bight itself, that grab-bag of a body of water, becomes a symbol of the poet's mind. Through the creative labor of dredging, what is least promising, what is nondescript to the point of invisibility, what is in fact buried under a shifting load of psychic debris becomes visible, tangible, and fraught with possibility. The poem provides an artfully staged but privileged glimpse of the poetic imagination in process.

Nelson Hathcock

BINSEY POPLARS

Author: Gerard Manley Hopkins (1844-1889)
Type of poem: Meditation
First published: 1918, in *Poems of Gerard Manley Hopkins, Now First Published, with Notes by Robert Bridges*

The Poem

Gerard Manley Hopkins's "Binsey Poplars" contains two irregular stanzas of eight and sixteen lines which mourn the loss of a stand of poplars to the woodsman's axe. These remembered trees, which are addressed in the first line, grew along the bank of the Thames River as it meandered from Oxford to the small village of Binsey, a charming walk of two miles that Hopkins often followed as a student at Balliol College, Oxford. The Thames, sometimes called the Isis in the Oxford area, is very narrow in the Binsey area; hence Hopkins recalls the slow-moving water and "weed-winding bank." The poet depicts the trees as "airy cages" that captured the sun in their leaves and supported a child dangling a sandal over the water, then reports their utter destruction, with none spared.

The second stanza chastizes humanity for its destructive impact on nature, which the poet calls "country" and personifies as both a young girl and an eyeball. Just as pricking an eyeball renders it sightless and unable to perform its proper function, even minor alterations to nature, including ones intended to aid it can destroy it and render it selfless. By investing nature and the Binsey poplars with "self," Hopkins exemplifies one of his most important concepts, that of the "inscape" of all living things, a sort of fluid DNA, which is made dynamic by the "instress" of God in the world. Hopkins emphasizes that it takes so little to irreparably alter nature; just ten or twelve strokes create a landscape that is unrecognizable and make the original pristine state unimaginable to those who come after. The last three lines celebrate the beauty and tranquility of the "sweet especial rural scene" before the trees were felled in 1879, and perhaps captures the "emotion recollected in tranquility," which the poet William Wordsworth, a poetic mentor of Hopkins, espouses.

Although Hopkins rarely returned to Oxford after his graduation, he became a Roman Catholic there under the influence of John Henry Cardinal Newman. This intense religious experience, combined with a search for poetic expression, helped him evolve his ideas of inscape and instress. During his years of preparation for the Jesuit priesthood, he made a deep study of Duns Scotus, a medieval theologian, who laid great stress on individuality and uniqueness in each person and all nature. "Binsey Poplars" reflects a synthesis of Hopkins's intense religious faith, his deep study of Duns Scotus, his growing understanding of inscape and instress, his happy memories of walks on the tow path of the Thames from Oxford to Binsey, and his horror at learning that his beloved poplars had been cut down. These ingredients combine to make "Binsey Poplars" an intense poem that both celebrates and mourns.

Forms and Devices

Perhaps because Hopkins's poetry was not published until 1918, under the aegis of his friend and classmate Robert Bridges, who was then poet laureate, his work has often been seen as more modern than its Victorian dates of composition would indicate. Indeed, many twentieth century poets cite Hopkins as a strong influence on them, chiefly because of his experiments with "sprung rhythm" (his term) and his compressed imagery. Hopkins developed the idea of sprung rhythm, in which each poetic foot includes at least one stressed syllable and a varying number of unstressed ones; this form gives Hopkins's poetry more elasticity than traditional metric schemes while affording it a form not available in free verse. The indentations and overall shape of "Binsey Poplars," especially in the first stanza, suggest the number of stresses in each line.

The first stanza is written with the eye of an artist as Hopkins describes not only the trees themselves but also the negative space created by their branches, quelling and quenching the sun, which appears to leap as its angle changes and the leaves move. Negative space is suggested again in the image of a child swinging his legs and "sandalled" feet over the water from the branch of a tree, thereby creating a shadow in the river, which can be seen to sink or swim.

Hopkins uses end-rhyme, interior rhymes, and alliteration to tie the poem together. Many critics have noted that he uses more alliteration than any poet writing in English since the Anglo-Saxons, and this observation is certainly true of "Binsey Poplars," as may be seen in phrases such as "fresh and following folded rank" and "dandled a sandalled shadow." Hopkins, who had studied Old English, also shows its influence in his choice of such forceful words as "quell," "felled," "hack," "rack," "hew," and "delve." It is worth noting that all these words suggest the destruction or repression of natural beauty.

The second stanza introduces an unusual metaphor that compares the effect of cutting down the trees to pricking an eyeball; the eye, which is such a miraculous instrument of sight, can be rendered functionless with one prick, just as ten or twelve hacks deprive the rural scene of its identity. Again the idea of inscape is made manifest in the "self" of the trees and of their place in the landscape; the beautiful inscape of the Binsey waterway is "unselved" (robbed of itself) by the felling of the poplars.

Binsey is the site of an Anglo-Saxon holy well dedicated to St. Margaret and was often the destination of religious pilgrims in the Middle Ages. Binsey may have been a place of mending in earlier days, but Hopkins makes clear that modern efforts to mend the landscape only end it; once more Anglo-Saxon words such as "end" and "stroke" emphasize this loss with harsh sounds.

Themes and Meanings

"Binsey Poplars" is a poem whose meaning functions on several levels. Clearly it is a poem that examines nature from an ecological point of view. The often heartless industrialization of the nineteenth century prompted Hopkins and others to contemplate what was being lost to cutting and clearing as well as to improvement schemes that did more harm than good. The lovely rural quality of the Oxford environs was being threatened by bustling commerce on England's waterways, which led to the felling of the poplars. Hopkins notes how quickly and unexpectedly such destruction in the name of progress can take place and sees the irony in the finality of such hasty, heedless action. Nothing can bring the Binsey poplars back: They are gone forever.

Just as the poplars are gone, so are the happy days Hopkins spent at Oxford, days when he absorbed the beauty of the "sweet especial rural scene" along with the theology of Duns Scotus and discovered his own Roman Catholic faith and vocation to the priesthood. Because his life bore Hopkins far away from Oxford, it became a more special place in his imagination than it might have been had he stayed there. The news of the felling of his beloved poplars in 1879 hit him hard and led to the meditation on his loss, which became "Binsey Poplars." "Duns Scotus's Oxford," written in the same period of his life, also celebrates the connection of Oxford, the rural scene and his growing awareness of inscape, while "Spring and Fall, to a Young Child," written shortly thereafter, recognizes that the death of natural things foreshadows the demise of the individual. These three poems form a trio of Hopkins's early ideas concerning the connection of God's power and the beauty of nature and humanity's ability to both appreciate and destroy this perfection.

Because "Binsey Poplars" is both accessible and rich, it makes a good introduction to Hopkins's ideas of inscape and instress, sprung rhythm, Anglo-Saxon vocabulary, and alliteration. In the poem the reader experiences the mind of the poet as it grows and tests its wings. "Binsey Poplars" is well worth study for its own sake and as an introduction to Hopkins's more difficult poems, such as "The Windhover," "Carrion Comfort," and "No Worst, There Is None."

While "Binsey Poplars" mourns the loss of the "sweet especial rural scene" that existed before the cutting of the trees, the poem itself restores the image of the trees to the imagination. The airy cages quelling and quenching "in leaves the leaping sun," the sandaled foot whose shadow casts its reflection on the river, and the "weed-winding bank" are all restored to the reader in the poem. The rural scene unselved by the heedlessness of humanity is re-created by the art of the poet.

Isabel B. Stanley

BIRCHES

Author: Robert Frost (1874-1963)
Type of poem: Lyric
First published: 1916, in *Mountain Interval*

The Poem

"Birches" is an enduringly popular lyric by one of the United States' most celebrated poets. In fifty-nine lines of blank verse, the poem presents a description of birch trees in a New England countryside, scenes of a boy swinging from these trees, and reflections on the meaning that being "a swinger of birches" has in Robert Frost's life. He addresses the reader in an informal, conversational manner, using the first person "I" and addressing the reader casually as "you." Sometimes poets create first-person speakers who are quite different from themselves. In "Birches," however, Frost seems to be speaking in his own voice: as a grown man who has often observed and mused upon the birch trees he is describing, who remembers swinging from birches as a boy, and who has endured the adult tribulations he discusses late in the poem.

Frost reinforces the effect of conversational informality by casting the poem in continuous form. Rather than dividing the poem into stanzas or other formal sections, Frost presents an unbroken sequence of fifty-nine lines. Within this continuous form, however, Frost does shift his focus and tone, sometimes abruptly, as if he were digressing in a conversation with the reader. In this way, Frost's major shifts reveal five sections in the poem.

In the brief first section (lines 1-3), Frost muses that when he sees birch trees that are bent over, he "like[s] to think" it is because "some boy's been swinging them." Frost quickly rejects this pleasant thought as whimsical and inaccurate, though. In the second section (lines 4-20), he presents a more dismal and realistic explanation: Winter storms coat the birches with a heavy load of ice that causes them to grow in a bent-over position.

In the third section (lines 21-40), however, Frost playfully reverts to his original theory. In contrast to the ice-storm explanation, he "prefer[s]" to develop the myth of a boy who bends down all the birches on his father's land "by riding them down over and over again." Toward the end of this section, Frost's description vividly dramatizes the skill and exhilaration of the boy's play.

The fourth section (lines 41-49) returns to a tone of burdensome gloom that echoes section 2. Now, however, instead of the birches suffering, it is the poet. Frost reveals that he himself was once "a swinger of birches," and he ruefully admits that he now dreams of returning to this activity as a release from the worry, confusion, and pain of adult life.

In the fifth section (lines 50-59), Frost ends the poem on a note of hopeful reconciliation. He realizes that he does not wish for a total escape from the earth and the troubles he experiences there, but only for a temporary respite.

Forms and Devices

The key action described in "Birches" consists of swinging free of the constraints of the earth, up toward heaven and through the air, before landing on the ground again. Through his careful organization of imagery, tropes, and myth, Frost designs the poem as a delightful reflection of its content. That is to say, he takes the reader through a series of swings back and forth between earthbound realities and imaginative possibilities.

The first section of the poem, for example, swings from a real image that Frost has observed (birches bent over) to a myth he would like to believe (that the birches are bent because of a boy's play). In the second section, though, the poem swings back grimly toward reality, as Frost presents dismal images of how ice left by winter storms actually bends the birches: "They are dragged to the withered bracken by the load." Frost also observes ruefully, "once they are bowed/ So low for long, they never right themselves."

The grim power of reality in the second section seems to inspire Frost to assert the countervailing power of his imagination even more strongly. He thus begins the third section by playfully personifying reality as a rude interrupter that he can easily dismiss: "But I was going to say when Truth broke in/ With all her matter-of-fact about the ice-storm." Aware of his own impudence, Frost then imagines a mythical account of how the birches were bent by a boy whose powerful control over reality seems to reflect the power Frost is claiming for his own imagination. The boy "subdued" all his father's birches into bent-over arches until "not one was left/ For him to conquer."

Frost swings back to reality in the fourth section through the surprising revelation that he was once himself "a swinger of birches." The poet has not, however, enjoyed the satisfying mastery over his life that the mythical boy did over his father's birch trees, and Frost "dream[s] of going back to be" a swinger of birches once again as a release from the cares of adult life.

In the first four sections of the poem, then, Frost seems to be largely concerned with dramatizing the conflict between the harsh limitations of earthbound reality, and the more attractive possibilities of play and the imagination. The images of the last ten lines, however, present a surprising and harmonious synthesis of the two extremes. Frost emphasizes that he is no longer so naïve as to wish for complete escape from the earth and its cares. "Earth's the right place for love," he asserts, implying that it need not exist chiefly in heaven or in the imagination. Similarly, he does not take the regressive, whimsical route of imagining that he would swing up and out from a birch tree with the aggressive abandon he had exhibited as a youth. Instead, he imagines the milder pleasures of the gradual climb up the tree "*Toward* heaven" (not the impossible fantasy of soaring into it) and of the gentle descent as the tree would place him down on the ground. In this way, Frost imagines a birch-swinging experience that "would be good both going and coming back," without the conflict between imaginative flight and earthly reality that seemed to prevail earlier in the poem.

Themes and Meanings

"Birches" is a popular poem largely because it so satisfyingly represents the loveable side of Robert Frost. The poem neatly encapsulates much of what is most familiar and endearing about this poet: his vivid description of a New England natural scene, his folksy voice mixing plain talk with whimsy and imagination, and his clear development of simple images and actions into accessible symbolic meanings. Further, the conclusion of the poem is warmly reassuring, making the conflict between realism and romanticism seem reconciled so that earthly realities do not ultimately seem too harsh or discouraging, and playful imaginings do not seem too whimsical or quixotic.

Seen from another perspective, however, "Birches" also reveals a more sophisticated view of the theme of the relation between imagination and reality. Though in general terms the poem presents these two realms as in conflict, Frost also delights in showing that realistic and imaginative language often dissolve into each other, so that the dichotomy between them is not as clear as many people (including the speaker of the poem) seem to think it is. For example, in the second section of the poem (the one mainly concerned with the actual "Truth" about how ice storms bend the birches), the fervor of Frost's observations leads him into some wildly imaginative tropes. Ice shattered by the sun becomes the metaphor "heaps of broken glass to sweep away" that seem to have fallen from the "inner dome of heaven." A simile asserts that the birches with leaves hanging down to the ground are "Like girls on hands and knees that throw their hair/ Before them over their heads to dry in the sun." On the other hand, in the third section, Frost moves almost imperceptibly from imagination to reality—from the myth of the boy who bent down all of his father's birches, to precise images of what could well be an actual launch ("Then he flung outward, feet first, with a swish,/ Kicking his way down through the air to the ground"), to the poet's revelation that "So was I once myself a swinger of birches."

Thus, even in such a seemingly straightforward poem as "Birches," there are moments of subtle strangeness and surprise that show why Frost deserves his current reputation not only as a beloved popular poet in the United States but also as one of the great modern poets of the early twentieth century worldwide. "Birches" shows how the poetry of Robert Frost, perhaps more than that of any other great modern poet, is dedicated to keeping realism and romanticism in close touch with each other. As Frost puts it in the final line of the poem, "One could do worse than be a swinger of birches"—one who knows the pleasures of swinging back and forth between earth and sky and of moving between the realms of reality and imagination.

Terry L. Andrews

THE BIRD

Author: Louis Simpson (1923-   )
Type of poem: Lyrical ballad
First published: 1957; collected in *A Dream of Governors*, 1959

The Poem

In Louis Simpson's lyrical ballad "The Bird," the poet attempts to appeal to both the intellect and the fashion of the day. This poem was published in *A Dream of Governors* (1959), the first of Simpson's poetry collections to be divided into sections. The fourth section, "The Runner," contains "The Bird," one of the six poems relating to World War II in the volume. Because Simpson intertwines fantasy with the gruesome realities of war in "The Bird," it differs from the other five.

This ballad-like lyric of World War II is divided into seven parts and tells the tale of Heinrich, a German private assigned to a concentration camp. The poem has twenty-eight quatrains, and the second and fourth lines are in regular, iambic trimeter. The first and third lines use feminine rhymes and end, therefore, with an unaccented, additional syllable. The final result of the quatrains—the *abab* rhyme scheme, the three-stress lines, and the meters—is a rhythm that is singsong. The controlled result is appropriate for a poem about a soldier who has a prescribed military life and little say in or understanding of what is happening to him. The regular rhythm also suggests the structured cadence of marching, an activity common to most soldiers. The experiences are set in Germany, but the lack of control over one's life is a common occurrence for enlisted people everywhere.

The first part of "The Bird" presents the German soldier Heinrich as an idealistic young man who plays the zither and sings. His best friend Hans wants to be a soldier and goes to war; Hans dies. In the second division Heinrich is a young man who has been drafted and has been relegated to a Jewish extermination camp. The third section describes Heinrich's duties: sorting the clothing of those killed in the gas chambers. The fourth section depicts Heinrich as changed from a romantic youth to a hardened soldier who has volunteered to execute those whom he has learned to hate. Heinrich attends dutifully to his assignments, but he still plays his zither and dreams of escape as a bird.

The fifth part of the poem is one of tragedies: The Russians are rapidly approaching; the colonel kills himself; Heinrich discovers the major dressed in women's clothes; the prisoners demand vengeance upon Heinrich, "the Bird." The Russians search for Heinrich in the sixth part of the poem, but they do not find him; there is no clear image of him to use for identification. The Russian in charge of writing the reports, however, notes a bird that flits from tree to tree. The final part, consisting of only one quatrain, leaves the reader with an image of Heinrich still singing and dreaming of flying away across the sea; his sad song "makes his children cry."

Forms and Devices

Simpson commands meter, rhyme, and stanza to be used his way; he does not allow them to control his verse. He employs the tight lyric in traditional English form to separate himself from the material and to place more emphasis on the means of conveyance than on the tragic content. Like the soldier who alienates himself from life, the reader and poet can separate themselves from the horrors of the narrative by the structured form, which allows the story to unfold and reach its surprising climax with a minimum of emotion. As Simpson intended, the reader's interest is focused not on the narrator but on the poem and its story. The strictly regulated form reflects the controlled life of the German soldier—and soldiers universally.

The repetition of the German refrain "'Ich wünscht', ich wäre ein Vöglein'" ("I wish, I would be a bird") makes parts of the poem predictable and encourages the active participation of the reader in the unpleasant narrative. In contrast, part of the content of the poem is unpredictable and imaginative, the fantasy making it easier for the reader to bear the harrowing story.

The poet allows the sensitive character Heinrich to compartmentalize, or separate, his job and his life—an all-too-real occurrence for those who worked in the concentration camps of Germany. Heinrich continues to retreat into protective isolation, which even his children eventually mourn. The story comes full circle with the crying of Heinrich's children, rather than Heinrich's mother.

Using many stylistic devices in the poem, Simpson employs personification when he writes "The stars looked down from heaven," "The zither softly playing," and "The wind bore from the East." Foreshadowing is another important element in "The Bird." The sound of Heinrich's zither and the song of flight precede important events, such as Heinrich's leaving home, the death of the Jews, and Heinrich's escape. The same song foreshadows the escape through death of the Jews in the gas chamber. As a father, Heinrich continues to sing; his children cry as they hear the song that foreshadows Heinrich's separation from them.

Simpson provides the reader with realistic images, both visual and aural, of World War II Germany. Stacks of clothing ("Skirt, trousers, boot and shoe . . . For every size of Jew"), a bird that flits "from tree to tree," the envelope marked "Deceased," and the "'group snapshots, badly blurred'" become familiar images to the reader. Simpson also presents the sounds surrounding the events. He mentions the snap of a pocketknife, the birds that sang in the woods, and even "a drumming/ Of small arms that increased."

Simpson's use of contrasts makes the images and events even more real to the reader. For instance, he juxtaposes the banks "bright with flowers" with "a fence with towers/ On which armed sentries stood." He also makes use of metaphors in his narrative. For instance, the doctor calls Heinrich "Scamp." The sergeant refers to the gas chamber as a chimney, a metaphor that Heinrich recognizes immediately; in the poem the chimney is a tangible symbol of the destruction of human life. When Heinrich asks for a change in duties, he calls the officer "Herr Ober-Leutnant"; this title ("Over-Lieutenant") is both a hyperbole (exaggeration) and a metaphor. The most important metaphor, however, is the bird that symbolizes freedom and serves as a means of escape for Heinrich.

Themes and Meanings

"The Bird" presents the soldier's view of war and employs three traditional literary themes: reversal of fortune, survival of the unfittest, and the picaresque (or journey). Heinrich, the young musician and miner, must become a soldier (reversal of fortune), and he is able to escape from death and capture (survival of the unfittest) through his songs of flying away like a bird (picaresque).

Freedom is a common thread throughout the poem, set in Germany in the 1940's. Hans, in the beginning of the poem, longs to be free; this desire is evident also in Heinrich and in the prisoners in the concentration camp. Heinrich as a young man escapes through his music and through his dreams of a bird flying away; later he literally escapes, like a bird.

Although Simpson vividly portrays images to the reader, he does not focus on the characterization; most are flat characters about whom the reader knows little. The people that Heinrich thought he knew were actually veiled to him. For instance, he does not expect to find the body of the colonel with "[a] pistol by his head." Heinrich is also surprised when "He [finds] the Major drinking/ In a woman's party dress."

Alienation is typical of many of the characters in the poem. Heinrich does not talk with his mother, who cries; his attempt to contact Hans through a letter is unsuccessful. Heinrich's officers do not know him. When Heinrich asks to fill the vacancy, they ask to see his dossier. His commanding officer does not even care to get to know him: "Dismissed! Don't slam the door." The fact that Heinrich does not know his officers— still more evidence of alienation—is evidenced by his surprise at the suicide and the cross-dressing. Heinrich's alienation from the prisoners is evident by the matter-of-fact method in which he is able to kill them. Later, he is able to alienate himself from the search party by literally taking flight as a bird. Even with his own family, later, he separates himself through song.

The most enduring themes in "The Bird" are the ideas. Humans are executed, take their own lives, and die; material possessions, like clothes, are discarded. The song, however, remains; through creativity Heinrich finds escape from the pressures of war and life. The poem leaves one with a sense of sorrow for the life that others— Heinrich's mother, the government, Heinrich's own family—prescribed for the young soldier. The reader can take consolation, however, in the fact that Heinrich is able to escape through fantasy.

Despite Heinrich's escape and the release of some of the prisoners from their confinement, the poem ends sorrowfully. Heinrich's song "makes his children cry"; he appears lost to himself and to others. Whether Heinrich ever finds himself and whether his pursuers ever find him remain unclear. Simpson leaves the readers with an open denouement and with the freedom to create an ending that they deem acceptable. They may choose a realistic ending or, like Simpson, they may employ fantasy.

Anita Price Davis

THE BISHOP ORDERS HIS TOMB AT
SAINT PRAXED'S CHURCH

Author: Robert Browning (1812-1889)
Type of poem: Dramatic monologue
First published: 1845, in *Dramatic Romances and Lyrics*

The Poem

As the subheading "Rome, 15—" explains, the setting is sixteenth century Rome, Italy. A Catholic bishop lies on his bed, near death. He has summoned his nephews or sons—he is not always sure which—to impart his instructions for his burial in his present church, Saint Praxed's.

The Bishop's primary consideration is that his tomb must outshine the tomb of his old rival, Gandolf, presumably his predecessor as bishop, now dead and buried inside the church, as was customary for high-ranking church leaders. The speaker cherishes the idea that old Gandolf always envied him, especially for his beautiful mistress. The Bishop wants Gandolf to envy his superior tomb as well and plans to enjoy this envy throughout eternity.

The monologue opens with a garbled quote from Ecclesiastes about the vanity of worldly interests. Yet the rest of his long speech reveals him as vain, greedy, and hypocritical, interested only in possessions, pleasures, and besting his rivals. On occasion the Bishop interrupts his instructions about his tomb to utter pious phrases that a bishop would be expected to say, but he himself has not followed these precepts.

Gandolf has already beaten the Bishop to the choice location for his vault, much to the Bishop's annoyance, but he consoles himself that his own spot is satisfactory and that his vault will be much more elaborate. He knows exactly what he wants for every detail. It should be made of the best antique black basalt, with nine peach-blossom-colored marble columns around it, arranged similar to the way the listeners are standing around his bed. When his former church had burned, the Bishop whispers, he had taken from it a huge lapis lazuli gemstone, and now he wants them to dig it up from the vineyard where he had hidden it and use it to adorn the effigy of himself atop his vault. Around the vault he wants a continuous band of bronze sculpture depicting various scenes, including Christ giving the Sermon on the Mount, Moses with the Ten Commandments, and—unsuitable for the Christian theme but totally suitable as a reflection of the Bishop's character—a scene depicting pagan Greek Pans and Nymphs, including one Pan about to "twitch the Nymph's last garment off." Even his epitaph on the vault must be "choice Latin" from Tully (the classical writer Marcus Tullius Cicero); it should clearly outdo Gandolf's epitaph from the less notable Ulpian.

The Bishop hears the young men talking and turns to his son Anselm as though he were the only one he might hope to trust. He worries that they will take his riches for themselves rather than use them for his tomb. He alternately bribes and threatens. He tells them he can pray to Saint Praxed to send them horses and rare old manuscripts and mistresses. If they disobey his wishes, however, he will disinherit them and leave his villas to the Pope instead.

The Bishop becomes increasingly confused as death approaches. He is unable even to remember which author he wanted quoted for his epitaph. As the nephews/sons start to leave, he tells them to leave him in his church, where Gandolf still envies him.

Forms and Devices

Robert Browning shows his mastery of the dramatic monologue form in this poem. Browning had an early interest in playwriting, and the poem is a compressed play with one speaking role, that of the Bishop. The minor characters, the nephews/sons, move together and function almost as a Greek chorus, with only Anselm named. The reader is the audience. Dramatic irony enables the audience to know more than the speaker intends to reveal, and as the Bishop unmasks himself he is inadvertently didactic, instructing the audience in the folly of worldly corruption. Stage directions and props are indicated through the Bishop's remarks about the positioning of the other characters and the lighted candles.

The basic verse pattern of the poem is unrhymed iambic pentameter (blank verse); the central device is irony, created by clusters of images, shifts in tone, and the sense of movement throughout the poem. The poem immediately establishes the scene, with the central character calling reluctant listeners around his deathbed. The other characters (nephew was often a euphemism for a priest's son) seem as preoccupied with selfish interests as does the Bishop. He calls them closer as he whispers his theft of the lapis lazuli from the burned church (he may even have started the conflagration), and they listen as he tells where the treasure is hidden. Soon he hears them whispering among themselves and exclaims, "Ye mark me not!"

The sense of physical movement throughout the poem is supported by tone shifts. The Bishop gloatingly recalls his worldly triumphs and fondly details his lavish tomb. His description of it, however, increasingly becomes a desperate need to communicate both the instructions and the urgency of carrying out his orders.

As the candles burn down, the Bishop's words show that his mind is drifting into delirium. He seems almost to be speaking to himself as he says, "strange thoughts/ Grow, with a certain humming in my ears." He mutters a biblical reference about personal evil but immediately stops that thought with a reminder that he wants the lapis. When he has a horrible vision of the body in a coarse, crumbling gritstone box, whose sides "sweat/ As if the corpse they keep were oozing through," he can no longer console himself with thoughts of lapis; the listeners are walking away. The Bishop asks them to arrange the candles in a row so that he can "watch at leisure" if old Gandolf leers at him in envy of his fair mistress.

The central image of the poem is the tomb, the Bishop's obsession, which merges with his revelation of character. Numerous references to stone—marble, travertine, onion-stone, jasper, and pure basalt—rich, rare, hard, and flawless, mingle with images of sensuality, as in the "great smooth marbly limbs" of mistresses or his sacrilegious metaphor that the lapis lazuli is "Blue as a vein o'er the Madonna's breast." Other clusters of images indicate his thorough familiarity with Renaissance art and his thorough immorality. Every word in the poem contributes to the reader's understanding of the total drama.

Themes and Meanings

A major theme of the poem is moral decay. Although this is seen most obviously in the hypocritical and worldly Bishop, similar immorality is also suggested in the greedy and untrustworthy young men, in the envious and conniving Gandolf, in the material wealth of the churches, and in the implication that the Pope himself would welcome new villas to add to his riches. The total effect indicts the dominant Renaissance religious institution as corrupt and spiritually dead.

A bishop should guide his flock and be exemplary in Christian compassion and charity. This bishop, however, devotes himself to personal ambition, wealth, and pleasures. Rather than chastity, poverty, and obedience to God's will, he relishes his memories of his mistress and the thought that Gandolf envied him. His villas and his indulgent luxuries show that he is no follower of Saint Praxed, who gave all she had to the poor. Even now, on his deathbed, rather than repenting his sins and thinking of God's judgment, the Bishop concerns himself only with his earthly remains. Given the example he has set, it is no wonder that he suspects that his nephews/sons will not fulfill his instructions.

The Bishop's closest human tie seems to be his hostile rivalry with Gandolf, which he assumes will continue after death; Gandolf will know the Bishop's tomb is superior to his and will still envy him. The fact that the Bishop is a learned man who has had many privileges makes his attitude and actions especially reprehensible. To him, the Church has meant power, material goods, and sensual stimulation. In a particularly gross perversion of the central Church doctrine of transubstantiation (Holy Communion), he says that from his tomb he will "hear the blessed mutter of the mass,/ And see God made and eaten all day long."

The poem is one of Browning's finest of many dramatic monologues, and Browning has again created a character whom readers love to hate. The poet has also given readers a means of seeing beyond the surface. The judgment of the Bishop is complicated by one's acquaintance with him. The reader recognizes that it is only because of his dying haziness that he reveals himself, that the nephews/sons will betray his dying wishes, and that the Bishop is only following the example of other ecclesiastics.

This literary example of moral corruption implies the need for change both in institutions and in individuals. Part of the solution is contained in the poem itself—the idea that man's years are short, and the material things of this world are less important than creating a worthy soul.

Lois A. Marchino

BITCH

Author: Carolyn Kizer (1925-   )
Type of poem: Satire
First published: 1984, in *Mermaids in the Basement: Poems for Women*

The Poem

The speaker of Carolyn Kizer's "Bitch" provides a satiric account of a typical encounter between her and a former lover during the unspecified period since the end of their relationship. In a single, thirty-four-line stanza, the speaker engages in a comic monologue that displays a quintessentially ironic duality: the speaker's two simultaneous but divergent dialogues, one consisting of the speaker's external conversation with her former lover and the other of silent admonitions, threats, and explanations to her inner self, represented in the poem as a female dog, or "bitch."

Over the course of the monologue, the reader learns the range of the speaker's intensely ambivalent feelings toward the ex-lover, from vicious hostility to cowed devotion to dismissive self-deprecation. Throughout the conversation with the ex-lover, the speaker masks her true feelings with unfailing politeness.

The speaker's initial hostility whenever she and her former lover meet reveals itself in the immediate warning she gives to "the bitch inside [her]" not to start "growling"; while once the man may have been a "trespasser," she says, he is now merely an "old acquaintance." The conflicting feelings suggested by this conversation with her inner self are quickly dramatized: The speaker offers a first pleasantry, but "the bitch starts to bark hysterically." However, as the pleasantries continue, "a kind word" from the man produces a dramatic change in the reaction of the inner self: "she begins to whimper./ She wants to snuggle up to him." Now the roles are reversed as the speaker must threaten the "bitch" not to be too approachable.

The shift in the inner self's reaction to the man, producing a consequent, if not as dramatic, shift in the speaker, doubles the layers of ambivalent emotion the speaker feels toward her former lover. Now she must explain, in apparent defense of her inner self—of her own forgetfulness of "the casual cruelties, the ultimate dismissal"—that a thoughtful word has simply reminded the "bitch" of her former devotion and of the man's past "small careless kindnesses." While these seem, momentarily, more important than what produced a strong but hidden enmity, the speaker maintains an external equilibrium, against both anger and forgiveness, as the pleasantries with her former love continue.

She instructs her inner self—herself—that she was not right for the man, dismissing herself as "too demonstrative, too clumsy,/ Not like the well-groomed pets of his new friends." At that, the speaker utters some last, cheerful but hurried words of goodbye as she drags the "bitch" off "by the scruff," perhaps in fear of any further weakening of her will—perhaps, too, in shameful discomfort at her inner weakness.

Forms and Devices

Kizer's feminist poetry is often discursive, directly addressing those issues in male-female relations and of gender roles and characteristics that were at the core of late twentieth century feminist thought. On other occasions, as with "Bitch," she abandons discursiveness in favor of narrative and dramatic representations of relational and emotional issues as they play themselves out in brief encounters or over long periods of time. In "Bitch," Kizer approaches the narrative in the form of a satiric-quasi-dramatic monologue. Although the satire is in the gentler Horatian mode, without bitter anger or invective, it offers, perhaps, even more compassionate understanding for the subject of the folly it exposes than is typical for that mode. Kizer, the satirist, is not here ridiculing some "other"; rather, she is incisively poking fun at the very women whose lives she has championed.

The fundamental element of the poem's satire is the representation of its speaker's inner self as a "bitch." The word has dual meanings. Most immediately, the word suggests men's historical characterization of what they have perceived as harsh, complaining, even angry women as bitches, much as the inner self in the poem seems to be in her initial reaction to the former lover, or in a milder but shrewder sense, as the speaker might be characterized when excusing her inner self's sudden obsequiousness on receipt of a kind word.

Kizer satirizes not only the male use of the word but also female acceptance of it, by playing off its original meaning in reference to a female dog, a dog that might "whimper" and "snuggle up" to its master, even one that has mistreated it. Kizer's appropriation of the derogatory term from its male owners to stand as the title of the poem satirizes in itself the implicit victimization men claim when characterizing a woman as a bitch.

Kizer further satirizes women like her speaker in the ironic contrast between the polite banality of what the speaker actually says to her former lover and the tumultuous inner dialogue that simultaneously takes place. While the notion of split selves—external and internal—may be commonplace, it is represented in the poem to particular comic effect because of the breadth of the split and because the emotional extremes are expressed in doglike behavior. Unique locutions evincing the split self also produce comic effects, such as "I say, as I say" and the near personification of "My voice says. . . ."

The inner dialogue with the "bitch" is balanced by the outer dialogue with the former lover, and the speaker recounts both in something close to a dramatic monologue. There is no apparent silent interlocutor other than the reader to whom the speaker addresses herself, as is usually present in the form, but in the manner of dramatic monologue, the reader learns much about the speaker from the way in which she purposely and inadvertently reveals herself while speaking. These revelations are manifold. They emerge from the direct narrative account, from the separate dialogues with her inner self and her former lover, and from the final, subtle, but odd redirection of the speaker's voice that takes place in the final three lines.

Whereas the speaker's remarks to the "bitch" through most of the poem have always been part of the dialogue during the encounter with the former lover, in the final three lines they become, instead, part of the narrative account of the incident: "You gag/ As I drag you off by the scruff,/ Saying, 'Goodbye! Goodbye! Nice to have seen you again.'" This displacement of the silent interlocutor from the reader to the inner self makes uncertain precisely to whom the speaker has been addressing herself, to what end, and to what ultimate conclusion on the part of the reader about the speaker.

Themes and Meanings

Throughout much of her poetry, Kizer seeks to elucidate the historical and contemporary situation of women in a male-dominated world. She does this not only by noting and representing the destructive characteristics of male behavior and drives but also by calling attention to what, in "Pro Femina" (1964), she calls the independent but "maimed" condition of women. In "Bitch," this wounded condition of the speaker is everywhere and increasingly present. It is in the title, in which a truly felt sense of belittlement confronts demeaning male name-calling. It is in the speaker's own representation of her inner self as a "bitch," one that not only "bark[s] hysterically," as men posit but also, more profoundly, may "whimper," even "cringe," at the most insignificant of kindnesses. It is also in the bitch's forgetfulness, her easy willingness to remember past adoration and "the small careless kindnesses" in the face of the former lover's greater self-absorption, boredom with her devotion, and "casual cruelties," indeed, his "ultimate dismissal" of her.

The conceit of the "bitch" and her behavior provide the poem's greatest, most obviously self-directed feminist satire. An easier satire lies in the speaker's masking strong emotion with external pleasantry. While the masking is a common behavior, what draws particular sympathy from the reader is the very existence of the still unresolved, warring emotions. The speaker carries her wounds still, against much evidence in her own mind that would deny their emotional sense. Even when the poem presents the speaker as a strong woman, a woman so determined to maintain her independence from a destructive emotional attraction that she threatens to give her own inner self, the "bitch," a "taste of the choke-chain," the fervency of her resistance to the man reveals her wounded condition. The anger toward the ex-lover is reflected back on herself.

The speaker does express compassionate understanding for the bitch's quick reversion to obsequious behavior, yet that compassionate tone slips all too easily, almost unnoticeably, into self-deprecation. She apparently consoles the bitch:

> He couldn't have taken you with him;
> You were too demonstrative, too clumsy,
> Not like the well-groomed pets of his new friends.

After this dismissal of herself, the speaker's leave-taking is a desperate getaway: She drags the gagging bitch off before all self-restraint is lost. That the speaker offers the account of this act to the bitch herself, and not to the reader, suggests the speaker's continuing inner dialogue; she contests with herself not only during the period of the encounter with the former lover but also, perhaps, at other times. The internal conversation of wounded women who seek emotional independence from unhealthy attachments to men, Kizer tells us, is not easily ended, and the "bitch" a woman may be is not the one men call her.

A. Jay Adler

THE BLACK ANGEL

Author: Henri Coulette (1927-1988)
Type of poem: Lyric
First published: 1963; collected in *The War of the Secret Agents and Other Poems,* 1966

The Poem

"The Black Angel" is a distilled version of a longer poem by Henri Coulette about a memorial statue of a black angel that stands in the midst of an Iowa City cemetery. A number of Coulette's contemporaries also wrote poems about this statue, though his contemporaries did not publish their poems. Coulette seems to have been uncertain about what he wanted to do with the figure; he wrote at least three versions of the poem, eventually condensing it so far as to make the reference of the title and the line "I will not meet *her* eye" somewhat obscure.

The metrical form of the stanza is the same in all the versions of the poem. It follows a pattern of beats that repeat 5-2-3-4-5-3 in each stanza—a metrical form invented, according to poet Robert Mezey, by Peter Everwine. The first version, of nine stanzas, was not published, but it was printed privately on a double folio that held nine pen-and-ink drawings of the figures invoked by the poem, done by a fellow student. The 1963 version published in *The New Yorker* consisted of the first eight stanzas of the poem, without the original ninth. It was published in *The War of the Secret Agents and Other Poems* (1966) as the four-stanza poem that is discussed here.

The whole poem is in the first person, and while sometimes a poet uses first-person singular even when he or she is writing in the persona of an imaginary speaker, this poem gives no indication that the speaker is anyone but the poet himself. While he is thus speaking of his own thoughts and experiences, the use of the pronoun "I" invites the reader to see through the "eye" of the speaker, to see and experience vicariously what he does.

The stanzas that Coulette excised describe the graveyard statue and muse about those who lie buried about it. He then shifts the focus of his musing from the historical past of prosaic pioneers to ask about others who are gone, or will be gone one day, whose lives were of a different scope. These are the stanzas that make up the poem.

The first stanza begins with a query that, by asking about people of great beauty and longings, draws one's attention to the inevitability and obscurity of their end. The second stanza is more specific, in that it refers to particular friends of Coulette: The "friend too much moved by music" is Donald Justice; "that one too much moved by faces," Robert Mezey; and "that marvelous liar," Philip Levine. All these friends were living, and in fact fairly young men, when this poem was written, so their fates were unknown then.

The third stanza has more to say about these friends: their activity as poets, what it is like to be them, how their lives may end. In the last line of this stanza, the reference to "*her* eye" signals a return to the contemplation of the figure of the black angel.

The fourth stanza describes some very immediate images, things that are found around the speaker as he is standing in the grassy cemetery—"but here's a butterfly,/ And a white flower." He even describes a bit of himself as one of those immediate things: "the moon rising on my nail" refers to the small, crescent-shaped, white cuticle at the base of the fingernail.

Forms and Devices

Coulette places his poem in a classical context by the use of allusion and conceit. He makes a reference to Thomas Gray, which tells the reader that he understood himself to be writing a poem that on one level was part of the long tradition of graveyard elegies. In those elegies, primarily written in the eighteenth century, the meditation on death stands for a contemplation of the sublime—that which is beyond human comprehension. The use of the Renaissance conceit of *ubi sunt* (Latin for "where are they now?") in the first line ("Where are the people") both reinforces this meditative tone and emphasizes the placement of the poem within a long poetic tradition.

Another connection to poetic tradition is made by the poem's allusion to figures of mythology (if one sees the "idler whom reflection loved" as Narcissus and the "woman with the iridescent brow" as Psyche) and its proposal to "bring them flowers." These references together introduce echoes of John Keats's "Ode to Psyche" (1820). Like Keats's poem, it proposes to do something it never actually begins to do. The speaker who "would" bring flowers, "thinks" of friends, and "will not" but someday "shall" meet the eye of the black angel is very much like the speaker of Keats's poem promising to build a bower to a deity who never arrives.

This poem progresses from very metaphorical to very concrete imagery. The repetition of images of reflection in the first stanza ("mirrors," "oceanic," "reflection," "iridescent") creates a sense of something not plainly visible, but rather something that shimmers and wavers. At the same time, such things as "oceanic longings" and an "iridescent brow" are purely imaginative: While one can have a sense of what is meant, one cannot picture it in the mind's eye.

The image of the "old streetcars buried at sea" is very strong but strange; the intended oddity is plain. Such things are possible, but incongruous. At the same time, to be "buried at sea" is to be beneath the level of shimmer and reflection of the surface of the water. With this image, the poem progresses; it moves from the elusive to the more tangible.

The objects in the fourth stanza are concrete almost to the point of being prosaic but also seem to represent something more than themselves. Their whiteness is an opacity that is the opposite of a reflecting surface. Yet none of these variations—mirroring, murky, or opaque "elements"—implies clear, direct vision, so the impression one gets through the poem is of something not quite comprehended. This sense is made even stronger by the final image, which pairs two seemingly opposite senses of motion.

Themes and Meanings

The figure of the black angel, whether specifically meant or as a general reference, is a signal of death. Combined with the *ubi sunt* theme of the first stanza, one can understand this poem as a contemplation on the passing away of things. The shift from the first stanza to the second stanza, a general query to thoughts of friendship, tells the reader that the poet is contemplating the end of life as he knows it.

In the third stanza, it could be the friendships mentioned in the second stanza that are "the past of what was always future"—that is, friendship is based on what came before but is defined by its lasting forward into time. This line also could place those friends, and thus Coulette himself along with them, among those to be lamented by some future *ubi sunt*. It may be that when others look back upon them, maybe even during their own time, the differences that distinguished them as poets made them as strange as "old streetcars buried at sea"; the experience of being "in the wrong element" may be a kind of death even while they are living.

Further, these lines may also be about poems (which people are "as beautiful as"). It could be that poetry itself, speaking "in tongues,/ Silently, about nothing" is what is so strange, and it is what these friends do that is "what was always future."

In all these possibilities revolve questions about death: Where are those who are gone? Where will my friends be? Where will I be? Will something about me exist in the future? Even the turnings of the friends in the second stanza pose a similar question: Are the turns—from music to games, from faces to the wall ("turned his face to the wall" is in one sense a paraphrase for suicide), from lies to truth—positive change or progress, or are they merely preludes to the final turn to the face of death?

The refusal in the last line of the third stanza puts off that final turn, but the fourth stanza, acknowledging the inevitability of that final meeting ("Although I shall" meet her eye), attempts to put it off by focusing on the "presence of things present" (the butterfly, the flower, the moon). Then death intrudes again, this time as a simile for the hardship of life: "Flying woefully" (life) is like "closing sweetly" (death). Between these two possibilities—living that is as woeful as death and death that may be as sweet as life—which are always all that is present and in everything that is present, "there is nothing else."

"Closing sweetly" also carries a sexual overtone that is not implausible when people's "oceanic longings" and the "woman with the iridescent brow" are considered. This changes the meaning of "I will not meet *her* eye . . ./ Although I shall" somewhat as well. To read the images this way is also not inconsistent with the classical associations of the poem, as the oblivion of the moment of sexual abandonment has been, from the Renaissance on, linked with the "nothing else" of death.

Laurie Glover

BLACK HAIR

Author: Gary Soto (1952-   )
Type of poem: Lyric
First published: 1985, in *Black Hair*

The Poem

Gary Soto's "Black Hair" is a short poem in free verse, its thirty lines forming three equal stanzas. The opening poem of the anthology, this poem is an eight-year-old's explanation of how he connects with baseball, through players who look like him.

"At eight I was brilliant with my body," Soto begins, describing the innocence and bravado of youth. Despite the oppressive heat of July, the speaker "sat in the bleachers" to see a "figure—Hector Moreno/ Quick and hard with turned muscles." He comes to memorize the stance of Hector, his hero, to match it: "His crouch the one I assumed before an altar/ Of worn baseball cards, in my room."

The reader wonders why this player, Hector, is so significant. The speaker answers in the second stanza, "I came here because I was Mexican, a stick/ Of brown light in love with those/ Who could do it." The speaker comments on his own size, "What could I do with 50 pounds"; on a personality trait, "my shyness"; and in the next line, on a more obvious physical characteristic, "My black torch of hair." The speaker wants to watch a player who can and does "do it," "the triple and hard slide,/ The gloves eating balls into double plays." He needs the role models of those—like him—who can succeed, unlike his parents. The end of this stanza abruptly shifts away from the game of baseball to the realities of this young speaker's life. "Father was dead," he states, "his face no longer/ Hanging over the table or our sleep." As painful as such a revelation about his father might be, the portrayal of his mother may be even more painful as her actions continue. She "was the terror of mouths/ Twisting hurt by butter knives." While his father's actions no longer affect the speaker, his mother's appear to haunt him continually.

The poem shifts once again as the third stanza begins. The joy of the game returns to the speaker: "In the bleachers I was brilliant with my body." In the bleachers, the speaker knows how to be a great fan, using his body to wave "players in," showing his support by stomping his feet. As a fan in July, he grows "sweaty in the presence of white shirts," or white T-shirts, the uniform of stalwart fans. Intensely into the game, he chews "sunflower seeds" and drinks "water" and emotionally sweats out the end of the game, biting his "arm through the late innings." The poem ends hopefully as Soto parallels the game of baseball with the "game" of life.

The last half of the stanza describes Hector's prowess and the speaker's wish for the same ability. The speaker lives vicariously through Hector's accomplishments. He says, when Hector "lined balls into deep/ Center, in my mind I rounded the bases/ With him." When the speaker is running the bases with Hector, the imagined vision of "my faced flared, my hair lifting" is "Beautiful." This vision is critical to the young speaker's sense of well-being, for in Hector the speaker is powerfully aligned with "his people," Mexicans who succeed and are cheered in life. Mentally, running alongside Hector, he, too, is a victor who is "coming home/ To the arms of brown people," the people from whom the speaker most needs affirmation.

Forms and Devices

Beginning with the opening line, Soto immediately engages the reader by using words in unexpected ways to reinforce his meanings. The speaker says he was "brilliant." The reader typically associates brilliance with a level of intelligence, of cognitive ability; Soto surprises the reader by using it to designate physical talent, as he does again as he begins the third stanza: "In the bleachers I was brilliant with my body."

The word "brilliant" is also often associated with describing levels of light. Soto forges a link with light imagery in using metaphor to compare the speaker to a "a stick/ Of brown light." Color is linked with the goodness of light. Soto creates another metaphor to reinforce this connection when he states that the speaker's hair is a "black torch," which he fears is "about to go out" given the realities of his family life. However, Soto continues to use light imagery, with the word "flared" to describe the speaker's vicarious rounding of the bases with Hector. Concurrently, Soto says his hair lifts "Beautifully," in the shape of a lit torch. Despite the fact the speaker has dark hair, Soto uses it as an emblem of light, a symbol of promise, as in the first light of a new day, a symbol of tomorrow, of light that illuminates the future.

The poet squarely places the speaker at the game—"I sat in the bleachers/ Of Romain Playground"—and then uses movement to paint the setting of the game: "in the lengthening/ Shade that rose from our dirty feet." As the sun sets, the shadows grow, covering the "dirty feet," a typical trademark of an eight-year-old on a hot summer evening, but perhaps they are meant to be indicative of this young boy's plight: He has dirty feet because he is Mexican and has no shoes.

If so, the speaker's need for a hero in his life is heightened in the next lines when he admits to having created an "altar/ Of worn baseball cards" in his room. The word "altar" connotes religious imagery; before an altar, someone worships, as it appears this speaker does. Further, he does so in the image of the person he is worshiping; the young boy assumes "His crouch." Beyond living vicariously through his hero, he worships his hero in the form of his hero.

Soto uses personification as gloves "eat" balls into double plays. The image of hungry mouths that "swallow" catches and potential victories, juxtaposed with the metaphor of the temperature of July as a "ring of heat/ We all jumped through," creates a powerful picture of the speaker's position in life and his need for great accomplishment against enormous odds.

Themes and Meanings

Soto provided an anecdote explaining the poem's impetus. For "Black Hair" he wrote, "As a kid, I was no good at baseball. Many of my summers were spent watch-

ing games from the bleachers and rooting for a player who was Mexican, like me."
This longing for acceptance in a world in which being different, such as Mexican, was
not considered desirable, dominates this poem. The speaker craves positive reinforce-
ment as a person. While many children would experience in their homes this life-
affirming need, his home life clearly does not provide it. He did not receive accep-
tance from his father, who is now dead. His mother seems unable to fulfill her son's
needs as well; compared with a butter knife, her words wound, not nurture—even a
butter knife hurts when twisted.

This longing is not exclusive to Latino culture. Psychologist Abraham Harold
Maslow's hierarchy of needs places belonging just after the physical needs of food
and shelter. Soto has written a poem describing the need for community among hu-
mans. Human beings do not live in isolation from one another. They live in commu-
nity, and because of that, they consistently compare and contrast themselves with oth-
ers. If one is happy with oneself, one does not need to be the "best." For the speaker,
the evidence is in watching Hector and his athletic ability.

The title "Black Hair" creates a fitting image for the entirety of this poem. A most
noticeable physical feature, Soto compares "black hair" to a "torch." Soto makes this
feature, the hair on a human head, symbolic of light and the promise of the future.
This young boy wants to believe that he can be a player in the game of baseball, and
more importantly, in the game of life. Soto's poem provides powerful imagery and ev-
idence that he can. The young speaker can live this dream because someone like
him—a Mexican—can succeed; he has his longed-for role model. The speaker wit-
nesses Hector's athletic skill in person. While he is "in the bleachers" during this
poem, only a fan right now, he believes that he, too, is "brilliant with his body." In-
deed, his belief in himself will cause his success; ultimately, his "black hair" will be
his crown of victory. His "black torch of hair" is not "about to go out."

Alexa L. Sandmann

BLACK HILLS SURVIVAL GATHERING, 1980

Author: Linda Hogan (1947-   )
Type of poem: Lyric
First published: 1981, in *Daughters, I Love You*

The Poem

The setting for this poem is the Black Hills of South Dakota, specifically at the places where enormous holes drilled into the earth house missile silos. The sites contain nuclear warheads that are capable of traveling thousands of miles and destroying large cities. The occasion is an encampment of people protesting the existence and potential use of these weapons; the poem describes an early morning scene, as the people awaken and begin the day's activities.

In the first stanza, the reader sees Buddhist monks, familiar at peace and antinuclear demonstrations, in their orange-colored, togalike robes, outlined against the rising sun. The next two stanzas depict other people beginning to awaken, as bombers fly overhead. While the encampment stirs and comes to life, more people arrive on the dusty roads.

The speaker then turns, in the fourth stanza, from the panoramic view of the whole camp to speak of her family: her husband and two daughters, who are participating in the event with her. She describes her husband bathing their small daughter in a pail of water, then in the next stanza turns to the other daughter combing her hair. The speaker says that she makes coffee, and while doing so tells her daughter that they are camped in the land of the daughter's ancestors. She wonders about her daughter's reaction to this knowledge. The sixth stanza turns again to a slightly more distanced view, as the speaker places her family with respect to the sun and the hills and reflects on the names in her family: Thunder Horse and Dawn Protector for the daughters, and her husband's name, Hogan, which means "home" in Navajo.

In the last two stanzas, the speaker begins to speak first for all of her family, then for all of the people in the encampment. "We" stand, she says, at ground zero, the center of the bombs' target. Enormous power for destruction exists overhead and beneath the earth, in the flying bombers and buried missiles, and this sense is juxtaposed with the description of the people awakening and looking. The increasing light as the sun rises makes the earth almost seem to be on fire, and the speaker sees a mare standing on a distant ridge looking as if she might have been at Hiroshima. The speaker describes the veins within the people carrying life, sees her children's vibrant hair, and begins to hear and feel the monks mentioned at the beginning of the poem as they start to sing to the rhythm of their drums. The poem ends with a single word, "heartbeat."

Forms and Devices

Like almost all Linda Hogan's poems, "Black Hills Survival Gathering, 1980" is written in first-person free verse. The poet alludes directly and deliberately to her family, referring to her husband and daughters by name, and she reinforces the identification between the author of the poem and the voice or speaker within it. The poem proceeds by way of direct description, with very few examples of rhetorical devices such as simile or extended metaphor. One exception is the comparison of the mare seen on a distant hill, which looks like "one burned/ over Hiroshima." This practice of using plain language and straightforward description is in keeping with Hogan's philosophy of writing, which stresses the accessibility of her poetry to ordinary people; as she stated in an interview with Bo Scholer, which was published in *The Journal of Ethnic Studies* (1988), "I don't want my work to be something you can only read if you have gone to a university."

While the description in "Black Hills Survival Gathering, 1980" is unadorned by rhetorical figures, it is highly impressionistic. That is, the reader is constantly drawn to the appearance of things, to the way in which things strike the speaker's eye, and things are often described as if the way they appear is the way they are. In the opening of the poem, for example, the sight of the monks looking as if they are touched by the sun's fire is described in words that state that their bodies actually are "on fire." Later in the poem, the shining of her daughter's hair as it is being combed is portrayed in words that state that the "warm sun" itself is being combed across the hair. The effect of the device, which blurs the distinction between what appears to be and what is, is to suggest metamorphosis and transformation.

Colors play an important part in the description of the process of awakening in the encampment. The monks' orange robes correlate with other images of light and fire in the "fractures of light" (a metaphor for lightning) in the distance, the sulfur-colored grass, and the "burning hills" which appear to be on fire as the sun's light catches them. Close to the light/orange configuration is the red of the horse and the red veins the speaker imagines under the fragile skin of her children. The red of blood and flame contrasts in turn with the sky and the blue of veins. Within this pattern of color is the metaphor of the people's veins as "tunnels"—red and blue—carrying the pulsing life within the body, contrasted with the death-dealing tunnels containing warheads and destruction.

Themes and Meanings

"Black Hills Survival Gathering, 1980" is part of a group of poems that resulted from the Black Hills Alliance International Survival Gathering, the event commemorated in the poem. The poems, first printed in *Daughters, I Love You* (1981), are dedicated to Sister Rosalie Bertell, M.D., who inspired the poet with the words quoted in the dedication to the book: "Everywhere I go, women are grieving the death of the species. You can either turn it around or help it to die." The poem, like all the poems in the book, is a plea for life against death. The contrast between life and death, the image of life in the midst of death, permeates the description, imagery, and rhetoric of the poem. A secondary theme is the persistent memory, explicit in the description of the monks and the reference to Hiroshima, of the realization of the annihilating power of nuclear destruction. The poem calls for a moral awakening even as the process of awakening is documented in the description.

The life-and-death contrast begins with the description of the B52's leaving "a cross on the ground" over the heads of men awakening on the hilltop. The cross is the cross-shaped shadow of an airplane passing over the grassy hillside. The figure is also an oblique allusion to the crosshairs on the bombardier's sight, which will locate "ground zero," where the participants of the encampment stand as they assemble in the morning light. Finally, the cross on the ground suggests the association with crucifixion: the sacrificial death of innocent victims.

Throughout the poem, the speaker contrasts the homely, ordinary events of living—bathing children, making coffee, combing hair—with the imminent destruction buried within the earth and flying overhead. The specifically nuclear nature of the threat is woven through the description, from the monks "on fire" against the morning horizon to the dusty roads transforming matter into energy (the energy of the resisters), the electric breeze and, finally, the "radiant" morning. The literal description of people waking up after a night's sleep and beginning their day's activities becomes, in the circumstances, a figure for the moral awakening they undergo with respect to the beauty and fragility of the earth and the necessity for preserving it against the wanton and savage destruction threatened by the missiles and bombers. The poem's reiteration of "waking" constitutes a chorus on this idea: The men wake on the hillside, the speaker's husband wakes, one daughter wakes, then the other, and finally, the entire encampment: "We are waking/ in the expanding light."

Another thread of images links the people and their individual lives with common human life and finally with the life of the earth itself. The speaker reflects that her daughter, as she stands being bathed, contains "wind and fragile fire"—the breath in her lungs and warmth of her body—under her skin; the daughters find their union with the land through their ancestors, "blood and heart." The speaker suggests another potential transformation, speculating that the daughter's hair might become "a mane" in her identification with the plains and its horse culture; this image echoes later in the sight of the red horse, first drooping as if in sickness, but then "surging" toward the sky. Finally, the veins pulsing with life-carrying blood join with the singing and drumming of the monks and all the participants; the poem's final word, "heartbeat," then unites people, land, and inner soul in a single affirmation of life.

Helen Jaskoski

THE BLACK RIDERS

Author: Stephen Crane (1871-1900)
Type of poem: Book of poems
First published: 1895, in *The Black Riders and Other Lines*

The Poems

Stephen Crane was well launched into a career as a fiction writer before he ventured into poetry. As early as 1890, he was writing sketches for a college monthly, and shortly thereafter he began producing columns for the *New York Tribune.* In 1893 Crane published one novel, *Maggie: A Girl of the Streets*, began work on another, *The Red Badge of Courage* (1895), and ventured into poetry. Since at that time he had only seven more years to live, it is hardly surprising that in all Crane produced only 136 poems. Half of these appeared in *The Black Riders*, another thirty-seven in a later volume, *War Is Kind* (1899). Only eight more poems were published during Crane's lifetime; the remainder were collected and printed after his death.

Though Crane's important first collection is usually referred to as *The Black Riders*, it actually appeared under the title *The Black Riders and Other Lines*. His poems deal with serious issues, but they are not based on a systematic theology or philosopy. Instead, they are speculations, born of fleeting thoughts or experiences, that the poet jotted down and then shaped into a coherent form. Like lyrics, each of the poems in *The Black Riders* is clearly tied to a moment, and therefore there are often marked differences between various poems on the same subject. Crane's poems are not intended to express emotion as a lyric does, but to be little essays in poetic form— or, as the author also described them, "pills" to remedy the spiritual and intellectual ills that afflict humanity.

One reason Crane used words such as "lines" or "pills" to describe his poems was that, while he was happy to be classified with fiction writers, he did not want to be considered a poet. For him the term implied effete bohemianism. On the other hand, Crane was proud of his own works in the genre. He even admitted liking *The Black Riders* better than *The Red Badge of Courage*, explaining that the novel was limited in scope, whereas the poetry covered all areas of human existence.

The sixty-eight poems in *The Black Riders* are all written in free verse. They are very short, many of them no more than three to six lines in length. Only four are over twenty lines. Moreover, because most of Crane's lines are themselves so short, sometimes consisting of just a word or two, even the longest of the poems in the collection (number 49) does not seem as lengthy as its forty lines might indicate.

Despite their brevity, however, Crane's poems have internal conflict and move to a conclusion. For example, the first poem in the collection begins with a dramatic description of the "black riders" and ends with a startling explanation: The ride of the mysterious men, readers learn in the last line, is like that of "Sin." By contrast, the drama in the second and third poems involves a contrast in perspective, in one case between the judgments of birds and human beings, and in the other between the persona and a "creature, naked, bestial," who may or may not be human but in any case is acting in a very peculiar fashion, at least as far as the narrator is concerned. Crane introduces his unnamed persona for the first time in number 3; though he does not appear in all of the poems, he does so frequently enough to provide a degree of unity to the collection.

The book does not have the same tight structure as the poems within it or as any of Crane's fiction, however. While a dozen themes or motifs appear, disappear, and reappear as the collection proceeds, no thematic divisions are evident, nor does the work as a whole move toward any conclusion. It has been suggested that *The Black Riders* is meant to represent a journey through life, perhaps that of the persona, whose presence could be imagined even when he does not appear. If so, the journey is circular rather than linear, for though each poem moves toward some discovery, the work as a whole does not move toward any transforming vision or redeeming certainty. This may be exactly the point Crane is making—that while one may appear to be progressing in life, making one discovery after another on the way to some final understanding, actually one ends where one began, except that one's mind is now crowded with conflicting truths, flooded with metaphors that still refuse to form a coherent pattern.

Forms and Devices

Crane's experiments with poetic form came as a direct result of his exposure to the work of another highly original poet. In the spring of 1893, Crane had been invited to call on the prominent novelist William Dean Howells. During their visit Howells read Crane several of Emily Dickinson's poems, and almost immediately thereafter Crane began writing the poems that would appear in *The Black Riders*. It is not difficult to see why this exposure to Dickinson, along with Howells's obvious admiration for her, so inspired Crane. Like her, he decided to ignore the conventions of the genre, even in so superficial a matter as the way his book would look. For instance, Crane insisted that his poems be given no titles, only numbers, and that they be printed, one to a page, in capital letters throughout. As a result, they looked at least as strange as Dickinson's dash-filled lines.

There was also much in Dickinson's style that appealed to Crane, notably her terseness and her use of epigrams. In number 34, for example, Crane's persona spurns those who are attempting to foist their own images of God upon him: "I can't buy of your patterns of God,/ The little gods you may rightly prefer." In number 62, a final epigram denies the significance of a man's entire life: "Yet when he was dead,/ He saw that he had not lived." One of the antiwar poems, number 5, describes how a well-intentioned suggestion by a single individual led to a bloody and long-lasting conflict. In time, readers are told, the man died, broken-hearted. The poem ends with a memorable epigram: "And those who stayed in bloody scuffle/ Knew not the great simplicity." The shortest poem in the collection, number 56, does not just contain an epigram, but is an epigram in its entirety: "A man feared that he might find an assassin;/ Another that he might find a victim./ One was more wise than the other."

In other ways, however, Crane's poetry is very different from that of Dickinson. Instead of meter and rhyme, he used the looser rhythmic patterns of free verse. Moreover, where Dickinson's references to the natural world—a snake, a bird, a fly—were always exact and particular, Crane's images are general, used primarily for allegorical purposes. The "little birds" in number 2, for example, have no individuality, and, except for his grin, the "fat, stupid ass" in number 55 is as unrealized as the "green place" where he is standing. Often Crane mentions mountains, deserts, gardens, and stars, but he does not describe them. Instead, he uses the words as stimuli which will prompt his readers to sketch appropriate landscapes from their own experience, while he proceeds to indicate the metaphorical implications of his imagery.

In *The Black Riders* Crane uses imagery to reinforce the statement he makes so often in his poems: that the world is, above all, a place of suffering and conflict. Even when his point about the seeming inevitability of human conflict is not made explicitly, as it is in number 27, where an encounter turns into a murder, and in number 5, where killing seems to be humanity's favorite pastime, it is implicit in such images as the "clang of spear and shield" in the title poem and even the "noise of tearing" that threatens the persona in number 40. There is no refuge. If various gods do not attack a man, as in number 19, the mountains will, as in number 22. In number 41, the very landscape, with its rocks and briars, seems malevolent. Frequently the world is described as a hostile desert (number 3, number 42) or a place of "snow, ice, burning sand" (number 21).

Crane's use of color imagery in *Black Riders* is particularly significant. At least a dozen times, the poet refers to red or to such associated images as fire and blood, and about as often, he mentions black or darkness. Thus blackness symbolizes not only sin (number 1) and death (number 68), but also existential fear (number 10) and the unknowable nature of the universe (number 29). This earth is indeed "a place of blackness" (number 23).

Though red is sometimes associated with life and hope, in Crane's poems it symbolizes pain, torment, and, like black, inevitable death. There are specific references to the color red, such as the red demons in number 46, but red is also associated with fire, with the desert heat, with the "crimson clash of war" (number 14), and with blood. In number 30, for example, the "red sword of virtue" means virtual suicide. In the final analysis, it does not much matter whether one dies on a "burning road," on the bloody field of battle or, more quietly, in black despair. In *The Black Riders* the serene, green gardens all lie "at impossible distances" (number 26). Red and black are the colors of this world, and there is no comfort in either of them.

Themes and Meanings

The Black Riders begins with an affirmation of the existence of sin and ends with an affirmation of the existence of God. While the title poem demonstrates the power of sin, it does not offer any hint as to its origin or indicate a possible remedy. One cannot derive any more comfort from the final poem in the collection, for although God finally strikes down a spirit for denying him, thus proving that he exists, he would not aid the spirit or even admit his presence during the spirit's long and anguished search for him. Thus what seem to be certainties are not certain at all, and what appear to be answers merely direct one toward more questions.

It is not surprising, then, that one of the dominant themes in the collection is that of the search for truth. Crane does not minimize the difficulty of this quest. Too often, he thinks, the overconfident find themselves in the position of the "learned man" in number 20, who confidently leads the persona into the unknown, only to find that he himself is lost. Crane is skeptical of people like the man in number 28, who insists that he has ascended to the "mighty fortress" which is truth and viewed the world from his unassailable position. In Crane's opinion, it is more likely that truth is a "shadow, a phantom" that he may never discover. Nevertheless, Crane knows that something in the human spirit yearns for truth. It may be that one is a fool for seeking it, like the man in number 24, who keeps "pursuing the horizon" even though he is told his quest is utterly "futile." It is interesting to compare this poem with number 7. Here the searcher is pictured not as a fool but as a person of some courage: "Fear not that I should quaver,/ For I dare—I dare./ Then, tell me!" Perhaps the difference between being a fool—one of Crane's favorite terms—and being a brave man is simply the difference between pride and humility. A fool does not know his limitations, either as an individual or as a human being; a brave man acknowledges them but refuses to embrace despair.

Whatever his uncertainties about truth or the possibility of discovering it, Crane did have firm opinions as to what constitutes human error. High on his catalog of sins was pride. Sometimes he points to this epitome of folly by contrasting human beings with animals, as he does in number 2, when the birds mock a man who cannot sing anywhere as well as they can, and in number 55, where anyone can see that the "stupid" ass who is enjoying himself in an earthly paradise is really cleverer than the man working so hard on the "burning road." In number 18 Crane sums up the issue in the form of a parable. Brought before God for judgment, various little blades of grass boast of their achievements. One of them is diffident, confessing that he cannot remember his good deeds, whereupon God praises him as being best of all.

If human beings possessed the humility of the diffident blade of grass, they would not be so certain of their own infallibility. In number 47 an insufferably arrogant man insists that the persona think just as he does, threatening that if he does not, he is "abominably wicked," a despicable "toad." After due deliberation, the persona decides that under those circumstances, he would prefer to be a toad. However, as Crane points out in number 17, it is far easier to be a conformist. Very few people are brave enough to think for themselves. As a result, the poet suggests, they are herded into church (number 32), where they worship other people's gods (number 34), or go willingly to war in order to kill those they have been told are their enemies (number 14).

Even though the poet can see the weaknesses of humanity, he does not himself fall into the trap pride sets for nonconformists. Thus in number 45, he reveals his scorn for tradition, which he says is "milk for babes," not "meat for men," but then he admits quite honestly that "alas, we all are babes."

While Crane seems firm in his ethical principles, he still wonders whether God exists, and if he does, how he relates to his creation. Sometimes the poet inclines toward nihilism (numbers 10, 66, and 67); at other times he taxes either an omnipotent God or some lesser divinity with being unjust (number 12, number 19). In number 6, he compares the world to a ship, marvelously made by divine hands, that slipped away before it could be equipped with a rudder and now drifts aimlessly through space. In this interpretation, God is not evil, just a bit careless and much too busy—it was his need to remedy a wrong that caused him to turn aside just when the world most needed him. Elsewhere, however, Crane is more hopeful. Clearly he would like to believe in a God of compassion (number 33) and of tender, "infinite comprehension" (number 51). Perhaps, the poet muses in number 49, there is a "radiance/ Ineffable, divine" that would give meaning to the universe. Perhaps it is only his own spiritual blindness that causes the vision to elude him. At the end of *The Black Riders* Crane is as uncertain about the existence and the nature of God as he was at the beginning.

Although Crane's fiction has long been admired, his poetry has been largely neglected both by readers and by critics. It deserves better. The poems in *The Black Riders* are worth reading for the surrealistic landscapes alone, but they have other virtues as well, including stylistic originality, profound subject matter, and, above all, uncompromising honesty in their search for truth.

Rosemary M. Canfield Reisman

BLACK TAMBOURINE

Author: Hart Crane (1899-1932)
Type of poem: Lyric
First published: 1921; collected in *White Buildings*, 1926

The Poem

"Black Tambourine" is written in three stanzas, each a quatrain with end rhymes on the second and fourth lines. This poem, brief as it is, is like much of Hart Crane's poetry: It carries suggestiveness to an extreme, never openly revealing its hand. The poem, though it appears to take a lyrical pleasure in measure and imagery, is told rather than spoken, allowing the reader to imagine that it may be a meditation rather than a lyric. The words seem to be said for their own sake. There is, in a sense, no definable speaker or audience.

The poem begins with the image of "a black man in a cellar." The second line states, in language reminiscent of a newspaper editorial espousing racial equality, that the black man's downtrodden living conditions "Mark tardy judgment on the world's closed door." The stanza concludes with starkly realistic images of gnats flying in a bottle's shadow and a roach running across the floor.

The second stanza changes the scene so abruptly that the reader struggles to find a connection. The speaker tells about Aesop, the ancient Greek fabler whose moral tales involving animals may have delighted children but clearly pointed at adult behavior. Aesop is generally regarded as a legendary figure, but the most prominent of legends makes him a slave who earned his freedom, or at least a measure of human dignity, through his capacity to tell stories.

There is the hint of a connection here in a double measure: African Americans were brought to the New World as slaves; those who are dehumanized and brutalized by the institution of slavery must, in a sense, "sing for their supper." In a 1921 letter to a friend, Crane offered a further connection between Aesop's fables, with their disarming simplicity, and the sentimental conception of African American romance, as was popularized by such Caucasian Southern writers as Joel Chandler Harris in his Uncle Remus tales.

The last stanza states that "the black man, forlorn in the cellar,/ Wanders in some mid-kingdom." He is truly no longer of his original world, yet he has not been fully assimilated into the mainstream of the culture in which he and his people were first introduced as slaves. Thus, his tambourine—conforming to a common racist notion that the "childlike" black loves music and dance—is not an active part of his life. Instead, the instrument is "stuck on the wall," while back in his ancestral home, Africa, there is nothing left but a decayed and corrupted—and irrevocable—past symbolized by "a carcass quick with flies."

Forms and Devices

In this poem, Crane works chiefly with two forms of poetic shorthand—metonymy and synecdoche. Synecdoche, the substituting of the part for the whole, is the easier of the two to define, and it is regarded by some as a special case of metonymy. An example of synecdoche is to use the word "sails" for "ship" or "ships." Metonymy is more complex: offering someone a "mug" when the item being served is actually coffee is one example—the container is substituted for the contained. One might argue that everything in this poem is what it seems to be—and less, and more. "The world's closed door," for example, covers a multitude of socioeconomic injustices, but it is also a door keeping the black man in his cellar (at the bottom of the socioeconomic ladder). Aesop is the fabler, but he also stands for the vision that sees through adversity to higher truths. The tambourine is a real instrument, but it is also the body of African American culture, that is, the beauty that African Americans managed to salvage from the detritus of the slave culture into which they were forced. The "carcass quick with flies" is a vivid image in concrete terms, but it also stands for what remains of black culture on its native soil as a consequence of the slavers' rapine.

If the carcass is the body of the past, and the tambourine is a token of the slave mentality, which he can put aside but not escape, then Crane wants the reader to see the black man as someone who can neither return to his origin nor advance beyond the figurative cellar of the Europocentric culture into which he has been introduced.

Themes and Meanings

Crane was rather explicit about his intentions for this poem, and although one should generally treat a poet's stated intentions gingerly, in this instance, one may learn from what Crane said he was hoping to achieve.

Referring to the last stanza's "mid-kingdom" analogy (the black man "wanders in some mid-kingdom"), he wrote in a letter to his close friend Gorham Munson in the spring of 1921 that the poem was a "bundle of insinuations, suggestions bearing out the Negro's place somewhere between man and beast." He stated that his only personal "declaration" in the poem was that he found "the Negro (in the popular mind) sentimentally or brutally 'placed' in this midkingdom." Crane also noted that a "propagandist for either side of the Negro question could find anything he wanted to in it," insisting that "the value of the poem is only, to me, in what a painter would call its 'tactile' quality—an entirely aesthetic feature."

It is not easy to know what to make of Crane's statements or, therefore, of the poem itself. What may sound, at the one extreme like the most dispassionate of racist attitudes can also sound, at the opposite, like the most dispassionate of aesthetic detachment. Putting those two ends together, however, one can possibly see what Crane means. He is neither depicting the black man as a generic entity nor portraying a particularized African American so much as depicting perceptions of blacks in America—neither from his perspective, nor from theirs, but from the perspective of the dominant white culture of his day.

Although the poem is filled with concrete socioeconomic details and, as noted earlier, a virtual editorial fervor for elucidating the "Negro question," the poem is not "about" the so-called "Negro question." Even that aspect of the poem is a part, not of its theme, but of its texture—its "tactile" quality, as Crane called it.

This is not to say that the poem has no "meaning." Crane is representing something as elusive as attitudes and values, and by evoking them accurately and authentically, he is exposing them to all. As Crane asserts, he does not want to take sides so much as to show the human element at the heart of the matter.

Russell Elliott Murphy

THE BLACK WALNUT TREE

Author: Mary Oliver (1935-   )
Type of poem: Lyric
First published: 1978; collected in *Twelve Moons,* 1979

The Poem

"The Black Walnut Tree," written in free verse, is a short poem of thirty-five lines. The title immediately draws the reader's attention toward the natural world and the center of emotional conflict in the poem. Like the large branches of an ancient walnut tree, Oliver's poem is shrouded in the shadow of her family tree. Using the first person, Oliver makes no distinction between the speaker of the poem and herself; in fact, the poet's family history is the source for the events described. In this poem, as in much lyric poetry, the speaker addresses the reader directly about her personal experience, and, by using this poetic form, Oliver makes the reader part of the events she describes, forcing one to consider the poem's dilemma as if it were one's own.

"The Black Walnut Tree" concerns the poet's and her mother's struggle to decide whether they will have a tree on their property cut down. If they decide to have the black walnut tree removed and to sell it for lumber, they will be able to pay off their home's mortgage; however, if they remain faithful to everything the tree represents, they risk a limb falling through the roof of the house in some storm or, worse, foreclosure and the loss of the house itself.

The poem opens with this general dilemma but moves quickly to its inevitable consequence: the two women trying to sort out what is really the best course of action in such a situation. Part of the poem's strength originates in what Oliver, in typically understated fashion, calls a "difficult time." While the responsibilities of home ownership are often thought too mundane to be the subject of poetry, Oliver manages to make a connection with her audience by plumbing the joys and burdens of owning a home or, more precisely, exploring how a home becomes more than a physical property.

In an attempt to convince each other that the only logical and financially responsible action is to cut down the tree, the poet tells her mother that the tree's roots are in the cellar drains, to which the mother replies that she has noticed the leaves growing heavier in the fall, when they must be raked, and the tree's fruit becoming increasingly difficult to gather. Clearly, however, the fruit this tree bears represents strong and essential connections to the past, an issue with far greater consequence than the tree's present inconveniences.

Thus, in the sixteenth line of the poem, there is a shift: The speaker realizes, in the process of her deliberation over the physical problems the tree presents, that "something brighter than money/ moves in our blood." At this point, the problem evolves from merely a physical dilemma to a spiritual one, and Oliver's insight is confirmed that night as she sleeps. Her dreams are populated by her Bohemian fathers—men who worked the "blue fields/ of fresh and generous Ohio"—and she wakes with the knowledge that she can never remove the tree. However, even though the poet is reconciled to the threat of high winds, heavier leaves, and falling fruit, she still hears "the whip-/ crack of the mortgage" as the poem closes.

Forms and Devices

Poet and novelist James Dickey suggests that Oliver's poems are "graceful and self-assured, serene even when they treat the ordinary agonies of life . . . richly complex without throwing complexities in the way of the reader." In "The Black Walnut Tree," Oliver does indeed suggest the complexity of what might be overlooked as merely mundane. She does so, however, without obscuring the events of the poem. As in much of Oliver's poetry, she achieves clarity in this poem by using common language to develop a short poetic line and metaphor that grows naturally out of her subject matter, all couched in a domestic narrative.

In "The Black Walnut Tree," as in much of her work, Oliver makes use of the lyric as plainsong, never allowing traditional verse forms to intrude on her subject. The short line she favors appears to have little to do with phrasing; rather, it establishes white space for contemplation. By placing so few words in each line, Oliver insists that the reader account for each word and the possible connections that the word may offer within the line and then within the poem as a whole. Perhaps this formal consideration culminates most dramatically in the final two lines of the poem, when Oliver hyphenates and splits the word "whip-/ crack," placing the emphasis equally between the two. The split allows the word to take on the physical characteristics of a whip: On one line it is drawn back; on the next it comes forward to lash its subject, the "crack" of the mortgage sounding.

At the same time that this "crack" relates to the mortgage, it also suggests the movement of the walnut tree's limbs. By constructing her metaphors from the very fabric of her narrative, Oliver gracefully and unobtrusively pushes the reader toward a recognition of the many levels at work. Truly, one might best describe Oliver's use of metaphor as organic or holistic, a practice that suits her spiritual perspective nicely. However, because of this practice, upon a first reading of the poem, it is relatively easy to overlook the extended conceit that Oliver carefully constructs.

The conceit grows from the black walnut tree at the center of the poem, taking on three interrelated meanings that function on significantly different levels. First, the black walnut tree exists on the physical plane, creating tangible, concrete problems for the poet and her mother. The tree has grown old, making inroads into the foundation with its roots, its falling fruit is more of a nuisance than a blessing, and its leaves pile higher with each passing autumn, becoming more difficult to dispose of.

Second, the tree exists on a spiritual plane that involves the deeply entwined history of the family. The walnut tree, like any other living organism, has started from a seed, and the poet realizes that "an edge/ sharp and quick as a trowel/ that wants us to dig and sow" moves in her blood. She is beckoned by this tree, in her own and her "fathers' backyard," to remember her fathers who filled the fields of Ohio with "leaves and vines and orchards." Thus, the tree in her yard comes to represent both the spiritual and physical call of her heritage.

Finally, as the poem closes, the tree takes on yet another meaning. The tree, limbs moving in "leaping winds," becomes a symbol of the mortgage that threatens to destroy the poet's own life with her mother, as well as the memory of her fathers. This final move allows the reader to recognize the complex and potentially tragic dimensions of this situation. The metaphor coalesces, encompassing both the physical and the spiritual, both the past and the present, to profound effect.

Themes and Meanings

"The Black Walnut Tree" is a poem about connection. Like her fellow Ohio native James Wright, to whom she dedicated her Pulitzer Prize-winning volume, *American Primitive* (1983), Oliver continually strives to illustrate the ties between people and place, often ending in some transcendent moment or epiphany. As the title of the collection *Twelve Moons*, in which "The Black Walnut Tree" first appeared, suggests, Oliver often discovers the connections between people and place in the primitive, natural order.

Oliver's search for elemental connections, like those associated with the moon, occur in "The Black Walnut Tree" when the poet and her mother are confronted with the demands of the present. However, the true conflict in this poem, which leads more toward insight than epiphany, is the undeniable hold that the past has on the present.

What prevents the poet or her mother from having the tree removed and paying off the mortgage is the knowledge of the tree's connection to a past that includes generations of men and women working the fields of Oliver's Ohio home, where the vines of their lives were woven into the very soil that they lived upon. To remove a visible symbol of this past connection—a living history told in the limbs, leaves, and fruit of this looming tree—would be to ignore and, in a sense, betray the universal truth that people are known and come to know others by recognizing the lines of history and their intersection in the present, pushing ever on toward an unknowable future. Consequently, with this insight, after dreaming of her fathers working the orchards they had planted, Oliver explains what she and her mother both know, "that we'd crawl with shame/ in the emptiness we'd made," a truly profound insight for what appears to be a rather modest poem.

Todd Davis

BLACK WOMAN

Author: Léopold Senghor (1906-   )
Type of poem: Lyric
First published: 1945, as "Femme noire," in *Chants d'ombre*; English translation collected in *Selected Poems*, 1964

The Poem

"Black Woman" is a short poem in free verse, with eighteen lines divided into three stanzas of five lines each and one stanza of three lines. It is written in the first person and is addressed directly to the woman of the title, the black woman who gives the poem its theme.

This was one of many poems written when Léopold Senghor was living abroad, away from his own country of Senegal. During this period, he was a student in Paris and wrote about his childhood, which he viewed as a kind of paradise. These poems abound in his memories of Africa—an Africa seen in his mind's eye—and are an imagined return to an idealized Africa.

Having experienced a feeling of estrangement amid Western society, he set out on a poetic quest for his homeland. He looked back to the time of his childhood and to the place where he was reared. The main themes in his first collection of poetry are a longing for his homeland, a nostalgia for his childhood, and especially an affirmation of his African heritage. "Black Woman" is one of the best-known poems from this collection. When Senghor writes of Africa, it is frequently in terms of a woman, a woman who is both wife and mother; she is the "promised land" mentioned in the poem.

The first stanza gives the theme of the poem: the natural black woman whose color is life and whose form is beauty. The poet has grown up in her shadow and has felt the gentleness of her hands. Now that he is grown, he returns to find her as if he were coming upon the promised land. He views her through a mountain pass at noon in the midst of summer, and her beauty strikes him directly to the heart, like the flash of an eagle.

In the second stanza, she is seen as a lover, a woman with the flesh of ripe fruit, a woman who can transport the poet with somber ecstasies of black wine, a woman with a mouth that makes his own mouth lyric. The poet elaborates, finding her a woman who is like a limitless savanna that shudders beneath the caresses of the east wind; a woman who is like a tight, well-sculpted drum that resounds under the fingers of the conqueror; a woman whose solemn contralto voice becomes the spiritual song of the loved one.

In the third stanza, she is almost a goddess, so perfect that even her skin is smooth as the oiled skin of an athlete or a prince. She is like a graceful gazelle with celestial adornments. Pearls become stars on the darkness of her skin. The reflections of the setting sun on her glistening skin are delights on which the mind can exercise itself.

The poet's anguish is lightened by the sunlike glance from her eyes, when he is in the shadow of her hair.

In the fourth and last stanza, the poet—more philosophical—informs the black woman that he is celebrating in verse her beauty, which is passing, and her form, which he establishes eternally in his poetry, before fate can turn her to ashes in order to nourish the roots of life.

Forms and Devices

The poem is a hymn of praise to the black woman—not only as an individual, but also as a symbol of African women and as a representative of her race. The first two lines serve as a statement of the poem's theme: the beauty of the natural black woman, who though naked, is "clothed" in her color, which is life. There is also the poet's response to this beauty, as the black woman is perceived in both sensory and emotional ways. The poet has experienced the touch of her hand, and he is struck to the heart by her beauty.

Even though the musical language and the rhythm of the original poem may lose something in translation—and many of Senghor's poems were written to be accompanied by African musical instruments—one nevertheless perceives the impact of this poem through the imagery, metaphor, and personification that the poet employs.

In an enumerative style, similar to that of a litany, Senghor presents a series of images that are, in effect, the attributes of the black woman. He thus seems to summarize her qualities, beginning with a description of the natural woman, then—elaborating metaphorically—he describes her as the promised land, a plain that rustles, and the nocturnal sky. The poet thereby sees her not only in terms of a person, but in terms of the earth itself, and even the universe.

There are other metaphors: In the second stanza—more erotic than the first—the black woman is seen in terms of ripe fruit, black wine, a savanna that shudders beneath the "caresses" of the east wind, and an object—a sculpted drum—that responds to the touch. Even her voice is the song of the loved one. In the third stanza, the oil on her skin is seen by the poet as the oil on the limbs of an athlete or on those of the princes of Mali. She is now more of a goddess, a graceful but celestial gazelle, perhaps a totem for her people.

Associating her with eternity, the poet uses terms dealing with things eternal: earth, wind, summer, noon, stars, night, suns. The poet thus sees the woman not only in terms of a person, not only in terms of the earth, but also in a more cosmic sense. The poet also employs words dealing with color, many of which are synonymous with black—shadow, dark, and somber. These words that are images of darkness are contrasted with words that are images of light: brighten, gold, stars, and suns.

The poet also uses the device of inversion. The first line of the first stanza—"naked woman, black woman"—becomes "naked woman, dark woman" in the second stanza, and these words are inverted in the first lines of the last two stanzas. Inversion is again used, as the repetition of the theme in the final stanza uses the words of the first stanza—life, form, and beauty—but in inverted order.

Use of punctuation is sparse, the ends of the lines serving as the ends of the word groups. A change of tense occurs only in the third line of the first stanza, where the poet uses the past tense in order to recall the comfort that black womankind has given him. He immediately resumes the present tense for the rest of the poem. This effect helps to connect the past with the present. He had grown up under the black woman's shadow; now he seeks solace again in the shadow of her hair.

Personification is another device, as the poet writes in the fourth stanza of Fate, which is jealous and capable of reducing one to ashes. It is in this stanza that he reveals his vocation of poet, as he informs the black woman that he is celebrating her beauty and her form in poetry, before she returns to ashes in order to nourish the roots of life. Thus the poet has moved, by means of description, metaphor, and personification, from praise of the black woman herself to an affirmation of the continuation of life. He has saved the best for last as he ends on a note of optimism.

Themes and Meanings

The meaning of this poem revolves around Senghor's contemplation, description, and glorification of the natural black woman. Woman holds a place of importance in Senghor's life and in his poetry. When he writes of Africa in his poetry, it is frequently in terms of a woman. His glorification of the black woman is quite different from that of Western poetry, which had so often glorified women of Western society. The black woman of this poem is more than an individual person; she is also the progenitor of his race, and thus symbolic of Africa itself and an embodiment of Senghor's African heritage. Senghor takes pride in his race, and here especially, he shows his love and respect for the black woman. He uses her very color as part of his praise and seems to abstract her characteristics into an idea of a black woman in order to praise her.

This deservedly famous and often-quoted poem was written when he was away from his homeland. The nostalgia that one finds in the other poems of his collection *Chants d'ombre* is reflected in this poetic return to an Africa that was almost unspoiled by the ways of the Western world and that was, for him, a sort of paradise where all seemed to be in harmony and at peace, where he felt secure in his place in the world. In this Africa of his childhood, there was a sense of a life spent in common with his family, his village, his clan, his tribe, and even his ancestors.

In this poem, he sees, in his imagination, an idealized African woman in several roles: in the first stanza, as mother, and thus comforting; in the second stanza, as lover, and thus erotic; and in the last line of the last stanza, as nourisher of life. There is a certain sweetness in this poem, a contemplative quality, a quiet appreciation of the African woman, and the emotions the poet experiences at her sight and at her touch. He details his pleasure in contemplating her and the comfort he experiences in her presence.

He realizes that life is transitory, that even though beauty seems permanent, time works on the individual woman. He is a poet, however, and he informs this woman that he is celebrating her beauty and her form in poetry, before she returns to ashes. The final stanza affirms the gift and the mission of the poet as someone who can relate the temporal to the eternal; as Pierre de Ronsard wrote to immortalize the passing beauty of his Helen, or Cassandra, or Marie, so can Senghor immortalize the beauty of the black woman. Thus the last stanza, even though potentially tragic as to the fate of the individual black woman, ends on a note of hope. These very ashes will be used to nourish life anew.

George Craddock

BLACKBERRY EATING

Author: Galway Kinnell (1927-   )
Type of poem: Lyric
First published: 1980, in *Mortal Acts, Mortal Words*

The Poem

"Blackberry Eating" is a short poem in free verse, its fourteen lines (in one stanza) all parts of one compound-complex sentence. One-sentence poems are not uncommon for Galway Kinnell. The title plunges into the immediacy of the context of the poem by focusing on an action as subject. The poem is written in the first person. There is no indication that the speaker's persona is someone other than the poet, so the poem fits into the classic tradition of lyric poetry wherein the poet directly informs the reader about a personal experience.

A subject that is clearly in the realm of the ordinary is the starting point of "Blackberry Eating." Kinnell introduces the activity of picking blackberries by grounding the experience in a particular mood, love, and a particular season, autumn. Autumn suggests the time of harvest, when the prospect of impending death weighs heavily on the mind. No drape of melancholy is allowed here, though; the enthusiasm of love keeps it pushed aside.

A descriptive series of words, a vibrant picture of blackberries begging to be picked, helps the reader see, smell, and feel the clusters of fruit. A blending of wilderness and civilization follows when the speaker links his exploration of nature with humankind's regularity and demands: The blackberries are for breakfast.

When Kinnell draws attention to the prickly stalks, he focuses on the significance of small details and comments on the mystical process of creation. He suggests that the stalks earn their prickles as a penalty for "knowing the black art of blackberry-making," a parallel with the myth of Adam and Eve's loss of Eden for "knowing" too much. The "knowing" here has mysterious and sexual connotations, as well as moral ones, since what is referred to as a "black art" is the knowledge of reproduction, which requires a penalty that serves as a flag of warning or an obstacle to be overcome for the speaker. Standing among the prickly stalks, the speaker raises clusters of blackberries to his face. The berries are framed in a close-up now, so ready to enter his mouth that they almost drop in, but the inclusion of "almost" qualifies the relationship of berry and tongue so that the necessity for deliberate involvement on the part of the eater remains.

The poem shifts away from the actual wilderness setting when blackberries are compared to a certain class of "words" in the latter portion of the long sentence. Kinnell limits these words to those with many letters and one syllable, and then, keeping blackberries within sight, he calls the words "lumps." The poet suggests "strengths" and "squinched" as examples of words that invoke a sensory experience like that of the provocative berries when such words, like the berries, engage the tongue. The interaction between the words and the poet, described in a series of actions of increasing intensity, emphasizes the sensory experience. In the last two lines, Kinnell returns the reader to a vantage point distant enough to glimpse the relationship between his satisfaction in encountering nature's empowering impetus in the creative wild and his satisfaction in realizing the same empowering impetus in his own creative impulse. The familiar blackberry-eating terminology in the description is not what it seems, however, since it now describes an inner place in which the black art of language making resides.

Forms and Devices

Its fourteen-line length demonstrates that "Blackberry Eating" is an unrhymed, free-verse sonnet in the style of Robert Lowell. The strict sonnet forms specify definite patterns of meter and rhyme but can also be interpreted on the basis of spirit and passion. The poem's first eight lines, or octave, consistent with the Italian sonnet form, serve as an introduction of the theme, developing the theme in the direction of the sensory experience of blackberry eating. Also true to form, the poem's last six lines, or sestet, introduce a new development or application of the proposition, wherein words are substituted for berries as sensory objects. This flow and ebb are sonnetlike, even though none of the other aspects demanded by the sonnet form is present.

The controlling image of the poem is a simile: the comparison of blackberries and words. Each element of the simile, however, has a specific definition. The blackberries are "fat, overripe, icy," and the words are "many-lettered and one-syllabled." In the first instance, Kinnell uses a series of somewhat hyperbolic adjectives to enhance the reader's appreciation of the sensate function of the blackberries. The "words" of the simile, restricted by Kinnell's imposition of rules, are heightened in meaning as well, since they directly relate to "strengths" and "squinched" by being the kind of words that sound "strong" because they "squinch" their few vowels among an abundance of consonants.

Kinnell's simile is framed by an analogy between the mysterious "art of blackberry-making" and the mysterious power of words. By use of a mirroring syntax including the repetition of the phrase "in late September" in the first and last lines of the poem, and the repetition of the adjectives "icy, black" in the second and next-to-last lines at the end of a series of adjectives modifying blackberries and language, respectively, the poem conveys the message that, in the same way that the blackberry bush produces blackberries, language produces succulent words that, when boldly embraced by the tongue, introduce sensations akin to the pleasure derived from devouring luscious blackberries.

The very sounds of "Blackberry Eating" underline its sense-oriented theme. The alliteration of *b*'s and long *e*'s, and the repetition of *p* in the first four lines, together with the *s*'s sprinkled generously throughout, work the lips and tongue. Especially involving are the *l*'s and *s*'s of line 9 followed by "squeeze, squinch . . . splurge" and then "silent, startled, icy"—words that infuse both energy and surprise into the images they evoke.

Themes and Meanings

With a Whitmanesque receptivity to experience, Kinnell transmits his wonder and delight in nature's creative power, and his own, in "Blackberry Eating." The speaker, frank about his love of nature, provides an idealized picture of rural life by describing a fall morning's experience that he implies he has repeated many times. The experience is not an end in itself, however, but acts as a sounding board for a more personal phenomenon: the eruption of words into his consciousness to be manipulated into their most effective mode.

"Blackberry Eating" concerns the origin of creative power, a playful presentation of the creative process as evidence of what Andrew Taylor has called the positive aspect of darkness that appears throughout Kinnell's work. This positive aspect, writes Taylor, "is the nonself, the unconscious, the preconscious, the unpredictable source of vitality, the Mystery."

Kinnell's mysterious "source of vitality" here touches the speaker in the form of inspiration, in compact words that bring with them a fullness of experience that awakens the speaker's senses to a mysterious void that lies just beyond the knowable. The void, however, does not loom in its "silent, startled, icy" blackness as a pit of destruction, but becomes, through its dramatic association with the extreme sensory pleasures of blackberry eating in the wild, a communicator of a life-affirming bias in the inexplicable design of the universe.

From its opening clause, "Blackberry Eating" reveals its Romantic underpinnings. Its form, that of a nature lyric replete with intimate observations of the beauty and bounty of the wild, displays Romanticism in the exaltation of detail and in the relationship imposed by its comparison of the speaker's sensory interaction with the physical world to his spiritual interaction with his own inner world. The influence of Austrian poet Rainer Maria Rilke on Kinnell's poetic vision shines through in this poem's organic vehicle. Although Rilke's emphasis is on transformation and Kinnell's is on empathetic participation, both poets use contact with the earth to penetrate the surface of things in order to achieve an understanding of the life/death cycle.

When Kinnell writes of the blackberry stalks "knowing the black art of blackberry-making" and later describes "the silent, startled, icy, black language of blackberry-eating," he is hinting at a metaphysical philosophy of a kind of Jungian collective unconscious that employs sensory, or even sensual, experience as its messengers. In *Walking Down the Stairs* (1978), Kinnell comments that "language itself comes from the deepest place, from sex." "Blackberry Eating" introduces this "deepest place" in a wider, yet still sensory and sensual context, and invites one to realize such ecstasy for oneself.

Virginia Starrett

BLACKCURRANT RIVER

Author: Arthur Rimbaud (1854-1891)
Type of poem: Lyric
First published: 1886, as "La rivière de Cassis," in *Les Illuminations*; English translation collected in *Complete Works, Selected Letters*, 1966

The Poem

"Blackcurrant River" is a short poem, composed in May, 1872, that was not published by the author. It remained a manuscript until 1886, when it was published together with a number of other pieces, entirely without the poet's knowledge. By the time "Blackcurrant River" appeared, Arthur Rimbaud had abandoned poetry and left Europe to live as a trader in Ethiopia.

The poem is composed of three rhyming six-line stanzas. In the French original, the lines are of unequal lengths, alternating eleven-syllable lines with lines of five to seven syllables. The rhyme scheme is also slightly irregular. While the rhymes of the first and third stanzas alternate in a simple *ababab* pattern, the second-stanza rhyme repeats a single nasalized vowel (*revoltants, temps, importants, entend, errants, vent*). Formal deviations such as these are difficult to render in a translation; their effect in the original French is considerable.

"Cassis" is a fruit, a popular flavor of sweetened syrup, and a liqueur. Thus the French title suggests a stream of sweet liquid, an inviting counterpart to the Big Rock Candy Mountain. When translated into English, the title contains a pun (currant-current) that is absent in French. Rimbaud spoke English, however, and may have been conscious of the possibility. In any case, the title helps establish a deceptively mild tone for the poem, although "black currents" run throughout.

The opening stanza evokes a pastoral landscape of a stream that rolls unknown through strange valleys. The stream is accompanied by the voices of a hundred ravens (or crows), and these are true, good "angel voices." Another element of this scene is the great movements of fir thickets in plunging winds. An undercurrent of tension troubles the ideal countryside: Why is the river unknown? Why are the valleys strange? How can the cawing of crows be hailed as angel voices? Even the winds, in the verb "plunge," are characterized with unusual violence.

The second stanza adds picturesque references in a guidebook tone. Everything rolls (as the river rolls), with mysteries of campaigns of ancient times, visited dungeons, important parks. All the elements of a country ramble in château country are here, yet the poet compromises his pastoral by terming his mysteries "revolting." Within these boundaries are heard the passions of knights errant, but the passions are dead. Again, the stanza ends with the wind, here set in opposition to the rest of the scene: "But how salubrious is the wind!"

The final stanza brings human figures to the landscape, a foot-traveler and a crafty peasant. An impersonal voice directs the hiker to look at latticework fences; if he does so, he will feel braver. Ravens are called soldiers of the forests, sent by the Lord. They are "dear, delicious ravens," directed to chase away the peasant. The peasant figure, crafty and guzzling (the verb used can also mean offering a toast), has the old stump of an amputated limb. In its final image, the poem offers a degraded figure, deformed by some old injury, a blot upon the fairy-tale pastoral landscape. Disturbing undercurrents in the description of that landscape suggest, however, that the sympathies of the poet lie with this "crafty peasant."

Forms and Devices

"Blackcurrant River" was written during the young Rimbaud's close early association with fellow poet Paul Verlaine. This was a very productive period, and several poems from roughly the same time, such as "Larme" ("Teardrop"), "Bonne Pensée de Matin" ("Good Morning Thought"), and the four "Fêtes de la Patience" ("Feast Days of Patience"), show the poet's formal experiments.

One element of experimentation is the length of the lines. Rimbaud's earliest poems are often written in formal Alexandrine (twelve-syllable) lines—even sonnet form. The poems of May, 1872, use shorter lines, although they rhyme and use regular verse form, sometimes inconsistently. In the "Fêtes de la Patience," for example, three of the four poems are written in lines of five syllables, the fourth in lines of eight.

The uneven rhythm of "Blackcurrant River" is one of its most distinctive features; it halts briefly after each shorter line, suggesting a limping step or the irregular flow of water over stones. This effect may not be rendered in all translations. The longer lines could be read separately and produce a legible text. The shorter lines throw the poem into its essential imbalance, and their content is emphasized. These lines often carry the more unsettling thoughts and images of the poem. In the briefer lines, crows' croaks are qualified as "angel voices," winds plunge and are praised, crows are called "dear" and "delicious," and an amputated limb serves to lift a toast or guzzle. These lines are longer by two syllables in the last two stanzas, adding to the irregularity of the poem.

Rhythm is not the only element that unifies "Blackcurrant River." The two first stanzas of "Blackcurrant River" are bound by an internal echo; both have the same main verb, "roll," and both evoke the wind. The first and third share the image of crows and their qualification as angels or soldiers of the Lord. Within the overall rhyme structure, which tends toward "rich" rhymes (that is, rhymes in which two or more elements of the word ending are the same), the rhyme scheme of the second stanza, which is built around the same nasalized vowel for all six lines and has a full syllable rhyme for the first four, produces a closed atmosphere. It emphasizes the suggestion of confinement that is thematic within this stanza, with its dungeon keep, river banks, and formal park.

Themes and Meanings

If the image of a "blackcurrant river" evokes a vagabond's paradise, the development of the poem expands that image by coupling it with medieval, fairy-tale commonplaces and a little faintly ironic advice to the timid hiker. This pastoral thematic is, however, accompanied by hints of violence. The wind, for example, is not always a tame breeze, but sometimes a violent one. In the first stanza, the movement of the fir thickets is produced by several winds "plunging." In the second stanza, the wind is set in contrast to the enclosed atmosphere of revolting mysteries, ancient campaigns, dungeon keeps, important parks, and dead passions. It is "salubrious," healthy and unconfined.

Also important in "blackcurrant river" are the ravens or crows, harsh-voiced birds of ill omen, which frequently devour dead heroes in traditional ballads. Within a poem that stresses the theme of medieval romance, this link cannot be denied, yet the birds are addressed positively as the forest's soldiers, sent by the Lord, "dear . . . delicious." Rimbaud's poem "Les Corbeaux" ("The Ravens"), published in September of 1872, deals directly with crows as scavengers of the battlefields of the Franco-Prussian War. He uses the same positive language, calling the birds "dear . . . delicious" and addressing them as "saints of the sky." In both poems, the use of quasi-religious vocabulary is ironic. Nature's imperative of decay and destruction is carried out by scavengers, and the carrion birds fill this role. They are addressed positively in opposition to traditional values, as the violent unconfined wind is valued above the romantic figures of the second stanza in "Blackcurrant River."

The third stanza presents the reader with two more figures in opposition: the hiker and the peasant. The first is only hinted at, in a manner suggesting that he is both threatened and in need of reassurance. What danger he fears is not explicitly mentioned, but wicker-work fences seem scant protection. He may be the eye that observes the picturesque features of the earlier stanzas, the tourist in these strange valleys.

The peasant figure completes the disintegration of the picturesque scene. While the knights errant of medieval romance are noble figures, and their ruined castles, formal gardens, and ancient wars and passions are popular clichés for elevated sentiment and beauty, the peasant is common, crafty, and deformed. The ravens are ordered to make him flee, but their role is an ironic one, and the peasant still holds the emphasized position at the end of the poem. It is he, after all, who actually drinks from the blackcurrant river and does so with gusto.

As for the stream from which he guzzles, if it is made of cassis syrup, it is thick and dark red, suggesting blood, another stream that flows unseen in dark valleys. Ravens and crows, as eaters of flesh and blood, reinforce this equivalence. One could go further and see, in the references to ancient romantic and military themes, a source of the river of blood from which the deformed peasant drinks, as well as an attempt to discredit the romantic glorification of war.

Any deliberate step-by-step logical interpretation, however, would directly oppose the declared intentions of the poet. In May of 1871, Rimbaud had formulated a poetic theory that envisioned a direct assault on the senses and sensibilities of his reader through manipulation of poetic form. The reader is, in some sense, placed in the position of the timid foot-traveler, seeking reassurance behind a wicket gate but faced with the uneasy knowledge that the sympathies of the poet lie with the powers of disintegration: the crows, the wind, the crafty peasant with his old stump of a limb. All the forces of the poem, from the unsettling rhythm and uneven rhyme to the seditious and troubling images, combine to provide a vivid landscape that is undercut by an unpredictable black current.

Anne W. Sienkewicz

THE BLESSED DAMOZEL

Author: Dante Gabriel Rossetti (1828-1882)
Type of poem: Ballad
First published: 1850; revised and collected in *Poems*, 1870; revised again for *Poems*, 1881

The Poem

There are four versions of "The Blessed Damozel," which was written in 1847, when Dante Gabriel Rossetti was eighteen years old. The first version was published in *The Germ* in 1850, the second in *The Oxford and Cambridge Magazine* in 1856, the third in 1870 in Rossetti's collection *Poems*, the fourth in *Poems*, 1881. The changes appearing in the second and third versions are generally regarded as improvements.

Many years after the poem was written, Rossetti is said to have attributed it to his admiration of Edgar Allan Poe's "The Raven" (1845). Rossetti is reported to have said that Poe had done the most that was possible to do with the grief of a lover on earth longing for a lover in heaven and that he (Rossetti) was determined to reverse the conditions in "The Blessed Damozel."

Both a poet and a painter, in 1848 Rossetti, along with Holman Hunt and John Everett Millais, established the Pre-Raphaelite Brotherhood. The term "Pre-Raphaelite" was first used to describe a group of German artists who early in the nineteenth century formed a brotherhood in Rome to restore Christian art to the medieval purity of the great Italian masters preceding Raphael. The German group was short-lived, and the term was later used to designate the English school founded by Rossetti and his followers. In general, the English Pre-Raphaelites reacted against the neoclassic tendencies and low standards of the art of their day. Both their painting and their literature are characterized by an interest in the medieval and the supernatural, simplicity of style, love of sensuous beauty, exactness of detail, and much symbolism.

Not only is "The Blessed Damozel" Rossetti's best-known work, but it also epitomizes the Pre-Raphaelite school. He used the medieval form of damsel, "damozel"— a young, unmarried woman of noble birth—in the title to emphasize the medieval setting and visionary aspects of the poem. He was commissioned in 1871 to do a painting of the poem and by 1879 had given it a *predella* showing an earthly lover (wearing a cloak and a sword) lying under a tree in the forest looking up at his beloved. The poem is presented as his reverie. He dreams that she leans out from the golden bar of heaven. Although she has been in heaven ten years, to her it scarcely seems a day. In the forest, the lover imagines that the autumn leaves are her hair falling on his face. Around her, lovers, met again in heaven, speak among themselves, and souls ascending to God go by "like thin flames."

Her gaze pierces the abyss between heaven and earth, and she speaks. (Her lover imagines that he hears her voice in the birds' song.) She wishes that he would come to her, for when he does they will lie together in paradise and she herself will teach him the songs of heaven. She will ask Jesus that they be allowed to live and love as they once did on earth—but for eternity. She sees a flight of angels pass by and lays her head on the golden barrier of heaven and weeps. The lover asserts that he has heard the tears.

Forms and Devices

Originally, the ballad was a narrative lyric poem preserved by oral tradition. The ballad meter of England derived from the *septenarius*, a rhymed Latin hymn meter of seven feet or accents. These long lines, technically known as "fourteeners," as they often numbered fourteen syllables, were afterward broken up into four shorter lines of iambic tetrameter alternated with iambic trimeter, which accounts for the alternating unrhymed lines.

In the case of "The Blessed Damozel," Rossetti has broken three long septenarian lines into six shorter lines of alternating tetrameters and trimeters. Thus, the second, fourth, and sixth lines in each stanza rhyme, as in stanza 2: "adorn," "worn," and "corn." The ballad was predominantly a medieval poetic form, and Rossetti's use of it exemplifies the Pre-Raphaelite preoccupation with medievalism.

Another important aspect of Rossetti's poetry is his "painterly" style. It is often said that reading one of his poems is almost like looking at a painting. Rossetti himself said that the supreme perfection in art is achieved when the picture and the poem are identical—that is, when they produce the same effect. Rossetti achieves this effect by paying meticulous attention to detail and by using concrete images. The damozel's eyes are as deep as waters "stilled at even" (at twilight); she wears seven stars in her hair, which is yellow like corn; holds three lilies in her hand (seven and three are mystical numbers); and wears a white rose on her robe. The earth spins in the void "like a fretful midge"; the "curled moon" is a "little feather" in the gulf—all of these are concrete images that present a portrait of the damozel, the earth, and the moon.

Finally, the poem abounds with Christian imagery and symbolism. Arising from the tradition of courtly love, one of the great medieval themes was an idealized, platonic, spiritual love. Although this tradition had its carnal aspects, the spiritualized love and adoration are best exemplified by Dante Alighieri's mystical devotion to Beatrice and his portrayal of her in paradise. True to his intention, Rossetti has reversed the roles in this poem. By setting the poem in heaven, within a medieval Christian framework, he has tried to suggest the spiritual nature of the damozel's love for her earthly lover. The heavenly lover wears the white rose—a symbol of virginity—and is therefore fitted to be in the service of Mary, who is the ultimate symbol of pure, chaste love. It is Mary herself who will approve their love and bring the lovers before Christ (lines 115 to 126).

Themes and Meanings

The reader can see in "The Blessed Damozel" the expression of an ancient and well-known theme: the desire of an isolated, separated lover to achieve unity with the beloved. Rossetti has framed this vision as a reverie, a daydream, a wish-fulfilling dream in the mind of a lover. The heart of the poem is the ironic conflict between the earthly bodily desire and the tradition that heaven is a place of disembodied souls, comforted and joyful in the presence of God. This irony is emphasized by the poem's religious framework.

The earthly, fleshly dimension of the lover in heaven is unconsciously revealed in several places in the poem: Her bosom "warms" the bar of heaven (line 46); she imagines taking her lover's hand (line 75), lying together in the shadow of the mystic tree (lines 85 to 86), laying her cheek against his (line 116), and, finally, living in heaven "as once on earth" (line 129).

These are all images of touching in the earthly sense. Yet, by the standards of medieval theology—which the whole framework of the poem implies—she ought to be contemplating the joy of God and exhorting her lover to lay aside grief and remember that she now enjoys the real reward of life: eternal life with God.

The Christian imagery, which is largely derived from Dante and other medieval Italian poets, is used decoratively and in this context does not support the sensuous desires of the lover. As much as Rossetti tried to emulate the austere spiritual idealization of Dante, his own sensuousness prevented him from achieving it.

The heavenly lover yearns passionately, intensely, for her earthly companion. In her yearning, she moves from a vision of their reunion, to hope of everlasting unity, and finally to doubt and despair. The void between heaven and earth is immense. What is emphasized is the separateness of the lovers: The wish is not the thing itself; the traditional Christian sops about being in heaven hold no comfort for the bereaved lover, for without the beloved, the heaven becomes a hell.

Dean Davies

A BLESSING

Author: James Wright (1927-1980)
Type of poem: Lyric
First published: 1963, in *The Branch Will Not Break*

The Poem

Like many of the nature poems of the English Romantic poets, James Wright's "A Blessing" begins with the close observation of the natural world and moves toward a startling moment of self-revelation. Consisting of a single stanza of twenty-four un-rhymed lines, the poem begins by announcing its geographic setting—"Just off the highway to Rochester, Minnesota"—and the time of day—twilight. The speaker and his friend watch two Indian ponies emerge from a group of willows and walk toward them. Then the two humans "step over the barbed wire into the pasture" and approach the ponies, who show no fear. In fact, not only are the ponies unafraid, but also, ac-cording to the speaker, their eyes are dark "with kindness," they come "gladly" for-ward to "welcome" the two people, and "they can hardly contain their happiness/ That we have come." Watching the ponies, the speaker decides, "They love each other."

The speaker's evident pleasure in the ponies and the positive emotions he ascribes to them seem almost sentimental, but the hint of sentimentality is undermined at the center of the poem when, just after asserting that the ponies love each other, the speaker says, "There is no loneliness like theirs." In line 8, the speaker states that the ponies have been grazing all day "alone," which might explain the delight they take in their human visitors, but the "loneliness" in line 12 is not a temporary or circumstan-tial phenomenon. Rather, this loneliness sets them apart from both the humanlike emotions with which the speaker initially characterizes them and the human world in which the speaker normally lives. Theirs is the "loneliness" of the nonhuman, natural world, not the frightening loneliness of the human world.

As line 13 makes clear, the ponies are very much "At home" in their world, "munching the young tufts of spring in the darkness," and the speaker is beginning to feel at home there as well. One of the ponies nuzzles his left hand, and as he caresses her ear, he begins to imagine her as a human girl. "I would like to hold the slenderer one in my arms," he says, and then describes her ear as "delicate as the skin over a girl's wrist."

At this point the speaker has forgotten all about Rochester, Minnesota, and the highway he had been on. He has even forgotten his friend. In the darkening twilight of this pasture, in physical contact with this pony, the speaker comes unexpectedly into contact with another level of his consciousness. He becomes aware of a visionary, spiritual truth about himself, the revelation of which marks the poem's climax: "Sud-denly I realize/ That if I stepped out of my body I would break/ Into blossom."

Forms and Devices

Unlike the poems of Wright's first two books, most of which exhibited iambic me-
ter and end rhyme, "A Blessing" relies on the rhythms of ordinary speech, and none of
its lines rhyme. Syntactically, the poem employs simple sentence structures, many of
which follow the bare "pronoun and verb" model, such as "They have come . . . ," "We
step . . . ," "They ripple . . . ," "They bow . . . ," "They love . . . ," "I would like . . . ," "She
is. . . ." The first ten lines of the poem are composed of five sentences, each of which is
two lines long, so that every other line ends with a period. This syntax of short, declar-
ative observations or assertions reveals a voice that is assured and confident, a voice
that the reader is willing to trust, so that as the poem moves from the description of the
ponies to the speaker's confession of his desire "to hold the slenderer one," and finally
to the climactic moment of visionary insight, the reader follows the speaker's experi-
ence each step of the way.

The poem makes relatively little use of conventional tropes or devices. The most
obvious is personification—the speaker's ascribing of human emotions such as kind-
ness, gladness, happiness, shyness, loneliness, and love to the ponies—which domi-
nates the first half of the poem and suggests his empathy with them. Some readers
have suggested that Wright carries this personification so far that it becomes senti-
mental, or an example of the pathetic fallacy. This is an important point, for the poem
concerns the individual's communion with the natural world. Whether that commu-
nion is actually achieved in the poem—whether the reader believes it—determines
whether the personification connotes genuine empathy or mere sentimentality.

Simile occurs twice in the poem: The ponies "bow shyly as wet swans," which sug-
gests their grace, and one pony's ear is "delicate as the skin over a girl's wrist." This
simile is significant, for it adds a sensual, or even subtly erotic, connotation to the
speaker's desire to hold in his arms the slenderer pony, whose "mane falls wild on her
forehead." Yet the simile's suggestion of sensuality is finally less important than its
emphasis on the delicacy of the pony's, or a girl's, skin. Such delicate skin is a mem-
brane or border between outside and inside, but it is so thin that to cross it would be
quite possible, and that possibility leads to the startling revelation expressed in the
poem's dominant and concluding metaphor: "Suddenly I realize/ That if I stepped out
of my body I would break/ Into blossom."

Formally, the poem is structured around a series of juxtaposed images: the inno-
cent, welcoming ponies as they approach from the willows; the speaker's caressing
one of the ponies and imagining her as a girl; and finally, the speaker's stepping out of
his body and breaking into blossom. The poem derives much of its energy from the
tension between these clearly drawn, powerful images and the plain, simple syntax in
which they are presented.

Themes and Meanings

"A Blessing" is a visionary nature poem; it begins with a careful description of the
natural world, with the speaker's gradual immersion into that world, and then moves
suddenly and unexpectedly to a moment of spiritual revelation. At first, the speaker is

caught up in the mundane world of human activity; he has been traveling on "the high-way to Rochester, Minnesota." Yet something has caught his attention, has led him to pull over and to get "off" the highway. He and his friend have seen the two Indian po-nies, and they begin to leave the human world of highways and cities and enter the nat-ural world, the world from which twenty-first century Americans are typically es-tranged. Human alienation from nature is the starting point of this poem, and the capacity to undo that alienation is its topic. The boundary between the human world and the natural world is of central concern, and images of crossing boundaries are fre-quent. In the second line, for example, the twilight "bounds softly forth" on the pas-ture grass, but it would seem that the ponies, and not the twilight, are doing the bound-ing forth. Already boundaries are blurring. As the speaker and his friend "step over the barbed wire" fence and cross into the pasture, their movement into and participa-tion in the natural world become clearer.

Often nature appears indifferent to human beings, and animals are typically fearful of people. In this case, however, the natural world as embodied in the ponies ap-proaches the speaker with what seem to be feelings of welcome and happiness. The speaker is delighted by the ponies, yet he recognizes what, in human terms, one would call their "loneliness." That is, to human beings living in society, playing socially pre-scribed roles and understanding themselves and the world in terms of that social net-work, anyone who is not a part of that social network must be "lonely." Henry David Thoreau in his hut on Walden Pond or a religious mystic living alone in the desert is "lonely" as these ponies are. Yet this "loneliness" is not the frightening thing that most people think it is. The ponies "love each other," and they are quite "At home" in the pasture, in the darkening spring twilight, in the natural world.

Recognizing the true nature of their loneliness, the speaker's relationship with the ponies shifts from simple observation to desire. As one of the ponies walks over to him and nuzzles his left hand, he imagines holding the pony in his arms. He begins to caress the delicate skin of its ear, and in that moment of intimate, physical contact, he is struck with the sudden realization that if he were to step out of his body, to cross the boundary of his physical, mortal existence, he "would break/ Into blossom."

He does not step out of his body, nor does he break into blossom. The "if" is signifi-cant. Yet he has received "a blessing," a spiritual insight: The social world is not the only source of meaning in life. Although humans have alienated themselves from na-ture, they can undo that alienation and find deeper sources of meaning. Finally, be-yond the border of this life, a spiritual blossoming is possible, and the awareness of that possibility infuses the moment described in this poem with a visceral, palpable joy.

Gary Grieve-Carlson

THE BLINDMAN

Author: May Swenson (1919-1989)
Type of poem: Lyric
First published: 1965; collected in *Half Sun Half Sleep*, 1967

The Poem

"The Blindman" unfolds in six stanzas consisting of three lines each. Its irregular meter is not without rhyme. The poem consists of rhyming couplets, some of which span the stanza breaks, as the last line of one stanza is completed by the rhyming first line of the next. The title prepares the reader for an experience without sight. As a blind person must rely on other forms to "see," those with sight are shown how color can be more than an abstract concept for someone who has never witnessed rainbow hues.

Those who are born with the ability to see take color for granted. Children learn color at a very early age without much difficulty. This simple lesson is recorded, and for the remainder of one's life the brain recognizes various colors with no need for translation. In May Swenson's "The Blindman," the speaker watches as a blind man uses his other senses to "see" colors. The poem begins with the man tasting the color purple by placing "a tulip on his tongue." In the second stanza, feeling the blades of grass against his cheek, the man construes the color green.

In the third stanza, the blind man's tears are described as "fallen beads of sight." This image leads one to believe that the blind man is not quite satisfied with his limited grasp of color. Nonetheless, he continues to grope for answers and lets the reader know that he is aware of these descriptive words.

The poem shifts from the third person to the first as the blind man speaks for himself, continuing to solve the mysteries of color by using objects for comparison. These clues give the man a basis for imagining what color means. He uses the sense of touch to feel the fibers of a scarf for the color red. His association of red with the warmth of the sun matches his interpretation of orange as he feels this color from the heat of a flame. These bright, vivid colors must be strong, like the intensity of fire.

He realizes that there is a multitude of colors; the "seven fragrances of the rainbow" are interpreted through various scents. In the last stanzas the use of all the senses is complete when the blind man tells how he can hear certain colors through the sounds of instruments. Even the sound made by rubbing the smooth surface of a piece of fruit—"a pomegranate lets me hear crimson's flute"—allows the blind man to conjure up an idea of deep pink. He must use everything around him in his attempt to capture the mysterious phenomenon of light. The second half of the last line, "Only ebony is mute," ironically sums up his concept of color, for black is the only color he truly understands.

Forms and Devices

Poetry is an imaginative expression of consciousness, and in this poem Swenson illustrates an acute awareness of something that is taken for granted by those fortunate enough to see. The poet and the blind man are similar in being able to reach beyond what is directly in front of them. In the words of Dylan Thomas, poetry is "the movement from an overclothed blindness to a naked vision." In "Blindman," rather than lifting the cloth to see more clearly, Swenson shields the eyes for a better look. The poem magnifies the colors as they take on a new dimension.

Just as art dates back to the beginning of humankind, imagery and metaphors have been used for centuries to describe vision. Poetry has been a part of human expression since antiquity. The Greek lyric poet Simonides of Ceos defined poetry as "painting with the gift of speech." A painting is said to be "worth a thousand words," and in poetry only a few words are needed to tell an entire story. Swenson once noted that a "poem must be rich and evocative, but at the same time compact and exact."

Her imagery in "The Blindman" provides a masterful peek into the blind man's world. Seeing an image is difficult enough without looking at it. Seeing color without sight is impossible, but the blind man compensates for his missing sense of sight by fully using the remaining four. He tastes and feels the ocean: "In water to his lips,/ he named the sea blue and white." Stimulated further by sound, he notes that his sightless world is embellished by music: "Trumpets tell me yellow." Again, the crimson flute of the pomegranate may come from the squeaky sound heard from the hard shell of that fruit when he rubs the skin and listens with his ear. The colors that the blind man sees are imaginary, but the poet tries to expand his world with different ways of imagining. It is typical of Swenson to draw upon nature for her imagery, and the nature imagery is especially appealing in this poem.

Themes and Meanings

While the blind man discovers ways to see color in this poem, the sighted person experiences something that is equally unimaginable: how one can *not* know what color is. In the only way he knows how, the blind man must taste, touch, smell, and hear the different colors of the spectrum, knowing that there is a vast array from which to choose. He holds and runs his fingers all over an object to know its shape and texture so that he will recognize it the next time. He will know the scent of a rose after the first time he smells the sweet fragrance of that flower; likewise he will know the sound of the piano. Color is used extensively in language, but it can be neither touched nor heard. Whatever he is told about the color green, the blind man can know only what an object feels or tastes like. He has been told that grass is green, so he feels that color by rubbing the smooth blade across his cheek.

Human curiosity forces the man to try in every way he can to seize some kind of understanding. He creates his own interpretations, but he realizes their limitations. The poet includes the blind man's tears of defeat in the only line of the poem that expresses any kind of emotion. The blind man desperately longs to see the colorful world that he hears so much about. In the last line of the poem, "Only ebony is mute," he tells the reader what he actually knows—blackness, darkness.

Swenson has written other poems about color that are strictly visual. In "Colors Without Objects," for example, her "painting" has no shape, but it becomes a kaleidoscope of colorful images that blend from one scene into the next. In "The Blindman" color has an entirely different meaning. What is implicitly known by a sighted person is totally perplexing to the blind man, yet he refuses to allow his blindness to shut him out from the brilliant world.

The sighted person has never had a reason to question what color is, but this poem urges readers to think how blind they may have been in not considering the experience of the person they see walking with a cane or seeing-eye dog. He is not only someone who is disabled but also someone with an awareness that goes beyond the obvious. If one looks a little deeper than usual, the world can be even more colorful than it appears.

Mary Ann Hoegberg

THE BLUE DRESS

Author: Sandra Cisneros (1954-   )
Type of poem: Meditation
First published: 1980, in *Bad Boys*

The Poem

"The Blue Dress" consists of six short stanzas of brief lines in free verse. In spite of its brevity and informality, the poem successfully conveys a multitude of feelings. Cisneros looks at a young man's breakup with his girlfriend, the events precipitating it, and his consequent anxiety and pain. The poet narrates the details of two final visits between the former lovers, suggesting metaphorically the distance and the lack of commonality the young man feels at separating from the woman for whom he had once felt a close bond but who now goes her way alone to wait out the final days of a pregnancy. The speaker of the poem is an observer uninvolved in the actions of the couple, so she identifies with both, understands the dynamics of their relationship, and urges the reader to meditate on the situation. By describing little more about the woman than the blueness of her dress, Cisneros makes her fuse with the horizon. Inherent in this fusion is a sadness about how the events of life have turned.

In the first stanza the focus on the "curve of the belly" is the first clue to the details of the pregnancy that will be alluded to repeatedly. The emphasis is on external details, on objects: the bulging dress, the farewell, and the bouquet, all of which fuse and fade into the background. Nothing is stated directly about facial expressions, about feelings. The inexpensive (and possibly artificial) flowers from the "Five & Ten" (stores such as Woolworth, known for stocking myriad domestic products and clothing at inexpensive prices), point to the overall paucity or meagerness of the scene at all levels. The "you" referred to in the second stanza is the young man, who is living out the final details of his obligation to the young pregnant girl. His ambivalent emotions are made clear: "You . . .// Want to tell her that you love her/ You do not love her."

In the next two stanzas one sees that each person lives in a different setting and world. They meet for a few hours on Sunday, each commuting to a common meeting place, going through the motions of socializing. Each offers a topic for conversation, but they no longer know the same places or the same people. The only moment of sharing occurs when she eats the food he cannot swallow because of his discomfort.

The last two stanzas seem to describe the final visit and parting. The woman has summoned him by letter, requesting that they meet at a museum, away from the residence for females, operated by nuns, where she is staying. The image of the whale exhibit in the museum parallels the gravid and sluggish image of the young woman's final stages of pregnancy (the "curve" of her stomach has become a "swell") as she arrives dressed again in the blue dress. Once again, the reader only perceives the appearance of the dress rather than a person with specific characteristics.

This rhetorical device of using the part to represent the whole (her blue eyes, her white skin), helps more to depict the situation than to portray characters and their sentiments, as would be more common in a lyric text. The poem describes the man as dressed formally, according to societal norms, wearing "your best suit/ and the tie your mother gave you," signifying that this formal meeting is also only a polite ritual—more form than substance. No conversation, no details of sharing. The farewell and rupture become more definitive, as he purchases the airline ticket that will put even greater distance between the two. The speaker of the poem need say no more. This chapter is now closed.

Forms and Devices

Sandra Cisneros began her writing career as a poet and continued to write poetry as she progressed into the writing of short stories. (In a later book of short prose, *The House on Mango Street*, 1983, one finds pithy stories in a prose so full of sound and visual images that they are akin to poems.) The reader senses that every word, every turn of phrase, is carefully chosen for sound, for metaphorical capacity, and for the image it can convey. "The Blue Dress" is among Cisneros's earliest published work, written during her years in graduate school. It is the only poem in a brief chapbook entitled *Bad Boys* that does not reveal specific details of Cisneros's Mexican American roots.

In this particular poem, the color blue of the dress is the dominant image. The color and garment evoke the image of the young woman. She is only a vague, fading image that fuses with the color of the surroundings, particularly the air ("blue wind") and the horizon. The weight of the burden both people carry (their separation, single parenthood, guilt, imposed obligations, and the ruptured relationship) is in contrast to the poem's brief, fragmentary lines, which are like brush strokes that barely suggest the essentials of the story. Cisneros's style has been aptly described as minimalist.

The constant understatement of details serves to emphasize the impossibility of communication, reunion, or a positive outcome. The speaker takes the position of the young man as actor and observer. There is paucity at every moment, whether in the meagerness of the flowers, the lack of dialogue, the man's lack of clear vision as he watches the approaching figure of the woman, or his oversight of surrounding details ("Someone offers his seat/ You never noticed").

The tension mounts as the couple attempt to eat; the man does not know what to say, and when he speaks, he blurts out a statement about himself (his upcoming birthday). Both people seem to act as if directed by the norms and constraints of proper societal behavior. He wears the suit and tie given to him by his parents, the prescribed clothing for formal encounters. She, in turn, has only a few hours away from the rules of the institution and the nuns who house her. This portrait is dominated by the cool blue color of detachment, vagueness, and sadness. The blue and painful feelings of the protagonists and the situation are well represented by the repetition of the color.

Themes and Meanings

"The Blue Dress" is concerned with the pathos of broken relationships and promises. By representing a couple who meet occasionally, constricted by a variety of rules (transportation schedules, house rules, codes of dress and behavior), and who convey no joy during their brief encounters, Cisneros makes the reader sense and empathize with their discomfort and anxiety. The events and situations that lead to the birth of an infant are usually associated with excitement, anticipation, and joy. None of that is suggested in the poem. The reader must conclude that the young woman will become a single parent or that her new baby will be given to the nuns for adoption.

Both protagonists were involved in this event initially, but at the time and place in which they are represented in this text, their ties are strained and untenable. While the young woman is left in the background in a swath of blue, she demonstrates more tranquillity in her situation than he, by eating heartily and by stating in the last stanza, "I am fine." The young man, however, is burdened, ambivalent, and anxious at each meeting and departure. Finally, he buys the airline ticket which will take him far from these duties.

Eduardo F. Elías

BLUE GIRLS

Author: John Crowe Ransom (1888-1974)
Type of poem: Lyric
First published: 1924; revised and collected in *Two Gentlemen in Bonds*, 1927; completely rewritten for *Selected Poems*, 1945

The Poem

John Crowe Ransom's "Blue Girls," a four-stanza lyric in iambic meter, explores the traditional theme of the transitory nature of beauty. The final and now-standard version of the poem reflects Ransom's attempts to perfect his poetry through revision. Although some phrases ("Practise your beauty, blue girls") appear in both the original and the final versions, only the second line is identical in the two poems: "Under the towers of your seminary." In fact, the final version of the poem is so significantly different from the original, especially in its shift from a somewhat sentimental to a detached, stoic tone that it is really a different poem and far superior to its predecessor.

In the first stanza, the speaker (generally assumed to be an elderly man, perhaps even a teacher at the seminary) watches a group of young women walking across the grounds of a private school and in a gently ironic tone mentally admonishes them to listen to their "old and contrary" teachers without believing anything they hear. Stanza 2 continues with another command that the speaker clearly expects the girls to heed even though he apparently never actually voices it. He urges them to concentrate on their appearance and to show no more concern for the future than bluebirds fluttering on the grass or through the air.

In the third stanza the tone becomes more serious and impassioned as the speaker implores the girls to practice their beauty. He also introduces for the first time a reason for his commands: the transitory nature of beauty. His focus then shifts from the girls to himself as he pledges what he will do if the girls obey his wishes. He, as speaker— as poet—will proclaim loudly, write about, and celebrate beauty. In the concluding stanza the speaker offers a specific example of beauty's frailty by referring to a women he knows and perhaps lives with. Age has rapidly destroyed her beauty, but her loveliness once surpassed that of any of the young women he has been admiring.

Although the speaker is generally assumed to be an elderly male, the poem does not limit itself to that interpretation. The speaker could instead be a female, even the woman with the "terrible tongue." Such a reading makes the conclusion even more poignant as the lost beauty is experienced personally, not merely observed.

Forms and Devices

Colors are Ransom's most frequently used symbols, and "Blue Girls" effectively depicts his tendency to begin with a color used in a descriptive manner and then to imbue it with additional meaning. The first line of the poem suggests that the term "blue girls" originates with their blue skirts, most likely the navy uniforms frequently worn by females at private schools in the first half of the twentieth century, but the color blue rapidly takes on a different hue and attached symbolic values. Connecting the girls with a "seminary," an old-fashioned word for a private girls' school, evokes an association with blue blood and suggests upper-class society girls attending a finishing school, girls traditionally expected to be more interested in physical beauty and outward appearance than in sharpening their minds or receiving a classical education.

More important, however, the color blue conveys a sense of youthfulness, carefree innocence, and playfulness, especially when coupled with the metaphor of bluebirds in stanza 2. The description of the bluebirds on the grass and "on the air" further contributes to an atmosphere of spring, youthfulness, and lightheartedness. The use of the word "girls," rather than "young women," and the image of "white fillets," which suggest lace as well as headbands or ribbons, also enhance the sense of youthfulness and innocence. The alliterative verbals "twirling" and "travelling" and the rhythm of the opening lines contribute lightness and lyricism.

The contrasting touch of negativity introduced in the first stanza with the phrase "teachers old and contrary" is momentarily dismissed in stanza 2 with the only completely regular iambic line in the entire poem: "And think no more of what will come to pass." The word "pass" obviously not only embodies the idea that the girls are to be unconcerned about the future but also reminds the reader that these are schoolgirls unconcerned about passing academic subjects.

Although vocabulary associated with schools ("towers," "seminary," "teacher," "pass") abounds in the first two stanzas, any interest in academics is overshadowed by the emphasis on the girls' carefree enjoyment of the present. When the demands of school do come into focus in stanza 3, they do so with an ironic twist. Rather than concentrating on academics, the girls are commanded to "practise" their beauty "before it [not "before they"] fail." Instead of practicing their language or mathematical skills, they are to "practise" their appearance. The British spelling calls special attention to the word and suggests, along with other vocabulary used by the speaker ("sward," "seminary," "fillets," "establish"), the "bookish" nature of the speaker, perhaps confirming that he is a teacher.

As the focus shifts from the girls to the speaker in stanza 3, the lightly ironic and carefree tone becomes quite shrill with the assertion "I will cry with my loud lips and publish/ Beauty which all our power shall never establish." The words "cry" and "loud" both emphasize the force of his proclamation, but "cry" also conveys the sense of weeping or mourning.

The lighthearted chattering of the young girls in stanza 2 degenerates to the "terrible tongue" of the elderly woman in stanza 4. Likewise, "Blear eyes [have] fallen from blue" and "perfections tarnished." The use of the word "fallen" not only indicates the loss of physical beauty but also conveys a sense of corruption, particularly when coupled with "tarnished" and "terrible tongue." Beauty has been blemished and besmirched; reputation and honor have been destroyed. The imperfect rhymes of lines 13 and 15 ("tongue" and "long") reinforce this idea.

The shift in the speaker's voice from stanza 3 to stanza 4 is crucial in understanding his or her attitude. From an assertive "I will cry with my loud lips and publish," the speaker moves to an unsure "I could tell you a story." The implication is that the speaker could, but will not, tell the girls the story because he realizes they will not listen and also because he knows the hopelessness of the situation even should they listen. Even if they practice their beauty, time will destroy it. Nothing he can say or do will change that; yet he continues to value beauty despite, or perhaps because of, its transience.

Themes and Meanings

"Blue Girls," like most of Ransom's best poetry, is a poem of antithesis, of an ideal, but impossible, world of beauty and joy in conflict with a real world of violence, decay, death, and pain. It focuses particularly on the contrast between the desirable but evanescent world of youth and beauty and the undesirable but inescapable world of age and decay. The tension of the two worlds of youth and age introduced briefly in stanza 1 with the phrase "Go listen to your teachers old and contrary" moves progressively to culmination in the final stanza, with the blue girls set in contrast with the once-beautiful woman with "all her perfections tarnished." Though the speaker longs for that ideal world, experienced briefly, he resigns himself to the real world of degeneration. His detached resignation makes the feeling all the more poignant for the reader, who senses the deep emotion beneath the stoic surface, the pain masked by wit and irony.

Because the speaker urges the girls to practice their beauty, the poem is inevitably associated with the Horatian *carpe diem* tradition. Yet Ransom's poem varies significantly from this tradition in that the speaker is not a young man who has a personal goal of seduction or pleasure in mind. Rather, he is an elderly man who, despite his urging the young girls to enjoy the moment, seemingly has only a casual relationship with them and is interested in them not as individuals but as representatives of youth and beauty.

The speaker does not seek any kind of personal relationship with the "blue girls." In fact, he does not even promise, in the fashion of many Renaissance poets, to keep them forever young and immortal in his poetry. He vows instead to publish, write about Beauty, yet he does so with the clear knowledge that it is beyond his or anyone else's power to "establish" beauty. He stoically accepts the frailty of beauty, the only way tension between the ideal world and the real world is resolved in Ransom's poetry, but he continues to appreciate that beauty both as presently viewed in the young girls and as remembered from the past in the woman who once was "lovelier" than any of them.

Verbie Lovorn Prevost

BLUE WINE

Author: John Hollander (1929-   )
Type of poem: Meditation
First published: 1979, in *Blue Wine and Other Poems*

The Poem

"Blue Wine" comprises eleven numbered sections. They vary in length from the three-line seventh section to the twenty-nine lines of the eighth section. Each line in the poem is fourteen syllables long. One key to the poem is its dedication: "for Saul Steinberg." The inspiration for the poem was a visit by John Hollander to Steinberg's home, where Steinberg (an artist, humorist, and cartoonist) had done a drawing of several bottles of "blue wine." The whimsical names Steinberg gave the bottles in that initial drawing are given in the poem's eleventh section. From there, Hollander "thought about blue wine, and what it might mean." He was also thinking about Steinberg's art, specifically the 1979 second edition of *The Passport*, to which Hollander contributed the introduction. *The Passport*, a melange of real and false immigration documentation, is similar in tenor to Hollander's *Reflections on Espionage*; both acknowledge by undertone that authority is always authority, but it is not always correct.

As "Blue Wine" opens, a winemaker "worries over his casks," but the wine has its own consciousness. Red wine or white wine "broods on its own sleep." One cannot learn anything about blue wine, however, by looking in the barrels; "a look inside . . . would show/ Nothing." The difficulty of understanding blue wine is established.

The next four sections delineate methods of apprehending the wine. These result in mutually exclusive conclusions and arrays of half-truths. The second section presents intellectual approaches ranging from the scientific to the contemplative, while the third evokes the sensual, emotional reactions of the wine itself, such as "a blush of consciousness/ (Not shame)." By the final two lines of the third section, neither emotional nor intellectual interpretations are seen as more than convenient representations, unable to fully comprehend "immensities like blue wine."

The fourth and fifth sections show modes of "high" and "low" culture, respectively. The scholar translating Plutarch stands in sharp contrast to Hollander's rearranging of the "bluing for extra whiteness" of a television advertisement. Again, neither is in itself sufficient. In the sixth section, the names tell the tale: The name of the wine may translate as "The Blue Heart," but the wine comes from a nobleman whose title translates as the "marquis of silliness." What follows is a preposterous description of personal revelation. By the end of this section, the reader will trust in no one's authority on the matter of blue wine.

Sections 7 through 9, like section 6, are tales of personal encounters. They are, respectively, apocryphal, epic ("Homeric"), and naturalistic. The eighth section, with its blatant evocation of Homer's *The Odyssey*, anchors the poem solidly in the poetic tradition. The ninth both returns the reader to the contemporary world and links the arts to the world around them.

Section 10 is the only part of the poem to present the first-person experience of the author with "blue wine," which he remembers as only occasionally (with "domestic reticence") being poured at family meals. The last section ties the various perspectives together, and the poem's final four lines concurrently reject and affirm their own incomplete nature. The last words, "to see what he will see," refers to drawing one's own conclusions and having one's own encounters. The final line's evocation of Ralph Waldo Emerson's essay "Nature" brings the poem to a close.

Forms and Devices

Connections and evocations abound in Hollander's poetry. Nowhere is this shown more clearly than in the linkages (the following examples are by no means all-inclusive) between sections 3 and 8 of the poem. The concluding word of the eleventh line of section 3, "surmise," while appropriate in and of itself, also evokes the similarly phonemed "sunrise" as an element of the wine itself. This schemata of structural linguistics would not be so effective had not Hollander set it up by invoking "the dark moon of the cork" and "the bottom over which" the wine has come: The reader is subtly led to expect the sun beginning to broach the horizon. Hollander makes further connections. He has described poetry as an ongoing dialogue with poets previous, and the phrase "mild surmise" evokes the "wild surmise" in the penultimate line of John Keats's "On First Looking into Chapman's Homer." The explicitly "Homeric" eighth section is thus linked to this section.

Once the first link is noticed, the appearance of others comes as no surprise. One is especially delightful: The wine's "blush of consciousness/ (Not shame)" in section 3 invokes Adam and Eve in the Garden. Hollander uses this reference obliquely to reinforce the fourth and fifth lines of section 8. Even as the "gnashing rocks to leeward" evoke the Scylla and "the dark vortex" Charybdis from *The Odyssey* (book 12), so that which Charybdis "display[s] in its whorls/ . . . what it could never have/ Swallowed down from above" is a fig tree—the type of tree whose leaves Adam and Eve used to cover themselves after their first "blush of consciousness."

In Hollander's reconception of *The Odyssey's* book 12, Odysseus's crew, instead of eating Helios's cattle, drinks blue wine. As with Hollander's more complex poem "Spectral Emanations," the blue is evoked through the colors leading to it. The spectrum is described, from "Brightness of flame" to "flavescent gold," with both all colors (white, "blinding bleakness") and the absence of color ("the shining black of obsidian") limned. What remains on the island is the "constant fraction" of blue that abided "even after every sky/ Had been drenched in its color." The final phrase of section 8, the joyous "the sea-bright wine," is an inversion of "the wine-dark sea" of *The Odyssey*.

Themes and Meanings

The theme of the poem has been identified by many people as how people react to art. This conceptualization is a rather broad stroke, yet it is arguably incomplete, as it disregards Hollander's omnipresent consciousness that the line between art and life is a chimera.

Hollander's development as a poet follows a predictable arc. An ardent admirer of W. H. Auden in his early days, Hollander published his first book, *A Crackling of Thorns* (1958), under Auden's aegis as a volume in the Yale Younger Poets series. As Hollander developed, Auden's influence ebbed, while Hollander's admiration for Wallace Stevens grew, leading to the explicit "Old W. H., get off my back!" in "Upon Apthrop House" from his collection *Spectral Emanations: New and Selected Poems* (1978), immediately previous to *Blue Wine and Other Poems*. Possibly even more telling is the Auden-like poet Myndal from Hollander's *The Quest of the Gole* (1966), a bard who values his powers so much that he rewrites that which needed no changes solely because he can. It is not Myndal who succeeds in the quest, but rather his younger brother who saves the kingdom through his heart, good will, and attention to the world around him. The transition from the verse of Auden to the work of Stevens is a movement from art for its own sake to art as part of the world around it.

The contemplative sections of "Blue Wine," notably sections 2 and 5, emphasize the reactions that people filter through their senses—taste ("vinosities"), sight, and smell are considered at length, with contradictory conclusions. It is not that the senses are inadequate; rather, people use them in preconceived ways, thereby failing to realize the wine's essence. Similarly, the personal narratives (especially 6, 7, and 9) minimize the sensory for the sake of the experience, leaving conclusions that are ultimately unsatisfying because of their uniqueness ("reality is so Californian").

The key sections are those that show art (as exemplified by blue wine) and life as coincident, most notably sections 4 and 10. The "heavy leaves of the rhododendrons" are complemented by the "quickening leaves" of the scholar's translation, while the father's "abashed/ Smile" and the narrator's having "hid [his] gaze" emphasize interactions and influences, each making the other seem more real.

The final meaning that should be considered is the explicitly and implicitly Jewish nature of the poem. Critic Harold Bloom observed that Hollander "has no way back to Judaism, but is ruggedly and constantly aware of his almost-lost tradition." Knowing that the Zohar compares the Torah explicitly to wine, it is not a great leap to the realization that "Blue Wine" is, in many ways, an exploration of the Jewish experience in America.

Section 10 is the most explicit in this regard, evoking as it does the holiday of Passover, a celebration of the Jews' attaining freedom from oppression. Hollander expresses his own position in lines 3-5: He honors the tradition even though he abjures some of the halachal laws ("commandments"). When the final stanza lists wine bottles with German, French, and even Romanian ("*Vin Albastru*") names, the reader may think of those who have left Europe for this continent, leaving behind their laws but not their traditions.

Written during the period of Hollander's works that most explicitly deal with the role of the Jewish poet ("Spectral Emanations" being the other most noteworthy),

"Blue Wine" is a poem to make Saul Steinberg, himself a Jewish immigrant from Europe, proud of the path that he and Hollander have chosen, in making their experiences with the world into art—and making both the world and the art the better for it.

Kenneth L. Houghton

BOBO'S METAMORPHOSIS

Author: Czesław Miłosz (1911-   )
Type of poem: Lyric
First published: 1965, as "Gucio zaczarowany," in *Gucio zaczarowany*; English translation collected in *The Collected Poems, 1931-1987*, 1988

The Poem

"Bobo's Metamorphosis" is a 102-line poem—or cycle of poems—in eight sections, each having its own style, subject, and structure. Despite the differences, the poem develops cohesiveness on the basis of recurrent imagery and consistent thematic focus.

Drawn from an eighteenth century Polish text entitled *Zabawy przyjemne i pożyteczne* (1776; entertainments pleasant and useful), the poem's epigraph, "The distance between being and nothingness is infinite," serves as an excellent introduction to both the poem and the six typographically distant lines that make up its opening section. In this section, which resembles Wallace Stevens's "Thirteen Ways of Looking at a Blackbird," the first three lines are lyrically intense but only barely sketched word-pictures. The fourth and longest line introduces a narrative "I." The fifth is the most abstract, as an annunciation of the reader's dilemma and the poem's theme: "Life was given but unattainable." The sixth line, a reprise of the preceding five, transforms seeing into feeling and telescopes time and space into a single, fragmentary transtemporal moment: "From childhood till old age ecstasy at sunrise."

Dawn and dusk serve as ways of establishing a painterly and almost mythic frame of reference and of creating an odd continuity between the poem's otherwise discontinuous parts. Section 2, for example, begins with a fragment which almost seems an afterthought to section 1, an attempt to complete what was left unfinished: "As life goes, many of these mornings." Section 2 also reintroduces the "I" who only fleetingly appeared in section 1. Again there is a telescoping of time ("I was grown up and small"), but now this telescoping is contextualized as the seemingly random recollections of a narrator who may be Miłosz, as suggested by the geographical references in line 9, but who may also be an insect, as suggested by the fourth line of section 1, the fifth line of section 2, and the seventh section of the poem.

Section 3 presents, in a highly naturalistic yet semifantastic manner, a solitary "consciousness" hiking somewhere in California. The relative continuity gives way to the complexity of the poem's fourth and longest section, which begins with a mention of the story of Philemon and Baucis from Ovid's *Metamorphoses* (c. C.E. 8). The mention of the "wandering god" and the "advancing weevil" recalls the hiking consciousness earlier and prepares the way for the return of the wandering, advancing "I," who will recall his own version of Baucis in a jumbled sequence of images ending with her sudden aging and departure. In the final two stanzas of section 4, the narrator's cinematic memory jump-cuts from autobiographical recollection back to literary fantasy:

to Prospero's island from William Shakespeare's *The Tempest* (1611) and more specifically to Miranda, the sorcerer's daughter. Miranda is seen briefly against a backdrop which includes spirits looking strangely like skin divers, another of the poem's many temporal and spatial discontinuities.

The narrative "I" abandons the role of Prospero and returns to autobiographical recollection in the next two sections, the only time in the poem that a single narrative is carried over from one section to the next. The subject is the unnamed artist whom "I liked . . . as he did not look for an ideal object"—he commits himself to the impossible art of painting things as they are.

Section 7 clarifies the poem's title even if it does not identify its source: Zofia Urbanowska's children's book of the same name in which, as the poem points out, "Bobo, a nasty boy, was changed into a fly." In the novel, Bobo is restored to human form and given the opportunity to reform. The poem's version of Bobo's metamorphosis is equally humorous and fantastic but less moralistic. It is far more lyrical and is also, in its hint of death, a bit somber.

"Bobo's Metamorphosis" is a poem of dust and death but also of excess and ecstasy. Nowhere are the two combined so effectively as in the final stanza, which serves as a reprise and distillation. The table introduced in section 2 takes on a more overtly important role, separating the narrative "I" from the woman who sits across from him. The efforts of the "I" to know this minutely observed person recall the realist artist's desire to draw both object and essence in sections 5 and 6. The distance between "I" and "other" is imaged in terms of Zeno's arrow moving across an infinitely divisible space of time. The image creates a paradoxical sense of both the despairingly impossible and the joyously inexhaustible. Looking across that endless expanse, the narrator believes that the woman knows what he knows. From this mutual knowledge of endless separation comes what the poem affirms, that "humanness, tenderness" which may not be two distinct qualities at all.

Forms and Devices

Although it refers specifically to a single children's story, the title "Bobo's Metamorphosis" implies a profusion of endlessly metamorphosing autobiographical materials (people, places, events, as well as literary texts), which in turn implies Miłosz's belief that poetry comes from personal experience, not from other poetry. For Miłosz, however, poetry must never be merely personal, or merely historical. A poem is not a confession but a distillation and transformation of life into art through form. By form, Miłosz means something quite different than meter, rhyme, and the other trappings of conventional verse. He means the "search" for "direct forms," a search which may, as in the case of "Bobo's Metamorphosis," involve the bringing together of many different forms, including (as in the first section) ones that may be mere notes or jottings.

The language of these notelike lines, and indeed of the entire poem, is simple and direct—surprisingly so given the range and depth of Miłosz's religious and philosophical interests. This simple speech is well suited to what Miłosz has called his "struggle to seize hold of fragments of reality." His need to capture in words "something that actually happened" becomes most clearly articulated in section 5. There, Miłosz takes exception to Poland's other great contemporary poet, Zbigniew Herbert, for claiming in one of his own poems that "The most beautiful object/ is the one that doesn't exist." The artist who appears in the fifth section of "Bobo's Metamorphosis," like Miłosz, rejects the privileging of abstraction and metaphor over reality. Miłosz and his artist (anonymous but, by virtue of "his tobacco-stained beard," not abstract) choose a more realistic approach in their efforts "to name, paint, draw" existing objects. This naming implies something more than mere photographic depiction. It implies that contemplative state toward which Miłosz's "realistic" yet highly meditative poetry is invariably drawn and against which he feels as invariably compelled to offer the counterweight of events in all their immediacy and time in all its fluidity.

The immediacy and fluidity of "Bobo's Metamorphosis" are most artfully apparent in the repeated metamorphoses of subjects, scenes, styles, and time, such as the frequent shifts from present to past tense and the change of mood in section 4 from indicative to subjunctive. Objects, people, places, and certain key words appear, disappear, and suddenly, almost randomly, reappear in a text which strikes the reader as specific in detail yet strangely elusive in meaning. The poem is realistic in approach yet fantastic, even magical in effect, like the original *Bobo's Metamorphosis*. Overall, the poem operates within the opposing claims established by the two forms of what, after "metamorphosis," is its most important word: the kinetic physicality of the verb "to attain" and the static spirituality of the noun "the attainable."

Themes and Meanings

The ideal task of the poet, Miłosz pointed out in his Nobel Prize lecture, "is to contemplate the word 'is.' " In Miłosz's case, this "is" encompasses ontology (over the more fashionable contemporary preoccupation with epistemology), on the one hand, and a preoccupation with "the complexity and richness of the visible world," on the other. Conceiving the world as indissolubly double—as objective existence and ontological essence—and drawing on Urbanowska's children's story about a boy turned into a fly, Miłosz embodies in his poem that "basic curiosity about the world" which he, both as "witness to poetry" (the title of his Harvard lectures) and as witness to history (the German occupation of Poland and the rise of the Stalinist state), warns is fast disappearing. About "flying into the center of things" and exploring "reality from various angles, in various guises," according to the poet, "Bobo's Metamorphosis" conforms to Miłosz's definition of poetry as "the passionate pursuit of the Real," but a Real which remains stubbornly, magically unattainable.

Against history's generalizations and its annihilation of the individual, Miłosz posits the sensuous apprehension of the world in all its immediacy as it is experienced, remembered, or contemplated. Although experience and memory act as checks on each other and so would appear to have more or less equal status, memory in fact occupies a special place in Miłosz's philosophical scheme, mediate between the experiential and the eternal. Marked by two temporal worlds, memory exhibits the duality of humanity's at once timebound and timeless existence.

The linkage of the sensual and the spiritual in "Bobo's Metamorphosis" derives at least in part from the Catholicism in which Miłosz was trained and to which he continued to subscribe. The essential paradox at the very heart of the poem, however, summed up in the line "Life was given but unattainable" and even more succinctly in the phrase "the eternal moment" from "Notebook: Bon by Lake Leman," written a decade earlier, derives in large measure from a quite different source: the writings of Simone Weil, and her thoughts on contradiction in particular. One must not become "at home" with contradiction too easily, Weil has warned; rather, one must struggle against it with all one's intelligence and only then admit to its inevitability. In "Bobo's Metamorphosis," the contradictory forces do not merely oppose one another: They meet and merge (or metamorphose) one into the other. The "eternal moment" that is the poem "Bobo's Metamorphosis" develops from the fluid movement of various styles, forms, subjects, and the "passionate pursuit of a Real" which is at once ephemeral and eternal, fragmentary and whole, "given" and "unattainable."

Robert A. Morace

BODY OF SUMMER

Author: Odysseus Elytis (Odysseus Alepoudhélis, 1911-1996)
Type of poem: Lyric
First published: 1943, as "Soma tou kaloukariou," in *Ilios o protos, mazi me tis parallayies pano se mian ahtidha*; English translation collected in *The Sovereign Sun: Selected Poems*, 1974

The Poem

"Body of Summer" is a free-verse poem of four stanzas. The poem can be divided in half: The first two stanzas describe a landscape in the voice of a third-person narrator; the last two stanzas address the personified landscape directly in the song of the "little siren."

A deceptively simple description of midsummer opens the poem: "A long time has passed since the last rainfall was heard." The landscape is dry, parched from long drought. "Now the sky burns endlessly." Populated by ants and lizards, the landscape seems inhuman, yet the fruit trees "paint their mouths" with the colors of overripe fruit splitting in the sun, and the earth is slowly opening its thirsty pores. Instead of the elemental sound of rain from above, the "syllabic" drip of water is heard from a hidden spring below that trickles the rudiments of language, as though the earth itself is beginning to speak.

Beside the spring, a "huge plant" gazes into the eye of the sun. Like the fruit trees and the water, which are nonspecific (neither pears nor pomegranates, neither fountain nor stream), the plant is generic and anonymous. Perhaps it is a sunflower, which, like the soul of man (especially Greek man), follows the sun.

The second stanza compares this landscape to a personage, not really a person, that is reclining sensuously on the shore, huge and naked, smoking olive leaves, like Gulliver stranded on the beach. Like Lilliputians, cicadas are in his ears, ants are on his chest, and lizards are in his armpits. He swarms with life. The question is asked: "Who is this who sprawls on the far beaches?"

This is the body of summer. The reader discovers this in the second half of the poem, an apostrophe sung by the "little siren," who addresses the personified season directly: "O naked body of summer." Unlike the aloof narrator of the first two stanzas, the singing siren is celebratory, admiring, perhaps even seductive, and certainly erotic. Her catalog of physical traits gives the abstract season substance, weight, and texture. His skin is eaten by oil and salt, his body is rock, his heart throbs. His hair is the willow, and his breath is as fragrant as "basil on the curly groin." Like a sailing ship, his body is a "vessel of day!"

This lazy eroticism gives way to a violent sexual coupling in the final stanza, as winter returns to descend on this vessel-rock, whose "hills plunge into thick udders of clouds." Winter is depicted as a "savage" beast with claws and udders, the female equivalent of the masculine body of summer. When this period of strife is over, however, the body of summer reemerges, smiling "unconcernedly" in its "deathless hour" and reasserting its "naked health" and vigor under both sun and sky.

Forms and Devices

In an interview with Ivar Ivask (March, 1975), Odysseus Elytis cites "Body of Summer" as an example of the way in which he has kept "the mechanism of myth-making but not the figures of mythology." In this poem, he says, it is "the idea of summer which is personified by the body of a young man." Such transformations are typical of his first period of poetry, which was influenced by Surrealism and written before and during World War II. "In my first period nature and metamorphoses predominate (stimulated by surrealism, which always believed in the metamorphosis of things)."

Elytis is a visual artist as well as a poet, and his collages are reminiscent of his poetry in the way they transpose various photographic images. In "Body of Summer," for example, there are visually surprising images that could occur only in the literal medium of collage—cicadas in the ear, lizards in the grass of armpits—images that employ synesthesia, using one sense to evoke another, the visual evoking the tactile: one hears, sees, and also feels the cicadas' warmth and the lizards' glide.

The figure of the little siren animates the physical world of the first two stanzas, in which the transformations are merely metaphorical, with the mythical world of the last two stanzas. By addressing the body of summer directly, the little siren turns the poet's metaphorical language into living myth. She is the poem's animating soul (its anima, in Jungian terms).

This is what connects Elytis's poetry with the Surrealism of Paul Éluard (1895-1952), for whom the poem exists as a vehicle by which to discover the erotic link between landscape and the human psyche. Elytis felt such a sensuous and loving connection between the language and the landscape of his native Greece.

Elytis insists on the untranslatable significance of objects named in their own language. "If I say in Greek, for example, 'olive tree' or 'sea,' these words have completely different connotations for us than, say, for an American." The poet's private associations are similarly untranslatable. Lizards are, for example, creatures who thrive in a parched landscape; they are, for Elytis, personal symbols. In the Ivask interview, he tells how "once, at high noon, I saw a lizard climb upon a stone . . . and then, in broad daylight, commence a veritable dance, with a multitude of tiny movements, in honor of light. There and then I deeply sensed the mystery of light."

Themes and Meanings

"Body of Summer" aims, as does all Elytis's poetry, to reveal what he calls the mystery of light: limpidity, clarity, transparency. This is why the sun (*hylios*) and sky (*ouranos*) figure so prominently in his poems. Some translators have exchanged the two terms, as in line 3: "Now the *sun* burns endlessly," although Elytis has written *ouranos* (sky or heavens) and not *hylios* (sun).

This is a key difference in this poem because it points out the distinction between the pagan Greek sun worship and the Byzantine Greek yearning for heavenly transcendence. Elytis would hope to unite the two, the Christian and the pagan, in his modern poem.

The final lines of the poem illustrate this theme, which can best be seen by comparing two translations. The Keeley-Sherrard translation reads: "As the sun finds you again on the sandy shores/ As the sky finds you again in your naked health." The pagan sun beats down, earthward, while the Byzantine sky lifts up, heavenward. The final emphasis is on the sky's approval of "naked health."

The poem ends with the word *ouranos*, however, which in Greek (like the French *ciel*) means both sky and heaven. This detail is captured in Kimon Friar's translation: "As once more you are found on the beaches by the sun/ And amid your naked vigor by the sky." Here, the final position of the subject of the verb (which is active in Greek syntax) makes the sky's discovery more forceful and memorable. The naked vigor and health of the body is approved by both the sun and the sky (*hylios* and *ouranos*), the final word turning the emphasis away from the pagan "naked health" of the Keeley-Sherrard translation toward the Christian "sky" of Friar's. It is important to end the poem on this high note, because it turns a poem of hedonistic sun worship into a poem of spiritual transcendence.

Elytis calls this movement upward in his poems "meteorism" or "a tendency to mount up to the sky, to rise toward the heights." This is why he denies being a pagan or Dionysian poet, insisting always on the "clarity" of his poems—not *la belle clarté* of French rationalism, but rather what he calls "limpidity." "What I mean by limpidity," he notes in the Ivask interview, "is that behind a given thing something different can be seen and behind that still something else, and so on and so on. This kind of transparency is what I have attempted to achieve. It seems to me something essentially Greek."

This double-exposure or montage effect is what attracted Elytis to Surrealism. The Surrealist juxtaposition of images allows the emanative essence of a thing to break through, to rise above the surface of things. This is particularly evident in the poet's collages, in which certain images, a Greek *kouros* statue or a naked girl, seem to be emerging through a rip in the surface of the colorful Greek postcard landscape.

Yet it is not only the classical world that emanates through Elytis's poetry, as it is for example in that of his contemporary George Seferis, but also the Christian heritage of Byzantine Greece. The collage that serves as frontispiece to *Odysseus Elytis: Analogies of Light* (1981) is a good example. "Votive Offering" shows a Byzantine angel rising above a cluster of whitewashed island rooftops as though bestowing a blessing on the village; from the village blossoms a cluster of shells. Clearly, the elements of water, earth, and sky are connected in these figures that represent the animal, human, and divine worlds.

This benediction of the Byzantine that is bestowed on what is sensuous and "pagan" is at the heart of Elytis's erotic poetry, which is always striving to change the world "through continual metamorphoses more in harmony with my dreams," and to create "a contemporary kind of magic whose mechanism leads to the discovery of our true reality."

Richard Collins

BOGLAND

Author: Seamus Heaney (1939-   )
Type of poem: Meditation
First published: 1969, in *Door into the Dark*

The Poem

"Bogland," a short poem of seven four-line stanzas (quatrains), is the final work in Seamus Heaney's second collection of poetry, *Door into the Dark*. Heaney was born in the small town of Mossbaum, in County Derry, and is considered one of the most accomplished of the "Ulster poets," or writers from Northern Ireland. As is much of his early poetry, "Bogland" is heavily influenced by the writer's rural upbringing and reflects his close ties to the Irish landscape. The title originates from Ireland's often swampy countryside and from Heaney's childhood memory of the local interest generated by the discovery of an elk's skeletal remains in a bog near his hometown. The event was significant because, as he writes, "I began to get an idea of bog as the memory of the landscape, or as a landscape that remembered everything that happened in and to it." The poem's link to issues concerning the Irish countryside is further emphasized by its dedication to Thomas P. Flanagan, who authored several novels that reflected the political turmoil and class struggles in rural Ireland during the late nineteenth and early twentieth centuries; he also wrote influential critical texts on Irish prose. Flanagan taught at the University of California at Berkeley when Heaney was a guest lecturer there from 1970 to 1971.

"Bogland" opens with the poet comparing the landscape of the American West to that of Ireland and contrasting the vastness of the prairie to the close horizon of the Irish countryside, which seems to "encroach" upon the poet. Unlike American history, which in its westward expansion seemed to explore limitless horizons, Irish history turned inward, toward the center. The poem's perspective moves inward from the horizon to a nearby "tarn," or mountain lake, and the poet imagines that all of Ireland is reflected in the pool and its swampy surroundings, as if it were the eye of the Cyclops, a mythical, one-eyed giant.

The poet's attention focuses more closely on the marshy land around the lake and its "crusting" surface, which appears firm but is in reality unstable. Continuing to turn inward, the third stanza moves the poet's imagination back to the time when the elk's carcass was discovered in the bog. Readers are led to the edge of, and then into, the bog itself. For Heaney, the elk raises the question of what other articles are suspended in the bog's "black butter." He remembers childhood stories of people storing food in the peat for long periods of time; the bog therefore becomes a repository, not only of archaeological artifacts, but of Irish culture, history, and identity. Ireland's mythic past, suggested by the Cyclops reference, is joined in the bog with its physical, organic past. The swampy landscape, soft and unstable, swallows anything laid to rest on it yet preserves and combines these objects into an amalgamation of personal and cultural histories.

The poet is led deeper into the peat, as if he were sinking in quicksand, and sees objects suspended in the bog. The poem concludes with Heaney attempting to strip away all the layers of soil and history that have accumulated over thousands of years. He discovers that there is no bottom, as if the swampy hole were so deep that the Atlantic Ocean itself had seeped up through the Irish landscape. If he should go farther down, he would ultimately go below the island itself and straight through the earth, never reaching the bottom.

Forms and Devices

Written in free verse, the poem's progression depends largely on the lines' enjambment, which pulls readers down the page as the poet is drawn deeper into the landscape. For example, stanza 1 concludes with the image of the poet's eye surveying the "Encroaching horizon," which is completed in the opening lines of the second stanza as his eye is "wooed into the cyclops' eye/ Of a tarn." Similarly, the last line of stanza 4, "The ground itself is kind, black butter," is continued in the first line of the fifth stanza, which echoes the theme of the bog's "Melting and opening underfoot." Just as stanzas 4 and 5 are linked syntactically by "butter/ Melting," so the grammatical distinctions between stanzas and sentences become blurred.

"Bogland" presents the poet as historical, cultural, and artistic archaeologist. Heaney had been influenced by P. V. Glob's *The Bog People* (1966), an account of a Danish excavation of a first century settlement in Windeby, Germany. The marshy German terrain had nearly perfectly preserved several bodies and artifacts, and Heaney recognized the swamp's potential to serve as a metaphor for human experience. Instead of civilization progressing linearly along a time line, cultures were built upon each other like the layers of sediment in the bog. This treatment of history is reminiscent of T. S. Eliot's description in part 5 of *The Waste Land* (1922) of how civilization is built upon the ruins of previous cultures. Heaney observes that "Every layer they strip/ Seems camped on before." For Heaney, the layers are not easily distinguishable because, unlike the layers of solid ground, the bog is continually "melting and opening underfoot." What was long past mingles with what has recently found its way into the marsh, and distinctions between time periods become unclear.

As the poet-archaeologist of "Bogland" digs deeper into the peat, he travels back not only through historical time but also into the collective human consciousness. The artifacts uncovered in the upper layers give way to increasingly primitive objects: the butter, the "waterlogged trunks" of ancient trees, and finally a primordial sea deep below the surface where the "wet centre is bottomless." Leaving the historical, physical world, the poet enters the realm of myth and the supernatural. Here he seeks to reveal the foundations of culture and the roots of identity by literally penetrating below the surface and identifying previously obscured social and artistic origins. In the end, though, the poet is unable to reach a solid beginning, having found instead a vast ocean of experience that is beyond humanity's knowledge and power of understanding.

Themes and Meanings

In part, "Bogland" illustrates the poet's quest to break free from artistic conventions and traditions. Historically, poets have struggled with the need to create their own identities as artists, and this struggle has been difficult for twentieth century Irish poets living in the shadow of influential writers such as William Butler Yeats (1865-1939). Searching for his own artistic roots, Heaney followed the advice of fellow Irish poet Patrick Kavanagh (1905-1967), who believed that the local, or parochial, could transcend its mundane, or provincial, limitations to represent universal themes. The close scrutiny of the landscape in "Bogland" provides the poet with a metaphor for exploring larger cultural themes.

One of the most omnipresent themes in Irish literature is the search for a national identity. Having lived in Northern Ireland during the "Troubles" (the political and religious conflicts between unionists and separatists, with origins that trace back hundreds of years), Heaney is keenly aware of the difficulties associated with establishing a national identity. The poet avoids the problems of essentializing his definition of Irish culture by presenting culture as a landscape in a perpetual state of metamorphosis. Ireland and the Irish are not a single, simply identifiable entity determined solely by political or religious affiliations. Rather, they are the accumulation of thousands of years of history, which becomes jumbled and confused in multiple layers of collective cultural consciousness. The bog serves as the landscape's archetypal memory, preserving everything that has occurred. It contains an organic record of each generation that has lived on it. Therefore, Ireland's identity is constantly redefining itself as successive generations add to the bog and are made part of the whole.

For Heaney then, the bog functions as a metaphor for the search for significant patterns, a means of unifying a fractured, postcolonial society. Establishing what it means to be "Irish" is possible, but only as an accumulation of meanings that reverberate back and forth from present to past to present again. While Heaney's search terminates in the vast, bottomless center of the world, the poem's conclusion is neither pessimistic nor nihilistic. As he digs deeper, the poet uncovers increasingly ancient levels of culture and consciousness until he verges on the mysterious origins of history itself. Here, in the dark roots of Ireland, the poet can explore his origins free from the political, religious, and artistic limitations that confine him on the surface.

Thomas F. Suggs

BOMB

Author: Gregory Corso (1930-2001)
Type of poem: Dramatic monologue
First published: 1958; collected in *The Happy Birthday of Death*, 1960

The Poem

"Bomb" is an extended dramatic monologue presented as shaped verse in the form of the mushroom cloud of an atomic blast. The title refers to the object addressed in the poem. The speaker talks to the silent atomic bomb, comparing it with the other works and practices of humankind, declaring the bomb worthy of laughter, admiration, and love.

"Bomb" opens as the speaker begins the address, exclaiming, "You Bomb/ Toy of Universe   Grandest of all snatched-sky   I cannot hate you." How, the speaker wonders, can he hate the bomb in particular when no similar hate is felt for the thunderbolt, the caveman's club, Leonardo Da Vinci's catapult, or Cochise's tomahawk? Indeed, the speaker asks, "[H]ath not St. Michael a burning sword   St. George a lance   David a sling[?]" The bomb is, after all, "no crueller than cancer."

To all others, death in any other form, whether "car-crash lightning   drowning/ Falling off a roof   electric-chair   heart attack" or "old age   old age," is better than death by the bomb, but to the speaker, the bomb is "Death's jubilee/ Gem of Death's supremest blue." The speaker imagines the effect of the atomic blast on pedestrians and subway riders in Manhattan but quickly lets imagination soar, envisioning "Turtles exploding over Istanbul" and "The top of the Empire State/ arrowed in a broccoli field in Sicily." With the atomic blast, the ruins of antiquity, the structures of the present, and the possibilities of the future shall all be at an end, and the bomb can "tee-hee finger-in-the-mouth hop/ over its long long dead Nor." Even God will be gone: "A thunderless God   A dead God/ O Bomb   thy BOOM His tomb."

The speaker justifies the unusual perception of the bomb, announcing, "I am able to laugh at all things," adding, "I say I am a poet and therefore love all man." As a poet, the speaker does not need to be "all-smart about bombs," for if "bombs were caterpillars" the speaker would "doubt not they'd become butterflies."

The poem continues with a comic vision of "a hell for bombs," where they remain after being blown to bits, singing German and American songs, longing for songs in Russian and Chinese. There is also comic sympathy for the "little Bomb that'll never be," the Eskimo bomb, with whom the speaker longs to frolic in play. The comic effect reaches a peak when the speaker becomes the bomb's suitor, arriving at its doorstep with flowers in hand, pleading to be allowed to enter, saying, "O Bomb I love you/ I want to kiss your clank   eat your boom."

The poem climaxes with a crescendo of sound:

> BOOM   BOOM   BOOM   BOOM   BOOM
> BOOM ye skies and BOOM ye suns

```
BOOM BOOM ye moons      ye stars BOOM
nights ye BOOM      ye days ye BOOM
BOOM BOOM ye winds      ye clouds ye rains,
go BANG ye lakes      ye oceans BING
Barracuda BOOM and cougar BOOM
Ubangi BANG  orangoutang
BING BANG BONG BOOM      bee bear baboon
ye BANG ye BONG ye BING
```

This orchestration of words signals the thunderous arrival of the bomb, but the poem's last lines take a serious and prophetic turn. Simply to say that the bomb will explode and all the world will yield to its force is insufficient. "Know that the earth will madonna the Bomb," the speaker declares, and "in the hearts of men to come more bombs will be born/ magisterial bombs wrapped in ermine   all beautiful/ and they'll sit plunk on earth's grumpy empires."

Forms and Devices

The most obvious device in "Bomb" is the shaping of the poem to give it the pictorial impression of a nuclear mushroom cloud. The top section of the poem is round like the top of an atomic blast, while the portion beneath is tapered like the stem of the cloud rising from the earth. In using shaped verse, Corso makes the design of his poem conform to the object of the poem's focus. If the poem is read as part of *The Happy Birthday of Death* (1960), the illustration of the atomic blast on the volume's cover provides additional emphasis on the appearance of the detonated bomb. Furthermore, the title of the volume suggests that "Bomb" is about the birthday of the bomb, or "Death's jubilee," the anniversary of the explosion of the nuclear weapon over Japan in August, 1945, and that this birthday, at least in the surprisingly playful mind of the speaker, is a happy occasion. However, if the poem is read in *Mindfield: New and Selected Poems* (1989), the visual impression of the original broadside or the subsequent foldout is lost.

A second feature of "Bomb" is the dramatic situation, in which Corso exploits the apostrophe, making the speaker address an object that cannot literally answer. With the apostrophe, the poem becomes a dramatic monologue well suited for a live reading, especially by Corso himself, whose talents as a reader lend themselves well to comedy based on the improbable personification of a nuclear weapon.

A third feature of the poem is Corso's juxtaposition of antiquity with modernity. The speaker refers to St. Michael, St. George, David, Hesperus, Homer, and Zeus, but also mixes in Rathbone, Dillinger, Bogart, Boris Karloff, and Harpo Marx. He pits Hermes, the mythic messenger with winged shoes, against Jesse Owens, the track star of the 1936 Berlin Olympics. The interruptive, conversational lines often marked by the informality of contractions are juxtaposed with archaic words such as "hath," "thy," "false-talc'd," and "ye." There is a "final amphitheater/ with a hymnody feeling of all Troys," but for the "Ritz Brothers from the Bronx caught in the A train/ The smiling Schenley poster will always smile." This juxtaposing of the old and new is characteristic of many of Corso's poems, including "Marriage," his most famous work. Corso's experience as an abandoned child, an imprisoned thief, and a streetwise young man gives him dominion over contemporary idiom, but he is also proud that he devoted much of his time in jail to studies of the classics and antiquity. He enjoys demonstrating his erudition.

The subtlest feature of "Bomb" is its ironic confounding of standard expectations. One might expect a poem about atomic weaponry to denounce the bomb and its power to destroy humanity; instead, the speaker loves and celebrates the bomb. He is protective and sympathetic; he even tries to woo the bomb. One might expect images of horror and death, but Corso mutes the horror with comic effects, such as the "top of the Empire State/ arrowed in a broccoli field in Sicily." One might expect the onomatopoeia of the climactic outburst of sound to underscore the thunder of the bomb, but the selections of sound include "Barracuda," "cougar," "Ubangi," "orangoutang," and "bee bear baboon," steering the poem toward humor. One might expect the bomb to be associated with the work of the devil, but the poem concludes with a reference to the Madonna and the birth of the savior. This last twist deflates the previous comic antics, giving special impact to the closing prophecy that not only the speaker, but all others as well, contribute to the birth of the ultimate blast.

Themes and Meanings

"Bomb" asks the reader to reconsider his or her understanding of nuclear weaponry. Is the bomb the most terrible thing that humankind has ever developed, or is it the natural progression of destruction signaled by all previous human behavior, and will the progression continue until the ultimate bomb arrives? Corso is prophetic, but he is also cautionary, warning all readers and listeners that the ultimate bomb will be all-powerful and even capable of dispatching God. If Corso were to deliver this warning in a straight and serious tone, he might not hold the reader's attention. However, Corso uses the surprise of the speaker's declaration, "O Bomb I love you," the comic effect of juxtapositions of the ancient and the modern, and a tumult of sound to seize the reader's attention and make him or her think in new ways. The final turn in the poem, however, demands reflection. Is all humankind, despite the lip service people give to peace, actually courting the bomb? By adopting the lifestyle that suppresses fear, even awareness, of the pending apocalypse, do people tacitly revere the bomb?

The poem also reflects strongly on poetry and the role of the poet: Does a poem have to be printed on a standard page in a book with its lines aligned at the left margin, or can it work on the scale of an illustrative poster with its lines arranged to depict its subject? Does the poet have to strive for consistency in tone and reference, or can the poet blend ancient culture and language with contemporary references and informal idiom? Does the topic of the end of the world and the entombing of God require absolute solemnity, or can humor and playfulness successfully serve to issue an urgent warning?

William T. Lawlor

THE BOOK OF THEL

Author: William Blake (1757-1827)
Type of poem: Narrative
First published: 1789

The Poem

The Book of Thel is one of William Blake's early "Prophetic Books," illustrated and printed by Blake himself on eight plates, in a process he invented. The poem itself consists of a motto followed by four sections of blank-verse paragraphs of varying lengths.

After the motto has posed some cryptic questions about how knowledge and wisdom might be acquired, the reader is introduced to Thel, a young girl wandering in a mythological pastoral setting, the vales of Har. The unhappy Thel is asking many questions about the purpose of her life. She is particularly distressed about the transience of existence. Why must everything in creation, including Thel herself, fade and die?

Various nonhuman aspects of nature, appearing to her in human form, try to answer her questions. First, a "Lilly of the valley" explains that although it is small and weak, it receives continual blessings from heaven during its brief span of life. When it fades away it flourishes again in "eternal vales." The Lilly tells Thel that she has no reason to complain. Thel replies that although she can see how the Lilly plays a useful part in nature—providing nourishment for the lamb and, with its perfume, reviving the cows after milking—she cannot see that her own life has any useful function. The Lilly tells her to ask the Cloud.

Thel asks the descending Cloud why it does not complain, even though it fades away so quickly. The Cloud replies that when it vanishes, it is to a far richer life, "to love, to peace, and raptures holy." It gives up its separate existence and merges into the morning dew which then provides food for all the flowers. Thel is still not comforted. She fears that she is not like a cloud. She does not provide food for the flowers, even though she can enjoy the sweetness of their smell. She will die and become the food of worms, and there will have been no purpose to her life.

The Cloud replies that this is not so, because "every thing that lives,/ Lives not alone, nor for itself," and calls to a worm to confirm this. Thel sees a worm on the Lilly leaf, and thinks it is weeping like a newborn baby. A Clod of Clay emerges and repeats that nothing lives merely for itself. The Clod may appear to be the least significant thing, but God pours blessings on her as mother of all the children of the earth. The Clod does not understand how this can happen, but she lives and loves without questioning. Thel, still weeping, replies that although she knew that God might cherish a worm, she did not not realize the full extent of the divine love. The Clod of Clay invites Thel to enter her domain and play her full part in earthly existence. Thel has nothing to fear and will be able to return to her vales.

Thel enters the domain of earth, but she discovers it to be "A land of sorrows & of tears where never smile was seen." She wanders around in a distressed condition until she sees her own grave. She hears a voice coming from the grave, asking a series of questions about why the five senses are permitted to register such intense and horrifying experiences in life. Thel is terrified and rushes back to the peaceful vales of Har.

Forms and Devices

The Book of Thel is the gentlest of Blake's illuminated books, a complete contrast to the harshness of *Tiriel*, which was written at about the same time. The poem is written in iambic heptameters, usually with a caesura after the third or fourth foot of each line. Blake adapted the ballad form, in which lines of three feet and four feet alternate, consolidating this pattern into one line. The meter is fairly regular, although there is enough variation to avoid monotony. The repetition of soft consonants, such as *l* and *f*, in the opening sections create the dominant tone of the poem's language. The overall effect is one of sweetness and femininity; the word "gentle," for example, is repeated four times in lines 12-13.

The only major change in the musical, flowing language and meter comes in the last few verse paragraphs, when Thel contemplates the harshness of earthly existence. The line length becomes irregular, varying between five feet and eight feet. There is an increased use of trochees rather than iambs. In addition, the insistent and cumulative repetitions in the questions Thel hears about the roles of the senses (a technique Blake used frequently in his later prophetic books) impart a feeling of intensity and urgency that has not been felt in the languid and passive atmosphere of the poem up to that point.

Unusual names and settings, such as the river of Adona, Luvah's horses, and the vales of Har, create a mythological atmosphere. Thel herself is described as a daughter of Mne Seraphim, a name Blake may have found in the work of the Renaissance magician and alchemist Cornelius Agrippa. The mythological elements provide an appropriate background for the poem's major device, the pathetic fallacy, which allows the elements of nature, both animate and inanimate, to find a voice.

All Blake's illuminated books involve both text and designs. The illustrations do not merely illustrate the text; sometimes they provide a counterpoint, a new angle on the matter of the poem, or put the text in a wider context. *The Book of Thel* has six illustrations, the most interesting of which is the final one. It shows a young girl, possibly but not necessarily Thel, and two smaller children, riding on a serpent. Thel holds the reins in her hands and appears to be in control of the beast, and the children look as if they are enjoying themselves.

The serpent is an ancient symbol with many meanings. In alchemy, the serpent is often shown with its tail in its mouth and symbolizes nature in its unregenerate or untamed form. Seeing the young figure riding the serpent of nature with such ease gives the reader another perspective on the ending of the poem. Perhaps Thel is needlessly afraid of the powers of nature, which may be more benevolent than she realizes.

Themes and Meanings

The Book of Thel has been variously interpreted. Some commentators believe it is a Neoplatonic allegory. According to this view, Thel is an unborn soul contemplating its descent from the eternal, spiritual world into the realm of matter. For the Neoplatonists the material world was only a shadow, a reflection, of the eternal world, and life on earth was a kind of death, or imprisonment, of the soul. Blake was familiar with Neoplatonic theory, which he would have found explained in Thomas Taylor's translation of Porphyry's *Cave of the Nymphs*, which was published in 1788. Much of the imagery of the poem is of water in its various forms, and water is a Neoplatonic symbol of the material world.

According to the Neoplatonic view, Thel would be showing some wisdom in rejecting her incarnation; however, the philosophies espoused by Lilly, Cloud, and Clod of Clay are very different. They are closer to the worldview Blake would have found in alchemy, with which he was also familiar through the writings of Paracelsus and Jakob Böhme. In the alchemical philosophy, the divine spirit interpenetrated the natural world, and every particle of creation served a spiritual purpose. Blake expressed this idea many times in *The Marriage of Heaven and Hell* (c. 1790-1793), especially in the phrase, "Every thing that lives is holy." Thel's rejection of earthly life shows that she has failed to grasp this principle.

A more naturalistic interpretation of the poem views Thel as a young girl in a state of innocence, who is reluctant to enter the state of experience. In his *Songs of Innocence and of Experience* (1794), Blake called these the "Two Contrary States of the Human Soul"; the unreflective joy and naïveté of innocence had to give way to the more somber realities of maturity before innocence could be recaptured at a higher level. Thel's intellectual questioning and her unhappiness show that she has already outgrown innocence, but her refusal to move on to the next stage in life shows her lack of maturity. She is refusing to grow up; her egotism and selfishness block her progress. The name Thel was probably taken from a Greek word meaning "will," and this may imply that Thel is also showing a deficiency of will.

Thel would cease her lamentation if she could learn to go beyond seeing life solely in terms of the individual ego and absorb the philosophy taught by the Lilly, Cloud, and Clod of Clay. They all take delight in what Blake was later to call "self-annihilation"; they willingly give up their individual identities so as to serve the larger purposes of creation. In doing so, they feel constantly blessed and fulfilled. This is the central paradox of all religious faith: He who loses his life shall save it. Blake's achievement in *The Book of Thel* is to have expressed this view with such charm and delicacy, giving a voice to the humblest and apparently most insignificant aspects of creation.

Bryan Aubrey

BOOKBUYING IN THE TENDERLOIN

Author: Robert Hass (1941-   )
Type of poem: Verse essay
First published: 1967; collected in *Field Guide*, 1973

The Poem
   Having originally published "Bookbuying in the Tenderloin" in *The Hudson Re-view*, Robert Hass included it in his first collection, *Field Guide*. A thirty-four-line poem employing a complex rhyme scheme punctuated by a scattered series of couplets, "Bookbuying in the Tenderloin" is vintage Hass: blunt, direct, and vivid in language and imagery but also profound in its larger social and philosophical implications. The title is straightforward enough; Hass's poem does indeed describe a book-buying junket in the seedy Tenderloin district of San Francisco and details the thoughts about modernity that such an excursion occasions. The title is also ironic; buying books is not an activity normally associated with the decadent Tenderloin.
   Indeed, the poet's urban meanderings through the Tenderloin constitute something of a symbolic quest for meaning—perhaps even transcendence—not unlike the kind described by T. S. Eliot's *The Waste Land* (1922), although Hass's poem is, in every way, on a much more modest scale than Eliot's epic. Ultimately Eliot was able to make a leap of faith and embrace Anglo-Catholicism in order to avoid the terrifying nihilism that marks the *Zeitgeist* of the twentieth century. Writing almost half a century later, after the horrors of World War II concentration camps and the atomic bomb, and at the height of the Vietnam War, Hass had less reason to be sanguine about humanity's prospects. For American intellectuals in the 1960's, Hass among them, theology was too quaintly remote to offer any comfort. Political idealism and hard-nosed scientific positivism offered nothing better as a way out of the agonizing cultural crisis that has engulfed the Western world.

Forms and Devices
   "Bookbuying in the Tenderloin" is cast in the form of a peripatetic meditation that employs precise descriptive detail, a sardonic tone, and a flair for ironic, even grotesque, juxtaposition. At the outset of his wanderings through the Tenderloin, Hass's speaker passes St. Boniface Church, a 1902 city landmark at 133 Golden Gate. In the Church's Gethsemane Garden "a statuary Christ bleeds sweating grief" in a distinctly secular neighborhood "where empurpled winos lurch to their salvation." Because "incense and belief" no longer suffice in the modern age, the drunkards' port in the storm of urban decay is, literally, port: a self-defeating psychic defense that produces "muscatel-made images of hell" out of the quotidian chaos. St. Boniface's "Christ in plaster" suggests an injured deity or a cheap and fragile icon. In either case the image underscores the increasing irrelevance of religion in contemporary America, an institution that has lost its legitimacy as a means of spiritual redemption.

Just as the Church has been reduced to moribund parcels of real estate that no longer harbor the spirit they were meant to tend, so too has the union movement ceased to exist as a vital force for social change. Continuing onward, the poet notices Longshoreman's Hall, across the street from St. Boniface's. A hotbed of radical politics in the 1930's and 1940's, the hall has become something of a historical mausoleum since the ouster of "the manic Trotskyite/ screwballs from the brotherhood" three decades earlier. De-radicalized after World War II, the unions have "closed their ranks,/ boosted their pensions, and hired the banks/ to manage funds for the workingman's cartel." For the most part, unions have been robbed of their revolutionary promise and are now docile upholders of the capitalist status quo.

After the church and union hall, the third type of symbolic structure the poet encounters on his walk is the secondhand bookstore. Here he finds works by "Comte, Considerant, [and] Fourier . . . thick with dust in the two-bit tray[s]." Hass chose these particular writers for a very specific symbolic effect. French positivist Auguste Comte was a passionate adherent of rationalism. He sought nothing less than a sweeping reorganization of the social order in accord with scientific principles. Charles Fourier, French philosopher and a leading proponent of revolutionary socialism, was author of the "universal principal of harmony" between the material universe, organic life, animal life, and human society. Nineteenth century American Fourierists founded a number of short-lived utopian communities, among them Brook Farm in Massachusetts. Victor Considerant was a follower of Fourier. Hass cites these utopian thinkers to tacitly argue that, in contemporary America, the intense optimism and social idealism of the Enlightenment is long dead; its obscure traces can be found only in secondhand bookstores.

To reinforce and extend a pervasive sense of hopelessness, Hass infuses the poem's closing lines with street images of "Negro boy-whores," "noisy hustler bars," "girls who sell their bodies for a dollar/ or two, the price of a Collected Maeterlinck." The allusion to Maurice Maeterlinck, Symbolist dramatist and the 1911 winner of the Nobel Prize in Literature, is particularly apt inasmuch as his work was famous for its melancholy and pessimism.

Themes and Meanings

In his magnum opus, the six-volume *Course of Positive Philosophy* (1830-1842), Auguste Comte theorized that, because of the nature of the human mind, each science or field of knowledge passes through three major states of development: the theological or fictitious state, the metaphysical or abstract state, and the scientific or positive state. At the theological stage, all phenomena are naïvely explained by appealing to the will of some deity or deities. At the metaphysical stage, events are explained with reference to fixed, abstract philosophical categories. In the final, scientific stage of epistemological evolution, any attempt to arrive at absolute causes is relinquished in favor of empirical explanations as to how events interrelate, arrived at not inductively, by some a priori conceptual fiat, but deductively, through careful observation of real world events.

Comte further posits that each of these epistemological stages can be correlated to political stages of development in human history. The theological stage is manifest is such notions as the divine right of kings. The metaphysical stage is reflected in such Enlightenment concepts as democratic government, social equality, and the social contract. The positivist stage, which Comte hoped to inaugurate, would involve a rigorously scientific or "sociological" approach to political organization, conceived and managed by a scientific elite.

In theme and structure "Bookbuying in the Tenderloin" brilliantly parodies Comte's tripartite epistemological-political schema. Surely, St. Boniface's Church epitomizes Comte's theological state of knowledge, a superstitious worldview massively superseded by modernity's scientific and technological revolution. Longshoreman's Hall represents the metaphysical stage, an Enlightenment-inspired attempt to order human affairs on abstract principles of justice and social equality, also doomed to failure. The secondhand bookstores symbolize Comte's third or scientific state in the sense that they are repositories of knowledge apart from any unifying ideological agenda. One is free to read anything and draw one's own conclusions. Hass slyly spoofs Comte's Positivism by placing him and related utopian thinkers in history's dustbin, emphatically reminding readers that empiricism has also failed to usher in a golden age.

What is left after Comte's three states have been exhausted and found wanting? There is nothing except the sybaritic anarchy of the street. Hass's speaker admits that, in the places he haunts, he has "no power/ to transform the universal squalor/ nor wisdom to withstand the thin wrists" of the prostitutes who ply their trade in the Tenderloin. Lust, greed, and the blind instinct to survive defeat all utopian aspirations. The poet can name modernity's malaise with moving eloquence but is at a loss for solutions. In the end, he can only utter an exasperated sense of wonder at the historical predicament in which he is caught: "My God, it is a test,/ this riding out the dying of the West."

Robert Niemi

BORN OF WOMAN

Author: Wisława Szymborska (1923-   )
Type of poem: Lyric
First published: 1967, as "Urodzony," in *Sto pociech*; collected in *Sounds, Feelings, Thoughts: Seventy Poems by Wisława Szymborska*, 1981

The Poem

"Born of Woman" is a poem in free verse, containing forty-five lines divided into sixteen stanzas of varying length. The ending on the Polish word of the original title, "Urodzony," makes it clear at the outset that the subject is a man; the poem represents the musings of his wife or lover, who has just caught her first glimpse of his mother. Her words are directed inward; she is talking to herself.

The first stanza begins abruptly, as if the speaker were somewhat surprised or bemused: "So that is his mother." What follows is barely a description, for the only physical details offered are that she is gray-eyed and small. Small she may be, but she is the cause, the "perpetrator" of the man's existence. From "perpetrator" Wisława Szymborska moves into one of her controlling metaphors. The mother is the boat in which he floated to shore and out of which he struggled into this temporary world. The fourth stanza finally defines the relationship between the speaker and the man— between the "I" and the "he" of the poem—but does so in the barest of terms. The mother is "the bearer of the man/ with whom I walk through fire."

The next four stanzas focus on the mother, who, unlike the wife, did not choose him but rather created him. She seems to be complete in herself, the ultimate beginning, the "alpha" who molded him into the form and shape that the wife now sees. She gave him the gray eyes that in turn looked at the woman who would be his wife. This section ends with a question that might be plaintive, annoyed, or simply rhetorical: "Why did he show her to me."

The next section shifts the focus to "him" and to the speaker's discovery that he is like everyone else and most of all like the speaker herself. He was born and must die. Here Szymborska returns to her metaphor of the journey and describes the man as a newcomer to this world, a traveler on his way to his omega, his end. As a newcomer he is confused by the world and moves through it dodging, bobbing, and weaving, hoping to avoid the inevitable. While he may not yet understand the inevitable, the speaker does. She knows that he has passed the halfway mark on the road to omega. Returning to the beginning, she reminds the reader and herself that he himself never said so. All he said was, "This is my mother."

Forms and Devices

The poem's short, sometimes incomplete sentences, short lines, and short stanzas create the impression of a woman talking to herself, trying to cope with what seems to be an unpleasant surprise. However, the tone is more reflective, wry, and controlled than it is overtly emotional, and the thought process does not seem fragmented or disjointed. Szymborska uses both repetition and metaphor to connect the thoughts, moving the poem coherently from beginning to end.

Stanzas often begin with parallel constructions. "So that is . . ." introduces three stanzas describing the mother and is used one last time midstanza when the speaker comes to the crux of the problem: "So he too was born." The same construction may link the opening lines of two successive stanzas; for example, stanza 13 begins with "And his head," and stanza 14 begins with "And his movements." Although there is no rhyme or fixed meter, there is rhythm.

Single words, too, are repeated, most strikingly in Szymborska's use of pronouns—or more accurately, in her repeated avoidance of specific nouns. The speaker names no one; the poem is dominated by "his," "she," "her," "I," "my." (This effect is even more exaggerated in the English translation, because Polish verbs indicate gender in the past tense. So "he floated" in Polish can leave out the actual "he," with the verb ending making it clear whether the subject of the verb is male or female.) The nouns used to refer to the personages are among the most basic, such as man, woman, mother, son, or parts of the body, such as eyes, skin, bones. The rest is metaphor.

The overarching metaphor of the poem is of life as a journey. The mother is the boat that has carried the man to this shore, "from body's depths." He begins by struggling out of that boat, and ever afterward the journey is a difficult one. A newcomer to this world, he walks, wanders, dodges, and bangs his head against a metaphorical wall. Regardless of whether he accepts or understands the fact, he is already more than halfway down the road. On a more abstract level, his mother is "his alpha"—the beginning not of life but of "non-eternity," and if there is a beginning, then there must be an end. He is "a wanderer to omega" whether he likes it or not.

The speaker certainly does not like it, and Szymborska brings in a smaller metaphor (smaller in the sense that it is less developed), that of a trial. The first noun used to describe the mother is "perpetrator." Toward the end of the poem it is not the mother but the son to whom an inevitable "universal verdict" applies.

Themes and Meanings

"Man that is born of a woman is of few days, and full of trouble. He cometh forth like a flower, and is cut down. He fleeth also as a shadow, and continueth not." So says the Bible's Job, and the Western lyric tradition has been saying so ever since. The fleeting nature of human life has preoccupied poets for centuries, sometimes expressing itself in calls to "gather ye rosebuds while ye may," other times expressing itself in somber contemplation of the dust of kings.

Szymborska's theme, then, is not a new one, and neither is her metaphor of life as a journey. The notion that, side trips and accidental detours notwithstanding, everyone is heading toward the same destination is as old as the story of Gilgamesh and as new as the latest "road movie." What makes Szymborska's treatment interesting is her choice of emotional framework. She places these meditations on "non-eternity" within a set of ordinary human relationships that, like the theme itself, are as ancient as they are troublesome.

Szymborska's speaker takes her own ordinariness for granted. She is like everyone else; she was born and she will die. Yet so far she has managed to avoid the idea that the man she loves is subject to the same eternal law as ordinary people. She does not idolize him; her problem has more to do with the human tendency to take loved ones for granted.

The first line, "So that is his mother," might set the stage for either a tragedy or a comedy; in either case two women have claims on one man. So on one hand the speaker is coolly sizing the mother up, taking the measure of a rival. She has a certain advantage, because the encounter is one-sided. The reader has no idea whether the mother sees the speaker, let alone what she might think of her. On the other hand, the measure is an intimidating one, because the mother is not only the means by which the man came to exist but also the very reason for his existence. She not only brought the man to this shore, she created him. Having "bound him to the bones hidden from me," the mother knows things that the speaker does not. Not only that, his gray eyes are his mother's eyes as well. She has knowledge, and therefore power, that the speaker lacks.

The tension between wife and mother-in-law is implied in the words used to describe the latter. "Gray-eyed perpetrator" is an accusation. Many a wife or lover has leveled accusations at her husband's mother, but this poem contains what might be the ultimate one, which could be paraphrased as, "He is mortal, he is going to die, and it is all your fault." At the same time, as Szymborska knows perfectly well, mortality is no one's fault; it is simply a fact of existence.

Jane Ann Miller

BRAHMA

Author: Ralph Waldo Emerson (1803-1882)
Type of poem: Lyric
First published: 1857; collected in *May-Day and Other Pieces*, 1867

The Poem

"Brahma" is an excellent reflection and representation of Ralph Waldo Emerson's work as a whole. Though he is more widely known as a writer of essays, several of his poems may be seen as keys to his use of style and theme in all of his work, and this is one of those poems. Stylistically, he uses the same spiral or circular method that he does in his prose, rather than the more straightforward linear development used by most poets of his time. Thematically, he insists on the same spiritual and physical unity and harmony in the universe, expressed in a similarly intensive and dense language, as he does in his essays. These qualities demand much from the reader.

"Brahma" is a poem of sixteen lines, divided into four quatrains. In order to understand and appreciate this poem fully, one must know something about Eastern religion, especially Hinduism. In Hindu theology, Brahma (or, more commonly, Brahman) is the supreme spirit or divine reality in the universe, the eternal spirit from which all has come and to which all shall return (similar to what Emerson more commonly called the Over-Soul). The "strong gods" (line 13) are secondary gods who, like all mortals, seek ultimate union with the supreme god, Brahma: They include Indra, the god of the sky; Agni, the god of fire; and Yama, "the red slayer" (line 1), or god of death. The "sacred Seven" (line 14) are the highest holy persons or saints in Hinduism, who also seek union (or reunion) with Brahma.

In stanza 1, Emerson insists that in the creative spirit of the universe, nothing dies; if death thinks that in fact it kills, or if those who are killed think that they are really dead, they are wrong, for death is maya, or illusion. Brahma is subtle; the patterns of life and death, of eternal return, are not always obvious to the human eye or mind. Through the intuition, however, a person can see and understand his or her role in these patterns and can accept and learn from them.

In the second stanza the reader discovers the essential unity of opposites—what Emerson called polarity. The physical and spiritual are intimately intertwined, with the physical being the concrete representation in the material world of the spiritual, which alone is real. In Emerson's terms, "both shadow and sunlight are the same" (line 6); in other words, light and dark, good and evil, life and death, happiness and sadness, and "shame and fame" (line 8) are all the same. They are illusions which mortals believe to be real but which are not. In the same way, all human experience is one and is eternally present; what is "far or forgot" (line 5) is in fact near, and both past and future are encapsulated in the present moment.

Stanza 3 suggests that one can never escape this creative energy, since it is present everywhere in the universe. Humans ignore it at their own peril, since it alone is real, and it encompasses both "the doubter and the doubt" (line 11). It is the song of creative joy sung by the Brahmin, the highest caste in Hinduism. Fortunately, however, even if one does ignore the creative spirit, it remains present in one's life, and eventually one's spiritual eyes will open and one will recognize it. Both the person who doubts and the doubts themselves are essential parts of the universal plan.

Stanza 4 states that all seek union with this eternal spirit—whether lesser gods, saints, or those persons who are considerably farther down on the spiral of spiritual enlightenment. If one loves the good, regardless of one's faults, one shall find it. Even if one is insecure or "meek" in one's beliefs, one should turn away from the illusion of the Calvinist Christian heaven, where entrance is limited to the very few elect, and all others are rejected and damned. One should seek the Brahma, or Over-Soul, the eternal spirit of creativity and life in the universe, from which all have come and to which all will return.

Forms and Devices

"Brahma" reflects Emerson's periodic use of the standard poetic meter and rhyme of his time: The four quatrains are in iambic tetrameter, and his use of coupled rhymes (*abab*) is a reflection of his thematic sense of the inescapable polarity in the universe.

The central figure in the poem is the speaker, who is Brahma, or the Over-Soul, the creative spirit in the universe. Having the Brahma as the speaker allows Emerson to posit the unity within the world's polaric structure; though contradictions seem to exist, he suggests, they are in fact meaningful paradoxes and not meaningless contradictions. Emerson makes extensive use of irony in his poetic strategy; he indicates that death is not really death, that shadow and sunlight are the same, and that both the doubter and doubt are contained within the Brahma, to which all persons aspire to return. There are other ironies as well: It is clearly implied that it is the abode of Brahma (line 13) which is to be sought rather than a Christian heaven and that those who adopt the Darwinian perspective of the survival of the fittest miss the realization that, in reality, all survive.

Emerson has, in "Brahma," used a series of images borrowed from Hindu scriptures (many of which he translated in the issues of the Transcendentalist magazine *The Dial*, which he co-edited with Margaret Fuller for two years and then edited himself) to reflect the coordinated pattern and unity in the physical universe, which is itself a reflected pattern of the same unity in the spiritual universe.

Themes and Meanings

Emerson insists in his writings that it is only the spiritual world which is "real"; the material world is simply an illusion, created by human senses, that must eventually be transcended. He frequently used one segment of the world (as did Henry David Thoreau, who learned the method from him) as a microcosm of the universe as a whole, believing that if one could but understand all of one aspect of the reality, one would have a clear entry into understanding the whole.

Another central Emersonian theme is implied in this poem, one that has to do with the relationship between people and nature: Physical nature can be a mirror to reflect back to humankind the spiritual facts which lie behind and inform all physical facts. Shadow and sunlight, for example, can reveal that they are inescapable parts of one phenomenon and thus one spiritual reality. Just as a person may come to realize that shadow is only the absence of light, so may one come to realize that evil is only the absence of good.

Other central themes in Emerson's work are reflected in this poem: the idea of compensation, for example, which shows that there is a principle of balance in the universe, since for everything that is given, something is taken away, and vice versa. In the whole (or spiritual) sense, nothing is ever lost. There is also a commentary on the nature of experience, which Emerson saw—in a metaphor which he used in several works—as being like beads strung on the string of one's temperament. In other words, what one sees and finds in the world is directly connected to one's perspective, or point of view, since how one looks at things determines what one sees. It is much like holding up a string of colored beads to the light and looking through them with all their varied colors—except, as Emerson states in his essay "Experience," that these beads are named desire, reality, temperament, succession, and subjectiveness. It is also the case, as he argued in his essay "Fate," that the universe is structured as much or more by one's internal fate or destiny as it is by any external fate. Since everyone desires to return to the Brahma or Over-Soul, from which they have come (whether they realize it or not), and since the Brahma, Over-Soul, or creative principle in the universe is waiting to accept or re-accept them when they are ready, the purpose of free will is to lead people to choose what has already been chosen (another paradox, and another polarity), to return to the ultimate unity and harmony from which everyone originally came.

Clark Mayo

BRANDING THE FOALS

Author: Padraic Colum (1881-1972)
Type of poem: Lyric
First published: 1930, in *Old Pastures*

The Poem

Padraic Colum's richly evocative seven-line poem "Branding the Foals" compares the fire of amorous passion that a man feels for his beloved with the fire necessary for the branding tool to clearly mark foals as the farmer's possession. In this first-person narrative, the unnamed male farmer is speaking to himself. At first, he asks himself a paradoxical question: He wonders why he needs fire to brand his foals. This seems incomprehensible to readers who realize that cold tools cannot be used to brand farm animals, but by the second line of this short poem readers come to suspect that the fire of which the farmer speaks should be interpreted figuratively and not literally. In the second line, the farmer asserts that the only fire he truly needs is his intense physical attraction for his lover, with whom he would like to make love. She is also a farmer, and they live together on their simple farm.

In the third and fourth lines, the male farmer makes reference to the "lighted coals" and the "branding tool," which she is bringing to him. These physical objects serve to remind him of their intense love for each other. Although both lovers are hardworking farmers, their major concern is their mutual "desire." Although they are accomplishing mundane agricultural tasks, they think constantly of their strong attraction to each other.

In the fifth line, the male farmer assures his readers that he has no needs for the coals and tool that the woman is carrying. His true need is more profound. He requires her physical love so that his life can have meaning. The physical pain inflicted on foals who are branded serves only to remind him how much he suffers internally whenever he cannot touch his lover. Her "hands," which hold the branding tool, remind him that those same "hands" can also be used to caress him during moments of intense physical passion. The final line in this short poem conveys to Colum's readers another paradoxical insight. He writes, "And grass, and trees, and shadows, all are fire!"

Trees and grass can burn, but the shadows of trees and high grass do give lovers relative privacy to make love in the open air. Everything in nature inspires in lovers a reason to express their passionate love for each other, no matter where they may be.

Forms and Devices

Colum was a deceptively simple poet. Unlike more famous Irish writers, such as William Butler Yeats, James Joyce, Lady Augusta Gregory, and Oliver Joseph St. John Gogarty, who created with Colum the literary movement called the Irish Renaissance during the first decades of the twentieth century, Colum was from a very poor peasant background. He grew up in poverty in the Irish countryside, and his formal education ended in eighth grade. He was largely a self-educated writer, but he never forgot his childhood as an Irish peasant, although he lived in Dublin from 1901 until his departure in 1914 for New York City, where he lived with his wife and fellow writer, Mary Colum, until shortly before his death on January 11, 1972, in a nursing home in Connecticut. Many critics mistakenly concluded that Colum was little more than a sentimental poet who re-created in his finely crafted poems and short stories daily life in the rural Ireland of his youth. Such critics, however, did not realize that Colum strove to express keen insights into universal human experiences through the Irish peasant culture which he knew so well.

It is not essential that readers even know that Colum was an Irish writer. The two lovers in "Branding the Foals" could live in any agricultural society, and their mutual passion can certainly be understood by readers from any country or century. In "Branding the Foals," Colum makes very effective use of seemingly straightforward words and images to convey to his readers the intensity of the lovers' passion. He stresses the levels of meaning in the words "look," "need," "fire," and "desire." A lover "looks" for his beloved just as a farmer must "look" for the fire needed to heat branding tools. When this lover "looks at" the branding tool, he sees not just a physical object and his beloved but also his inner love for her. He "sees" an invisible reality that only lovers can understand.

Colum also uses the word "need" in a richly suggestive manner. A farmer "needs" fire so that foals can be properly branded, and foals "need" to be branded so that they can be returned to the rightful owner if they are stolen. The two lovers, however, have more profound "needs." Without the joy of physical love based on mutual respect, their lives will have no meaning for them and there will be major voids in their existence. These farmers could certainly live without their foals. They would be poorer, but their lives would continue. Without their physical and emotional "needs" being satisfied, however, they could not experience true satisfaction and ecstasy, which would make their emotional lives poorer.

Like water and air, fire is essential for human existence. Fire is needed to prepare meals, heat cottages, and brand farm animals, but fire can also destroy houses, livestock, forests, and lives. People must somehow learn to control "fire" so that it brings pleasure and not destruction. This is relatively easy to do when dealing with real fires that can be extinguished with fire equipment or water, but these two lovers realize that there are much more dangerous fires within them. These are the fires inspired by passion, which people cannot and do not want to extinguish because they enrich life completely, even though they expose people to great risk and may result in intense emotional suffering. These two farmers "desire" a better quality of life on their farm so that they no longer have to live in poverty, but in "Branding the Foals," the male farmer refers to his beloved as his "desire." She is the one who gives true meaning to his life, and he cannot imagine life without her.

Themes and Meanings

Colum was a very refined poet who relied on suggestive images and abstract ideas to help his readers appreciate the intense "desire" of these two lovers. In this poem, they do very little. The male lover thinks about his beloved while she brings him "lighted coals" and a branding "tool." The most erotically charged poems are often not pornographic poems that depict the sexual act itself but rather those that convey to the reader in an understated and elegant style sexual desire itself. Unless the physical act of love manifests mutual love, respect, and equality, love is debased and is nothing more than a form of physical conquest. The very scene in this short poem strongly suggests that the woman shares with her beloved not just the physical pleasures of love but also the mundane responsibilities a farming couple must share.

She heated the coals and then brought them in a pot to him with the appropriate branding tool. He could not have held the foals had she not done this preliminary work. They had to cooperate so that their foals could be properly branded and thus protected from theft. By their very cooperation they are able to be together almost all the time. This enables their mutual "desire" to increase in intensity because they are always "looking" at each other, whether they are in bed or working in their barn or on their farm.

Sexual desire is obviously not something that can be described with mere words. A poet must suggest its force to readers through thoughts or actions. Both farmers in this poem dutifully accomplish the necessary daily tasks on their farm, even unpleasant ones, such as branding foals, but their thoughts are always elsewhere. Physical objects such as "lighted coals," branding "tools," "trees," and "grass" constantly remind them of their mutual desire, but the desire itself is more meaningful and universal than the physical act of love. All readers understand the emotional and psychological reality of sexual desire, but the actual physical manifestation of this desire depends on personal preferences and the specific circumstances in which the lovers find themselves. If they are in the company of others, they can express their desire by flirting or holding hands, but if they are alone, they can leave more flight to their imagination and creativity. "Branding the Foals" is a powerful and evocative poem that explores the complexity of the rich psychological and emotional passion that Colum refers to as mutual "desire."

Edmund J. Campion

BRASS FURNACE GOING OUT

Author: Diane di Prima (1934-   )
Type of poem: Ode
First published: 1975; collected in *Selected Poems, 1956-1975*, 1975

The Poem

"Brass Furnace Going Out," subtitled "Song, After an Abortion," is a direct address by the poet to the spirit of an aborted baby who functions as a comforting, though haunting, presence throughout the work. It consists of twelve irregular sections written in variants of open verse ranging from three to forty-three lines. In categorizing it as a "Song," Diane di Prima is using the term in the classical sense of an ode—a song composed for performance at a public occasion. Her intention is to take a private struggle and make it accessible to a large audience. The prevailing mood of the song is elegiac as it laments the death of the baby as well as the lost possibilities of life, but there are radical shifts in mood as the poet works through stages of grief and guilt, richocheting from section to section in a pattern of abrupt emotional reversals. The first section finds the poet already part of a world both absurd and horrible:

> and what of the three year old girl who poisoned her mother?
> that happens, it isn't just us, as you can see—
> what you took with you when you left
> remains to be seen.

This question introduces a pattern of reversal by juxtaposing the horror of an abortion with an equally chilling alternative: the child killing her mother. The poet acknowledges her place in the drama but does not yet know what the impact of her actions will be. The second section provides one possibility, a lurch to emotional extremity as the poet expresses resentment toward both the father (now absent) and the baby, accusing the child of "quitting/ at the first harsh treatment." This vindictive bitterness is countered by the motherly tone of the third section, as she imagines a letter to the child, who seems to be merely away at school or on a trip. "I want to/ keep in touch" she writes, "I want to know how you/ are, to send you cookies." This comforting dream is interrupted by a nightmare in section IV in which the poet is consumed, not by anger as in section II, but by guilt. She has a vision of a rotting fetus in a river surrounded by animals who reject the baby just as the poet has. This is the longest section of the poem, a surrealistic picture of a return to origins as the abortion itself is revisited in terms of the natural world absorbing the life-spirit of both the mother and the child.

The harrowing scene in section IV leads to a defensive burst of anger in the next part as the poet attempts to find someone or something to share the blame and then begins a kind of preparation for burial as if ordering the baby out of her mind. There is some sort of release in this action, as the end of the section introduces a feeling of partial acceptance for the first time, the baby relinquished to be reborn in another setting but carrying a message to the new mother warning her away from shared communication.

Section VI reinforces the emotional see-saw pattern by destroying any attempt to come to terms with the baby's absence. Horrific images of the baby's rotting corpse ("your goddamned belly rotten, a home for flies/ blown out & stinking, the maggots curling your hair") actually reflect the poet's disgust with herself. The depth of her feeling is emphasized by the suggestion that a child grown to be a criminal, or one doomed to be starved or shot, would still "have been frolic and triumph compared to this." The agony implicit in her declaration represents the degree to which she has been wracked by the entire process.

Section VIII is pivotal and only three lines long. Here the poet asks for forgiveness from the child, an initial step toward some semblance of recovery. Taking on the responsibility she formerly rejected, the poet's feelings turn in a new direction. Her realization that she may be exiled from the cosmos of reason if she cannot be absolved of the burden of guilt leads her to beg, "forgive, forgive/ that the cosmic waters do not turn from me/ that I should not die of thirst."

Part of this absolution comes in section IX, where a mystic ritual takes place, bringing about the release and transference of the baby's soul. This ritual permits the poet to imagine what could have been. Returning to the motherly stance of section III, the poet revels in the imagined baby's happy infancy in a fantasy projection balancing the awful images of decay with a tender, touching portrayal of domesticity. Inevitably, another reversal occurs, but this time it is overridden by a vision of her young child living a happy, normal life. Section XII concludes with an invitation to the child to come to her again and promises to make the child comfortable, offering her body now ready to nurture again: "my breasts prepare/ to feed you: they do what they can."

Forms and Devices

The poem's title is a symbolic representation of its subject. It suggests the extinguishing of the life of the fetus and eventually of the poet's guilt as well, setting the course which the poem follows. The "Brass Furnace" is a controlling image for the physical and emotional being of the speaker. As a heated enclosure, it objectifies the womb, warming and generating the fetus. When the abortion removes the developing baby, the "Going Out" refers to the extinguishing of its life's fire as well as the literal departure of the fetus from the mother. It also represents the direction of the poet's emotional journey. As a furnace shuts down, it cools over time. The poem chronicles the cooling process that the poet goes through. She is very hot at first—her wrath ignited by her pain. As she works through her feelings, occasional sparks leap up to rekindle her passion before the body image of a fiery forge is replaced by one of a liquid carrying the promise of regeneration.

While the striking image of the brass furnace controls the progress of the poem, the range and variety of the images di Prima uses sustain the high emotional pitch at which it operates and makes each switch in mood convincing. In section II, when di Prima blames the baby for "quitting// as if the whole thing were a rent party/ & somebody stepped on your feet," the reduction to the colloquial grounds the action in the familiar and tempers the pain with bizarre humor. The vision in section IX, in contrast, is written as a version of a transformative rite, the images of "orange & jade at the shrine" symbolizing the necessities of the reproductive process as di Prima utilizes sacred objects (the orange suggesting fruitfulness, the jade an emblem of celestial semen) from a hidden feminine subculture.

Throughout the poem, liquid images counter the fire of the furnace, continuing the pattern of reversal, first as manifestations of a polluted river, then as a healing balm, then as the water associated with birth. Similarly, animal imagery which often directly mirrors the poet's feelings is the central motif of many sections. For instance, the dogs playing trumpets in section I reflect the distortion of reality that is part of the poet's confusion; the giraffes "mourning cry" in section IV echoes the poem's tone of lamentation, and the fish in section XI resemble the aquatic state of the baby prior to birth. In addition, the animal imagery enables di Prima to explore her own animal nature as a being whose physicality is always a prime concern.

Themes and Meanings

Although men such as Jack Kerouac, Allen Ginsberg, and William Burroughs have dominated the public's attention in studies of Beat writers, Diane di Prima's close association with them brought her minimal acclaim. She is not only the premier woman poet of this group but also a writer whose prototypical feminist thought introduced an underground feminist mythology to American literary culture. "Brass Furnace Going Out" is a highly personalized poem depicting a shattering experience that transformed the consciousness of the poet as the experiences reflected in "Howl" did for Ginsberg. Both works are intense renderings of emotional responses that explore dimensions of a subject not previously considered appropriate for literary discourse.

As were many of her contemporaries, di Prima was quite familiar with conventional literary forms but recognized that it was necessary to create a distinctly singular voice to capture the full range of her subject. Her inventive employment of the rhythms of speech and thought, combined with an artful insertion of items from an arcane mythological base, not only made her exploration especially vivid but also created new ways of seeing. Her avoidance of easy judgment, her disinclination to preach or moralize, has kept the poem relevant, whereas propaganda for either pro-choice or pro-life positions on abortion can easily become strident and stale.

As Ann Charters observed, di Prima has been "dismayed that her eloquent meditation on her early abortion has been read by antiabortion groups as supporting their cause." Beyond the compelling nature of a charged subject, di Prima's poem is about loss and acceptance in both a specifically personal and a universal sense. Di Prima has not understated the particularly feminine aspects of the experience in tracing the process of grief that follows a traumatizing event, but the poem is not bound by any definitions of gender.

Amy R. Walter and Leon Lewis

BREAD AND WINE

Author: Friedrich Hölderlin (1770-1843)
Type of poem: Elegy
First published: 1894, as "Brod und Wein," in *Friedrich Hölderlin: Sein Leben und sein Dichten*; English translation collected in *Poems and Fragments*, 1966

The Poem

"Bread and Wine" is a nine-stanza poem written in an elegiac form based on Greek and Roman elegies—a form used to express a sense of tragedy. Written by Friedrich Hölderlin in 1800, it is often cited by critics as a poem that marks the culmination of his younger period. That is, it is the work of a poet who is reaching the peak of his powers.

The nine stanzas that constitute the poem divide easily into three sections of three stanzas apiece. The first section begins in contemporary times (that is, Hölderlin's times) by looking at a town at night. As people head home from their work, night is presented as a time of rest, a time of quiet reflection when one can think of love and of distant friends. When the moon and the stars come out, however, night becomes "Night, the fantastical," "Night, the astonishing, . . . the stranger to all that is human."

The second stanza develops the view of night as "astonishing." "No one," the poet says, "Knows what it is," and not even the wisest understand what the purpose of night is; the reason of day is better suited to humankind. Nevertheless, people find the darkness of night attractive. To the mad and the dead, night is sacred, but even to other people night offers a hint of "holy drunkenness" and "frenzied oblivion," of "a life more intense and more daring" than the life of day. It should be noted that the original dedication of this poem was to the "Wine god"—traditionally, Dionysus. Associating night with the idea of holy drunkenness is thus also a way of associating it with Dionysus, who will become an important figure as the poem progresses.

In the third stanza, the narrator associates the attraction of night with a divine fire that, day and night, urges people to be gone. "Let us go then!" he says, and later adds, "Off to the Isthmus," referring to the Isthmus of Corinth where the ancient Olympic games were held, and "Off to Olympian regions." He will guide the reader to ancient Greece, because "back there points the god who's to come."

The middle section, stanzas 4 through 6, describe an imaginary journey to ancient Greece, a journey that begins when the narrator laments the loss of ancient Greece, with its festival halls and its temples dedicated to singing to the gods. He then goes on to imagine the beginning of Greek culture, which begins with a visitation of gods, especially "Father Aether," conceived of by Hölderlin as the father of the gods.

It is this visitation of the gods that the fifth stanza, which is structurally and thematically the center of the poem, details. When the gods first appear, they are not immediately recognized, except by children. Nevertheless, the gods offer gifts to humankind, which humankind is pleased to receive but immediately begins to waste. At that point, the gods appear "in truth," meaning in their corporeal persons, and people grow accustomed to joy and to "the sight of godhead revealed." For the first and only time, humankind is completely happy, with every desire satisfied by the presence of the gods. Humankind remains blind to the value of this enormous gift but does find words "like flowers" to name these gods.

The sixth stanza records the heyday of Greek civilization, which Hölderlin conceives of as a civilization whose art and achievements were dedicated to praising the gods. Again the poet asks: Where are the heavenly temples and cities of the Greeks? What happened to the sacred theaters that celebrated joy, and why do the gods no longer appear at the feast with humankind?

The seventh stanza opens the section of the poem that returns to contemporary times. The gods are still living, Hölderlin says, although not in this world, because humanity can no longer stand a direct encounter with godhood. Humanity must be hardened through its encounters with night and frenzy before it will be able to face the gods again. In the meantime, Hölderlin wonders, "who wants poets at all in lean years?"—that is, the job of poets is to praise present gods, but there are no gods present. Poets, an imaginary listener responds, are today like the priests of Dionysus who once roamed the night. That is, poets (as Martin Heidegger comments in an essay inspired by these lines, "What Are Poets For?") are the ones today who stay on the trail of the absent gods, trying to find the traces of their movements.

In stanza 8, Hölderlin explores this comparison. When the gods disappeared, they left behind a few gifts that would remind humanity of the time of spiritual joy. Bread and wine, which were used in sacraments to Dionysus in much the same way that they have been used in Christian Communion ceremonies, are two such gifts, and when people taste them in religious ceremonies, they can experience a taste of divine joy. Similarly, poets in another way provide a small taste of this divine bliss.

In the final stanza, Hölderlin prophesies the ultimate return of the gods. In the meantime, however, even though humankind lives today as a mere shadow of its past and future self, the wise can find the "Son of the Highest"—which is a reference to Dionysus but is presented as a Christlike figure—whose torch can bring light to wise men and who will eventually lead the way to a second golden age.

Forms and Devices

The form of the elegy came to Hölderlin ultimately from Classical literature but was in fact being invigorated in German literature at the time Hölderlin was writing by Johann Wolfgang von Goethe and Friedrich Schiller. Traditionally, an elegy entails a poet looking at the tragic aspects of life but finding consolation in some principle. As the critic Richard Unger notes in his remarks on "Bread and Wine" in *Friedrich Hölderlin* (1984), Hölderlin also follows Schiller's lead in using the form to express a longing for an absent ideal—in this case, to lament the absence of divine presence.

In Hölderlin's hands, however, the elegy also becomes a prophecy. In this regard, Michael Hamburger, a critic and translator of Hölderlin, notes that a fruitful comparison can be drawn to Hölderlin's English contemporary, William Blake. Like Blake in such prophecies as "America," Hölderlin in "Bread and Wine" foresees a time when humankind will be able to see the divine world directly. Unlike Blake, though, who created an enormous system of his own in his poetry, Hölderlin worked closely with existing religious systems in "Bread and Wine"—primarily the ancient worship of Dionysus but also the modern worship of Christ, which he presents as similar.

Images of light and darkness play a key role in the prophetic aims of this poem. The description in the opening stanza of night falling in a contemporary village plays a crucial role, drawing the reader into Hölderlin's prophecy with its very homeliness. Night is a time of rest, a time for reflection, and a time for drunken celebration. As the poem develops in the second stanza, however, the problem being presented is that there is something about the night that is foreign to human reason. To an extent, Hölderlin seems to be accepting the common opposition by which day is associated with reason and darkness is associated with madness and lack of reason.

Darkness, however, is also associated with the "holy drunkenness" granted by the wine god (Dionysus). Thus night offers a lack of reason that, rather than being disabling, is in fact enabling. The night not only allows the poet to travel imaginatively to ancient Greece but also provides the divine inspiration, in the form of holy drunkenness and madness, that will prepare humanity for its ultimate encounter with the gods.

At the end of the poem, Hölderlin is clearly trying to resolve this opposition. The "Son of the Highest" is already among human beings, who live as shadows; he is holding his torch to lighten the "gloom." Although the night allowed Hölderlin to travel back to ancient Greece in spirit, what the night revealed was the light of this torch, which is the light of inspiration, not of reason. This light will not eliminate the shadows—humankind—but allow humankind to become fully real.

Themes and Meanings

Much of this poem's meaning can be found in the title. The bread and wine mentioned are important not only to the Hellenistic feasts of Dionysus but also to the Christian ceremony of Communion. This is merely one of several hints throughout the poem of a subtle but crucial aim of this poem—to reconcile the ancient worship of Dionysus with the modern worship of Christ.

Toward this end, the view of Dionysus that this poem presents is not the view that Friedrich Nietzsche (who was nevertheless much influenced by Hölderlin) was to present later in the nineteenth century in *Die Geburt der Tragödie aus dem Geiste der Musik* (1872; *The Birth of Tragedy Out of the Spirit of Music*, 1909), a work that in the twentieth century did much to shape views of Dionysus. As Richard Unger points out, Nietzsche's Dionysus is a god of orgiastic violence; Hölderlin's is a god of drunken inspiration. Both writers present gods who are associated with the uncanny, but (as is shown in Hölderlin's description of the night, in which he associates the "inhuman night" not only with madness, death, and inspiration but also with rest and reflection) Hölderlin's view of an encounter with this god—while not devoid of the fearsome—is gentler, reconcilable with views of Christ as a bringer of comfort.

The eighth and ninth stanzas of the poem especially call attention to this comparison. The identity of the "Genius" who in stanza 8 dispenses divine comfort and then leaves is left deliberately vague; it could be either Christ or Dionysus. The bread and wine, which are all that remain to contemporary humanity of divine grace, also promise that the "Heavenly who once were/ Here . . . shall come again," another reference that seems to have been deliberately constructed to invoke Christian promises of a divine return.

Similarly, in the final stanza, the poet promises that the "Son of the Highest" is already among humanity, bringing his torch to dispel the gloom of people living in an age devoid of the gods. The "Son of the Highest" could be Dionysus, a son of "Father Aether," or Christ.

It is important to recognize, however, that while Hölderlin takes pains to present a Christlike view of Dionysus, the fundamental sensibility underlying the poem is not particularly Christian, and Hölderlin was not, when he wrote this poem, a conventional Christian. As Richard Unger points out, what the taste of bread and wine remind one of today is that all the gods—Hellenistic as well as Christian—were once here, and all shall return. Furthermore, the time of this return, as Hölderlin conceives it, will be marked by a society based on the ancient Greek model, a society that—when humankind is once again able to endure the direct presence of the divine—will live among and for the gods.

Finally, a related theme in "Bread and Wine" (which remains important in Hölderlin's later poetry) concerns the relationship between man and language. While the visitation of the gods to the Greeks is not presented as the origin of language, that time is presented as a time when language lived most fully, "like flowers leaping alive" to name the gods. For Hölderlin, the most vital task for language—and poetry especially—is to name the gods; however, as he acknowledges when he asks "who wants poets?" in a time when the gods are absent, all a poet can do is trace the potential presence of these gods. By performing this role, this poem can serve the same purpose as the bread and wine of its title. It cannot bring the gods back, but it can provide a taste of the divine presence that is absent from the world.

Thomas J. Cassidy

BREAD WITHOUT SUGAR

Author: Gerald Stern (1925-   )
Type of poem: Elegy
First published: 1989; collected in *Bread Without Sugar: Poems*, 1992

The Poem

"Bread Without Sugar" is a long fifteen-page poem in eight unnumbered parts that function not so much as stanzas as discrete sections (each approximately thirty to sixty lines in length). To further complicate the picture, the poem is written in memory of the poet's father, contains an epigraph from Grace Paley ("This is what makes justice in the world—to bring these lives into the light"), and, at its conclusion, is dedicated to the writer and editor Ted Solotaroff. It is necessary to keep these three aspects in mind as the poem unfolds.

The setting for "Bread Without Sugar"—and there usually is an external setting for a Gerald Stern poem—is his father's gravesite in Miami, and it is his father's life that Stern wants to "bring to light." Kneeling in wet December sand to see the headstone, the speaker travels through memory to the day of his father's funeral; he sees the cantor, the boring rabbi, the Jewish businessmen from Newark and Flatbush who, like his father—a retired tailor and buyer—had come to Miami. He then goes back through a cross-section of his father's life ("born in Kiev, died in Miami"), to a cross-section of his own life (memories of Pittsburgh, the "bread without sugar" he had eaten as a boy, his eventual travels), to a day in "1940 or 1941" when the family had first visited Florida. Simultaneously, the governing sensibility of the poem travels outward, embracing the whole of Jewish history, the scattered past that in the end can bring such different people together in the same place.

As the poet contemplates his somewhat strained relationship with his deceased father, what he calls an "odd vexation," he also recounts his interaction with his aging mother and begins to wonder where he himself will be buried. He considers a variety of his favorite places, going from "country/ to country in search of a plot." These imaginative gestures move him into what might be termed "speculative time." Thus Stern is able not only to select several possible burial sites but also to create his death scene (hit by a taxi in Poland). His expansive imagination embraces the future: "I want/ to live with the Spanish forever. I love/ their food and I love their music; I am/ not even dead and I am speaking/ their language already; I hope their poets/ remember me." There is a complicated mix of tenses so that chronological time becomes meaningless. In this way Stern allows himself, at least figuratively, more than one life.

Further, the poet is able to move quickly from remembered time (the family in the Charles Hotel) to his projected old age in the same hotel; he envisions himself drawing his pension, cooking on a hot plate, losing his glasses on the sand, not being able to find his towel. The poem ends with incantation, an individual prayer for the self, fully realized because of its all-inclusive, all-embracing journey through concomitant histories: "May the turtles escape/ the nets: May I find my ocean! May/ the salt preserve me! May the black clouds instruct me!"

Forms and Devices

Over the years Gerald Stern has developed an idiosyncratic voice—one that readers can recognize instantly as belonging to him alone. It is not simply conversational; it is a voice which seems to come from the most visceral center of the man: personal, engaging, spontaneous, often breaking free in impromptu associations. To read Stern is to accompany him on a sort of spiritual autobiography. This voice is not that of a confessional persona pretending to "tell all"—it does not invite or even seem to need the reader. Readers participate fully, but as bystanders. Each poem embodies a thought process—a scattering of real moments and personal connections, a twist of particular synapses, then new observation, new wiring, odd pairings that lead to more memories, more connections.

"Bread Without Sugar" proceeds on just such a circuitous associative route. The sentences seem to spill into one another, a jumble of questions and observations, punctuated by dashes and semicolons, commas linking one fleeting thought to another, one memory to its outlandish extrapolation. A good example is the section in which the speaker is thinking about the people buried near his father:

> The sky
> is streaked tonight; I love the tropics,
> the orange underneath the blue; green parrots
> are flying out of the sun, voices
> are rising out of the ground, it must be
> Yaglom and Sosna, those are his neighbors,
> And Felder and Katz; some are New Yorkers,
> one is from Cincinnati, one
> was born in Africa, one is from Turkey—
> he would know grapefruit. When they sing
> they do it as in the movies or they
> do it as if they were sitting down there
> in Lummus Park, on Wednesday afternoon.
> Schmaltz was our downfall, schmaltz was our horror,
> we wept on the streets or walked to the swimming pool
> weeping, we drove to the bakery weeping.
> What was it for? What did we long for
> so much, what had we lost?

The reader is inside the speaker's head. The poem functions more like a meditative lyric than a narrative, yet its length allows it room to range through the father's history, the poet's own story, and even the ongoing saga of Jews in the Diaspora, regaining Spanish, "remembering words/ they hadn't thought of for five hundred years." The interest is as much in what the poet is thinking and feeling as in any "story" he might tell.

An interesting aspect of "Bread Without Sugar" is the use of the sense of smell. Each section contains some reference to a memory of a stench—seemingly brought on by a garbage dump near the cemetery in Miami. The poet's associations are held together by smell; it crops up as a memory of a rat-strewn bakery where he had to cover his mouth as a boy, the heavy syrup of his parents' fruit salad sundaes, the "disgusting smell" of the clinkers in the yellow cloud of air at Union Station in Pittsburgh, the burning city, pigs "rolling in shit" in Mexico, the angel who "stank from the sun," each image just a bit more exaggerated than the last.

Themes and Meanings

Many of Gerald Stern's poems are about loss. They hinge on a before and after—his love poems often have an elegiac note at their inception. "Bread Without Sugar," however, contains two simultaneous presents—the one of the immediate, felt world and the one of his active imagining. Yet the poem is not so much about the present as it is about the past and the future that are opened by present circumstances. Just as the poet is able to reflect on several distinct pasts, he confidently projects a variety of futures.

Because there are fleeting moments of direct address, as though the poem were intermittently spoken to Ted Solotaroff, it implies a shared history. It documents the experience of the wandering Jew, but it is also about the simple sustenance—the bread without sugar—of family, neighborhood, country. In the end the poem pays homage to America and its immigrant experience. In celebrating his own family's history, Stern speaks for all the forgotten, for those who died in the Holocaust, producing a kind of "justice."

"Bread Without Sugar" begins with the speaker standing "between two continents" and ends with him fixed (in his imagination) on the sandy beach of his past. The poem is concerned with balance—one version of life versus another, one impulse set against its opposite, a veritable scale on which justice will be weighed. In every instance, thought itself is at stake, presenting as it does alternative ways of approaching any subject. Stern's tentative, self-interrogating voice inevitably complicates the issue. Thought turns on itself, finally isolating the poet. By questioning itself, this voice accepts all of human nature, so "Bread Without Sugar" is able to range through personal and cultural history in order to lay Stern's father to rest. Only through the written word can they finally be "at peace with each other."

Stern's previous work has fashioned a special relationship between his readers and the personal (and sometimes very intimate) details he shares with them. The self presented in "Bread Without Sugar" is created almost exclusively by his poetic voice: its passions, its peculiar energy, its exuberance and humor. Contrary to what seems a pervasive critical response to his work, Stern is not a contemporary version of Walt Whitman. His voice is lonelier, more independent, closer to the bone. It sweeps readers along in its self-questioning, and fundamental, urgency. It manages to speak movingly for something larger than itself without pretending to speak for everyone's lives.

Judith Kitchen

BREAK OF DAY IN THE TRENCHES

Author: Isaac Rosenberg (1890-1918)
Type of poem: Lyric
First published: 1916; collected in *Poems*, 1922

The Poem

As its title suggests, Isaac Rosenberg's "Break of Day in the Trenches" is a poem in which time juxtaposes with setting to create a new poetic perception of life and death. It is a short free-verse poem of twenty-six lines, capturing the bemusement of an ordinary infantryman confronting the harshness of existence in the trenches during World War I. It is also a reverie on life and the persistence of life in the midst of war.

Almost every line contains some reference to violent death, sometimes death on a grand scale. Yet even in the midst of mass warfare, Rosenberg notes, there is life of a sort. For instance, the poetic speaker's casual act of plucking a poppy—an act of killing—is juxtaposed with his observations on a living creature, a rat, that approaches close enough to touch the speaker's hand.

With sardonic humor, the speaker compares the rat's situation with that of ordinary soldiers, observing that the "Droll" animal is able to survive in the fields of battle. He observes that the trenches and the other demarcations of war that separate the English soldiers from their "enemies" matter little to the rat, which will perhaps cross no-man's-land to continue its feast on German corpses.

It is this free act of crossing a few miles of open space that figures in the next section of poem. The speaker marvels at the rat's ability to survive, while "haughty athletes" with "Strong eyes, fine limbs" are so easily slaughtered. If the dominant fauna of this environment is the rats that feed on the corpses, the common flora is "Poppies whose roots are in man's veins," flowers of blood from wounded soldiers.

This reduction of humans to mere objects is reinforced later in the poem when the movement of the rat is contrasted with the prostration of soldiers, who are "Sprawled in the bowels of the earth." From the description, the soldiers could be either living or dead; perhaps it does not matter much to the speaker. At least the speaker knows that he himself is still alive, although the slight dust on the poppy he has put behind his ear prefigures the dust of the grave that always stands waiting.

Forms and Devices

Much in "Break of Day in the Trenches" is characteristic of English World War I poetry. For instance, while many English poets wrote in the traditional poetic genres—in this case, the pastoral—they enriched the genres and played on the expectations of their readers by introducing wartime experience as new subject matter. Further, some poets used unconventional meter and rhythm to approximate the broken rhythms of life during war. While "Break of Day in the Trenches" draws on both conventions of war poetry, its visual imagery is its most important aspect.

As a young man, Rosenberg showed considerable natural talent for drawing. Later he studied art at Birkbeck College and the Slade School of Art in London. Although he ultimately gave up the visual arts for poetry, the pictorial quality of some of his poems is particularly notable. In "Louse Hunting" (1917), for instance, Rosenberg first presents his readers with an image of naked soldiers, "Yelling in lurid glee," who have stripped off their clothes to kill the vermin infesting them. This initial image is strongly rendered, dominated by the "Grinning faces/ And raging limbs" that "Whirl over the floor one fire."

Similarly, two strong visual images dominate "Break of Day in the Trenches": the grinning rat and the poppy. In the first place, the rat imagery encompasses both the animal and the speaker who notices it. The line "A queer sardonic rat" refers to the animal, but it also indicates the speaker's tone and situation: He, too, is a sardonic rat. Although the rat imagery is important in establishing connections between these two unwilling victims of the war, the considerably more dense poppy imagery universalizes the situation of this individual soldier. The poppy is both image and metaphor. The plucked poppy serves as an example of the casual killing that accompanies life in the trenches. The poppy is also a well-chosen way to indicate this death, since the flower was normally planted alongside graves.

Metaphorically, the poppy indicates ways of dying. The speaker's placement of the red flower behind his ear points to a considerable more brutal image, the "flowering" of blood from a head wound. That Rosenberg had this subtlety in mind is suggested by his repetition of the poppy imagery a few lines later, where one reads that the poppies grow from "roots [that] are in man's veins." Blood is both flower and fertilizer in this vivid wordplay.

In his early twenties, Rosenberg had felt forced to choose between writing and painting, remarking that art requires "blood and tears." He chose poetry, as Jon Stallworthy points out in *Lost Voices of World War I* (1987). Thereafter, Rosenberg strove to write "Simple *poetry*,—that is where an interesting complexity of thought is kept in tone and right value to the dominating idea so that it is understandable and still ungraspable." While Rosenberg achieved this balance in his greatest poems, it is also true that the concentration on evocative pictorial images renders "Break of Day in the Trenches" as inscrutable and immediate as visual art.

Themes and Meanings

The themes of "Break of Day in the Trenches" emerge from Rosenberg's inversion of the traditions of the pastoral poem. Generally, pastorals take place in stylized, idyllic rural settings, often early in the morning; their central figures are usually innocent shepherds, whose comments on life are intended also as pointed criticisms of larger social issues. Although the speaker of the poem does not share the rural background of shepherds, he—presumably, like Rosenberg, an urban poet from the East End of London—unselfconsciously emphasizes three main themes: the horrors of war, the artificiality of political barriers, and the necessity of maintaining human values, especially humor, to endure trench warfare.

In "Break of Day in the Trenches," the speaker clearly thinks of the war as mass slaughter, hardly a situation where one man's life—or one man's effort—amounts to much. The inversion of pastoral conventions indicates this. In the second line, daybreak is called the "old druid Time," a time of human sacrifice—that is, something to be endured, not welcomed. To the soldiers, day is a time to be dreaded; the horrible reality of war is once again visible when darkness starts "crumbling." This pastoral is not concerned with idyllic moments but with "shrieking iron and flame/ Hurled through still heavens." Finally, the rat's closeness to the speaker is another buried hint of the conditions that prevail, implying that the living speaker has been mistaken for a corpse, the animal's food supply. This would suggest that the central animal of the pastoral—the sheep—has been replaced in this poem by a rat. This setting is stylized but hardly idyllic.

Further, while it is a part of the horrors surrounding the war, the literary rat also marks a second theme: the artificiality of human barriers. The speaker describes the rat as "cosmopolitan," implying that it is free of the political barriers that, like trench lines, scar the human landscape. While the English and Germans are physically separated as enemies, they are joined by their subjection to the rat and by their victimization in the war.

Finally, Rosenberg explores a third theme in "Break of Day in the Trenches" growing out of his inverted pastoral: the necessity of humor in the midst of horrors. Rosenberg's contemporary, the English poet Wilfrid Owen, also used pastorals to throw the horrors of war into high relief. Although his poems are compassionate, Owen's tone is almost uniformly bitter. Rosenberg, for his part, makes use of a lighter tone, although his social criticism is as severe and often as biting. The speaker refers to the grim humor of the trenches several times in the poem: The rat is "sardonic" and "Droll," and it "inwardly grin[s]" as it crosses no-man's-land. Juxtaposed against this grim humor, the charnel images have all the more power. For instance, the speaker asks questions of the rat that no one, certainly not the soldier himself, can answer: "What do you see in our eyes/ . . . What quaver—what heart aghast?" In the face of these unanswerable questions, it is easy to believe that the soldiers are the butt of some hideous cosmic joke. Only the speaker's humor and his relief at a temporary moment of safety enable him to pose these questions.

Michael R. Meyers

THE BRIEF JOURNEY WEST

Author: Howard Nemerov (1920-1991)
Type of poem: Meditation
First published: 1950, in *Guide to the Ruins*

The Poem

"The Brief Journey West" is a meditative poem of twenty-eight lines divided into seven stanzas. The title suggests not only a particular journey, but a frontier push and, most important, the brevity of human life. The iambic pentameter of the poem gives it a formal, almost elegiac quality, which suits the subject of aging and death.

Written in the third person, the poem features an omniscient speaker with the stately quality of a court storyteller, an Anglo-Saxon "scop," or bard. The "fathers" of the poem represent the fathers of any nation, movement, or race; the decline refers both to the pioneers and to their visions.

The poem opens with a description of the fathers coughing and spitting in a room by a "dry road." Both the illness of the fathers and the arid land outside their "room" convey impotence and sterility. The reader is reminded that these ineffectual men once so conquered and crushed their environment that they "hung/ That bloody sun upon the southern wall." Now, however, as the second stanza reveals, they are so old that the wrinkles of their skin duplicate the maps they made when, forging new territory, they drained wild swamps. They wanted to make a place for themselves in history, but now youth and discovery have vanished—they are only history's "cracked precipitate."

The poem's third verse describes the decay of youth and vision through images of shattered glass and a sun that "burn[s] the prosperous flesh away/ Of the filthy world, so vilely fathered on/ The fathers." These lines suggest that decay results in part from corruption of the fathers' ideals. These fathers are now so old that they are only "black cinders, sitting there."

In the fourth stanza, the poem's speaker then addresses the fathers, asking them what vitality, specifically "lecheries," remain. He comments mournfully that nothing flows in the blood of the old fathers except, "When schoolgirls pass," the "custom of desire." Instead of being disturbed by passion, the fathers now enjoy "the sarcastic triumph of the mind . . . letting their lust alone," because age has robbed them of passion.

"The Brief Journey West" becomes increasingly somber in the final two stanzas. The sixth stanza states that the aged fathers, no longer naïve or passionate, wish neither for "reformation of the past" nor for inevitable disease. Instead, in the silence of the wise, they recognize a world that is "A shrivelled apple in the hand of God." The last verse shows these once impassioned trailblazers routinely hanging their "somber flags" and pursuing "their theme/ Of common images," through the night in sleep. Completely spent, these old men hope for nothing more than sleep. They want to be through with all crises but "the one," the inevitable disaster of death.

Forms and Devices

References to destruction and a somber tone give "The Brief Journey West" its power. Words that convey aridity and heat express both the shriveling of the fathers and of the world as "apple in the hand of God." The first three stanzas contain varied images of sterility resulting from lack of moisture. There is the "dry road," and the fathers' skin, which is "seamed and dry" as a drained swamp, presumably now so dry that all that is left is "cracked precipitate"—like the fathers themselves, who are now so scorched with age that they are "black cinders." The "cracked precipitate" image refers to both swamp and man. As a drained swamp leaves deposits, so the "black cinders" of the fathers are the aged residue of history. Not only are the fathers scorched into black cinders, but their triumphs are also withered because the "bloody sun" has burned "the prosperous flesh away/ Of the filthy world."

These references to withering heat are followed by equally harrowing images of cold, hardness, and brokenness. Metaphors of hardness and cold imply death through the deadening of desire. The "black cinders" of the fathers are so lifeless that they are no longer moved by much of anything. When women pass, their flesh are "Cold gleams" that provoke only the "custom of desire" in the fathers' eyes, which have hardened into the likeness of cold gems. The triumph of the mind over lust is "sarcastic," because the fathers have no choice but to twist the cooling of desire into a triumph. These images of cold stones coupled with those of brokenness, crushed beetles, "the cracked precipitate," and shattered glass add to the poem's desolation.

The most powerful metaphor of the poem, however, is of the world as a "shrivelled apple in the hand of God," a comparison that functions on several levels. The world is round like an apple, and it has become old and corrupt as a withered apple. This line is also a biblical allusion to the Garden of Eden apple, the consumption of which led to the Fall.

The poem's concluding images refer to sleep and the oblivion it brings. In the last stanza, the fathers desire only sleep. Sleep, as a symbol for oblivion, emphasizes not only the old men's disintegration but also their resignation. They want only to sleep, not to fight or blaze new trails. The words "somber," "dark," and "sleep" suggest the old men's slide into death. They are unwilling to deal with any other challenges, but "the one"—death.

The images in "The Brief Journey West" progress from active to passive images of decay, an advance that imitates the sequence of aging. The poem starts with coughing and spitting, a road, a room, and trophies in the room. Glass shatters, sun burns. Thereafter, the images slowly become more passive: cooling desire, silence, sleep, death.

Themes and Meanings

"The Brief Journey West" is about, in the poet's own words, man's transitory life span. Many poets have addressed mutability in their work, specifically the transience of man, and Howard Nemerov is no exception. There are at least two ways, however, in which the poem differs from many on the same theme. The first is in the darkness of its vision; the second is the poet's outrage.

"The Brief Journey West," written when Nemerov was twenty-six, indicates what was to be a hallmark of the poet's work, his pessimism. In this poem focusing on aging and death, man's lot is portrayed as the anguished Macbeth termed it, "Full of sound and fury, signifying nothing." The poem's tone is one of bitterness and rage; all comes to nothing—all heroics, all heroes. There is no implication of either personal or collective immortality.

What sets this meditative poem apart from other poems on the same subject is the darkness of Nemerov's vision. The only surcease offered from the relentless process of decay is the oblivion of indifference through sleep, and the bitterness of the poet's tone suggests that, to the speaker, such a solution is unacceptable. The anger of the speaker suggests that there should be more than aging, death, and oblivion to follow all of man's efforts. Implicit in the bitter tone is an angry spiritual question: Why?

The unacceptability of death as a fitting end to man's strivings is emphasized through the painful, often violent images of burning and brokenness ("shattered," "cracked"). That life is not as it should be, that it is metaphysically flawed, is further suggested by the biblical allusion to the apple, which led Creation to groan and to Fall.

Although Nemerov's later work on the same subject expresses some serenity, there is none in "The Brief Journey West." It has not only an outraged but a hopeless quality. Despite the biblical allusion, there is no redemption, either by God or man. Man is alone; he strives, conquers, only to be conquered by the same sun that he hung (or thought he hung) on the southern wall. The poem's elegiac quality, resulting from the sonorous tone of its stately rhythms, recalls the Anglo-Saxon bard's sad ballads, but it has none of the Old English sense of man's collective solidarity in the midst of a bad fate. There is no sense of brotherhood present among the "black cinders, sitting there," nor does the poet suggest hope in a kind of collective consolation. There is not even God to rage against; life has a useless, mechanistic quality to which the speaker cannot adjust.

The poem is saved from complete misery by the grandeur of its rhythms and language. No matter how absurd man's fate, "The Brief Journey West" implies, by its sweeping pictures of man's triumphs before his inexorable demise, that man has dignity. "The Brief Journey West," written in Nemerov's youth, is both an example and a presage of later work in which the speaker questions but receives no answers.

Mary Hanford Bruce

BRIEF PAUSE IN THE ORGAN RECITAL

Author: Tomas Tranströmer (1931-   )
Type of poem: Lyric
First published: 1983, as "Kort paus i orgelkonserten," in *Det vilda torget*; English
translation collected in *Tomas Tranströmer: Selected Poems: 1954-1986*, 1987

The Poem

"Brief Pause in the Organ Recital" is a lyric poem that contains twelve carefully
balanced, four-line stanzas of free verse. The immediacy of the experience recounted
in the poem is emphasized by the fact that almost all the verbs in the poem are in the
present tense.

The poet/speaker is attending an organ recital in a medieval cathedral. The sudden
silence during a brief pause in the program breaks into his elevated mood and makes
him aware of the traffic noises—"that greater organ"—outside the cathedral. He per-
ceives that though it lacks the rigidly formal structure of the organ music to which he
has been listening, the traffic noise has a freer rhythm of its own. Next, he becomes
aware, as if it were part of the street noise, of the pulsing of his own blood, what he
calls "the cascade that hides inside me." The passing of a trailer-truck heavy enough to
shake the six-hundred-year-old walls of the cathedral brings to mind an experience he
had as a child of four: Seated on his mother's lap, he listened to the distant voices of
contending adults ("the winners and the losers"). Though he initially appears to reject
the idea, he senses a similarity between the mother's lap and the sheltering church. In
effect, he is reinventing a metaphor that became a cliché in an earlier age of firm reli-
gious faith: the Church as the believer's mother.

Gazing at the pillars that support the roof of the cathedral, he appears to rediscover
a common Romantic symbol, that of nature (the forest) as a vital, protective force. The
mental image that likens the interior of the cathedral to a forest serves as a transition to
a remembered dream with an outdoor setting. The poet vividly relives this dream: He
is standing alone in a churchyard that is surrounded by blooming heather; he is wait-
ing for someone, a mysterious friend who is never identified, even though the dreamer
soon notices that this friend has already arrived. The setting (a graveyard) and the
heather (a familiar portent of death in Swedish folk tradition) suggest that the awaited
friend might be Death; indeed, in the following lines, when the dream reaches its cli-
max, the reader learns that "death turns up the lights from underneath, from the
ground." If what the dreamer is experiencing is a vision of his own death, however, it
seems to hold no terrors for him. When death intensifies the purplish (heather-
colored) light, that light is transformed into a color that is beyond human experience.
Finally, this hue converges with the rosy light of dawn that "whines" in through the
eyelids of the dreamer and awakens him. This example of synesthesia (in this case,
color becoming sound) finally gains semantic content and is articulated as a word:
"PERHAPS." Tentative though it may seem, this message from beyond the grave (or

from the depths of his own self) gives the poet enough hope to sustain him in this unstable world and to persuade him that he must not expect to be able to reduce it to an abstract picture—anymore than he could hope to find the blueprint of a storm.

This acceptance of uncertainty and earthly mutability leads to the poet's final reinvention of a traditional symbol: the world as a book. He remembers that he learned to read by scanning the pages of the family encyclopedia, a book that intends to reduce the world to an abstract picture, to certainties. As a result of his dream experience, he now realizes that each individual produces a personal encyclopedia, a book of contradictions that is constantly being updated and revised by each new wave of experience. Returning to the positive image of the forest that he likened to the interior of the cathedral, the poet now uses the same image to characterize the vitality of this internal encyclopedia that is growing inside each person, as near to one as one's blood, as dynamic as the sea. In Swedish, the poem ends with an incomplete line, as wave succeeds wave, and an ellipsis, indicating the continuation of the process.

Forms and Devices

One of the most striking features of this poem is its extremely regular formal structure. As he frequently does in his poems, Tomas Tranströmer carefully establishes a distinct rhythmic pattern in the first stanza that he repeats with little variation throughout the remainder of the poem. The first two sentences of this poem fall into a stanzaic pattern in which two long lines (the first and the third) alternate with much shorter lines (the second and the fourth). These expanding and contracting lines may be thought of as imitating the diastolic and systolic actions of the heart, a bodily rhythm that figures importantly in this poem. (Robin Fulton's English translation of this piece achieves a similar effect by sharpening the rhythmic contrast between the long and the short lines.) One can only guess whether the rigid metrical order of this poem is meant to suggest that the universe too has a meaningful structure.

The speaker of this poem clearly longs for some proof that life has meaning and purpose, that there is some basis for religious belief. Though Tranströmer makes little mention of overt religious observances in his poetry, many conventional religious values seem to correspond not only to his own deepest personal needs, but also to his poetic intuitions. In an interview with Richard Jones in 1979, Tranströmer speaks of his "religious longing" and of the direction in his poetry toward "some sort of cosmic feeling" (*Poetry East* 16, 1980). In this poem, he expresses the "cosmic feeling" by adducing a series of analogies that tend to show that nature is a nest of boxes: During a pause in the music, the speaker hears first the pulse of society, then his own pulse; finally—in the dream he so vividly relives—he thinks he hears the pulse of the universe. The traffic circulating around the cathedral is a "larger organ" that produces a music of its own, a music that is echoed in the circulation of the blood through the poet's vascular system. The rhythmic pumping of his heart also corresponds to the regular surge of the seas, the ebb and flow of the tides that metaphorically wash through the text of the reader's inner encyclopedia at the end of the poem. The correspondences he perceives between the rhythm of his own body and the rhythms of the outer world—evidence, in other words, that man is a harmonious part of nature—might have led Tranströmer to the facile conclusion that "God's in his heaven—/ All's right with the world" (Robert Browning, *Pippa Passes*, 1841). What prevents him from doing so is his awareness that the order he perceives is constantly at risk: Potentially disruptive or destructive energies (the cascade that hides inside him, the storm that cannot be mapped) may at any moment be unleashed.

The moment of insight comes, therefore, not from the poet's perception of outer correspondences between man and nature but from within his own psyche—at the end of the dream that is the spiritual climax of this poem. Tranströmer, a trained psychologist, has more than a clinical interest in dreams. He believes, as one can tell from many of his poems, that dreams not only link one's inner with one's outer self but also enable one to penetrate more deeply into one's essential self than is possible in the waking state. The manifest content of this dream (the churchyard, the heather, the friend he is awaiting, the way in which death "turns up the lights from underneath, from the ground") might lead one to conclude that the dreamer has an overwhelming awareness—if not fear—of death. Tranströmer is, however, more interested in conveying the emotional impact of the dream than in interpreting it.

Themes and Meanings

"Brief Pause in the Organ Recital" is a poem about religious experience. Though the words "mystic" and "mysticism" are often applied to Tranströmer and his work, it is important to notice that no revelation, no vision bringing certainty, is vouchsafed to the speaker of this poem. The dream that leads him to affirm the world with "an unshakable PERHAPS" can best be characterized as a secular epiphany or a moment of extraordinary insight.

The cessation of the music enables the poet to hear the traffic outside the cathedral. In Tranströmer's poetic vocabulary, "traffic" usually symbolizes human intercourse at all levels—the social order and its contextual situation in time and space. The vaguely disturbing murmur of the traffic outside becomes more threatening when the rumble of a heavy trailer-truck causes the cathedral walls to tremble, and the poet immediately associates this with a similarly jarring experience that he had when he was four: Then, safely seated on his mother's lap, he was protected from social discord. These two images (the sheltering cathedral walls and the mother's lap) help the poet define the barrier between the safe inner world and the menacing world outside, a characteristic concern of Tranströmer's. In the interview mentioned above, he said, "I like border regions. I am interested in borders and I am always writing on the borderline—the borderline between the inner world and the outer world. I call this borderline 'the truth barrier' . . . because that's the point where you can see the truth."

The sudden silence also enables him to cross another border. Listening to the beating of his pulse, he becomes aware that, like the music, it too will someday stop. Will it be only a short pause? Placed on the borderline between life and death, the poet finds new meaning in a dream he once had: Alone in a churchyard, surrounded by heather, he is waiting for a friend who, he soon realizes, is already there; death begins turning up the purple light until, becoming a hitherto unknown hue, it merges with the light of dawn and becomes articulate. Is the mysterious friend death or—as one Swedish critic suggests—Christ? Does the purple heather portend death, or does the liturgical association of the color purple with Christ's passion suggest the idea of resurrection? There is not enough evidence to enable one to answer "yes" or "no" to any of the questions that the poem raises. The most positive answer Tranströmer can give is PERHAPS, which is unshakable.

In crossing the border between dreaming and the waking state, Tranströmer appears to have glimpsed the divine, timeless world that has always been at the heart of religious belief. He senses—but cannot verify—a meaningful order in the universe. This is the point at which humankind usually takes refuge in belief, but Tranströmer seems to feel that it is as limiting to believe in the existence of meaning where none may exist as it is to deny its existence on the grounds of insufficient evidence. Seen in this light, PERHAPS (which is understood to include contradictions and uncertainties) is neither a defeat nor a compromise but a proclamation that the poet chooses to remain open to all possible blueprints of reality.

In the last three stanzas of the poem, Tranströmer uses the image of the book to justify his endorsement of uncertainty. He thinks of the family encyclopedia, with which he taught himself to read as a child. He now realizes, however, that because it attempts to give an abstract picture of the world, to reduce it to a closed and static system, this kind of encyclopedia—ironically described as "all-knowing"—is an inadequate guidebook to the world. His dream experience has convinced him of the supreme value of uncertainty, and he sees that each person contains his or her own individual encyclopedia, one that is written from birth onward on the tabula rasa (or formatted disk) of the mind. No book of certainties, this is one that encompasses contradictions; its pages, as vital as the quivering leaves in a forest, are—like a database—always being updated and restructured by each new wave of information. Although this "open system" is subject to constant revision, however, its basic structure is never destroyed. Would one be justified in seeing the permanence of this inner encyclopedia's essential structure as somehow analogous to the medieval notion that nature is a book written by God to show humankind how He works in the world? Undoubtedly, Tranströmer's answer would be "PERHAPS."

Barry Jacobs

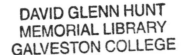